Third Edition

Soviet Political Society

Leon P. Baradat
Mira Costa College

Library of Congress Cataloging-in-Publication Data

Baradat, Leon P., 1940–
    Soviet political society / Leon P. Baradat.
        p.   cm.
    Includes bibliographical references and index.
    ISBN 0–13–824962–8
    1. Soviet Union—Politics and government.   2. Soviet Union—
Economic conditions.   3. Soviet Union—Social conditions.
I. Title.
DK43.B29   1992
947.084—dc20

91–18143
CIP

Acquisitions editor: Karen Horton
Editorial/production supervision and
  interior design: Colby Stong
Copy editor: Linda B. Pawelchak
Cover design: Ben Santora
Prepress buyer: Debra Kesar/Kelly Behr
Manufacturing buyer: Mary Anne Gloriande

Acknowledgment is gratefully made for permission to use material from the following sources: Photos pp. 7, 16, 30, 156, 184, 214, 234, 379: Louis and Helen Van Moppes. Photo p. 80: Leslie Deeb. Photo p. 13: AP/Wide World Photos. Photo p. 309: Harriet Norris. All other photos: Leon P. Baradat. Maps pp. 19, 36, 41, 78: from Basil Dmytryshyn, *A History of Russia*, © 1977, pp. 4, 35, 410, 567. Reprinted with permission of Prentice Hall, a Simon & Schuster Company, Englewood Cliffs, NJ.

© 1992, 1989, 1986 by Prentice-Hall, Inc.
A Simon & Schuster Company
Englewood Cliffs, New Jersey 07632

Printed in the United States of America
10 9 8 7 6 5 4 3 2 1

ISBN 0-13-824962-8

Prentice-Hall International (UK) Limited, *London*
Prentice-Hall of Australia Pty. Limited, *Sydney*
Prentice-Hall Canada Inc., *Toronto*
Prentice-Hall Hispanoamericana, S.A., *Mexico*
Prentice-Hall of India Private Limited, *New Delhi*
Prentice-Hall of Japan, Inc., *Tokyo*
Simon & Schuster Asia Pte. Ltd., *Singapore*
Editora Prentice-Hall do Brasil, Ltda., *Rio de Janeiro*

For my wife, Elaine

And for the memory of
Marguerite Largenté, my beloved grandmother
Olley L. Coté, a genuinely good person
Maxwell H. Norman, a wise mentor
Michael K. Becker, a dear friend

Contents

Preface

Since the first edition of this book was published, the Soviet Union has entered a period of reform that is bringing about fundamental changes in the society. Yet, at least until recent events, Mikhail S. Gorbachev and his fellow reformers are struggling with an institutionalized inertia so great that one can only guess at this point whether their programs will succeed. To fully appreciate the magnitude of their task, one must carefully study the Soviet political society.

Replete with paradox and contradiction, Soviet society is populated by a people who reflect the nation's geopolitical development. They are stoical and suspicious in the presence of strangers, but emotional and gregarious among friends. Often characterized as people without style or grace, the Soviet people have made ballet their own, and no other people appreciate poetry as they do. This is a land where, for want of private automobiles, people walk a great deal, yet they cannot produce good shoes. The Soviet economy is among the largest in the world, yet people in the provinces lead lives resembling those of their counterparts in the Third World more than those of people in an advanced state. Pioneering space travel and setting many records in space, the Soviets on earth find computers rare, calculators scarce, and the abacus ubiquitous.

These contradictions only scratch the surface of the Soviet paradox, but they remind us how difficult a task understanding the Soviet Union can be. Yet understand it we must if we are realistically to hope for an improvement in world affairs.

It is not enough to confine oneself to the narrow parameters of political parties and the Soviet government if one is to comprehend in full measure the substance of Soviet political society. Accordingly, I have gone beyond this limited scope into a broad exploration of other factors in Soviet life, aspects that also do much to impel political beliefs and activities. Thus, I examine such features as geography, history, social institutions, economics, and cultural phenomena in an effort to bring the reader a more complete understanding than can be drawn from a more restricted approach. Although the subject is treated with a rather broad brush, I have endeavored to make clear the relationship of each feature to the political realities of the Soviet Union. I have also tried to help the reader understand the Soviet Union better by introducing several anecdotes or descriptions of Soviet life that may be left out of other texts on the subject.

Further, following the Soviet people's own example of trying to underscore certain aspects of their lives with humor, I have included many jokes that circulate on the streets of the Soviet Union. Humor can be a powerful tool. It can be used to relieve boredom, to emphasize absurdities, to humiliate opponents, to hazard political comment and social observation that would be better left unsaid in any other way. The political potential of humor has been long appreciated in Russia. It was, after all, Nikolai Gogol, the famous Russian novelist of the nineteenth century, who wrote, "Laughter is feared even by the man who fears nothing," and the renowned British analyst of twentieth-century totalitarianism, George Orwell, wrote that political jokes are "tiny revolutions."

Above all, I have made every effort to be evenhanded and objective about the subject, to sort through the many myths Westerners hold about the Soviet Union. Partially based on truth, the picture of the Soviet Union commonly held in this country is often overgeneralized and inaccurate. To the extent that it is possible, I have tried to give an accurate picture of Soviet politics, conditions, and motivations. Hence, the positive as well as the negative aspects of the subject are included for the readers' consideration so that they can develop their own attitudes about the Soviet political society.

Note on Transliteration

The Cyrillic alphabet used in the Russian language is quite different from the alphabet used in English. Hence, certain problems are posed in transliteration. Complications are increased because certain Russian words commonly appear in a particular English form that may not be consistent with the system of transliteration one chooses to use. Furthermore, certain people's names are commonly translated into their English equivalent, while other, less well-known people are referred to by their Russian names: Pyotr I is referred to as Peter I or Peter the Great, while Theodore I, a less well-known tsar, is usually referred to as Feodor I.

Although consistency is generally a good idea, absolute consistency in this case would be more confusing than allowing some modification of the chosen transliteration system. Accordingly, I have tried to maintain the following regimen: All names appear in their Russian form except those that are very commonly translated into English: Vasily is used instead of Basil, Feodor instead of Theodore, and Yekaterina instead of Catherine, unless these names are commonly translated into English, as in Catherine the Great.

Secondly, for the English "ee" sound, there are two Russian vowels, commonly translated as *y* or *i*. I have chosen to use the *i*. Yet there are some exceptions. For example, I write of the *Stanovoi* rather than the *Stanovoy* Mountains. But *Dostoevsky, Tolstoy,* and *Vasily* are commonly spelled with a *y* in English, so I have followed that tradition. Similarly, *Bielorussia* is spelled *Byelorussia* in this book because of common English usage.

Plurals present problems of a similar nature. It is not uncommon to see the word *Bolsheviks* spelled with an English plural—*s*—rather than with the Russian plural—*i*—as in *Bolsheviki*. I have again tended toward common usage rather than insisting on absolute consistency, thinking that such a modification will be less confusing for the reader.

Acknowledgments

No project of this scope can be accomplished without the help and support of many people, and one of the greatest pleasures of publishing is that one is permitted to publicly thank the people who have contributed to a book's completion.

To begin with, my most important debt is owed my wife, Elaine, who shares the dedication to this book. Having learned the intricacies of the word processor, she spent untold hours typing and correcting the manuscript. Further, her criticism and suggestions were invaluable. Indeed, her contributions to this work are so enormous as to make her as responsible for its completion as I am. I simply could not have done it without her. Our sons, Pierre and René, also deserve much appreciation for willingly sacrificing so much time with their parents—time that might have been spent in more pleasurable pursuits.

I am also pleased to thank Professor Susan Critchfield, who labored long and hard correcting my sloppy prose, my tortured syntax, and my "creative" spelling. Susan deserves the lion's share of the credit for whatever lucidity this book enjoys.

Speaking of spelling, I am also deeply obliged to Ms. Deborah Wenck, who carefully proofread the numerous Russian terms used. Despite my unintentioned but persistent attempts to frustrate her at the task, Debbie succeeded in reducing the work to a consistent transliteration.

My appreciation also goes to Louis Van Moppes, Helen Van Moppes, and Harriet Norris, whose photographs are featured in several places in the book. Others to whom I am indebted for help with this project are Professors Mohammed G. Rajah, Gail Prentiss, Gloria Floren, Larry Jorgensen, Leland E. Russell, Janet Megill, and Gwendolyn M. Greene. Also Sherry L. Hiltz and Marilyn D. Kimsey deserve mention for their aid in completing the book.

Last, but certainly not least, I want to thank the people of Prentice Hall for their vital help in making this project a reality, especially Karen Horton, Stan Wakefield, the late Walter Welch, Colby Stong of P. M. Gordon Associates, and copy editor Linda B. Pawelchak.

Leon P. Baradat

The Attempted Coup and Its Aftermath

On August 19, 1991, after this book was well into the process of being printed, right-wing elements in the Soviet Union attempted a coup d'etat. Mikhail Gorbachev and his family were held incommunicado, but Gorbachev defiantly refused demands that he resign. Conspirators, including USSR Vice President Gennady I. Yenayev, Interior Minister Boris K. Pugo, KGB chairman Vladimir A. Kryuchkov, Minister of Defense Dmitri T. Yazov, and USSR Premier Valentin S. Pavlov declared a state of national emergency and formed a committee to govern the country. The media, political parties, and government agencies were ordered to obey the new government, or see themselves abolished. Meanwhile, Boris Yeltsin, President of the Russian SFSR, courageously resisted a siege at his Moscow headquarters, and probably thus saved the situation.

As events unfolded, people took to the streets in the major cities to resist the would-be dictators, and many workers answered Yeltsin's call for a general strike. Although orders were given to crush the protests, key officers and military units refused to fire on their compatriots, and some troops even defected to Yeltsin's side. Hence, the coup collapsed, the conspirators were arrested—except for Pugo, who committed suicide—and a new era has arrived.

The hard-liners are being swept from the KGB, MVD, military, and government. Gorbachev has crippled the Communist Party by resigning as General Secretary and expropriating the assets of the Party. All Party activities were suspended by the Supreme Soviet while an investigation is conducted regarding the Party's culpability in the coup. Gorbachev is trying to form a new government and has pledged to accelerate reforms to develop a market economy. Meanwhile, the Union itself seems in jeopardy of collapsing as Estonia, Latvia, the Ukraine, Byelorussia, Moldavia, Kirghizia, and Uzbekistan have joined Lithuania and Georgia in declaring their independence, and other republics also appear on the verge of doing so. An effort to forge a new, less centrally controlled government is being made, but at this point no one can be sure that it will succeed. The hero of the hour, Boris Yeltsin, has gained enough power to challenge Gorbachev's political dominance, but many leaders in the non-Russian republics and in Russia itself are increasingly hesitant about allowing this Russian nationalist to become too powerful.

With people in the streets demanding that the Party, the KGB, the MVD, the military, and the government be drastically purged, the situation is very unstable. Clearly, if the state is to be saved and if deprivation and hunger this winter are to be averted, Gorbachev and Yeltsin—who were rudely reminded by the attempted coup that they are indeed in the same camp—will have to develop a new spirit of cooperation. They have already agreed to succeed one another should one of them be illegally removed again. Yet, Yeltsin has unwisely bullied Gorbachev and humiliated him publicly.

Political chaos looms. Although the right wing has suffered a severe setback, another coup is not beyond the realm of possibility if the social and economic conditions are not improved and if ethnic violence is not quieted. The threat of civil war among rival nationalities is also palpable. If the situation is not improved soon, the cry for strongman government could go up, a militaristic regime could be forcibly imposed, and fascism could be visited upon this beleaguered country.

On a more hopeful note, the coup instilled in many Soviet people, especially the youth, a greater appreciation for their new liberties, and gave them confidence in themselves as a people who need no longer rely upon imperious leadership. A new tradition for democracy in the Soviet Union was born when the liberals prevailed in the tense August confrontation. In these few exciting days, democracy stood bare-handed against Soviet tanks—and democracy won. As a consequence, the country may have changed in a fundamental way. Whatever the case, Soviet political society will never be the same again.

Leon P. Baradat
September 3, 1991

chapter 1

Geography

"Russia is a freak of nature."
Dostoevsky

Although the field of geopolitics is currently out of fashion, few would argue that geography is not an important influence upon a people, its history, and its socioeconomic-political system. Perhaps no better example of this relationship among place, space, people, and posterity can be found than in the Soviet Union. Hence, no study of Soviet political society is complete without at least a glance at Soviet geography.

GENERAL GEOGRAPHIC FEATURES

Topography

Beyond doubt the most striking feature about Soviet geography is its **size.** In a skit in which he referred to a map of "Mother Russia," Tommy Smothers once commented, "Russia is a really big mother!" That, as we shall learn, was an understatement.

Almost from its founding, Russia has been among the largest countries in the world, and its vast expanse has long presented problems to its governments. Today it is better than twice the size of its nearest competitor, occupying over 8.5 million square miles—about one-sixth of the land area of the entire globe. By contrast, the United States comprises only about 3.5 million square miles. Spanning two continents, the Soviet Union is more than two and a half times the size of China, the second largest country in Asia, and it dwarfs France, Europe's second largest country. Moreover, the Soviet Union is bigger than the continents of Antarctica, Australia, Europe, or South America.

Lacking only ten degrees from stretching halfway around the world at its northern latitude, this mammoth nation is served by 11 of the world's 24 time zones. Consequently, as a Soviet family in Kaliningrad begins its day with an 8:00 A.M. breakfast, its counterpart in Uelen on the Bering Strait is preparing to eat dinner.

Another remarkable feature of the Soviet Union is its **flatness.** Virtually the entire interior of the country is a huge, flat surface interrupted only occasionally with formations that barely exceed the description of rolling hills. Indeed, Soviet Europe is but the eastern extension of a great European plain. Beginning at the northern slopes of the Pyrenees Mountains in southwestern France, these lowlands travel north, skirting the Alps and Carpathian Mountains and reaching across Belgium, Holland, and northern Germany, through Poland, and into the Soviet Union. The vast and flat expanse is gently interrupted by the Ural Mountains, which also form the border between Europe and Asia. Beyond the Urals, which in themselves hardly constitute an impediment to travel, lies another enormous flatland, the Great Siberian Plain, which stretches beyond the Ob River to the Yenisei River. This area is probably the largest single level land expanse on the globe. East of the Yenisei the terrain becomes somewhat more dramatic, but the geological uplifts certainly do not deserve the designation of mountains. Finally, only miles before the continent ends at the Sea of Okhotsk, a thin spine of mountains known as the Dzhugdzhur Range ends the otherwise monotonous flow of flatland to the sea.

Mountains make up approximately 20 percent of the entire Soviet land area and are usually found on the periphery of the country. In Europe, there are three important ranges. In the far north, at the top of the Kola Peninsula, is the eastern portion of the Khibin Mountains, which seldom reach heights of more than 3,000 feet. Much more significant are the Carpathians. This crescent-shaped range runs through portions of Rumania, Hungary, and the Ukraine. In fact, it forms the boundary between the latter two states. The Caucasus, a narrow ridge of peaks running basically east and west between the Black and Caspian seas, is the only European range standing totally within the Soviet Union. Although it is a thin range, it rises abruptly from the lowlands and reaches significant heights. Indeed, several summits in the Caucasus exceed the height of Mont Blanc. The Caucasus's loftiest peak, Mount Elbrus, which rises to 18,481 feet, is also Europe's highest point.

Although they do not qualify as a mountain range, the Valdai Hills are a significant highlands in the Soviet Union. Located south and slightly east of Leningrad, these hills barely muster 1,000 feet at the highest point; their average height is closer to 300 feet. Although of inconsequential elevation, these hills have played a crucial role in the geography and history of Russia and the Soviet Union, and due to the heavy rainfall in the area, they are the headwaters of the Western Dvina, Dnieper, and Volga rivers, as well as several lesser waterways.

Soviet Asia is much more mountainous than its European counterpart. Yet, the Soviet Asian highlands also tend to hug the hems of the country. Almost the entire Soviet frontier adjoining the rest of Asia is protected by high mountain ranges that run from the base of the Caspian Sea east, swooping northward at the Mongolian border. These highlands slope toward the north until they disappear in the great flatlands of Siberia, where they form a giant "amphitheater" facing the northwest.

The Elbrus Mountains skirt the southern slope of the Caspian Sea and continue eastward until they join the Kopet Range, thus sealing the Soviet frontier between the Turkmen SSR and Iran. Tadzhikistan and Kirghizia embrace the bulk of the Pamir Range, which is often called the "roof of the world." The Pamirs—where the *yeti* (abominable snowmen) are supposed to stalk—run east and north along the Chinese border until they meet with the majestic Tien Shan Mountains.

Beyond the Dzungarian Gates, a narrow pass leading to China and Lake Ala, another mountain system rises to form the border with Mongolia. The Altai Mountains plunge deep into Mongolia, but their width in the Soviet Union is not great as they quickly give way to the Sayan Mountains, which form the headwaters of the Yenisei River. East of Lake Baikal, the Yablonovy Range protrudes, stretching north and east until it links with the east-running Stanovoi Range. Suddenly, the Stanovoi Mountains meet the Dzhugdzhur Range, which abruptly drives north and then turns northwest, becoming the Verkhoyansk Range, which ends at the mouth of the Lena River on the Arctic Ocean.

Rivers and Canals

Few countries have been favored by such large and numerous rivers. The Soviet Union is served by 190,000 miles of navigable rivers, and recently many of them have been connected by canals, thus increasing their utility. Among the most important Soviet canals are the Baltic-White Sea Canal, the Moscow-Volga Canal, the Don-Volga Canal, and the Ob-Yenisei Canal. These canals, together with an extensive system of rivers, lakes, and dams, have been forged into an integrated system of water transportation that handles a large percentage of Soviet commerce and travel even today. River travel is as old as history in Russia, and today one can see virtually every imaginable water conveyance, from primitive crafts to the most sophisticated hydrofoils. Another canal of note, although it is used for irrigation rather than navigation, is the Kara-Kum Canal. This aqueduct stretches across the desert for 850 miles—the world's longest canal—and carries water from the Amu Darya River to the desert of the Turkmen SSR.

The **rivers** are particularly important historically as they were the arteries for Russian culture and political organization. Indeed, because of the flatness of the Russian terrain and its broad meandering rivers, movement has always been inordinately easy in Russia. Accordingly, during

times of political or economic adversity, masses of people have wandered the land looking for better conditions. Unfortunately, however, such mass migrations tended to contribute to instability, thus encouraging Russian rulers to prohibit free travel of their subjects. As a consequence, the internal passport or its equivalent has been required of the Russian people since the seventeenth century. Perhaps because Russian rivers symbolize a freedom that the people have never been allowed to enjoy, they have been the focus of many nostalgic stories and songs, making some of their names among the best-known features of Soviet geography in the West.

In Soviet Europe, the rivers flow basically north or south, thus facilitating travel in those directions. Beginning in southeastern Soviet Europe, the Ural River rises from the Ural Mountains and flows west until it bends to the south and empties into the Caspian Sea. Only a few miles to the west is the mouth of the mighty Volga River, "the mother of Russia." Europe's longest river, this great watercourse begins in the Valdai Hills north of Moscow and flows southeast, then turns south, and empties into the Caspian Sea. The river flows for 2,300 miles and spreads out to a width of 25 miles in some places. It is fed by a number of major tributaries, the most important of which is the Oka River, which lies south of Moscow and flows basically west to east. The Volga drains about 590,000 square miles, making its basin larger than any Soviet republic except Russia and Kazakhstan. Of all Soviet rivers, the Volga carries the greatest volume of traffic and commerce. Its importance to society is attested to by the affectionate place it holds in Russian song and literature.

Coming very close to the Volga at one point, then turning abruptly southwest and meeting the Sea of Azov, is the Don River. The Don has its headwaters south of Moscow in the same general area as the Oka. It flows southeast to within only a few miles of the Volga. It is at this point that the two rivers are joined by a canal. At about the same point the river changes course, bearing southwest; it is then joined by the Donets River, its major tributary.

On the opposite side of the Crimea peninsula is the mouth of the Dnieper River, the second most important river in the country. The Dnieper shares the same point of origin as the Volga. Rivaling the Volga for the title "mother of Russia," this river spawned the first modern Russian state. It was on the lower reaches of the Volga, Don, and Dnieper rivers that the Cossack tribes organized in defiance of the major powers surrounding them during the fifteenth, sixteenth, and seventeenth centuries. Also flowing into the northern end of the Black Sea are the Dniester and the Prut rivers—the latter becoming the border between the Moldavian SSR and Rumania.

In the north there is another significant, if somewhat less important, group of rivers. There are two Dvina rivers: The Western Dvina empties into the Gulf of Riga, and the Northern Dvina flows to the White Sea, meeting it at Archangel. Situated between these two watercourses is the Neva River, which flows from Lake Ladoga, through Leningrad, to the Gulf of Finland. Although this river carries a substantial amount of com-

A young boy baits his hook as he prepares to fish in Kiev on the banks of the Dnieper River. (Photo provided by Louis and Helen Van Moppes.)

merce and flows through the second largest Soviet city, it is far more notable for historical reasons. In the eleventh century, the Neva was the site of a great battle in which the forces of the city of Novgorod, led by Alexander Nevsky, Russia's greatest military hero, defeated the attacking Swedes, thus saving the Orthodox believers from the Catholic invaders, in 1240.

Most of the rivers in Soviet Asia follow a northerly course. Just beyond the Urals flow the mighty Ob and its great tributary, the Irtysh. The Ob springs from the watershed of the Altai Mountains and runs the entire length of Western Siberia, draining a huge area. Making its way northwest until it is met by the Irtysh, which also begins in the Altai, the Ob then bears north and empties into the Gulf of Ob, a huge inlet from the Arctic Ocean. In all, the Ob travels some 2,500 miles, 200 miles farther than the Volga.

To the east of the Ob lies the Yenisei. Originating in the Sayan Mountains, the Yenisei makes its way north to the Arctic, draining over one million square miles of territory and traveling 2,365 miles. The Ob-Yenisei Canal joins the two giant rivers at their closest point on the floor of the Great Siberian Plain.

The north-flowing Ob and Yenisei present a serious problem to transportation on the Great Siberian Plain. At the outset of winter, the rivers freeze at the mouth first. The waters, running downhill from their origins in the mountains bordering Mongolia and China, continue to flow long after the outlet to the sea has turned into an impenetrable barrier of ice. The water begins to back up, quickly covering the almost level Great Siberian Plain with a shallow layer of water that penetrates the thawed topsoil, creating an enormous quagmire virtually halting all land travel in the area. As winter progresses, the entire region becomes frozen, and travel across the hard surface again becomes feasible.

With spring comes another thaw, however, and the whole process takes place in reverse. The thaw occurs at the headwaters first, while the mouths remain frozen. The water again fills the enormous flatland between the Urals and the Yenisei, creating yet another impenetrable swamp. The same phenomenon takes place among the north-flowing rivers of the arctic region to the west of the Urals, but the scale of the western swamps is considerably smaller than in the east. Even when the arctic surface thaws, however, the subsoil, but a few inches from the top, remains solidly frozen. This permanently frozen soil, called **permafrost,** can reach a depth of 1,000 feet and poses obvious problems to farming, drilling, and mining.

The third great Siberian river that empties into the Arctic is the Lena. The longest of all Soviet rivers, it became an apt basis for the revolutionary name adopted by Vladimir Ulyanov (Lenin) while he was in exile in Siberia. Coming to life behind a small ridge of mountains west of Lake Baikal, the Lena flows northeast until it is turned to the northwest by the spiny Verkhoyansk Mountains. Flowing through the city of Yakutsk, the Lena follows the contour of the Verkhoyansks until it fans into a huge delta before entering the Arctic. This immense river runs a course of almost 3,000 miles, expands to a width of 20 miles in some places, and drains a land area of 1,169,000 square miles, which is almost as great as that of the Mississippi River. Its water flow has created several natural curiosities, including the largest arctic delta and a 25-mile-long Russian "grand canyon," with walls vaulting as high as 2,000 feet above the river.

South of the upper Lena is the Amur River. Beginning at the junction of the Shilka and Argun rivers, the Amur flows basically westward to form part of the border between China and the USSR. At the western slopes of the Sikhote-Alin Range, the Amur is joined by the north-flowing Ussuri. From that point, the Amur turns north and flows into the Strait of Tatar, which is located between the Soviet mainland and Sakhalin Island. The Amur and the Ussuri, which also separates China from the Soviet Union, were the sites of the territorial conflicts between the two giant states during the 1960s and 1970s.[1]

Central Asia, composed of Kazakhstan, Uzbekistan, Kirghizia, Tadzhikistan, and Turkmenistan, is also in the Soviet Union. The three lifelines of Central Asia are the Chu, the Syr Darya, and the Amu Darya (or Oxus) rivers. Each of these rivers flows northwest from the Tien Shan Mountains. The Chu River eventually disappears into the sands of the Muyun Kum, a desolate desert. The Syr Darya and the Amu Darya, flanked by deserts, provide thin greenbelts along their course to the Aral Sea. Much of this water, however, is being siphoned off to irrigate the cotton fields of Central Asia.

[1]Alvin Z. Rubinstein, *Soviet Foreign Policy Since World War II* (Cambridge, MA: Winthrop, 1981), p. 127.

Lakes

The Soviet Union boasts the world's oldest, largest, and deepest lakes. Indeed, when the volume of all its rivers and freshwater lakes is combined, the Soviet Union is estimated to possess about one-quarter of the world's fresh water. In the northwest the most important lakes are Onega, Ladoga (Europe's largest lake), and Peipus. These lakes, of historical as well as commercial importance, are close to the Gulf of Finland. South of the Ukraine, the Sea of Azov opens into the Black Sea, which, in turn, leads through the Bosporus and the Hellespont to the Aegean Sea.

The Caspian Sea separates Soviet Europe and Asia in the south. This, the home of the famous Russian sturgeon caviar, is the largest lake on earth. Covering some 170,000 square miles, the Caspian is a shallow body lined with oil fields. Owing to the consumption of water on the upper Volga River, the water level of the Caspian is dropping at an alarming rate. East of the Caspian, the Aral Sea is depleting even more rapidly. In fact, it has become an ecological disaster of unparalleled proportions. Once larger than any of the American lakes except Lake Superior, the Aral Sea has shrunk dramatically because the Syr Darya and Amu Darya rivers, which replenished it, were diverted to irrigate the desert. Since the 1960s, the Aral has lost 40 percent of its almost 11,000 square miles. Never before has such a large body of water disappeared within a single generation.

Once abundant with fish, the vanishing lake is now too saline to support life, and former fishing villages find themselves 20 miles from shore, their boats stranded on salt-encrusted sands. The lake's disappearance has had an egregious effect on the 35 million people in the surrounding area. The summers have become hotter and the winters colder, as the shrinking lake exercises a less temperate influence on the area's climate. An estimated 43 million tons of salty lake bed sand is annually blown by the winds to distant parts of the Soviet Union. Traces of it have been detected as far away as the arctic coast. People in the vicinity of the lake suffer as their eyes and mouths are assaulted by the salty grit. High rates of throat cancer and infant mortality in northeast Uzbekistan (the highest in the country) are attributed to the effects of the sand-fouled air. In 1984 it was decided to divert water from the Ob River to replenish the lake, but the plan was later scrapped due to complaints by Russian nationalists and to ecological concerns.[2]

East of the Aral Sea are two major lakes: Issyk, a huge lake in the Tien Shan Range above Alma-Ata, and Balkhash, a long shallow lake north of Alma-Ata. Further east still is one of the world's great natural wonders. Lake Baikal is the world's oldest and deepest lake. Sprawling over an area of 12,150 square miles, it is larger than the entire country of Belgium. Fed by 330 rivers and streams, it is drained by only one river, the mighty Angara. With a known depth of 5,400 feet, Lake Baikal holds more water than all of the Great Lakes combined and is the largest freshwater reservoir

[2]Vladimir Bukovsky, "The Political Condition of the Soviet Union," in *The Future of the Soviet Empire*, ed. Henry S. Rowen and Charles Wolf, Jr. (New York: St. Martins Press, 1987), p. 36.

on the globe, containing about one-fifth of the world's supply. A lovely body of water, it was saved from industrial pollution by the efforts of scientists and ordinary citizens whose protests kept its waters from becoming a dump for industrial waste.

Ports

Historically, Russia has been landlocked, being denied access to the great oceans by frozen waters or by alien governments dominating the exits from interior seas. Today, however, the Soviet Union owns one of the world's largest fleets and has established a permanent presence on the high seas.

Bordering on the Baltic, Arctic, and Pacific oceans, the Soviet Union boasts the longest coastline in the world, almost 25,000 miles. Its major ports at Riga, Tallinn, Kaliningrad, and Leningrad on the Baltic are ice-free seven to nine months of the year. On the Barents Sea, the northernmost major port in the world, Murmansk, enjoys open water during most of the year because of the warm current of the Gulf Stream. Archangel, on the White Sea, though considerably farther south than Murmansk, is not so favored and remains frozen for several months of the year. At the other end of the country, Vladivostok rests on the Sea of Japan; ice-free for nine months of the year, the port is kept open in winter by ice-breakers. The major commercial centers of Odessa, Poti, Batumi, Sukhumi, Novorossisk, and Sevastopol on the Black Sea also remain ice-free year-round.[3]

Climate

The Soviet Union is a land of violent climatic contrasts caused by its unique geographical setting. To begin with, it is a nordic country. Eighty-four percent of the country lies in the north temperate zone, while the remainder is north of the Arctic Circle. The bulk of the country occupies the same latitudes as Canada, Alaska, and Scandinavia. The continental United States lies between 20° and 49° N lat., whereas the continental Soviet Union occupies a space between 36° and 78° N lat. The most southerly part of the Soviet Union shares approximately the same latitude with Norfolk, Virginia; Joplin, Missouri; and Fresno, California. Ashkhabad, the capital of the Turkmen SSR, is no further south than Sacramento, California, or Topeka, Kansas. Vladivostok is about even with Chicago, Illinois; Odessa with Bismarck, North Dakota; Kiev with Vancouver, British Columbia; and Moscow with Goose Bay, Labrador. Leningrad, the nation's second largest city, is only a degree or so south of Anchorage, Alaska, and Murmansk, at 69° N lat., has no commercial equivalent anywhere at its latitude.

Clearly, the Soviet Union's northern location is apt to cause its winters to be very cold. Other important geographical features compound the problem, however. Because it is situated inland from the warm ocean cur-

[3]John S. Reshetar, Jr., *The Soviet Polity*, 2nd ed. (New York: Harper & Row, 1978), p. 26.

rents, the Soviet Union is assured a continental climate. Although some warm air does reach Soviet Europe, the highlands of Scandinavia and the land's expanse prevent much of it from reaching the interior. At the same time, the absence of mountains in the Soviet Arctic means that the violent arctic winds continue unabated from their point of origin south to the Black Sea, the Caspian Sea, and the Tien Shan Range.

Since a little warm air from Western Europe manages to reach European Russia, the western part of the country tends to be warmer than Siberia. Yet, because the arctic winds are not arrested anywhere in the country, Odessa is only a little warmer than Leningrad during the winter, and Irkutsk, near Lake Baikal, suffers a winter only slightly less severe than towns in north-central Siberia. In other words, the climate is about the same from north to south, but it grows increasingly colder the farther east one travels.

Winters are long in the Soviet Union, stretching from October to April or even May. Siberians boast that their winter lasts for 12 months, but that the rest of the year is summer. Although some places in the United States, Canada, and Scandinavia suffer temperatures as low as those in the Soviet Union, the Russian winter is thought most severe because it lasts so long and is seldom interrupted by warm periods. Spring is usually very brief, and, for the same reasons that the winters are so cold, the summers tend to be quite hot. The highest temperatures are recorded in Central Asia. It is not unusual to find the thermometer reaching 105°F in Turkmenistan, and temperatures as high as 120°F are not unknown. Yet, there is a surprisingly narrow variation in temperature from north to south. In the summer the lower regions of the Arctic, which only a few short months before were frozen between −80° and −90°F, often report highs in July and August of 90° to 100°F.

The extremes of temperature are duplicated by extremes in rainfall. Most of the Soviet Union receives less than 16 inches of rain per year. Under ordinary circumstances, the volume might be enough to sustain a viable agricultural industry, but Soviet precipitation tends to be erratic. Large areas can go for months with little or no rain. Then, in the spring, sheets of precipitation fall, ending in little percolation, much runoff, and serious soil erosion. Hence, Soviet irrigation projects are seen as a vital feature for agriculture in much of the country. If the rains come at the wrong time, entire fields can be beaten down by a heavy downpour, or, on the other hand, crops can wither and die for lack of water. If the snowfall is too heavy or too light, too early or too late, the vital crop of winter wheat can be ruined. Indeed, few countries are subject to such precarious weather conditions as those experienced in the Soviet Union. These conditions play havoc with the foundation of the Soviet economy—its agriculture.

Resources and the Environment

Perhaps no other country enjoys the bounty of natural resources as does the Soviet Union. A major producer of virtually every mineral, it is more self-sufficient in raw materials than any other industrialized nation, and it is a major exporter of vast quantities of precious commodities upon which other nations are dependent. Yet, since only about 75 percent of its territory has been geologically explored, the true extent of its wealth in resources is not known.

The Soviet Union has the largest stands of timber in the world. Its forests produce enormous quantities of lumber and wood by-products. The Soviets are almost equally rich in metallurgical minerals. The USSR has the largest iron deposits on earth, and it exceeds all others in the production of manganese. Additionally, it is a noted producer of nickel, aluminum, chromium, lead, mercury, mica, and tin. Although the Soviets guard exact production figures as state secrets, they are known to produce large amounts of gold, silver, and diamonds. The country also turns out substantial quantities of copper, graphite, phosphorite, potassium, salt, sulfur, sodium sulfate, and zinc.

Virtually every section of the country produces important resources. The least productive, as one might well imagine, are the arctic region and the deserts of Central Asia. Yet, Siberia is a veritable treasure chest of precious material, containing about 25 percent of the world's known mineral resources. The engineering problems of extracting Siberian resources are understandably complex: Wrenching resources from the permafrost is an extremely expensive endeavor.

Rich in energy, the Soviet Union has some of the world's largest hydroelectric plants (Siberia produces more electricity than it can use). Having even greater potential for hydroelectric power, the Soviet Union has vast quantities of energy-producing minerals. It is the world's largest producer of oil, and it has 40 percent of all known reserves of natural gas, with major fields along the Caspian Sea; in the Caucasus Range; in the Ukraine, between the Volga River and the Ural Mountains; and in Siberia.[4] Its coal reserves are the world's largest, comprising 30 percent of the world's known supply. At the current rate of use, these coal reserves will last for 200 years. Enormous deposits are located in the Ukraine, along the southern Volga, in the Caucasus, and in Central Asia. In Siberia major coal deposits are concentrated just east of the Urals, near Irkutsk, between the Yenisei and Lena rivers, and in the eastern Yakutsk region. The Pripet Marshes in Byelorussia and the bogs of Estonia have abundant supplies of peat, and an ample quantity of uranium is produced in Tadzhikistan.

Enjoying a ready source of uranium, Soviet planners embarked on a massive increase in nuclear power–generated electricity. Currently, about 12.7 percent of all electricity used in the Soviet Union is produced in nuclear power plants. The accident at Chernobyl in April 1986 stymied Soviet plans to double the amount of nuclear power–generated electricity by the year 2000. Although the government continues to claim that only 31

[4]It should be noted that as oil fields in Soviet Europe become exhausted, reliance on Siberian sources becomes heavier. The remoteness and extreme weather conditions of Siberia make exploitation of its rich oil deposits extremely costly. Reliance on these fields forces the Soviet Union to become more heavily dependent on Western technology, since many of the machines and equipment necessary for Siberian exploration and drilling are not produced in the Soviet Union.

Damage to the reactor and surrounding buildings at the Chernobyl nuclear power station can be seen at center. (AP/Wide World Photos)

people were killed when a Chernobyl RBMK reactor partially melted down, members of the Soviet parliament and some Soviet news sources claim that the immediate death toll reached 250 to 300 persons, and Dr. Robert Gail of UCLA, who is helping the Soviets deal with the disaster, estimates that between 5,000 and 150,000 cancer cases worldwide will result from the accident. Some Ukrainian political authorities claim that the death toll has already reached 10,000.[5]

It is estimated that perhaps 1.5 million people, including 160,000 children, received large doses of radiation from the accident. Scores of thousands have been evacuated from the most contaminated areas, creating a severe housing problem, while millions of others are forced to remain in areas less seriously contaminated. The incidence of leukemia has doubled in some places, and in March 1990 51 children were sent to Israel for treatment for radiation poisoning. Authorities estimate that the cleanup and relocation efforts may cost a total of $415 billion, and Byelorussia has appealed to the United Nations for aid. The government has evacuated people from 580 square miles in the Ukraine and Byelorussia, abandoning the area to the stray dogs, pigs, and poultry left behind. Scientists who study development in these areas have found mutations in animals and plants they believe attributable to the radiation, including usual-sized pine needles that are 10 times heavier than normal.

[5]"Chernobyl Fatality Toll Being Compiled," *The Los Angeles Times,* March 19, 1991.

The national government's reaction to the Chernobyl disaster was far from exemplary. It failed to publicize the accident for several days after it happened; its evacuation of people was inexplicably slow, causing needless exposure to dangerous doses of radiation; and it delayed for three years in warning the people of the true risks—all that time these people consumed contaminated food and water. At the same time, it continued to operate two reactors at the Chernobyl site and planned to construct others until forbidden by a recently assertive Ukrainian Supreme Soviet. Meanwhile, 16 of the Soviet Union's remaining nuclear reactors are of the same design (BRMK) as the Chernobyl plant. Although the Soviets continue to use them, claiming that the energy they produce is essential to the country's economic reforms, Western experts warn that their continued use threatens another nuclear power plant disaster.[6] Indeed, the core at Chernobyl is still active, and the concrete sarcophagus in which it has been entombed cannot be expected to remain leak-proof for much longer.[7]

Public reaction to the government's irresponsible policies continued to build until finally "radiophobia" reached near hysterical proportions. Mass protests across the country have prevented nuclear-powered commercial vessels from docking at Soviet seaports; several reactors and reactor construction sites have been closed; and plans to build several new reactors have been scrapped—including the projected expansion at Chernobyl. In 1990 the Ukrainian parliament ordered that the remaining active reactors there be shut down within five years. On the other hand, a Ukrainian tourist agency, Kievturist, is now conducting tours of the Chernobyl area, including the concrete entombed reactor where the accident occurred.[8] Whether or not public resolve will remain high enough to continue to check a government that has traditionally exhibited a cavalier attitude toward the safety of its nuclear power plants is impossible to know. One thing is clear, however: Chernobyl, besides being an environmental calamity, was a political disaster destroying much of the public's confidence in the government.[9]

The debacle at Chernobyl gave important impetus to the Soviet people's growing concerns about the environment. One might think that an economy and a society so centrally controlled would be able to maximize the use of resources and minimize the adverse effects on the environment, but unfortunately this is not the case. As in the United States and other industrial countries, the air and water have been fouled with industrial pollution until fish and caviar are dangerous to eat and over 100 Soviet cities have 10 times more air pollution than is considered safe; Soviet rivers dump 20 times the pollution into the Baltic Sea as the Rhine River delivers to the North Sea. Soil erosion has destroyed about 243,180 square miles of land, about 400 square miles are destroyed annually by strip mining, and

[6]Randy Abramson, "Chernobyl 'Replay' Seen as Likely," *The Los Angeles Times*, April 25, 1991.

[7]Michael Parks, "Chernobyl," *The Los Angeles Times*, March 23, 1990.

[8]"Chernobyl a Hot Tourist Attraction," *The Los Angeles Times*, Feb. 4, 1991.

[9]See Zhores Medvedev, *The Legacy of Chernobyl* (New York: W. W. Norton, 1990).

Soviet forests are rapidly deteriorating because of acid rain and air pollution.[10]

In response to public outrage at the rape of Soviet resources and official disregard for the environment, the government has taken several remedial steps. It created the Environmental Protection Committee to police ministries and enterprises, and it has backed away from several projects including offshore oil drilling in the Baltic, construction of an early warning radar system in the Ukraine, and construction of a chemical weapons destruction plant on the Volga River. It has even been forced to slow the progress of several joint ventures with the West because of protests by environmentalists, and the Soviet press announced in 1991 that the Committee for State Security (KGB) has been charged with helping to restore the environment and with combating "ecological crime." Even though these and other steps are certainly not enough to reverse the environmental deterioration of the Soviet Union, they are a beginning. How successful they and other efforts will be remains to be seen. The economic need for vast improvement in Soviet agricultural and industrial production, however, does not bode well for the environment.

GEOGRAPHICAL DIVISIONS

Because of its varied and enormous proportions, Soviet geography can perhaps be best appreciated if it is described on three different bases: continental, vegetational, and political.

Continental Divisions

Culturally, the Soviet Union has three distinct parts: the European Soviet Union, Central Asia, and Siberia. The western part of the country is in Europe. In fact, the **European Soviet Union** totals about 42 percent of the continent and serves as the base connecting the European peninsula to the Asian land mass.

Separated from Asia by the Urals, a narrow rounded spine of mountains, the European sector of the country enjoys many important advantages. About 75 percent of the Soviet population resides in this area, and it is home to the heaviest concentration of industry and economic bounty in the country. Though much smaller than Siberia, Soviet Europe not only includes the greatest diversity of people and cultures but also is the location of two-thirds of the union republics—the major geopolitical divisions in the country.

Central Asia is the second principal continental division. Straddling the ancient trade route between China and the West, Central Asia is largely desert, interrupted abruptly by high mountains in the southeast. Lying north and east of the Caspian Sea, this portion of the Soviet Union stretches from the lower Volga to the Ob River in the east. The northern

[10]Bukovsky, pp. 35, 36.

border of Central Asia extends almost to Omsk, and the southern boundary reaches the southernmost point of the Soviet Union, the frontier of Afghanistan.

Although still backward when compared to the European part of the USSR, Central Asia has made important strides since the Bolshevik Revolution and boasts many modern advances, including an extensive irrigation and canal system, which has made the desert bloom and the city of Tashkent a showcase for Soviet architecture. Its predominantly Muslim populations enjoy a distinguished history and a rich cultural heritage. Its ancient buildings and the traditional costumes still worn by many of its inhabitants create an atmosphere more similar to the Middle East than to what is normally thought of as the Soviet Union.

The third and largest area in the Soviet Union is **Siberia.** Except for Central Asia, Siberia constitutes all of the Soviet Union east of the Ural Mountains. Siberia in the Buryat language means "sleeping land," but Maxim Gorky, remembering its sad history, called it "the land of death and chains." Today, however, Soviet workers call it "the land of the long ruble" because of the bonuses they receive to work there.

Incredibly vast, Siberia spans seven time zones and is larger than Soviet Europe and Central Asia combined. It is even larger than the lighted surface of the moon. When Siberia is combined with the area of Central Asia, Soviet Asia comprises about 43 percent of the entire continent. Yet, unlike Central Asia, Siberia does not resemble Asia. Rather, covered with evergreen trees and blanketed with snow for much of the year, Siberia looks much more like Alaska or western Canada, and its vast treasure of natural resources enhances the comparison.

Uzbek men haggle over prices in a Samarkand market. (Photo provided by Louis and Helen Van Moppes.)

Siberia's rigorous climate and remote location assured its isolation from Russia until the sixteenth century. Protected by the elements, Siberia's few Turkic inhabitants remained free of tsarist control until the allure of animal pelts drew Russian trappers and explorers eastward. Since the sixteenth century, however, Siberia has posed a compelling challenge to the Russians; even today it is seen as a huge frontier to be tamed and reduced to the service of the Soviet people.

Although vast, Siberia accounts for only about 11 percent of the Soviet population. Life here is very hard, and workers are paid as much as three times the ordinary wage to brave its elements. Winter lasts for nine and one-half months, and the cold is legendary. The village of Ust Nera in Central Yakutia is the coldest regularly inhabited place on earth. In 1959 it recorded a temperature of −94°F. In this deeply frozen land, milk is sold in unwrapped frozen blocks, rivers freeze to depths of 20 feet, spit turns to ice before it hits the ground, moisture from breath freezes and cracks in the air, combining with vehicle exhaust to form a haze called "ice fog." Solid steel can crack like a match stick, truck tires explode, and children blow bubbles from spittle to throw at each other.

Construction is very difficult in Siberia. Roads disappear beneath the surface during the short spring and summer thaw. Portions of the trans-Siberian rail lines have sunk, forcing reconstruction of whole sections. Log cabins slip into the melted ooze until the windows are at ground level. Modern buildings are constructed on 40-foot piles, which are seated in ground melted by steam blasts. The "ground floors" are build four feet above the surface to prevent the building's heat from melting the surface, thus causing the building to sink. Walls are double insulated, and each window is shielded by three thick panes. It costs about three times as much to build a structure in Siberia as it does in Europe.

Travel is difficult and often impossible except during the summer. Virtually without permanent roads, Siberia travelers use trains, aircraft, sleds, and boats, depending on the season. Siberia is far from self-sufficient: As much as 80 percent of all food and manufactured goods must be imported by the people extracting the region's gold, diamonds, coal, and oil.

Spring vanquishes the cold, but its thaw creates thousands of square miles of swamp on the Great Siberian Plain. Taking advantage of the momentary warmth, insects breed quickly, infesting the groundwater and blackening the sky. In the oil-rich Tyumen region of west-central Siberia, winter's departure leaves 80 percent of the oil fields blanketed with stagnant water, in which 111 pounds of mosquitoes are estimated to inhabit each acre.

As summer ends and autumn rains subside, the approaching winter freezes the surface first. The weight of the ice at the surface bears down on the soggy turf below and squeezes out the water, which runs in sheets along the surface. This creates a treacherous condition: The surface is frozen, but between the surface and the permafrost is a deep layer of ooze. Heavy equipment working on the surface can break through, sinking in the mud and endangering drivers. Some vehicles are equipped with ejection seats to hurl drivers free of their sinking vehicles. Finally, even the ooze is frozen by winter's cold, and the cycle begins all over again.

Vegetational Divisions

A second perspective by which to study Soviet geography is to focus on the remarkable variety of vegetation. Basically, this immense country is girdled by five great belts of vegetation running generally east and west on a transcontinental course: the tundra, taiga, steppe, desert, and Mediterranean zones.

The **tundra** is found in the far north and completely traverses Siberia. It begins on the northern reaches of the Kola Peninsula and stretches beyond the Urals. Occupying approximately 15 percent of all Soviet land area, this arctic region spans the entire distance between the White Sea and the Pacific Ocean.

"Tundra" is a versatile term, used sometimes to describe the vegetation found in the arctic and sometimes to signify the northern latitudes of Canada, Scandinavia, and the Soviet Union. The word "tundra," which comes from the Finnish language, roughly means "barren land."

During the long winter months the entire tundra is frozen; the thick blanket of snow yields to the land only briefly from June to August. The northernmost latitudes are certainly deserving of their Finnish name, being void of vegetation except for moss and lichens, which cling precariously to soil found in the cracks of rocks or among the gravel. But in the southern reaches of the tundra the summer months reveal grasses, scrub brush, cranberries, heather, and a profusion of gaily colored wildflowers, as well as an occasional stunted black spruce, birch, fir, or willow trees. The permafrost substrata, which underlies the entire tundra, prevents the development of a root structure necessary to support plants of any substantial height. Shallow-root trees, which might otherwise survive the surface frost, are discouraged by the gale-force winds that sweep from the north across to the flat terrain.

The tundra is incapable of sustaining many large animals. It is sparsely populated with Laplanders, Samoyeds, and Yakuts, who herd reindeer into this inhospitable region to feed on its scarce foliage. Besides humans and reindeer, some polar bear and a few herds of musk ox and caribou eke out their survival at this latitude. In the summer months, the tundra attracts a wide variety of birds, including ducks, geese, plovers, buntings, longspurs, and pipits.

To the south, the tundra gradually gives way to a huge forest land called the **taiga.** About one-fifth of the world's timber is found in the Soviet Union; this startling statistic gives pause until one surveys the size of the taiga. The only vegetation zone spanning the entire country, this belt of woodlands sweeps across Soviet Europe from the Baltic and the Polish border, across the Urals, and through Siberia to the Pacific. At the Yenisei River basin—virtually the center of the country—the "green sea," as the natives call it, widens to embrace the entire area of Siberia except for the tundra in the far north.

The **northern taiga** is composed of mostly softwood trees, including pine, spruce, fir, larch, and cedar. These lands rest largely on permafrost, and the forests are dense and dark, with soil too poor in nutrients to allow

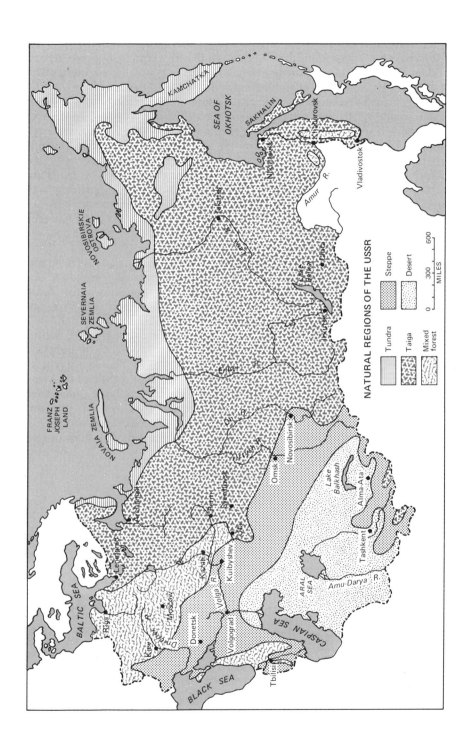

NATURAL REGIONS OF THE USSR

Steppe

Desert

Tundra

Taiga

Mixed forest

MILES

0   300   600

SEA OF OKHOTSK

KAMCHATKA

SAKHALIN

Khabarovsk

Nikolaevs

Amur R.

Vladivostok

Iakutsk

Chita

Lake Baikal

IRKUTSK

Enisei R.

NOVOSIBIRSKIE OSTROVA

SEVERNAIA ZEMLIA

Ob R.

Irtish R.

Novosibirsk

Omsk

Lake Balkhash

Alma-Ata

FRANZ JOSEPH LAND

NOVAIA ZEMLIA

Sverdlovsk

Perm

Tashkent

Arkhangel

ARAL SEA

Amu-Darya R.

Leningrad

Volga R.

Kuibyshev

Kazan

Moscow

BALTIC SEA

Riga

Dnieper R.

Kiev

Donetsk

Volgograd

CASPIAN SEA

Tbilisi

BLACK SEA

19

much farming. Although the taiga sustains more people than the tundra, it is still extremely sparse in human habitation and is commonly considered a wilderness. Rich in fur-bearing animals, the area is host to trappers pursuing the region's bear, wolf, sable, squirrel, fox, ermine, and lynx.

The **southern taiga** is sometimes described as a mixed forest. Considerably smaller than the northern taiga, it consists of two parts. In the west, it occupies a triangular space, with the base stretching from the western Baltic coast to the Soviet-Polish frontier and the apex reaching the southern part of the Ural Mountains. This area, which is as large as France, includes the city of Moscow as well as the Pripet Marshes on the Polish border. A smaller area is found in the far east, basically conforming to the Amur and Ussuri river basins. The southern taiga enjoys sparser stands of the coniferous trees that are so abundant in the north, but a large variety of deciduous trees fill in the spaces. These forests include groves of oak, elm, ash, birch, and alder.

Besides being hospitable to a larger variety of trees, the southern taiga is also well suited for farming, for which vast stands of trees have been cleared. Its climate and rich soil provide suitable conditions for raising winter wheat, rye, and flax. Together, the northern and southern taiga comprise more than half of the entire Soviet land area.

Southwest of the forest lands lies the famous **steppe.** In stark contrast to its northern neighbor, the steppe is virtually treeless. Covering about 14 percent of the Soviet territory, the steppe begins in the vicinity of the Dnieper River and includes most of the Ukraine. Beyond the Sea of Azov, it spreads to the south, coming to rest at the Caucasus. Reaching almost to the shores of the Caspian Sea, the steppe sweeps north, crossing the lower reaches of the Ural Mountains and fanning out to straddle the frontier between Central Asia and Siberia until it ends against the Altai Mountains.

The taiga in a Latvian forest.

The arid climate in summer and the sweeping winds in winter prevent trees from taking root naturally. Instead, the essentially flat steppe was covered each spring with tall grasses that became parched and dried out during summer and were blanketed with snow in winter. Today, however, the massive grasslands have been conquered by the plow. With virtually all of the steppe now under cultivation, it represents a vital resource for the Soviet Union, accounting for about two-thirds of all the arable land in the country. The soil quality and climate are not uniform throughout the steppe, but clearly it is the most important food-producing area in the country. In the east the arid climate and sandy soil necessitate extensive irrigation to sustain production. But to the west, especially in the Ukraine, the steppe is blessed with a rich black soil and adequate rainfall, making the area so fertile that it was once called the breadbasket of Europe. Besides winter wheat, the steppe produces the bulk of the country's sugar beets, hay, sunflowers, and potatoes. Cotton and rice are also becoming important to the area.

Gradually the fertile steppe grows increasingly arid until it becomes the Soviet **deserts.** Beginning with a thin strip on the western shores of the Caspian Sea and then reaching across its northern edge, a huge expanse of semidesert lies beyond the Aral Sea and Lake Balkhash, finally ending on the slopes of the Pamir Mountains. This region comprises almost 20 percent of Soviet territory and includes almost all of Central Asia.

Between the Caspian Sea and the Sea of Aral lies a semidesert usually referred to as the Ust Urt Plateau. Although marked by scanty rainfall and poor soil, the plateau bears irregular amounts of grass and shrubs capable of sustaining a hardy breed of sheep native to the area. South of these uplands are three deserts: the Kara-Kum, between the Caspian Sea and the Amu Darya River; the Kyzyl-Kum, between the Amu Darya and the Syr Darya rivers; and the Muyun-Kum, between the Syr Darya and Lake Balkhash. Nature has denied enough water to these forbidding sand deserts to sustain more than the numerous snakes, lizards, rodents, and scorpions that populate the area. Yet, ambitious irrigation projects have made large tracts of former wasteland productive. This is especially true of the Kara-Kum, which now has large farms producing grapes, melons, fruits, and—especially—cotton. The Soviet Union is one of the world's largest producers of cotton, and the irrigated deserts of Central Asia account for over two-thirds of the crop. Yet, the desert area remains largely untamed. Small tribes of nomads still wander it in search of water and grass for their sheep, much as their ancestors did in past millennia.

Tucked away in the southwestern corner of the Soviet Union is its fifth vegetational region. Tiny by comparison with the other four regions, the **Mediterranean zone** (roughly conforming to the mixed forest area to the north and east of the Black Sea depicted on the map on page 19) is nonetheless an important part of this huge country. The Mediterranean region hugs the coast of the Black Sea. Its northern extremity is located on the southern portion of the Crimea peninsula, and the region then generally follows the crescent contour of the eastern shore of the Black Sea. Enjoying a relatively temperate climate, this area is the vacationland for Soviet citizens who are fortunate enough to journey there. Proximity to the

Soviet citizens enjoy the Black Sea beach at Sochi.

Black Sea and its latitude combine to create a humid, subtropical atmosphere that is much sought after by the sunstarved people of the north.

These same pleasant conditions give the Soviet people access to domestically produced exotic foods, such as olives, oranges, lemons, grapes,
nuts, apricots, and peaches. The pleasant spa-studded area along the Black
Sea is interrupted by the Caucasus, which lift from the lowlands to form a
spiny ridge connecting the Black and Caspian seas. Even though the elevation of these lovely and rugged mountains acts to lower the temperature of
the region somewhat, it enjoys a modified Mediterranean climate and is
thus covered with a lush blanket of trees and foliage.

Political Divisions

The historical circumstances that led to the creation of the Soviet
Union are discussed in a later chapter, and will not be explained in great
detail here. Today the Soviet Union is divided into 15 separate union
republics.[11] Each of the 15 union republics is designed to incorporate the

---

[11]Between 1940 and 1956 there were 16 union republics. The Karelo-Finnish SSR
stretched from Lake Ladoga north along the Finnish border to the Komi Peninsula. Its
southern border ran on a line between Lake Ladoga to Lake Onega, and its eastern frontier
followed the Onega River to the White Sea. In 1956 the Karelo-Finnish SSR was abruptly
reduced in status, being made the Karelia Autonomous Soviet Socialist Republic. The reasons
given for this change suggested that the area had been unable to establish an economic base
sufficient to sustain an independent political unit. Separatist stirrings among the area's Finnish
population have also been suspected of causing the unprecedented change.

traditional lands occupied by 15 of the largest national groups in the country. It should be noted, however, that several large national groups were not so favored despite their size. The Tatars, who now rank as the sixth largest national group, and the Jews, whose numbers make them the thirteenth largest national group in the country, have no union republic to call their own. Soviet Germans, Chuvash, Mordvas, Bashkirs, and Poles also exist in numbers ranging between one and two million people, yet they have no union republics of their own in which to nurture their cultures. Each of these ethnic groups, except the Poles and Germans, do have smaller political units, ostensibly designed to reflect its national identity and to preserve its culture, but several of these units have failed in their purpose.

The 15 union republics can be clustered into four groups: Slavic/Rumanian, Baltic, Transcaucasian, and Central Asian. The **Slavic/Rumanian** cluster accounts for the largest population (74.5 percent of the total) and the greatest expanse of territory (81 percent of the total land area). It embraces the country's greatest industrial and agricultural wealth and the bulk of its political power. The groups consists of four union republics: the Russian Soviet Federated Socialist Republic (RSFSR), the Ukrainian SSR, the Byelorussian SSR, and the Moldavian SSR.

Russia is mistakenly thought by many people to be the name of the country properly referred to as the Union of the Soviet Socialist Republics (USSR) or the Soviet Union. The confusion stems from the fact that the present country is virtually identical to the Russian Empire ruled by the tsars until 1917. With the revolution of that year, however, the Russian Empire was destroyed, and the Soviet Union was gradually built to replace it. What is today named Russia—formally, the Russian Socialist Federated Soviet Republic (RSFSR)—is only one of the fifteen union republics.

Russia is the largest union republic, constituting about 77 percent of the USSR's total area. It stretches from Europe to the Pacific coast. It includes all of Siberia and most of Soviet Europe, dwarfing the other union republics individually and collectively. Its population of 147.4 million is 51.4 percent of the total of the USSR. Indeed, even without the other 14 union republics, Russia would remain the largest country in the world, and its population would far exceed any other European nation.

The capital of Russia is Moscow, which doubles as the capital of the USSR. Russia also includes a large assortment of political subdivisions that mark the territories of important ethnic groups within its borders, but these more local jurisdictions will be explained in a later chapter.

Russia produces 57.8 percent of the country's gross national product (GNP). Its Siberian region alone provides 3.5 times more raw materials than the rest of the country put together. Russia produces 78.7 percent of the country's natural gas, 88.8 percent of its oil, 56.2 percent of its coal, 61.2 percent of its electricity, 90.3 percent of its paper, 60.6 percent of its cement, and 58 percent of its steel. It produces 55 percent of its poultry, 48 percent of its wheat, 48 percent of its beef, and 26 percent of its corn. Clearly, besides having the largest expanse of territory and the greatest population, Russia is also the economic giant of the Soviet Union.

The **Ukrainian Soviet Socialist Republic,** sometimes called Little Russia, is the second most populous union republic in the country, with a population of almost 52 million. However, it ranks third in land area, making it quite densely populated. Like Russia, the Ukraine is dominated by a Slavic people. Its capital city, Kiev, was the capital of the earliest

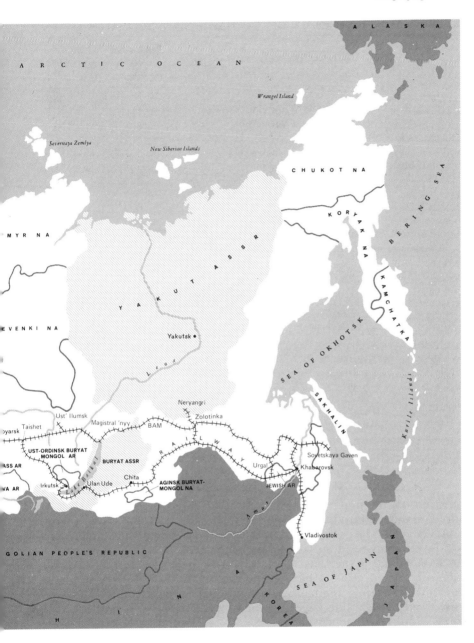

modern state in the land. Today, Kiev is the nation's third largest city, behind Moscow and Leningrad, respectively.

As previously mentioned, the Ukraine has rich steppe black soil, the most productive farmland in the country. It produces 25 percent of the country's wheat, 24 percent of its beef, and 22 percent of its poultry. The re-

TABLE 1-1   Union Republics

Union Republic	Capital	Area (sq. mi.)	Population (millions)	Percentage of Total Population	Population Density (per sq. mi.)
Slavic/Romanian					
Russian SFSR	Moscow	6,600,000	147.4	51.4	22
Ukrainian SSR	Kiev	240,000	51.7	18.0	215
Byelorussian SSR	Minsk	80,000	10.2	3.6	128
Moldavian SSR	Kishinev	13,000	4.3	1.5	334
Subtotal		6,933,000	213.6	74.5	31
Baltic					
Estonian SSR	Tallinn	17,000	1.6	0.6	93
Latvian SSR	Riga	25,000	2.7	0.9	107
Lithuanian SSR	Vilnius	25,000	3.7	1.3	148
Subtotal		67,000	7.9	2.8	119
Transcaucasian					
Georgian SSR	Tbilisi	30,000	5.5	1.9	182
Armenian SSR	Yerevan	12,000	3.3	1.2	274
Azerbaijan SSR	Baku	33,000	7.0	2.5	213
Subtotal		75,000	15.8	5.6	210
Central Asian					
Kazakh SSR	Alma-Ata	1,050,000	16.5	5.8	16
Uzbek SSR	Tashkent	156,000	19.9	6.9	128
Kirghiz SSR	Frunze	77,000	4.3	1.5	56
Tadzhik SSR	Dushanbe	55,000	5.1	1.8	93
Turkmen SSR	Ashkhabad	187,000	3.5	1.2	19
Subtotal		1,525,000	49.3	17.2	32
Total		8,600,000	286.6	100.00	33

Source: 1989 Soviet Census.

gion is also rich in mineral deposits, with large reserves of iron ore, phosphorite, manganese, potassium, and salt, as well as some oil and a large amount of coal. A large industrial capacity in the area takes advantage of its proximity to so many important natural resources.

Byelorussia is the third Slavic union republic. Because its frontier abuts with Poland, it has long been on the invasion route from the west. Accordingly, its landscape has been the frequent site of battles. Both Byelorussia and the Ukraine were governed by nations other than Russia for several centuries. Byelorussia, however, was generally weaker than the Ukraine and was thus unable to sustain the long periods of political independence enjoyed by the Ukraine. Hence, although the Byelorussians manifest a distinct identity, they do not equal the passionate nationalism of the Ukrainians. However, since 70 percent of the radiation from the Chernobyl accident fell in this union republic, its population has recently mobilized politically.

Byelorussia, meaning White Russia, has a population of 10.2 million. It is the fifth most populous republic but ranks only sixth in land area. Minsk, the capital, was virtually leveled in World War II, but it has been rebuilt and is again a cosmopolitan city with a large industrial and trade base; in fact, its workers generate the highest industrial per capita productivity in the Soviet Union.

The fourth republic in the Slavic/Rumanian group is **Moldavia.** Containing 4.3 million people in only 13,000 square miles, Moldavia is the most densely populated union republic. Still, Moldavia is principally an agricultural area, producing fine wines, fruits, grain, sugar beets, and tobacco.

Moldavia—or Moldova, as it now wishes to be called—is bordered on the west by Rumania, and its principal ethnic group is of Rumanian origin. Its capital city, Kishinev, is close to the center of the union republic, which, during most of its history, was known as Bessarabia. Bessarabia had long, close ties with Rumania, Hungary, Turkey, and Poland, as well as with Russia. In 1940 it was annexed into the Soviet Union.

The three **Baltic** states of Estonia, Latvia, and Lithuania, which are tucked into the northwestern corner of Soviet Europe, constitute the second group of union republics. Each of these enjoyed a history as an independent country before being brought under the domination of the Russian Empire. After the 1917 revolution, the three states became independent of Russian control, but they were reannexed in 1940.

The Baltic states are the most prosperous republics in the Soviet Union. They are the most Western as well, clearly portraying a Scandinavian image. Their people, however, are of distinct races that are neither Scandinavian nor Slavic. Each Baltic race differs from the others, although they are often dealt with as a unit. **Estonia,** with its capital in Tallinn, has the smallest population of all the union republics. Ethnically most closely related to the Finns, the Estonian people number about 1.6 million, or just over one-half of one percent of the total Soviet population. Since much of the land is marshy, with about 20 percent of the area composed of peat bogs, land is a precious commodity. Still, agriculture is Estonia's principal industry. The republic is a major producer of dairy goods, flax, oats, barley, rye, and potatoes, as well as timber, paper, and meat products.

Latvia and **Lithuania** are about the same size in land area, but Lithuania's population of 3.7 million is about one million more than Latvia's. The capital of Latvia, Riga, is a major manufacturing center, specializing in electronics. Yet, the union republic is still heavily dependent on its agricultural base. Today, Latvia is the Soviet Union's most important producer of meat, with a per capita production better than that of France or West Germany.

Lithuania, with its capital at Vilnius, is the most heavily industrialized Baltic state, although it sorely lacks raw materials. It boasts a large number of industries, including machine tools, furniture, textiles, cement, and ship building. At the same time, however, Lithuania has one of the most efficient agricultural industries in the Soviet Union, producing sugar beets, potatoes, wheat, corn, flax, and livestock. Having driven out its German occupiers, the Teutonic Knights, Lithuania built a vast East European empire in the twelfth century. Today its empire is no more, of course, but its language survives as Europe's oldest living tongue.

Wedged between the Black and Caspian seas are three small union republics collectively referred to as the **Transcaucasian** Union Republics. West clearly meets East in this tiny region. The **Georgian** SSR is home for an ancient people who are Christian and European. Next door, we find the **Armenian** SSR, whose people belong to one of the world's oldest Christian sects but are a Middle Eastern people. On either side of Armenia is the **Azerbaijan** SSR, the only union republic besides the Russian SFSR to be divided into two parts. The Azerbaijans share Armenia's eastern heritage, but they are devoutly Muslim and thus have a cultural heritage more similar to that of the people in Central Asia than to that of their fellow Transcaucasians.

Georgia and Armenia are very similar in a number of ways. Commercially oriented, both republics produce wines, citrus fruits, and other crops rarely found elsewhere in the Soviet Union. Their cultures easily predate the birth of Christ: Both peoples founded ancient kingdoms that carried on relations with the Greeks and were conquered by the Romans. Possessing only about 12,000 square miles, Armenia is the smallest union republic. Yet with 3.3 million inhabitants, it has a population density second only to that of Moldavia. Furthermore, of all the union republics, Armenia has the smallest Russian community in its midst—about 2.3 percent. Its capital, Yerevan, which has a population of almost one million, stands in the shadow of Turkey's Mount Ararat, where Noah is said to have beached the Ark.

The capital of Georgia, Tbilisi, is not far from Gori, the birthplace of Joseph Stalin. The Georgians are freewheeling commercial people who seldom feel comfortable in the collectivist Soviet society. Yet they are fiercely proud that Georgia is Stalin's homeland and tend to ignore the fact that Stalin abandoned the traditional Georgian nationalism in pursuing ruthless russification programs throughout the land—including in his own homeland.

The Georgian SSR hosts two autonomous soviet socialist republics—the Abkhasia ASSR in the northwest and the Adzharia ASSR in the southwest—and one autonomous oblast—the South Ossetia AO in the northeast. The precise legal and political status of such subsections will be more fully developed in a later chapter, but for now suffice it to note their existence within the Georgian SSR and that each has recently demanded more autonomy from Georgia. Outbreaks of violence between the Georgians and the Adzharians and South Ossetians have resulted in dozens of deaths.

Georgia ranks with Armenia as one of the Soviet Union's most prosperous republics. Its people are enterprising; its agriculture produces a wide variety of crops; and it has a thriving livestock industry, providing beef, pork, and lamb for its fellow Soviet citizens. Georgia also possesses several important raw materials. Its lovely mountains contain deposits of manganese, coal, baryta, diatomite, tungsten, mercury, gold, iron, lead, and oil. The republic is also rich in clay deposits, marble, alabaster, and cement.

The Azerbaijan SSR is the largest and most populous of the three Transcaucasian Union Republics. Its territory was historically part of the Persian Empire, and even today there is a large Azerbaijan population in Iran. Yet, the Azerbaijan people are not Persian; they are ethnically Tatar, and their language is closely related to Turkish. Its Muslim culture and its semidesert region along the western shores of the Caspian Sea make Azerbaijan more similar to the lands of Central Asia than to Georgia and Armenia, with whom it shares the Transcaucasian area. Azerbaijan is quite mountainous in some areas; its population and most of its economic activity are concentrated in the semiarid lowlands.

Azerbaijan's principal crop is cotton. It also produces wheat, fruit, silk, tea, rice, and tobacco. Yet, by far, Azerbaijan's most important product is oil. Its capital, Baku, is the center of one of the world's largest oil fields, and Azerbaijan has about 90 percent of the oil refining capacity in the Soviet Union. Indeed, oil has been a major industry of this area since as far back as the late tsarist period. Not only do the skeletonlike derricks hug the coast of the Caspian, but numerous wells have been sunk beneath the lake as well.

The fourth group of union republics comprises the five republics in **Central Asia:** the Kazakh SSR, Uzbek SSR, Turkmen SSR, Kirghiz SSR, and Tadzhik SSR. By far, the largest of the five republics is the **Kazakh SSR,**[12] the second largest union republic in the country. Kazakhstan is dwarfed by the RSFSR, but even so its expanse approximately equals about one-third of the continental United States.

Prior to 1917, the people of this region were basically poor nomadic herdsmen. Today, however, Kazakhstan is a prosperous area with rich harvests of oats, barley, rice, wheat, cotton, sugar beets, and tobacco. Beef and lamb are produced as well. Although Stalin's collectivization policies wreaked havoc with its native population, the area has benefited from the enormous investment in its agricultural production. Irrigation canals built since the revolution bring water, without which the region would remain barren and sparsely populated.

Along with its agricultural potential, the rich mineral deposits of Kazakhstan have been extensively developed. Since the revolution, Kazakhstan has become a major producer of coal and oil. It also produces substantial quantities of copper, lead, and zinc. The exploitation of tungsten, nickel, salt, silver, gold, bauxite, and manganese is also notable.

Alma-Ata, Kazakhstan's capital city, is located south of Lake Balkhash. Situated in the shadow of the Zailisky-Alatau Mountains, this modern city boasts a population of 1.1 million. Many of its people are rather recent arrivals. Kazakhstan has experienced a great increase in population since World War II, as have other parts of Central Asia. Because most of the

---

[12]Because its northwestern corner is found in Europe, Kazakhstan is not included in Central Asia by some authorities. However, since the bulk of the union republic is in Asia and because the Kazakhs are a Turkic, Muslim people, it seems appropriate to include Kazakhstan in Central Asia.

newcomers are from Soviet Europe, the Kazakh people are now not only a minority population in their own republic, but they also comprise a smaller percentage of the population than the Russians: 36 to 41 percent respectively.

Sharing Kazakhstan's distinction as a prosperous Central Asian republic is the **Uzbek SSR.** The Uzbek SSR hosts Central Asia's most fabled cities. Khiva and Bukhara are famous for their historical roles as religious and intellectual centers of the ancient Muslim world. Rich in architectural treasures, they are reminders of a distinguished past. Even more spectacular is the ancient city of Samarkand. Once the capital of a great empire, this lovely city, with its beautifully restored mosques, madrasahs, tombs, and ancient observatory, is a showplace for Muslim culture. Tashkent, Uzbekistan's capital and the Soviet Union's fourth largest city, enjoys an imaginative and colorful architecture that is atypical of modern buildings found elsewhere in the country.

Uzbekistan, like Kazakhstan, is largely semidesert flatland dotted with oases. Soviet irrigation projects have brought water to the otherwise parched land and have made it a very productive agricultural area. Cotton is the union republic's principal crop, with Uzbekistan alone being responsible for 60 percent of the entire Soviet production. The reclaimed desert also yields rice, wheat, sugar beets, grapes, alfalfa, and fruit. Uzbekistan produces wool, silk, and rubber rendered from the guayule plant. Although Uzbekistan is not as rich in mineral deposits as Kazakhstan, coal, iron, oil, lead, and silver are extracted from its subterranean reserves.

Southwest of Uzbekistan lies the **Turkmen SSR.** Poorer than its north-

An Uzbek woman enjoys the shade of a Samarkand garden. (Photo provided by Lois and Helen Van Moppes.)

eastern counterparts, Turkmenistan is almost totally desert land of the most barren sort. The Kara-Kum Desert, which covers the republic, reluctantly yields to the plow and irrigation. The Parthian Empire flourished in this area 2,200 years ago, sustained by an extensive canal system. Upon its decline, however, the desert reclaimed the land and would sustain only tiny tribes of nomadic herdsmen. With the construction of the Kara-Kum Canal—850 miles long, 15 feet deep, and 100 yards wide—enough water is now brought into the area to make a portion of the desert fertile again.

Although a few nomads still lead their herds from oasis to oasis, Ashkhabad, Turkmenistan's capital, is now the center for a considerable agricultural base which yields cotton, melons, wheat, vegetables, and fruit. Additionally, the traditional production of wool and silk has not only continued but has been increased with the help of modern technology.

East from Turkmenistan, on the other side of southern Central Asia, is the **Kirghiz SSR,** a rough mountainous region populated by a hardy people who—like the Kazakhs, Uzbeks, and Turkmen—speak a Turkic tongue. Although the Kirghiz are still the largest population group in the republic, like the Kazakhs, they fail to equal a majority, accounting for only 48 percent of the population. Although life in Kirghizia is perhaps no longer primitive, it is still rugged; travel is easier by horse than by motor vehicle in many parts of the republic. Its people are still largely nomadic, and although they are peaceful folk, they amuse themselves with rough equestrian sports that call for cunning, agility, and strength.

An example of the unusually beautiful Soviet architecture found in Tashkent. A publishing house stands on the left, the Lenin Museum on the right.

Agriculture is not an important activity in Kirghizia. The economy is much more dependent upon livestock herds, which have grazed the region's lush mountain valleys since before recorded history. Mining is also becoming relatively important; the republic produces coal, gold, lead, and tin.

The capital of Kirghizia, Frunze, was named for the famed revolutionary general Mikhail Frunze, who was born in the city. It is located on the Chu River, at the base of the Tien Shan Mountains. The city is only about 100 miles west of Issyk-Kul, a large lake dominating the eastern part of the republic.

To the southwest of Kirghizia is the **Tadzhik SSR.** Its people are unique in Soviet Central Asia in that they are of Persian lineage and not Turkic; moreover, they remain adamant about preserving their unique culture in the face of being encircled by Oriental people. Their land, like Kirghizia, is very mountainous. In fact, Tadzhikistan has the distinction of possessing the highest peak in the Soviet Union, Mount Communism, which reaches 24,584 feet. Tadzhikistan's ample water supply and mountainous terrain give it great potential as a source of hydroelectric power. Soviet engineers speculate that construction of dams in strategic places could result in the production of as much as 300 billion kilowatt-hours of electricity annually, about one-third of present Soviet consumption. The Tadzhiks, however, resist dam construction because they want to preserve their precious mountain valleys.

Basically an agricultural area, Tadzhikistan produces cotton (its per acre yield of cotton is the highest in the Soviet Union), silk, fruit, rice, and grain. Livestock is also important to its economy, and it specializes in raising cattle, sheep, and yak. Its mineral resources are significant; it produces substantial yields of tin, gold, lead, coal, uranium, zinc, and salt.

The capital of Tadzhikistan is Dushanbe. Formerly called Stalinabad, the city has a population of about 616,000. Even though the union republic has a population of only 5.1 million people, it grew by 34.5 percent between 1979 and 1989—the fastest rate of growth in the country.

One can only stand in awe of the natural and cultural phenomena that constitute the Soviet Union. It is perhaps impossible to describe it accurately without using superlatives. Its size is the greatest, its water resources the largest, its natural resources the richest, its latitude the highest, its topography the flattest, its climate the coldest, its culture among the most diverse in the world! Clearly, a geography so powerful must have important and lasting effects on the historical and political development of the people who must deal with it. So it is appropriate that we now turn to the history of Russia and the Soviet Union in an effort to understand its political society.

chapter 2

Russian History

Contemporary Soviet society is not an aberration, nor is it solely a product of communism. The result of centuries of human development, the present Soviet system is, like most societies, an intricate mosaic. Even those societies that are products of revolution consist of pieces that were created by previous generations. A civilization is the product of innumerable and largely unknown people who, each in his or her time, contributed to the whole, thus, perhaps unknowingly, preconditioning the future—someone else's present, someone else's past.

Accordingly, many policies that are attributed to the country's communist rulers are actually traditional practices antedating the lifetime of Marx himself, to say nothing of the current Soviet leaders. Institutions and practices such as the secret police, domestic passports, and terrorism are not of communist but of Russian origin. These policies were used long before Lenin's time and may well have been continued had the Bolshevik Revolution never occurred. Because the customs, policies, and aspirations of contemporary Soviet society are rooted in the past, this chapter will review Russian history—a necessarily concise account, as the space available allows for only an overview.

ANCIENT ORIGINS

Compared to most European lands, Russia has a relatively recent political history. Because Russia rested far beyond the reach of ancient civilizations

that recorded early history—places like Rome, Persia, India, and Greece—
we know little about the ancient peoples inhabiting the forests and grassy
plains of the land that came to be known as Russia. Sketchy records of the
area south of the forest, the great Ukrainian steppe, tell of waves of invaders breaking into the rich grasslands. These people—Scythians, Sarma-
tians, Alans, Huns, Avars, and others—did little to civilize the area. Their
constant raids were early manifestations of a problem that would plague
Russia and the Ukraine for two thousand years. Barbarian hordes from the
southeast threatened Russian society by cutting off its access to the advanced civilizations on the shores of the Black and Mediterranean seas.
This insecurity partially accounts for the traditional Russian distrust of
strangers and fierce resistance in the face of foreign invasion.

The Slavs, who dominate Russia today, are not indigenous to that vast
land. Originating in the environs of the Vistula River in present-day Poland, this sturdy people began to expand beyond their ancestral home.
Some of them went south, eventually congregating in what is today
Yugoslavia; a second group consolidated its control over modern-day Poland and Czechoslovakia. A third contingent moved east and settled a large
area bound by the Carpathian Mountains on the southwest, the Oka River
on the east, and Lake Ilman on the north. It is this East Slavic people who
brought the rudiments of political organization to Russia.

Firmly established in their newly adopted home by A.D. 600, the East
Slavs were divided into a number of tribes. Their political organization,
however, was not well established, and the East Slavs found themselves in
perpetual turmoil, constantly at war with one another. Complicating these
circumstances were the pressures felt from recurrent raids by warlike
hordes driving toward the Byzantine Empire from the east.[1]

The Kievan Period (862–1200)

Plagued by intertribal feuding and molested by periodic barbarian
plundering, the territory of the East Slavs was by A.D. 800 a sad place
indeed. At about that time, pressure from the Khazars, the latest maraud-
ing people to arrive from the southeast, threw the East Slavs into new
disorder.

In 862[2] the chaos attracted Viking warriors, whom the Slavs called
Rus.[3] These Nordic interlopers established the first modern state in Russia,
and their children became the rich and powerful nobility called **boyars.**
Centered in Kiev, the state stretched from Novgorod southward to the
Black Sea. Over the years the grand princes of Kiev created a wealthy and
powerful realm. Although Kiev traded with much of Western Europe, its
embrace of the Greek Orthodox faith drew it closest to the Byzantine

---

[1]Otto Hoetzsch, *The Evolution of Russia*, trans. Rhys Evans (San Diego, CA: Harcourt
Brace Jovanovich, 1966), pp. 7–12.

[2]Some historians place the date at 856.

[3]It is believed by some historians that the name *Rus* could be the source of the word
Russia.

Looking down on the Dnieper River from the bluffs of Kiev, one can see a statue of Vladimir I (978–1015), who converted his people to the Orthodox faith in 988. Perhaps ironically, the Soviets held a series of gala events celebrating the millennial anniversary of Russian Christianity in 1988.

Empire. The economic and cultural ties between Kiev and Constantinople profoundly influenced the Russian people—their religion, alphabet, and architecture, as well as other elements of their culture.

Having reached its "golden age" during the reign of Yaroslav the Wise (1019–1054), the Kievan state entered a long decline after his death. Civil wars between contending princes and pressures of raiding tribes from the southeast eventually stimulated a migration of Slavic people from the center of the Kievan state to the north and east during the twelfth century. Eventually Kiev was eclipsed, and political power gravitated to the northern city-empires of Novgorod, Vladimir, and Suzdal. Disunited and weakened, the Russian principalities were no match for the onslaught of the Mongols in the thirteenth century.

Sweeping over Russia from the depths of the Asian land mass, the generals of Jinghis Khan fell upon the hapless land with unprecedented savagery. City after city was leveled until all of Russia was made subject to the "Tatar yoke." Disseminated by the Mongols, the Russian people found themselves governed by masters who cared little for anything save tribute. Hence, although the conquest was cruel, Russian culture remained relatively undisturbed as the people rallied to their religion and traditions to preserve their identity.

The Rise of Moscow

During the Mongol rule, a line of ruthless and cunning princes transformed an obscure village on the Moskva River into a powerful Russian principality. After a period during which the grand princes of Moscow served the Mongol Khans as tax collectors and policemen, Ivan the Great

KIEVAN RUS
ca. 1050

•   Major towns
—·—·—   Frontiers
Rus Tribes
Rus Neighbors

WHITE SEA

Pechora

Perm

L. Onega

Korelians

L. Ladoga

BALTIC SEA

Chud

Slavs

Cheremis

Novgorod

Pskov

Kors

Suzdal

Murom

Bulgars

Zhmud

Dvina R.

Krivichians

Oka R.

Prussians

Litva

Polotians

Smolensk

Viatichians

Mordva

Poland

Dregovichians

Radimichians

Volga R.

Derevlians

Chernigov

Volynians

Severians

Dulebians

Kiev

Pereiaslav

Don R.

Halych

Dniester R.

Polianians

Dnieper R.

Polovtsians

Magyars

Ulichians

Tivercians

Pechenegs

Vlakhs

Danube R.

Tmutorokan

Kasogians

BLACK SEA

Constantinople

AEGEAN SEA

Byzantine Empire

(Ivan III, 1462–1505) turned on his Asian lord and liberated Russia in 1480.

Not content with his victory over the Khan, Ivan III adopted the trappings of the defunct Byzantine Empire, centralizing political power at the expense of the boyar class. These policies were continued by Ivan's heirs until a titanic struggle between the tsar and the boyars ensued during the reign of Ivan the Terrible (Ivan IV, 1533–1584). Crazed by boyar treachery and personal tragedy, Ivan IV was the first to take the title "Tsar" as he ravaged his country with a reign of terror in order to cow his dissident nobles. Other classes suffered grievously as well, especially the peasants. Although they loved the tsar, viewing him as a stern father who had to be harsh to control the hated boyars (their landlords), the peasants were heavily taxed to pay for Ivan's eternal wars. Falling into hopeless debt, many peasants were forced into serfdom, while others fled to the south, joining the Cossacks at the mouths of the Don, Volga, and Dnieper rivers.[4]

When Ivan's death left the succession in question, a long period of chaos and civil war, called the **Time of Troubles,** ensued. During this tumultuous period, Russia was ruled by Boris Godunov, various brigands and usurpers, and even the king of Poland. The land so weakened by Ivan IV's excesses was again ravaged by incessant civil wars until order was finally restored when Mikhail Romanov was elected tsar by the boyars in 1613.[5]

The Time of Troubles represented the final spasm of bloodletting that fatally weakened the boyars. Their ultimate demise awaited only a strong ruler. Meanwhile, the realm was rocked by two other segments of the society. First, a religious schism occurred when the *raskolniki,* or Old Believers, refused to comply with certain liturgical modernizations. Then a serf rebellion was led by Stenka Razin, who called on the people to rise up and kill their masters in their beds. Although the serf rebellion was soon suppressed, the restoration of order did not improve Russia's deteriorating social conditions. Isolated and sullen, Russia was a backward land with little influence on the events in Europe.

The Russian Empire

Peter the Great (Peter I, 1682–1725) came to the throne determined to modernize his country. Upon his return from a tour of Western Europe,

[4]Fleeing serfdom, oppression, or hard times during the sixteenth and seventeenth centuries, people from every adjunct area congregated close to the mouths of the Don, Dnieper, and Volga rivers. Wedged between the effective control of Russia, Turkey, or the Polish-Lithuanian Empire, these hardy people filled a power vacuum in the area and established their own societies. They were collectively called Cossacks. Fiercely independent, the Cossacks became the best cavalry of their day, gradually pushing their control into the Ukraine. Alternately allying with the Poles, Turks, and Russians, they managed to remain free of foreign domination for some time. Gradually, however, opposing pressures grew too great, and the Cossacks became attached by treaty to the Russian tsar. They were granted autonomous status and rewarded with other special privileges. Hence, the Cossack regiments, once dangerous enemies of Russia, became the most reactionary element in the country, a mainstay of the tsarist system.

[5]Melvin C. Wren, *The Course of Russian History,* 3rd ed. (New York: Macmillan, 1968), p. 188.

Peter insisted that his subjects change their antiquated ways. Peter reformed the government and army. He forced Russia into the center of European politics by defeating Sweden in a long war, and he built a new capital on the Baltic, St. Petersburg. By the time of his death, Peter had made Russia a European power—but at great cost. Although his modernization had left the boyar class permanently subjugated to the tsar, the peasants, as under Ivan the Terrible, suffered from taxes, debt, serfdom, and squalor. Yet, unlike Ivan, Peter had institutionalized the tsar's power.[6] Regardless of how dismal the qualities of Peter's successors, the power and authority of the monarchy went unchallenged, awaiting another person of talent and ability.

Catherine the Great (Catherine II, 1762–1796) was such a person. She ascended the throne after the murder of her husband, Peter III, a plot in which she was almost certainly involved. Catherine completed many of the policy objectives Peter had established. She recovered the long lost territories of Byelorussia from Poland, and she forced Turkey to vacate permanently the lands north of the Black Sea. Yet, her reign was plagued with domestic strife. Accommodating the aristocrats, she created the "golden age of the nobility;"[7] at the same time, her policies forced virtually every peasant into serfdom. An archetypical enlightened despot (one who talks about reforms but never quite carries them out), Catherine flirted with French radicalism. Yet her unhappy people were so oppressed that they eventually followed Emilian Pugachev in the most destructive and terrorizing serf rebellion in Russian history.[8] Although Pugachev was finally defeated, the term *pugachevshchina* became synonymous with the serf rebellions that haunted Russia from that time. By the time of Catherine's death, virtually all Russian peasants had become serfs, a legacy that plagued Russia for a century.

REFORM AND REACTION

Catherine's era ended as the fury of the French Revolution engulfed all of Europe. A central player in the tumultuous events of the Napoleonic wars was Alexander I (1801–1825), Catherine's grandson. Like his distinguished grandmother, Alexander toyed with reform but found his efforts interrupted by the disruptive events in Western Europe. Defeated by Napoleon on the field, Alexander negotiated the Treaty of Tilsit in 1807. The treaty divided Europe between the two emperors, but it imposed upon Russia certain economic conditions that Alexander found he could not abide. Relations between France and Russia deteriorated until Napoleon disas-

[6]An excellent recent biography of Peter I is Robert K. Massie, *Peter the Great: His Life and World* (New York: Ballantine, 1980).

[7]Marc Raeff, *Origins of the Russian Intelligentsia* (San Diego, CA: Harcourt Brace Jovanovich, 1966), p. 10.

[8]Daniel Field, *Rebels in the Name of the Tsar* (Boston: Houghton Mifflin Co., 1976), p. 167.

trously decided to send his "Grand Army" into the Russian expanse. Scorching the earth and waiting for the harsh winter to take its toll, Alexander's forces fell back until Napoleon occupied Moscow. Waiting for a surrender that never came, Napoleon's army became threatened by cold and hunger. Soon the French emperor had no choice but to retreat westward over the frozen Russian landscape. Harassed by partisans, the French commander staggered out of Russia with only a fraction of his 600,000 invaders and was ultimately vanquished by converging European forces.[9]

Post-Napoleonic Europe was a reactionary, repressive place. Europe's monarchs joined Alexander in a pledge to use their armies to suppress democratic rebellions wherever they erupted. Inspired by the liberating ideas of the French Revolution, the people of Europe found their dreams of reform crushed again and again by the powerful and intransigent monarchs.

In Russia young nobles returning from the war to their backward land began to demand change but were rebuked and repressed. After Alexander's death in 1825, these enlightened soldier-nobles rose up against the new tsar, Nicholas I (1825–1855), and demanded a constitution. The **Decembrist Revolution** was easily quashed, and the would-be reformers were confronted by a reactionary tsar whose only response to pleas for change was to crush the "dangerous leftists." Thus, Russian radicals became increasingly extremist, until finally many became captivated by the hopeless dream that all would be better if only they could assassinate the tsar. Accordingly, the terrorist rule of the tsar inspired terrorism among the radicals.

At the same time, although faced with censorship laws that someone quipped "made it almost illegal to read," Russia produced its first great writers. Pushkin, Gogol, Turgenev, Bielinsky, Dostoevsky, and Tolstoy made Russian literature, hitherto undistinguished, a treasure of Western civilization. From this time forward, Russian writers performed the vital role of social and political critics.

Europe breathed a sigh of relief when Nicholas, called the Gendarme of Europe, died in 1855. The old bully had bungled a disastrous war with Turkey, England, and France. The Crimean War (1853–1856), the first of three military conflicts that eventually toppled the monarchy, presaged Russia's decline. Plagued by corruption, ineptitude, and stupidity, the Russian state, previously viewed as a colossus, revealed itself to be an archaic relic whose institutions were hopelessly outdated.

Even so, as a glance at the map of Russian territorial expansion on page 41 reveals, Nicholas continued the drive eastward begun by his ancient predecessors. During his reign and that of his immediate successor, Russia annexed vast lands in Central Asia and in the Far East, virtually completing the expansion of the Russian Empire. Pictured in the West as a menacing, insatiable octopus whose tentacles clutched lands in all direc-

[9]Jesse D. Clarkson, *A History of Russia*, 2nd ed. (New York: Random House, 1969), pp. 258–261.

tions, Russia was viewed with great suspicion by its European, as well as its Asian, counterparts.

At the same time, social conditions in Russia deteriorated. Its fledgling industry became centered in crowded cities. Workers—little more than displaced serfs—were jammed together in dingy factories and filthy slums, forced to work for 14 and 15 hours a day. In the countryside, the serfs lived in squalor made inevitable by the fact that they—perhaps 85 percent of the population—were producing the wealth that their masters squandered.

Faced with repeated serf violence and confronted by the declining profitability of serfdom, Alexander the Liberator (Alexander II, 1855–1881) emancipated the serfs in 1861—four years before the United States freed its slaves. After the euphoria over their new freedom subsided, the peasants found that they were not really free but had only been transferred to a new master. Denied the right to own land themselves, the former serfs were forced to live on communal farms called *mirs*. It was to the mir that land was sold, and too little land was sold at that: As the former serfs put it, "not enough to turn a chicken around." Although the peasants were allowed only meager parcels—usually the worst available land—extortionate prices were charged. Thus, the emancipation actually resulted in a severe decline in the peasant standard of living.[10] Centuries of exploitation, augmented by this new brutalization, lost the monarchy one of its strongest mainstays. Numbed by their plight, the peasants lost their ancient and naive love of the tsar, the "Little Father." Thus, when the revolution came, the peasants did not rise to the tsar's defense. Revolution, however, had to await the development of Russian radicalism.

Russian Radicalism

The first Russian radicals to develop a coherent ideology were the *narodniki*, idealistic populists who became prominent between 1850 and 1880. They romanticized peasant life, claiming it was the source of all wisdom and goodness in Russian culture. Being socialists, they saw the mir as an institution that naturally prepared the peasants for the advance to a new collectivist human existence. How ironic that these idealists would see the mir, the new exploiter of the peasants, as the institution offering their salvation. Although the **narodniki** were hopelessly romantic about the life of the peasant, their leaders produced theories of revolution that Lenin later adopted to bring down the state.

Sharing no illusions about the mir with the *narodniki* were the **anarchists.** These socialists saw government as the major instrument of oppression and as an impediment to human development. Thus, they sought to eliminate the state in order to free people from needless restrictions. Some anarchists, including Leo Tolstoy (1828–1910), hoped for a nonviolent transition to anarchism, while others, including Mikhail Bakunin (1814–1876) and the nihilists, called for the violent destruction of government.[11]

[10]Wren, pp. 372–379.

[11]Basil Dmytryshyn, *A History of Russia* (Englewood Cliffs, NJ: Prentice Hall, 1977), pp. 357–380.

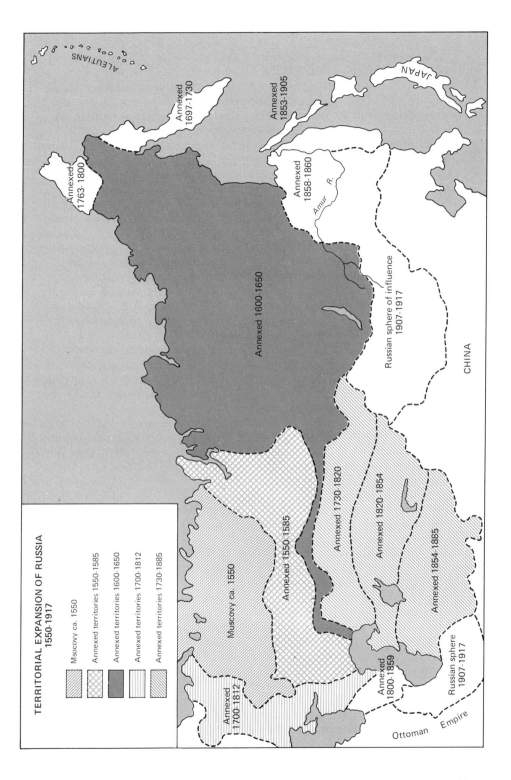

TERRITORIAL EXPANSION OF RUSSIA
1550-1917

Mscovy ca. 1550

Annexed territories 1550-1585

Annexed territories 1600-1650

Annexed territories 1700-1812

Annexed territories 1730-1885

Muscovy ca. 1550

Annexed 1550-1585

Annexed 1600-1650

Annexed 1700-1812

Annexed 1730-1820

Annexed 1820-1854

Annexed 1854-1885

Annexed 1800-1859

Russian sphere 1907-1917

Annexed 1697-1730

Annexed 1853-1905

Annexed 1858-1860

Amur R.

Russian sphere of influence 1907-1917

Annexed 1763-1800

ALEUTIANS

JAPAN

CHINA

Ottoman Empire

41

Marxism.   Both the *narodniki* and the anarchists concentrated their efforts on the rural masses in Russia. Russian Marxism, which developed a bit later than the other two radical movements, focused its attention on the urban workers—the proletariat. Also, unlike some elements of the other two movements, the Russian Marxists tended to eschew terrorism as a revolutionary technique, thinking it counterproductive.

Karl Marx (1818–1883) advanced the theory that economics forms the most fundamental human motivation. Accordingly, he joined other materialists who believed that the environment predisposes people's ideas and behavior. Marx maintained that each era of history is preconditioned by the dominant economic activity of the period. In this, his theory of **economic determinism,** the German scholar opined that every particular social system is built upon an economic foundation consisting of the relationship of available technology to available resources. This relationship, according to Marx, determines the society's economic system. The people who own the means of production (the resources and the technology) dominate the social and political elements in the society as well. Using its control of society, the dominant social class (the owners) employs every available means to keep itself in power at the expense of less fortunate people. Thus, a **superstructure,** consisting of every institution and every means of establishing and communicating values, is built on society's economic **base.** The superstructure, made up of government, education, religion, ideology, art forms, and values, is created and controlled by the class that owns the means of production and is used to perpetuate the dominance of the ownership class.

Marx reasoned that regardless of how effective a governing class may be in denying power to other classes of the society, it could not prevent changes in the economic base upon which the society is founded. That is to say, even plentiful resources tend to become depleted and new technology is developed, causing modifications in the means of production. As the means of production begin to change, a challenging social class arises to control the new economic base. Tension grows between the two classes until the new challenging class rises up in revolution, putting out the formerly dominant class. According to Marx, revolution is necessary to complete the process because the old dominant class will never willingly surrender power to its challenger.

The process of economic evolution creating a new dominant class and of political revolution vanquishing the obsolete social class is called **historical materialism.** Developing his analysis, Marx identified several historical eras. Each era is distinguished by an economic system peculiar to itself, and each preceding era was destined to be supplanted by the next as the economic conditions upon which it was based changed through time. The era of bourgeois democracy was the period in which Marx found himself, but he perceived that capitalism, its economic form, was fraught with contradictions that would inevitably lead its exploited workers (the proletariat) to rise up against it, bringing themselves to power.

When the proletariat did succeed in taking control of a political system, Marx advised a two-step progression into the final and most advanced historical era: a **democratic utopia.** In the first stage, the proletariat is to establish a dictatorship that is to eliminate all antagonistic social classes, creating a classless society in which labor and its product are to be shared by each individual. As the antagonisms created by class differences disappear and the classes themselves vanish, the need for the **dictatorship of the proletariat** would also dissipate. Hence, when all social classes are eliminated, the second stage emerges: People will live in common, work in common, and share in common. Each individual will govern himself or herself according to the good of all, and the state will "wither away." In this manner, Marx would have humankind evolve an idyllic social system in which people willingly engage in collective labor and individuals *govern themselves* according to his dictum "from each according to his ability, to each according to his need."

There is little doubt that Marx expected the first proletarian revolution to occur in an advanced, industrialized state—Germany perhaps. Certainly he did not anticipate that Russia would develop the first socialist state. Yet, Marx was learning Russian at the end of his life because he wanted to study the revolutionary developments in Russia. He became persuaded that a revolution might indeed occur in Russia first. This, however, he expected to be a peasant revolution that at best might unsettle Europe, thus tripping off proletarian revolutions in industrialized states. Since he died in 1883, some 34 years before the Bolsheviks seized power, we cannot know what Marx's view might have been about the potential for a successful socialist revolution in Russia.[12]

The Development of Russian Marxism

Marxist ideas had begun to filter into Russia during the 1870s, but the rational, "scientific" approach of Marx held little appeal in Russia as long as the more romantic *narodnik* movement was dominant among leftists. The popularity of Marxism in Russia emerged when a former *narodnik* leader, Georgi Plekhanov (1856–1918), abandoned the populist ideology and adopted Marxism as his new creed. Accordingly, in 1883, the year of Marx's death, Plekhanov founded the first Russian Marxist group, earning him the title "Father of Russian Marxism." Soon, however, he had to flee to Switzerland to avoid arrest. Although he was a talented theorist, Plekhanov was not capable of providing the kind of practical political leadership necessary to carry off a revolution. The movement had to await yet another leader.

Vladimir Ilyich Ulyanov (1870–1924), better known as *Lenin*, is perhaps history's most important revolutionary. One of a number of children in a well-to-do family, Lenin, like his brothers and sisters, became an active revolutionary even though his father was a superintendent of schools, a job that earned him the status of a petty noble. Quickly rising to a position of leadership among St. Petersburg's radicals, Lenin was closely watched by

---

[12]Avrahm Yarmolinsky, *Road to Revolution* (New York: Collier Books, 1962), p. 324.

the police and was finally arrested in 1895. Imprisoned for over a year, Lenin was then sent into Siberian exile until 1900.

While Lenin was in exile in Siberia and Plekhanov was in Switzerland, an attempt was made to organize the disparate Marxist factions in Russia. At a meeting in Minsk (the First Party Congress) in 1898, the delegates (nine in all) formed the Russian Social-Democratic Workers' Party, but their work was soon undone by police infiltrators.

In 1900 Lenin was released from Siberian exile. He and his wife, Nadezhda Krupskaya, joined Plekhanov in Switzerland and immediately entered into a debate with him over the structure and function of the party. The issue was joined in 1903 in Brussels at the Second Party Congress. Insisting on the viability of his views, Lenin refused to compromise, thus alienating those who disagreed with him. Finally, some of the exasperated comrades abandoned the meeting, leaving only Lenin's followers (who took the name **Bolsheviks,** meaning "those in the majority") and Plekhanov's adherents (whom the Bolsheviks called **Mensheviks** or "those in the minority").

In succeeding years, the split between the Bolsheviks and the Mensheviks became increasingly bitter and ideologically distinct. Plekhanov insisted that the dialectic had to proceed as Marx had suggested; thus, a feudal society had to first pass through the bourgeois capitalist stage before developing socialism. Therefore, he argued that feudalistic Russia had "two stages" ahead of it before socialist could be achieved and that the ultimate revolution was probably far in the future. He also insisted that the party should be open to everyone and should be democratically managed. Perhaps most interestingly, Plekhanov argued that since Russia was still in the feudal stage and since capitalism had to exist before socialism could emerge, Marxists would do their best service by assisting the capitalists to come to power. The bourgeois would then "dig their own graves," by establishing an economy that cruelly exploited the proletariat, forcing rebellion and the subsequent establishment of a socialist system.

Note the absence of any important role for the peasant in Plekhanov's revolution. Marx himself had been strangely silent on the question of what part the peasantry could play in a socialist revolution, but Plekhanov was quite definite on the point. He believed that the peasants were too much a product of the feudalist era, too intimidated by their exploiters to be an important revolutionary force. At worst they would support the ruling class, while at best they could be expected to be neutral in the coming struggle.

Lenin countered Plekhanov's position by suggesting that although some peasants were immobilized by their feudal consciousness and others—the wealthy peasants called *kulaks*—were tainted by capitalism, the great majority of peasants were the equivalent of an agrarian proletariat and, under the leadership of the industrial workers, could become part of the ultimate revolutionary movement. Drawing upon an essay he wrote in 1902, *What Is to Be Done?* (the title of which he took from *narodnik* Nikolai Chernyshevsky's earlier work), Lenin went on to argue that Russia could hope to have a socialist revolution only by following the leadership of an elite—a small, disciplined, and absolutely dedicated group of revolutionaries—the Bolsheviks. Resurrecting a relatively obscure concept in Marxist theory, Lenin called his followers the **vanguard of the proletariat.**

Explaining how he and other bourgeois people could be the leaders of the proletarian movement, Marx had claimed that some people, usually intellectuals, perceived the forces of history before others did. These people were to act as the proletariat's vanguard, educating the worker about the forces of history. The vanguard of the proletariat was to teach "class consciousness" to the workers, thus helping to create the conditions for revolution but not actually leading it.

Lenin's concept was quite different. He would have the tiny Bolshevik Party actually direct the revolution. This activist, elitist notion, combined with the view that the peasantry could play an important part in a socialist revolution, constituted fundamental modifications of Marx's original ideas. Lenin's ideas were more consistent with traditional Russian revolutionary thought than with Marx's theories. Rather than letting history take its natural dialectic course, as Marx had advised, Lenin *took* power by an elitist-led coup, but once he controlled the state, he *used* power to bring Marxism to Russia.

Another brilliant revolutionary, Leon Trotsky (1879–1940), emerged as a separate force between the Mensheviks and the Bolsheviks. An independent thinker, Trotsky tried to steer a middle course and encouraged the quarreling factions to settle their differences. As time passed, however, he began to devote his energies to his own theory, **permanent revolution,** also based on a relatively obscure concept in Marxism. Rejecting Plekhanov's two-stage theory, Trotsky suggested that the workers could seize control of the state and use its institutions to continue the revolution until society passed through all the historical eras to enter the socialist phase. Thus, once in power, the workers should use their authority to make the revolution a permanent feature until the conditions for a perfect society had been created. Lenin rejected this "revisionist" notion until only months before the Bolsheviks, whose ranks Trotsky then joined, took power in October 1917.[13]

THE REVOLUTION (1905–1917)[14]

By 1905 the Russian Marxist movement was but a tiny, splintered, quarreling body that received most of its leadership from intellectuals in exile. How such a disorganized group of malcontents could eventually take control of the world's largest state is a fascinating story of governmental stupidity and ineptitude on the one hand and ruthless, dedicated, fanatical revolutionary zeal on the other.

[13]For an exhaustive treatment of the development of Russian Marxism, see Thornton Anderson, *Masters of Russian Marxism* (Englewood Cliffs, NJ: Prentice Hall, 1963).

[14]For an excellent treatment of this period, see Harrison E. Salisbury, *Black Night, White Snow: Russia's Revolutions 1905–1917* (New York: Doubleday, 1978).

Alexander III and Nicholas II

Alexander II's liberation of the serfs and other reforms were at first met with popular approval. Yet, as the wretched conditions of the peasants' emancipation became apparent, the tsar's popularity dwindled until he was finally assassinated by terrorists in 1881. His assassination brought to the throne Alexander III (1881–1894), a 36-year-old narrow-minded man who allowed himself to become the tool of the reactionaries in his realm. Alexander III was honest and hard-working but lacked compassion for his suffering people. Like his grandfather, Nicholas I, Alexander III exhibited a passion for reactionary authoritarianism.

Alexander III plunged Russia into a new round of repression. Censorship was increased, and liberals as well as radicals were jailed. The peasants found themselves controlled by newly appointed land chiefs, who exercised vast powers, thus tightening the grip of the central government on the rural masses. Russification policies saw minorities oppressed, Old Believers persecuted, and Jews brutalized by *pogroms* (mob violence). These severe policies caused many Jews and other minorities to join the ranks of the radicals.

The political consequences of these intolerant polices were serious enough without further complication, yet Russia's social and economic problems aggravated the situation enormously. By 1890, Russia's industrial sector was rapidly developing; it was producing textiles, steel, oil, various ores, railroads, and chemicals. Having received large amounts of foreign investment, it had skipped over the usual stage of light industry to develop heavy industrial production for export.

Leningrad, a city with many canals, is sometimes called the Venice of the North. In the background is the Church of the Resurrection, built on the spot where Alexander II was assassinated in 1881.

The number of industrial workers was not great in the period just preceding the revolution, totaling only about two million in a country of well over one hundred and twenty million inhabitants. But the conditions of labor were among the worst in the industrialized world. Workers were forced to stay at their machines for 14, 15 and even as many as 16 hours a day for miserably poor pay. Women and children were not spared from these horrible working conditions. Indeed, they were often selected over men because they were less apt to resist the deplorable circumstances. Social Security, workers' compensation, and unemployment protection were unknown. Little or no effort was made to provide adequate lighting or ventilation for the factories, to say nothing of assuring that the machines were safe.

The living conditions of the laborers were hardly more pleasant. Their houses, usually built of wood, were old or hastily constructed. There was no plumbing or electricity. Not infrequently, workers were housed in dormitories where people of both sexes and of all ages slept on the floor. Since there was little sanitation, disease was a constant menace, striking the weak and fatigued.

Although the number of proletariat was not large, it became a potent political factor as the nineteenth century ended. These people became committed to city life and assimilated into a new laboring class, one that rather quickly developed the self-awareness that Marx called "class consciousness." Another factor adding to the strength of the proletariat was that the industrial workers were usually concentrated in or near large cities, which had always been the center of political activities in Russia. Hence, although the vast majority of the Russian people remained on the farms, the political potential of the proletariat became far greater than its raw numbers seemed to suggest.

The peasants' conditions had become even worse than those of the industrial workers. The peasant population increased by 50 percent between 1860 and 1900. But the amount of land the peasants were allowed to purchase after liberation increased by only 10 percent. Hunger and malnutrition became the constant state of affairs, and when crops failed—a frequent occurrence—widespread famine set in, causing suffering and death for hundreds of thousands, even millions, of people. Crushed by the burdens of providing for their families, of paying extortionate taxes, and of making hated redemption payments (payments for the purchase of the land they farmed), the peasants lashed out against their oppression. Hundreds of peasant rebellions had to be brutally suppressed by the tsar's troops during the closing years of the nineteenth century. Failing to win improvements in their conditions, thousands of peasants fled to the cities or lost themselves in Siberia's expanse.

By 1900 the social dichotomy had created an explosive political situation. The tsar had proved himself as callous and uncaring toward the common man as the nobles had been. The huge governmental bureaucracy remained insensitive to the people's needs and governed with a cruel arrogance. The Russian Orthodox Church, while still exerting enormous influence over the simple folk of the provinces, was also viewed by many as no more than another oppressive instrument of the state. The long-suffering peasants were brooding and rebellious over their hopeless squalor; the workers developed a growing rage over the despicable lives they led. The ancient, stabilizing myths about the tsar's benevolence had evaporated among the people. Meanwhile, the aristocracy and capitalists went on with their greedy, exploitive, socially carnivorous lives, failing to study the popular mood long enough to see the terrible fate awaiting them.

Into this era of almost hopeless complexity stepped Nicholas II (1894–1917), a man of shallow intellect and archaic values, a weak man whose personal kindness and love of family obscured an utter inability to transform his genuine compassion for Russia's suffering people into meaningful social changes that might have prevented disaster.

The Revolution of 1905

The domestic turmoil of Russia was brought to crisis because of its foreign wars. Modern wars caused Russia extraordinary hardship. Although the tsarist system somehow managed to govern its backward people, it was a vestige of an extinct era and proved itself unable to meet the challenges from more advanced industrial societies. The first serious challenges to tsardom arose at the time of Nicholas I in the wake of the Crimean War in the 1850s. For his part, Nicholas II undertook the disastrous Russo-Japanese War (1904–1905), partially in an attempt to distract Russian public attention from domestic problems. What would be a better distraction than a "little victorious war"? But this strategy backfired as the war with Japan turned out to be neither little nor victorious. Failing to record a single victory against its tiny opponent, Russia was humiliated by stinging defeats, which saw its armies destroyed and its fleet sunk. Instead of distracting the Russian people, the Russo-Japanese War focused public attention on the incompetence of the government.

As discontent grew, an Orthodox priest named Georgi Gapon led a huge but peaceful march in St. Petersburg on January 9, 1905. The procession was headed toward the Winter Palace, where Gapon planned to deliver to the tsar a petition asking for needed reforms. Instead of meeting with his subjects, however, the tsar sent his Cossacks against them. The tsar's soldiers rode down the icon-carrying petitioners, mercilessly killing thousands of people. The day came to be called Bloody Sunday, and the cruel events of that day destroyed forever the myth of the tsar's benevolence toward his people. The revolution had begun![15]

A wave of violence and disobedience swept the country when news of the massacre reached the provinces. Peasants vandalized the gentry's property and killed the hated landlords. Strike after strike brought the industrial sector to a virtual standstill. As the year wore on, the crisis was complicated by serious food shortages. Even the military, the institution that the tsar could not afford to alienate, showed shocking signs of discontent.

[15]David MacKenzie and Michael W. Curran, *A History of Russia and the Soviet Union* (Homewood, IL: The Dorsey Press, 1977), pp. 396–398.

Meanwhile, the workers organized informal governing bodies called **soviets** (councils). To coordinate the efforts of the soviets throughout the county, the Soviet Workers' Deputies was established in St. Petersburg. One of its elected leaders was the young Marxist Leon Trotsky,[16] who led the workers in a general strike that paralyzed the country.

Stunned by these events and enjoying too little support to control the situation, Nicholas promulgated the **October Manifesto** on October 17, 1905. The document gave Russia a constitution, which included provisions for a legislative assembly and guaranteed freedom of association, speech, assembly, and conscience. The document took the steam out of the revolutionary movement temporarily, but it proved to be woefully insufficient. At this time in Russian history, the demands for the revolution contained three major points. First, the leaders called for a legislature, or Duma. Second, they demanded a constituent assembly for writing a constitution. Third, and perhaps most significant, the radicals agitated for land and capital redistribution. The October Manifesto partially addressed the first two points but ignored the third. The last goal was social and economic in nature, and it represented the most fundamental change for the society as a whole, as it would have substantially modified the ownership structure in Russia. The halfway measures of the October Manifesto managed to defuse the 1905 revolution, but the tsarist system was clearly obsolete and proved unable to survive the next national crisis.

The years between 1905 and 1917 were marked by a mixture of repression and reform. Nicholas dismissed Duma after Duma until one was elected that suited his conservative views. While the political parties of the Duma struggled with the tsar, Pyotr Stolypin, the tsar's minister, moved to suppress the violence that still plagued the countryside. Although Stolypin treated the revolutionary leaders harshly, he developed a reform that dissolved the hated mir and sold land directly to the peasants. By 1915 almost 14 million peasants farmed land that they personally owned, and the worst examples of government domination and exploitation of the peasant were eliminated. Yet, although many peasants were now freeholders, they still were not allowed enough land to make a decent living.

World War I (1914–1918)

As Russia grappled with its domestic problems, foreign events drew it toward war in Europe. Russia's traditional goals of gaining control of the entrance to the Black Sea and of expanding its influence toward the southwest under the guise of **Pan-Slavism** (Russia's claim to being the protector of the Slavic, Orthodox people in the Balkans) became urgent as the political situation in the Balkans deteriorated. Meanwhile, Austria, Germany, France, and England each sought to turn European events to its advantage. Matters came to a head on June 28, 1914, when Austrian Archduke Francis Ferdinand was assassinated. Motivated by alliances of mutual assistance and by a military doctrine calling for quick offensive action, the great

[16]Trotsky's real name was Lev Davidovich Bronstein.

European powers virtually rushed into a needless and senseless blood-letting.[17]

News of the war was met with nationalistic enthusiasm, but World War I proved the undoing of old Russia. Because the conflict was massive in scale and long in duration, it placed incredible strain on even the most modern political and economic systems, let alone semifeudal Russia. The war was the first large engagement since Europe had industrialized, and the demand for resources and material was enormous. Russia, an un-developed economic state with a moribund social and political system, sim-ply could not stand the strains imposed by the war. As historian Jesse D. Clarkson put it: "The marvel is not that the regime collapsed but rather that it survived so long."[18]

Within a year and a half, Russia had lost millions of troops, and its armies were in retreat. Stunned by these reversals, the Russian people were given pause to question their involvement in the war and the competence of those managing the effort. Peasants began to hide from conscription officials, and thousands of soldiers deserted the front to return home. Tales of the hopeless situation at the front sent a chill through the land, and people began to grumble about the seemingly senseless slaughter.

The mobilization of 15 million men put a severe strain on both agri-cultural and industrial production. The transportation network began to disintegrate with the collapse at the front because the empire's best railroad system was abandoned to the enemy. As the armies retreated, hundreds of thousands of refugees left their homes in ashes and fled before the advanc-ing enemy. Strikes increased with the growing unpopularity of the war. These disruptions, combined with government mismanagement and the demand from the front for industrial goods, began to cause serious short-ages of goods and, subsequently, spiraling prices. Finding less and less for which to exchange their goods, the peasants began to refuse to produce more than they needed themselves.

Nicholas, however, had little time for domestic problems as he became preoccupied with the conduct of the war. Encouraged by Tsarina Alex-andra, the tsar decided to leave the government in her charge while he went to the front to take personal command of the troops. Confident that God guided his hand, the tsar left the capital to take charge of the imperial forces, an act with truly disastrous consequences.

Alexandra was a headstrong simpleton prone to mysticism and there-fore an easy target for religious charlatans. In 1905, after already having become the partisan of a number of holy seers, she met Rasputin. An uneducated self-proclaimed monk, this Siberian fanatic managed to gain Alexandra's confidence by using his hypnotic powers to stop the bleeding of her hemophiliac son, the heir apparent. As time passed, Alexandra became devoted to the "holy man," who repaid her attention with advice and prophesies, which she in turn took to Nicholas.

[17]For a full account of this era, see Barbara Tuchman, *The Guns of August* (New York: Dell Pub. Co., Inc., 1962).

[18]Clarkson, p. 424.

An ancient Russian Orthodox church in Suzdal.

Unmindful of Rasputin's notorious reputation arising from sexual indiscretions, Alexandra installed him as her most trusted adviser. With his encouragement, she replaced ministers with outrageous frequency, substituting even more incompetent and corrupt administrators for those Nicholas had appointed.

Rasputin's evil and wanton ways scandalized the empire. People from every class, already discouraged by the tragic events caused by the war, began to lose confidence in the tsar and his government. Support for the regime became seriously eroded. Because he remained the favorite of the tsarina, Rasputin used his advice to justify military maneuvers, government purges, and domestic arrests. All the while, his indiscretions and greed almost certainly led to depositing vital state and military secrets in German hands.

Finally, even the most reactionary tsarist supporters realized that this "dark force" in the Winter Palace threatened the monarchy itself. In December 1916 a small group of very high-placed nobles murdered Rasputin. But their desperate deed came too late to save the monarchy. By the end of 1916, Russia had suffered the loss of 12 million people, who had been killed, wounded, and captured in the war.[19] Disgusted by this tragedy, the

[19]Dmytryshyn, p. 417.

traditional mainstays of the regime all agreed that the autocracy had led them to disaster. Brutalized and humiliated by Rasputin's arrogance and Alexandra's incompetence, the nobility and the bureaucracy were both appalled. Even the Church, although the least disenchanted of the major institutions found itself unable to justify Nicholas's rule any longer. The army had completely lost confidence in the tsar, and its ranks were being depleted by desertions. No social class could support the tsar any longer, and some, like the workers, were often openly defiant of his authority. Yet, Nicholas managed to remain blissfully oblivious to the fact that his government had lost institutional and popular support.

The February 1917 Revolution

With Rasputin gone, public attention focused on the tsar himself, and he began to receive the full blame for the disasters at the front as well as the privation at home. Fed up but cautious, members of the Duma and the military met secretly, each assuring the other of support in instigating a coup but neither having the courage to act. In the end, neither the army nor the politicians made the first move. The revolutionary leaders also failed to seize the opportunity of driving the monarchy out of Russia. It was the ordinary people who began the revolution in Petrograd on March 8, 1917, in an unplanned, leaderless protest over the scarcity of bread.[20] The disorder soon spread throughout the city, and the industrial workers went out on strike to join the protesters. Troops were dispatched to restore order, but as often as not they joined their comrades as social discipline began to disintegrate. While looting, strikes, and protest marches consumed Petrograd, disorder rapidly spread to other sections of the country.

Finally, on March 11, with the capital city in flames, the tsar demanded that the Duma dissolve. It refused to do so, and at the same time, the Cossack troops (usually the tsar's most loyal supporters) refused to take command of the city. On the following day, the Duma elected an Executive Committee to establish a government, while the workers and soldiers independently created a new soviet. Although the Executive Committee of the Duma, dominated by liberals, claimed to represent the "sovereign Russian people," the socialist-dominated soviets clearly enjoyed the support of the people. The relationship between the two competitors was curious. The Duma's Executive Committee had legal justification, but it had little popular support. The soviet enjoyed popular support, but it hesitated at forcing the legally elected Duma out. Hence, an uneasy stalemate, or dual government, existed while the various leaders waited and watched developments. Finally, accepting his hopeless position, Nicholas abdicated in mid-March, leaving the government in the hands of a cabinet created out of the Duma's Executive Committee.[21]

---

[20]St. Petersburg was renamed Petrograd during World War I because the original name was thought too German. In 1924 the city was renamed Leningrad in honor of the great revolutionary leader. In an anti-Communist pique, the majority of Leningrad's citizens adopted a 1991 nonbinding referendum issue to readopt the name St. Petersburg. To date, no action on the name change has been taken by the authorities.

[21]MacKenzie and Curran, pp. 446–447.

So in March 1917 the ancient Russian monarchy came to an end. Maintaining its control for centuries by force, the monarchy passed from the scene quietly, while the new political leaders tried to bring some order to the chaos that had befallen their land. The liberals who controlled the government received the immediate support and recognition of Russia's war allies. Yet, the Russian people withheld their support, assuming a cautious wait-and-see attitude. Although the monarch had been discredited and expelled, monumental problems still confronted Russia. Some of the goals of the revolution were not unlike those that had been articulated earlier in Russian history: to create a constituent assembly that would draft a constitution and redistribute the land and capital on an equitable basis. Now, however, new cries went out from the people: "All power to the soviets" and, above all, "End the war!" The liberal government's failure to heed the social and economic needs of its people meant that the political situation had to change—and change it did!

MARCH TO OCTOBER 1917

The fall of the tsarist regime visited a heady spirit on Petrograd. Temporarily united in their joy, few revolutionaries noticed that the disparate groups of the new Russia were united by little but the euphoria of success. The enthusiasm of the first days of the Provisional Government was soon dampened, however, by the stark reality of the monumental problems facing Russia. The war dragged on, food and goods were in short supply, the workers demanded reform, and the peasants craved social justice. Facing these enormous difficulties was a group of well-meaning but inept people who were thrust into leadership more by an accident of history than by the force of their political acumen.

Unsure of itself, the Provisional Government, led by Prince Georgi Lvov, failed to take the decisive steps necessary to satisfy the country's needs. It delayed calling a constituent assembly, it hesitated at instituting land reform, and it acceded to the demands of its Western allies that Russia remain in the war.

Reacting to the power vacuum, workers, soldiers, and peasants across the land organized soviets. Because these impromptu bodies responded to public whim, they usually enjoyed more popularity and authority than the official government. However, the soviets were usually informally organized and often became captive to the most articulate and dedicated faction. The Bolsheviks were such a faction; between March and October 1917, they gradually assumed leadership of this popular base, using it as a platform from which to attack the government.

The revolutionary events in March caught the Bolsheviks off guard. Most of their leaders were in exile.[22] Both Lenin and Trotsky were in the West when the tsar abdicated. Trotsky, who was in New York with Nikolai Bukharin, reached Petrograd in May. Lenin, who had been in Switzerland, had arrived in the Russian capital courtesy of the German government the

[22]David Shub, *Lenin* (Middlesex, England: Penguin Books, 1966), p. 206.

previous month. Quick to appreciate the advantage of flooding Russia with revolutionaries, the Kaiser's government approached Lenin and other radicals, offering money and guaranteed passage across German territory to Russia. Lenin and many other revolutionaries jumped at the chance to return to Russia at such an opportune moment. Accompanied by Grigory Zinoviev and Karl Radek, Lenin crossed German territory in a sealed railroad car and entered Russia from the north. He was met at Finland Station in Petrograd by a large crowd, which greeted him as a returning hero.

Only days after his return to Russia, Lenin published his platform known as the ***April Theses***. This document eventually became the cause the Bolsheviks advocated in gaining power and served as a blueprint for the basic programs they implemented once the Provisional Government was driven from the Winter Palace. Declaring the Provisional Government incompetent, the *April Theses* exhorted the Bolsheviks to take control of the soviets and to use these popular bodies as a base from which to take control of the government, end the war, socialize the land and wealth, and replace the army and the police with a people's militia.[23]

Even as the Bolsheviks were deciding the course they were to follow, Lvov's government faltered. Failing to withdraw from the war, the government collapsed under public pressure. Lvov managed to remain premier, but Alexander Kerensky became the dominant member of the cabinet. The new government convened in May, but it was unable to effect policies that differed substantially from those of its predecessor. The war went on, food shortages beleaguered the cities, and striking workers forced fearful owners to close factories.

Meanwhile, following the instructions of the *April Theses*, the Bolsheviks concentrated on taking over the leadership of the soviets and on pressing their program by circulating slogans: "Workers take the factories," "Peasants take the land," "End the war," "Bread and peace," "All power to the soviets!"

Pressure on the government built throughout May and June. The Allies demanded that Russia launch an offensive to take pressure off the western front, and Kerensky hoped to quiet the dissidents in Russia by showing progress in the war. Hence, on July 1, 1917, the Russian Command threw its forces against the Central Powers in a new offensive in Galicia. This "Kerensky Offensive," however, collapsed against the German defenses, and Russian armies were again in retreat.

Prompted by the new disaster at the front, the Bolsheviks thought the moment for revolution was at hand. They appealed for action to the sympathetic Petrograd garrison and exhorted the workers to rise up against the government. But the government acted decisively for a change, using the police to smash the Bolshevik party headquarters and its press, *Pravda* (Truth). Kerensky then appealed to the troops and the workers not to follow Lenin, claiming he was a German agent. The coup failed, and many Bolsheviks were jailed, including Trotsky, who had thrown his support to

[23]Shub, pp. 221–225.

Lenin's party only earlier that month. Lenin himself managed to escape capture; he went into hiding in Finland and did not reemerge until the eve of the October Revolution.

Shaken by the failure of the July offensive and by the attempted Bolshevik coup, Lvov resigned his post, leaving Kerensky in control. Now premier, Kerensky opened his government with his usual oratorical brilliance, but conditions in Russia had deteriorated too much to be buoyed by words alone. The conservative elements in the country became convinced that Kerensky could not control the leftists. Supported by the Western Allies, they conspired to wrest power from the socialist demagogue. The man they chose to carry out these plans was the Cossack general Lavrenti Kornilov.

Kornilov's attempted coup forced Kerensky to seek support from leftist groups, including the Bolsheviks. Seizing the leadership in defense against Kornilov, the Bolsheviks helped save Petrograd from a reactionary counterrevolution. Kornilov's defeat, however, also spelled the inevitable demise of Kerensky himself. Proving themselves decisive leaders and organizers, the Bolsheviks gained the confidence and support of the soviets. The charges that they were dupes of the Germans were forgotten, and their leaders were hailed as saviors of Petrograd. Additionally, the Bolshevik supporters who had been armed in preparation for the defense of the city were organized by Trotsky into the Red Guard. Hence, when Kornilov's attack from the right failed, the Bolsheviks stood poised to seize power for the left.

The Bolsheviks Take Power

The Bolshevik seizure of power was almost bloodless. The government had lost support because it simply failed to meet any of the demands for change. The war had dragged on, the land and capital had not been redistributed, and no constitution had been drafted.

Exploiting their new popularity, the Bolsheviks consolidated their power over the soviets, the Petrograd garrison, and the sailors at the Kronstadt naval base.[24] Concerned that he was still in danger of being arrested, Lenin surreptitiously reentered Petrograd from his hiding place in Finland on October 20.

In the meantime, the Petrograd Soviet, at Bolshevik urging, moved to take control of the Russian military. It organized a Military Revolutionary Committee, with Trotsky as its chairman, and called upon the military to refuse to obey any order not sanctioned by the committee. By accepting the committee's authority, the military rendered the Kerensky government, headquartered in the Winter Palace, virtually helpless, its demise all but accomplished. Sensing the government's vulnerability, Lenin called for his

---

[24]The Kronstadt naval base is located on an island in the Gulf of Finland just a few miles from Petrograd. Its sailors were among the staunchest supporters of the Bolsheviks and later played an important role in forcing Lenin to reconsider his early economic policies.

followers to attack the Winter Palace on November 7.[25] After only a brief skirmish, the government was theirs.

Thus the movement that would indeed shake the world came to power by a virtually bloodless coup. Six people were killed storming the Winter Palace, but the rest of the city slipped into Bolshevik control without a struggle. Indeed, the Bolshevik seizure of power had been so quiet that the audience at the Petrograd ballet that evening, undisturbed by the battle, watched the performance to its conclusion. This seemingly tranquil takeover certainly does not deserve the designation of revolution. The *revolution* actually took place *after* the Bolsheviks had taken power, when they attempted to impose socialism and Soviet power on a relatively unwilling population.[26]

[25]The calendar used in Russia before the Bolsheviks took power was that to which the Orthodox Church subscribes and is 13 days behind the Gregorian calendar used in the West. Hence, the Bolshevik seizure of power took place in October by the Russian calendar but in November according to the Gregorian calendar. This explains the seeming contradiction of the Soviet celebration of the October Revolution on November 7. The Bolshevik leaders adopted the Gregorian calendar in 1918.

[26]A detailed account of the Bolshevik coup can be found in Alexander Rabinowitch, *The Bolsheviks Come to Power* (New York: W. W. Norton & Co., Inc., 1976).

chapter 3

Soviet History

On the morning of November 7, 1917, Lenin and Trotsky met in the Winter Palace to congratulate each other on their victory. The revolution had come at long last. Now it remained to them and their followers to create a "new world." Steeped in theory but inexperienced in government, the Bolsheviks embarked upon their historic task with enthusiasm and idealism. The complexities of Russia's enormous political and social problems, however, soon combined to awaken the Bolsheviks to the realistic strictures of practical politics.

LENIN'S GOVERNMENT

Early Policies

When the euphoria about their success receded enough to permit rational reflection, Russia's new masters set themselves the difficult task of organizing a government. This endeavor was not easy, for the revolutionary elements were far from united. After several disputes with other leftist groups, the Bolsheviks formed a coalition with the Left Socialist-Revolutionaries (the radical wing of the Socialist-Revolutionaries, or S-Rs) as junior partners. The important seats in the government were held by the Bolsheviks, however. Lenin was the chairman of the people's commissars;

Trotsky, the people's commissar of foreign affairs; Alexei Rykov, the people's commissar of interior; and Joseph Stalin, the people's commissar of nationality affairs. The Extraordinary Commission for Combating Counterrevolution and Speculation (*Cheka*—the secret police) was established in late December 1917 and headed by Feliks Dzerzhinsky. Under Dzerzhinsky's leadership, Cheka carried out the first Bolshevik purges, which came to be called the Red Terror.[1]

The immediate task of the new government in Petrograd was to consolidate its control over the rest of the land. Determined resistance in Moscow was overcome, and the local governments were replaced by Bolshevik-controlled soviets. The non-Russian minorities remained a problem for Lenin, however.

In an effort to undercut the authority of the tsarist regime, the Bolsheviks had always advocated national self-determination for the minority peoples in the empire. So on November 15, 1917, the new government issued a proclamation sanctioning secession of those minorities who chose to establish separate states.

This proclamation had unexpected international ramifications, however. Seeing the opportunity to capitalize on the chaos in Russia, the German government lent its support to the separatist movements in Estonia, Latvia, Lithuania, Finland (formerly part of the Russian Empire), Byelorussia, and the Ukraine, while the French and British were quick to protect their commercial and strategic interests in Georgia, Armenia, Azerbaijan, and Central Asia.

Startled by these defections and affronted by the minorities' willingness to use foreign support in gaining independence, Lenin's government quickly modified its position. Declaring that while it continued to support national self-determination, the Soviet government found that the anti-Bolshevik governments in the provinces were counterrevolutionary and therefore must be quashed. The resulting nationalistic resistance to Bolshevik power was the first major opposition to the new regime, one that tended to encourage other Bolshevik opponents to engage eventually in civil war.[2]

A second controversy centered around the election and function of a Constituent Assembly. Perhaps the oldest revolutionary goal in Russia was for a constitution to be drafted by a freely elected body. Indeed the date for an assembly's election had already been set by the time the Bolsheviks came to power. The Bolsheviks had been as vocal as any other group in advocating for a constitution, so when they seized power they were obliged to conduct the elections even though it had become clear that they would not win a majority of the seats.

The election that was held on November 25, 1917, constitutes the only freely contested national election (an election in which more than one candidate was allowed to run for each office) in the history of the Soviet

---

[1]David Shub, *Lenin* (Middlesex, England: Penguin Books, 1966), pp. 348–352.

[2]Isaac Deutscher, *Stalin*, 2nd ed. (New York: Oxford University Press, 1967), pp. 182–185.

Union until the late 1980s. True to their expectations, the Bolsheviks managed to win only about a quarter of the seats in the Constituent Assembly; the S-Rs captured almost 60 percent. The remainder of the seats was divided among other socialist parties (the Mensheviks won only 16 of the 707 seats) and the Cadets (liberals). Viewing their weak position in the assembly as a threat to the revolution, the Bolsheviks suppressed it after only one meeting. Many who might have otherwise remained uncommitted in the approaching civil war took this abrupt squelch of democracy as a dark omen and became alienated from the Bolshevik cause. Yet, at the same time as the party was rejecting the authority of representative democracy and as Dzerzhinsky's Cheka was intimidating the reactionary opposition by arresting more and more "enemies of the revolution," radical reforms were being pursued with great fervor, thus bringing liberation to millions who had been suppressed socially and politically.

Indeed, in the first weeks of Bolshevik rule, sweeping changes were instituted. Capital punishment was abolished the day after Lenin's takeover. Decrees redistributed the land; laws divested the Church of property, privilege, and power; and edicts proclaimed the equality of women. Vast reforms were sponsored in education, divorce and abortion procedures were liberalized, and artists and intellectuals were encouraged to express themselves openly. Beyond question, the Bolsheviks had set in motion a revolution that piqued the imagination and attention of leftists throughout the world, as idealists dreamed of the dawn of a new human era.

At the same time, Lenin was well aware that the immediate future of his government depended on one overriding factor: ending the war. More than any other issue in these early days, the question of the war divided the Bolshevik camp. Some revolutionaries wanted to continue the war. Others, including Trotsky, preferred a "no war, no peace" policy; that is, they advocated refusing to fight the Germans while holding the lines at the front so that no more territory would be lost.

Lenin summarily rejected continuing the war, and he gave Trotsky's ambivalent tactic scarcely more consideration. Consistent with his pre-revolution stance, Lenin argued that the war was a capitalist fight and that the socialists should not participate in it. Reinforced by the realization that the Russian people would not support the war any longer, Lenin called for a negotiated peace at almost any price.

Lenin's argument that the mass desertions from the front amounted to the soldiers' "voting with their feet" was persuasive. Over the objections of Trotsky, Bukharin, Dzerzhinsky, and the Left S-Rs, the Bolsheviks agreed to accept the extortionist peace terms the Germans offered. They also decided to move the capital to less vulnerable Moscow, thus escaping potential German capture.

The **Treaty of Brest-Litovsk,** signed in March 1918, represented a total capitulation to German demands. Surrendering all the lands occupied by the German army, the Soviets ceded virtually all the European territory amassed by Russia since the Romanov ascension to power in 1613. The territorial gains made by Peter the Great, Catherine the Great, and Alexander I were abandoned to the Hun. Although the dissident Bolsheviks accepted the decision, the Left S-Rs refused to support the treaty and withdrew from the coalition government. Since this defection, the Bolsheviks, soon to be renamed the Communist Party of the Soviet Union, never again shared power.[3]

The Civil War (1918–1921)

Disillusionment over the squelched Constituent Assembly, opposition to the radical social changes being pursued, resistance to the terrorist tactics of Cheka, revulsion over the terms of the peace treaty, and general discontent with political and economic conditions caused various groups to reject the Bolshevik government by the spring of 1918. Some leading military personalities abandoned the areas held by the Bolsheviks altogether, going into provinces and attempting to raise armies to oppose the regime in Moscow. The beginning of the Russian Civil War was signaled in Siberia when a group of former prisoners of war called the Czech Legion refused the Bolshevik order to disarm.[4] Seeing this confrontation as an opportunity to seize power, Admiral Aleksandr Kolchak hastily formed a "**White**" government in Omsk, Siberia. Soon the Bolshevik "**Reds**" found themselves surrounded by hostile counterrevolutionary White forces. Besides Kolchak in the east, other armies organized in the north, west, and south.

As if not sufficiently threatened by armies of its own people, the Bolshevik government also found itself besieged by the invasion of expeditionary forces from Great Britain, France, Japan, and the United States. The fact that the Western powers invaded their country at such a desperate time is one that the Soviets have never forgotten, and one they remind us of from time to time.

The Civil War was a brutal and destructive bloodletting during which both sides engaged in wanton slaughter and inhumane reprisal. As the armies swept back and forth across the country, millions of people were killed or died of hunger and exposure. Millions more found themselves caught up in the savage carnage, scarcely understanding the causes for which they were being asked to surrender their goods or give up their lives. Left homeless in the wake of the titanic struggle, people followed the action, killing and looting because someone had previously brutalized them. It was this aimless killing and destruction that Boris Pasternak so dramatically sketched in *Doctor Zhivago*.

Although the Reds were outnumbered—in troops, generals, and guns—they managed to defeat the Whites by 1921. Lacking ideological unity, the Whites were badly divided. Many of their leaders were ambitious people who were seldom troubled by moral principle and who arrogantly refused to cooperate with one another for fear that their competitors might profit more than they. Hence, the Whites were unable to agree on military

---

[3]J. P. Nettl, *The Soviet Achievement* (San Diego, CA: Harcourt Brace Jovanovich, 1967), pp. 51–54.

[4]Georg von Rauch, *A History of Soviet Russia*, 6th ed., trans. Peter and Annette Jacobsohn (New York: Praeger Publishers, 1972), pp. 90–91.

or political objectives. Moreover, their rape of the Russian land, coupled with the aristocratic arrogance of their officers, assured that little popular support sustained their cause.

By contrast, the Bolsheviks enjoyed an ideological focus and also advanced a specific economic and political program, which was viewed by many as a welcome change from the tsarist regime. Additionally, the Reds benefited from a crucial strategic advantage. Occupying the political and industrial center of the country, the Red Army was not pressed to attack until it was prepared to do so. Thus, the Bolsheviks had the luxury of being able to defend against the Whites, who had to mount attacks in efforts to dislodge them from their stronghold.

Ill-prepared for the conflict at first, the Bolsheviks gave ground to the Whites and the invading Allies. Their position became so jeopardized in Siberia that on July 16, 1918, Nicholas II and his family, who were in Bolshevik hands, were executed in Yekaterinburg to prevent their possible rescue by the Whites.[5] Gradually, though, Leon Trotsky made an efficient fighting force of his army, and the Reds began to carry the field, sending their domestic enemies into retreat, a fact that persuaded the foreign invaders to grudgingly withdraw also. One front after the other collapsed.

By 1920 the Whites were all but completely defeated, with just one sizable element remaining in the south. But the danger was not yet ended, as the right-wing government of Poland under Marshal Joseph Pilsudski, in a bid to expand its territory at Soviet expense, launched an invasion on the Bolshevik state. Following advances and retreats by both sides, the line was stabilized, and the Soviet government agreed with Poland to accept borders that were considerably farther east than they had been before World War I. (These territories would be recovered by the Soviets shortly before World War II.)

With the end of the Polish war, the Soviets quickly defeated the Whites in the south, and peace was restored in 1921. Although some of the minority territories of the old empire were not yet under Soviet control and eastern Siberia was yet to be repatriated, the Soviet Union had survived its ordeal. With the Civil War ended and foreign invasions repulsed, attention had to be focused on domestic policy.

War Communism and the NEP

The Civil War had been a consuming event. Every effort was bent to its cause; other pressing but less immediate problems had to await its end for solutions of their own. The economy was one of those problems.

Flush with success in 1917, the Bolsheviks plunged into nationalizing industrial production without adequate thought or preparation. Factories and mines were turned over to the workers. "The expropriators were expropriated," according to the dictum of Marx. But this policy, referred to as **war communism,** proved foolhardy as former owners and managers

---

[5]Basil Dmytryshyn, *A History of Russia* (Englewood Cliffs, NJ: Prentice Hall, 1977), p. 494.

were brushed aside by the workers' councils. Lacking the necessary skills to run the industries and plagued by incessant bickering, the workers' councils failed to sustain the productivity that tsarist industry had managed to generate. Hence, industrial yields plummeted, and Lenin's government responded with centralization techniques that dissolved the workers' councils and ended forever worker control of the factories in the Soviet Union.

At the same time, the war disrupted the transportation system, thus hindering communications and shipping between the industrial and farming centers and causing even greater scarcities than the declining food and industrial production ordinarily would have brought. Some of the greatest fighting during the Civil War was in the south and west, areas where farming was most productive. The destruction of battle and the scavenging armies ravaged huge tracts of farmland, making useless any serious effort to plant and work the land on a large scale.

Repelled by the chaos in the cities, workers fled to the countryside, increasing the burden on the peasants, who had to share their scarce food with the city folk. In those places where farmers did have crops to sell, they found that the money was worthless because low production of consumer goods had inflated their costs beyond reason.

Responding to these perplexing circumstances, the peasants began to produce only enough to feed themselves and tried to ignore the confusion surrounding them. But such was not to be their lot. Desperately needing the foodstuffs for the cities and the fronts, the Red government sent collection gangs into the countryside to force the peasants to give up their produce. These confiscation forays took on a foreboding character. Poor peasants joined with government agents to despoil the lands of the kulaks, a harbinger of an even more lethal purge on the farms a decade later.[6]

By the end of the Civil War, the economy was in shambles. Inflation was rampant, unemployment was high, and the peasants had become sullen and uncooperative. Agricultural production was less than half of what it had been in 1913, and industrial production had fallen to one-seventh of the prewar mark. Because of limited production and transportation failures, all goods became scarce, and the reemergence of a black market was as inevitable as it was spontaneous.

Clearly, something had to be done to improve the economic situation. A sailor's rebellion at the Kronstadt naval base indelibly impressed Lenin with the urgency of the matter. The sailors of Kronstadt had long been among the most strident Bolshevik supporters. By March 1921, however, matters had reached such a state that these formerly loyal sailors rose up against Lenin's government. Trotsky himself rushed to command the troops sent to put down the rebellion, managing to subdue the naval base only after a fierce siege.[7]

Never slow to learn political lessons, Lenin moved quickly to take the necessary remedial economic steps. He admitted that because of the diffi-

[6]Alec Nove, *An Economic History of the U.S.S.R.* (Middlesex, England: Penguin Books, 1972), pp. 59–63.

[7]John Lawrence, *A History of Russia,* 2nd ed. (New York: Mentor Books, 1969), p. 248.

culties caused by the Civil War and because of its zeal to achieve socialism quickly, the party had made mistakes. Accordingly, he introduced the New Economic Policy (NEP).

In essence, the NEP returned to private ownership most retail operations and factories employing fewer than 20 workers. Heavy industry, transportation, communications, and finance all remained in government hands. In the countryside, peasants were assessed a tax to be paid in kind, but they were left to vend their surplus crops at whatever rates the market would bear.

Encouraged to produce a surplus, the peasants began to work the land with new enthusiasm. But although the NEP was a success eventually, a year of terrible suffering preceded better times. The winter of 1921–1922 brought a great famine to the land. The poor harvests had taken their toll, and the 1921 crop was particularly meager. Hunger set in and deepened until millions were starving. The proportions of the famine were so great as to alarm world public opinion, and several international efforts were mounted to bring relief to Russia's helpless people. Exhibiting a much different attitude than when it invaded the Soviet Union, the United States sent Herbert Hoover, the man who had engineered the relief of Belgium during World War I, to organize the aid efforts in Russia.[8] (Unlike the United States invasion of their homeland, Hoover's relief efforts receive little mention by Soviet historians.)

Official estimates put the deaths at five million before the famine eventually passed and the incentives of the NEP brought greater productivity on the farms as well as in the cities. By 1927 the Soviets could announce that the prewar level of production had been restored.

Political Questions

Even as the economy was being freed, however, the Bolsheviks began to address a number of touchy political questions. When the revolution took place, radicals across the globe flocked to Russia; their presence created certain administrative and theoretical problems. An immediate question confronting the new state was what the nature of the government was to be. Was it to include all the radical elements that milled about in Soviet politics, or was it to be limited to the Bolsheviks alone? At first Lenin tried to govern in coalition with the other radical elements, but they refused to cooperate with the Bolsheviks after the demise of the Constituent Assembly and the controversy over the Brest-Litovsk Treaty. Although Cheka began to attack the reactionaries as early as July 1918, radicals enjoyed substantial freedom in the Soviet state, to the extent of even being allowed to criticize the government publicly until 1921.

Seizing upon the Kronstadt rebellion as a pretext, Lenin took the opportunity to rid his regime of some of his most severe leftist critics. Employing Cheka, he had hundreds of dissenting radicals arrested, impris-

[8]Nove, p. 86.

oned, and even executed. By 1923 there was no question that the Communist Party was to monopolize Soviet power, refusing to share it with other political parties or even with the trade unions.[9]

On the international front, a particularly troublesome question evolved concerning the disposition of Soviet power. Should Soviet power be used to ignite revolution throughout the world as Trotsky proposed, or should it be used to build a strong base for "socialism in one country" as Stalin would have it? Taking a middle course, but clearly leaning toward Trotsky's position, Lenin agreed to the 1919 creation of the Communist International (**Comintern**). Led by Grigory Zinoviev, the Comintern trained revolutionaries and fostered revolutions throughout the world. Two of the most famous Comintern agents were Josip Broz Tito of Yugoslavia and Mikhail Borodin, who played such a large part in the early stages of the Chinese revolution.

The Russian Orthodox Church also posed a problem to the revolutionaries. From the beginning of Bolshevik rule, the Church found it difficult to function. The Bolsheviks saw the ancient religious institution as an instrument of oppression, "an opium of the people," as Marx had suggested. Accordingly, Church lands and buildings had been confiscated and religious services discouraged immediately following the Bolshevik coup.

Resisting Bolshevik control, the Church had encouraged the faithful to oppose the Reds during the Civil War. When the war ended, Lenin again focused his attention on religion. Turning the dreaded Cheka loose, he arrested, imprisoned, and executed the clergy and many of the faithful. Seminaries were closed, ornaments and relics were confiscated, and services were forbidden.[10]

STALIN

Having survived a 1919 assassination attempt and a series of strokes in the early 1920s, Lenin died on January 21, 1924. Before his death, however, the Bolshevik leader dictated a letter to his colleagues, which has since become known as his "Political Testament." The letter candidly analyzed the strengths and weaknesses of the leading contenders for succession. Complaining about Stalin's rudeness and declaring him unfit for the post of party general secretary,[11] Lenin recommended that Stalin be removed.

Succession

Lenin's death brought to the fore the power struggle that had been going on behind the scenes since his first stroke. The contest for succession

[9]David MacKenzie and Michael W. Curran, *A History of Russia and the Soviet Union* (Homewood, IL: The Dorsey Press, 1977), p. 480.

[10]Lawrence, pp. 260–265.

[11]The post of general secretary of the Communist Party was created at the Eleventh Party Congress in April 1922, and Stalin was then elected to the office.

was waged on very important ideological and political issues, but personal jealousies and animosities were also crucial factors.

Leon Trotsky seemed to be the most likely person to assume leadership of the Soviet Union. Although he became a Bolshevik only a few months before the October coup, no other person besides Lenin himself could boast an equal role in making the world's first communist state a reality. Revered though he was, however, Trotsky had many detractors in high places within the party because of his personal arrogance and his radical, idealistic politics. Foremost among Trotsky's opponents were two of Lenin's old comrades, Lev Kamenev and Grigory Zinoviev. This pair did not greatly differ with Trotsky on ideological grounds. Instead, they opposed Trotsky's leadership because they did not want this arrogant genius to assume control of the regime. Accordingly, Kamenev and Zinoviev joined in an alliance with Joseph Stalin in 1923.

Once described by Trotsky as "the most eminent mediocrity in the Party"[12] because of his innocuous role in party affairs, Stalin originally had been commissar of nationalities but in 1922 assumed the newly created post of general secretary of the party. Perceiving the new office as a bureaucratic position laden with mundane administrative chores, the other Bolshevik leaders avoided it and willingly elected Stalin to the job. This act was but one of numerous miscalculations that the ruthless Georgian's colleagues lived to regret. Slowly and methodically, Stalin used his control in the party to elevate his own supporters to positions of power. Unfortunately, the significance of Stalin's maneuvers escaped the attention of most of his colleagues, although Lenin was the first to sense the danger and warned about it in his Political Testament.

Despite Lenin's warning to his comrades to depose the general secretary, Kamenev and Zinoviev thought Stalin could be used as an ally to defeat Trotsky's bid for dominance. So it was that they played crucial roles in perhaps the most fateful decision in the history of the Soviet Union. At their urging, the Central Committee voted to suppress Lenin's testament after his death.[13] Had Lenin's condemnation been published and Stalin deposed, Soviet history would have followed a very different course.

The struggle for power between Trotsky and his three opponents centered on three major issues. First, attempting to play on Lenin's warning, Trotsky attacked Stalin's management of the party. He accused the Georgian of dictatorial and centralist policies that contradicted the basic "democratic" nature of the party. Second, Trotsky advanced his theory of **permanent revolution,** insisting that Soviet power should be used to instigate revolutions in the advanced industrial states of Europe with the idea that such revolutions would complement and support the communist regime in the Soviet Union. Displaying a paranoia that later characterized him, Stalin argued that the Soviet Union was under siege of a "capitalist encirclement" and that by "building socialism in one country," the Soviet

[12]von Rauch, p. 167.

[13]Deutscher, pp. 272–273. Lenin's testament was not officially published in the Soviet Union until 1987.

Union should make itself invincible before becoming a catalyst for revolution abroad. Third, Trotsky wanted to end the NEP and resocialize the Soviet economy, industrializing it with all haste. Stalin advocated a more cautious, gradual approach to industrial and agrarian reform.

While Trotsky's condescending and arrogant attitude alienated many Old Bolsheviks, Stalin's appointment of hundreds of supporters to pivotal positions clearly gave him a decisive edge in the party. Further, the people Stalin promoted were far different from the original Bolsheviks. When the party was firmly in power, it needed plodding, methodical bureaucrats to administer policy; the brilliant revolutionaries had become obsolete and even embarrassing to the new regime. Hence, although Trotsky's position of permanent revolution was probably more consistent with Marxism, Stalin's cautious, defensive approach was much more attractive to people who were reluctant to jeopardize their new positions with revolutionary adventures abroad.

Displaying techniques that he would use to advantage in the future, Stalin mobilized party opposition through meetings at which Trotsky was vilified and maligned by speakers who led the assembly in chants and unthinking protestations. Finally, at the end of 1924, Kamenev and Zinoviev realized that it was Stalin, not they, who had profited most from embarrassing Trotsky. In a desperate attempt to redress the balance of power they gravitated toward Trotsky—but alas, too late.

Stalin's control of the party was becoming too strong to resist. To seal his victory over the "left" (Trotsky, Kamenev, and Zinoviev), the general secretary allied with the party's "right," personified by three men—Nikolai Bukharin, after Lenin, the party's leading theoretician; Alexei Rykov, chairman of the people's commissars; and Mikhail Tomsky, the leader of the trade unions.

The "rightists" of the party wanted to continue the gradualist socialization policies of the NEP. They argued in favor of sustaining the private ownership of small business and farmlands, at least until Soviet production had regained its prewar level, and they emphasized producing consumer goods and raising the people's standard of living. They contended that once productivity was raised, the economy could be gradually socialized to the exclusion of private ownership.

The struggle between right and left progressed over the next two years. Inextricably, the Stalin-Bukharin faction gained strength and support, while the opposition slipped from favor. By 1927 the left was completely defeated; Trotsky, Kamenev, and Zinoviev were expelled from the party along with many of their supporters. Having refused to bow to his Georgian adversary, Trotsky was expelled from the Soviet Union and ultimately settled in Mexico, where he carried on the struggle by pelting Stalin with stinging criticism. Finally, in 1940, Trotsky was assassinated by a Soviet-trained agent of Spanish origin. Ironically, the erstwhile revolutionary managed to outlive most of his comrades, who perished in the great purges of the 1930s. For their part, Zinoviev and Kamenev recanted their "errors" and were restored to the party. This act managed to save them for only a few years, however, as they were among the first to be shot during the purges.

Not satisfied with the extent of his victory, Stalin reversed himself again, this time accusing Bukharin, Rykov, and Tomsky of harboring capitalist tendencies. Once more, the compliant party members met to denounce the new offenders, removing them, too, from party membership. By late 1929, Stalin could content himself in the knowledge that he was without peer in the Soviet Union.

The Five-Year Plans

Having discredited and demoted the Old Bolsheviks, Stalin turned to Soviet economic problems in earnest. With astounding suddenness, the general secretary reversed his position once again, this time adopting several policies that Trotsky had advocated only a few years before. Abandoning Bukharin's modest approach to industrial and agrarian reform and proclaiming the end of the NEP, Stalin launched the Soviet Union on a crash program meant to accomplish two things: The economy was to be industrialized and resocialized. The capital for this bold venture was to be appropriated from a reduced defense budget and, more importantly, squeezed from the peasants who were to produce more goods even as they were allowed less of the material benefits of the society.

Stalin's economic transformation was to be accomplished through planning and the centralization of control. The details of the planned economy will be discussed more completely later; fundamentally, it consists of a central agency providing that estimated resources be allocated to the production of targeted products either directly or indirectly through capital investment.

The First Five-Year Plan (1928–1932) called for impossible goals. Its objectives could have been reached only if no difficulties were encountered. Such was not to be the case, however. Harvests were poorer than anticipated, major construction projects were delayed, and quotas in essential raw materials went unmet—factors that tended to detract from successful completion of the plan. The 1931 Japanese invasion of Manchuria also caused the Soviet leaders serious apprehension, and they found it necessary to divert resources and capital into defense projects that had not been originally anticipated. In the same year, Stalin made a prophetic statement about the urgency of modernization: "We are fifty to one hundred years behind the advanced countries. We must cover this distance in ten years. Either we do this or they will crush us." Scarcely a decade later, the Nazis invaded the Soviet Union.[14]

Even though the First Five-Year Plan failed to reach all of its objectives, it was generally considered a success. Although many quotas went unfulfilled, others were exceeded, and, overall, the Soviet economy made giant strides forward. Perhaps even more importantly, the party managed

[14]MacKenzie and Curran, p. 506.

to mobilize the population, calling upon sincere popular enthusiasm for the projected advances. An atmosphere of excitement ran through the people, creating an enthusiasm that had not been known since the tsar abdicated. Indeed, so great were the accomplishments and changes during the 1930s that historians refer to the period as the "second revolution."

Successes of the plan did not occur without accompanying problems, however. Dire consequences often attended failure in reaching the quotas set forth in the plan. Failure could mean the loss of one's job or, in serious cases, arrest, exile, and even execution. These hazards, coupled with the often impossible quotas, encouraged officials to resort to "creative" means by which to avoid punishment. Production shortfalls saw figures falsified and other statistics manipulated, causing warps in the data used to develop the next plan. By contrast, if all went well and a plant managed to produce above its quota, the surplus was usually hidden away, both as insurance against a time when the plant fell short of its goal and as a precaution against encouraging planners to increase the plant's quotas.

Sadly, the economic system became riddled with bribery, lying, cheating, and theft—all to accomplish the goals of the plan. At the same time, labor camps bulged with people who violated the dictates of the state and, even more tragically, with people who were guilty of no misdeeds whatever. The camps, run by the secret police (called the NKVD at the time), quickly became an integral part of the Soviet economy. Indeed, they became so important to the state's productivity that their existence was perpetuated long after the political need for them had disappeared.[15]

Collectivization of the Farms

At the same time that he instituted forced industrialization, Stalin also reversed his former position on agricultural organization. As pointed out earlier, the capital for Soviet industrialization was to come largely from the peasants; consequently, their income could not follow on par with the growth in other parts of the economy. The peasants met this imposed sacrifice with stubborn resistance. Hoping to force prices up, they refused to sell their crops at the artificially low figures mandated by the government. This defiance stimulated a grain shortage that threatened food supplies in the cities in 1927 and 1928.

In 1928 only about 20 percent of the Soviet farmers were located on collective farms; the bulk of the peasants worked on privately owned land. The huge estates owned by the gentry before the revolution had been destroyed in 1917–1918, and the land was shattered into more than 25 million small farms. Production tended to lag because the small farms were unable to mechanize, fertilize properly, or utilize other modern agricultural techniques sufficiently. Accordingly, when the farmers withheld their crops from the market, shortages quickly became severe.

Perhaps in an effort to relieve the food crisis, Stalin took a decisive step toward ending the economic freedom enjoyed by the peasants during

[15]Nove, pp. 266–267.

the NEP. In the fall of 1929 he commanded a cadre of thousands of urban party members to go into the countryside to institute collectivization and, at the same time, to bring confiscated farm goods to the cities. The result was catastrophic. Virtually invading the rural areas, these party zealots ravaged the villages, ruthlessly forcing the peasants into collective farms and extorting crops with brutal, sometimes even lethal, methods. Desperately hoping to weather the onslaught, millions of peasants resisted with such force that in some places the Red Army was sent in, leveling whole villages with artillery and killing many of the inhabitants.

The simple peasants were no match for their assailants, so they decided to strike back with the only means at their disposal. They burned harvested crops, left standing grain to rot in the fields, and slaughtered as much of their stock as possible. Yet, despite their resistance, almost half of the Soviet peasants found themselves on collective farms within a few months.

The massive collectivization continued for several years. By 1932 the disruption had become so complete as to create a great famine that resulted in the loss of five to ten million lives.[16]

Hence, the collectivization of Soviet agriculture, fostered to force the peasant to pay for industrial modernization, sacrificed millions of people. Sadly, many of the land's most efficient farmers were among those who perished. The survivors found themselves on state-controlled tracts, occupying the lowest priority in the planned distribution of goods.

The Stalinist Society

At the same time, however, Stalin was also a great modernizer. His policies, wretched as they were, catapulted the Soviet Union into the twentieth century. By 1939 the Soviet Union not only boasted the world's first socialist economy, but it also had become a leading industrial power. And these changes were made during a decade when the Western economies suffered their most serious setbacks in modern history.[17]

Accompanying the economic transformation was a social revolution. At the close of the 1930s, the Soviet social structure had assumed the basic form it retains to this day. A simplistic though useful classification of Soviet society of 1939 would find it divided into three basic categories. The **peasantry,** which found itself split between the collective farms and the state farms (the distinction between these units will be explained later), continued to occupy the base of the society. The workers, or **proletariat,** populated the cities and generally enjoyed a higher standard of living than those people on the farms. Then there was the **intelligentsia,** consisting of leading party members, high-ranking military personnel, and leading scientists, athletes, and artists. The intelligentsia was clearly a privileged class, enjoying the best the society had to offer. Stalin was careful to reward his sup-

[16]Dmytryshyn, pp. 534–536.
[17]Nove, p. 223.

porters with undisguised bounty, but those whom he perceived as enemies suffered grievously.

The Great Purges (1934–1938)

Since it came into power, the Communist Party felt the need to "dress" its ranks from time to time by a process that became known as the *purge*. The party had grown from only a few thousand in 1917 to about three million in 1930. Many of those who joined late were opportunists who were not as dedicated to the Marxist cause as the original Bolsheviks had been. Consequently, periodic efforts were made to rid the party of hangers-on. Additionally, Lenin had used Cheka to rid the government and the state of Mensheviks, Anarchists, Syndicalists, and other radicals who refused to conform to the discipline thought necessary to the survival of the new government. Although they had never been pleasant, the purges before Stalin had not been massive, nor did they have the character of personal vindictiveness that they came to symbolize later.

Stalin's early purges against Trotsky, Zinoviev, Kamenev, Bukharin, and others in the 1920s have already been discussed. These episodes were the result of raw power politics but they did not end in the death of the participants. Indeed, even though Trotsky was banished, the others were reinstated to the party and to important positions after their admission of transgressions. Yet, events took a tragic turn in 1934.

Late in that year, Sergei Kirov, Leningrad's popular party chief, was assassinated. Although the assassin was quickly apprehended, the exact details of the killing and the people behind it have remained a mystery. Khrushchev and others later suggested that Stalin was responsible for the elimination of Kirov, whom he saw as a rival. Whatever the truth of the matter, the interrogation of the assassin and his alleged coconspirators purportedly implicated Zinoviev and Kamenev in plots to assassinate several Soviet leaders, including the general secretary himself.[18]

This startling "revelation" electrified the party and launched an unprecedented repression. Zinoviev and Kamenev were arrested, as were many of their associates. Meanwhile a Special Commission was created to ferret out the spies and traitors in the party and to bring them to "justice." The NKVD, led by Genrikh Yagoda, threw out a net in search of enemies of the state. Soon, the country was terrorized with the spectacle of mass arrests, executions, and shipments of thousands of people to labor camps.

When he felt strong enough to make a move, Stalin ordered the first of several show trials. During these disgraceful circuses, prosecutor Andrei Vyshinsky shamelessly browbeat the accused, many of whom were among the country's leading revolutionary figures. Charged with the most outrageous crimes, tortured, and abused, many of the prisoners confessed to crimes they did not commit; others either committed suicide or went to the shooting wall, defiant to the end. Regardless of their conduct, during the

[18]See Robert Conquest, *Stalin and the Kirov Murder* (New York: Oxford University Press, 1989).

trials, they were all convicted, and they all met death—either by their own hand or before a firing squad.[19]

The list of victims in his hideous episode reads like a "who's who" among Soviet revolutionaries. Zinoviev and Kamenev were early victims of the madness. Later, Bukharin and Rykov were tried and shot. Even NKVD chief Yagoda fell victim to the purge and was replaced by Nikolai Yezhov, who later was also shot. In addition to those executed, a large number of prominent Old Bolsheviks committed suicide, disappeared, or died under mysterious circumstances. Among these were Maxim Gorky, Mikhail P. Tomsky, V. V. Kuibyshev, and G. K. Ordzhonikidze (Stalin's fellow Georgian who was at one time his closest associate).[20]

The appalling statistics go on and on. Only 15 of the 140 Central Committee members who were serving in 1934 survived the purges, and 65 percent of all military officers above the rank of captain died. Yet, however enormous its impact on the leadership, the purge had equally far-reaching effects on the civilian population. An estimated 5 or 6 percent of the total Soviet population was arrested between 1934 and 1938. Some of these people were released, but between eight and 23 million people were either executed or sent to the camps. The NKVD administered a huge network of labor camps in such desolate, frozen places as Karelia, the Kola Peninsula, and Siberia.[21]

At first, people were arrested for specific political or economic crimes. Citizens were encouraged to be vigilant against counterrevolutionary activity. Many responded by reporting friends, relatives, and even complete strangers to the authorities. The people's motivations for such actions were often founded in the sincere wish to protect the state. Yet, sometimes less noble reasons compelled their "cooperation" with the police. People were reported by their neighbors for petty spite or by their enemies for selfish reasons; some, hoping to prove their own loyalty and thus escape the camps themselves, would bear witness against others.

The entire affair is a sordid, dismal chapter in Soviet history punctuated with tragedy, hypocrisy, and irony. The end of the purges left a thoroughly cowed population and a party whose ranks had been thinned of its best members. Gone were the brilliant ideologues, the daring and courageous revolutionaries whose exploits had rocked the world and ushered in a new era of history. A phalanx of independent thinkers and activists gave way to echelons of yes-men who owed their positions to the largess of Stalin and who therefore dared not question him.

The Great Patriotic War

Because of the party's absorption with domestic events, foreign policy received second billing in Soviet politics after the Treaty of Brest-Litovsk.

[19]Deutscher, p. 373.

[20]Roy A. Medvedev, *Let History Judge* (New York: Vintage Press, 1971), pp. 170, 180, 193.

[21]MacKenzie and Curran, pp. 490–493.

Soviet foreign policy took various turns during the interwar years depending on how national interests were viewed at the time. The Comintern was used to infiltrate foreign labor unions, education, and leftist movements, and it carried on large propaganda campaigns in efforts to incite workers' revolutions in the non-Marxist states.

For a time in the 1920s, Germany and the USSR found themselves isolated and outcast nations sharing compatible needs. Accordingly, they cooperated on a limited basis, the Germans secretly training troops on Soviet soil in exchange for German technological shipments to Moscow.

The Soviet Union continued to play the part of a loner in Europe until it became clear that no successful leftist rebellions were likely in the West. Then the Soviet Union cautiously moved into the mainstream of international politics and, moderating its aggressive-defensive posture, joined the League of Nations in 1934.

When Hitler came to power in 1933, the growing menace of the Third Reich induced Moscow to call for all governments to join in a "popular front" to resist Nazi aggression. However, Western reluctance to resist Germany's occupation of the Rhineland in 1936 and the fascist involvement in the Spanish Civil War forced Stalin to reassess his position. Suspecting that England and France might never stand up to the Nazi tyrant or, even worse, that the capitalist states might encourage Hitler to expand eastward, Stalin tried to chart a more cautious course in 1937, recoiling from his former anti-Nazi stance despite sending aid to the republican cause in the Spanish Civil War (1936–1939). When England and France invited the German invasion of Czechoslovakia by surrendering the Sudetenland at Munich in 1938—a conference to which the Soviet Union was pointedly not invited—Stalin felt he had little choice but to strike his own deal with Hitler.

Moscow was not convinced that the capitalist states hoped that Germany would spend its energy on an invasion of the USSR. But the Soviets desperately needed time to build their strength since the purges had all but destroyed their officer corps. Consequently, feverish efforts were made to find an accommodation with Germany. Finally, in August 1939, a nonaggression pact was signed between the Soviet Union and Nazi Germany. Reminiscent of the Treaty of Tilsit, the accord secretly divided Europe between its signatories. Hitler was to be left alone in the west, while the USSR was free to collect Bessarabia, part of Finland, and the Baltic states of Estonia, Latvia, and Lithuania. Poland was to be divided between Germany and the Soviet Union.[22]

The Soviet-German agreement shocked the world. Denunciations about Soviet duplicity rang throughout the West. Yet, with the perspective of time, it is clear that the Soviet policy was a vital step if Hitler was to be put off. Following a policy of appeasement, the Western powers showed no inclination to confront the Führer. Instead, every sign seemed to point to a clear Anglo-French policy of turning the German blitzkrieg toward the

[22]Alvin Z. Rubinstein, *Soviet Foreign Policy Since World War II* (Cambridge, MA: Winthrop, 1981), pp. 15–17.

Soviet Union. Coupled with Stalin's already well-developed mistrust of the capitalist intentions, the Soviet-German Nonaggression Pact makes sense from the Soviet perspective.

With the pact concluded, the two tyrants set out to claim their respective spheres. Hitler's invasion of Poland in September 1939 signaled the beginning of World War II. Stalin, in the meantime, attacked his western neighbors. The Soviet army invaded Finland on the cynical pretext of securing its frontier, but it was deeply embarrassed when the stiff Finnish resistance caused the aggressors to falter. Eventually, however, the tiny nation had to withdraw, leaving the Soviets with a large portion of Finnish Karelia. Losing its League of Nations membership over the incident, the Soviet Union next turned on the Baltic countries, compelling them into submission, and then on Rumania, easily forcing it to surrender Bessarabia in 1940.

Meanwhile, the German military machine swept through northwestern Europe until only England remained free of Nazi domination. Pounding England with continuous air strikes, Hitler considered it defeated by the late spring of 1941. Hence, violating the Nonaggression Pact, he turned to the invasion of the Soviet Union. Gathering three million troops in Poland, the Füher launched Operation Barbarossa on June 22, 1941. The Soviet forces were stunned by the attack, and the German army penetrated deep into Russia and the Baltic states.

Many people who found themselves in the path of the invading force met the Germans with joy, thinking they were being liberated from Stalin's Great-Russian domination. The sad truth quickly became evident, however, as SS battalions brutalized people, forced them into slave labor camps, or murdered them by the hundreds of thousands. Nazi cruelties to civilian and military personnel soon convinced the non-Russian Soviet citizens to join their Russian comrades in resisting the invaders rather than welcoming them. This turnabout proved costly for Hitler's forces. By 1942 a full-fledged resistance movement vexed the Germans behind the line of battle. Tying down thousands of troops that could have been used at the front, Soviet partisans sabotaged factories, ambushed columns of troops, and disrupted the thinly stretched supply lines of the invaders.

Meanwhile, it had become clear that the Soviet people would respond more willingly to nationalistic pleas than to calls for the defense of communism, so Stalin deemphasized ideology and the party to concentrate upon themes of Russian unity. Harkening back to prerevolutionary memories, Stalin called upon his people to rise up in a patriotic effort to destroy everything in the path of the advancing Teutons in what came to be called the Great Patriotic War. The Soviet army donned insignia and formed regimental units reminiscent of the tsarist era, and the Russian Orthodox Church was reinstated to full prominence in return for its support against the invader.

Even as the German army advanced and the Soviet people resisted, a massive migration of people and equipment was put in motion. Consistent with the ancient Russian tradition of scorching the earth while retreating, the Soviet leaders decided to save what industry they could while destroying anything that would otherwise fall into German hands. In a monumental effort, more than 25,000 factories were dismantled and shipped east beyond the Ural Mountains. Enormous sacrifices were imposed at the front and among the people in order to spare the personnel and resources necessary for such a huge project.

Besides factories and equipment, the Soviet government also moved a huge number of people east. Thousands of children and other defenseless people were sent beyond the Urals and into the Central Asian republics, and skilled workers were also required to follow the factories into Siberia. The largest number of people shipped east, however, were deportees. Several dissident national groups aroused the government's suspicions that they might welcome the Nazi advance. Others were accused of collaboration after the Germans had been vanquished. Accordingly, millions of people were deported to Siberia and Central Asia. Crimean Tatars, Volga Germans, and Kalmyks were forcibly evacuated from Russia and the Ukraine. From the Caucasus, the Chechen-Ingushs and the Karachai-Balkars were evacuated en masse. Sadly, many of these people were never repatriated and remain in the lands of relocation.[23]

Sweeping over Byelorussia, Smolensk, and Kiev, the Nazis prepared to conquer the Soviet capital. As Japanese planes rained bombs on Pearl Harbor, bringing the United States into the war, the Germans launched their attack on Moscow. This time, however, they met a better prepared, more determined enemy and were forced to fall back from the capital. The new year, 1942, greeted the Soviet army with other victories as well. The unusually cold winter caught the Germans unprepared. Lacking proper clothing and adequate equipment for the severe Russian winter, the German war machine stalled while Soviet troops counterattacked. In the south, Rostov was retaken by the Red Army, and in the north a link with Leningrad was established across Lake Ladoga, probably preventing that besieged city from succumbing to the Nazis.

Interfering with his generals, Hitler insisted that the 1942 offensive be concentrated on the oil fields in the Caucasus. In the meantime, Stalin's alliance with England and the United States provided him with billions of dollars worth of food, clothing, weapons, munitions, and equipment. Thus, the Soviet army met the full brunt of the German advance and managed to deny it its goals. The Allied aid was absolutely crucial to the Soviet effort, probably representing the difference between ultimate success or failure against the attackers. Yet, in all, the U.S. Lend-Lease Program amounted to only about $11 billion worth of goods, a fraction of the total Soviet effort.[24] Unfortunately, some Western chroniclers of the war have tended to overemphasize the importance of the Allied aid, thus denying the Soviet people their just due. It must never be forgotten that the Soviet Union absorbed the full fury of the Nazi war machine, and its people, suffering unspeakable hardship and cruelty, incurred ghastly losses repelling the fascists.

[23]Nettl, p. 163.
[24]MacKenzie and Curran, p. 561.

As the war progressed, the question of a second front became an issue. Seeing his country take unspeakable losses and remaining suspicious of the West, Stalin became increasingly concerned about his allies' intentions. Indeed, speculation among some irresponsible Western publishers, military men, and politicians caused Stalin concern that the Allies might bide their time while the two totalitarian giants bludgeoned each other.[25] Accordingly, pushed back to a front extending along a line from Leningrad to Moscow to Stalingrad, the Soviet leader began unrelenting pressure for an Allied invasion of France.

The Allies had their own strategy, however. Instead of opening a second front in Europe, as they had promised Stalin they would do, they chose to fight in North Africa. Stalin took the news of the Allied invasion of North Africa as confirmation of his suspicion about the capitalists' intentions. Europe was the target; Europe was the key to ending the war! Yet, rather than invading Europe, the British and Americans assaulted North Africa, accomplishing two things as Stalin saw it. First, conquering North Africa did much to secure British colonial and commercial interests in the Mediterranean. Second, the Allies could claim the second front had been opened while still leaving the Nazis and the Soviets to battle each other alone in Europe.

Stalin assessed the Allied invasion of Sicily (July 1943) and Italy (January 1944) similarly, in that Germany was protected by the Alps from a southern attack. Further, he found Churchill's scheme of attacking Europe's "soft underbelly" by invading Yugoslavia and Greece equally obnoxious. Again, such a strategy would work to the commercial interests of Great Britain, and Churchill was quite open with his argument that the southern route to Berlin included the advantage of denying much of Eastern Europe to the Soviet Union after the war.[26] Although Stalin allowed these facts more credence than perhaps they deserved, his interpretation contained an element of truth, and one should keep it in mind when trying to understand Soviet postwar policies.

However, 1942 was not a year for ideological polemics: Too much was left to be done in the war. By August the Germans had begun their assault on Stalingrad. As in the Civil War, when it was called Tsaritsyn, this city was a vital rail and river center, linking Russia to the oil of the Caucasus as well as to the food of the steppe. The Nazi panzers reached the outskirts of the city on September 1, signaling the beginning of a pitched battle that became the turning point of the entire war. Fighting heroically, the Soviet troops stopped the Nazi advance at Stalingrad.

Stymied by a lack of fuel and by the stubborn Soviet defense, the German Sixth Army found itself in serious trouble. The Soviet generals launched a massive counteroffensive that broke through the enemy's left and threatened to encircle the entire German army. The German commander might still have saved his army, except that Hitler refused to hear

[25]von Rauch, p. 336.
[26]Deutscher, pp. 506–507.

"Mother Russia," calling her people to rise to her defense, stands defiantly at the top of Mamaev Hill, the scene of the fiercest fighting in Volgograd (then Stalingrad) during World War II. This is the tallest free-standing statue in the world, taller even than the Statue of Liberty in New York harbor.

of a strategic retreat. Hence, the Soviet pincers drew tightly around the entire Sixth Army, which surrendered after unsuccessful efforts to resist.

The loss of a half million crack troops complete with equipment and arms was a fatal blow to Hitler's fortunes. The Soviet army maintained the offensive, pushing the Nazis back into the Ukraine and away from Moscow, even as the grisly 900-day siege of Leningrad was finally lifted.[27]

Battling through 1943, the Soviets pushed the Nazis back across Byelorussia and the Ukraine. The winter and spring of 1944 brought new German defeats, and by June the German lines had been forced all the way back to Rumania.

It was then, in June of 1944, that the Allies landed in France—*finally,* from the Soviet point of view! Having forced the Axis armies to retreat into their own territory, the Soviet leaders considered them defeated and regarded the long-delayed invasion of France as a belated Allied bid to share the spoils.

[27]For a detailed account of the siege of Leningrad, see Harrison E. Salisbury, *The Nine-Hundred Days: The Siege of Leningrad* (New York: Harper & Row, 1969).

The Piskarevskoye Cemetery and War Memorial outside Leningrad. Embankments to the sides of these walks are mass graves entombing the bodies of over 400,000 people who perished in the 900-day siege of Leningrad during World War II. The number buried here totals more than all the American casualties during World War II. (Photo provided by Leslie Deeb.)

The winter of 1945 saw the Germans falling back on two fronts. Allied and Soviet forces raced toward each other across Europe and closed in on Berlin. Using some of his most fearsome divisions, Marshal Grigory Zhukov attacked the Nazi capital after a heavy barrage by his artillery. Block by block, street by street, building by building, the city grudgingly fell to the Soviet troops. Hitler shot himself in his bunker on April 30, but the city did not surrender until May 2, only five days before the European war itself ended.

Meanwhile, the war continued to rage in the Pacific. Neither one wishing to fight the other, Japan and the Soviet Union had signed a nonaggression treaty in 1932. By 1942, however, the picture had changed considerably. The United States, seeking help in its struggle, pressured Stalin to join the Allies against the militarists in the Orient, but Stalin consistently avoided the issue. As the European war came to a close and the United States feared the conquest of Japan would claim a million American lives, Roosevelt pressed hard for Soviet help in the Pacific and finally secured Stalin's commitment at the Yalta Conference of February 1945. In exchange for several important territorial concessions in Asia, Stalin agreed to enter the Pacific war three months after the fighting in Europe ended. True to his promise, Stalin declared war on Japan exactly 91 days after

SOVIET TERRITORIAL GAINS IN EUROPE, 1939-1945

Acquired between 1939-1945

Soviet satellite states

Communist but not Soviet satellites

hostilities had ceased in Europe. The fact that the Americans dropped an atomic bomb on Hiroshima only two days before the Soviets entered the war has led some observers to suggest that Stalin rushed to enter the Japanese war only after he saw that they were defeated. Little evidence supports this assertion, however, since Stalin's actions were perfectly consistent with his commitments to the Allies.[28]

[28]Jesse D. Clarkson, *A History of Russia*, 2nd ed. (New York: Random House, 1969), p. 676.

The Cold War

Throughout the war the Allies had consulted in a number of high-level conferences. Although relations between the Soviets and the West were never really warm, they were cooperative, especially during the early stages of the war. Yet, as victory became apparent, the participants in the alliance began to maneuver for postwar position.

Primary in Stalin's mind was the objective of securing the Soviet Union against another attack. It must be remembered that his country had been invaded by Germany twice within a quarter century. Each time the country had suffered greatly and had lost huge amounts of territory. Thus, Soviet policy was intent upon ringing the USSR with buffer states to guard against invasion from a world that it still regarded as hostile. Hence, Soviet troops installed communist regimes in the countries they occupied.

In Yugoslavia it was not necessary to force a communist into power since Josip Tito had already emerged as the nation's leader by the time Soviet troops arrived. Czechoslovakia was another exceptional case. It was unique among East European countries in that it had enjoyed a strong industrial base and a well-developed democratic tradition. After the war, a coalition government was formed with strong communist representation. With Soviet help, the communists managed to take advantage of the postwar economic and social dislocation, thus plunging the country into turmoil. The communists, who controlled the police, gained a greater and greater share of the government until finally they were in command, and they promptly transformed Czechoslovakia into a Soviet satellite.

Poland, of all of Eastern Europe, was the most serious point of contention between East and West. Except for East Germany, Poland was more important to the Soviet leaders than any other satellite state because it had always been the natural invasion route to Russia from the west. Consequently, Stalin was determined to have his way there, although he later promised at Yalta to sponsor democratic elections in Poland. As the Russian army approached Warsaw, an uprising of partisans attempted to drive the Nazis out of the capital. Knowing that the partisans were anti-communist as well as anti-Nazi, Stalin halted his forces, refusing the insurgents aid and ultimately seeing them crushed by Hitler's forces. Only then did the Soviet generals drive the Nazis out and establish a puppet regime.[29]

Consistent with the policies of Franklin D. Roosevelt, Harry S. Truman, who became president after Roosevelt's death in April 1945, tried to develop a lasting cordial relationship with the former ally. Yet, the Soviet policy of establishing satellite states in Eastern Europe, coupled with Soviet meddling in the unstable countries of Iran, Greece, and Turkey, were incompatible with Western postwar aspirations. Consequently, relations continued to disintegrate between East and West until 1948, the year that signaled the beginning of the Cold War. In that crucial year the West was outraged by events in Czechoslovakia, Tito withdrew Yugoslavia from the Soviet orbit with Western support, the Soviets blockaded the Western-controlled sectors of Berlin, and the communists seemed about to take over

[29]Nettl, pp. 171–172.

China. Unable to resolve their differences, the former allies faced each other as antagonists. In 1949 the North Atlantic Treaty Organization (NATO) was forged to prevent further communist aggression in Europe, and the following year North Korea invaded South Korea with Soviet support, tripping off a major conflict in Asia. The world was tense and strained; the specter of atomic annihilation haunted the globe.

Reconstruction and Re-Stalinization

By any measure, Soviet losses during World War II defy available adjectives. Destruction came in five separate waves: (1) The Soviet people themselves scorched the earth as they retreated east before the Nazi advance; (2) the German invasion and occupation brutalized the populace; (3) the partisans sabotaged rails, factories, buildings, and bridges; (4) the Soviet reconquest of the land added to the demolition and death; and (5) the Nazis deliberately destroyed what they could not carry as they withdrew. Suffering far more destruction than any other country, the Soviet Union lost between 20 and 27 million people, and a full quarter of its national wealth was destroyed or stolen by the Nazis. The psychological damage to Soviet citizens and the impact of the number of maimed and injured have never been effectively calculated. For perspective, one should remember that not a single enemy bomb fell, nor was a belligerent bullet fired, in the United States during the war, and more than twice as many people died in the city of Leningrad alone than the United States lost in the entire war.

When the fighting stopped, the European portion of the Soviet Union lay in ruins. Historian Melvin Wren records that 1,700 towns and 70,000 villages were laid waste, 25 million Soviet people were left homeless, and half of the country's production of steel, cement, rolling stock, and electric power was gone. Farms were destroyed by the tens of thousands; schools, railroad tracks, factories, and telegraph lines were laid waste; and on, and on, and on.[30]

Exhausted and crippled, the Soviet people faced what must have seemed a monumental task—reconstructing their homeland. Food, fuel, and clothing were rationed, and housing was unbelievably scarce. Huge segments of the population were displaced. Soldiers returned from the army to find their families had moved east, as had the factories. Prisoners of war and Nazi labor camp internees staggered home to find their houses demolished, their friends dead or dispersed, their loved ones gone. Everyone carried the debilitating physical and psychological scars attendant to such a horrible experience.

Faced with the United States economic might and its monopoly in atomic weapons, Stalin was determined to rebuild Soviet industry and to develop an atomic capacity in record time. Hence, the Soviet Union was once again subjected to the rigorous sacrifice of the planned economy. In

---

[30]Melvin C. Wren, *The Course of Russian History*, 3rd ed. (London: Macmillan Company, 1968), pp. 664–665.

this atmosphere, the government announced its new Five-Year Plan (the fourth). The plan was one of extremely ambitious proportions. Again emphasizing heavy industry rather than consumer goods, it called for huge increases in coal, oil, electricity, pig iron, and steel production. Even though relatively modest increases were anticipated in the production of most consumer goods, a major effort was launched to construct housing.

Having cooperated in the defeat of the Nazis, many Soviet citizens hoped that the political situation would be more relaxed than it had been during the prewar era. After all, the party's role in the society had been reduced, and traditional institutions like the Church had been allowed more latitude than before. Unfortunately, these expectations went unfulfilled. In order to meet the challenge of reconstruction, the system returned to many of its prewar practices. The party apparatus tightened its grip on the system as economic centralization increased. Labor discipline was redoubled in the factories and most particularly in agriculture while Soviet society entered a new round of exploitation for the good of the state.

Instead of emptying the forced labor camps at the end of the war, Stalin continued to operate them. The Soviet deportees were kept in place, to be joined by new trainloads of people who fell afoul of the regime. Prisoners of war were not released immediately but instead were kept at their tasks of building public works in Siberia and the arctic region. Although hundreds of thousands finally made their way back home, thousands of others perished amid the snowdrifts of the east.

Forced to rebuild its economy a second time in a quarter century, the Soviet Union now enjoyed one major advantage it had lacked during the first era of industrialization. Eastern Europe was under Soviet control, and the Soviets took advantage of the satellites' economic productivity to help rebuild the USSR. Encouraged by the knowledge that Bulgaria, Rumania, and Hungary had been German allies and that the latter two had sent troops to the invasion of the Soviet Union, Stalin made extortionate demands on their economies. They were required to make enormous sacrifices at home so machinery, fuel, minerals, and advanced technology could be shipped east. Food, scarcely more available in Eastern Europe than in the USSR, was also shipped to the Soviet Union in huge quantities.

As in the previous five-year plans, the objectives of the fourth and fifth plans were not reached. The emphasis on quantity rather than quality caused the same problems in production that had been experienced before. The inefficiencies of centralization and compulsory quotas were as debilitating in the late 1940s and early 1950s as they had been before the war. Yet, as in the previous era, the shortcomings of the plans did not obscure the enormous gains achieved. The Soviet Union entered the 1950s as the second greatest industrial power in the world—and one that had developed an atomic capacity as well.

Such great economic advances came only at an enormous price. In an effort to mobilize and direct the populace, Stalin sponsored a new era of political centralization that resulted in a corresponding loss of individual liberty. At the same time, the Soviet dictator, Georgian by birth, embarked on a veritable binge of Great-Russian nationalism. Perhaps in an attempt to bolster the morale of his exhausted people, Stalin pursued a "Russia first" policy that assumed laughable proportions. Scholars were ordered to emphasize Russian contributions to history and to lionize Russian cultural achievements. Russia was credited with the original invention of practically every modern innovation and technological advance. Free artistic expression, tolerated somewhat during the war, was halted as Andrei Zhdanov demanded a return to the strictures of **socialist realism** (requiring artists to portray the Soviet Union in the most flattering light).

Ultra-Russian nationalism and socialist realism formed but two of three ideological pillars of the postwar Soviet state. The third and most prominent buttress supporting the regime was the personality cult that glorified Stalin. Although well-developed during the 1930s, public adulation of Stalin was whipped to gigantic proportions during and after the war. Stalin was portrayed as an infallible leader—the father of his people, who, though stern, was unfailingly tending to the people's best interests. Buildings, monuments, cities, various geographical phenomena, technology, government programs, youth organizations, and even battle plans were named after him. Virtually every speech attributed to him the most monumental achievements. Stalin was all-knowing, faultless, the epitome of the "new Soviet man."[31]

The party, like the rest of society, was reorganized after the war, but Stalin was apparently not content with only mild reform. In 1953 rumors began to spread that a new purge—the **doctors' purge**—was in the making. It was alleged that a group of doctors, most of them Jewish, had systematically murdered Zhdanov and other high Soviet officers and were preparing to kill even more people, including Stalin. Stalin's closest associates quaked at the thought that they might be slated for extermination. Even so, they were unable to take precautionary steps. Khrushchev suggested that his colleagues were mesmerized by the great dark personality whom they called *Vozhd* (leader). Fortunately for them, however, the old dictator suddenly died of a cerebral hemorrhage at age 73 on March 5, 1953.

SINCE STALIN

At the time of Stalin's death, the bulk of the Soviet population had known no other leader. He had ruled the country virtually single-handedly for a quarter of a century and had led it through two economic transitions, as well as through its most devastating war. The thought that he would someday not be at the helm of state had scarcely been entertained by many Soviet people. News of his death therefore was greeted with shock and disbelief. Perhaps remembering only that Stalin had guided the state

---

[31]Deutscher, pp. 609–610.

through many seemingly impossible hazards and forgetting the cruelty of his methods, peasants were seen weeping for the departed *Vozhd*.[32]

The reaction to Stalin's death was considerably different among the Kremlin's occupants. The Politburo members (the leading people in the Communist Party) buried the dead tyrant with great honor but with no tears, and they were quick to begin maneuvering for positions of power.

Khrushchev's Rise to Power

Three people enjoyed stature enough to warrant hope of succeeding the fallen leader. Party Secretary Georgi Malenkov, Stalin's chosen successor, on the face of things seemed the easy favorite to win a power struggle with his colleagues. But Malenkov was not very popular among the party membership and tended to represent the interests of the economic managers instead.

Lavrenti P. Beria, the head of the secret police, was the most feared person in the Soviet Union. Once Stalin's faithful hatchetman, Beria worked closely with Malenkov in developing policy immediately after the dictator's death.

The person about whom least was known in the West but who managed to emerge victorious in the ensuring struggle for power was Nikita Khrushchev. Possessing keen native intelligence and driven by raw ambition, Khrushchev overcame his humble beginnings as a coal miner's son and worked his way through the party ranks to become Moscow's party chief, a member of the Central Committee, and a member of the Secretariat, the party's leading administrative organ. Dutifully carrying out Stalin's orders during the 1930s, 1940s, and 1950s, Khrushchev participated in the purges and in the executions of thousands of Ukrainians accused of collaborating with the enemy. Throughout his career he had established many important contacts and had managed to advance a covey of protégés to positions of influence, including one Leonid Brezhnev. By the time of Stalin's death, Khrushchev enjoyed the reputation of an expert in agricultural matters and was noted as a devoted party worker.

Stalin's sudden passing from the scene released in Soviet politics a complex power struggle that had remained obscured as long as the all-powerful *Vozhd* lived. No longer dominated by the overbearing presence of the old tyrant, several institutions emerged as power bases from which individuals could launch bids for personal leadership. The major institutions that confronted one another in 1953 were the economic managerial group, led by Malenkov; the secret police, headed by Beria; the party, soon to be led by Khrushchev; and the military, headed by Marshal Grigory Zhukov.

[32]The impact of Stalin's personality cult was far-ranging, indeed, since many Western Sovietologists seemed convinced that the Soviet Union could not survive Stalin's death. See Stephen F. Cohen, *Rethinking the Soviet Experience* (Oxford: Oxford University Press, 1985), pp. 25–26.

Although Malenkov was made premier and wanted to lead the party as well as the government, he was not trusted by the party. Thus, the cry of "collective leadership" went up, and Khrushchev was elected first secretary of the party only days after Stalin's death.[33] Soon afterward, Beria was arrested and tried for treason. He was convicted and executed along with several of his closest collaborators in the secret police.[34]

With Beria removed, Khrushchev attacked Malenkov's economic policies as impossibly visionary, and in 1955 Malenkov was forced to resign as premier. He was replaced by Nikolai Bulganin. Throughout 1955 and 1956, Khrushchev continued to consolidate his position. Reminiscent of Stalin before him, Khrushchev quietly but methodically replaced his rivals' supporters in the party with his own cadre. Although Soviet leaders maintained the principle of collective leadership, it was increasingly obvious that Khrushchev was the first among equals on the Politburo, the ruling party body. Still, there was an opposition element in the party that awaited an opportunity to attack this shrewd peasant politician.

This Anti-Party Group, as it came to be called, included Malenkov, Vyacheslav Molotov, Lazar Kaganovich, and Dmitri Shepilov. In 1957 they thought they recognized an opportunity to oust Khrushchev. Supported by the military—led by Marshal Zhukov—and by the Party Central Committee[35] which Khrushchev had packed with supporters, Khrushchev prevailed, and by 1958 the Anti-Party Group had been completely defeated. In another, more brutal time, such a defeat would have meant death for the vanquished. But Khrushchev, once a loyal executioner for Stalin, was a different sort than the old tyrant. Eschewing a blood purge, he contented himself with seeing his rivals assigned to obscure posts far from Moscow.

Once most of his rivals were out of the way, Khrushchev turned his attention to a man with whom he had cooperated but did not trust. Suspicious that Zhukov was trying to make the military an independent political force in the Soviet Union, Khrushchev demanded his ouster from power. That accomplished, Bulganin, who was in the Anti-Party Group, was demoted in 1958, and Khrushchev himself replaced him as chairman of the Council of Ministers. From that time on, Khrushchev's power, although never absolute, was by far the greatest among Soviet leaders of his time.

Nikita Khrushchev was an extremely complex person. He was shrewd and clever but also crude and impulsive. He had been a loyal supporter of Stalin while the old dictator lived, but when he came to power he managed to rise above the limitations of his background and became a political innovator who led his country away from the despotism of Stalinism. Although many mistakes were made, Khrushchev's reforms were crucial for

[33]Edward Cranshaw, *Khrushchev* (New York: The Viking Press, 1966), p. 189.

[34]Roy A. Medvedev and Zhores A. Medvedev, *Khrushchev: The Years in Power*, trans. Andrew R. Durkin (New York: Columbia University Press, 1976), p. 12.

[35]The Central Committee of the Communist Party of the Soviet Union was given unique authority on this occasion. Technically the agency that elects the Politburo, it actually has always been denied a crucial role in making policy except for this episode and perhaps for the present era.

the political maturation of his country. Relegated to the category of a non-person by Brezhnev, Khrushchev was largely ignored until recently. Since Gorbachev has come to power, however, the Soviet media has been more judicious in its treatment of Khrushchev.

Khrushchev's Reforms

As the leader of the party, Khrushchev was anxious to minimize the trend toward developing several independent power bases in the system. A prime institution asserting independence from the party was the technocratic establishment, which was responsible for economic planning and administration. Led by Malenkov, this cadre of technocrats found their interests jeopardized with his downfall.

Hoping to increase industrial productivity while at the same time reducing the independence and power of the technocrats, Khrushchev advocated a program of decentralization in the economy. He divided the country into more than 100 economic regions, which were to develop and administer economic programs instead of relying on Moscow alone for the task. This move took control of the economy away from the managers and put it into the hands of the local party bosses, who were under Khrushchev's influence.

Although Khrushchev's political goal of reducing the technocrats' independence and power succeeded, his drive for increased productivity failed miserably. Local party bosses tended to put provincial interests above those of the national economy. At the same time, the technocrats were understandably disgruntled at their loss of prestige and power, as well as by the fact that many of them were forced to move from Moscow into the provinces to ply their skills in the new system.

Khrushchev's agricultural reforms met a similar fate, although some of them proved to be successful in the long run. The most spectacular of his agricultural reforms was the exploitation of the **virgin lands** east of the Urals. Correctly assessing the potential of vast tracts of semiarid lands in southwestern Siberia and northern Central Asia, Khrushchev committed enormous amounts of capital and energy to their development and unleashed a national effort of epic proportions. Many people were relocated in these lands against their wills, but thousands of others enthusiastically joined the effort in an idealistic drive to push back the frontier. Within two years of the program's 1954 inauguration, almost 90 million acres had been reduced to cultivation. At the same time, huge irrigation networks were constructed to bring life-giving water to the otherwise parched region. Plagued by unfavorable weather conditions, the project produced disappointing results at first. With the passage of time and continued development, however, the area has become a rich asset for the country.

A second series of reforms was designed to improve the standard of living for farmers who had been forced to pay the lion's share for Stalin's economic policies. In a series of changes, Khrushchev reduced the expenses for production borne by the peasants, abrogated a portion of the debts incurred by the farming class, and raised the prices of farm goods in order to increase the peasants' income. The net result of these policies was to improve the standard of living on the farms and to narrow the gap between the income of the peasants and that of the city dwellers.

Less sanguine was Khrushchev's policy of closing the *Machine Tractor Stations (MTSs)*. Established by Stalin as a means to control the collective farms, the MTSs concentrated heavy agricultural equipment and rented it to the collectives. Bureaucratic and political, the MTSs were inefficient and resented by the peasants. Khrushchev's plan was to sell the MTS machinery to the collective farms. Unfortunately, the short-term result of this policy was not as pleasant as he had hoped. Many collectives, although happy to get out from under the thumb of the MTSs, found it very difficult to spare enough capital to buy the machinery. Also, the collective often lacked the skill to use or maintain the machines properly; thus, many machines were prematurely lost to production as they sat rusting at the edge of the fields for want of an operator or spare parts.

Another reform of dubious wisdom was Khrushchev's attempt to consolidate the collective farms into huge state farms. The precise difference between these two institutions will be discussed more fully in Chapter 9, but for now suffice it to say that the state farms were larger and more bureaucratic than the collective farms, and their growth at the expense of the smaller farms caused a decrease in productivity. As part of the same program, the severe reduction in private plots farmed by the peasants resulted in lower agricultural production.[36]

Refusing to occupy himself totally with economic change, Khrushchev turned his attention to a number of political reforms as well. Attempting to make the party more efficient, he tried to streamline it in a number of ways. He objected to the economic privileges Stalin had let party members enjoy. Accordingly, he reduced their salaries and attempted to stamp out bribery and other forms of corruption common in party circles, and he initiated a bloodless purge by which he hoped to rid the party of this undesirable element. Unhappily, the lower echelons of the party, resenting the loss of privilege and the threat to their jobs, refused to cooperate with the cleanup campaign and were content to see it fail.

At the same time, the first secretary attempted to reorganize the party in an effort to increase agricultural production by sharpening the party focus on that aspect of the economy. Khrushchev ordered that the party be divided into agrarian and industrial sectors. The response to this reform within the party was, like the reaction to the other changes, overwhelmingly negative. Hence, met with bureaucratic foot-dragging and subterfuge, Khrushchev's attempt was stymied. Indeed, the most dramatic result of Khrushchev's endeavors to reform the party was that they caused deep-seated discontent with his leadership and greatly contributed to his ouster.[37]

[36]Medvedev and Medvedev, pp. 85–93, 109–116; Nove, pp. 362–468.
[37]Medvedev and Medvedev, pp. 153–158.

De-Stalinization. Even as he tried to find innovative solutions for the economic and political difficulties of the system, Khrushchev embarked on his most important reform of all, liberalization. Although some steps toward liberalizing the system had already been taken by Malenkov, the Soviet Union was still mired in the stifling political conditions incumbent in the Stalinist regime. Genuinely committed to modernizing the country, Khrushchev launched a policy of liberalization, which is generally referred to under the rubric of *de-Stalinization.*

In a secret speech to the Twentieth Party Congress in February 1956, Khrushchev left his audience thunderstruck as he condemned Stalin in the most explicit terms. Lashing out against the dead leader, Khrushchev decried government conduct by terrorism and the secret police. He charged that Stalin was guilty of using the purges to cow rivals, of murdering opponents, and of making needless blunders that caused the war to be even more destructive than necessary. As part of his de-Stalinization program, Khrushchev ordered the labor camps emptied; eight million victims of Stalin's tyranny were rehabilitated and even given public apologies.

Additionally, the previous restraints on social commentary, literature, and the arts were somewhat alleviated. The condemned novel by Boris Pasternak, *Doctor Zhivago,* was rehabilitated and, more importantly, Alexander Solzhenitsyn's *One Day in the Life of Ivan Denisovich* was published, unedited, on Khrushchev's express orders.[38] It should be pointed out that Khrushchev was not consistently tolerant, however. Late in his career he found it necessary to order a reversal of the most liberal policies. Yet, the straightjacket into which Stalin had forced the arts and letters was never fully reimposed.

Foreign Policy

Displaying his best and worst qualities in foreign policy, Khrushchev made an impact in international relations equal to his domestic accomplishments. Viewing Stalinist foreign policy as archaic and counterproductive, Khrushchev was quick to mend fences with Tito. To do this, Khrushchev had to accept the Yugoslav leader's view that socialism could be reached by several different paths, and Khrushchev promised to send Yugoslavia substantial foreign aid.

The liberalization inside the Soviet Union, coupled with Khrushchev's accommodation of Tito, led to moves in East Germany, Poland, and Hungary to liberalize those systems. By assuring the Soviet Union of their loyalty, East Germany and Poland averted Soviet intervention, but such was not the case in Hungary.

In 1956 the Hungarian government, led by Premier Imre Nagy, called for free elections and announced that henceforth Hungary would be a neutral nation. Such independence on its western frontier could not be

---

[38]MacKenzie and Curran, p. 605.

tolerated by the Soviet Union. Accordingly, on November 4, Khrushchev ordered Soviet tanks into Budapest to put the Nagy government out. Several thousand people were killed resisting the Soviet invasion, and more than 200,000 refugees fled the country for the West. Earlier, the Eisenhower Administration had recklessly promised aid to any East European state that rose up against Soviet domination, but when the Hungarians rebelled, the United States refused to send the help it had promised because the confrontation with the Soviet Union it had disdained in theory seemed more serious when it became an immediate possibility. The unwillingness of the Western democracies to aid Hungary dampened other potential risings in the Soviet bloc, and a general stabilization developed in Europe.

The year before the Hungarian uprising, several important events occurred. In a belated answer to NATO, the Soviet leaders created the Warsaw Pact, a mutual defense agreement among Soviet bloc countries in the event of an invasion from abroad. Although the Soviet Union clearly remained the senior partner in its relationship with its Eastern European allies, the Warsaw Pact signaled the end of the satellite status of these states. Organizing an integrated economy among the pact's participants, Khrushchev ended the raw economic exploitation that had characterized Stalin's relationships with his allies in favor of a more egalitarian mode.

In the same year, Khrushchev tried to defuse the relationship between East and West by unilaterally granting two important concessions to the West. Extracting no *quid pro quo* or reparations payment, the Soviets voluntarily evacuated an important naval base in Finland. Next, satisfied that Austria would not become an antagonistic power, Khrushchev voluntarily withdrew Soviet troops from that country.[39]

These policies were but a continuation of previous Soviet efforts to stabilize East-West relations. In little more than a month following Stalin's death, the Soviets allowed an armistice in the Korean War. Then, shortly afterward, they renounced Stalin's long-held claim to territory in Turkey.

Khrushchev was also quick to realize that nuclear weapons had made warfare between the Soviet Union and the United States unthinkable. He logically concluded that East-West tensions were simply too dangerous in 1955. Accordingly, he launched a policy that constituted a major ideological innovation. Declaring that a direct armed conflict between socialism and capitalism was impractical, he proclaimed the doctrine of **peaceful coexistence**. He took the position that Lenin's theory that socialists and capitalists could not long endure side-by-side may have been valid at one time but was no longer an unquestionable truth. Pointing to wars of national liberation and to economic competition as alternative sources of victory over capitalism, Khrushchev modified the doctrine of **permanent revolution**, making it less confrontational.

Consequently, Khrushchev became a leading proponent of reduced tensions between East and West. Ironically, at the same time, John Foster Dulles, secretary of state for the Eisenhower administration, developed the

[39]Rubinstein, pp. 75, 104.

doctrine of **massive retaliation** as the cornerstone of United States–Soviet relations. Frustrated in attempts to stop the spread of communism, Dulles warned that the United States would respond to the slightest communist intrusion in the noncommunist sphere with a massive nuclear strike at the Soviet homeland. This bellicose policy not only constituted an unpersuasive deterrent to communist expansion, but it also made the United States appear as an irresponsible, bloodthirsty aggressor compared to Khrushchev.

Toward the end of the 1950s, however, Soviet policy began to shift again. Buoyed by Soviet accomplishments in space, Khrushchev began to assume a more belligerent and forceful stance in world affairs. In 1960 he threatened to destroy the United Nations by refusing to support the election of a new secretary general. Later that year, he spoiled chances for a summit talk with President Eisenhower by making a cause célèbre of the downing of a United States spy plane more than 1,000 miles inside Soviet territory. The following year, the Berlin Wall was built in an effort to prevent the exodus of so many young, skilled East Germans to the West. Each of these events caused a crisis that seemed to threaten the peace of the world. Then, in 1962, Soviet missiles capable of delivering nuclear warheads to the United States were discovered in Cuba. The ensuring crisis saw Khrushchev and President Kennedy squarely facing each other in a frightening test of wills. Fortunately, Khrushchev blinked, although he must have realized that backing down from the United States placed his own career in jeopardy.[40]

Meanwhile, Soviet ties to China began to unravel. Despite very close cooperation between China and the Soviet Union since the 1949 founding of the People's Republic, the two communist giants began to draw apart shortly after Stalin's death. Political, territorial, and ideological issues divided them. The ideological problems between the liberalizing Soviet Union and the doctrinaire China are expressed in an old Soviet joke.

> Khrushchev complains to Chinese Premier Zho Enlai: "The difference between us is that I rose to power from the peasant class, whereas you came from the privileged Mandarin class."
>
> Zho quickly retorts: "True. But there is this similarity. Each of us is a traitor to his class."

Khrushchev's truculent attitude toward China exacerbated the problem, but the differences between the two states were deeper than personality problems and persisted after Khrushchev's removal. In the early 1960s, however, Khrushchev's colleagues felt he had mishandled relations with China, and the issue was added to a growing list of complaints about his policies.

[40]Nettl, p. 227.

Khrushchev's Fall

The reasons for Khrushchev's ouster from power are numerous and complex. His economic reforms had caused great disruption and were accompanied by only limited success. His liberalization policies disturbed political stability at home, alienated China, and encouraged independent stirrings in Eastern Europe. His foreign policy was not unsuccessful, but it became increasingly dangerous, bringing the world to the brink of annihilation and ending in a humiliating Soviet retreat in the face of American nuclear might. He was also criticized for being impulsive, for embarking on reforms and changes without ever developing a format for integrating the changes into the system as a whole. And perhaps most importantly, his attempted reforms threatened too many powerful people within the party and government, people who eventually supported the removal of their former chief.

On October 14, 1964, the Central Committee unanimously ratified a previous decision of its Presidium (Politburo) to oust Khrushchev from power. Removed from all his party posts, he was forced to retire to a comfortable but obscure life as a "nonperson." Although at the time the coup came as a bitter blow to Khrushchev, late in his life he mused that among his greatest legacies was his own peaceful retirement rather than an execution, which would almost certainly have been his fate if Stalinist methods were still being used.[41] Ignored by the press after his fall, little was heard from him until he smuggled his memoirs to the West.[42]

Khrushchev's Successors

Khrushchev was replaced by a quadrumvirate who pledged to respect the principle of **collective leadership** and who were committed not to continue Khrushchev's disruptive policies. The principal figures among the new leadership were Leonid Brezhnev, Alexei Kosygin, Nikolai Podgorny, and Mikhail Suzlov.

The collective government continued until, in the late 1970s, the quartet began to disintegrate. Brezhnev elbowed Podgorny aside, and Suzlov and Kosygin died. Yet Brezhnev never achieved the power of Stalin or even Khrushchev. In 1976 he suffered a debilitating stroke. According to Roy Medvedev, he was actually clinically dead but was revived by doctors. For the next few years, until his death in 1982, he was largely managed by his advisers, sometimes actually being led by the hand at public appearances.

Early on, Kosygin attempted to decentralize the economy in an effort to stimulate productivity, but the reform was defeated by the same kind of bureaucratic resistance that foiled Khrushchev's reforms. Following that failed policy, the Soviet economic and political systems began to ossify. The

---

[41]Medvedev and Medvedev, pp. 172–179.

[42]See Nikita Khrushchev, *Khrushchev on Khrushchev*, trans. and ed. William Taubman (Boston: Little, Brown and Co., 1990).

bureaucracy expanded to over 100 ministries—under Stalin there had been only 25. Official corruption became rampant and economic growth began to slow, even as the people became cynical and bereft of ideological commitment.

Perhaps the most dynamic aspect of the era was in the growth of the military. Committed to developing military parity with the United States, the Brezhnev administration poured resources into the navy, missiles, air power, and land forces. At the same time, the government-controlled media and education system lionized the military by endless accounts of its contributions during World War II. Brezhnev, who actually played a relatively minor role in the war, was also repeatedly honored and decorated as a great hero. The farce became so obvious that wags quipped:

> Did you hear about Brezhnev's surgery? He had a chest expansion to make room for all his medals.

The propaganda hype about Soviet military might was not often duplicated with action, however. In general the Soviets were very cautious in foreign affairs, avoiding a repetition of Khrushchev's incredible gamble that led to the Cuban Missile Crisis. Even though Soviet tanks were sent to crush the 1968 Czech attempt under Alexander Dubcek to free itself from Soviet control, more temperate later liberalizations in Poland and Hungary did not bring Soviet intervention. Relations with China, however, continued to harden, and in 1969 serious border skirmishes broke out along the Ussuri and Amur rivers.

United States–Soviet relations warmed considerably during the early 1970s, as President Richard M. Nixon and Brezhnev entered into a period of **détente**. The Soviet Union signed the Helsinki Accords in 1975, pledging to expand human rights in its territory, and two Strategic Arms Limitation Treaties (SALT) were agreed to by Brezhnev and American presidents. Relations, however, cooled again in 1979. In December of that year, the Soviet Union sent troops into Afghanistan to quell a rebellion against its socialist government. Not only did this act destroy détente, but it involved the Soviet Union in a long, costly, and futile bloodletting, one which Gorbachev later brought to an end by a unilateral withdrawal.

The Afghanistan war was an albatross around the Soviet Union's neck. Its enormous cost in lives and money further disenchanted the people. Even without it, however, Soviet society was becoming moribund. Brezhnev's conservatism stabilized the society—but stability soon became stagnation. Official slovenliness and corruption were duplicated in the behavior of the general public. As productivity slowed, the black market, always a factor in the Soviet Union, expanded—as did theft of state property.

Brezhnev's death brought Yuri Andropov to power, and briefly it seemed that the decline might be reversed as he announced campaigns against corruption, poor work habits, and alcoholism. Soon, however, Andropov himself became very ill and he finally died in 1984. He was succeeded by Konstantin Chernenko, a Brezhnev hack, so the downward slide continued until he too died in 1985.

So it was that Mikhail S. Gorbachev rose to the pinnacle of a system that was already in an advanced state of exhaustion. His obvious task is to rejuvenate it. As Khrushchev learned, however, change can be threatening, and resistance to it can bring the reformer down. Keeping this historical lesson in mind, we can move on to a study of the contemporary situation, confident that this perspective will help us develop a fuller appreciation of the complexities of the Soviet political society.

chapter 4

The Communist and Other Parties

Although many changes have recently taken place to challenge its dominance, the Communist Party (CPSU)[1] is still the most powerful institution in the Soviet Union. Founded by Lenin in 1903, the Communist Party remains central to the development and execution of policy. This view is not held by all people, of course. Until recently it was an incontestable fact, but within the past few years, so many changes have occurred in the party's structure and function that many people now question its efficacy. A June 1990 poll by *Pravda* (the Communist Party newspaper) showed that 53 percent of those surveyed believed the party was no longer the society's leading force, while only 18 percent said that it was. Although these results reveal a clear decrease of the party's stature in the public view and the reduced power of the party, no other institution has yet been able to challenge its dominance in Soviet political society.

The Communist Party of the Soviet Union has no precise parallel in Western societies. Consequently, comparing and contrasting the functions

---

[1]Following their successful seizure of power, the Bolsheviks renamed themselves *The Russian Communist Party* in 1918, but in 1952 they took the title *The Communist Party of the Soviet Union (CPSU)*, which remains the party's name to this day.

of the CPSU with Western political parties will help us appreciate the unique character of the Communist Party.

THE CPSU AND WESTERN PARTIES

Western political parties perform a number of tasks that normally relate directly to electoral politics. Their primary function is to recruit, nominate, and elect candidates to office. In the process, they generally try to articulate the issues, to educate voters about their particular views, and to point out the weaknesses in the opposition. If defeated, Western political parties organize the "loyal opposition," criticizing the party in power and offering alternative policies that they hope will check the "ins" while advancing their own chances of winning in the next election. If elected to power, they organize the government and institute policies reflecting their view of the course government should take on the issues. At the same time, the Western parties, to greater or lesser extent, strive to hold their own members and officers accountable for their political conduct.

The CPSU performs each of these roles, but it has yet to become very comfortable with one of them: the role of the loyal opposition. Between 1920 and 1990 the Communist Party disallowed all competitors, reserving for itself a monopoly on the mantle of authority, and even today it dominates most political, social, and economic institutions. Some significant exceptions to this political homogeneity exist, however, such as the city governments of Moscow and Leningrad, and the union republic (province) government of Georgia which are controlled by other parties or political groups.

Contested elections are also new phenomena in the Soviet Union. Even though many recent elections have been fiercely fought, a true multiparty contest has yet to occur nationally, and many seats still have but one candidate. Even so, the party has had to change its previous approach to recruiting candidates (selecting the "right" people for the job)—it has become more concerned with nominating candidates who are attractive to the voters. This transformation is still in its developmental stage, however.

Another modification the party has undergone relates to its interaction with the government. Before the governmental reforms of 1989 (discussed in the next chapter) created meaningful legislatures, the Communist Party actually made the major decisions about government policy, and the nominal legislatures rubber-stamped the policies. Today, the CPSU functions much more as Western parties do in this regard. It still has great influence on government policy, to be sure, but it no longer completely dictates what legislation will be passed.

Also changed, albeit less so, is the party's supervision of government. Until recently, every level of government was directly responsible to a corresponding party institution, and the party could manage the government's administration of policy. This function has been somewhat muted as the government has become increasingly independent of the party. However, since most government officials are still party members and subject to its discipline, the independence of government from party is far from complete, especially at the local levels.

The CPSU probably takes the matters of articulating the issues and educating its citizens far more seriously than do Western parties. Maintaining an elaborate network of publications, lectures, and schools, the party is extremely careful to inculcate its attitudes in the body politic. Also, Soviet politicians and bureaucrats are far more accountable to the CPSU than their Western counterparts are to their parties. It is possible for a Western bureaucrat to largely ignore partisan politics. Indeed, many governments insulate their functionaries against undue political pressure. Such independence does not exist in the Soviet Union. Further, even though some CPSU politicians have acted independently of the party and the party itself has struggled with how much latitude to allow its members, the most prominent mavericks have left the party rather than be shackled by its required orthodoxy.

One of the most striking facts about Soviet politics is that officials are inordinately dependent on the party for their jobs and authority. In the Western democracies, people of several different power bases support various officials while contesting one another for control. Included among these power bases are not only the public and competing political parties, but also trade unions, corporate concerns, and such social institutions as churches, conservation groups, the elderly, and numerous other interest groups. Although it would be simplistic to suggest that the CPSU is the only institution with political power in the Soviet Union, it is appropriate to point out that the party easily has more power than any other Soviet institution and that it exercises an extraordinary amount of control over the other institutions, as it does over the society as a whole. Further, even though elections have become more meaningful in Soviet politics and public opinion cannot be ignored, the party is so deeply burrowed into the political system, and its opposition is as yet so weak, that the party remains insulated from the public will to a large extent.

The internal administrative functions in the CPSU are far more extensive than those of Western political parties. In this and following chapters we shall discover that the party officiates over virtually every aspect of Soviet life. The extent of its activities and the number of people it employs and supervises involve it in extraordinary administrative details, consuming massive amounts of energy, resources, and time.

Beyond the functions that Western parties perform, there are a variety of tasks the CPSU engages in that make it unique. The most prominent of these functions is the party's insistence that it alone holds the monopoly on determining the definition of Marxism-Leninism. Since the party contends that all truth is revealed through Marxist analysis, it reserves to itself the sole power to determine truth. From Stalin's time until 1990, the party insisted that its way was the only true course, and it systematically crushed opposition inside and outside its ranks. At present, however, opposition parties are tolerated, but the party still holds that its view of the truth is the only correct interpretation.

The party's self-bestowed monopoly on truth also involves it in an

A statue in Kishenev, Moldavia, of Marx and Engels debating a fine point of ideology. Behind them stands the Communist Party headquarters of Moldavia.

extraordinary relationship with individuals in the Soviet Union. Party members are responsible for teaching their fellow citizens the latest interpretation of Marxism-Leninism and for explaining the government's policy. This process is ongoing. It is known as **propaganda** if the message is intellectually sophisticated and complex and as **agitation** if the line is reduced to simple, repetitive slogans. Party members are expected to "spread the word" by giving lectures, distributing literature, and visiting neighbors. One might wonder how successful party members are at this task given this joke making the rounds in Moscow:

> In capitalism—man exploits man. Ah, but in communism—it's the other way around.

Besides their propaganda task, party members are expected to lead their fellow citizens to the socialist way by becoming role models. Party cadre are supposed to be the first to volunteer extra time and labor for socially approved projects, to be the first to sacrifice when called upon to do so, to demonstrate their patriotism by turning out for national holidays or volunteering for hazardous work assignments.

Finally, the party considers itself the *vanguard of the proletariat*, and as such it is to be ever vigilant against counterrevolutionary activity. Party members are to be alert to possible transgressions by fellow party members, government officials, or private citizens. Violations, when encountered, are to be dealt with appropriately. Minor infractions usually evoke stern criticism and instructions about proper conduct, while more serious problems are reported to the appropriate authority. By introducing this function, however, it is easy to give one an exaggerated notion about the party. I do not wish to lead the reader to believe that behind every door, around every corner, listening to every phone call, and watching every move, a party member can be found waiting for but a false step. Such is certainly not the case. In fact, most activities common to everyday life proceed in the Soviet Union much as they do in any other society. Yet, the CPSU exercises an extraordinary degree of protective and reactive control in the Soviet Union. It is, indeed, a major fact of life in Soviet political society.

PARTY HISTORY AND GOVERNANCE

Early in 1917 the Bolshevik Party counted only slightly more than 20,000 members. Although they were soon to return, the bulk of the leadership had spent long years in exile before the revolution while the ordinary members carried out their orders or executed their own initiatives inside Russia. Lacking strong central control, the party adopted policy only after long and often bitter debate. Indeed, Lenin himself often encountered opposition to his ideas. Yet, the independence within the party contrasted sharply with the ambivalence in Kerensky's Provisional Government.

As 1917 wore on and public frustration with the ineptitude of the Lvov and Kerensky governments mounted, the Bolshevik alternative became increasingly popular. The party grew rapidly, until by October 1917 it boasted a membership of 200,000. The phenomenal growth of the party obviously was essential to its ultimate success in seizing power, but the infusion of such large numbers of people over so brief a time forced a fundamental change upon it. Although many of the new members were committed Marxists, many more were opportunists who saw their chance to join the winning side, thus advancing themselves considerably.

Once in power, the party continued to grow rapidly, as it needed personnel to help coordinate policy. By 1922 party membership had reached over 420,000, and management of such an enormous number of functionaries presented a considerable problem. Hence, in that year the party created the leadership post of general secretary and, in a fateful decision, Joseph Stalin was appointed to the new position.

Because the revolutionary intellectuals of the party—Trotsky, Bukharin, Zinoviev, Kamenev, and others—viewed the general secretary's job as tedious and bureaucratic, they were content to leave it in the hands of the plodding Stalin. As mentioned earlier, they failed to appreciate the advantage Stalin enjoyed by being able to appoint his supporters to key party positions.

Following the collapse of its coalition with the Left Socialist-Revolutionaries, the Bolshevik Party increasingly centralized power, attempting to find a formula for successful governance. Besieged by opponents in the Civil War, it outlawed all opposition parties, purging their leaders. At the same time the trade unions were forced under party control.

In 1919 the party invoked the governing principle of **democratic**

centralism. Attempting to combine centrally controlled discipline with the party's accustomed independence at the local level, democratic centralism was composed of four principles. First, the leaders of each echelon in the party were to be elected by the membership they served. Second, policy options were to be freely debated by the membership prior to decisions. These two principles constitute the "democratic" half of the concept. The "centralist" portion of the rule included two additional principles. First, party members were obliged to exhibit unquestioned obedience to their superiors. Second, although debate on an issue was supposed to be open to all party members, the decisions were to be made by the leadership; once the decision was made, it was to be followed without dissent.

Although democratic centralism has never been completely successful, earnest attempts were made to apply each of its principles during Lenin's era. Very quickly, however, the democratic aspects of the rule became dominated by the centralist principles, and the elections and debates became largely pro forma exercises. Since Gorbachev became general secretary, some party elections and debates have become more meaningful as the lower echelons of the party are given more to say about its management. However, the party still continues to be dominated by its leadership, and abiding by decisions made by the higher-ups is still the most important part of democratic centralism.

Despite his initial willingness to abide some dissent, Lenin took steps to dampen a growing opposition in the party in 1921. Dissatisfaction with the management of the economy and the Civil War resulted in mounting criticism in several sectors of the party. Feeling Bolshevik power jeopardized by such internal strife, Lenin pushed through the Tenth Party Congress a resolution condemning "factions" in the party as "bourgeois" and unacceptable in the new regime. Thus, by 1921, Lenin had laid the groundwork of centralization, which Stalin and his successors later used to stifle attempted challenges to the leadership. The accumulation of power at the center did not pass without this observation by cynical jokesters:

> A party leader tells a worker: "When we have achieved communism, everyone will eat strawberries and cream."
>
> The worker replies: "But I don't like strawberries and cream."
>
> Undaunted, the party leader insists: "When communism is achieved, you *will* like strawberries and cream."

In the meantime, the party continued to grow as its grip on the Soviet state tightened. Lenin's death in 1924 and the struggle for power in the second half of the decade saw Stalin consolidating his power. Using his control of the party apparatus, he recruited new members who possessed the managerial and technical skills needed to implement the five-year plans that he introduced.

As the Communist Party grew, its character continued to evolve. Outmaneuvering his adversaries one by one, Stalin managed to exile, demote, or cow all of the Old Bolsheviks, the intellectual lights of the regime. In their place he appointed bureaucratic technocrats who followed his orders without question. Thus, the party gradually changed from an exciting revolutionary movement to an administrative machine managed by relatively dull-witted hacks.

By 1933 the party had grown to include some 3.5 million members. Stalin was in firm control of the party, but dissatisfaction over some of his harsh economic policies mounted. Sensing danger, he initiated a series of purges that eventually took the lives of more than 1.5 million party members, including virtually every Old Bolshevik. In 1939 the party membership stood at only 1.9 million, and the Soviet Union teetered on the brink of World War II.

During the Great Patriotic War, party membership increased to about six million, but immediately following the war Stalin purged many workers and peasants, replacing them with a new wave of technocrats, to whom he gave the task of rebuilding the economy. The party continued to grow, but in 1952, when its membership totaled almost seven million, the party braced itself for what appeared to be the beginning of yet another purge. Fortunately, however, the grisly dictator died before launching a new round of killings.[2]

Khrushchev's subsequent ascent to power was accompanied by a considerable amount of turmoil in the party. Breaking with Stalin's lethal policies, Khrushchev did not execute his enemies, preferring instead to retire them in disgrace. At the same time, however, he pursued reformist policies, attempting to replace corrupt and inefficient party members with younger, better educated people. These policies, as well as others, caused serious discontent in the party ranks. Resisting pressures of his opponents, Khrushchev began to take more and more actions unilaterally, ignoring the principle of **collective leadership** that had come into favor in the post-Stalin period. Disgruntled with his policies and resentful of his leadership style, Khrushchev's subordinates, many of whom he had promoted, replaced him in 1964.

By that year the party had grown to over 11 million members. Weary and resentful of Khrushchev's disruptive policies, the new collective leadership, headed by Brezhnev, pledged to promote stability and consistency in the party and government. True to its commitment, the Brezhnev regime was singularly devoted to maintaining the status quo within party ranks. When Yuri Andropov assumed power, a new emphasis on honesty and efficiency was heralded throughout the whole society, including the party. Several high officials were dismissed, and some were even executed for corruption and inefficiency. Yet, while Chernenko gave nominal support to Andropov's reforms, he took a somewhat less strident position, and during his short tenure the party lapsed into the same stifling stability afforded it by Brezhnev.

[2]Roy A. Medvedev and Zhores A. Medvedev, *Khrushchev: The Years in Power*, trans. Andrew R. Durkin (New York: Columbia University Press, 1976), p. 13.

Gorbachev's party reforms.   In 1985 Mikhail S. Gorbachev found himself at the head of a huge, conservative, and self-indulgent party bureaucracy that had lost much of the public support it once enjoyed. At first he thought it could be reformed by a simple puritanical campaign against corruption, negligence, and inefficiency. He eventually learned, however, that the immense economic and social problems of the Soviet Union could be adequately addressed only by a massive liberalization of the society and by profound reform of the Communist Party. Unfortunately, however, the political liberalization ran far ahead of the party reforms, with the result of fostering deep political fissures in the society, greatly worsening the economic problems (each of these will be detailed in later chapters), and generating ideological and political splits within the party.

Essentially the conservative, or neo-Stalinist, wing of the party has pulled back from support of Gorbachev's policies, while the radical wing has become frustrated with what it views as Gorbachev's cautious posture. The right, populated by committed Marxist dogmatists, party functionaries—especially from central Russia (some of them want "Volgograd" renamed "Stalingrad"), Russian Nationalists, military people, and the trade unions, condemn Gorbachev for abandoning socialism and enfeebling the party at home, for giving Eastern Europe away, and for being too accommodating with the West. The left, on the other hand, is largely composed of intellectuals. They see Stalinist totalitarianism and Communist Party hegemony as evil and want the rule of law, respect for individual rights, multiparty competition, and a market economy. Some even want Lenin's body removed from public display in the Red Square Mausoleum, and they mock the orthodox Marxists by sarcastically volunteering that:

> Socialism is the synthesis of the stages of mankind's development. From prehistory it takes the method. From antiquity, slavery. From feudalism, serfdom. From capitalism, exploitation. From socialism, the name.

Gorbachev finds himself sandwiched between these two extremes. He has tried to foster change in the system, while supporting party authority. In what is perhaps an impossible task, he has not succeeded. Striking out against party functionaries who were corrupt and inefficient, by 1986 he had changed almost half of the government ministers, central committee members, and provincial party leaders. Publicly demanding that the party leaders be honest and respectful of people's rights, he encouraged popular opposition to official abuse. Subsequent popular protests forced resignations of regional party leaders in Kuybychev, Kaluga, Sverdlosk, Chernigov, Baku, and dozens of other places. Meanwhile, striking coal miners demanded that party offices at the mines be removed. The popular disquiet did not stop at the lower levels, however. Gorbachev himself was heckled and criticized by people who were losing confidence in his policies.

Moved by this dissatisfaction, Gorbachev resolved that the party had to be reorganized at the top and democratized if it was to survive the looming political, social, and economic problems facing the country. Consequently, in a series of party meetings from mid-1988 to mid-1990, he pushed through a number of changes he hoped would restore the people's confidence in the party. The reforms included electing delegates to party conferences and congresses. Regional party first secretaries became subject to party ballots and were forced to resign party leadership if they were not also elected by the general public to lead the government that corresponds to their party level. (Several high-ranking party leaders, including Politburo member and Leningrad Party First Secretary Yuri F. Solovoyov, failed to be elected to the government and were forced to resign from their party posts as a result.) Privileges for party officials were to be reduced so that they might suffer the same problems in everyday life the ordinary people endure. The party bureaucracy was reduced in size, and it is being removed from the day-to-day management of the government, the economy, and other institutions in society. Total socialism was abandoned as a goal of the party, and top party personnel and institutions were reorganized. Most significantly, in 1990 the party voted to abolish its monopoly on power so that opposition parties are now legal.

All of these reforms have not yet been completely implemented, and they were not approved by leading party groups without anguished and heated debate. However, they were ultimately adopted because party leaders saw little choice. In 1989 the communist governments of Eastern Europe either collapsed or, in the case of Rumania, were driven out by popular revolts. At the same time, hundreds of thousands of Soviet citizens took to the streets in Moscow, Leningrad, Kiev, and elsewhere demanding party reforms. Some signs threatened, "Party Bureaucrats, Remember Rumania!" and some people even campaigned for outright abolition of the Communist Party. Such massive public protests had not been seen in the Soviet Union for a half century.

Party splits. The political unrest, the social stirrings, the nationalistic impulses, the economic difficulties, and the party reforms have combined to shatter the once monolithic CPSU. Despite vigorous efforts by Gorbachev and the CPSU to stop it, the Lithuanian Communist Party, led by Algirdas Brazauskas, declared its independence from the CPSU in December 1989. The Lithuanian communists claimed that only through independence could they continue to govern their separatist compatriots. Only a small group, composed principally of Russian residents in Lithuania, remained loyal to the CPSU. Organizing late at night, after the bulk of the party members had declared independence and gone home, this tiny loyalist group was dubbed the "night party." Although the Lithuanian communists' separatist action was condemned by the CPSU, it could not be prevented, and in 1990 the Estonian and Latvian Communist parties followed suit.

Complex rifts have also occurred within the CPSU. On the left, the **Democratic Platform** urges an end to democratic centralism and a more democratic party governance system. It also favors human liberties, legal restraints on government, a multiparty system, and private property. It claims between 60,000 and two million members organized into 162 local clubs in over 100 cities. In July 1990, during the Twenty-eighth Party Congress (technically the highest party organ), some of Democratic Platform's most important leaders, including Boris Yeltsin, Moscow's Mayor Gavril Popov, and Leningrad's Mayor Anatoly Sobchak, resigned from the party, and in 1991 Edward A. Shevardnadze and other leading figures quit the party calling for a democratic party.

On the right, the **Marxist Platform** calls for an end to most of the reforms and a return to direct party control of the society. This movement has been gaining strength since the summer of 1990. The most dramatic example of the right wing's mobilization is the organization of the Russian Communist Party in June 1990. Although each of the 14 other union republics had its own branch within the CPSU, Russia had not had a distinct branch of the CPSU since 1925. Reacting against the nationalistic and anti-Russian disorders in the other union republics, and to Gorbachev's reforms within the CPSU, the Russian communists—ignoring Gorbachev's protests—organized their own separate branch of the CPSU.[3] This move is significant for two reasons. First, the Russians constitute about 58 percent of the party and their decision to develop a separate identity within the CPSU could mean that Gorbachev and the central apparatus may have difficulty controlling the party in the future. Second, the Russian Communist Party is dominated by conservative zealots who elected Ivan K. Polozkov, a noted opponent of many of Gorbachev's policies, as the party's first secretary. In fact, the Russian party is so conservative that many Russian communists refuse to join it, although they remain affiliated with the CPSU. The Russian party has become a major forum for Gorbachev's party opposition.

The splintering of the CPSU has greatly complicated Gorbachev's task of uniting the Soviet political system and reinvigorating the economy. To make matters more difficult, the membership of the party began to become unstable in 1989.

PARTY MEMBERSHIP

The party membership has deliberately been kept small because Lenin prescribed that only the most dedicated people should be allowed to join its ranks.

Accordingly, the party maintains a relatively stringent entrance procedure. Most of its members are drawn from the *Komsomol*, a party youth group. A candidate must be a Komsomol member in good standing and be recommended by its leadership for party membership. A candidate may enter the party at 18 years of age if he or she is recommended by the Komsomol. Otherwise, he or she may not enter the party until the age of 23. In this case, the applicant must be sponsored by three party members,

---

[3]This action is not equivalent to what the Baltic parties did. The Baltic parties actually withdrew from affiliation with the CPSU, while the Russian Party has organized as a branch within the CPSU.

each of whom has been a full member for no less than five years. In either case, the applicant must serve for one year as a candidate member before being advanced to full membership. Advancement to full membership is not automatic; tens of thousands of candidate members have been refused full membership in the past 15 years.

The party is sustained by dues from its members and by revenue from its publications. The dues range from half of 1 percent of a student's income to as much as 3 percent of an employed member's income. The party's annual budget is about $3 billion and it officially lists its assets at $7.8 billion.[4] Opponents of the party claim that its holdings are much more extensive and they demand that the party turn over its assets to the government. Indeed, some local trade unions and cities have unilaterally expropriated party property. Gorbachev, however, was quick to outlaw such acts and he moved to restore the confiscated property.[5]

In January 1989 the party membership stood at about 19 million, but almost 200,000 more people resigned in that year than joined, and even greater numbers of resignations in 1990 and 1991 brought the membership down to about 16 million, or about 8 percent of the adult population. The party has often culled its own membership, but never before have so many party members voluntarily quit. The reasons for this exodus vary. Many members have joined the general public in becoming disgusted with the party, as it is blamed for the worsening political and economic conditions and for its association with the terror of the Stalinist era. Other members have deserted the party because they feel they no longer need it to get good jobs or promotions, while others resent having to pay party dues. Additionally, many people are dropping out for ideological reasons, with some leaving because the party has become too liberal, while others complain that it is not changing fast enough.

The popularity of the party has dropped so low and the number of people leaving it has become so great that people have begun to joke that:

> In order to leave the party and join the ranks of the more honest general public, one must secure the recommendation of two nonparty members.

Duties and Privileges

It is commonly thought that party members enjoy great power and privilege in Soviet society. It is undoubtedly true that the ranking party members are the beneficiaries of such perks, but, in fact, the bulk of the membership is asked to make considerable sacrifice for the cause. Only about one million of the party members are paid for their services—the

[4]Carol J. Williams, "Majority of Party Members Turn Deaf Ear to Share-the-Wealth Faction," *The Los Angeles Times,* July 4, 1990.

[5]Carey Goldberg, "Gorbachev Bars Confiscations of Communist Property," *The Los Angeles Times,* Oct. 13, 1990.

vast majority are volunteers who hold down regular jobs and perform party tasks during their spare time. Hence, for the most part, party members who commit to their assumed roles are relatively dedicated people. This, of course, is not to say that all members work for the cause to their full potential.

The party rules call upon members to perform a number of specific functions, including the following:

1. To be dedicated to self-improvement
2. To foster and increase productivity and prosperity
3. To implement party policy
4. To teach the people the party line
5. To be courteous, respectful, and responsive to the people
6. To participate actively in political and cultural life
7. To set an example for the people
8. To master the principles of Marxism-Leninism
9. To combat bourgeois ideology wherever it is found
10. To place public interest above self-interest
11. To be patriotic
12. To remove shortcomings through "criticism and self-criticism"
13. To report all actions injurious to the party and the state.

The list of duties goes on and on and could easily consume all the time of its members if they committed themselves to these functions completely.

The degree of commitment, of course, varies among members. Their attitudes range from very intense devotion to their responsibilities, through relatively casual, eyewinking attitudes, to cynicism. The differences among party members stem from a variety of factors. The younger members, a rapidly dwindling group, often seem more idealistic than their seniors. Party position frequently appears to influence the members, with those directly in charge of others assuming a more officious and strict posture than subordinates. Obviously, people who join the party because of ideological commitment take their obligations more seriously than those who join to assure professional advancement.

Although the party takes reasonable precautions to assure that its new members join out of devotion to the cause, it would indeed be naive to suggest that this is the sole motivation. Although one does not wish to detract from those who join the party out of a sincere wish to further socialism, it must be recognized that there are other inducements as well.

As indicated earlier, it is easy to overestimate the privileges accruing to party membership. Stalin was careful to see that party loyalties were reinforced by the granting of many special privileges. Khrushchev embarked on a policy to bring the party closer to the people, which meant the elimination of many, although certainly not all, of the privileges its members enjoyed. During the Brezhnev era the party became more self-indulgent than ever. For his part, Gorbachev recently called for a reduction of party privileges, but it is prudent to wait to see if this admonition will be taken seriously. In any event, the extra benefits enjoyed by party members do not extend on an equal basis; the leadership clearly gets a greater slice of the privilege pie than ordinary members, and even Gorbachev himself has been criticized for high living.

Nevertheless, several advantages do accrue to low-ranking members. Party membership usually assures decent jobs and working conditions. Being closer to the governing elite than most people, party members often learn when scarce items are coming to town and where they will be sold. They may find it easier to get an apartment of their own, thus not having to share space with in-laws or parents for as long as other people must. They are also less often obliged to live in apartments where bathrooms and kitchens must be shared with neighbors. Party members can also be fairly confident of enjoying an advantage in educational opportunity, job advancement, and vacation accommodations. Although most of these advantages are only minor, they can make life more convenient, comfortable, and enjoyable, thus compensating for the extra tasks required.[6] Such advantages for the select few, to say nothing of the much greater benefits going to the ranking party members, lead to considerable public cynicism, as reflected in this popular joke:

> "Comrades," a party agitator is supposed to have said, "in the next five-year plan we shall have more to eat. We shall have more cars. We shall get better treatment. We shall see our living standards rise."
>
> At that point a worker in the back of the crowd shouted, "So much for you, what about us?"

Public skepticism aside, the greatest advantage to party membership is that it is a prerequisite for advancement into the elite, the very few high-ranking people who enjoy the greatest privileges in the society. It must be kept in mind that only a small percentage of the rank and file actually reach this exalted status, but the rewards are indeed bountiful for those who do. Among the benefits enjoyed by these elite are access to summer cottages (dachas), automobiles, personally owned apartments, educational advantages, special medical treatment, and foreign travel opportunities. Another benefit is access to stores that sell otherwise unobtainable merchandise, including luxury perfumes, jewelry, clothing, and Western-made radios, televisions, and tape recorders. The party elite often obtain supplemental income from secret bonuses or even lucrative salaries for spouses who perform no work.[7] An important status symbol for the party and government elite is found on their office desks—the more telephones on the desk, the more important their owner is assumed to be. For the most important people there are very high salaries: The average monthly salary for a

[6]Mervyn Matthews, *Privilege in the Soviet Union* (London: George Allen & Unwin, 1978), pp. 91–130.

[7]Matthews, pp. 36–55.

worker is about 200 rubles, while Politburo members receive between 1,209 and 1,513 rubles per month. Gorbachev is the highest paid official, earning 3,750 rubles per month. The highest officials also have many other privileges that no one else in the country enjoys. For example, each Politburo member has an airplane available for his or her use.

As economic conditions declined in 1988–1989, the question of privileges for the elite—never popular—became a major issue. Then, in January 1990, a minor automobile accident in the Ukrainian city of Chernigov, involving a high local party official, popped open the trunk of his chauffeur-driven limousine. A crowd gathered and noticed that the trunk was brimming with choice foods and unobtainable delicacies. The people became enraged; they dragged the car three miles to the center of the city and rioted. The upshot of this episode was that six top party officials, including the first secretary of Chernigov, resigned. Even so, riots and protests against party privilege spread to other cities, forcing more party officials to resign, and the issue became a major factor in the government elections in Russia and other union republics. Responding to public pressure, Gorbachev announced that some of the party's special stores would be closed. In addition, party medical clinics began to take regular patients, the number of government limousines was reduced, and many party vacation resorts were opened to the public. These reforms followed previous efforts in 1986–1987 to reduce public animosity over party privileges by making the special stores less conspicuous.[8] Such reforms during Khrushchev's time, however, were ultimately unsuccessful in curbing party excesses, so more time will have to pass to learn if these new measures have the desired result. Certainly the people are not optimistic, as is made clear in this joke:

> Olga asks Sasha: "Have you heard this joke? Two party officials are riding on a streetcar."
>
> "Yes, go on," says Sasha.
>
> "That's the joke," replies Olga. "Who ever heard of party officials riding the streetcars?"

CHARACTERISTICS OF PARTY MEMBERS

Party membership can be viewed from a number of different perspectives. The most appropriate division is into four major groups from the standpoint of their party function. The first group, the **leadership corps,** is composed of about 250,000 people who occupy the top positions in the party, the military, and the government. These range from the most powerful—those in the Central Committee, the Politburo, the Secretariat, and the government ministers—down through the leading positions in the

---

[8]Walter Laqueur, "Soviet Politics: Current Trends," in *Soviet Union 2000: Reform or Revolution,* ed. Walter Laqueur (New York: St. Martin's Press, 1990), p. 33.

party and governmental positions in the provinces. These people are the decision makers, and they are responsible for supervising the smooth exercise of policy in the system. Needless to say, they are among the elite described in the previous section.

The second group consists of approximately 750,000 **professional party functionaries.** These people, generally salted throughout the bureaucracy, can be found in the secretariats at the various levels of the party and in the government and military as party agents. Their principal functions are to develop the technical data needed by the leadership corps for making its decisions, to supervise the implementation of policy, and to see to the internal mechanism of day-to-day party administration. The highest ranking members of this group share the great privileges enjoyed by the leadership corps, while lower-ranking people are less favored. Together the leadership corps and the professional party functionaries are sometimes referred to as the **apparatchiks.**

Third are the **celebrity members.** Precise data on this element in the party are not available, so the exact number of people who fit this description is impossible to discern. Presumably, however, their number is far smaller than that of the two groups previously listed. In any event, this sector is also among the elite of the society, although their status is earned in quite a different manner than the previous two categories. Attempting to maintain a prestigious place in public opinion, the party seeks out celebrated people in the society and encourages them to join the party. As an inducement, the party holds out many of the privileges mentioned above and is also able to deny such advantages to the uncooperative. Among the most important benefits to this group are the right to live in Moscow or another major cultural center, working conditions conducive to the person's endeavor, and foreign travel (which also includes benevolent customs inspectors who close their eyes when these people return with contraband luxuries). Celebrity members include dancers, musicians, entertainers, actors, artists, athletes, prominent scholars, scientists, writers, cosmonauts, and military heroes. This group enjoys one privilege that the others do not: Its members are usually exempt from any but perfunctory party tasks and obligations.

The last sector is the largest group in the party, comprising about 16 million people. These are the **rank and file,** the foot soldiers of the party. This group receives fewer of the benefits from the party, although its members carry out the party's most basic tasks. It is these people who must carry the policy and image of the party to the people. They are on the "front lines," the members who, in the last analysis, are expected to mobilize the society, exhorting the people to greater accomplishments, more productivity, better conduct, more sobriety, more honesty, increased mutual courtesy, safer driving and working habits, and better family relations. The rank and file are supposed to differ from their neighbors only to the extent that they are model citizens who show the people the way to a better society.

Obviously, not every party member meets the expectations of his or her superior. But without this huge foundation, the CPSU would indeed fail to govern the society as it presently does and would probably have to fall back on more repressive means of control. The party tries to maintain a positive image among the Soviet people. It presents itself as the best of the best, the leaders, the model socialists. As indicated earlier, it has not been very successful in this endeavor recently.

As an indication of the amount of commitment demanded of the party members, consider the following complaint to *Pravda* by a local party member:

> Each of us is obliged to attend in the course of one month: two sessions of the party bureau, one meeting for all party members in the garage, two sessions of the People's Control group and one general meeting each of the shop party organization's communists, the column trade union, and the brigade.
>
> To this we must still add the quarterly meetings of the People's Control groups and of the party organization *aktiv*, conferences, etc. Add participation in ad hoc commissions and People's Control inspections— sometimes lasting several days—and there goes your week! All our month's free days turn out to be taken up by volunteer work.
>
> Of course, each of us has a family, too, for which time must be allotted.[9]

Social Class Structure in the Party

The Soviet Union recognizes only three social classes in its society today: workers (including state farm workers), collective farmers, and intelligentsia (white-collar workers). These classes, official ideology insists, are "nonantagonistic" because each is equally devoted to building socialism. Hence, until the classless society Marx envisioned is created, these three nonexploitative classes can live side by side in a peaceful environment.

By the mid-1950s the effort to bring the technocrats into the party resulted in the intelligentsia enjoying a slight majority (50.9 percent) in the party. Workers were listed as the second most numerous class (32 percent), with collective farmers accounting for only 17.1 percent. Since 1956, however, the party leadership has pursued a deliberate policy of increasing the percentage of workers at the expense of the other groups. According to official Soviet statistics, the workers' proportion has risen to 45.3 percent of the party, while intelligentsia and collective farmers account for 43.1 percent and 11.6 percent, respectively.[10]

Because of the emphasis Soviet ideology places on social class, great importance is accorded to the sociological composition of the party by its leaders. This distinction, however, is less significant than might otherwise

[9]Gail Warshofsky Lapidus, *Women in Soviet Society* (Berkeley: University of California Press, Ltd., 1978), p. 225.

[10]*USSR Yearbook '90* (Moscow: Novosti Press Agency Publishing House, 1990), p. 174.

be the case. The social class of party members is registered at the time they enter the party. No attempt is made to adjust the designation as members change jobs or advance in the society. Thus, even though a given person may have been a worker when he or she entered the party, promotions or party work may have deposited him or her in a white-collar job; yet the party list of social class categories remains unchanged. Further, the designation of worker or collective farmer can be misleading. Far greater percentages of the skilled workers in these categories are admitted to the party than their brethren in unskilled jobs.

Similarly, a far greater percentage of the party membership holds higher education degrees than is reflected in the population as a whole.[11] Indeed, almost half of all college graduates are party members. By contrast, although slightly over half of the total Soviet population, as well as its work force, are women, they make up only about 30 percent of the party and are allowed only a tiny percentage of the top leadership posts.

The ethnic characteristics of party members are also revealing. Clearly, the Russians govern the Soviet Union. Making up only about 52 percent of the population, Russians hold around 58 percent of the party positions. Russians also occupy a much larger percentage of the leading party posts than is suggested by their proportionate share.

Only the Jews, Georgians, and Ukrainians join the Russians in enjoying a greater percentage of party positions than their share of the population would entitle them to have. The Armenians account for about the same percentage of the party as they do the population, but all other ethnic groups are underrepresented, with the Moldavians being the least represented and the Uzbeks second from the bottom of the list.

Hence, the CPSU is populated by an elite. A typical party member is likely to be male, Russian, and a college graduate or skilled worker. This fact should not surprise us since the party makes no pretense of being a mirror reflection of the population. Party members are supposed to be the best of the best, and their membership cards describe the party as the "wisdom, honor, and conscience of the epoch." On the other hand, it is somewhat unusual to find a nation's political elite so similar to its population in demographic terms. The United States Congress, for example, is proportionately far more male, wealthy, white, and educated than the people it represents.

ALL-UNION PARTY STRUCTURE

True to Russian tradition, the CPSU is a highly complex bureaucracy composed of a bewildering variety of committees, bureaus, secretariats, and other bodies (See Figure 4–1.) Equally typical of the country that spawned

[11]Matthews, pp. 114–119. Many party members hold degrees from party schools, and others earned degrees from correspondence courses that, according to Matthews, are sometimes of questionable academic quality.

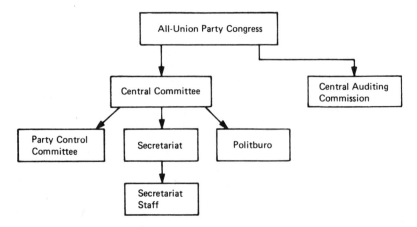

FIGURE 4–1   Structure of the All-Union Party *on paper.* Arrows indicate the flow of power.

it, the CPSU is a centralized institution, tightly controlled by its leaders and allowing for little individual variation among its members and institutions. Power inevitably gravitates to the top of the party structure; thus, it is appropriate that we first turn our attention to that level.

All-Union Party Congress

Theoretically, the highest organ in the party is the **Party Congress,** which is supposed to be the ultimate repository of power in the party and its legitimatizing authority.[12] In the early days of the party, the Party Congress indeed equaled its constitutional authority. The First Party Congress met in Minsk in 1898, at which time the party was founded and named the Russian Social-Democratic Workers' Party. After this secret meeting of nine delegates on Russian soil, the party leaders were forced to go into exile, where the next six party congresses were held. The most important of these was the Second Party Congress in London in 1903. It was at this meeting that the tiny party split into the Menshevik and Bolshevik factions.

While Lenin lived, the Party Congress met almost each year and was characterized by relatively freewheeling debate. As Stalin's grip tightened on the party, however, the Party Congress met infrequently (the congress did not meet at all between 1939 and 1952) and echoed the "party line."

After Stalin died, the congress was convened more regularly, but its power over party policy did not increase. Meeting once every five years, the congress' 5,000 delegates sat for days listening to speeches that ranged from the lauding of the glorious work of the party in a particular locality to the heroic efforts exerted during the last grain harvest. Between the long and redundant oratory, the delegates were afforded the exercise of raising their hands to vote in favor of the issues laid before them. The votes were

[12]Article IV, clause 30, of the Rules of the Communist Party of the Soviet Union.

inevitably unanimous. Delegates would vote approval of party programs, party rules, the Five-Year Plans, foreign policy positions, and resolutions of commendation. Met with great media fanfare, the congresses were principally forums for publicizing the latest policies and attitudes of the party and for stimulating the public interest. In fact, they were rarely significant political meetings. Even their elections of Central Committee members and the Central Auditing Commission were scripted. Occasionally, the congress was used for something truly important, as when the Ninth Congress in 1920 voted to subordinate the trade unions, the Tenth Congress in 1921 adopted the principle of nonfactionalism in the party, and the Twentieth Congress sat spellbound in 1956 during a secret speech by Khrushchev in which he excoriated the deceased Stalin for "crimes" against the people.[13] Normally, however, the proceedings have been quite mundane.

Although the Twenty-sixth Congress in 1986, the first presided over by Gorbachev, was not much different from its predecessors, matters changed shortly afterward. Disturbed by the slow pace of his political and economic reforms, in June 1988 Gorbachev attempted to counter party bureaucratic resistance with a direct appeal to the party. Yet, since the Party Congress was not scheduled to meet again for more than two years, he resorted to the unusual step of calling the Nineteenth **party conference,** a substitute for the Party Congress, last used in 1941.

In this extraordinary public meeting, delegates engaged in open debate, some publicly criticizing Politburo members—including Gorbachev. Others called for the resignation of old leaders, charged some officials with corruption, demanded disclosures of the finances of Central Committee members, challenged a personnel decision of the Central Committee, and even recommended the creation of a stock exchange in this socialist country. In the end, the reform package submitted by Gorbachev was adopted, but not without considerable debate and some important amendments.

Such openness and public dispute in the party had not been seen in the Soviet Union since its founding, but it was soon to be duplicated in the Twenty-eighth Party Congress of July 1990. Originally scheduled to meet in February 1991, the congress was convened seven months early because Gorbachev wanted to secure approval of several new structural changes. Meanwhile, however, the conservatives in the party had mobilized and they too wanted to meet early, albeit not for the same reasons as Gorbachev. Scheduled to meet for seven days, the contentious session actually lasted for 12.

Previous congresses had been firmly controlled by the leadership. The various constituencies had been represented proportionally on the list of hand-picked delegates. This time, however, the delegates were elected by the local party organizations, so the delegation of 4,683 was heavily weighted with leading party officials, economic managers, bureaucrats, and military officers. (See Table 4–1.) Hence, another 350 workers and farmers were invited to attend so as to better balance the delegation.

The meeting was a factious affair. The reformers, although struggling

[13]Medvedev and Medvedev, p. 69.

TABLE 4–1   Delegates Attending Party Congresses

Class	27th Congress	28th Congress
Peasants	9%	5.4%
Workers	42	11.6
Party Officials, Economic Managers, Military	49	83.0

Source: Central Committee CPSU

to hold their own, were outnumbered by the conservatives. The Democratic Platform warned that unless the party liberalized, it would suffer the same fate as the communist parties in Eastern Europe. Some members of the Democratic Platform even went so far as to demand that the CPSU change its name to the Party of Democratic Socialism. Such a title was anathema to the Marxist Platform, and it was easily rejected.

For their part, the conservatives lashed out at the reformers. They heckled prominent Politburo liberals, demanding their resignation. When these officials (Alexander Yakovlev, Vladim Medvedev, and Eduard Shevardnadze) rose to speak, they were interrupted by booing and rhythmical handclapping. Even Gorbachev himself had to threaten to leave the podium unless hecklers quieted themselves during his speech, and he too heard a conservative delegate demand his resignation. Marxist Platform speakers decried the failed Gorbachev reforms, although the general secretary's name was not usually invoked; they lamented the party's loss of public support, and they railed at the loss of Eastern Europe—which Shevardnadze reminded them was made up of independent countries, not Soviet trophies.

The spectacle of the general secretary and his closest supporters being reviled continued for days. Although the conservatives were obviously more powerful than before, they did not have enough votes to defeat Gorbachev or his proposed changes. The moderates held out for Gorbachev, and the left also supported him. Accordingly, he was reelected general secretary—with one-quarter of the delegates voting against him.

Another struggle took place over the election of the deputy to the general secretary. This new post was created to take over some of the day-to-day party chores that Gorbachev could not handle as long as he also served as president of the Soviet Union. The conservatives supported their leader, Politburo member Yegor K. Ligachev, for the post, while Gorbachev backed Ukrainian leader Vladimir Ivashko. Considerable drama surrounded the election because even though Gorbachev and Ligachev are personal friends, they are political adversaries. Forcing the general secretary to take on a deputy who opposed many of his policies would be a crippling handicap. As it turned out, however, Ivashko won even more heartily than did Gorbachev, with only 776 votes cast for Ligachev. The right wing did not lose completely, however, as the Latvian conservative Boris Pugo was elected to continue as chair of the Party Control Commission. Significantly, however, the secret ballot election of the general secretary was the first time the Party Congress had elected the leader. Previously, the Central Committee had done so. With Gorbachev and Ivashko elected by the Party Congress, they may be somewhat more independent of the Central Committee than was the case previously.

Gorbachev's other proposals were also adopted, although modified somewhat. The most important was the reorganization of the Politburo, which will be discussed later. Perhaps as revealing as what was adopted by the congress is what was not proposed. Unlike most of its predecessors, the Twenty-eighth Party Congress focused upon personalities as much or more than upon issues and programs. Although Gorbachev managed to emerge the winner in the party struggle, fending off a revolt by party conservatives, his victory may have been a hollow one. Even though the country found itself in desperate economic straits and deeply divided along ideological and nationalistic lines, no new programs or reforms were adopted by the congress to deal with the strife. Thus, like George Bush after his 1988 presidential victory, Gorbachev emerged from the Party Congress without an articulated consensus about what should be done.

A sense of futility pervaded the country at the end of the congress. All of the vitriol and leadership struggles did not pass unnoticed, but they were seen by many people to be largely irrelevant, as the country prepared to enter one of its history's bleakest peacetime winters. Capturing the mood of a disenchanted people, a Moscow truck driver described it as "a congress of the dead."[14] Another ominous note was struck at the end of the congress when Boris Yeltsin, the country's most popular politician, took the lectern to announce his resignation from the party. Yeltsin had previously warned that unless the party reformed itself profoundly, it would lose its relevance to the people. His resignation was quickly followed by that of several other prominent Democratic Platform delegates.

The resignations were greeted with regret by the left and with glee by the right. Thus reconstituted, this extraordinary congress proceeded to its final substantive act—electing the members to the Party Central Committee.

The Central Committee

Each Party Congress elects a *Central Committee,* which is charged with exercising its powers when the congress is not in session. As with the Party Congress, the nominees for the Central Committee are selected by the top party leaders. Although the Twenty-eighth Party Congress elected 412 members instead of the planned 398, there has seldom been any dispute with the leadership over its nominees.

In the early years the committee met frequently and actually made party policy. It was the only executive committee of the party. Gradually,

[14]C. S. Manegold, Andrew Nagorski, and Carroll Bogert, "'Congress of the Dead,'" *Newsweek,* July 23, 1990.

however, the committee became less and less important, until it suffered from abject neglect under Stalin. The size of its membership grew steadily, and turnover was relatively frequent, reaching a peak between 1934 and 1939, when Stalin purged 125 of its 140 members.

Khrushchev continued the policy of purging the Central Committee, although he merely demoted his enemies rather than liquidating them. True to his promise to stabilize conditions, Brezhnev did not call upon his supporters on the Central Committee to purge Khrushchev's loyalists from the body. Instead, he simply added his own supporters to it, letting attrition gradually remove Khrushchev's stalwarts. Brezhnev's conservative personnel policy assured that age and corruption eventually afflicted the Central Committee. Andropov and Chernenko were not in power long enough to effect many personnel changes, but Gorbachev quickly asserted his authority, calling for "radical changes" in the system and sweeping many of the oldest and most corrupt persons from the Central Committee at the Twenty-seventh Party Congress. In 1989, about one-third of the members were removed in another Gorbachev purge, and the Central Committee bureaucracy was reduced by half, to about 3,000 functionaries. These maneuvers, however, do not yet seem to have assured Gorbachev of incontrovertible authority over the Central Committee.

The Central Committee used to meet twice a year, but Gorbachev has convened the body more frequently to deal with the multitudinous problems bearing down upon the party and the society. The economy and the nationalities questions have been areas of special focus. The Central Committee's official function is to approve party policy in the absence of the Party Congress and to elect the members of the Party Control Committee, the Secretariat, and the Politburo. However, since the candidates for these posts are supplied from above and since the Central Committee meets only briefly at infrequent intervals, it clearly does not enjoy the dominance suggested by the list of its formal functions.

It would be unwise, however, to hastily discount the power, or at least the potential power, of this body. The Central Committee is composed of the leading party officials throughout the country. In addition to members of the Secretariat and the Politburo, its ranks include party leaders from the provinces, the ranking professional functionaries and staff personnel in the party, and leading members of the government, military, trade unions, and the academic community. Although its precise role and authority remain unclear, we know that it has been quite significant in the past, and indications are that it may be more influential now than a casual glance may reveal.

In an apparent effort to dominate his colleagues on the Politburo, Khrushchev skillfully manipulated the Central Committee for his own advantage. In 1955 and again in 1957 he used his control of the Central Committee to foil his opponents. Most dramatically, he rallied the Central Committee to repeal a Presidium (Politburo) vote for his removal in 1957 and to remove his enemies from the party. Whether the Central Committee has ever successfully contradicted the Politburo a second time is not known, but the fact remains that in at least one instance it has been used to negate the work of the Politburo, which is usually seen as the system's most powerful institution. Hence, the potential power of the Central Committee is a matter that cannot be kept too far back in the minds of the party leadership.

Although we cannot be sure, it appears that the Central Committee is a force with which to be reckoned. Whether or not it ever dramatically impacts Politburo decisions is open to conjecture. Certainly it does not regularly check the leadership through its votes. The possibility, and some scholars believe the likelihood, remains, however, that Politburo decisions are somewhat tempered by the knowledge that the Central Committee, the collection of the country's leading politicians and technocrats, could exercise its constitutional powers. The Central Committee is no doubt even more influential during periods like the present when the system is destabilized by leadership changes. For example, consistent with his call for democratization of the system, Gorbachev proposed to the Central Committee in February 1987 that contested elections of party leaders be instituted. Yet, displaying unprecedented independence of its general secretary, the Central Committee passed a resolution giving only vague and diluted support to the idea. Such a contradiction is extremely unusual.

Even more unusual, in the April 1991 Central Committee plenium, the conservatives mounted an apparent attempt to oust Gorbachev. For weeks before the meeting, rumors circulated that the Central Committee might vote no confidence in the general secretary. When the meeting finally convened, Gorbachev was lambasted by speaker after speaker for three days. Gradually, however, it became apparent that the opposition was in the minority. Finally, an angry Gorbachev took the rostrum and called the conservatives' bluff by offering to resign. By this maneuver Gorbachev proved that he has not lost his incomparable intra-party political skills. The Central Committee recessed following his sobering announcement, while the Politburo convened to discuss the matter. (Russian party leader, Ivan K. Polozkov—a vocal conservative critic of Gorbachev's who had led the attacks against the general secretary, sits on the Politburo.) After some time, the Politburo announced its *unanimous* support for Gorbachev remaining general secretary: The conservatives found themselves defeated. Later, the Central Committee reaffirmed its confidence in Gorbachev with only 13 members voting in the negative and 14 abstaining.

The authority of the Central Committee remains ambiguous. Since the Twenty-eight Party Congress elected Gorbachev as general secretary, it is questionable whether it could legitimately force him out. Still, as Gorbachev's threat to resign demonstrates, should he ever lose the Central Committee's support, he may find remaining at the head of the party impossible.

Since 1988 the Central Committee has been augmented by six standing commissions. Each commission is assigned to study and report on an area of concern to the party: party affairs and personnel, ideology, economic and social questions, agriculture, international affairs, and legal affairs. This new structure replaces a much more complicated apparatus and it, together with other structural reforms in the Secretariat and the Politburo, are intended to reduce the party's involvement in the day-to-day governance of the Soviet Union and to focus the party more on long-range planning. The commissions are headed by top party leaders and they report to the Politburo as well as to the Central Committee.

"Independent" disciplinary agencies.   Before discussing the most powerful institutions in the party, some attention should be given to two less prominent bodies: the Central Auditing Commission and the Party Control Committee. The **Central Auditing Commission** is elected directly by the Party Congress. As its name implies, it is supposed to function as an independent accounting agency, a watchdog for party funds and their use. In fact, however, although the commission makes regular reports to the Party Congress and the Central Committee, it seems to lack any significant power and certainly enjoys little independence from the leadership of the party.

The **Party Control Committee,** elected by the Central Committee, is charged with "verifying the observance of party discipline" and punishing members who violate party rules, programs, or ethics. Because actual disciplinary action is usually carried out by the local party agencies, the committee is also directed to review appeals of contested cases.[15]

The Secretariat

The Central Committee elects two executive committees[16] to exercise its authority in its absence: the **Secretariat,** for administrative detail, and the **Politburo,** for policy development. The precise relationship between the Secretariat and the Politburo is not clearly understood by Western scholars. The constitutional functions of the two bodies are not clearly stated, and the power relationship between their members tends to shift with circumstances, thus modifying the status of the two organs. It is generally agreed, however, that the Secretariat is probably less powerful than the Politburo. Even so, the degree of responsibility the Secretariat owes the Politburo is not at all clear.

The general secretary[17] captains the Secretariat of the Central Committee and is unquestionably the most important official in the Soviet Union. First created in 1922, the general secretaryship has been the platform from which Stalin, Khrushchev, Brezhnev, Andropov, Chernenko, and Gor-

[15]Article IV, clause 39, of the Rules of the Communist Party of the Soviet Union.

[16]Russian government has always been heavily bureaucratic. The Communist Party is no different, as testified to by its compounding of executive committees. The Party Congress elects the Central Committee to function in its absence, then the Central Committee elects two additional committees, the Secretariat and the Politburo, to run party affairs when the Central Committee is not seated. This kind of bureaucratic duplication is consistent throughout the party and government.

[17]The same position was titled First Secretary from 1953 to 1966.

[18]Although he was clearly the leader of the party during his lifetime, Lenin never actually assumed the formal position of general secretary. Instead, he recommended that Stalin assume the post when it was created in 1922, only to reverse himself a year later, recommending that the Georgian be removed.

Mikhail S. Gorbachev, general secretary of the Communist Party of the Soviet Union. (Photo provided by AP/Wide World Photos.)

bachev dominated the political system.[18] Both Stalin and Khrushchev also took the position of premier (head of government), and Brezhnev, Andropov, and Chernenko became the president of the Soviet Union (head of state). But the real source of their power rested in their control of the party. A major objective of Gorbachev's reforms, however, has been to reduce the party's dominance over the government. Although the general secretaryship is still a critical position, the new powers of the Soviet president, together with the declining centrality of the party, give the presidency great significance, and it may soon become more important than the general secretaryship itself.

Besides the general secretary, there are several subordinate secretaries who are elected by the Central Committee. There is no set number of secretaries; the Secretariat has been as large as 14, but it currently numbers 11. The Secretariat meets in secret about once each week in the Communist Party headquarters a few blocks from the Kremlin. Its function is basically to administer and supervise the work of the party. The Secretariat used to be of central importance to the system, but Gorbachev's reforms seem to have reduced its significance. The work of the Secretariat can be divided into four main functions: internal party administration, government oversight, ideological development, and staff work for the decision makers.

Seeing to the internal administration of the party is a massive job in and of itself. Technically, the Secretariat is the administrative arm of the Central Committee, and as such it is supposed to supervise the party in every aspect of its responsibility. Hence, the Secretariat has 16 million people—the party members—under its direct supervision. About one million of these are full-time functionaries, and it is they with whom the Secretariat works most closely.

A large part of the Secretariat's administrative role is taken up in personnel matters. Each level of the party is responsible for assuring that the level below carries out its assigned task and is led by loyal and efficient party members. The Secretariat caps this massive system and has the authority to intervene directly to assure the smooth function of the party at any level.

The party has traditionally exercised close supervision over the government and the economy. Although this role is currently being deemphasized, the party is still very active in overseeing the government. Each level of government—national, union republic, oblast, krai, raion, city—is shadowed by a corresponding party institution. In fact, the top governmental offices are usually headed by leading party officials, and each party first secretary is expected to hold a leading government position. Even so, the party is gradually relaxing its grip on the various institutions in the society.

Until 1990 the party used the **nomenklatura** lists to assure that only politically trustworthy people held positions of importance in the system. These lists included every significant position in the government, military, trade unions, press, police, courts, economic management, and the academic community. Aspirants for these posts had to get the approval of the party in order to be promoted. Although being a party member was not technically essential for such promotions, most of these jobs went to party members. In August 1990, however, the party announced plans to abandon the *nomenklatura* lists, stating that it would continue to exercise control only over those jobs that were directly related to the party itself. What this change will ultimately mean to the party's relationship to the government and other institutions in the society remains to be seen, but it could lead to a significant reduction in the party's control in the Soviet Union.

Early indications are that party officials are reluctant to lose control of key government positions. For example, the Moscow city soviet, led by radicals who have abandoned the party, appointed Vyacheslav S. Komissarov chief of police in 1991. Although a member of the party, Komissarov is also one of its critics and is pledged to reform the Moscow police force. However, the ministry of interior, headed by orthodox party member, Boris K. Pugo, refused to confirm the appointment. Instead, the Moscow police was placed directly under the ministry of interior by presidential decree in an attempt to control anti-government protests brewing in the capital.[19] Whatever the problems with relaxing its control over the society, the Communist Party must eventually abandon the *nomenklatura* system or risk the growing ire of the public. Such a transition, however, is not easy, so one can expect many frustrations before it is complete.

Another indication of the party's backing away from exercising day-to-day control of the system is the reorganization of the Secretariat's department structure. Until recently, the Secretariat had 21 departments devoted to virtually every economic, political, and social aspect of the society, and it exercised significant influence in the administration of policy through these departments. Now, however, its departments have been reduced to nine: Six parallel the Central Committee commissions and do staff work for them, and the remaining three are devoted to other broad areas, including defense. This reorganization seems to reflect the party's shift from micromanagement of the society to more general, long-term planning activities.

Among the most important departments in the Secretariat is the one dealing with ideology. Indeed, the last three general secretaries served as head of the ideological department immediately before their promotions. Establishing the proper ideological line for the party is fundamental to the system. Once the party line is established, a great effort is made to publicize it. The Secretariat runs schools and seminars, publishes pamphlets and tracts, and organizes party workers to give lectures—all in efforts to spread the gospel. It is the party's unique ability to determine the appropriate ideological course that gives it its claim to legitimacy.

The departments within the Secretariat are also fundamental in accomplishing its fourth task: providing staff work for the decision makers. Expert in particular areas, the Secretariat staff does research and analysis for the secretaries and for the Politburo as well. The importance of this work in the administration of party affairs is obvious, but it is no less important in matters of government policy. The Secretariat staff makes a separate information source available to its superiors. Thus, the leadership is not totally dependent on the government bureaucracy for technical information.

The Politburo

The first Politburo was created in 1917 just before the Bolsheviks took power. Its authority grew at first, but under Stalin the Politburo was neglected as his personal rule became the dominant fact in Soviet political life. Under Khrushchev, the authority of the Politburo (renamed the Presidium between 1952 and 1966)[20] was revived as Stalin's successors emphasized collective leadership. Indeed, Khrushchev's growing tendency to ignore the

---

[19]Carey Goldberg, "The Komissarov Affair: Just Who Is Moscow's Police Chief, Anyway?" *The Los Angeles Times,* April 27, 1991.

[20]Be careful not to confuse the Presidium of the CPSU with the Presidium of the Supreme Soviet discussed in the next chapter.

counsel of his colleagues on the Politburo late in his term helped provoke his being replaced by a vote of that body. For his part, Brezhnev was always careful to consult with the Politburo, and after Stalin's death—although it is a party organization—the Politburo made the basic policy decisions for the Soviet government. That role has been significantly modified by Gorbachev, however.

The Politburo used to meet once a week, but since 1990 it has met only monthly, and although its proceedings have been tersely publicized since 1982, little of substance is known about them. Before 1990 the size of the Politburo fluctuated but was usually kept at around 20 members, divided between full and candidate members. It was also characterized by an **interlocking directorate,** which included the leading party and government officials. Besides the general secretary, who still presides over the Politburo, its leading members were usually some people who also sat on the Secretariat: the party heads of important areas like Moscow, Leningrad, and the Ukraine; the premier (head of government); the foreign and defense ministers; and the head of the KGB.

Gorbachev's rise to power not only brought significant personnel changes to the Politburo, but it also ultimately led to dramatic changes in the Politburo's function. Between March 1985 (when he became general secretary) and 1989, virtually every position on the Politburo changed hands. Then, in July 1990, the Central Committee adopted his proposal for a wholesale restructuring and restaffing of the body.[21] Consistent with Gorbachev's scheme for removing the party from the "command-and-administer" role that it had previously performed over the society, for the first time in history, with the exception of Gorbachev himself, the leading government officials are no longer on the Politburo. Hence, the basic government policy decisions will be made by the government itself, rather than by the Politburo. Although the new role of the Politburo is not yet clear, presumably it will be confined to making policy decisions for the party, and the Secretariat will carry them out.

The current membership of the Politburo consists of 24 people, including Gorbachev and his deputy Ivashko, the first secretaries of each union republic party, the party leader of Moscow, the editor of *Pravda,* and the presumed core of the Politburo—five party secretaries. Perhaps the most interesting things about the new focus of the Politburo are its effort to unite the party by including each of the union republic first secretaries and its new emphasis on women. Galina V. Semyonova, a philosopher and editor of the popular magazine, *Krestyanka* (Peasant Women), was elected to both the Secretariat and the Politburo in 1990. Only two women before her had reached such high party posts: Yekaterina Furtseva during the Khrushchev era and Alexandra P. Beryukova who retired from the Secretariat and the Politburo in 1990. Yet, neither of them was charged, as is Semyonova, with the express task of focusing on improving the lot of

---

[21]The nominations for the Secretariat and the Politburo are self-generated; that is, the Central Committee elects to its executive committees the people those bodies instruct it to vote for.

women in the society. The most fundamental change of all, however, is the tacit commitment to withdrawing the party from actively governing the country by the removal from the Politburo of the government officials who previously were regular members. This move, if it is sincere, immensely changes the nature of the Soviet political society.

Whatever the relationship between the party and government, it is clear that the real power relationship among party agencies does not conform to what is represented on paper. (See Figure 4–1.) In fact, one would get a clearer impression of the Soviet power structure by simply inverting Figure 4–1. Perhaps Figure 4–2 will be helpful in giving an accurate picture of the power relationship within the CPSU. Care, however, must be taken not to overgeneralize the point. The present power relationships, at least between the Central Committee, the Secretariat, and the Politburo, appear to be more fluid than any chart could convey. Although it seems clear that the Politburo is the decisive body in most cases, it also appears that it is influenced at times by the Central Committee and by the Secretariat.

REGIONAL AND LOCAL PARTY STRUCTURES

Sandwiched between the All-Union Party structure and most local party organizations are a series of party institutions that organize and coordinate party activities within their jurisdictions. Essentially, the various party levels parallel the numerous divisions of government, and the party structure is fundamentally the same at each level. (See Figure 4–3.)

FIGURE 4–2 Structure of the All-Union Party *in practice.* Arrows indicate the flow of power.

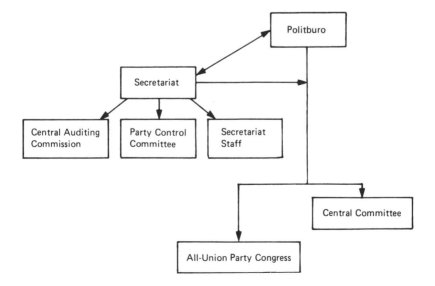

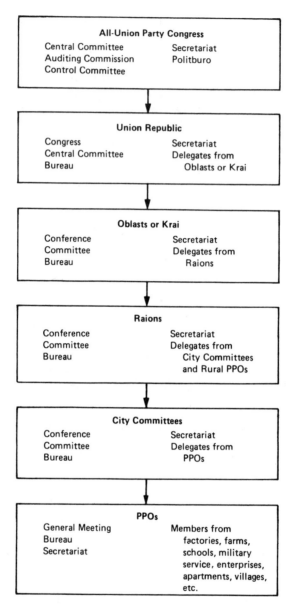

FIGURE 4–3 Structure of the CPSU.

Each of the Soviet Union's constituent members, the union republics, has a centralized party structure of its own. Each union republic elects a party congress, which elects a central committee. The central committee, which elects a bureau, a first secretary, and a second secretary, employs a professional staff. The bureau is divided into several departments corresponding to the government and party functions they monitor. The union republic party officials are elected by the next lower party agencies (oblasts or raions), and although the union republic party offices usually include some nonprofessional party members for the sake of appearance, most of them are either professional party functionaries or ranking union republic government officials. The union republic party organizations are very powerful and are responsible for basically five functions: to implement policy made in Moscow; to monitor the union republic governments; to encourage the appointment or election of loyal communists to office; to render service to the citizens in its jurisdiction by way of propaganda, agitation, and arbitration of disputes between the people and the government; and to administer the party structure within its jurisdiction.

Organizations below the union republic level share the same responsibilities and obligations for their respective jurisdictions as do the union republic party organs. The equivalent of the Party Congress at the oblast (province), krai (territory), raion (rural district), and city levels are called conferences, and their equivalent for Central Committees are simply called committees. Delegates to the conferences are elected by the next levels, and the conferences then elect their committees, bureaus, and secretaries.

With literally thousands of these congresses, conferences, committees, bureaus, and secretariats, one can appreciate the tedious and awkward bureaucratic nature of the system. Yet, even though the system is highly centralized and laden with quadruplicate forms, the secretaries at each level are enormously powerful. These "little Stalins," as Alexander Yanov terms them,[22] hold enormous power within their jurisdictions. These provincial party leaders are often even more powerful over their regions (some of which are larger than some European countries) than are people in Moscow—even though there are many authorities in Moscow who can be imposed upon to countermand orders, the regional first secretaries are uniquely dominant over their jurisdictions.[23] Yanov and others suggest that besides their power over the people, the local secretaries exercise considerable influence over their superiors as well. Being responsible for executing party policy, they perform a central role, and their satisfaction with the leadership is crucial to its success. It is well to keep this fact in mind lest we overgeneralize about the degree to which the top party leadership controls the system.

Primary Party Organizations (PPOs)

All higher party organizations parallel the various levels of government and are thus geographically based. Only the Primary Party Organizations (PPOs) are functionally based, thus insinuating the party into the very

[22]See Alexander Yanov, *The Russian New Right: Right-Wing Ideologies in the Contemporary USSR*, trans. Stephen P. Dunn (Berkeley: Institute of International Studies, University of California, 1978).

[23]Stephen F. Cohen and Katrina VanDen Heuvel, *Voices of Glasnost* (New York: W. W. Norton & Company, 1989), p. 257.

mainstream of the society. These local organs are essential to the party's success, since they deal directly with the ordinary Soviet people. Although some PPOs are established in apartment houses or in villages, most of them are organized at the work place. Every member of the CPSU must belong to a PPO, and a PPO can be created wherever there are three or more party members. Some PPOs have hundreds of members, but the vast majority are very small. Theoretically, the highest PPO organ is the General Meeting of all its members. PPOs with 15 or more members elect a bureau and secretaries to administer their work; smaller PPOs are simply headed by a first secretary and perhaps a deputy secretary. Most secretaries go unpaid, but some get time off from their regular jobs for party work. PPOs with 150 or more members, however, are entitled to a full-time professional secretary. Prior to Gorbachev's democratizing reforms, the PPO leadership was chosen by the leadership of the next higher level and then dutifully elected by the PPO in a *pro forma* procedure. Now, however, as at all levels of the party, the PPO leadership is elected in contested elections. Yet, many of these elections, like party elections at higher levels, are "managed" to assure the results. Most of the "little Stalins" (those ranking members of the party structures in the provinces) worked their way up as volunteer PPO members and unpaid PPO secretaries.

Numbering about 440,000, the PPOs are found on farms or in factories, mines, schools, military units, government offices, stores, hospitals, service enterprises, police departments, train depots, airports, entertainment troupes, athletic clubs, and Komsomol headquarters. Recent public pressure may eventually force the party to vacate offices (or rent them) in facilities the party does not own, but for now, the PPOs are usually headquartered at the place of employment. Called "cells" prior to 1939, the PPOs are the most basic unit of the party. The bulk of the party's membership scarcely have any regular contact with any party body save their PPO. The PPOs recruit new members, and with permission from above, they may also expel members. They are the true vanguards since they are in direct and constant contact with the rest of the society. The PPO members are responsible for the political and ideological education of their neighbors. They are expected to lead exemplary lives, working hard and engaging in useful cultural and recreational pursuits during their leisure. They are sensory organs for the leadership. Although some of the party authority to interfere with the government and the economy has been reduced, party members are still expected to encourage economic enterprises to meet production contracts, to agitate workers to act responsibly on the job, to exhort plant and farm managers to treat employees fairly and to remind government officials, managers, and citizens to be loyal, honest, courteous, and efficient. They are expected to report corruption, hooliganism (vandalism or loitering), antisocial conduct, and disloyalty. Entering even the home, party members can be asked to help settle family disputes; cut government red tape; and intercede for citizens for draft exemptions, job changes, and new apartments.

For those of us who were raised in a society revering individualism, the constant presence of party members might seem like an intrusion, but

Russian culture has spawned a large variety of busybodies in the past, be they priests, matchmakers, or grandmothers. Thus, the local party members' function seems quite natural, and only where it is done badly is it usually found offensive. Besides, party members often perform a service to the people by giving them a way to report an oppressive foreman, a tyrannical schoolteacher, noisy neighbors, or a teenage delinquent, thus solving many frustrating problems that might otherwise go unattended. Regardless of whether they provide a service or are a nuisance to the people, the rank and file—the grounding rods of the party—perform an irreplaceable task in the governance of the society.

OTHER POLITICAL PARTIES

Long enjoying the sole right to organize politically, the Communist Party's monopoly began to crumble as Gorbachev launched his glasnost (openness) and democratization reforms. Responding to his thinly veiled invitation to do so, suddenly thousands of groups organized to further particular causes. Before 1986 no group, regardless of its nature, could organize without official sanction; but Gorbachev's policies saw tens of thousands of groups created by enthusiasts of ecology, bicycling, photography, science fiction, the theater, and so on. The 400-year-old Russian Order of Sorcerers even reappeared.

Emboldened by the success of these nonpolitical groups, political organizations also began to emerge. First appearing in the Baltic, these groups called themselves **popular fronts** and claimed to be created for the purpose of supporting Gorbachev's reforms. In fact, however, many of these groups quickly evolved into nationalist forums, advocating more cultural freedom and political autonomy, and eventually some of them struck out for complete independence.

Finally, **Sajudis,** the Lithuanian popular front, ran a slate of separatist candidates and won control of the union republic parliament in late 1989. Its success encouraged nationalists from virtually every union republic to attempt to do the same. Among the most successful to date have been the popular fronts in the Ukraine, Byelorussia, Estonia, Latvia, Moldavia, Azerbaijan, Armenia, and Uzbekistan. In Russia, Civil Action and Democratic Action won control of the governments of Leningrad and Moscow, and their candidate, Boris Yeltsin, was elected president of the Russian SFSR government by a popular vote in 1991.

Not content to front as "voters clubs," some organizations actually formed political parties—although until 1990 these groups were illegal. *Plyrualism,* a word taken from English and meaning *pluralism,* became the battle cry for these groups as they demanded the right to legally field candidates against the Communist Party. At first, Gorbachev opposed a multiparty system, but eventually he relented, and early in 1990, opposition parties were legalized. The resulting parties cover the full political spectrum—from reactionary to radical. Table 4–2 presents a partial list of parties that organized either before or after this legalization.

TABLE 4–2   Political Parties in the Soviet Union

Christian Democratic
Confederation of Anarcho-Syndicalists
Constitutional Democratic
Democratic
Democratic Party of Russia
Democratic Union
Free Labor
Greens
Islamic Democratic
Liberal Democrats
Orthodox Constitutional Monarchy
Russian People's
Russian Republican
Socialist
Social Democratic
United Workers Front

Following the Twenty-eighth Party Congress in July of 1990, some members of the Democratic Platform resigned and organized the **Democratic Russia party** to challenge the Communist Party in the next national elections. In 1991, Shevardnadze also quit the party to form an opposition party. Meanwhile a coalition of separatist parties called the **Round-Table-Free Georgia** won control of the Georgian SSR's government in October 1990, and in 1991 the Georgian parliament followed Lithuania in declaring independence from the Soviet Union. Neither has yet been able to effect complete separation, however.

With the exception of those in Georgia and the Baltic, opposition parties remain weak and disorganized, but if multiparty elections are allowed to continue, their strength is almost certain to increase. Such a circumstance would eventually present a formidable problem to the Communist Party. Indeed, matters have come to such a state that jokesters have asked:

What is the difference between the United States and the Soviet Union?

The United States will soon be the only country with a Communist Party.

Although it is unlikely that the Communist Party will disappear anytime soon, events are occurring rapidly in the Soviet Union, and there is real potential for the evolution of a viable multi-party system. Even though minor parties have scored some significant electoral victories, the Communist Party remains in control of almost all Soviet governments and the minor party legislators have had difficulty in translating their electoral victories into parliamentary strength. Yet the growing unpopularity of the Communist Party among the general public reduces its legitimacy considerably. Poll after poll since 1989 indicates that only a minority of the nation's people believe that the Communist Party is able to successfully lead the country. This political ambiguity has contributed to the general stagnation in which the government and economy find themselves.

For over a year, various political leaders, including Gorbachev and Russian SFSR leader Boris Yeltsin, called for "round table" discussions including representatives of all political parties. It was hoped that these sessions would lead to agreements among the competing factions that could be used to solve the country's political and economic woes. Such a meeting finally did occur in 1991. It included the leaders of nine union republics, and an important agreement was reached concerning a treaty that will forge a new, revitalized Soviet Union. While this accord was made in the absence of six of the union republics, the uncooperative entities (Estonia, Latvia, Lithuania, Moldavia, Georgia, and Armenia) are small and far from essential to the well-being in the society. As matters stand now, they may very well become independent soon. The agreement for a new union is not only important for its content, it is also very significant as a model by which the political leaders of the Soviet Union might develop solutions to other problems facing the society. It also holds out the possibility that multi-party government may indeed develop since at this point the Communist Party is clearly incapable of governing without the cooperation of many people who do not associate with it. It must be pointed out, however, that because of the country's profound social and economic problem and because the political situation is still terribly fluid and volatile, overly optimistic expectations are premature. More time must pass before a clear picture of what is likely to happen will become apparent.

chapter 5

Soviet Government

Having studied the CPSU and other political parties, we now turn to an examination of the institutions of Soviet government. Just as the CPSU has undergone enormous change in the past few years, so too has the government. It has been rapidly transformed from a strongly centralized system to one that seems on the verge of disintegration. Its legislature and courts, once dominated by the Communist Party, are now more independent. Its executive, once technically limited but actually overbearing, has recently been given extraordinary power, yet it seems incapable of taking the dramatic steps necessary to deal with the society's problems.

FEDERALISM

The Constitution of the USSR[1] establishes a federal system. The constituent members of the federation are its 15 union republics: the Armenian SSR, Azerbaijan SSR, Byelorussian SSR, Estonian SSR, Georgian SSR, Kazakh SSR, Kirghiz SSR, Latvian SSR, Lithuanian SSR, Moldavian SSR, Russian SFSR,[2] Tadzhik SSR, Turkmen SSR, Ukrainian SSR, and Uzbek

---

[1]The present constitution was adopted in 1977, but it has recently been amended numerous times. Previous constitutions were adopted in 1918, 1924, and 1936.

[2]Since the Russian union republic is also a federation, it presumably compounds the federal structure on a more local basis.

SSR. (See map, pp. 136–137.) As their names imply, the union republics embrace the principal ethnic groups in the country, with the exceptions mentioned in Chapter 1.

The constitutional authority of the union republics is indeed impressive. They are described as "sovereign Soviet socialist states" and are guaranteed the "right freely to secede" from the USSR. Their territorial integrity is assured, and each is left to determine the political structure within its own territory. Further, each union republic "has the right to enter into relations with other states, conclude treaties with them, exchange diplomatic and consular representatives, and take part in the work of international organizations."[3]

Until recently, none of these provisions was taken seriously. The Soviet government, although *federal* in form—giving constituent members considerable autonomy—actually operated as a *unitary* entity—with the central government dominating any aspect of local policy it chose. The few movements that advocated greater local autonomy or independence were suppressed, sometimes brutally. The constitutional right of union republics to secede was never accompanied by a statute detailing the procedure by which separation could occur; and no union republic maintained diplomatic relations with other countries. Byelorussia and the Ukraine join the USSR in holding seats in the United Nations, but they never acted independently of the USSR.

Indeed, the Soviet Constitution seems to contradict itself regarding union republic sovereignty. The term "sovereign" refers to the highest legal authority within a given territory. A spirited debate continues among legal scholars as to whether sovereignty can be divided between two authorities. In the United States, states' rights advocates claim that sovereignty can be divided and that each state enjoys sovereign powers. Others argue that the states can exercise autonomy in certain areas but that sovereignty resides only at the national level. Be that as it may, the Soviet Constitution declares each union republic "sovereign," yet Article 74 declares that any union republic law that contradicts national law is void.[4] This article is not unlike our own Constitution's Supremacy Clause, but our Constitution does not proclaim the sovereignty of the states.

In Article 75 of the Soviet Constitution, the sovereignty of the union republics is again jeopardized in quite specific terms:

> The territory of the Union of Soviet Socialist Republics is a single entity and comprises the territories of the Union Republics. The sovereignty of the USSR extends throughout its territory.[5]

Such ambiguity over a concept so fundamental as sovereignty would invite a veritable avalanche of court challenges, judicial opinions, and scholarly tracts in the United States. In the Soviet Union, however, controversy over this issue was virtually unheard of, until recently.

[3]Articles 73 and 76–80 of the Soviet Constitution.

[4]Robert Sharlet, *The New Soviet Constitution of 1977* (Brunswick, OH: King's Court Communications, Inc., 1978), p. 99.

[5]Sharlet, p. 99.

Looking across the Moskva River at the Kremlin. The large building on the left is the Grand Kremlin Palace, where the Supreme Soviet of the USSR meets. The church at center right is the Cathedral of the Archangel, where all tsars up to Peter the Great are buried. The tall structure on the right is the bell tower built by Ivan IV (Ivan the Terrible).

Some of Gorbachev's reforms were taken by various national groups as an invitation to mobilize, and the question of union republic rights has become one of the most volatile issues in the society. By 1991 every union republic had declared its sovereignty and two, Lithuania and Georgia, had actually declared themselves independent of the Soviet Union. What exactly is meant by sovereignty differs slightly in each union republic, but at minimum, it is used to convey the union republic's right to quit the union if it chooses; to hold its law above all others, thus negating national laws with which it disagrees; and to own and control all economic resources within its territory.

Clearly, if such a circumstance were allowed to prevail, the Soviet Union would not be unitary or even federal in form. Rather, it would be a confederacy, a compact among sovereign entities. Since few confederate systems have been successful historically, and because the USSR government would be extremely weak under such an arrangement, Gorbachev is not likely to accept it. Quite beyond internal political preferences, presumably the United States and other major powers would not be content to see Soviet nuclear might in the hands of such an amorphous entity.

Yet, to date the union republics continue to press for more autonomy. Reacting to the pressure, Gorbachev has taken several steps to assuage the restive union republics. After laying down an economic embargo against Lithuania in an attempt to force it to retract its declaration of independence, he negotiated with its government to postpone its separatist move until a process for secession could be agreed upon. In the meantime the national legislature passed a statute detailing the procedure by which a union republic could become independent of the USSR.[6] The statute is very controversial because of its rigid provisions. It requires three steps. First, a proposal to secede must be adopted by a two-thirds majority in a republic-wide election. Second, a five-year period must elapse while the terms of secession are worked out. The seceding union republic must pay the resettlement expenses of all those who wish to move from it to the Soviet Union, all USSR properties would have to be purchased by the exiting union republic, and all territory not belonging to the union republic before it entered the Soviet Union would have to be ceded to the USSR. The third and final step requires that the Congress of Peoples' Deputies (the highest USSR legislative body) must vote to accept the terms of secession. Gorbachev has since hinted that a less stringent secession statute may be developed in the future.

In other moves to deal with the union republics' demands for greater authority in the society, Gorbachev devised a new structure for the Politburo which, as you know, includes the party leaders from each union republic. Similarly, a government body, the Council of Federation, was created to help him formulate policy. It is composed of the chief executive of each union republic.

Finally, with the advice of a commission established by the Council of Federation, he is trying to develop a new "treaty of union" that will expand the rights and powers of the union republics. The original treaty of union which created the present federal system dates from 1922. A new treaty was first suggested by the renowned physicist, Nobel laureate, human rights activist, and statesman, Andrei Sakharov, shortly before his death in 1989. Gorbachev at first resisted the idea but later changed his mind. The terms of the proposed treaty were published in November 1990, and they provide for voluntary acceptance by the union republics (although no procedure is stipulated for giving or withholding assent) which will enjoy much greater control over the political, social, and economic affairs within their jurisdictions. Their laws will be binding within their jurisdictions unless they contradict national law. Conflicts between the two levels will be settled in court or by special commissions created for the purpose. They will also be allowed to establish their own taxes, the proceeds of which will go toward the administration of their policies. The national government will retain control over foreign policy, the police force, defense, and the frontiers. It will also retain some control over taxation, general economic policy, and foreign trade, and will be able to coordinate transportation, regulate the environment, and guarantee citizens certain human rights and liberties. Also, the name of the country will likely be changed to the Union of Sovereign Soviet Republics, or perhaps some other title.

As broad as the powers of the union republics would be under the new treaty, six of them rejected the proposal outright and others, including the Russian SFSR, expressed strong reservations. To settle the issue, a national referendum was conducted in March 1991. The ballot proposition

---

[6]Lithuania claims not to be bound by this or any other Soviet law, since it was annexed to the Soviet Union against its will in the first place.

was far from put in the form of a neutral question. It read "Do you think it is necessary to preserve the Union of Soviet Socialist Republics as a renewed federation of equal, sovereign republics in which human rights and freedom will be fully guaranteed for all nationalities?" Critics wondered out loud whether a no vote would be construed to mean that the union was not necessary, or whether human rights, freedom, and equality for the nationalities were unnecessary.

Whatever the case, the measure received a strong positive vote, yet the results were not unmarred. Six of the union republics (Estonia, Latvia, Lithuania, Moldavia, Georgia, and Armenia) refused to participate in the election. Polls were opened by the federal government in those republics on military bases and in other federal establishments, but the turnouts were sparse. Furthermore, although the rural areas heavily supported the issue, the urban areas were less positive, with barely a majority voting for it in Moscow and Leningrad, while the people of Kiev and Sverdlovsk actually failed the issue.

Following the referendum election, Gorbachev negotiated an agreement with the leaders of the nine union republics that had held the election. The agreement was a major victory for the beleaguered president. It included several provisions, the most important of which was a commitment to adopting the new treaty of union. Other important provisions of the agreement were that a new constitution would be developed within six months of the signing of the treaty, new elections of the national parliament and the presidency would be held, political strikes and ethnic violence were discouraged, and the parties to the agreement pledged to extend favorable trading conditions to each other. Also, Gorbachev promised to repeal the unpopular sales tax the government had levied earlier in the year.

Although this agreement is an important step forward in forging a new union, it was not signed by several union republics, and their continued membership is certainly questionable. As matters stand, Alex Alexiev, of the RAND Corporation, and some other scholars see the possibility that the Soviet Union—at least as presently constituted—will not survive this decade. The Baltic republics, Moldavia, Armenia, and Georgia are currently the most likely candidates for secession. Even if they do withdraw, their share of the population and land area is not great. Russia, however, is a different matter, and if it refuses to remain in the Union, one wonders what would be left.

In any event, for the present the union republics remain the basic units in the administrative structure of the Soviet Union. The structure of their governments will be examined later in this chapter.

Sub-Union Republic Structure

Below the union republic level, one finds a bewildering profusion of governmental structures. It is not necessary to deal with each separately because such governmental structures are almost camera copies of the union republic governments. It is worthwhile, however, to touch on the most important sub-union republic governmental levels.

The most homogeneous union republics usually enjoy the most un-complicated structures of government. In these simplified systems, the political level below the union republic government is the city and the rural *raion*. There are actually two kinds of raions. The rural raion is similar to a county, incorporating a given rural area of only villages and small towns. The second kind of raion is quite different. The largest Soviet cities are divided into urban raions, or boroughs; these in turn are subordinate to city-wide governmental units. In any event, the homogeneous union re-publics consist of rural raion governments, city governments, and the governments of towns, villages, and settlements.

More ethnically diverse union republics house considerably more complex governmental structures, which are sandwiched between the union republic governments and the most local governments. The raion, city, town, village, and settlement governments are not only local institutions. They are also based solely on geography and, unlike the union re-publics, are not intended to correspond to any particular ethnic group. The largest union republics, notably the RSFSR, also host larger administrative units that are based upon geography alone. These are the *krai* (territory), found in large but remote and sparsely populated areas, and the *oblast* (province), which generally includes larger populations but smaller areas than the krai. It should be noted that krais and oblasts are mutually exclusive areas and never overlap.

Besides the jurisdictions based strictly on geography, there are other political subdivisions based on ethnic criteria. The *autonomous soviet socialist republics* (ASSRs) serve the homelands of relatively large ethnic groups, for example, the Tatars and Karelians. Although these republics have their own constitutions, they are not considered sovereign and are subordinate to the union republics in which they are located. Some ASSRs, however, like the Adzharian ASSR in Georgia, have recently demanded that they be given union republic status. The **autonomous oblasts** envelop even smaller ethnic groups within several union republics. One of these areas, **Nagorno-Karabakh** in Azerbaijan, has tried for several years to free itself from the Muslim union republic and join with its Christian Armenian siblings. The **okrugs** (national districts) serve even smaller ethnic minorities in the far north and east of the Russian SFSR.

It should be reiterated that the Soviet federal structure basically refers to the relationship between the central government and the governments of the union republics. All other government levels (raions, cities, villages, krais, oblasts, autonomous republics) are subordinate to their respective union republic. For a visual concept of the government structure of the Soviet Union, see Figure 5–1.

THE LEGISLATURE

The Soviet government is a modified parliamentary system. This basic fact holds at every level of government, from the most local (the urban raion or settlement) to the central government of the USSR. Basically, a parliamentary system is one in which the people elect the legislative body and the

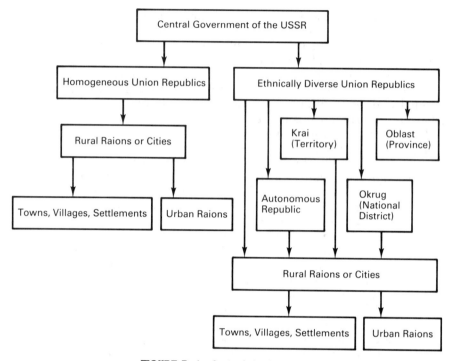

FIGURE 5–1   Soviet federal structure.

legislature elects the executive. The executive is then held accountable by the legislature for its actions. An example of a classic parliamentary system can be found in the government of Great Britain. In 1994 the president of the Soviet Union is scheduled to be elected directly by the people. If this election goes forward, the Soviet government will become less like the British parliamentary system and somewhat more like the American presidential-congressional system.

The Legislature of the Central Government

Until 1989 the "highest body of state authority" was the *Supreme Soviet.*[7] It was composed of two houses: the *Soviet of Union,* to which its 750 deputies were elected from equally populated districts throughout the country, and the *Soviet of Nationalities,* to which its 750 deputies were elected

---

[7]The term "soviet" means "council," and, as explained earlier, it became the appellation for spontaneous organizations of workers just prior to the 1905 and 1917 revolutions. Competing for power with the Lvov and Kerensky governments, the soviets were powerful institutions that the Bolsheviks eventually came to dominate. Upon seizing power, the Bolsheviks applied the term "soviet" to their government in an attempt to demonstrate the legitimacy of their regime. Accordingly, all legislative bodies in the USSR are called soviets, as in the official name of the country: The Union of Soviet Socialist Republics. Local governments are also referred to as soviets.

from the various ethnic jurisdictions in the country (union republics, autonomous republics, autonomous oblasts, etc.). Although the Supreme Soviet was supposed to be the ultimate legal authority in the country, in fact, it was little more than a rubber stamp for the party. Meeting only twice a year for three or four days each session, the Supreme Soviet was incapable of performing a true legislative role. In its absence, legislative power was exercised by the *Presidium,* a committee it elected from its membership. Then, when the Supreme Soviet met again, it would ratify the Presidium's edicts. The Supreme Soviet also elected the executive branch (the Council of Ministers) and major judicial agents like the members of the Supreme Court and the procurator-general (the chief legal prosecutor of the country). As with its legislative duties, however, these positions were always given to the people whom the leadership of the party chose.

This elaborate pretense ended abruptly in 1989. The year before, Gorbachev had proposed the creation of a new national legislature to be chosen in contested elections. The issue was widely debated throughout the country and supported by the Nineteenth Party Conference in March 1988. Then, after a spirited debate, the Supreme Soviet adopted an amended version of Gorbachev's proposal. Meanwhile, the once compliant Supreme Soviet was energized as deputies, thinking about the coming elections, began to reflect their constituents' interests in their votes. Accordingly, the body which had previously always voted unanimously[8] began to cast some no votes. This independence was so unprecedented that *Vremya,* the leading evening news program, gave five minutes to the dissenting votes the first time they were cast.[9]

Congress of Peoples' Deputies. The new system actually establishes two legislative bodies: the **Congress of Peoples' Deputies (CPD)** elected by the people and by certain powerful organizations in society; and the **Supreme Soviet,** elected by the CPD. The CPD has 2,250 members elected to five-year terms. The members were elected in one of three ways: 750 were elected from constituencies of equal populations throughout the country, and 750 were elected from the national constituencies (1 from each okrug, 5 from each autonomous oblast, 11 from each autonomous republic, and 32 from each union republic). Each voter casts one vote for each office. The third group of 750 were elected by about 30 public institutions. These institutions were apportioned different numbers of deputies based on their size and importance. (See Table 5–1.) Giving certain organizations in society the right to elect deputies was a controversial issue, and the constitution was subsequently amended to eliminate this method of choosing deputies in the future.

The election of members to each of the three groups brought surprises. Although about 87 percent of the deputies are Communist Party

[8]Konstantin M. Simis, *U.S.S.R.: The Corrupt Society,* trans. Jacqueline Edwards and Mitchell Schneider (New York: Simon & Schuster, 1982), p. 24.

[9]Michael Parks, "Glasnost Spreads to Soviet Parliament as Lawmakers Cast Unheard-Of Vote: 'No,' " *The Los Angeles Times,* Oct. 29, 1988.

members, the majority of them are rank-and-file members. Many of the leading party personnel were defeated in the CPD elections—including one member of the Politburo, Leningrad Party First Secretary, Yuri Solovoyov. Consequently, this hapless conservative was later removed from his party post. A number of radicals were elected, including Boris Yeltsin,

Yuri N. Afanasyev, Gavril Popov, Andrei Sakharov, and Victor Palm. A reasonable number of workers and farmers were successful as was a large contingent of the military. Even several churchmen were elected, including Pimen, the Patriarch of the Russian Orthodox Church; Alexi, the Metropolitan of Leningrad and Novgorod until Pimen's death, when he became

TABLE 5–1   A Partial List of Institutions That Elected
Deputies to the Congress of Peoples' Deputies

Organization	Number of Deputies
Communist Party	100
Trade Unions	100
Komsomol	75
Women's Committees	75
Veterans	75
Academy of Sciences	20
Soviet Peace Committee	5
Temperance Society	1
Stamp Collectors	1

the Patriarch; and Catholkos Vaskin I, the head of the Armenian Apostolic Church. On the other hand, only 352 women were elected. Comprising only 15.6 percent of the CPD, women are significantly less well represented numerically in the new legislature than they had been in the old Supreme Soviet, where the leadership seemed to maintain a quota of women at about 30 percent.

The CPD is required to convene at least once each year, but in its first two years it met four times. Its inaugural session was a spectacle that riveted the country's attention. Broadcast live, it was originally scheduled to meet for four days, but actually the session continued for two weeks (from May 25 to June 9, 1989). So many people took time to watch it that production was estimated to have fallen by 20 percent during that period.[10] Speaker after speaker rose to complain about the economy, the foreign policy, the environment, the strife among national groups, and so on.

The leftists quickly organized themselves into the **Inter-Regional Group.** Led by Yeltsin, Andrei Sakharov, and Yuri N. Afanasyev, this group became the first legislative opposition group tolerated in the Soviet Union since 1922. Their belief, as Afanasyev said, is that "parliament must be a legal opposition to the party apparatus and state bureaucracies."[11] They claim to have about 500 supporters in the CPD and they advocate a strong set of reforms, including workers' owning the factories in which they work, abolition of internal passports, freedom of foreign travel for all citizens, and several other liberalizing objectives. Several items that the Inter-Regional Group advocated have already become realities, including the legalization of a multiparty system, the popular election of the president in 1994, the legalization of independent labor unions, and an end to the state monopoly on television.

[10]"Soviets End TV Coverage of Congress," *Escondido Times Advocate,* July 27, 1989.
[11]Stephen F. Cohen and Katrina Vanden Heuvel, *Voices of Glasnost* (New York: W. W. Norton & Company, 1989), p. 109.

On the right wing, a group called **Soyuz** (Union) has developed. It claims a membership about as large as that of the Inter-Regional Group, but since mid-1990, it seems to be gaining strength. It is dominated by military personnel and Russian nationalists. Soyuz opposes many of Gorbachev's reforms: It is stoutly pro-defense, and it is opposed to the breakup of the Soviet Union. Joining Soyuz on the right are most of the deputies from Central Asia, while many deputies from the other union republics are reform-oriented. Between the right and the left, however, is a large moderate contingent that usually supports Gorbachev's proposals.

Like the old Supreme Soviet, the CPD not only has the powers to conduct hearings (American Secretary of State James A. Baker testified before the CPD in February 1990) and to legislate, but it also amends the constitution by an absolute two-thirds majority (1,687 votes) and confirms certain appointments (premier, procurator-general, members of the Supreme Court, the Peoples' Central Commission chair). The CPD also elected Gorbachev president of the Soviet Union when the office was created in 1990, but subsequent presidential elections are supposed to be by direct popular vote. In late 1990 the CPD amended the constitution to create the office of vice president, and it elected former trade union leader Gennady I. Yanayev on a second ballot after first narrowly refusing to elect him. Yanayev was Gorbachev's choice.

Supreme Soviet. Another critical function of the CPD is to elect members of the new *Supreme Soviet* from its own membership. The Supreme Soviet is elected for a five-year term, but as many as one-fifth of its 542 members may be exchanged for other CPD members each year. Members of the Supreme Soviet are not only members of the CPD, they may also be members of a union republic or other legislatures, and they can even be part of the executive branch. Boris Yeltsin, for example, was a member of the CPD, the Supreme Soviet of the RSFSR, and its chairman before he was elected president of the RSFSR by a direct vote of the people. The Supreme Soviet meets on a regular basis year-round. It is a bicameral body with its membership split evenly between the **Council of the Union** and the **Council of Nationalities.**

As a legislative body its structure is not unusual; it has a number of organs similar to those the American Congress calls joint committees, composed of members of both houses. Each house also has standing commissions, which deal with topics in which the particular house is interested; the Council of Nationalities, for instance, has standing commissions on nationality policy, culture and language, and regional affairs. As do the American congressional committees, the Soviet committees and commissions analyze legislation, modifying it when necessary, and they also investigate issues in which their parent body is interested. The Inter-Regional Group, Soyuz, and other coalitions are active in the Supreme Soviet, just as they are in the CPD.

Nominees to the government ministries, the Supreme Court, and so on usually come to the Supreme Soviet first for confirmation. However, the

CPD can countermand Supreme Soviet confirmations if it chooses, although it has not yet done so. By contrast, the Supreme Soviet has refused to confirm several people nominated to head ministries or state committees. Nine of 70 were rejected by the independent-minded body in its first session alone. Although the constitution does not specifically provide that the Supreme Soviet can remove appointees by a vote of no confidence, as can the British Parliament, in May 1990 it took up a motion of no confidence against Premier Nikolai I. Ryzhkov. The motion failed, so no action became necessary, but apparently the legislature believes it can force a resignation in the executive. Later, in March of 1991, the Supreme Soviet handed Gorbachev himself a stinging blow by twice refusing to confirm one of his nominees to the new National Security Council. In another move to hold the executive accountable, the Supreme Soviet holds **question time** on the last Wednesday of each month. Similar to the British parliamentary procedure—although that body holds question time virtually every legislative day—government ministers must answer questions from the deputies. The original questions must be submitted in advance but follow-up questions may be asked from the floor.

The Supreme Soviet is responsible for ratifying treaties, and its legislative calendar is, of course, much more active than that of the CPD, which meets less often. Although the Supreme Soviet has usually supported Gorbachev and the government, it has not infrequently refused to approve some measures, unlike its compliant predecessor, the old Supreme Soviet. For example, it rejected a plan to give limited autonomy to local governments, it refused to outlaw strikes, and it ignored objections of the minister of defense and authorized draft exemptions for students.

Still, creating a bona-fide legislature in a country that has almost never had one is a complicated process. In the fall of 1989, a small delegation of deputies from the Supreme Soviet visited the United States Congress to study its procedures. It seemed especially interested in the Ways and Means Committee (the taxation committee), intelligence oversight, and the work of the General Accounting Office (Congress's watchdog on public expenditures).

The present legislative structure, with its two separate bodies, is seen by many to be redundant. Many people inside and out of the legislature question the continued utility of such an awkward system. One of the two bodies may eventually be absorbed by the other. If the Supreme Soviet takes over the powers of the CPD, then the system will have to be changed further to provide for its direct popular election. In fact, the constitution has already been amended to allow the union republics and lower governments to elect their supreme soviets directly and not create a duplicate congress of deputies.

Presidium.   Seemingly, another anachronism is the **Presidium.** A holdover from the old Supreme Soviet, this body not only used to legislate during the long absence of the Supreme Soviet, but it also acted as head of state. Composed of 39 Supreme Soviet members, it appointed ministers of government, it could invoke martial law and declare war, and it accredited diplomats. It also exercised certain judicial powers, including granting clemency (pardons and amnesty) and voiding actions of the procurator-general and government ministers.

As the government has been changed, however, the Presidium's functions have become eroded. Between the CPD and the Supreme Soviet, a legislature is now almost always in session, so little need for the Presidium's edicts exists, and one wonders if the new independent legislatures would accept the Presidium's edicts even if it had occasion to promulgate them. Additionally, most of the executive functions of the Presidium are now held by the new office of President of the Soviet Union. With so many of its functions now handled by other agencies, one can expect that the Presidium will be either given other duties or eventually abolished.

Lower Legislatures

All of the lower legislative bodies follow essentially the same form as the national legislature, except that the lower levels do not have to elect a congress of deputies if they wish only to create a supreme soviet. Also, most legislatures below the national level are unicameral rather than bicameral bodies. It should be kept in mind that each of the sub-USSR divisions of government is either of two kinds: (1) based on nationality, which is supposed to enjoy some form of autonomy, or (2) based solely on geography, which is subordinate to higher levels in law as well as in practice.

Nationality divisions.   You will recall that the nationality divisions include the 15 union republics; 20 autonomous republics, 16 of which are found in the RSFSR; 8 autonomous oblasts, of which there are 5 in the RSFSR; and 10 national districts, or okrugs, which are all located in the RSFSR. Each union republic has a popularly elected legislature, with deputies representing electoral districts of equal populations. Most of the union republics have decided not to elect congresses of deputies, preferring instead to elect their supreme soviets directly. Lithuania for example, not only ignores the people's congress, but it calls its legislature the *Supreme Council* using the Lithuanian language, thus avoiding the word *soviet* altogether. The Russian SFSR, however, has a system that duplicates the national legislative structure, but there is growing support for dissolving the Russian Congress of Peoples' Deptuies and the disorderly Russian Supreme Soviet which is now elected by the Russian Congress of Peoples' Deputies and creating only a new supreme soviet that is elected directly by the people. Furthermore, in 1991 the RSFSR parliament expanded the republic's chief executive's powers and provided for the office to be elected directly by the people. Boris Yeltsin, who was subsequently elected president, stridently supported the RSFSR's government alterations, even though they closely paralleled changes successfully sought only a year before by Gorbachev at the national level. Ironically, Yeltsin opposed those changes, accusing Gorbachev of seeking dictatorial power. Not surprisingly, Yeltsin's opponents accused him of the same ambition when he sought expanded powers for his office. Whatever the case, unlike their predecessors, the current union republic legislative bodies meet regularly and have demonstrated considerable independence from the central government.

As already mentioned, each union republic legislature has declared its jurisdiction sovereign, and Lithuania and Georgia have declared independence. The Azerbaijan government refused to declare martial law in 1990 to quell ethnic violence, thus forcing the national government to intervene, and Estonia has taken over the police force within its territory. Of all the union republics, Russia, because of its size, economic power, and intractability, has become Gorbachev's greatest problem. Three days after Boris Yeltsin narrowly won election to the chairmanship of the RSFSR's parliament in mid-1991, he entered into separate negotiations with Lithuania, threatening to develop a separate trade agreement with it and thus break Gorbachev's economic boycott of that defiant republic. Russia also established its own police force, and in December 1990, it even refused to pay 85 percent of its taxes, thus threatening to bankrupt the USSR.

Each union republic legislature elects a presidium, a premier and government ministers, and a supreme court. Each of these institutions exercises powers equivalent to like bodies at the central level, but there is considerable controversy, as you know, about their relationship with the government of the USSR.

The RSFSR, Azerbaijan, Georgia, and Uzbekistan have autonomous republics within their territories. The autonomous republics have their own constitutions, which supposedly give them a degree of autonomy from the union republics. In actual fact, this autonomy amounts to very little. These governments have popularly elected supreme soviets, which in turn elect presidiums, ministers, and supreme courts; but these institutions are actually responsible to higher levels of the government.

Autonomous oblasts are found in the RSFSR, Azerbaijan, Georgia, and Tadzhikistan. They and the okrugs have similar structures. Even though these divisions do not have their own constitutions, provision for them is found in statute. These levels of government enjoy popularly elected soviets, which elect executive committees and district courts. As with the other units of government, all institutions of government in the autonomous oblasts and the okrugs are subordinate to governments above them.

Each of the legislative bodies at the intermediate level tends to be fairly large. Members are elected from constituencies that have equal numbers of people within each jurisdiction, and each is supposed to be the deciding authority within its jurisdiction. Although the union republic governments have demanded more autonomy from the national level, few local governments have been given the same courtesy by the union republics. Presumably, however, it is only a matter of time before the more local governments begin to stretch their wings as well. Although party membership is not required for election to a soviet, the majority of deputies in all soviets at the intermediate level are party members. The percentage of party members tends to decrease, however, in the more local governmental units.

The Supreme Soviet building of the Ukrainian SSR in Kiev.

Territorial divisions.   There are several other divisions of government that are somewhat more familiar because they are drawn on territorial bases. It should be noted, however, that not every union republic is structured in precisely the same fashion. As indicated in the section on federalism, most of the smaller union republics do not have intermediate territorial divisions, so they deal directly with the local governmental units. The larger union republics, however, include intermediate-level governmental units based strictly on territorial divisions. The Soviet Union includes 6 krais (territories) and 120 oblasts (provinces)—not to be confused with the autonomous oblasts that are governments based on nationality. Virtually identical with other Soviet governmental structures, the oblasts and krais are served by popularly elected soviets, which in turn elect executive committees and district courts. There are also more than 200 major cities, including Moscow and Leningrad, that elect city soviets, executive committees, and courts. Owing no responsibility to either oblast or krai, the city soviets are immediately subordinate to the union republic government.

The large cities are subdivided into urban raions, which duplicate the

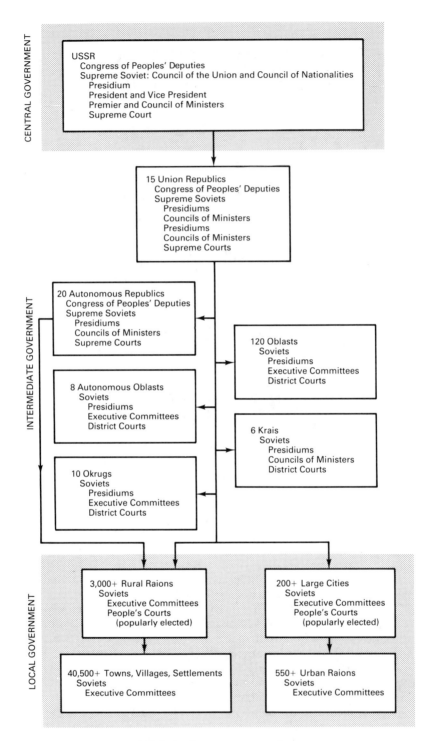

FIGURE 5-2 Soviet governmental structure.

familiar governmental pattern. The oblasts and krais are subdivided into rural raions, which have towns, villages, and settlements below them. Predictably, each of these local governments has soviets elected by the voters. Deputies to the local soviets are elected to terms of two and one-half years, in contrast to the five-year terms of higher soviets. The local soviets create executive committees, which do most of the government's business. The lowest Soviet courts, the people's courts, are elected directly by the voters of the large cities and the rural raions.

The local soviets (city, rural raion, and urban raion) are the only level at which the Communist Party does not usually hold a majority of the deputies. The local soviets meet on a regular basis, although the bulk of their business is executed by their respective executives. Sub-union republic government remains highly centralized, however, even at its most local levels, thus severely mitigating the amount of discretion available to the local soviets. (See Figure 5–2.) Even so, some local governments have asserted their independence. The cities of Moscow and Leningrad, as well as others, elected governments dedicated to pushing reform faster than Gorbachev is willing to go. The Moscow city soviet, for example, voted to give renters title to their apartments free of charge. In more provincial areas, four Pacific Coast ports refused to allow a nuclear-powered container ship to dock at their ports.

It should be remembered, however, that under normal circumstances, the Communist Party is most powerful at the local levels, even though it does not necessarily hold a majority of the local soviets, thus inhibiting local independence. But, party control is wearing thin even here. For example, in Zaporozhye, in the Ukraine, 150 party members walked out of a city soviet meeting to protest that they were being asked to rubber-stamp a party decision. The meeting was left without a quorum and had to be adjourned.[12]

NOMINATIONS AND ELECTIONS

When all the levels of government are totaled, we find more than 50,000 soviets, to which approximately 2.3 million Soviet citizens are elected. It should be recalled that, true to the parliamentary model, only the legislators are elected by the people. The executive bodies, except for the presidents of the RSFSR and USSR (starting in 1994), are elected by their respective legislators. People's court judges, also elected, will be discussed later in this chapter. All told, the number of elected officials in the Soviet Union is easily among the largest in the world.

Until recently, Soviet ballots contained only one candidate per office. Each candidate, although not necessarily a Communist Party member, was

[12]"Ukrainians Show Some Sole to Protest Rubber-Stamp Role," *The Los Angeles Times,* Oct. 16, 1988.

approved by the party after having been suggested by a trade union, a military unit, a Komsomol group, a collective farm, some other party-controlled organization, or the party itself. Considerable amounts of money and effort were expended to publicize the candidates' qualifications and to get out the vote on election day. When the voters arrived at the polls, they confronted a room containing a table with a stack of ballots at one end and a ballot box at the other. As secret ballots were guaranteed, polling booths were provided for those who wished to use them. Voters seldom took advantage of the privacy offered because usually there was only one candidate per office on the ballot. In such cases, the voters presented their identification, picked up a ballot—which was sometimes conveniently pre-folded—and dropped it into the ballot box. If there was a contested election, or if voters wished to vote against a candidate by striking out his or her name, they could use the polling booth. If a candidate failed to receive a majority of the votes cast, which happened—though rarely—in some local elections, a new candidate was submitted in a by-election. Write-in votes disqualified the ballots on which they appeared.

One might wonder why these elections were so important to the Soviet rulers. In the first place, regular elections anointed the regime with "democratic" legitimacy. They also demonstrated the people's unity and commitment to the state. Further, elections bathed the voters in campaign rhetoric and rationale for government policy. Although elections in the Western democracies are primarily used to select leaders, a glance at any good government text will reveal each of these other justifications as well.

Declaring in 1987 that "We need democracy to breathe," Gorbachev called for contested elections (where more than one candidate for each office is listed). Although only local offices were involved and the party still could deny someone a place on the ballot, contested elections were held in several areas, and a new interest and energy among voters accompanied the change. In 1989 the law provided that the elections for the CPD were also to be contested, and a flurry of excitement ensued as candidates were nominated and eventually ran against one another for legislative seats.

All citizens 18 years or older (except the insane) may vote, and each person's vote is equal to any other person's. The nomination process was similar to the system previously used. Organizations, including trade unions, collective farms, military units, and so on, held public meetings to select potential candidates. (Although anyone 18 years or older may run for local posts, candidates for the CPD must be at least 21.) Their names were submitted to election commissions, largely made up of party members, in each of the 1,500 CPD electoral districts from which one candidate was to be elected by popular vote. (Remember that 750 deputies were elected by about 30 public institutions.) The commissions applied rather vague and complicated rules to determine whose names were placed on the ballot. Almost 3,000 candidates were nominated to run for the 1,500 seats, and about 85 percent of them were party members. In most districts two or three candidates faced each other, but many districts had larger ballots with a few having over 20 candidates for a single seat. The election commissions of 384 CPD districts approved only one candidate for their respective districts. These commissions often approved only the name of a prominent party official.

The candidates for the 750 seats going to public institutions were nominated by either local units of the organization or by its executive committee and were elected by votes at nation-wide meetings of the respective groups. In some cases, the executive committees of these groups tried to rig the nominations. For example, the leadership of the Academy of Sciences had at first excluded the names of Andrei Sakharov and several other liberal members from the list of potential candidates. After an embarrassing protest by members of the academy, Sakharov and his colleagues were added to the list and subsequently elected to the CPD by a vote of the academy membership.

The election of the 100 Communist Party members took place in a meeting of the Central Committee. Over 35,000 candidates were submitted by local party groups, and the Secretariat reduced that number to 314. The Central Committee then elected its deputies. Predictably, the Politburo members who were candidates won, but surprisingly, not unanimously. The Soviet people were astonished when in March, the Central Committee published its vote totals; Central Committee votes had never before been made public. The returns indicated that 12 of 641 had voted against Gorbachev, 59 voted against Alexander Yakovlev, 78 against Yegor Ligachev, and so on. The Central Committee had never before been portrayed as divided in its decisions. Besides the Politburo members, the Central Committee elected others, including 26 workers, 22 professionals, 21 other party officials, and 7 workers.

As with the British electoral system, the candidates for the CPD need not be residents of the districts in which they are candidates. For example, Andrei Sakharov was nominated in over 30 constituencies, but he chose to run as a candidate for an Academy of Sciences slot. The state paid all the campaign costs. Each candidate was given a budget allowing for up to 10 aides and for printing and travel expenses. All candidates were also given television time and leave with pay from their jobs during the campaign, which lasted only a few weeks. However, the party did not engage in its usual campaign to get out the vote. In previous elections, Soviet officials claimed that over 97 percent of the electorate turned out.[13] These figures were no doubt exaggerated, but there is no question that the turnout was heavy. In 1989 the returns were much lower. Moscow recorded a 64 percent turnout, for example. However, other areas claimed higher percentages—some as high as 90 percent. By contrast, the turnout for the 1988 U.S. presidential election was 50.2 percent, and it was only 36.4 percent for the 1990 congressional elections.

The Russian word for voting is *golosovat* and comes from the same root (*golos*) as does *glasnost*. However, most Soviet voters had no experience

---

[13]On March 4, 1984, 99.94 percent of the eligible voters cast ballots, according to the Soviet press.

with contested elections, and some, usually older voters, simply picked up their ballots as before and dropped them into the ballot box unmarked. Most others, however, understood how to use the secret ballot and the private voting booths. Each voter had to vote in two elections: one for the deputy from his or her territorial district and one for a deputy representing his or her nationality.

Soviet election law allows citizens to vote "no" by scratching out the candidate's name, and candidates must receive a majority of all votes cast in order to win. These rules caught some powerful party leaders in the embarrassing position of losing the election even though they were unopposed. Thus, Valentin Zgursky, the mayor of Kiev, was defeated as was Yuri Solovoyov, the party first secretary of Leningrad and Politburo member. Solovoyov's name was scratched off on almost two-thirds of the ballots in his district. In such cases, by-elections were held with new candidates, and in 275 districts with multiple candidates where no one received a majority of votes, the highest two ran off. Solovoyov and his compatriot from Kiev were not the only party dignitaries to lose. Several who were uncontested and still others also went down to defeat, including almost one-third of the regional party leaders, the premier of Lithuania, the mayor of Moscow, and the KGB head in Estonia.[14] Gorbachev took the public's rejection of so many high party officials as proof that the old system was passé and that the party needed to reform itself.

Although about 87 percent of the deputies elected are party members, the majority of them are not in the party's leadership and, as it turns out, they were unwilling to march in absolute lock step with the leadership. Additionally, some of the party members are noted reformers. Boris Yeltsin, who won with 89 percent of the vote, has since left the party, as did Yuri Afanasyev and some other reformers. Yet, many have remained in the party, including Roy A. Medvedev, a former dissident. Other nonparty reformers were also elected, and they have joined with party reformers in the Inter-Regional Group.

Although they did not act as political parties, many popular fronts supported candidates. The nationalistically oriented popular fronts were perhaps most successful, but other organizations, including the ecologically committed Greens, supported winners. Gorbachev apparently hoped that open and contested elections would produce a popularly supported parliament but that a multiparty system would not be necessary. Democracy, he said, "is not defined by the number of parties but by the role played by people in society."[15] Matters soon spun out of Gorbachev's control, however.

From December 1989 to March 1990, elections were held at the sub-All Union levels. In December 1989 the Latvian government, under the

---

[14]Walter Isaacson, "A Long, Mighty Struggle," *Time Magazine*, April 10, 1989.
[15]Michael Parks, "Gorbachev Links Party's Vote to Food Shortages," *The Los Angeles Times*, Dec. 26, 1990.

leadership of Communist Party reformers, passed a law legalizing multi-parties. Although no other union republic followed suit, the nationalist popular front movements had become so powerful that their candidates managed to win large numbers of seats, defeating high party officials across the country. Sajadis candidates dominated in Lithuania, but other popular front candidates did well in Byelorussia, the Ukraine, Kirghizia, Tadzhikistan, Moldavia, Uzbekistan, and elsewhere. In Russia, reformers did well enough to elect Yeltsin president of the republic, but the most striking popular front victories occurred in its two major cities: **Democratic Election 90** in Leningrad and **Democratic Russia** in Moscow, two reform-oriented popular fronts, took majority control of their respective cities and were later elected by the people. Faced with the reality that the Communist Party was being defeated anyway, and that the popular fronts were political parties in fact, if not in name, Gorbachev finally relented in his opposition to a multiparty system, and in March 1990 the seven-decades–old Communist Party monopoly was revoked. Since then, the party has lost control of the government of Georgia and the presidency of Russia, and one can expect that even more broad-based defeats await it in the next round of elections.

In only three years, the Soviet Union traveled political light years, from uncontested, party-controlled elections to a relatively open democratic process. Although these elections are still far from unblemished or completely honest, they have made enormous strides. Hopefully the progress will continue.

THE EXECUTIVE

Until 1989 the Soviet Union's executive was comprised of the chairman of the Supreme Soviet and the premier. Each was elected by the Supreme Soviet and responsible to it in a technical sense, although not in reality because it was not a true deliberative body. The chairman of the Supreme Soviet was considered the head of state and officiated over the Presidium of the Supreme Soviet, accrediting ambassadors and dispensing judicial clemency. The Presidium also had the authority to countermand actions by the premier and his Council of Ministers, although the function was usually left dormant. The premier headed the **Council of Ministers** (the Cabinet) and was responsible for executing policy made by the party and adopted by the Supreme Soviet.

As part of the constitutional reforms creating the Congress of Peoples' Deputies and the new Supreme Soviet, the office of head of state was vested in the CPD chairman, and Gorbachev was elected to that office. The post included few formal powers not already extant, however, and as 1989 passed, Gorbachev became convinced that a more powerful head of state was needed. Eventually he proposed that the office of president be created and that it have significant executive authority. After considerable debate and compromise, in March 1990 the CPD created the office of President of the Soviet Union. The office was given the power to

> Veto bills, requiring a two-thirds majority to override the veto, or to pocket veto them, thus avoiding a possible override
>
> Commute death sentences
>
> Negotiate treaties and represent the country abroad
>
> Appoint the leading military and government officials, including the premier and the heads of the KGB and the national police
>
> Dissolve the Supreme Soviet in the event of any unresolvable differences between the two houses
>
> Issue legally binding decrees, provided they are based on the constitution
>
> Declare a state of emergency in any region with the approval of the Supreme Soviet and the union republic soviets
>
> Suspend union republic parliaments, with the approval of the Supreme Soviet.

Some of these powers are not unlike those of the president of the United States, but many deputies were concerned that they gave too much authority to a single person. It is true that in the Soviet context, where no tradition for checks and balances and no strong opposition parties yet exist, these powers are potentially formidable.

Gorbachev countered his opponents by arguing that a strong presidency was needed because as the party relaxed its control over the society, a new authority was needed to assure that the massive state bureaucracy carried out the economic reforms of **perestroika** (restructuring), **glasnost** (openness), and **demokratisiya** (democratization), the three pillars of Gorbachev's program. Although the constitutional amendments were bitterly debated and considerably changed from what Gorbachev originally wanted, they easily passed with 1,817 votes.

An even more serious struggle ensued over how the new president was to be elected. Although subsequent presidents are to be elected by a direct popular vote, Gorbachev asked that the president be elected in 1990 by the CPD. Soviet public opinion polls showed 84 percent of the people wanting a direct popular vote for the first president, even as Gorbachev's approval rating plummeted. In any event, he pressed ahead and although several candidates were nominated to oppose him, one by one they each withdrew. In the end, Gorbachev ran unopposed. He received 1,329 CPD votes (1,126 votes were needed to win). Of the remainder, 495 votes were cast against him and 426 deputies abstained. A Gorbachev ally, Anatoly J. Lukyanov, was elected to succeed the new president as chairman of the CPD.

Two groups were created to advise the president: the Council of the Federation and the Presidential Council of the USSR. The **Council of the Federation** is chaired by the president and composed of the chairs of the union republic parliaments. It was created to give new emphasis to the problems of the nationalities and to give the governments of the nationalities a special voice in developing their solutions. The council was specifically charged with developing the new treaty of union, working out and implementing the Soviet Union's nationalities policies, suggesting legislation to the Council of the Nationalities in the Supreme Soviet, and coordinating the activities of the union republics. Whenever issues involving people in sub-union republic jurisdictions are being discussed, delegations from their governments may attend the council meetings.

The **Presidential Council of the USSR,** also chaired by the president, was less well defined in terms of both membership and functions. It was supposed that this body would become the president's think tank for domestic and foreign policy, and so it seemed to function for a time. Gorbachev appointed the most important government ministers, including the chairman of the Council of Ministers (premier), the foreign and defense ministers, and the chairs of the State (economic) Planning Committee (*Gosplan*) and the State Security Committee (KGB). He also appointed a trusted ally from the Politburo (Alexander Yakovlev), a regional party first secretary, and a manager of an agricultural collective. Additionally, he appointed an independent trade union leader, two internationally known writers, and three members of the Academy of Sciences—one noted in physics, another in economics (Stanislav Shatalin), and a third in international affairs (Yevgeni Primakov).

In an attempt to organize his new office, Gorbachev appointed a presidential press secretary. This kind of post was as unprecedented as the presidency itself, and it reflects both Gorbachev's willingness to be more open to the public than any previous Soviet official and his incredibly busy schedule, since he serves not only as president but also as general secretary of the CPSU. He also sent a small delegation to Washington, DC, to study the American executive. The group was particularly interested in the Executive Office of the President (the closest presidential aides and advisers); the departments of Treasury, Justice, and Agriculture; and the General Service Administration (the housekeeping agency of the executive branch). Following that visit, John Sununu, President Bush's chief of staff, visited Moscow to exchange information about executive management techniques with Soviet officials.

The new executive structure was not successful, however. As 1990 progressed, the problems among many nationalities continued to fester and the food distribution system virtually collapsed. By fall the situation was critical. Radical reformers, including Yeltsin, wanted to implement a 500-day crash program to transform Soviet state socialism into a market economy, but Gorbachev preferred to take a more measured approach. Faced with a decision between the two programs, the Supreme Soviet balked. Instead of making a determination, it voted in September 1990 to temporarily delegate to Gorbachev its legislative authority in economic policy, subject only to Supreme Soviet veto. By failing to execute its responsibilities, relying instead upon executive decree, the Supreme Soviet raised questions among many observers as to the future of democracy. *Komsomolskaya Pravda,* a widely read newspaper, described the default as "a virtual freeze in the development of the law-governed state" and "a step back from the separation of powers toward their concentration in the person of the president."

Despite the creation of the presidency and the Supreme Soviet's September expansion of its powers, the crisis was not quieted—rather, it became more aggravated. By the winter of 1990 the situation had become so difficult that the Orthodox Church, the military, *Soyuz,* prominent writers and professionals, a plurality of public opinion, and paradoxically, even some radical reformers were demanding that decisive measures be taken by Gorbachev to solve the economic crisis and to bring order to the growing ethnic strife in some of the union republics. At the same time most of the people who had played the largest role in helping Gorbachev launch his reforms either were removed from office or resigned in protest of Gorbachev's increasingly conservative mood. Alexander N. Yakovlev, who many people believe was the architect of glasnost, was relegated to obscurity, as was Vadim Medvedev, another committed progressive on the Politburo; Vadim V. Bakatin, the liberal interior minister (who controls the national police), was removed and replaced by a conservative. Bakatin was later appointed to the National Security Council; and Stanislav Shatalin, an economist who favored a quick leap to a market economy, fell from favor. Finally, Foreign Minister Eduard A. Shevardnadze, who shared with Yakovlev and Medvedev the distinction of being the strongest supporter of Gorbachev's reforms, resigned. Apparently without informing Gorbachev beforehand, Shevardnadze took the lectern at the CPD meeting in December 1990 and decried the "advance of dictatorship" in the Soviet Union. The speech stunned the deputies and evoked, from governments around the globe, statements of profound regret that this universally admired statesman was leaving the government.

The issue that the CPD was considering at the time, and that apparently motivated Shevardnadze's surprise resignation, was a Gorbachev proposal that the presidential powers be expanded even further. Passed by the CPD in late December 1990, the following changes were amended to the constitution:

The Presidential Council of the USSR was abolished.

The president of the Soviet Union would assume direct responsibility for the work of the Council of Ministers and appoint the premier, subject to parliamentary confirmation. The Council of Ministers, previously roughly equivalent to the cabinet in the United States, was reduced to an administrative agency and the premier was downgraded to merely a coordinator of the administration.

The Council of the Federation, with the president at its head and composed of the presidents of the 15 union republics, was given broad powers to oversee agreements between the central government and the union republics, but its decisions require a two-thirds majority vote.

A *National Security Council* was established and is chaired by the president. It is composed of 9 members, including Dmitry T. Yazov, the defense minister; Foreign Minister Alexander A. Bessmertnykh; Vladimir A. Kryuchkov, the head of the KGB; Vice President Gennady A. Yanayev; Boris K. Pugo, the interior minister; Prime Minister Valintine S. Pavlov; Yevgeny M. Primakov, Gorbachev's foreign policy adviser; and Vadim V. Bakatin, the former minister of interior. Presumably, National Security Council will become Gorbachev's chief advisory body. It will develop the most important foreign and domestic policies, including those on national security, economic development, law and order, and the environment. Matters affecting the union republics or specific national groups must be coordinated with the Council of the Federation. The National Security Council will also govern the country during national emergencies.

The office of vice president was created. Besides acting as president in the president's absence, the duties of this office were also left vague, but apparently it is to do the president's bidding. Gennady I. Yanayev, the man elected to the post by the CPD, said he would focus on economic and budgetary matters and that he would attempt to find solutions to ethnic conflicts. (See Figure 5–3.)

These new powers were occasioned by the need to take firm action in two areas. First, it is hoped that the increasingly assertive union republic governments will be encouraged to cooperate more fully with the central

FIGURE 5–3   The Soviet executive.

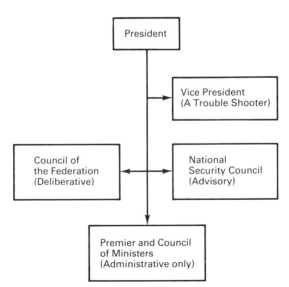

government if power over decisions affecting them is shared. At the same time, however, the central government is given more authority to bring order among the nationalities, several of which are seemingly verging on civil war. The second problem is that Gorbachev's economic reforms are often not implemented by the government bureaucracy. By taking direct control of the Council of Ministers himself and thus apparently reducing the premier to a mere coordinator of the ministers, Gorbachev hopes to be able to bring more discipline to the government bureaucracy—discipline that has been lacking since the Communist Party has withdrawn from its role of directly supervising the government. Although this move may give Gorbachev the leverage needed to make the bureaucracy work more efficiently, it also puts him up front on the matter. Under the previous executive format, the lines of authority between the president and the premier were unclear, so the president's right to oversee the administration of policy was questionable. At the same time, however, this ambiguity made it possible for Gorbachev to escape much of the blame for bureaucratic foulups. Premier Nikolai I. Ryzhkov became the lightning rod for complaints against the government, thus sparing Gorbachev much embarrassment. Now, however, Gorbachev is indisputably the person responsible for effective government. If he succeeds in making the system run smoothly and efficiently—a daunting task—he will be applauded; but if he fails, his reputation could decline even further than it has already. As Gorbachev himself put it while justifying this new authority, "We see that power has to become more effective, otherwise [political] processes will turn destructive—and so something must be done." He went on to assert that while some critics opposed his position, others demanded that he act. "People," he said, "have literally hounded these proposals out of me, so to speak."[16] Ultimately, this maneuver may be seen as one borne of desperation since few Soviet politicians would, if they had a choice, stake their futures on being able to effectively manage a previously unwieldy Soviet bureaucracy.

Although Gorbachev got from the CPD most of what he wanted, his waning influence was reflected in two defeats at its hands. Once described as "aggressively obedient" to Gorbachev's wishes, the CPD has become increasingly independent; the left has grown more and more cautious about the centralization of power in Gorbachev's hands, and the right has stepped up its criticism of his reforms. Even as the CPD accepted Gorbachev's proposal to create a vice president, it failed by 31 votes to elect to the post Gennady Yanayev, the man Gorbachev wanted. This forced the Soviet president to resubmit Yanayev's name and to lobby hard for the parliament to reverse its previous vote, which it eventually did. Much more significant is the CPD's refusal to create a "supreme state inspectorate" that Gorbachev hoped to use as a mechanism to regulate the bureaucracy. Many deputies opposed this agency out of concern that a new totalitarian mechanism might be created, but in failing to enact the proposal, the CPD denied Gorbachev the vehicle he thought necessary to gain control over the bu-

[16]Carey Goldberg, "Gorbachev Wins Broader Powers," *The Los Angeles Times*, Dec. 26, 1990.

reaucracy. Clearly, his task of assuring efficient government has been complicated.

The Council of Ministers

Until 1990 the **Council of Ministers** was the highest executive agency in the country. The chairman of the Council of Ministers (premier) was elected by the Supreme Soviet, as were the people he recommended as vice-chairs, ministers, and state committee chairs. In the mid-1980s there were about 115 ministries and a dozen vice-chairs on the Council of Ministers. Such a large number of ministers made frequent meetings of the council impossible, and although acts and statements were frequently published in its name, the entire council was not usually responsible for them. A smaller body, called the **Presidium of the Council of Ministers,**[17] met as an executive body for the council. Composed of the premier, some of the vice-chairs, and the most important ministers (foreign affairs, defense, interior, etc.), this body made most of the government's major administrative decisions. However, in urgent cases, the premier could unilaterally make decisions and represent them as the group's opinion. The Supreme Soviet was eventually asked to ratify decisions of the government, which it did without fail, of course.

The chairman of the Council of Ministers was a very powerful individual. Indeed it was one of the few positions that might have challenged the general secretary of the party for dominance. In the 1950s Premier Malenkov apparently attempted such a challenge of General Secretary Khrushchev by forging a coalition among government officials and industrial managers. His plan failed, however, and he was retired for his trouble.[18]

Both Stalin and Khrushchev held the posts of general secretary and chairman of the Council of Ministers simultaneously, thus aggregating great personal power. Apparently part of the agreement predicating Khrushchev's overthrow was that collective leadership would be guaranteed and that no person would again presume to hold the two offices simultaneously. Brezhnev kept his part of the bargain, and until 1990, Gorbachev showed little interest in heading the Council of Ministers.

The creation of a powerful presidency, giving Gorbachev direct authority over the Council of Ministers, even as he remains general secretary of the party, seems to constitute a violation of the old principle of collective leadership. On the other hand, the Soviet political system has changed considerably so that the power structure may not be at all what it used to be. The Communist Party is receding as a control mechanism over the government, the new rule that the Council of the Federation must vote by two-

---

[17]Care should be taken not to confuse the Presidium of the Council of Ministers with the Presidium of the Supreme Soviet. One should also keep in mind that during the Khrushchev era the Politburo of the CPSU was called the Presidium.

[18]Edward Crankshaw, *Khrushchev* (New York: Viking, 1966), pp. 250–252.

Perhaps the most famous of all sites in the Soviet Union, Saint Basil's Cathedral stands in Red Square just outside the Kremlin Wall. (Photo provided by Louis and Helen Van Moppes.)

thirds majority to adopt policy, the apparent growing independence of the CPD and the Supreme Soviet, and the growing independence of the union republic governments could each mean that Gorbachev is significantly checked in the exercise of power. Still, no previous person in Soviet history accumulated the vast formal executive authority that Gorbachev enjoys and the default by the Supreme Soviet on economic matters causes many critics to wonder if, indeed, the structure of a new dictatorship might have evolved.

The power of the bureaucracy. Long before the 1917 revolution, the government bureaucracy was a ponderous, powerful edifice. Lenin hoped that eventually the bureaucracy would be tamed by socialism and the development of the proletarian consciousness. This transformation never occurred, however; instead the bureaucracy became even more huge and dominant in the Soviet system. Not only did the government become a major factor in almost every conceivable human endeavor, but the Communist Party established its own parallel bureaucracy, thus compounding the awkwardness and insensitivity of the system. The bureaucracy became a self-aggrandizing and self-protective system that often paid scant attention to the needs of those whom it was ostensibly created to serve. "Of all the elements in Soviet society," wrote Vladimir Bukovsky, "the human being is the most neglected."[19] Instead of ideology overcoming bureaucracy, as Lenin foresaw, the reverse happened. Once the Communist Party took control of the government, party membership became obligatory for career advancement. Thus the party and the bureaucracy became inundated with **careerists** (people who joined the party not out of ideological commitment but because they wanted to advance in their careers).

Government functionaries have always been powerful because they control the administration of state policy, but in the twentieth century bureaucratic power has grown because governments have become active in more and more facets of daily life. The increasing dominance exerted by executive branches in controlling decisions is perhaps the most important single development in modern governments—be they democratic, authoritarian, or totalitarian. Issues and institutions of modern societies are so complex as to demand inordinate expertise from functionaries. The executive bureaucrats are the people who specialize in particular subject matter and are, therefore, sought after for specific detail when a matter of policy is being considered. Hence, virtually every modern government, including the Soviet Union, finds its executive initiating most policy issues, advising the decision makers on the issues, and administering policy once it is decided. This powerful combination concentrates enormous authority in the hands of the executive branch. In the Soviet Union the situation is exacerbated because the government is so omnipresent, controlling the economic and social factors in society as well as political matters.

When Gorbachev became general secretary, the government had almost 1,000 different agencies and it employed 17.7 million people, a figure that did not include the ministries of Defense and Interior, the KGB, and collective farm managers.[20] This leviathan was an onerous, clumsy bulk that had always been held in contempt by the people. As the poet Yevgeny Yevtushenko put it, "bureaucracy is war against people."

Attempting to exert control over this large amorphous mass, Gorbachev and Premier Ryzhkov began to pare it down. Thousands of government employees were dismissed and several ministries were eliminated; some were consolidated into other departments and some were abolished, their functions being turned over to the union republics.

Of course, these reforms were resisted by elements of the bureaucracy, as people resisted changes that contradicted their own interests. Others, however, particularly those whose jobs were not jeopardized and those who were task-oriented, supported the reforms and continued to advocate for more.[21] Finally, early in 1990, Ryzhkov proposed that the bureaucracy be

[19]Vladimir Bukovsky, "The Political Condition of the Soviet Union," in *The Future of the Soviet Empire,* ed. Henry S. Rowen and Charles Wolf, Jr. (New York: St. Martin's Press, 1987), p. 32.

[20]Cohen and Heuvel, p. 15.

[21]Walter Laqueur, "Soviet Politics: Current Trends," in *Soviet Union 2000: Reform or Revolution?,*" ed. Walter Laqueur (New York: St. Martin's Press, 1990), p. 23. Also see Cohen and Heuvel, p. 131.

further trimmed by layoffs and that the number of ministries be reduced by about one-third. Accordingly, in 1991 the Council of Ministers was now composed of the chairman; 13 vice-chairpersons (one was a woman, Aleksandra P. Biryukova), each of whom also headed a department; 38 ministers; and 17 state committee chairmen. The only other female minister besides Biryukova is Lyudmila Davletova, and only one minister, Nikolai Vorontsov, is not a Communist Party member. He is chairman of the State Committee of the USSR for Nature Protection (*Goskompriroda*).

Of the chairman and 68 other executive heads, only 8 are non-Russians. There is one Adygean, Armenian, and Kazakh, two Ukrainians, and three Byelorussians. Foreign Minister Shevardnadze is a Georgian, but he resigned his Council of Ministers post. Each of the other non-Russians heads only minor departments, although the Adygean, Vitali Doguzhiyev, is a vice-chairman of the Council of Ministers, yet he is not even a member of the CPSU Central Committee. Of the 69 people in the Council of Ministers, 36 are members of the Central Committee. There are also four generals on the council: Dmitri Yazov, minister of defense; Alexander Volkov, minister of civil aviation; Boris K. Pugo, minister of the interior; and Vladimir Kryuchkov, chairman of the State Security Committee (KGB).[22]

Any hopes that Ryzhkov's government would be more efficient than previous councils of ministers were soon dashed as a severe shortage of goods such as cigarettes developed in 1990. Smokers rioted in several cities because they were forced to buy jars of cigarette butts to satisfy their habits. Correctly blaming the bureaucracy for the shortage, the leadership fired the vice-chairman of the Council of Ministers who doubled as chairman of the State Commission for Foods and Procurements. Sacked for failure to produce and distribute cigarettes, this minister has a poetically just-sounding name, Vladimir *Nikitin*.

More significantly, despite bumper crops in 1990, poor management of harvests, transportation, and distribution visited a profound food shortage upon the state stores. Vexations of this sort, together with Gorbachev's suspicion that elements of the bureaucracy were deliberately sabotaging his reforms, led him to the politically risky step of taking personal charge of the government and downgrading the Council of Ministers from a policy-making body to a simple administrator of policy. Ryzhkov, who had threatened to resign several times because of lack of support in the parliament, was elbowed aside. Regrettably he suffered a serious heart attack, presumably brought on by the stress from his political demise, and was replaced by Valentin S. Pavlov, the former finance minister, a more conservative figure than Ryzhkov. Whether or not Gorbachev will have more luck than Ryzhkov in managing the government remains to be seen. For his part, Pavlov has become a thorn in Gorbachev's side, often leading conservative opposition to his reforms.

Structure and functions of the Council of Ministers.   The Council of Ministers functions much like the executive branches in other modern govern-

----

[22]*Who's Who in the Soviet Government* (Moscow: Novosti Press Agency Publishing House, 1990).

mental systems. It provides many of the social programs available to the public; it is responsible for maintaining public order and for guaranteeing security by maintaining adequate police and military establishments. The administration of foreign policy is also within its jurisdiction but, of course, the president and his National Security Council make foreign policy.

The Council of Ministers also presides over the formulation and implementation of the five-year plans and the annual budgets of every publicly controlled agency. This function alone involves it in most legal activities of any consequence in the society. Further, the Council of Ministers is involved in initiating most of the laws passed by the parliament or promulgated by the president. As a highly centralized system, and one that controls almost every legal aspect of economic and political activity, the Council of Ministers exercises enormous powers over credit, finance, employment, wages, production, distribution, prices, housing, and services. No individual or agency is untouched by its administration.

Besides supervising its own vast bureaucracy, the Council of Ministers also reviews the actions of the councils of ministers of the union republics. Although the union republic governments have recently been given more autonomy, the central government still claims to have the authority to void their laws if they contradict national statutes and policies.

The Council of Ministers is divided into three principal agencies: all-union ministries, union republic ministries, and state committees. The *all-union ministries* exercise powers exclusive to the central government, powers over which only the central government has authority. They are located in Moscow, but many of them maintain field offices, as appropriate, throughout the country. Although the reasons for some of these ministries being centralized is clear, the criteria for administering some other ministries exclusively by the central government remain obscure. For example, the nation's railroads are administered directly by the central government, yet highway construction and maintenance, as well as vehicular transportation, are administered by local agencies. On the other hand, each union republic has a ministry for foreign affairs, but foreign trade is exclusively administered by the central government, although certain enterprises have recently been allowed to trade directly with foreign corporations, thus circumventing the central bureaucracy. Examples of other all-union ministries are machine building, electronics, electrical engineering, aviation, shipbuilding, and chemicals.

The 30 *union republic ministries* administer areas that are shared concurrently by the central government and the union republics. (It is these ministries that have suffered the greatest reduction at the hands of Gorbachev's reforms, since many of their functions, like certain kinds of construction, were transferred to the sole control of the union republics.) The central government ministry, usually located in Moscow, deals directly with similar ministries in the union republics. Obviously, the ministries in the union republics that share jurisdiction with those of the central government experience the greatest scrutiny from the central government. Examples of union republic ministries are foreign affairs, agriculture, culture, finance, and public health.

Besides the two kinds of ministries in the central government, some categories of issues are handled by *state committees*. The criteria for making an agency a state committee rather than a ministry are not entirely clear, except that the issues with which state committees deal tend to span many, or even all, other government departments. In addition, there does not seem to be any precise ranking among the various ministers and state committee chairs. In fact, chairs of the state committees are often referred to as ministers in the Soviet press, and some state committee chairs double as vice-chairs of the Council of Ministers. Some examples of state committees are the State Planning Committee (*Gosplan*), the State Committee for Construction, the State Committee for Material and Technical Supply, and the State Committee for Science and Technology.

Consistent with the Leninist doctrine of democratic centralism and with Russian administrative tradition, each ministry is capped by a collective body (a sort of executive committee called a *collegium*), but the minister is vested with ultimate authority and responsibility. The collegia are composed of about a dozen deputy ministers and department heads. They have the right to advise the minister, but only the minister has the authority to make major decisions, issue orders, and promulgate rules. Accordingly, the minister remains responsible to the president for the success or failure of the ministry.

Intermediate and Local Executives

The structure of union republic, autonomous republic, autonomous oblast, okrug, oblast, and krai governments is so similar to that of the central government that a detailed description would only mire us in needless repetition. Basically, each soviet elects a council of ministers or an executive committee, and the executive committee divides into several ministries or departments. Union republics have basically two kinds of ministries: those sharing jurisdiction with the central government and those administering matters that are exclusive to their level.

Union republic ministers, therefore, owe responsibility to their own parliament and presumably to the Communist Party, of which most ministers are still members. In addition to these checks, the union republic minister is responsible to the national minister, whom he or she mirrors at the republican level.

The union republic councils of ministers enjoy the same powers over their subordinates as the central government exercises over them. Executive actions and rules promulgated by oblast or krai executive committees are subject to negation by the union republic executive should they be deemed inappropriate.

So it is throughout the system. Each intermediate executive branch exercises important powers over the next lower level. Yet each minister in turn must accept the administrative authority of the next higher executive, while, at the same time, remaining responsible to his or her own executive committee and to the parliament. As one might imagine, the complexity of Soviet policy administration involves its officials in innumerable bureaucratic delays, contradictions, and hassles. These problems encourage officials to be extremely cautious and slow to act, denying the system considerable decisiveness and spontaneity. Citizens or visitors asking a Soviet bureaucrat for something that falls outside of normal operating procedure will be met almost invariably with a response of *nyet!* The system can be very frustrating.

Local government levels (rural raions, cities, towns, villages, and settlements) are structured like their superior counterparts. The executive committees are usually headed by a chairperson, a deputy chairperson, a secretary, and several professional bureaucrats. These officials, the most powerful on the executive committees, are joined by several people who hold ordinary jobs outside of government. Bowing to the control of their local soviets, the executive committees are principally responsible for bringing the services of government to their citizens. This factor distinguishes them from other levels in the government, for they are the only agencies that regularly work directly with the masses of people in the society. Indeed, it is this level of government that Gorbachev is trying hardest to revitalize in an attempt to break the stifling influence of the party bureaucracy.

The number of functions performed by the local soviets would fill several pages and will not be exhaustively listed here. A partial summary of these duties might be helpful, however. Not unlike many local governments in the West, local Soviet governments keep public records; regulate land management and zoning; and provide public transportation, streets, water, and sewerage disposal. They coordinate medical, police, and fire services; and they maintain schools, playgrounds, libraries, cultural centers, and parks. As extensive as these services are, they scratch only the surface of local government involvement in the lives of their citizens. City governments manage and assign most housing; they maintain the wedding palaces (facilities in which civil weddings are performed); they run most local restaurants, movie theaters, markets, clothing stores, repair shops, hardware stores, bookstores, and other retail outlets. They provide the utilities, manage most construction, and even organize chess and stamp collectors' clubs. They run ice cream parlors, bistros, liquor stores, and the few night spots that exist in the country. Swimming pools, stadiums, tennis courts, skating rinks, and ski jumps are all run by the local government.

The list goes on and on. Except for the relatively small number of private or cooperative enterprises that have sprung up, there is virtually no building, no job, no store, no office, no apartment that is not owned, controlled, and operated by the government; and the local government is in charge of most of them. The next time you go downtown or to the local shopping center, imagine that everything you see is owned and operated by the government. You will then get some idea of the extent to which government pervades Soviet life.

Answering Gorbachev's call for change, the Party Congress approved an extremely controversial resolution that provides that the first secretaries of local jurisdictions (e.g., *oblasts, krais, cities,* etc.) are to stand for election to the chairs of the local soviets. The controversy surrounding this proposal is complicated. Many party functionaries resist it because, as you learned in the last chapter, it is the first time that party officials are to be subjected to votes of approval by the public. However, even some reformers object to the policy because they feel that it contradicts Gorbachev's effort to divorce the party from active involvement in the government. A third problem arises from the dilemma of a party first secretary who is rejected by the voters for the chair of a local soviet and must therefore resign the party post.

THE JUDICIARY

To an American, the Soviet judicial system might appear strange because it lacks many familiar practices and traditions found in the common law system used in Anglo-Saxon countries. Although there are several unique features to the Soviet system, it basically follows the format of the European civil law system and would therefore seem far less unusual to an Italian, German, Frenchman, Japanese, or Latin American.

Soviet law is divided into a number of discrete codes (civil law, criminal law, labor law, family law, etc.) containing statutes that are intended to be taken as complete statements of the social will. Hence, much less latitude and power are afforded Soviet courts than the American bench enjoys. For example, Soviet judges are expected to rule on the law solely for the case they are hearing. American judges, by contrast, can impose an interpretation from one case upon all similar cases in all lower courts. This power, *stare decisis*, or precedent, does not exist in either the European or Soviet legal systems. By the same token, American jurists, exercising the power of judicial review, can void a law on the grounds that it is unconstitutional, whereas European and Soviet judges lack this power. The combination of precedent (the power to bind lower courts to particular interpretations of the law through time) with judicial review (the power to declare a law void because it contradicts constitutional principles) makes the American judiciary extremely powerful as a social and political institution. Courts using the European code system, including the Soviet courts, lack these powers and therefore have far less impact on society.

Several other principles used in the European civil law system differ markedly from our own procedures. Holding the rights of the community paramount, the European system gives the individual fewer protections against state prosecutors than are enjoyed in the common law. Accordingly, persons can be held by Soviet authorities for as long as 10 days without being advised of the charges against them. The principle of *habeas corpus* is modified further by withholding the individual's right to an attorney until the trial stage. This provision can be crucial because, consistent with the European civil law system, the Soviets use an inquisitorial process during which investigators may subject suspects to questioning prior to an indictment. Thus, the state accrues a distinct advantage by being able to question suspects who do not have counsel present. It should be pointed out, however, that the Soviets have gradually relaxed on this point and now usually allow a suspect to engage counsel early on in the inquisitorial process. But given the premise of their legal system, that the good of the society super-sedes that of the individual, Soviet authorities could deny a suspect counsel during this inquisitorial stage.

Also similar to other systems using the European civil law approach, Soviet criminal courts enjoy a much higher conviction rate than is common in the United States. This is so not only because the prosecution can question suspects without defense counsel being present but also because defense advocates have little opportunity to carry out independent investigations, and surprise witnesses or new evidence is difficult to introduce. Further, great care is taken by the prosecution in screening the evidence so that questionable cases are not often taken to trial. Only about 35 percent of all initiated criminal cases reach Soviet courtrooms, but the conviction rate is in the high ninetieth percentile.[23]

The European civil code system does not provide for jury trials, and until recently, no juries existed in the Soviet Union either. Most cases are heard before tribunals, which then reach judgments among themselves. A unique feature of the Soviet system, however, is the use of *people's assessors* as jurists in cases that are being heard for the first time. People's assessors are private citizens who sit with professional judges in hearing cases. Thus, the Soviet system includes the aspect of a trial before one's peers within the tribunal procedure. However, unlike our system the judges and people's assessors do not act as impartial arbiters in the case. Rather, they actively participate in proceedings in attempts to find the truth of the matter.[24] In 1989, however, the Supreme Soviet passed laws providing that in murder cases and other serious criminal trials, juries would be used to determine the verdict.

The Soviet Approach to the Law

Soviet authorities have long seen the law in a somewhat idealistic fashion, even being quite naive about it at the debut of their system. Marx and Engels viewed the law as a vestige of capitalist and precapitalist societies and maintained that it was used, along with all other institutions, to keep the rulers in dominant positions. Thus, the law was considered an oppressive institution and was slated for elimination in the new socialist society. Lenin, himself a lawyer, had little trust or respect for his legal colleagues.[25] He theorized that the law was overburdened with jargon and ritual; he believed that courts and the bar could be eliminated to the general betterment of society. Accordingly, when he came to power, he eliminated the Russian legal system and banned the practice of law. Justice was

[23]John H. Minan, "An Introduction to Soviet Law," in *Law in the Soviet Union*, ed. John H. Minan (San Diego, CA: Professional Seminar Consultants, Inc., 1984), p. 5.

[24]Harold J. Berman, "The Comparison of Soviet and American Law," in *Law in the Soviet Union*, ed. John H. Minan (San Diego, CA: Professional Seminar Consultants, Inc., 1984), p. 18.

[25]Unlike in the United States, lawyers in the Soviet Union do not often go into politics. Gorbachev is the first person with a law degree since Lenin to reach the pinnacle of power.

dispensed by popularly elected "people's courts" and by revolutionary tribunals. It was not long, however, before it became evident that the judicial system would have to be reinstated if chaos were to be averted. Even so, the ultimate aim of someday eliminating the formal judicial structure was sustained in Soviet ideological statements.

Under Stalin, the law was put to the ominous purpose of bringing about the "second revolution." Much as during the time of Ivan the Terrible, the secret police were given free reign, cowing the people, the government, and even the party itself. Unique applications of law characterized the era. One example was the *doctrine of analogy*. Under this principle, citizens could be prosecuted for doing things that were not specifically against the law but were analogous to crimes. Giving vent to his paranoia and need for absolute power, Stalin used such legal mutations to fill labor camps with enemies, real or imagined. Millions of innocent people fell afoul of this terrible system.

After Stalin's death, the authorities abandoned the worst abuses, liberating hundreds of thousands—even millions—of prisoners. Khrushchev resurrected the "comrades' courts," heralding them as the harbinger of the new Soviet order. Since Khrushchev, however, Soviet officials have tended to place less emphasis on amateurish justice, and the legal profession is enjoying a rise in official and public esteem. Even so, it still lacks the status it enjoys in the United States and other Western societies.

To understand the Soviet approach to the law, one must keep in mind that the Soviet leaders believed they were building a totally new society—one where courts, police, and lawyers will ultimately be unnecessary. Once the Soviet authorities recognized that the law had to be continued in existence for a bit longer, they decided to use it, as they use all other institutions, as a tool by which to construct their new order. Perhaps ironically, therefore, Soviet authorities used the law for the same purpose as Marx, Engels, and Lenin condemned the capitalists—to preserve their power and to instill their values in society. Indeed, Lenin himself described the law as "a political instrument, it is politics."[26]

Thus, Soviet authorities view the law as a political tool. It is not seen as a reflection of social values so much as a propagator and teacher of values. The educational aspects of the law are paramount, and the entire legal system is bent toward teaching people the correct behavior in a socialist society. To this end, Soviet leaders place great store in public chastisement and embarrassment of offenders, as well as on repentance for social deviation. Gorbachev's reforms have brought an additional function of the law to the Soviet system. Since 1985, legislation has been in force which, as never before, subjects the state to the rule of law. In other words, the rule of law and not of leaders is supposed to be the guiding principle. Consequently, individual liberties have been given greater protection under Gor-

---

[26]John N. Hazard, "Legal Policy in the Soviet Union," in *The Soviet Union in the 1980s*, ed. Erik P. Hoffmann (New York: The Academy of Political Science, 1984), p. 57.

bachev than was imaginable during previous eras. As you will soon learn, Gorbachev himself has found that he has been restrained by the law and by the judicial system.

One of the most striking features of the Soviet judicial system is its participatory nature. Stemming from the long-felt bias against a professional judiciary, the wish to have people identify with the system, and the attitude that the courts are an educative institution, the Soviet judicial system includes several mechanisms encouraging public participation. Unlike the formal edifices in which our courts are housed, Soviet courts are found in ordinary, even dingy, buildings. Frequently, courts forsake their official seats, taking up session in the factory or apartment building of the defendant.

Judicial ceremony and procedures are kept to a minimum, encouraging an informality that might startle a Western observer. The rules of evidentiary admissibility tend to be very lax, and the judges and people's assessors often carry on a large share of the interrogation. Not infrequently, the audience is allowed to participate in the trial, and any social institution can send spokespersons to praise or criticize the character of the plaintiff or defendant.

Two institutions are particularly noteworthy with respect to popular participation in the judicial process. The *druzhina* is a voluntary police force of several million people who spend part of their leisure time patrolling the streets on the alert for minor offenders. These people may make citizens' arrests for such violations of public order as drunkenness and disorderly conduct. The *comrades' courts* are quasi-judicial institutions and not actually an official part of the judiciary. They receive cases from the *druzhina*, as well as from other social institutions. Originally begun by Lenin, they fell into disuse under Stalin but were resurrected with great fanfare by Khrushchev.[27]

The comrades' courts are elected by local public assemblies and sit *en banc* in groups of 25 jurists. They attempt to settle minor squabbles among families or neighbors. They hear cases of drunkenness, absenteeism, tardiness, laziness, disrespect, public cursing, and similar offenses. Comrades' courts can become judicial free-for-alls, with the jurists, litigants, and audience all taking part in the proceedings. No lawyers or professional jurists are present, and the court can (by a majority vote) reprimand, upbraid, or even fine those found guilty. If the comrades' courts find cases to be sufficiently severe, they can send them to the people's court, the lowest official Soviet court. Appeals from the comrades' courts can also be taken to a higher court. The real purpose of the comrades' courts, however, is not to punish offenders but to bring public pressure on them to conduct themselves in accordance with social norms.

---

[27]Roy D. Laird and Ronald A. Francisco, "Observations on Rural Life in the Soviet Union," in *Contemporary Soviet Society*, ed. Jerry G. Pankhurst and Michael Paul Sacks (New York: Praeger Publishers, 1980), p. 144.

The Legal Profession

In keeping with European values, the most respected legal pursuit is in the area of academics. Throughout Europe, education is universally respected, and scholars are among the most revered people in society. By contrast, largely because the European civil law system gives relatively little power to judges, jurists do not enjoy the high status in the Soviet Union that they receive in the United States. The policy of opening the judicial process to ordinary people also tends to discourage holding officials of the court in high esteem.

Soviet judges tend to be poorly paid. Technically, any citizen can become a judge, but in fact almost all judges now have some, although seldom more than four years, formal judicial training. Rather than capping a long career as an attorney with a seat on the bench, as is the practice in the United States, Soviet jurists usually take the bench early in their careers. Judges who leave the bench seldom go into politics, although most of them are party members. Those who change careers usually become practicing attorneys.

Practicing attorneys frequently follow one of three basic pursuits: They may become a legal counsel, an advocate, or a prosecutor. Legal counsels generally advise economic enterprises or governmental agencies, and they practice in civil litigation, which is quite common among Soviet enterprises. Their positions can be relatively important and they can have considerable influence with the management of their enterprises.

Advocates are trial lawyers who advise people about the law and defend them in court. Once admitted to the bar, Soviet attorneys may practice before any court in the land.[28] To be an advocate one must be permitted membership in an advocate's collegium of a large city or a rural raion. These collectives are ostensibly private associations, but they are supervised by the state, and lawyers are also responsible to the newly created bar association. Electing a presidium from their number to manage the collegium, the advocates take cases assigned to them for fixed fees. For example, a simple case involving no more than one day in court will cost the client about 50 rubles. The advocate receives about 30 percent of the fee and the rest goes to sustain the collegium's facilities.[29] Depending on client fees rather than government salaries for their livelihood, the advocates are among the very few independent employees in the Soviet Union. Advocate incomes are relatively low, about 300 rubles per month, thus some attorneys demand additional sums "on the left" (on the sly). Such a practice, if discovered, can result in disbarment, yet it apparently remains a fact of life, thus further eroding public confidence and esteem for practitioners of the law.

Advocates may defend people in criminal or civil procedures and they may advocate for plaintiffs in civil cases. People in the Soviet Union have

[28]Simis, p. 86.

[29]Alan Abrahamson, "Crime Lawyer from Ukraine Samples U.S. Legal System," *The Los Angeles Times*, Oct. 15, 1989.

always been able to sue one another, and they have recently been given the right to sue the government, when they feel it has violated their rights or done them harm. Advocates often find themselves in the delicate position of having to protect their clients in a system dedicated to giving collective rights first consideration. The adversarial system used in the United States assumes that defense attorneys will do everything within the law to aid their clients. The prosecution is expected to come forth with a similar effort on the other side, and justice will be served in the adversarial process. The Soviet system, by contrast, has traditionally assumed that the courts are political agents maintained to serve the interests of society and the state. Even though the individual enjoys protection in the law now, this pro-government attitude still pervades the system and introduces ambiguity into the role of criminal defense attorneys. If they suspect the guilt of their clients or if they discover incriminating evidence, they find themselves faced with a dilemma of some consequence to their conscience and careers. Additionally, most advocates are party members, a status that must have some bearing when they advise or defend such politically charged cases as draft evasion, political and religious dissidence, and certain economic crimes.

The third avenue that an attorney might pursue is the prosecution. The Soviets house prosecutors in a state agency, just as do most other systems. But the Soviet Union has created a completely unique institution for the purpose: the *Procuracy*. Headed by the procurator-general of the USSR, the Procuracy is technically independent of any element in the government. The procurator-general is elected to a five-year term by the Congress of People's Deputies of the USSR. He or she appoints the procurators of the union republics, the autonomous republics, the autonomous oblasts, and the okrugs. Officials at the lower levels of government are appointed by the union republic procurators until every judicial jurisdiction is served by a procurator. All lower procurator appointments are subject to the procurator-general's approval, and all procurators remain either directly or indirectly responsible to that office. The union republics want to abolish this centralized system and bring the procurators in their jurisdictions directly under their own control.

At first glance, one might be tempted to equate the procurator-general with the attorney general of the United States, but in fact the procurator's functions and powers reach far beyond those of the American office. Indeed, the two posts are not even structurally parallel: The attorney general of the United States heads the Department of Justice, while the procurator-general is not affiliated with the Soviet Ministry of Justice.

In criminal proceedings the procurator authorizes arrests and appoints and supervises the investigators who conduct the pretrial inquisitions. An investigator may indict a suspect, but the procurator can annul the indictment should he or she disagree with the investigator's findings. If the indictment is allowed to stand, the suspect is brought to trial and is prosecuted by the procurator's office. In civil cases the procurator may join either side of the dispute, thus lending the weight of that office to the favored party.

Court decisions of all kinds are regularly reviewed by the procurator. Should a discrepancy be found, the procurator may "protest" a ruling, thus forwarding the case to a new hearing at a higher level. In the Supreme Court of the USSR, the nation's highest court, the procurator may protest a ruling to the Presidium of the Supreme Soviet of the USSR. The power to protest a ruling extends to both criminal and civil cases; thus, there is no protection against double jeopardy in the Soviet Union even though such protection seems to be guaranteed in article 5 of the Soviet Constitution. If the procurator disagrees with an acquittal, defendants may find themselves facing new trials before higher courts. By the same token, however, convicted defendants may receive a second hearing by successfully appealing to the procurator to have their cases heard by a higher court.

The procurator also reviews all administrative laws, edicts, and decrees and can protest a ruling to the immediate superior of the offending agency if he or she finds it in violation of the law. By the same token, judicial administration concerns the Procuracy as well. Present at all plenary sessions of the USSR and republican supreme courts, the procurator may advise those bodies on judicial decisions and questions of procedure. The same consultative service is provided the soviets.

Beyond these vast powers, the procurator is supposed to supervise investigations by the militia (the regular police) and the secret police. The Procuracy is also charged with supervising the penal system, including detentions, prisons, labor camps, and executions.

Clearly, an office exercising such enormous powers is not ignored by the party. The procurator-general, and most lesser procurators and their staffs, are party members. Presently the procurator-general is a member of the Central Committee of the CPSU; this has not always been the case.

Influential though the Procuracy is, it does not function without controversy. Severe criticism of the way it was administering the judicial system led in 1970 to the creation of the Ministry of Justice. More recently, the Soviet press has complained that citizens are not getting a fair trial in some instances because the legal system gives such great advantage to the prosecution—the Procuracy.

In any event, with the Procuracy performing so many functions that are usually exercised by the Ministry of Justice in other systems, the Soviet Ministry of Justice is understandably a relatively low-ranking agency.[30] Its basic function is to serve as yet another monitor of the courts and the legal profession. Specifically, the Ministry of Justice of the USSR, in concert with the ministries of justice of the union republics, reviews judicial procedures and encourages their uniformity and consistency. The ministries of justice are also concerned with the political and ideological posture of the judiciary, and to this end they make suggestions regarding desirable interpretations and applications of the law. The ministries also serve the legal profession, promoting professionalism and ideological consistency. In these endeavors, the ministries of justice find themselves involved in the selection

---

[30]In most countries the Ministry of Justice ranks among the most prominent in the government. Such is not the case in the Soviet Union.

process of judges, as well as in the regulation of the membership and administration of the collegia of advocates.

The Judicial Structure

The lowest official court (remember that the comrades' courts are not officially part of the judicial system) is the **people's court.**[31] Judges to the people's court are elected by the people in their jurisdictions, but they may soon be elected by their respective soviets. This body hears the vast majority of civil cases and minor criminal cases in original jurisdiction. People's court judges are elected to five-year terms by the people of their jurisdiction (large cities and rural raions). The nomination process is similar to that for the people's deputies to soviets, and most judges are party members.

A typical trial in the people's court will find a judge flanked by two people's assessors, ordinary citizens who have been elected to two-and-one-half-year terms by the same constituency and in the same manner as the judges. People's assessors are given some instruction in the law and in judicial procedure, but they are far from expert. Although the judge presides over the trial, the people's assessors are supposed to have equal rights in deciding all questions before the court. Since they serve only two weeks each year, however, most of them tend to let the judge take the lead.

As mentioned earlier, courtroom procedure is very informal. Judges and people's assessors often become deeply involved in questioning witnesses, sometimes revealing their disposition in the case by the tone of their questions. This practice has recently drawn fire from the Soviet press, which has called for an end to the practice. *Literaturnaya gazeta* (Literary Gazette), a leading Soviet journal, contended that the practice of judges questioning defendants and attorneys before the witnesses are heard tends to imply that the accused is guilty before the trial is completed.

Trials are generally swift affairs, decisions being reached by majority vote and reduced to writing. Dissenting opinions are also written, but, although they are part of the court record, they are usually not read in court. The decision is usually accompanied by a judgment in a civil case or by a sentence if a guilty verdict is handed down in a criminal proceeding.

Dissatisfied parties in civil cases and convicted defendants in criminal cases may appeal a judgment to the next higher court. No further appeals are allowed, although a decision of any court may be protested by the procurator. The president of a higher court may demand a new hearing of a case within his or her jurisdiction. Hence, lower court cases may be forwarded to higher courts in three ways: on appeal, by protest of the procurator, or upon demand of a higher court.

The court immediately above the people's court depends upon the republic in which it is situated. Appeals in republics that have no oblasts or krais go directly to the republican supreme court. District courts, found in

---

[31]In addition to the regular courts there are three kinds of special courts: economic courts; labor courts; and administrative courts. These courts deal solely with the very technical law in which they specialize.

the oblasts and krais, are presided over by judges elected to five-year terms by their respective soviets. People's assessors are also elected by the soviet for two-and-a-half-year terms. District courts hear serious civil and criminal cases under original jurisdiction. In these cases, two people's assessors sit with a judge, just as in the people's court. Appellate cases go before a panel of three judges, however. Cases of the first instance may be appealed to the next higher court, but cases heard under appellate jurisdiction may only be forwarded upon a procurator's protest or upon the order of a higher court.

The republican supreme courts, whose members and lay assessors are elected by their respective parliaments, receive most of their cases from appeal, by procurator's protest, or upon their own demand. On rare occasions, republican supreme courts hear cases in original jurisdiction. These would normally be cases of an important nature to which the state wishes to give notoriety. The decisions of the republican supreme courts are final and may not be appealed to the Supreme Court of the USSR. An aggrieved party can, however, petition the procurator-general to protest the case, thus forcing it into the Supreme Court. As with the lower courts, the president of the Supreme Court of the USSR can also demand that a case be heard by his or her court.

The Supreme Court of the USSR is not only the highest court in the land, but it is also the only court maintained by the central government. Unlike lower courts, the membership of the Supreme Court is divided between *ex-officio* and elected persons. The Congress of Peoples' Deputies of the USSR elects a president, two vice presidents, and 16 other judges. It also elects 45 people's assessors. Added to this assemblage are the 15 presidents of the union republic supreme courts.

The Supreme Court of the USSR divides itself into three collegia: criminal, civil, and military. The collegia hear cases brought before them by protest of the procurator or by demand of the court's president. They may also hear cases in original jurisdiction, but this is extremely rare and employed usually only when the case is to be displayed as an example to the society. As with all lower courts, people's assessors are used by the Supreme Court only in cases of the first instance.

Following the decision by a collegium, the entire court convenes in plenary session to review the decision. The decision is final following approval of the plenary session, except that it may be protested by the procurator-general, in which case the matter is forwarded to the Presidium of the Supreme Soviet.

The Supreme Court of the USSR also meets in plenary session to adopt regulations for judicial procedure and interpretations of law that are then imposed upon the lower courts. The Supreme Court receives recommendations on these matters from the procurator-general, who must be present at all of its plenary sessions, and from the Ministry of Justice.

The Committee for Constitutional Compliance.   Prior to Gorbachev's rise to dominance, Soviet law, both constitutional and statutory, took second place to political expedience; the rights of individuals often suffered in the process. As a major step toward creating a system in which the law is above all other things, the **Committee for Constitutional Compliance** was created in 1990.

The committee, which is duplicated by similar bodies at the union republic and autonomous republic levels, is composed of a chair, Sergei S. Alexeyev, a vice-chair, and 21 members, including representation from each union republic. The members may not at the same time be members of any legislative, executive, or judicial body over which the committee has jurisdiction; they are elected by the Congress of Peoples' Deputies to 10-year terms.

The function of the committee is to assure that the acts of official institutions and individuals are consistent with the constitution and statute. Further, it has the right to submit drafts of law which it believes will improve existing codes to the CPD and the Supreme Soviet.

Although it is not technically a judicial body, it has the authority to void any law or act it finds in violation of basic human rights and freedoms. Astonishingly, the committee's first act of this sort was to invalidate an April 1990 edict by Gorbachev that directed the USSR Council of Ministers to decide which public demonstrations were to be permitted in the vicinity of the Kremlin. This edict, the committee concluded, illegally suspended provisions of a 1988 law giving such authority to city government and to the parliament of the Russian SFSR. In response, Gorbachev placed the Moscow police under direct control of the national department of interior, but undeterred, demonstrators manifested before the Kremlin in March 1991, demanding Gorbachev's resignation. At the same time, however, Gorbachev did not directly challenge the ruling or the authority of the Committee for Constitutional Compliance, and this check on the government's power is without precedent in Soviet history.[32] Indeed, since its first ruling, the committee has made several similar judgments, including ordering revision of a presidential edict authorizing army troops to patrol city streets, and in April 1991 it ruled invalid military regulations that bind the military to Communist Party policy.

The committee has less authority regarding matters that do not threaten individual rights. In such cases, the committee may publish its conclusion that a given law or act is unconstitutional. The opinion is served on the appropriate body and the law or action is suspended. The body involved is required to resolve the matter within three months. If the Council of Ministers or the Supreme Soviet refuses to repeal the offending action, the Congress of People's Deputies settles the dispute.[33]

The creation of such a body may prove to be among the most important developments in Soviet history. The committee's action successfully blocking presidential edict could become the Soviet equivalent of *Marbury v. Madison* (1803). In this case, the United States Supreme Court gave the judiciary the power to declare laws of Congress and actions by the execu-

[32]John-Thor Dahlburg, "Panel Rules Gorbachev Rally Decree Is Invalid," *The Los Angeles Times,* Sept. 15, 1990.

[33]Information provided by the Soviet Embassy in Washington, DC.

tive void on grounds that they violate the Constitution. The decision was fundamental, making the American judiciary a powerful check on the actions of the other two branches. It is much too early to conclude that the Committee for Constitutional Compliance may develop into an equivalent counterforce in the Soviet government, but it has taken extraordinary steps on a path that could lead to a significant modification of the Soviet political society.

Overview of the Soviet Judiciary

In broad terms, the Soviet judicial system has made a great deal of progress over the past few years. Although the Soviet Constitution assured that "judges and people's assessors are independent and subject only to the law,"[34] until recently the courts were seen principally as instruments of political control. Beginning with the Khrushchev era, the judiciary gradually became more protective of individual rights. Citizens whose cases were not political in nature could expect a fair resolution. When politics was a factor, however, the courts offered little solace. Today, however, Gorbachev's efforts to protect the rights of individuals further and to remove the party from interfering with the judicial system have considerably depoliticized the judiciary. This is not to suggest that the courts are completely fair and nonpolitical, because that is certainly not the case. "Telephone justice" (party or government officials fixing cases), bribery of officials, and other such problems persist, but enormous improvements have been made. Further, although the Soviet Union has an elite to whom it tends to give advantages, social prejudice and consequent uneven justice are now far diminished as compared to those of previous periods.

Proportional representation of gender has become a concern, and considerable effort has been made to increase the part women play in the law. At present, half of all people's assessors and about one-fourth of all judges are women. Once at the mercy of amateurs, the Soviet judiciary has become a professional institution, applying the law fairly throughout the society. Moreover, the government continues to reform its legal codes, albeit slowly. Among the reforms and intended reforms are a reduction in the number of crimes that carry the death penalty, a reduction in the maximum prison sentence from 15 to 10 years, and abolition of interior exile.

Crime and punishment. Soviet law prohibits virtually all the same acts that violate criminal statutes in the West, but as a society based on collectivist norms, it also exhibits some differences in the law and its applicability. Soviet law includes several criminal statutes not found in Western codes. Two of these are particularly noteworthy. The constitution dubs it a "duty and a matter of honor" for all able-bodied citizens to engage in socially

[34]Article 155 of the Soviet Constitution.

productive labor.[35] Thus, the *antiparasite* laws were implemented, making it a punishable crime not to work. In the 1950s and 1960s considerable abuse occurred in this area of the law; offenders were tried by ad hoc citizens' courts that could condemn convicted defendants to as many as five years at forced labor. Public outcries, especially from the legal community, about notorious abuses of these laws led to reforms in the late 1960s and early 1970s. Today, a person refusing to engage in socially productive labor can be tried in the regular courts and receive up to a year imprisonment if convicted.

Speculation, the purchase and resale of goods for profit, is also still against the law in many cases. Serious violation of this law can bring up to five years in prison. Although some market activity is now allowed, many forms of private ownership and making private profit are still viewed as an anathema in the society. More will be said about the legal forms of profit making in Chapters 8 and 9.

Punishment for crime is also somewhat peculiar in the Soviet system. Harkening to their assumed task of creating a new, more cooperative society and also perhaps influenced by the ancient Russian tradition of preferring contrition to punishment for social deviance, Soviet courts tend to be rather lenient with first-time offenders. Very minor crimes can be atoned for by an upbraiding from the judge and a sincere expression of remorse (self-criticism) by the defendant. Perpetrators of serious crimes and repeat offenders are dealt with more harshly, but recent reforms have reduced the penalties for certain crimes. Fines are not heavy in the Soviet Union, but, consistent with the Soviet work ethic, an offender can be sentenced to additional work at his or her regular employment or perhaps on some public project.

Relatively little is known about the Soviet penal system since it, as with so many other things, has long been shrouded in secrecy. Recently, however, Western media, human rights organizations, and individuals have been allowed to visit some Soviet penal institutions. The Soviet government maintains three kinds of detention centers: local prisons, labor camps, and penitentiaries. These institutions are administered by the Ministry of Internal Affairs and supervised by the procurator-general of the USSR.

Soviet authorities are fond of saying that rather than allowing their social deviates to languish in prison, they are put to productive labor while incarcerated. Apparently some outside observers agree with this approach. Charles W. "Chuck" Colson, a former aide to President Richard M. Nixon, who was imprisoned for his part in the Watergate scandal, has since worked to reform American prisons. He was invited to tour five Soviet prisons and emerged a devotee of the Soviet practice of requiring inmates to work. "One of the troubles with American prisons," he said after visiting Soviet prisons and labor camps, "is that we don't give prisoners meaningful labor." However, Colson was less complimentary about other aspects of Soviet prisons, claiming that visiting privileges are inadequate and punishment

---

[35]Article 60 of the Soviet Constitution.

Stark and lonely, Leningrad's Peter and Paul Fortress stands as a reminder of the Tsarist past. Originally used as a fortress, Peter and Paul's was converted into a prison that housed such personages as Feodor Dostoevsky, Sergei Nechayev, and Maxim Gorky. The chapel beneath the spire houses the tombs of the tsars since Peter the Great.

cells are "repressive." Colson heads an organization called Prison Fellowship, which gives Bible training to over 50,000 American inmates in 600 prisons. Interestingly, the Soviet government has invited him to establish a chapter of the organization in the Soviet Union.[36]

Local prisons are apparently used primarily for pretrial detention; yet, there are a number of penitentiaries to which some of the society's most incorrigible criminals are sent.[37] The bulk of those sentenced to imprisonment, however, are held in labor camps. A recent State Department report to Congress estimated that there are approximately 4 million people in the 1,100 Soviet labor camps, and although Gorbachev has released thousands of people classified as political prisoners, Amnesty International estimates that over 100 still remain behind bars, in mental institutions, or in the camps.

There are four kinds of labor camps: standard-regimen, intensified-regimen, strict-regimen, and special-regimen. Prisoners are assigned to the various camps on the basis of the seriousness of their crimes and their previous criminal records. Conditions in the camps—never pleasant—become more drastic as one approaches the special-regimen level. Receiving some of the worst offenders, the special-regimen camps assign the hardest

[36]George W. Cornell of the Associated Press as reported in "Crusader Sees Lesson in Soviet Prisons," *Escondido Times Advocate,* May 26, 1990.

[37]See Avraham Shifrin, *The First Guidebook to Prisons and Concentration Camps of the Soviet Union* (New York: Bantam, 1982).

labor and provide the poorest food, clothing, and shelter. Prisoners in the special-regimen camps are allowed one letter per month, two visits by relatives per year, and, after having served half of their term, one ten-pound package of food and clothing per year. Following two days of hearings in Moscow during 1990, the Vienna-based Helsinki Federation for Human Rights reported that conditions in Soviet prisons and camps are far below United Nations standards; beatings are common, there is overcrowding, and food and medical facilities are poor (over 70 percent of the country's tuberculosis cases are reputedly among former prisoners).[38]

Besides assigning fines, extra work, and prison sentences, Soviet judges can condemn convicted prisoners to death by shooting. The death penalty was abolished in 1947 but was quickly reestablished in 1950 as part of a general get-tough policy in efforts to re-create prewar discipline in the society. Through the 1950s and 1960s, more and more violations were added to the list of capital crimes. The Soviet authorities announce executions each year as they occur. Capital crimes in the Soviet Union include the usual array of serious offenses: murder, treason, terrorism, sabotage, espionage, heinous rape, and murder and attempted murder of a policeman.

Having completed our study of the legislative, executive, and judicial agencies in the Soviet Union, we now turn to an examination of other institutions that are also important in the Soviet political society.

---

[38]John-Thor Dahlburg, "Soviet Rights Violations Found to Persist," *The Los Angeles Times,* June 5, 1990.

chapter 6

The Military
and the Police

THE MILITARY

Not unlike other countries, the Soviet Union has been concerned with the potential political power of its military since its inception. During the tsarist period, Raymond Garthoff points out, the military influenced policy but was seldom allowed to formulate it. The great expansion into Central Asia and the Far East between 1860 and 1885 was accomplished largely because of Russian military prowess, but the impetus for it was primarily civilian.[1] Indeed, the greatest political significance of the military during the tsarist period was its steadfast loyalty and support of the system.

Interestingly enough, however, the reliability of the military under the Romanovs was, as with most of the rest of the population, seriously eroded—largely as a result of unsuccessful wars during the nineteenth and early twentieth centuries. Disgruntled military officers led the Decembrist revolt of 1825. The Crimean War in the 1850s and the Russo-Japanese War of 1904–1905 discredited and demoralized the military. Finally, the senseless slaughter of World War I (1914–1918) saw the military humiliated, and

[1]Raymond L. Garthoff, *Soviet Military Policy* (London: Faber & Faber, 1966), pp. 6–7.

its support of the Romanovs disintegrated. Consequently, elements of the military radicalized and eventually helped bring the Bolsheviks to power in 1917.

Inherently potent in a contest of power, the military posed serious problems for the Soviet leaders. Lenin and Trotsky were inclined to see the military dissolved and replaced with a citizens' militia. This plan, however, was truncated by the imperatives of the Russian Civil War (1918–1921). Desperate to prevail over the White armies, the Bolsheviks found themselves forced not only to organize the Red Army, but also to employ the services of about 50,000 officers and 200,000 noncommissioned officers from the old Imperial Army.

Insistent that the loyalty of the former imperial soldiers be monitored, Lenin appointed political commissars to each military unit. These party officials enjoyed considerable authority over military commanders, even to the point of the countermanding orders viewed as politically suspect. The Red Army was far from a duplicate of the tsarist force in other respects as well. Officers' privileges were severely reduced, rank was deemphasized, and the tsarist insignia and epaulets vanished.

The organizational genius of Leon Trotsky galvanized the Red Army into a formidable force. As it gradually destroyed its opponents, it often was responsible for establishing Bolshevik-controlled trade unions and local soviets. Thus, the Soviet military machine played a significant political role in addition to its martial task. Yet, after the Civil War, the military was cut back to about 600,000 troops, as the Soviet Union assumed a defensive posture in foreign policy. Isolated by the West in an effort to strangle the fledgling socialist state, the Soviet Union secretly cooperated with Germany (Europe's other "outcast" state) during the interwar period. The Soviet rulers provided locations for secret German maneuvers in exchange for weapons and officer training from 1919 to 1935.[2]

The Civil War had given stature to the Soviet military. It had produced a cadre of great leaders, including Tukhachevsky, Budenny, Bluecher, Frunze, and Voroshilov. Already enjoying special rations of food and goods, as well as preference in placing their sons in military schools, the officer corps won several concessions from Stalin by the early 1930s. Officers' salaries were substantially increased, separating them from the lower ranks. Insignia, epaulets, and rank—paraphernalia reminiscent of the imperial regime—were reinstated. Social groups, vacation spas, low rent, travel, educational advantages, and special recreation were also bestowed upon the officers, underscoring their growing elite status.[3]

Salutary as the officer corps may have considered these advantages, Stalin exacted a heavier toll from the military than from any other group in the blood purges of 1936 to 1939. Especially targeting the Old Bolsheviks in its ranks, Stalin expunged no less than one-fourth of the officer corps during these years, including three of the five marshals, all but two of the

[2]Garthoff, pp. 11–18.

[3]Mervyn Matthews, *Privilege in the Soviet Union* (London: George Allen & Unwin, 1978), pp. 68, 108; Garthoff, pp. 35–36.

15 army commanders, 57 of the 85 corps commanders, and 110 of the 195 division commanders.[4]

This frightening toll was accompanied by increased party control over the day-to-day operation of the military. The role of political commissars was gradually increased until combat in Finland discredited it. Following some experimentation with various methodologies, Stalin finally replaced the commissars in 1942 with the *Zampolit* (Deputy Commanders for Political Affairs)—political officers responsible for the morale and political training of the troops but having no right to interfere with questions of military significance.

The threat of Nazi conquest persuaded Stalin to allow the military a considerable amount of political independence while the war lasted. Once Hitler was destroyed, however, Stalin moved quickly to assure his own omnipotence by downgrading the influence of the military, stepping up secret police surveillance, and increasing party control. Paranoid to the end, Stalin threatened to evoke a new blood purge. This abortive purge—the Doctors' Purge—manifested every indication that prominent military leaders were slated for extermination.[5] Apparently, only Stalin's death forestalled a new round of hideous bloodletting.

Post-Stalinist Political Power of the Military

The political power enjoyed by the Soviet military has always been a matter of considerable debate among scholars. The fact that the imperial military was relatively apolitical, combined with early efforts by the party to control the military after the revolution, sufficed to keep the military from assuming great political power during the early history of the Soviet Union.

Stalin's death, however, ended two and a half decades of personal dictatorship, instantaneously elevating the political potency of several institutions, including the party, the economic managers, the secret police, and the military. A coalition between party leader Khrushchev and Minister of Defense Grigory Zhukov managed to prevail over Beria's NKVD and Malenkov's government technocrats. Khrushchev became politically dominant, the secret police was reorganized, and Zhukov was rewarded with promotion to the Politburo and a high military budget.[6]

With Malenkov and his allies defeated, Khrushchev took stock of the situation. While Khrushchev had been consolidating power in the party, Zhukov had done the same in the military and was pressuring for increased independence of the military from party control. Hence, Khrushchev decided that Zhukov had to be tamed and the military brought firmly under his thumb. Using Zhukov's adversaries in the military for support, Khrushchev removed Zhukov from both the Ministry of Defense and the Politburo in October 1957. Marshal Rodion Malinovsky replaced Zhukov as minister of defense but did not succeed to the vacant Politburo seat.

[4]Matthews, p. 36.
[5]Matthews, pp. 44–45.
[6]Garthoff, pp. 48–49.

This episode ended the era in which the Soviet military played its most active role in Kremlin politics. Although the military seems to have played no part in Khrushchev's ouster in 1964, it witnessed his fall with no remorse, since his politics had become unpopular with it as with other elements in the country.

The military's political influence rose significantly during the tenure of Leonid Brezhnev. Impelled by the policy of achieving military parity with the United States, Brezhnev channeled vast resources into the military and through the schools and media extolled its role as defender of communism. Brezhnev's decision to pursue a policy of détente also worked to the military's advantage because he promoted the minister of defense to the Politburo.

The year before he died, Brezhnev clearly lost influence in Kremlin politics. Responding to his weakness, contenders for succession began maneuvering for power. The winning alliance included Foreign Minister Andrei Gromyko, former KGB head Yuri Andropov, and Defense Minister Dmitri Ustinov, thus implicating the military in another significant role in Kremlin politics. When Andropov died, Ustinov and Gromyko again united to support Chernenko's bid for power.

Ustinov's death in 1984, however, seems to have marked a decline in the political fortunes of the military. He was succeeded as defense minister by Marshal Sergei L. Sokolov, an aging military man. But Sokolov was not given Ustinov's seat on the Politburo as a full member, having to content himself with no more than candidate membership. Only a few months later, Gorbachev was elected general secretary by a 5–4 vote in the Politburo. Anxious to subject the military to his will, Gorbachev jumped at the opportunity to purge the high command when it was embarrassed on May 28, 1987, by a 19-year-old West German pilot, Mathias Rust. Incredibly, the pilot eluded Soviet air defenses on a flight from Finland and landed his private plane in Moscow's Red Square. Sokolov and other ranking military personnel were fired, and Gorbachev bypassed several aging commanders and personally picked General Dmitri T. Yazov for defense minister and for a candidate seat on the Politburo. Under Gorbachev the military has been at a relatively low ebb politically, suffering serious reductions in its budget, troop strength, and activity. There are signs, however, that it is beginning to assert itself politically once more, which we will examine later in this chapter.

Military Structure and Party Control

The Soviet military has about 4.2 million persons and is divided into five branches, including Land Forces, Strategic Missile Forces, Air Defense Forces, the Air Force, and the Navy. These branches are augmented by logistical support and civil defense staffs and troops. Additionally, large contingents of troops are maintained by the KGB and the Ministry of Interior as border guards and internal security forces. These troops, however, are not technically part of the military and will be discussed later.

Ultimate command over the armed services is placed in the Defense

Council. Appointed by the Supreme Soviet and chaired by Gorbachev, this group is something of an enigma as little in detail is known about it. The Ministry of Defense administers the armed forces on a day-to-day basis, and each branch of the service is capped by commanders who hold the posts of deputy ministers of defense. Since most of the ranking Defense Ministry personnel are military people, civilian control of the military depends on its subordination to the Defense Council and to the authority the Communist Party has traditionally exerted over those in uniform.

The interlocking directorate that once so strongly existed between the party and government still exists in the military. An estimated 90 percent of all officers are members of the party or the Komsomol. Although a small number of specialists have achieved the rank of general without being party members, virtually every officer from colonel and above is in the party.

Simple party membership, however, may not assure the loyalty of any particular officer since it could be used as only a necessary step in career advancement. Hence four other major steps are taken to guarantee party control. First, the secret police carefully scrutinize the military, vigilant for potential problems with loyalty and commitment. Second, each military unit includes a PPO or Komsomol organization that carries out agitation and propaganda among the troops. Third, the Zampolit still directs political training and morale sessions among the troops while closely watching the officers for signs of political transgressions. Fourth, the Main Political Administration, technically part of the defense ministry but in reality controlled by the party, directs the work of the Zampolit, the PPOs, and the Komsomol units in the military.

The tradition in the military for political noninvolvement also serves as an internal check. Yet, the elaborate apparatus assuring party dominance indicates that the party takes no chances where this potentially powerful institution is concerned. As the party retreats from active involvement in the governance of the society's institutions, however, its dominance over the military will almost certainly relax as well. Indeed, the Committee for Constitutional Compliance has already ruled unconstitutional military regulations binding the armed forces to Communist Party policies, and the military has announced that it is reducing the number of its Zampolit by 37 percent.[7] Whether or not this evolution will necessitate developing new means by which to assure civilian control of the military is impossible to say at this point.

Privilege in the Military

Until Gorbachev became general secretary, no institution in Soviet society except the party enjoyed the vaunted position of the military. To sustain public support for massive military budgets, Brezhnev maintained a steady barrage of films, posters, literature, plays, and speeches reminding

[7]Michael Parks, "Communist Military Role Ruled Invalid" *The Los Angeles Times,* April 6, 1991.

people of the terror of World War II and of the glorious and victorious efforts of the military. Even though this propaganda effort has been considerably reduced under Gorbachev, the military still assumes a high profile in the Soviet Union. Children receive military training in school at an early age, young men are drafted upon leaving school, reservists are periodically called up for training until they reach the age of 50, and civil defense facilities permeate the society. In addition, millions of people belong to clubs sponsored by the Voluntary Committee for Assistance to the Armed Forces (DOSAAF); club members participate in parachuting, marksmanship, dog breeding, and dozens of other activities of military value.

Yet, the once positive public attitude about the armed forces has abated considerably. The defeat in Afghanistan, revelations of corruption and waste in the ranks, brutality against recruits and its attempted cover-ups, Gorbachev's own seeming indifference to martial ceremony and decoration, the new intense focus on domestic affairs, the disintegration of the Soviet bloc, and reduced global political tensions have combined to reduce public esteem and support for the military. Even at the height of its popularity, however, the military did not escape Soviet humor. Vasily Ivanovich Chapaev, a Civil War hero, was endlessly lauded as part of the propaganda effort on behalf of the military. In response, Soviet jokesters depict him and his loyal friend Pyotr as hopelessly stupid:

> Chapaev and Pyotr jump from a plane with the intent of opening their chutes only at the last minute. At 100 feet from the ground, Pyotr asks, "Shall we pull the cord now?"
>
> Not yet," replies the intrepid Chapaev.
>
> "Now, Vasily Ivanovich? It's only 50 feet."
>
> "Too soon," replies Chapaev.
>
> "We are only three feet from the ground!" screams Pyotr.
>
> "Ah then," Chapaev says confidently, "From here we can jump without a chute."

Esteemed or not, the Soviet military—or at least its officer corps—enjoys important advantages in the society. It should be noted at the beginning that a very clear distinction is made between officers and the soldiers in the ranks. Military service for the ordinary conscript can be a grueling, lonely experience, about which more will be said later. For officers, however, it is quite a different matter, regardless of how unegalitarian this dichotomy may be.

Except for a brief period immediately following the revolution, the Soviet military has long enjoyed privileged status. Among other concessions, early Red Army members were awarded Red Star Cards, entitling them to special rations. As time passed, officers saw their income augmented by the reduction of rent and tax payments and the extension of free education and travel privileges. Joseph Stalin pampered the military with rank and insignia; he even reinstated some of the old tsarist regalia, such as shoulder boards. To this day the Soviet military is the only martial organization in the world whose officers sport epaulets, velvet lapels, and dress daggers.[8]

In spite of Khrushchev's efforts to reduce privileges among the Soviet elite, including the military, the officer class has been among the most successful of Soviet institutions at accumulating special treatment. Officer pay is comparatively high, with salaries for colonels and higher ranks reaching elite levels.[9] Moreover, officers are entitled to shop in special stores featuring otherwise scarce or unobtainable items at cut-rate prices. Officers' clubs are lavishly appointed and staffed with efficient, polite service personnel. Field officers have personal orderlies, and their housing is far above average. The Ministry of Defense maintains a network of vacation and health spas in the country's best locations; military officials enjoy resorts equipped with excellent accoutrements, including elaborate recreational and entertainment facilities.

Authorities on the subject report an interesting social phenomenon taking place within the ranks of the officer corps. There is a growing tendency for military families to intermarry; the sons of these unions enjoy special entry to military academies. Hence, it is speculated that a military caste is beginning to develop as successive generations of the same families assume ranking positions in the armed forces. If this observation is correct, a new version of an old theme in Russian culture may be emerging: the stratification of society, with certain families providing the bulk of the high-level military leaders. The ever-active Soviet humor mill gives recognition to this phenomenon by telling of an army general answering questions from his grandson.

> Grandson: "Can I become a soldier grandfather?"
>
> General: "Yes you can, my boy."
>
> Grandson: "Will I ever become a general?"
>
> General: "I think you can become a general, if you work hard."
>
> Grandson: "Do you think I could even become a marshal?"
>
> General: "Not a marshal, my boy, the marshals have grandsons of their own."

Conditions in the Ranks

The comely benefits afforded the officer corps are far from duplicated among enlisted personnel, who are routinely conscripted for service. Upon arriving at their units, draftees find that they get the worst of a bad situation. Subjected to ***dedovshchina*** (rough hazing), they are assigned dou-

[8]Garthoff, p. 37.
[9]Matthews, pp. 27, 33.

ble shifts at the dirtiest details, the worst food, the shabbiest quarters, and the poorest sleeping accommodations. Even worse, gangs of roughs have formed, intimidating officers. Weapons are stolen and make their way to the black market. In other cases, soldiers actually rent their weapons and vehicles to the numerous ethnic national guard units that have organized illegally, while the Soviet commanders turn their eyes away from the larceny. These gangs also attack their fellow soldiers. Numerous homosexual rapes and torturous beatings of new conscripts are reported each year. Some critics claim that 15,000 young men were killed by such treatment between 1987 and 1990—as many deaths as the Soviets suffered in their 10-year war in Afghanistan.[10]

Seniority brings only marginal improvement, however, since discipline is strict and life is hard. Enlisted men's and, presumably, women's food usually consists of a gruel-like soup, cabbage, potatoes, dried or canned fish, tea, and black bread. Meat is infrequently available and is usually limited to salt pork. Enjoying but a single hot meal per day, recruits gain weight at about half the normal rate.[11]

On land, soldiers are housed in long, single-room, wooden barracks crowded with beds. At sea, sailors are often assigned to "warm bunks," beds shared in two or even three shifts. Although pay for noncommissioned officers is kept at reasonable levels, the men in the ranks are paid only a pittance.

Soviet military bases are often located in remote areas, affording little diversion for their troops. Denied long furloughs except for family emergencies, the men are given a single one-day pass each month. Receiving mail infrequently, isolated from wives and family, and having few recreational or entertainment facilities, the soldiers on base soon settle into a boring, painfully lonely existence. Off-duty hours are sometimes spent playing chess, playing soccer, or reading, but most often the men just drink.

Alcoholism is a mammoth problem in the Soviet Union, but nowhere is it as bad as in the military. Some authorities estimate that fully one-third of the people in uniform drink excessively on a regular basis. Earning so little, men are forced to resort to desperate methods to secure spirits. Favorite sources of alcohol are potent moonshine (*samogon*), eau de cologne (which often sells out on the day of arrival at commissaries), antifreeze and brake fluid pilfered from military vehicles, and de-icer drained from aircraft. There have even been reported cases of recruits spreading shoe polish on bread, allowing the sun to render the alcohol downward, and then eating the bottom portions of the bread. Such resourceful methods of providing relief from boredom not only result in drunkenness but sometimes end in blindness or even death for their hapless practitioners.

Occasionally, the dreary routine of camp life is relieved by films and by Zampolit-led tours of museums and monuments. Even less often, com-

---

[10]Elizabeth Shogren, "Red Army Killing Its Own?," *The Los Angeles Times,* July 31, 1990.
[11]Cullen Murphy, "Watching the Russians," *The Atlantic Monthly,* Feb. 1983, p. 30.

A group of Soviet sailors in Kiev. (Photo provided by Louis and Helen Van Moppes.)

manders may provide a "social evening" during which prostitutes are allowed on base.[12]

Racism is another serious problem in the Soviet military. The military has long been held up as an example of Soviet unity. It is considered to be one of the great assimilating institutions in society. Russian is the only language officially used in the ranks, and it is contended that young men are brought from all corners of the country in all their diversity and molded into a single united nation. The myth, however, is far removed from the reality.

Actually, racial bigotry is widespread in the ranks. Russian anti-Semitism is well known, but other minorities—especially the Central Asians, with perhaps 40 percent of these recruits speaking Russian poorly, if at all—have suffered Slavic prejudice as well. Central Asians have always been given menial tasks in the military. Indeed, even at the height of World War II, when the Soviets buckled at the furious Nazi onslaught, Stalin refused to arm his Central Asian legions, preferring instead to see them relegated to support roles behind the lines.

Today we find the situation changed only as it is seriously aggravated by demographics. Slavs are virtually at zero population growth, but the Central Asian population is increasing in unprecedented numbers. In the

[12]Moscow's Military Machine," *Time Magazine*, June 23, 1980.

mid-1960s, one of every 15 Soviet citizens was a Central Asian, but by 1980 the ratio had become one in six. This increase means that a very large percentage of the new recruits to the armed forces are from Central Asia. By the year 2000, almost one-third of the draft-age cohort in the Soviet population will be Central Asians. Until the present, most of these young men have been denied service in the air force, artillery, navy, and other high-tech areas. Almost 50 percent of the Soviet army consists of minorities because Slavs are given preference for more demanding service; perhaps as high as 75 to 80 percent of all Central Asians in the military are assigned to construction battalions.

The "yellowing of the Red Army" has grown to such proportions that reports of racial tension frequently surface. Often entering the service without an adequate knowledge of the Russian language or certain skills as basic to a modern military organization as driving, Central Asians frequently bear the brunt of jokes and harassment by their Slavic comrades. Name-calling, cruel pranks, and undisguised racial hatred combine to divide people in the ranks. These problems lead to unequal task assignments, low morale, and frequent fighting among enlisted personnel. The end result of these racial problems is that they erode discipline and seriously inhibit the effectiveness of many units.

The depth of this problem became obvious after the Soviet invasion of Afghanistan. A large number of troops in the December 1979 Soviet invasion force were Central Asians. Their poor performance betrayed a lack of training. Moreover, the Soviet Muslims alarmed their superiors by fraternizing with their Afghan co-religionists. By February 1980 the Soviet commanders had already begun to withdraw their Central Asian units, replacing them with European divisions. The loyalty of Central Asians has been seriously questioned as Russian soldiers returning from Afghanistan have complained that some Central Asians "would rather shoot Russians than Afghans."[13]

The draft, mutinies, and desertions.   As one might imagine, few young men volunteer for the service. Instead, all young men must register for the draft when they turn 17 years of age. At 18, they are inducted into the service: Those born in the first half of the year go in in May and those born later enter the military in November. Draftees into the navy serve a three-year hitch, all others serve for two years. Women are not drafted. Indeed only about 12,000 women are currently in the Soviet military.[14] In order to join, they must have had special training in medicine, radio operations, cryptography, cartography, clerical skills, and so on. Women soldiers perform clerical, medical, and administrative roles.

Because the overall Soviet population growth rate is declining, the military is expecting to encounter an increasingly difficult time in getting

[13]Robert Gillette, "Soviet Veterans Bitter after Afghan War Duty," *The Los Angeles Times,* Apr. 4, 1983.
[14]Jeff Trimble, Robin Knight, and Robert Kaylor, "Building a Military Machine," *U.S. News and World Report,* March 13, 1989.

the 1.5 million new recruits it needs annually. Deferments from the draft can be given for physical reasons and family hardship. Conscientious objectors are barely tolerated in the Soviet Union. They must enter the service, but they are assigned to construction battalions or other noncombat roles. If they refuse to serve, they may be imprisoned.

Although some young men look forward to military service as a way to escape the boredom and drudgery of rural life, the growing unpopularity of the military, its harsh conditions, diseases among the troops, and aggravated battle casualties from the Afghanistan war have encouraged vast numbers of youngsters to seek deferments. The current deferment rate is about 30 percent. Although the military is trying to reduce the deferment rate, the Supreme Soviet aggravated the situation in 1990 by adding attendance at post-secondary educational institutions to the list of deferment criteria, and it withdrew from the Ministry of Defense the right to determine the annual number of inductees.

This legislation was passed in response to the growing resistance to the draft. The newly assertive union republic governments want more control over the draft, the military bases, and the test ranges. They object to the practice of not allowing their youth to serve in military units in their home republics, and they decry racism and the brutality of *dedovshchina*. A group in the Baltic and Georgia calling itself Geneva-49 after the 1949 Geneva Convention claims that its members are occupied peoples, thus their children cannot be made to serve in the Soviet military. More officially, in the spring of 1990 the Armenian Supreme Soviet, after having formed its own military units to protect the republic in its struggle with neighboring Azerbaijan, suspended the national draft in its territory (an illegal move) until the USSR took measures to assure the safety of its young men in the ranks. Latvia, Lithuania, and Estonia each passed laws (again illegally) providing for alternative service to spending time in the Soviet armed forces.[15] In December 1990 Gorbachev decreed that efforts to form republican military units or to suspend the national draft would not be tolerated. At the same time, thousands upon thousands of young men risked prison terms by refusing to appear for induction. The problem became so severe that the government was forced to suspend all inductions for one month in the spring of 1990. By that time, draft evasion had increased eightfold since 1988.[16] In 1990 only 79 percent of the inductees called appeared for service, with the greatest number of no-shows coming from the Baltic, Georgia, Armenia, Moldavia, and the Western Ukraine. Accordingly, in 1991 Gorbachev ordered squads of soldiers to pursue the delinquent recruits, causing heated resentment in the union republics.[17]

Perhaps even more serious, the number of desertions by men already in the military rose precipitously, reaching 4,300 in 1990. Lithuania, having abortively declared its independence, encouraged its young men to leave

[15]Paul Hofheinz, "Heading for a Showdown," *Time Magazine,* Aug. 6, 1990.

[16]"Trouble Among Soviet Troops," *The Los Angeles Times,* May 10, 1990.

[17]John-Thor Dahlburg, "Troops Ordered to Baltics to Capture Draft Dodgers," *The Los Angeles Times,* Jan. 8, 1991.

their Soviet military units and come home. Pursued by the authorities, many of the youths who did so were hidden by the Lithuanian people and by the state. Indeed, the Ministry of Defense charges that some of the youngsters were given passports by the Lithuanian government to aid them in their escape from the military. Other recruits from Moldavia, Armenia, Azerbaijan, and the Ukraine have deserted in increasing numbers to escape the brutality and racism they encountered in the military. Additionally, several Russian soldiers sent to keep the peace in Georgia and other republics stricken with ethnic violence have deserted, claiming disagreement with the government's policies.[18] Several air force pilots have also defected, flying their top secret aircraft to the West. The most recent of these flew a MIG-29 to Turkey in 1989.

Mutiny has also been an enduring problem for the Soviet military. In 1985, 80 soldiers were reported killed in a day-long uprising of Tadzhik troops who rebelled after one of their number was executed for setting off an explosion in their base in Afghanistan. There have been several mutinies aboard Soviet military vessels, and in 1990, *Izvestia* (the government newspaper) even admitted that the cruiser *Storozovoi* had a mutiny in 1975, an event long suspected by Western intelligence experts. Stories of this mutiny became the basis of Tom Clancy's novel, *The Hunt for Red October*. Akin to mutiny is the alarming number of murders of officers, presumably by their own troops. In 1987 one officer was murdered, in 1988 two, but in 1989, 59 officers were killed.[19]

The USSR Supreme Soviet, in trying to deal with the mounting problems in the military, is considering several reforms. In an effort to put Afghanistan in the past, the Supreme Soviet voted in 1989 to give amnesty to soldiers who deserted to the West during the war.[20] Further, it is looking at a Gorbachev proposal to consolidate several of the branches; it is thinking about reducing the time of service for the ethnic minorities; and it is even considering eliminating the draft altogether. Although the senior military staff resists these ideas, the junior officers are more flexible.

Military Training

Officer training is apparently relatively good in the Soviet Union, and senior officers are respected in the West as highly skilled professionals. About 135 military colleges turn out approximately 50,000 junior lieutenants each year. Eleven staff colleges offer advanced courses to senior officers. Even so, experts have noted many deficiencies in Soviet training, among which is the tendency of officers to be reluctant to take the initiative, preferring the safety of "by-the-book" conformity.

Just as benefits differ between officers and enlisted personnel, so too

[18]Elizabeth Shogren, "For a Russian Deserter, Georgia's Fight for Independence Is Personal," *The Los Angeles Times*, April 2, 1991.

[19]"59 Soviet Officers Killed Last Year in Murder Wave," *The Los Angeles Times*, March 20, 1990.

[20]"In Moscow," *The Los Angeles Times*, Sept. 18, 1989.

does the training. Perhaps less severe than in the imperial days when the slogan was "beat two to death and train the third," Soviet training and discipline are still very harsh. Given only 30 days of boot camp, because they are already supposed to have had fairly extensive military training in school, recruits find themselves run through the same unimaginative maneuvers time and again. Consequently, Soviet troops learn little more than their own specific tasks and are unable to exchange roles. Taught to rely on orders from their officers, the Soviet soldiers' versatility under battle conditions is questionable. With a growing number of recruits coming from the minority populations, communications is a problem. Many minority youths are nonconversant in Russian, the language of the military. Hence, it takes inordinate amounts of time to train recruits for even the simplest tasks—driving, for example.

However, training under even the best conditions is far below the level received in Western military units. For instance, only Soviet officers and noncommissioned officers are trained in map reading, an absolutely essential skill on the field of battle. Moreover, the troops are given little practice with their weapons, which are usually locked away except when a unit is on maneuvers. Construction battalions often never see rifles at all, and Soviet tank crews fire an average of only six practice rounds per year. In contrast, American tank gunners average 36 rounds. Indeed, it seems that the recruits are kept so ignorant about their weapons and equipment that the officers find it necessary to perform the most difficult tasks themselves.[21]

Gorbachev and the Generals

In the mid-1980s Gorbachev called for the nations of the world to join him in exercising **new thinking** in military and foreign policy. As an important facet in this approach, he concluded that the political hostilities between East and West since World War II were counterproductive. Not only did the arms races fail to make either side more secure—in fact, the opposite could be argued, but the United States and the Soviet Union were also squandering their human and natural resources on exotic arsenals while Western Europe and Japan were becoming economic giants.[22] Further, he recognized that military superiority, or even parity with the West, was no longer necessary to deter aggression, given the magnitude of modern weapons. (See Table 6–1.)

At the same time, the Soviet Union found itself spending 15 to 17 percent of its gross national product (GNP, an estimate of the total value of the goods and services produced in a year) on defense. It was also using between 30 and 40 percent of its scientists, committing half of its machine-building capacity, and devoting the best of its production of almost every type to the military—when these resources could be put to the production

[21]Andrew Cockburn, *The Threat: Inside the Soviet Military Machine* (New York: Random House, 1983), p. 164.

[22]Mikhail Gorbachev, *Perestroika: New Thinking for Our Country and the World* (New York: Harper & Row, 1987), pp. 190–252.

TABLE 6–1   Balance of Strategic Weapons
(September 1985)*

	Delivery Vehicles	Warheads
Soviet Union	2,493	9,900
United States	1,935	12,200

*By 1983 the Soviet Union and the United States had a combined total of 9,852 megatons deployed in deliverable nuclear warheads. (A megaton is a measurement equivalent to the explosive power of one million tons of TNT.) It is estimated that the total amount of explosive energy released in the entire European theater of World War II equaled only 3.5 megatons.

9,852 megatons ÷ 3.5 megatons = 2,815

2,815 ÷ 365 days = 7.71

Hence, the United States and the Soviet Union in 1983 had enough nuclear energy in their combined arsenals to detonate explosive power equal to the European theater of World War II each day for the next seven years and 259 days. The megatonnage in the two arsenals is, of course, much greater now. With such destructive capacity in the hands of each superpower, the meaning of parity or superiority is moot, since each can easily destroy the other using only a fraction of its warheads.

of consumer goods and to the improvement of the competitiveness of the Soviet economy. Gorbachev also recognized that the playing field of international competition had changed from military might to economic prowess. Hence, he announced that "reasonable military sufficiency" rather than parity or superiority would be the Soviet defense goal; by word and deed, he set out to dramatically change Soviet military and foreign policy.

After Gorbachev took the opportunity of Mathias Rust's embarrassing flight to appoint new people to the general staff, the bellicosity of Soviet foreign policy and military statements toned down considerably, and Gorbachev announced that the Soviet Union would pull its troops out of Afghanistan. The withdrawal was completed by February 1989. Additionally, Soviet spokespersons began to reflect on the country's foreign policy, claiming that several mistakes had been made: for example, invading Afghanistan (actually the Soviet military had originally opposed the invasion but it was overruled by Brezhnev, and in fact a ranking general was fired for his negative position), deploying the SS-20 missiles in Europe, building an illegal military radar facility at Krasnoyarsk, continuing to amass toxic weapons after the United States stopped its own stockpiling of such weapons in 1969, and building up its military capacity far beyond what was reasonably necessary. The 1939 German-Soviet Nonaggression Pact was condemned as was the 1968 Soviet invasion of Czechoslovakia, and the Soviet Union, for the first time, disavowed the policy of exporting revolution.

An open debate about military matters was also encouraged for the first time in the Soviet Union. Some once-classified details are now in the public domain, and Gorbachev is trying to stir public support for his policy of reducing the size and arms of the military. Not only is the media encouraged to look critically at the military, but civilian academics are also now heavily engaged in analyzing military doctrine and advising political leaders as to their conclusions. These "defense intellectuals" are now found in many leading institutes and universities, when previously only civilians working for the Ministry of Defense or a few other key government agencies were allowed access to data needed for analysis. Furthermore, the ministers of foreign affairs and defense report regularly to the Supreme Soviet and the Congress of Peoples' Deputies, and these bodies have begun to investigate the operations of these departments. Beginning in 1989 the premier also reports to the parliament, detailing the nonclassified military expenditures of the government. Some of the strongest critics of the military in the Congress of Peoples' Deputies are themselves junior officers (military personnel may serve in the Soviet parliament). One of them, Army Major Vladimir Lopatin, has upbraided military officials and proposed far-reaching reforms of the armed service. The specter of a major publicly calling the generals to account is so bizarre that it has stimulated this riddle:

> What is the highest rank in the army?
>
> Peoples' Deputy.

Military exchanges have also begun between the Soviet Union and the West, especially with the United States. Soviet and American warships have visited each other's ports; groups of scientists have exchanged visits at the nuclear weapons production plants of the two countries; Minister of Defense Yazov visited the Pentagon, and the American Secretaries of Defense Frank Carlucci and Richard Cheney returned the call in the Soviet Union; and high ranking military people of each government have appeared to testify before the other's national legislature.

These ties, however, did not develop overnight. Perhaps justifiably, the Reagan administration and later the Bush administration approached Gorbachev's liberalization policies very cautiously. They wanted deeds, not words. Gorbachev's first gesture, a unilateral moratorium on nuclear weapons tests from August 1985 to February 1987 was ignored by the United States, as has been his offer to stop all further testing if the United States does the same. Gorbachev persisted, however, and in December 1987, the United States and the Soviet Union reached an historic agreement to reduce intermediate-range nuclear weapons (the SS-20s and Pershing-2s) in Europe and Asia. Although the INF (Intermediate-Range Nuclear Force) treaty is not militarily significant, since it reduced by only 4 percent the more than 50,000 nuclear warheads in the combined arsenals of the two superpowers, its political and symbolic importance are enormous. It is the first agreement that actually reduces the number of nuclear weapons. Further, it is an asymmetrical treaty with the Soviets destroying far more missiles and warheads than the United States. And last, it provides for stringent on-site inspection to verify compliance. In 1991 a preliminary agreement was announced to reduce by 30 percent the superpowers' strategic nuclear weapons.

True to the agreement, both countries destroyed the weapons according to schedule, and the Soviets sold off the surplus vehicles and other nonlethal hardware to elements in its economy. At the same time, a transformation was occurring in the military. The navy significantly reduced its blue water maneuvers, spending most of its time close to base, and the Soviets unilaterally removed all nuclear submarines from the Baltic Sea. Some of the aging Golf-II class nuclear submarines are being destroyed. The army too began to reconfigure, forsaking elements of its offensive stance for a defensive posture and reducing the number of its exercises and maneuvers. Then, in December 1988, Gorbachev made an astonishing announcement during a speech to the United Nations. He pledged that the Soviet Union would unilaterally reduce its land forces by 500,000 troops, 50,000 of which were to come from troops stationed in Eastern Europe, and that among these were crack assault troops that might be used in an invasion of Western Europe. This reduction amounted to a savings of 14 percent in the military budget, and he later announced his wish to cut the military budget by a total of 50 percent during the 1990s. As the reductions progressed, huge stores of surplus weapons, vehicles, and other commodities were sold off, and factories formerly producing military goods were converted to the production of consumer goods like television sets, plumbing materials, motorcycles, vacuum cleaners, and pasta. Furthermore, a nuclear weapons plant was closed, and the construction of an early warning radar station in the Ukraine was suspended. These closures were as much motivated by public concern for safety as by budget cuts, however.

Collapse of the Soviet bloc. The new Soviet moderation in military doctrine tripped off changes across the world. Soviet troop withdrawals from Afghanistan and Mongolia, together with its pressure on Vietnam to withdraw from Kampuchea (Cambodia), have seen relations warm between Moscow and the People's Republic of China. Soviet pressure on Angola caused Cuba to withdraw its 50,000 troops from that African country after an agreement was struck between the Angolan government and the rebel National Union for the Total Independence of Angola (UNITA). Soviet influence was important in helping to get an agreement from South Africa that its unwilling protectorate, Namibia, was to become independent. It also was instrumental in persuading President Daniel Ortega to hold elections in Nicaragua—elections that he lost to the non-Marxist, Violeta Chamorro. In the Middle East, Gorbachev has reduced his military support to Syria and significantly improved relations with Israel. He has also strongly supported the United Nations sanctions against Iraq after President Saddam Hussein's invasion of Kuwait. Although Gorbachev attempted to negotiate more favorable terms for the cessation of hostilities than were ultimately granted to Iraq, the Soviet Union never wavered in its support of the United Nations' effort to bring Hussein into compliance with international law.

However, the most significant change has occurred in Europe. Besides withdrawing Soviet troops from Eastern Europe—a policy that is causing considerable hardship since the returning Soviet troops have difficulty finding housing—he encouraged the liberalization of their governments, thus importantly aiding in the eventual collapse or overthrow of every communist government in the region. After some hesitation, Gorbachev even supported the reunification of East and West Germany and its affiliation with NATO (the North Atlantic Treaty Organization).[23] This remarkable phenomenon has, of course, dramatically changed the posture of Soviet defense strategy. The Warsaw Pact, the Soviet bloc military alliance, had all but collapsed by mid-1990. Finally, in February 1991 it formally renounced its military role entirely. (See Table 6–2.) Also, the economic association of the Warsaw Pact countries, the Council for Mutual Economic Assistance (popularly called *Comecon*) voted in 1991 to reorganize into the Organization for International Economic Cooperation. This new body is based on the exchange of goods through foreign (hard) currency (internationally exchangeable money, which none of its currencies is), its members are much more independent than before, and its purpose is to help its members integrate into the world economic system.[24]

At the same time as the Soviet military alliance system collapsed, Soviet martial pride took another humiliating blow. In the Persian Gulf War, the United States and its allies quickly established air superiority, Patriot anti-missile missiles successfully downed many Soviet SCUD missiles, and the Iraqi army was quickly defeated on the ground. The Soviet Union was the largest arms supplier to Iraq and although Iraqi soldiers and their commanders must bear much of the blame for the defeat, allied tactics against Soviet weapons and the inferior quality of the weapons themselves share responsibility for Iraq's rapid defeat. The poor showing of Soviet weapons and training among the Iraqi military is a source of profound embarrassment for the Soviet military.[25]

Meanwhile, negotiations between the Soviet Union and the United States for further troop and weapons reductions continued. After considerable negotiations, and significant concessions by the Soviet Union on disputed matters, Gorbachev and President Bush announced a troop reductions agreement for Europe with each side limited to 195,000 troops in Central Europe and the United States allowed to keep 30,000 more troops in Western Europe. The Soviets, of course, also keep troops in the European part of their country, and the East and West European states have their own forces. In June 1990 another agreement was reached. It pro-

[23]Shortly before East Germany joined West Germany, Erich Honecker, the longtime Communist Party leader of East Germany, sought asylum in a Soviet military base located in East Germany. In March 1991 he was secretly transported to the Soviet Union in order to escape prosecution at the hands of the German government. Tyler Marshall, "Honecker Flown to Moscow by Soviets; Bonn Protests," *The Los Angeles Times*, March 15, 1991.

[24]Michael Parks, "Soviet-Led Trading Bloc Will Be Scrapped for a New One," *The Los Angeles Times*, Jan. 6, 1991.

[25]Elizabeth Shogren," Allied Sweep Jars Soviets' Military Chief," *The Los Angeles Times*, March 1, 1991.

TABLE 6–2   NATO and the Warsaw Pact in 1990

NATO, founded in 1949	Warsaw Pact, founded in 1955
Belgium	Albania[a]
Britain	Bulgaria
Canada	Czechoslovakia
Denmark	East Germany[b]
France	Hungary
West Germany	Poland
Greece	Rumania[c]
Iceland	Soviet Union
Italy	
Luxembourg	
Netherlands	
Norway	
Portugal	
Spain	
Turkey	
United States	

[a]Albania withdrew from the pact in 1962.
[b]East and West Germany have become a single country which is now in NATO.
[c]Rumania became an inactive member of the Warsaw Pact in the late 1960s.

vided that the Soviet Union would reduce its chemical weapons stockpile by 90 percent while the United States would destroy 80 percent of its chemical weapons. Additionally, the agreement called for an 18 percent reduction in U.S. strategic weapons (those with a range of over 3,000 miles) and a 27 percent cut for the Soviets. (See Table 6–3.) It is hoped that further talks will result in a total reduction of strategic weapons of 50 percent.

Then in November 1990, the Soviet Union, declaring that it no longer wished to be a superpower but only a great power in Europe, signed the multilateral Conventional Forces in Europe Treaty (CFE) with other European states and the United States. The terms of this agreement bound NATO and the Warsaw Pact to 20,000 tanks, 20,000 artillery pieces, 30,000 armored cars, 6,800 aircraft, and 2,000 helicopters each. This treaty requires the Soviet Union to reduce its conventional weapons in Europe by about 50 percent while requiring NATO to make only marginal reductions because it had fewer weapons to begin with. (See Table 6–4.) To fully appreciate the degree of the Soviet concessions in this treaty, one must know that the NATO weapons are usually far better than most Soviet and Warsaw Pact weapons.

TABLE 6–3   1990 Strategic Arms Reductions

Weapons and Country	*Number of Warheads*		*Percent of Change*
	1989	1998	
Intercontinental Ballistic Missiles (ICBMs)			
Soviet Union	6,450	3,060	−53
United States	2,440	1,444	−41
Submarine-Launched Ballistic Missiles (SLBMs)			
Soviet Union	3,642	1,840	−51
United States	5,152	3,456	−33
Manned Bombers			
Soviet Union	1,228	3,350	+172
United States	4,885	5,280	+8
Total Number of Strategic Weapons			
Soviet Union	11,320	8,250	−27
United States	12,477	10,180	−18

Source: Adapted from data provided by the Natural Resources Defense Council and the Arms Control Association.

These spectacular advances have not come off without a hitch, however. At its current rate of modernization, the increased speed and accuracy of Soviet weapons by the mid-1990s will be formidable (as will be our own), even with the reductions planned. Further, in the two years it took to negotiate the reduction of conventional weapons in Europe, the Soviet Union moved thousands of tanks and other weapons east of the Ural Mountains, thus making them not subject to the treaty. Also, just before agreeing to the 1987 INF treaty, the Soviet Union secretly transferred a small number of its intermediate-range nuclear missiles to the possession of East Germany, Bulgaria, and Czechoslovakia in an apparent attempt to circumvent the treaty. When the fraud was discovered in 1990, the Soviets claimed to have done it because West Germany's INF missiles were not counted in the treaty. In the meantime, however, West Germany voluntarily destroyed its missiles. Finally, apparently because of growing anxiety within the military, the Soviets have begun to drag their heels on the agreement reducing troops in Europe.

The posture of the military in the face of all these changes is watched carefully. John Hines of the RAND Corporation and Stephen Meyer of the Massachusetts Institute of Technology (MIT), in a presentation to Congress, concluded that the Soviet military is demoralized and split in several ways. The loss of public support has hit badly. Also, the various branches are quarreling as each tries to minimize the impact of budget cuts on itself. There are deep divisions between the professional officer corps and the draftees, even as the recruits are divided against themselves by ethnic conflict and *dedovshchina*. Finally, the senior officers

TABLE 6–4   1990 Agreement on Reducing Conventional Arms in Europe

Weapons and Limit	NATO Amount	NATO Reductions	Warsaw Pact Amount	East Europe Cut	Soviet Cut	Soviet Weapons to Remain	East Europe Weapons to Remain
Tanks 20,000	22,230	2,230	36,798	5,050	11,748	13,150	6,850
Artillery 20,000	18,500	0	32,000	6,875	5,125	13,175	6,825
Armored Combat Vehicles 30,000	30,000	0	47,220	4,900	12,320	20,000	10,000
Aircraft[a] 6,800	5,700	0	9,840	0	3,040	5,150	1,600
Helicopters 2,000	2,235	235	3,550	200	1,350	1,500	500

[a]A total of 430 land-based naval aircraft is permitted, along with trainer craft. Carrier-based aircraft are not included in the treaty, a matter of discontent among the Soviet military, since the United States has a carrier fleet many times the size of the Soviet complement.

Source: The Arms Control Commission.

find themselves at odds with the junior officers over the proposed reforms.[26]

Stung by criticism among the public for its alleged waste and inefficiency, the military leadership complains that it is being made the scapegoat for all of society's problems. The Chief of Staff, General Mikhail Moiseev, publicly complained in 1990 that the political leaders were not doing enough to stem the growing antimilitary wave among the public. At the same time, Eduard Shevardnadze and the leading Soviet expert on the United States, Georgi Arbotov, engaged in bitter public debates with the generals over how much defense is enough and how the nation's resources might be used. As a measure of the acuity of this debate, Arbotov complained to the American press in December 1989 that the American invasion of Panama was "the best Christmas present the Americans could have given the Soviet military machine."[27] For their part, the junior officers are less defensive about the declining stature of the military and are more willing to consider reforms affecting it. Some of the radical junior officers have formed a group called *Shchit* (Shield) to resist the conservatism they see building in the military. The group first organized in 1988 after a commander ordered his troops to brutally attack protesters in Tbilisi, Georgia. Although the general was later relieved of his command, the

[26]Robert C. Toth, "Experts See Soviet Forces as Fractured and Demoralized," *The Los Angeles Times,* April 26, 1990.

[27]Masha Hamilton, "Washington Keeping Moscow Fully Informed about Invasion," *The Los Angeles Times,* Dec. 23, 1989.

damage had been done and several people were needlessly killed. Troops have also been used to quiet other ethnic disturbances, in Armenia and Azerbaijan in particular.

Shchit claims a membership of about 3,000 junior officers across the country, and its leaders believe that most of the men in the ranks support their objectives. "Our goal is to make sure that the army is never again used against its own people," said its founder, Vitali Urazhtsev. Most of *Shchit*'s leaders have been cashiered from the military and banished from the party, but they claim that others remain in the ranks and keep their *Shchit* membership secret. If this is true, the high command must wonder how long its troops will obey commands in new confrontations with protesters.

Despite the organization of reform-oriented officers, the conservatives are gaining ground. In February 1990, the commander of Soviet forces in Europe broke protocol and publicly complained that the projected Soviet troop cuts could endanger the national security. Since that time the military has become increasingly resentful of the policy and it may force Gorbachev to revise his plans. Also, the Soviet rumor mill repeatedly speculated during 1987–1990 about a possible military coup. These suspicions were given credibility when a senior NATO defense expert said that the military had mobilized an entire division in the Moscow region in February 1990 as a warning against further troop cuts.[28] This contention was denied, and although no known military moves have yet occurred, the rumors of their imminence persist. A name frequently mentioned as the possible leader of such a coup is Colonel General Boris V. Gromov. As the Soviet commanding officer of the Afghan, he was the last Soviet soldier in the invasion force to leave the country and was later assigned to command the Kiev military region. Gromov is a tough soldier, popular with his troops and the public. He repeatedly dismisses the rumors of his leading a coup as "rubbish." In any event, in a late 1990 shakeup of his government, one of several recent conservative moves, Gorbachev made Gromov the deputy minister of the Interior Ministry, which controls the national police force. Furthermore, in 1991 Gorbachev authorized the military to join the police on patrols of city streets. The Soviet president claimed that this unusual step was necessary to help stem the skyrocketing crime wave, but dissidents believe that the patrols are intended to squelch political movements for independence in the Baltic and elsewhere.

Whatever the circumstances of the Soviet military it must be carefully watched at all times, but most particularly during times of reform, because of its power and inherent conservatism. Other similar institutions, such as the police agencies, should also be examined.

THE POLICE

As with so many other institutions, the Soviet police apparatus has its origins in the tsarist government. The Soviet police is divided into two basic units: the militia and the secret police.

---

[28]Jill Smolowe, "This New House," *Time Magazine*, May 14, 1990.

The Militia

Upon coming to power, the Bolsheviks disbanded the tsarist police force, replacing it with a **militia** to perform the ordinary police work for the regime. This new police force was ostensibly controlled by the local soviets. In fact, however, the Russian, and even European, tradition for a centrally directed police force prevailed, and the militia was directed by the People's Commissariat of Internal Affairs. Stalin placed the militia under control of the infamous NKVD (secret police), but his successors were quick to divide the police and the secret police into separate organizations again. Consistent with his decentralization policies in other institutions, Khrushchev soon turned control of the militia over to the union republic governments. Shortly after Khrushchev was pushed aside, however, the government recentralized the militia under the Ministry of Internal Affairs (MVD), but with the recent rise of local autonomy, the union republics are demanding that they again be given control of the police.

The militia performs the usual array of police activities, including criminal investigation and apprehension, crowd control, traffic direction, and public order. Its functions, however, reach far beyond these mundane tasks. The MVD runs prisons, labor camps, drunk tanks, and sanatoria for drying out alcoholics. It is also charged with giving permission for and keeping track of all guns, explosives, photographic equipment, printing presses, and other items of potential political or military value.

In addition, the militia is responsible for administering the domestic passport system and thereby keeps track of all citizens residing in the Soviet Union. Since the time of the first Romanovs, the Russian people have been required to carry identification papers. Soviet citizens are required to register with the police at age 16. They are issued papers stating their name, place of residence, place and date of birth, nationality, family status, and military record. When visiting another town, Soviet citizens are required to register with the local police and to present their passports. In this way, the government not only attempts to know where each citizen is and what he or she is doing but also provides a mechanism for regulating the number of people living in the cities. This effort meets with less than complete success since virtually every city teems with "illegal" residents. To control the problem the police are now fining those who rent apartments to or employ people who are not registered with the police.

The militia has suffered a rather checkered history. Under Stalin it enjoyed privileged status along with the military and the party. Consequently, it became ladened with cronyism and inefficiency. Khrushchev's efforts to reform Soviet society brought to the militia a program of professionalization that was continued during the first part of Brezhnev's tenure. Attempts were made to recruit better educated youth into the police, and training was improved.

Unfortunately, these efforts were not sustained later in the Brezhnev era. Corruption set in as police began to accept bribes to overlook crime. (Cover-ups were also made to protect police records.) When Andropov came to power, he took several steps to rectify the situation. He changed the top leadership of the militia and served notice that corruption and slovenly work would no longer be tolerated.

Meanwhile, a major effort was launched to change the image of the militia. The number of patrolmen was increased to rout out drunks and loiterers in an effort to stem the rise of petty crime. At the same time, police visited the homes of citizens and asked for their cooperation in fighting crime and corruption. These efforts seem to have met with some success and perceptible support and relief among the population. Although Chernenko did not pursue the anticorruption campaign with Andropov's vigor, Gorbachev has given new impetus to these reforms.

Glasnost and perestroika expanded individual liberties and attacked the once sacrosanct authorities, but the new freedoms, together with the sharp decline in economic well-being, have seen the crime rate shoot up since 1986 by an aggregate of about 30 percent annually. Violence is also skyrocketing and police work is becoming very dangerous. In the 18 months from January 1987 to June 1988, 361 Soviet policemen were killed in the line of duty. In the same period only 106 policemen were killed in the United States.[29]

Demoralized by their inability to stem the crime spree, the police complain that Gorbachev's reforms are at fault. They also charge that they are underequipped to handle the new level of crime. Soviet yellow and blue police cars are ordinary, low-powered Soviet-made vehicles that cannot equal the souped up cars used by some criminals. Police cars are also often without radios and other equipment. Leningrad police cars, for example, are rationed to five gallons of gas per day, and any repair—even a minor one—usually takes a full day in the shop. Also, in Leningrad (the nation's second largest city), police have no computers to help them do their work. Consequently, it sometimes takes as long as three weeks to check on suspects' police records. The Soviet people spend about $17 per capita on the police, while in the United States the figure is $100 per capita.

Soviet policemen are also paid very little. Their average pay is 200 rubles per month, less than the national wage average. Bribery of policemen is commonplace. People pay them off for everything from forgetting to issue traffic tickets (three traffic violations in a year result in license suspension) to purchasing benign neglect for prostitution and other more serious crimes. Police authorities have also been found to cooperate with thugs and organized crime rings. It has become necessary for some cooperative businesspeople to pay the police for protection against gang vandalism, customer muggings, and arson. These felonious behaviors, combined with occasional police brutality in suppressing protests and the uninterrupted escalation in the crime rate, have engendered a renewed public contempt for the militia. A 1990 poll revealed that only 8 percent of the public expressed confidence in the militia, while neighborhood self-defense detachments are being formed to deter crime, and newly legalized private detectives are doing a land-office business, especially as bodyguards for prosperous cooperative businesspersons.[30]

[29]Masha Hamilton, "Crime in the Era of Glasnost," *The Los Angeles Times*, Oct. 13, 1989.
[30]Carroll Bogert, "On Reform: Prime Time for Crime," *Newsweek*, June 4, 1990.

Besides the regular police force, the MVD includes investigators, attorneys, archives, labs, and the usual complement of support services. Also, a new police unit was recently created, called the "black berets" because of its headgear. It is trained in crowd control and riot prevention and is being used as a flying squad to combat the growing number of incidences of violent ethnic and political protests. It was used in the 1991 suppression of the Baltic republics.

The militia also takes advantage of the age-old Russian tradition of busybodyism—people being overly interested in the affairs of their neighbors. The militia draws upon the services of large numbers of informers, including party members, the Komsomol, custodians, building superintendents, workers, and even *babushki* (grandmothers).

You will also recall the *druzhina* from Chapter 5. These private citizens, festooned with red armbands and occasionally sporting black-and-white night sticks, volunteer their services in a semi-official police force, patrolling streets, arresting drunks and rowdies, and giving lectures on "socialist legality." Although this institution has yet to meet Khrushchev's original goal of completely replacing the police, it remains an important part of the Soviet police system.

Apart from the regular police, support services, informers, and *druzhiniki*, the militia also maintains a quasi-military force. Composed of approximately 400,000 men, this internal security force is equipped with armored vehicles, tanks, and machine guns. Its stated function is to act against public disorder when the regular police prove incapable of containing a particular situation. It has recently been used, along with military detachments, to quell racial riots in Armenia, Azerbaijan, Moldavia, Uzbekistan, the Baltic, and elsewhere. Obviously, however, these troops, and a similar army under the KGB, can also be used to help check the military, should such action become necessary.

The infrastructure of the militia is typical of all other Soviet government institutions. The minister of internal affairs is usually a member of the Central Committee of the CPSU, and the leading positions in the militia are held by people with verified political dependability. In 1988 Vadim V. Bakatin was brought from a party first secretaryship in his native Siberia to head the MVD. A committed liberal, and a nationally popular person, he had no previous police experience, but he quickly became one of the nation's most prominent reform-oriented officials. He set to the task of rooting out corruption, and he demanded that the police exercise restraint in dealing with the public and in assuring that the rights of those arrested were not violated. These limitations were not well received by the police or the conservative elements, and no improvement occurred in slowing the escalating crime rate or calming the ethnic violence.

Pressed by growing conservatism among the public and in the military, Gorbachev removed Bakatin in December 1990, later appointing him to the National Security Council. Boris K. Pugo, a Latvian, replaced Bakatin as minister of interior. Pugo is seen as a hard liner. As a KGB general he distinguished himself by energetically trying to check Latvian separatism, and eventually became the party first secretary of his native republic. In 1988, however, he was forced from that office by the growing

Latvian nationalist movement, so he was brought to Moscow as the chairman of the CPSU Control Commission. In an apparent bow to the military, Gorbachev also appointed General Boris V. Gromov as Pugo's deputy at the MVD. The rise of these two conservatives to such strategic positions augurs ill for liberalization, and they have swiftly acted to clamp down on separatist movements. Moreover, in 1991 Gorbachev took personal control of all law enforcement activities, including the joint military and militia patrols. The full significance of this extraordinary step is not as yet completely understood, but it appears to be consistent with the Soviet president's drift toward the right of the political spectrum.

The Secret Police

The secret police has been a fact of life in Russia almost as long as the state itself has existed. The first well-organized secret police was established during the reign of Ivan the Terrible in the sixteenth century. In the eighteenth century Peter the Great reorganized and modernized the police, as did Nicholas I in the nineteenth century.

In this century the secret police under Nicholas II, the Okhrana, hounded the Bolsheviks and other radical groups. Lenin fought back with propaganda condemning the use of secret police, but the Bolsheviks were in power for less than two months when they established their own clandestine police force. The Extraordinary Commission for Combatting Counterrevolution and Speculation, popularly known by the acronym **Cheka,** was placed under the ruthless but capable leadership of Feliks Dzerzhinsky, a Polish aristocrat turned Marxist. During the Civil War, Cheka became an instrument for securing funds for the Bolshevik government and for ridding the regime of its internal enemies. To these ends, Cheka, the "sword and shield of the revolution," launched requisition drives, confiscating money, valuables, and farm goods from the people. It also arrested and purged S-Rs, Mensheviks, anarchists, syndicalists, and other non-Bolshevik revolutionaries. These activities and the additional policies of arresting and intimidating "enemies of the state" were labeled the Red Terror; similar travesties, called the White Terror, were perpetrated by the enemy camp.

Reflecting the traditional animosity between Russians and Poles, and noting the ruthless task which Dzerzhinsky so efficiently performed, a Soviet joke asks:

> "Why do the Poles revere Felix Dzerzhinsky so?" The answer: "Because he killed more Russians than any other Pole in history."

In 1920, when the danger of a White victory had diminished, the worst excesses of Cheka were suspended. Still, the secret police numbered about 30,000 agents, who remained actively engaged in protecting the regime against subversion and espionage. In 1922 the secret police force was reorganized, and its name was changed to the OGPU (Unified State Political Administration). Gradually it became the tool of Joseph Stalin, the head of the party. Sensing the utility of terror as a means of controlling the society, Stalin deployed OGPU agents in schools, factories, farms, and other institutions. The OGPU went unchecked by the ordinary judicial process, thus tightening Stalin's grip on the institutions in the land.

Yet another reorganization in 1934 saw the secret police incorporated into the agency that already administered the regular police, the infamous NKVD (People's Commissariat for Internal Affairs). Under Genrikh G. Yagoda, the NKVD's first leader, the great blood purges were begun. Yagoda himself eventually fell victim to the purge and was replaced by Nikolai Yezhov. Yezhov executed Stalin's bloody orders with such fervor that the purges became associated with his name and were called the *yezhovshchina*. Even the dogged loyalty of Yezhov could not spare him from Stalin's paranoia, however, and he too disappeared in 1938. Yezhov was replaced by Lavrenti Beria, a Georgian and the last head of the NKVD.

Stalin's principal instrument of government, the NKVD, become the most powerful institution in the country. Not only did it carry out the purge of the party, government, trade unions, military, and virtually every other important organization, but it also cleared people for employment, government posts, and party positions. Most importantly, it spearheaded Stalin's collectivization of agriculture and industrialization policies. These activities included mass arrests, deportations, executions, and the internment of millions in the labor camps that it administered. Indeed, the NKVD became the largest employer in the land. It is estimated that as many as 20 million people perished at the hands of NKVD firing squads or in the camps during Stalin's rule.

These camps, labeled by Solzhenitsyn as the Gulag Archipelago—a name based on the acronym for the Main Administration of Corrective Labor Camps—became an integral part of the Soviet economy. The hapless internees suffered from poor food, inadequate shelter, and brutal treatment. Yet they built roads, railroads, canals, and dams; they mined gold and coal; they cut timber. Mary McAuley estimates that by 1939 the labor camps may have accounted for as much as 10 percent of the Soviet work force and that they had become such an important factor in the economy that throughout the Stalinist era mass arrests were continued to provide needed laborers to the camps even though the purges were ended.[31] In 1953, the year of Stalin's death, approximately eight million people toiled in the camps, victims of the grisly dictator and his minions.

Stalin's death was quickly followed by Beria's arrest, trial, and execution. Many of Beria's henchmen followed him to the shooting wall. Brought firmly under control of the party, the secret police, which had been consolidated into the MVD in 1946, was reorganized again. Renamed the Committee for State Security (**KGB**), it was relegated to lower status in the infrastructure.

[31]Mary McAuley, *Politics and the Soviet Union* (Harmondsworth, England: Penguin Books Ltd., 1977), p. 131.

Trying to ensure that the secret police would never again become the dominant force it had been, the party leadership insisted that its officers and, most importantly, its leader be drawn from among loyal party members. Also, many powers formerly exercised by the NKVD and the MVD were denied the KGB. The labor camps were taken from its control; most of their inmates were released. The secret police found itself limited in its powers to arrest; its special boards, which had tried and sentenced millions, were abolished.

While Khrushchev remained in power, the KGB was not allowed to assume important stature, but its prestige was gradually increased during the Brezhnev era. Yuri Andropov, the leader of the KGB from 1967 to 1982, was promoted to a candidate member of the Politburo in 1967 and to full membership in 1973. In an apparent move to counter the growing influence of the military, Brezhnev also made Andropov a general of the army in 1976. This promotion indicates an interesting reversal of Khrushchev's policy of using the army to check the power of the secret police.

Andropov's administrative skills transformed the KGB from a discredited, distrusted institution to one of the most powerful elements in the Soviet government. From 1953 to 1978 the KGB, subject to the Council of Ministers, held a relatively undistinguished status. In 1978, however, it was elevated to the station of a state committee, thus acquiring more independence and prestige. At the same time, Andropov recruited some of the Soviet Union's most promising people, drawing them from the state's principal universities and from the families of ranking party, government, and military personnel. Noting the improvement in the quality of the secret police agents, Moscovites circulated the following joke:

> KGB agents must now travel in groups of three. One agent can read, the second can write, and the third keeps an eye on the two intellectuals.

Andropov's recruiting policies, along with reforms in training, transformed the KGB into a sophisticated and efficient organization. Although it still may employ relatively crude, thuggish methods against those who try to make public displays of discontent, it has increasingly resorted to more subtle techniques of intimidation and control. The terrorizing rap on the door at 3:00 A.M. has been replaced by an official summons to the KGB headquarters for questioning. Mass arrests of people to fill the labor camps have been abandoned. Instead, individuals who violate the social order are subjected to job discrimination, undesirable housing assignments, and denial of desirable but scarce consumer goods. Unfortunately, the most serious offenders still suffer imprisonment in labor camps or prisons, and even confinement in psychiatric hospitals, where drugs and electric shock are used to cow the most "dangerous" dissident element. The use of psychiatric hospitals to treat political dissidents has been curtailed in recent years, but evidence of such practices still occasionally becomes public.

Perhaps symbolic of the secret police's centrality in Soviet society, its headquarters, Lubyanka Prison, is located in central Moscow at #2 Dzerzhinsky Square—only a few blocks from the Kremlin. Ironically enough, Lubyanka is situated just opposite Children's World, the nation's largest toy store. In fact, one account relates that a shopper looking for the toy store became confused and inadvertently entered the wrong building. To the KGB's embarrassment, she was discovered frustratedly wandering around the first floor of the secret police headquarters.[32] A newer and larger KGB center, Lefortovo Prison, is located in northeast Moscow. The KGB also manages a vast network of agents, informers, investigators, and paramilitary troops. The KGB employs approximately 560,000 people officially and perhaps an equal number as informers.[33]

The KGB is divided into two main elements: the foreign directorate and the political security service, which handles domestic affairs for "the committee," as the KGB is called. Combining the roles performed for the United States by the FBI, the CIA, the Secret Service, the Immigration Service, and the National Security Agency, the KGB has a truly impressive number of functions, including the following:

1. Investigation and arrest for domestic political crimes such as espionage, political protests, anti-Soviet propaganda, criticism, and religious dissidence
2. Investigation and arrest for serious economic crimes such as counterfeiting, large-scale embezzlement or speculation, and smuggling
3. Censorship of the mail
4. Protection of the principal leaders in the country
5. Foreign espionage and counterintelligence.[34]

Most of the vast number of KGB agents work inside the country, as do the great bulk of its informers, thus constituting a major instrument of state control. The committee maintains offices at every administrative level in the country. Its agents can be found in every major enterprise: on the farms; in the military; in the trade unions and media; in the schools, institutes, and universities; in hospitals, vacation resorts, and stores; in the militia. In short, virtually no segment of society escapes its watchful eye.

Soviet law appears to limit strictly the powers of the KGB vis-à-vis its suspects. An arrest must be approved by the Procuracy within 24 hours after the suspect is taken into custody. If approval is not given, the law requires that the detainee be released. But if the arrest is approved, suspects may be held for as long as two months, during which time a preliminary investigation is conducted. Detention can be extended for up to six months with approval of the Procuracy. As with other criminal preliminary investigations, these inquisitions can be held in secret, and the accused has no right to counsel. The legal limitations on the KGB are the subject of serious controversy; many scholars suspect that the Procuracy is particu-

[32]John Kohan, "The KGB: Eyes of the Kremlin," *Time Magazine*, Feb. 4, 1983, p. 44.

[33]*The Soviet Union* (Washington, DC: Congressional Quarterly, Inc., 1982), p. 8.

[34]In 1989, the KGB was also given special responsibility for combating organized crime, a rapidly growing problem in the Soviet Union.

larly cooperative with it in matters of state security. Moreover, the laws regarding espionage and anti-Soviet propaganda are sufficiently vague as to allow the secret police great investigative latitude.

Although the majority of the KGB agents are engaged in domestic activities, the committee is very active in foreign countries. Just as it shares responsibility for police work at home with the militia, it is joined in foreign intelligence by the **Chief Intelligence Directorate** (**GRU**), the military intelligence agency, which maintains an extensive espionage network throughout the world. Indeed, having a budget several times that of the KGB for foreign espionage, the GRU is the major supplier of stolen foreign technology to the Soviet Union. Moreover, most Western authorities regard Aeroflot, the USSR's civilian airline, as a wholly owned subsidiary of the GRU since its planes are designed to be easily converted to military transport vehicles.

In any event, having agents in every major foreign country (as do most other major states' intelligence agencies), the KGB classifies its agents in two general groups: "legal agents" and "illegal agents." The legal agents are those who are assigned as diplomats, trade specialists, journalists, and the like. Although their clandestine activities are certainly illegal in the host countries, they use their real names and enjoy legitimate cover assignments. The illegal agents, sometimes called moles, assume false names and backgrounds and burrow deep within the governments, trade unions, industries, and other institutions of foreign countries.[35] United States naval intelligence analyst, Glenn Michael Souther, is suspected of having been a Soviet mole named Mikhail Yevgenevich Orlov. He defected, or returned, to the Soviet Union in 1989.[36]

The KGB does not rely solely upon its own agents, however. It has been very active in recruiting foreign nationals to provide information about their native land. Perhaps the most celebrated case of people betraying their country to the Soviet Union for ideological reasons occurred in England. In the 1930s four Cambridge chums—Donald MacLean, Guy Burgess, Harold "Kim" Philby, and Anthony Blount—agreed to pass secret information to Soviet agents.[37] They each remained dormant for a time while they rose in the ranks of the British government. Then, from positions of responsibility, they passed along information, some of which was important in helping Soviet scientists develop the atomic bomb. MacLean, Burgess, and Philby defected to the Soviet Union. Only Blount remained in England, undetected until 1979, by which time he had been honored by his appointment as the royal art adviser.

Ideological sympathizers aiding the KGB seem to have played out as the idealism of the Soviet experiment has dissipated. Even so, the KGB has

[35]Kohan, pp. 33–34.

[36]Michael Parks, "Soviets Hint Defector Was KGB Plant in U.S.," *The Los Angeles Times*, June 28, 1969.

[37]There is lingering suspicion that a fifth person was in the group but never discovered. Some authorities on the subject, a former KGB agent included, claim it is John Cairncross, a British diplomat, spy, and aide to the government minister. See Christopher Andrew and Oleg Gordievsky, *KGB: The Inside Story* (New York: Harper Collins, 1990).

Lubyanka prison, headquarters of the KGB, on Dzerzhinsky Square in Moscow. Diagonally to the left of this grim building, across the square, stands Children's World, the country's largest toy store. There is something poetic in the recent placement of a monument to Stalin's victims directly across from Lubyanka—it is a constant reminder of the role played in the terror by the secret police.

resorted to other means of recruiting foreign spies. The "honey trap" has sometimes been a successful means of securing information. This technique involves implicating individuals in sexual indiscretions and then threatening to tell all unless the victim cooperates with the secret police. In 1988 some Marine Corps guards stationed at American diplomatic posts in Moscow and Leningrad were accused of giving secret information to female Soviet agents with whom they became sexually involved. Later, in 1991, a Marine Corps corporal was convicted of trying to sell in the United States military secrets to FBI agents posing as KGB operatives, and real KGB agents, disguised as firefighters, searched offices and carried off several secret documents during a fire at the American embassy in Moscow.

The most effective method, however, is straightforward and simple: buying information. Lenin once said, "When it is time to hang the capitalist, he will sell us the rope." One would hope that Lenin was wrong, but there have been several recent episodes of American citizens agreeing to sell the KGB information and documents taken from their place of employment. Among the most celebrated recent cases are employees of American high-tech plants, several United States naval personnel, a disgruntled CIA agent who later defected, an errant FBI agent who was caught, some West German computer specialists, the Toshiba Machine Company of Japan, and the Olivetti business machine company of Italy. Additionally, Felix S. Bloch, a high-placed American diplomat, is suspected of selling the Soviets secrets, but he has not been charged with the crime.

The new freedom to travel abroad enjoyed by Soviet citizens has made American authorities more concerned about the increased opportunities for espionage. In 1989 San Diego, California, hosted a Soviet arts festival to which hundreds of Soviet artists and officials were invited. To the satisfaction of some and to the disgust of others, but to the apparent amusement of most, FBI authorities warned the locals to be on the lookout for any unusual behavior by suspicious-looking people—they might be Soviet spies.[38] No cases of spying were found to have taken place.

Not all has gone well for the KGB, however. Dozens of Soviet diplomats, journalists, and others have been expelled from the United States and other Western countries on spy charges. Additionally, KGB and other Soviet officials continue to defect to the West, bringing with them valuable intelligence information. Besides these reversals abroad, the Soviet press, responding to the imperative of *glasnost,* has begun to report on successful efforts of the CIA and other Western intelligence agencies infiltrating Soviet facilities and bribing Soviet officials to reveal state secrets. *Glasnost* has also led to disciplining at least one senior KGB agent, a step so extraordinary as to be considered unprecedented since Beria was removed in 1953. Attempting to aid in the cover-up of misdeeds by local government officials, the head of the KGB in the Voroshilovgrad area in the Ukraine tried to intimidate two journalists. The story broke on the front page of *Pravda* in January 1987, and the offending KGB officer was fired for "discrediting the high title of a Soviet officer."[39]

Border guards. The KGB is entrusted with another function considered vital to the security of the state. As you enter the Soviet Union, the serious and suspicious green-capped person who carefully inspects your passport is a KGB agent. Of the committee's 560,000 employees, approximately 340,000 are uniformed border guards. In addition to its role in passport control, this army patrols the 38,000-mile Soviet border, which is nine times that of the United States. Armed with tanks, armored vehicles, aircraft, and vessels, this security force is vigilant against saboteurs and spies. As with the militia security army, this heavily armed corps is also capable of serving as a check on the military.

Few other societies protect their borders with such enthusiasm. Sharing borders with 11 different countries—Finland, Poland, Czechoslovakia, Hungary, Rumania, Turkey, Iran, Afghanistan, China, Mongolia, and North Korea—the Soviet Union has girded itself with a "border zone" about 20 kilometers (12 miles) deep, in which Soviet citizens must carry special papers to live, work, or travel. Trying to cross the border without the appropriate papers can bring an offender as many as three years in a labor camp.

Such determination to protect its frontiers may seem a bit extreme, but the Soviet people, schooled by a history of invasion, blockade, boycott, and constant warnings about foreign spies, support their border guards

[38]Michael Granberry, "FBI Warning on Festival Spies Irks Soviets," *The Los Angeles Times,* Oct. 13, 1989.

[39]William J. Eaton, "KGB Says It Fired Official for Cover-up," *The Los Angeles Times,* Jan. 9, 1987.

with real verve. May 28 of each year is set aside for Border Guards' Day,[40] one of several national political holidays (Rocket and Artillery Day, Tank Day, Army and Navy Day, Victory Day, Revolution Day, New Years Day, International Women's Day, Christmas Day, and May Day are some of the others). Like our own Fourth of July, Border Guards' Day is accompanied by parades, fireworks, concerts, speeches, and editorials, all attempting to celebrate the brave men who patrol the borders to keep the state safe from real or imagined enemies. Gorbachev's liberalizing reforms, however, are changing even the traditional Soviet vigilance of its frontiers. Late in 1989, citing improved relations with its neighbors as the reason, the government announced it would reduce by 90 percent the border area patrolled by the KGB. It also dismantled the barbed wire and mines along portions of the frontier.[41]

The new—and the old KGB.   How much the KGB has changed is a matter of some debate. Since the time when Andropov headed the organization, the KGB has favored some reform in the system. It had more information than most others in the society and realized how much danger the Soviet Union was in of falling behind the West.[42] Andropov himself modernized the KGB, making it a much more sophisticated organization than it had been before. In 1988 Gorbachev replaced conservative Viktor M. Chebrikov as chairman of the KGB with Vladimir A. Kryuchkov, a lawyer and a former official in the USSR Procuracy. The following year, in an unprecedented event, Kryuchkov stood before the Supreme Soviet and answered questions in order to receive its confirmation, pursuant to the procedure outlined in the recently amended constitution. Never before had the KGB been subjected to such scrutiny by a Soviet legislative body, and some deputies seized the opportunity to bitterly criticize the committee. Although he drew titters from the deputies when he described the KGB as the people's servant, he riveted their attention when he outlined changes in the organization which had already been made or which would soon be made. He revealed for the first time that the infamous "Fifth Department" had been abolished. This KGB organization had been charged with "exterminating" ideological deviants. He promised that the operating rules of the KGB would be changed so that the committee would do less surveillance inside the Soviet Union. He also promised to be more open about the KGB's activities in the future, and he pledged to begin cooperative efforts with Western intelligence and police agencies in accomplishing mutual objectives.

Since his confirmation, Kryuchkov has apparently kept his part of the bargain, at least in the literal sense. He has held numerous press con-

[40]Ironically, Mathias Rust, the 19-year-old pilot who evaded Soviet air defenses during his flight from Finland to Moscow, landing his Cessna on Red Square, did so on Border Guards' Day, May 28, 1987!

[41]"KGB Plans to Cut Restricted Zones on Soviet Border by 90%," *The Los Angeles Times,* Oct. 21, 1989.

[42]Walter Laqueur, "Soviet Politics: Current Trends," in *Soviet Union 2000: Reform or Revolution,* ed. Walter Laqueur (New York: St. Martin's Press, 1990), pp. 35–36.

ferences—previously unheard of—discussing KGB policies. A publication, *KGB U.S.S.R.*, is released monthly and an hour-long film *KGB Today* publicizes the committee's new image. Some of these press conferences and publications go beyond image-building, however. The KGB has recently admitted that its predecessor was involved in Stalin's terror policies—an admission never before made by the organization—and it promised never again to become involved in such activities. It has confirmed that it foiled at least one attempt on Brezhnev's life and that it has stopped several attempts to assassinate Gorbachev, while admitting that security for the president could be tighter. It has even admitted errors of its own, like failing to catch several illegal shipments out of the country of Soviet military equipment. On a lighter note, Kryuchkov's efforts to improve the image of the committee even includes an annual contest for the selection of a "Miss KGB."

Apparently Kryuchkov has also focused the KGB's attention away from domestic political activity and more toward gathering foreign intelligence, preventing international terrorism, and combating organized crime. He has also initiated cooperative efforts with Western police and intelligence agencies, including the American Central Intelligence Agency and the Justice Department. These efforts are largely focused on combating drug running and terrorism, but late in 1990 the KGB shared with the United States some of its intelligence information on Iraq.

Despite these reforms, many people deeply distrust the KGB. Numerous public protests have been taken to the very door of Lubyanka Prison, with people shouting slogans and carrying signs expressing their animosity, such as "The KGB is the enemy of the people." Moreover, the Russian SFSR government wants to create its own security force, and President Boris Yeltsin claims to have secured permission, in principle, for such a move.[43] The most credible critic of the KGB, however, is former Major General Oleg D. Kalugin. Kalugin, the former KGB head of counterintelligence, was stripped of his rank, benefits, and pension and forced to retire in 1990, as he became increasingly disillusioned with KGB activities. Later he was elected to the Congress of Peoples' Deputies. He claims that the committee, contrary to its new image, still taps people's telephones and has agents in every farm, factory, office, and school. He even suggested that its agents had infiltrated the Russian Orthodox hierarchy and the highest councils of the Soviet government. He also charged that Kryuchkov is guilty of negligence and incompetence—the cause of mass resignations and defections by KGB agents.

Whatever the truth of Kalugin's accusations, it is clear that the KGB has not completely turned over a new leaf. In March 1990 a public letter penned by unmentioned KGB authors, but approved by the committee's headquarters, castigated "liberal politicians," accusing them of being power hungry, and ominously pledging that the KGB will act to protect Soviet security. Later, in December 1990, Kryuchkov spoke out against Gorbachev's reforms, claiming that they had failed and that the CIA and other

---

[43]John-Thor Dahlburg, "Yeltsin Gets Approval for Separate KGB," *The Los Angeles Times*, Sept. 20, 1990.

insidious forces were actively working to destabilize the Soviet system. He asked the Congress of Peoples' Deputies for the authority to crack down on "destructive political forces" in the economy and among the ethnic minorities. "No self-respecting state in the world," he said, "allows another to interfere in its domestic affairs." He also charged Western companies with selling the Soviet Union defective goods and spoiled food.[44]

Although Kryuchkov later tried to soften the impact of his remarks, the chilling tone of the supposedly concluded Cold War was heard once again by all. Whether he was simply acting as an agent for Gorbachev's recent turn to the right, or striking out on his own, is as yet unclear. For his part, Gorbachev seems to be relying increasingly on the KGB as well as the military and the militia. Late in 1990 he approved using KGB forces to prevent black market theft of the shipments of Western food and medical supplies sent to relieve the shortages during the winter of 1990–1991. Then, in 1991 the KGB announced that it had assumed responsibility for leading efforts to clean up the environment in several parts of the Soviet Union and for apprehending polluters. Perhaps more disturbing, in the same year Gorbachev empowered the KGB agents and the militia to enter any premises in the country, except foreign embassies. Gorbachev's decree allows the police to confiscate any documents from foreign or domestic businesses that might be needed in criminal investigations. Similar to their concerns about the joint police and military patrols, political activists fear that this policy may be used for political as well as civic police activity, and they charge that the Soviet Union is again becoming a police state.

Whatever the case, the KGB remains a powerful force in the society and we must await developments to determine its true course. Other elements in the society, once controlled by the party and used to control the society, have changed in varying degrees. Education, youth groups, the media, culture, and the trade unions are each in a state of flux, and we should now investigate them as to their importance to Soviet political society.

[44]Michael Parks, "Give Up Reforms, KGB Chief Urges," *The Los Angeles Times*, Dec. 23, 1990.

chapter 7

Instruments of Political Socialization

Until the late 1980s, every official institution in the Soviet Union was used for political purposes as well as for whatever else the institution was supposed to do. Schools, youth organizations, the media, cultural endeavors, and trade unions were controlled by the Communist Party and by the state, and they were used as life-long instruments of socialization (the process by which people are taught the values and norms of society) and mechanisms of political control. Gorbachev's efforts to open the system to new ideas and to democratize its institutions have brought immense changes to the social bodies so carefully controlled before. Suddenly, in a society that was allowed to learn only one "truth"—the party's interpretation of Marxism—the expression of a multitude of attitudes and ideas was encouraged. Before, only the party line was presented in the media and in art, now almost every possible interpretation of the society can be aired. Trade unions, which only a few years ago monopolized the labor movement and acted principally as vehicles for encouraging workers to meet government production quotas, now often oppose the government and economic managers, even as new unions are springing up everywhere. The changes in the party and government organizations discussed in previous chapters are of course very important, but the transformations occurring in the social institutions about to be examined are at least as fundamental, because it is these institutions that most closely affect the everyday lives of the people.

EDUCATION

Perhaps no institution is more important to a modern state than its educational system. Because education is the means by which the state first formally introduces itself to young citizens, all societies use their educational systems for political as well as instructional purposes. Socialization is vital to every political system. Education is a principal instrument by which socialization is implemented. Rarely are the society's norms presented in an objective manner. Rather, students are encouraged not only to learn about their political system but to revere it and support it above all others. This socialization process is particularly emphasized in the lower grades. In the United States we begin the elementary school day by pledging allegiance to the flag, and we learn about our presidents and other heroes. Our history is presented in the most positive light. Patriotism is encouraged. Our children are told stories (not all of them true, for example, George Washington and the cherry tree) that equate our nation, its leaders, and its people with good, justice, and happiness.

If the Soviet Union differs in any way from our efforts to inculcate the "right" ideas in students, it differs in degree but not in kind. The most politicized society on earth, the Soviet Union openly sets political indoctrination as the fundamental task for its schools. Making no pretense about this objective, Soviet authorities are far more direct about the political elements in their curriculum. Westerners sometimes criticize this forthright approach as evil, suggesting that schools should have no political role ·in society. In fact, however, the Soviet approach to political indoctrination is, if anything, more honest than our own. Soviet officials readily admit that they use the schools to train students politically. Our schools are perhaps somewhat hypocritical, however, because they clearly attempt to indoctrinate children but claim to encourage objectivity at the same time. Be that as it may, Soviet education is saturated with political indoctrination at every level, and its propagandistic efforts are obvious because they are so pervasive and no attempt is made to conceal them. Although ideological training has become an even greater part of the curriculum since 1984, the political presentations, while still clearly pro-Soviet, are more objective in their treatment of history and other subjects than they used to be. Today, both the positive and negative aspects are examined in textbooks and in the classroom—before the Gorbachev era, such objectivity was almost completely absent. Indeed, such great change has occurred in the interpretations of Soviet history that some people sarcastically say that

> The Soviet Union is the only country in the world with an unpredictable past.

History

Scant attention was given to education in Russia until Peter the Great (1682–1725), who focused on it as a way to modernize his realm. Yet, the first university in Russia was not established until 1755. Catherine the Great (1762–1796) shared Peter's appreciation for knowledge, giving considerable attention to Russia's educational system, even to the point of creating the Smolny Institute,[1] which offered women the best education in Europe at the time.

Remaining a low priority in the late period of tsarist Russia, education was available to only the wealthy classes until the 1860s. Generally speaking, the Church ran the primary schools, and the state sponsored the few existing institutions of higher education. Emphasis in the schools tended toward religious and classical training. Little attention was given to science or to the vocational fields studied in more advanced economic systems. During the 1800s the growing dissident movement often centered in the universities, causing reactionary tsars to regulate them closely, even closing them from time to time. Expressing his contempt for rationalism and the radical elements at the University of Moscow, Nicholas I (1825–1855) called it the "wolf's den." Although an effort to expand and modernize the school system was pursued by Alexander II (1855–1881), his successors generally ignored his reforms, causing Russia's people to languish in illiteracy and ignorance. At the turn of the twentieth century, only 24 percent of the total population was literate. Most of those who could read and write were aristocratic, Russian, and male. The lower classes, women, and ethnic minorities remained largely illiterate. Although some gains were made in the last years of Nicholas II's reign, the vast majority of the people had to await the revolution before they were taught their letters.

With the first decade of Soviet rule began an enormous effort to teach people to read and write. Virtually every literate person was set the task of teaching others these skills. Classes were held in the army, in factories, on farms, in apartment buildings, until seemingly every gathering of people became a school. By 1930 Soviet officials announced that no less than 81 percent of the population was literate. That many of these people were probably able to do little more than recite the alphabet and write their names should not detract from the government's remarkable accomplishment in raising the literacy rate.

The Soviet emphasis on education has continued; today virtually all Soviet people are literate. Rejoicing in their newly acquired skills, the Soviet people have become voracious readers. The average Moscovite, it is estimated, reads 15 or 16 books a year. On any public street, one can see people carrying books, newspapers, pamphlets, and magazines. People read at almost every opportunity: at bus stops, on the subway, in restaurants, at the theater during intermissions, in parks, in waiting rooms, in the

---

[1]The Smolny Institute was later used as a headquarters by Lenin prior to the revolution, and it was from there that he launched the march on the Winter Palace. Today the Smolny is popularly dubbed the "Heart of the Revolution" by Soviet officials.

ubiquitous lines before kiosks or in shops. It is indeed ironic that the people who read most should live in a society where censorship was strongest.

In addition to increasing the literacy rate, Soviet educators of the immediate post-revolutionary period also introduced an experimental era. The progressive ideas of John Dewey were invoked and the strict classroom decorum and curriculum of the tsarist age were rejected as leftovers from the capitalist era. Grades, exams, homework, papers, and degrees were jettisoned and classrooms became unruly. Soon, however, worried parents, quoting the Russian proverb that "repetition is the mother of knowledge," began to complain that their children were not learning. Finally, in the 1930s, when Stalin took control of the government and sought to train people in skills necessary for implementing his "second revolution" through the five-year plans, the Soviet Union reversed its educational policies. The euphoria of radical experimentation was abandoned, and the schools were returned to teacher-dominated classrooms with specific and traditional curricula. Four years of school became compulsory in 1930; the minimum has since been raised to 11 years, and about 89 percent of the adult population has completed at least 10 years of school.

Contemporary School Systems

Soviet education can be divided into basically four levels: preschool, primary, secondary, and post-secondary. The Soviet education system remains heavily centralized with the State Committee for Public Education being responsible for preschool through secondary institutions. Each union republic also has a Ministry of Education and there is a strong movement to decentralize education. Bowing to this pressure, the government has made several reforms, including creating local boards to participate in formulating school policy. These boards are composed of students, parents, trade union officials, and other community members. Even so, the central government continues to require a high degree of uniformity in curriculum, texts, pedagogical approaches, conduct, dress, and other details.

Preschool. Although most Soviet children still begin school at age seven, a major reform in the system is gradually requiring students to begin school at age six, thus extending by one the total number of years students must attend school. Since about 90 percent of all women of working age in the Soviet Union hold jobs, a large number of children (50–55 percent) enter preschool institutions before they reach their sixth or seventh year. There are over 145,000 preschools, accommodating 17.5 million children. Those not fortunate enough to attend preschool are looked after by grandmothers (*babushki*) or neighbors, or are sometimes left at home alone.

There are two basic preschool institutions: nursery schools and kindergartens. The nursery schools receive children as young as two months old and keep them until they reach three years. As in our own nursery schools, the children are taught to feed and dress themselves and to play games. They are also encouraged to take care of one another. They are

Soviet children walk together in a playground at a Volgograd kindergarten. (Photo provided by Louis and Helen Van Moppes.)

read stories; taught songs and simple folk dances; and taken on outings to museums, parks, factories, public buildings, and harbors. (See Figure 7–1.)

At age three Soviet children enter kindergarten. Although they do not have a formal course of study, kindergartens are more structured than the nursery schools. Political socialization begins in earnest at this level as students are read stories about the revolution, recent wars, and the national heroes. The children are told of legendary youths their age who did service to their country by helping the authorities catch spies or by directing Soviet troops to enemy locations. Each school is fitted with a full complement of flags, banners, emblems, and the ubiquitous picture of Lenin.

Besides political socialization, kindergarten students are also taught to live in a collective society. Most activities emphasize groups, although there is now a move toward encouraging some forms of individualism and creativity. Children are encouraged to share their toys and to help others who progress more slowly. Competition is also encouraged but never in an exclusionary sense. The winning groups in competitions are told that they won to further the interests of the whole society rather than to bring glory upon themselves. They are then encouraged to show the other groups how they might improve in the next contest. Moral training is also an important part of the curriculum. Students are taught the "socialist ethic" of honesty, truthfulness, hard work, comradeship, obedience, sharing, and modesty.

Parents are expected to take an active interest in their children's education from the very beginning. Contrary to some accounts, the schools do not presume to take over the upbringing of their charges. Rather, the

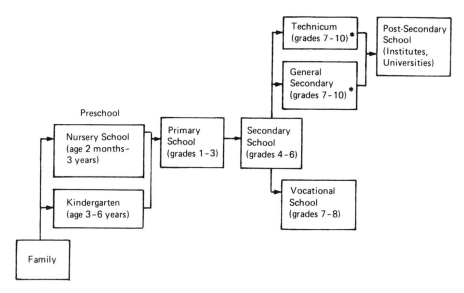

*As part of a major school system reform, Soviet students are gradually being required to increase their secondary education by one year. Hence, some students are now completing 11 rather than 10 years.

FIGURE 7–1   Soviet educational system.

relationship between parents and schools is more like a partnership. Schools send home frequent reports and schedule parent-teacher conferences in an effort to cooperate with the parents to encourage the children to conform with the discipline and activities of the school.

Preschools and kindergartens are far from uniform in quality. They are owned by trade unions, professional organizations, and economic enterprises. Some are well staffed and appointed (these usually belong to elite organizations), while others are less well financed. Unless special strings (political influence is called *blat*) can be pulled, parents must send their children to the institutions owned by their union or employers. Since these schools can be located at a distance from where people happen to live, getting children to and from school can be a hardship.

Each school is designed to handle between 100 and 120 students and is supposed to include trained staff (who have recently been allowed to experiment with the curriculum and to bring their own ideas and method to classroom activities) and medical personnel. Many schools, however, are overcrowded and understaffed. Salaries for preschool and kindergarten personnel are very low—usually set at about 130 rubles per month, much lower than the average wage. Perhaps because of the low salaries, the personnel in these institutions are often slovenly and corrupt. Stories abound about windows being left open all day so as to induce colds among the children to keep them home for a few days and skimping on the children's food so that the staff can take home the surplus. Sanitation in some of these institutions is also a problem; children often come home with lice and skin diseases.[2]

Youngsters usually spend the entire day at the school, having a hot meal for lunch and an afternoon nap before returning home. The socialization efforts of the preschools are relatively successful, but the efforts to prepare children for the school experience have mixed results. Studies indicate that children who attend preschool generally do better in school both academically and socially, yet they, like their less fortunate comrades, tend to suffer considerable trauma when faced with the severe regimen in regular school.[3]

Primary and secondary school.   At age six or seven, Soviet children begin their compulsory education. The 1984 school reform package, the first major school reform since the 1950s, provides that children will extend their education by one year, beginning school at the age of six. This proposal is very controversial among Soviet parents who oppose their children being forced to endure the pressures of the Soviet school system at such an early age.

Eight years is the minimum period of attendance, although the vast majority of children now complete 10 or 11 years of education. The primary schools comprise the first three years. Grades 4–6 are the secondary schools' responsibility. After secondary school, students complete their education in specialization schools, which will be discussed later. Because there are no private schools in the country, all students find themselves exposed to basically the same school experience.

Upon entering the first grade, students are subjected to a rather stern, businesslike atmosphere, although efforts are now under way to encourage teachers to be less strict and more compassionate. Attending from 8:30 A.M. to 1:30 P.M. each day, six days a week, they study required courses.[4] Electives are seldom allowed and are usually taken as overloads since the required curriculum is crowded. Discipline is firm. Students are to sit upright in their desks, to raise their hand if they wish to speak, and to stand until told to sit when the teacher enters the room. Misbehavior and poor study habits are handled by public reprimands and shaming, by peer pressure (usually the most effective method), and by enlisting the parents' support.

The required curriculum at the primary and secondary levels is heavily weighed toward mathematics, science, and vocational subjects. Soviet students average almost two courses in math per year, including algebra, geometry, and calculus. They study biology for five-and-a-half years, physics and geography for five years, chemistry for four years, and astronomy

[2]Francine de Plessix Gray, *Soviet Women* (New York: Doubleday, 1989), p. 37.

[3]Susan Jacoby, *Inside Soviet Schools* (New York: Hill & Wang, Inc., 1974), pp. 70–71.

[4]Some areas are experimenting with a five-day week. It has the support of the medical community, which argues that students who are less fatigued perform better during the shorter period. Many parents across the country are also enthusiastic about the idea, looking forward to more flexibility in their weekends when the children are out of school.

for one year. They also take courses in shop, home economics, or mechanical drawing each year.

Soviet students have heavy language requirements as well. All students study Russian. Students in non-Russian republics also study the national language of the republic (for example, Uzbek, Ukrainian, Lithuanian). Foreign language study, beginning in the sixth grade, usually includes English (there are more *teachers* of English in the Soviet Union than there are *students* of Russian in the United States), German, or French. Hence, Soviet students may study as many as three languages as part of the regular curriculum in school.

Concerned that the labor supply is dwindling and in response to a growing reluctance of students to go into the blue-collar trades, Soviet authorities have placed a new emphasis on vocational education. The regular academic curriculum is now more heavily integrated with vocational subjects such as growing plants, repairing appliances, and manufacturing basic items. Additionally, students 16 years old and above are required to spend some time during the school year and a portion of their summer vacations working on farms or in factories. In addition to these recent modifications to the curriculum, sex education and computer training have also been added to the already crowded schedule of classes for secondary students. Because sex has long been a forbidden subject in Soviet society, however, many teachers are uncomfortable with the topic and few are trained to teach it. Some parents and conservative organizations also oppose teaching the subject. Hence, sex education classes are often ignored; or they are taught as glorified home economics classes; or only the reproduction of plants is discussed, ignoring human subjects.[5] Computer courses are also slighted, but for a different reason. Computers are in very short supply, and although the government has set a goal of having one million computers in the schools by 1992, there is almost no chance of reaching this objective. Consequently, students usually learn about computers from textbooks and practice on dummy keyboards. If the schools they attend do have computers, students queue up on long waiting lines, preventing any single person from enjoying much time on the machine.

The humanities and social sciences generally receive little attention except as they relate to political instruction. Students study the history and culture of the republic in which they reside, the history of Russia and the Soviet Union, and the history of the CPSU. As already mentioned, however, classes now focus on the negative as well as the positive aspects of history. An emphasis on the brutality of Stalinism and the positive aspects of Khrushchev's term was so abruptly added to the curriculum in the late 1980s that the national history exams were canceled in 1988 because too many students had studied from textbooks that conveyed false information about the subjects. Later, textbooks were augmented with supplements that reflected new, more open treatments of the material.[6]

Like the preschools, primary and secondary schools devote consider-

[5]Michael D. Lemonick, "Rehabilitating Sex," *Time Magazine,* April 10, 1989.

[6]"Soviets to Fill-In Textbooks 'Blanks,'" *The Los Angeles Times,* Sept. 4, 1988.

able attention to the moral and social training of students. The same attributes of collectivism, frugality, hard work, and mutual consideration are taught. "Friendly competition" (also called socialist competition) is practiced as well. Competition between rows in the classroom, between classrooms, and between schools is established. These competitions are used to establish rewards for accomplishments and also to bring peer pressure upon sluggards. Winning groups are not only rewarded, but they are also encouraged to help other groups improve.

Military training is another area that receives serious attention in Soviet schools. Reminiscent of the 1950s in the United States, students from the second grade up are taught survival techniques in case of nuclear war. Boys also learn to march and drill, and girls study first aid. The ninth and tenth grades introduce students to even more sophisticated military training. Physical education is also considered important; every student learns to play sports and games. Team sports are emphasized, and interscholastic contests are also held.

Soviet schools are academically rigorous; students spend as many as four or five hours an evening doing homework. Discipline is also very important. Corporal punishment is forbidden, but students are kept in check by stern teacher recriminations, by being kept after school, and by peer pressure. Parents are also expected to help their children behave and learn. Parents are usually required to attend a lecture by school authorities before their children enter the first grade. This meeting is followed with a visit to the first-grade teacher within the first eight weeks of school. Throughout the primary and secondary years, parents attend parent-teacher conferences four times a year; at these meetings the teachers either compliment them or chastise them on the conduct and performance of their children. However, glasnost has encouraged parents to become more vocal about education as well as other issues, so parents have begun to stand up to tyrannical teachers and school authorities and complain if they believe the education system is not working properly. Even so, the school system appears to receive considerable support from the public. Teachers, although very poorly paid, enjoy considerable respect in the society.

Curricular options.   Soviet students usually follow one of three routes as they progress through school. They may remain in the *general secondary* school until completing the eighth grade; at this point they may choose to enter the labor force. Most students who remain in general secondary school beyond the sixth grade normally continue their education until they complete at least ten years of education, and then they enter the work place. After completing six years of secondary school, some students choose to enter **vocational programs** for two years and then leave school to work. A third alternative is for students to enter a *technicum* after their sixth or seventh year in the general secondary school. Technicums are advanced vocational schools that train people in specialized fields, such as nursing, medical technology, industrial management, machine tool technology, and some positions in education. Reversing the emphasis of the general secondary schools, the technicums spend roughly two-thirds of their time on vocational training and the remainder on standard academic courses. In any event, graduates from both types of schools may end their formal education upon graduation, or they may go on to post-secondary education.

The Soviets also maintain a number of *special schools.* There are special schools for the mentally handicapped and for the physically impaired. Some male students attend military academies in their last two years; destined to enter the officers corps, these students may, if they qualify, continue their education at one of the many military colleges in the country. The military academies are an important stage in one's military career, and competition for admission is fierce. The scramble for these scarce educational opportunities among young men from civilian families is exacerbated because sons of military officers enjoy priority for admission to the academies.

Finally, the especially talented student or the student with influential parents can attend special schools in mathematics, science, foreign languages, or the arts. These schools attract the best teachers and enjoy the most advanced equipment available. Here about 2 percent of the nation's students encounter curricula even more demanding than those in the regular schools, with special emphasis on the school's area of specialization. Owing to the prestige of these schools and their accelerated curricula, their graduates are three or four times more likely to enter post-secondary institutions than graduates of other schools. Although the advanced schools are designed for the most talented students, influential parents are often successful in securing places for their children even though the students may not meet the scholastic requirements of the school.

Post-secondary. The Soviets claim that 98 percent of their students finish the compulsory education, whereas only about 75 percent of all United States students complete high school. Yet, 54 percent of all high school graduates in the United States enter post-secondary institutions, whereas only 20 percent of the Soviet students are allowed to continue their studies. In 1988 almost five million students attended the country's 898 institutions of higher learning.[7]

There are basically two kinds of post-secondary institutions in the Soviet Union: institutes and universities. The **institutes** receive about 75 percent of all post-secondary students. These schools specialize in such fields as engineering, metallurgy, military science, pedagogy, and music. In addition to their teaching function, the institutes do the bulk of the research in the Soviet Union. Although some institutes, for example, the Moscow Power Engineering Institute (the equivalent of the Massachusetts Institute of Technology), enjoy great renown, the **universities** are generally the most prestigious institutions of higher learning. Similar to other universities throughout the world, Soviet universities are composed of several schools or faculties (for example, foreign languages, natural sciences, mathematics), which are divided into departments (for instance, the lan-

[7]*USSR '90 Yearbook* (Moscow: Novosti Press Agency Publishing House, 1990), p. 267.

guage faculty may be divided into French, German, English, and Chinese departments). Unlike in American universities, research is not a major task of Soviet universities; instead, they concentrate on teaching.

As might be expected, the competition for admission to the post-secondary level of education is fierce. Only about one-third of those who apply for admission are accepted. Applicants must enjoy the recommendation of their Komsomol units (membership in the Komsomol used to be an almost absolute prerequisite for admission to Soviet colleges), schools previously attended, or employers. Applicants then must sit for entrance examinations. These exams, given in January and June, have recently been made even tougher than before because of a growing feeling that the quality of higher education has declined over the past two decades. The exams must be taken at the school one hopes to attend. There is no central bank for examination scores, so if students are denied admission to the university where they took the exam, they will not be allowed to enter another school. Hence, care must be taken not only to score as well as possible in the exams but also to apply at a school and in a field where openings exist.

Besides the appropriate recommendations and exam scores, other factors often enter into the determination of who shall be admitted and who shall not. The state unofficially uses a quota system to assure that the desired number of women and minorities are admitted. Sometimes people resort to illegal means to assure success, like presenting forged recommendations or bribing admissions officials. Other students benefit from influential parents taking steps to guarantee their children's future.

Once admitted to an institute or a university, students have six years to complete the requirements for their diplomas. Although this period is sufficient for the 55 to 60 percent who attend full-time, it is considerably

The University of Vilnius, founded in 1570, is one of the oldest universities in Europe.

more difficult to meet for those who attend part-time or study through correspondence courses. About 50 percent of all full-time students live in government-supported dormitories, and close to 75 percent of all full-time students receive government stipends while in school. The amount of the stipend is determined by the level of school, parental economic status, field of study, and student performance. Generally speaking, the state pays more as students advance through their programs: Science and engineering students receive more than students of the humanities and social sciences, students with poor parents get more than others, and the better students receive more than those who perform less brilliantly. Only the very brightest and most accomplished students find their stipends reaching levels high enough to cover their total expenses, however, even though no tuition is charged.

As in the lower grades, the curriculum for each post-secondary major is filled mostly with required courses. Few electives are permitted, and then they are usually taken as overload subjects. All students take requisite courses in Marxism-Leninism for about 10 percent of the total class time. Physical education and foreign languages each absorb about 3 percent of the student's time. Virtually all the remaining time is devoted to the student's major subject. Various fields take varying lengths of time to complete. Journalism, law, and history, for example, usually require four years of full-time study. Science and engineering usually require five years, and medicine takes about five-and-a-half years to complete. All students in the same major study identical subjects during the first two or three years of college. Only in the last few years of study are they allowed to specialize.

Studies by Soviet sociologists reveal that students from "high-status" families dominate the ranks of those who are admitted to and successfully complete post-secondary studies. There seem to be several reasons for this trend, a trend that is also common in the West. Students from homes of high-status families are likely to have strong motivations to complete their college education. The more highly educated the parents, the more likely students are to be encouraged to read and develop necessary academic skills, to aspire to professional careers, and to study hard in preparation for college educations. High-status families can afford books or tutors to help their children with their studies and to prepare them for entrance exams. Students from high-status families are not likely to become discouraged or to drop out of school for financial reasons, the leading cause of Soviet dropouts. Finally, high-status families are most able to pay bribes to help their children succeed.[8]

In order to remain in school, students must maintain satisfactory grades in all subjects. There is no such degree as a baccalaureate. Successful completion of a college program is simply called a diploma, and most students stop upon earning the diploma. Only a very small number of the brightest students seek the post-graduate degrees of Candidate of Sci-

[8]Richard B. Dobson, "Education and Opportunity," in *Contemporary Soviet Society*, ed. Jerry G. Pankhurst and Michael Paul Sacks (New York: Praeger Publications, 1980), pp. 118–133.

ence (the equivalent of our Ph.D.) or Doctor of Science, for which there is no equivalent in the United States.

Upon graduation, students are required to accept assigned employment for at least two years in repayment for their free education. Of approximately 800,000 annual graduates from post-secondary institutions, however, tens of thousands refuse to report to their assigned jobs. Often these assignments are in backward provincial outlands that hold little attraction for these bright young people. Even though the law forbids plant managers to employ people who have been assigned to work elsewhere, this prohibition is often ignored because of the shortage of educated workers. Some students have even resorted to becoming pregnant in their last year of college to avoid being assigned to teach or work in the hinterland. In a recent attempt to prevent graduates from avoiding their compulsory service, diplomas are no longer being awarded upon completion of course work. Rather, the degrees are being withheld until the graduates complete their two years of compulsory work assignments.[9]

Appraisal of the Soviet Educational System

Like any other, the Soviet system of education receives mixed reviews. Given its basic objectives, however, one must conclude that it is quite successful at achieving the goals its leaders have set. Contrary to some expectations, liberal attitudes do not seem to increase among highly educated Soviet citizens. The politicization of the curriculum seems to assure that people generally accept collectivism as well as the Soviet regime. The emphasis on political propaganda, the sciences, and technical fields seem to assure that Soviet citizens are well trained but not well educated by Western standards. Lacking adequate exposure to the social sciences and the humanities, Soviet students usually do not exhibit much intellectual spontaneity, a matter of increasing concern among the leadership. For example, because the study of sociology focused on causes for social problems beyond economic ones, it met with disfavor during Stalin's era and was not revived until Khrushchev came to power. Even so, however, influential sociologist Tatyana Zaslavskaya reported that there are only three sociology departments in the whole country—and they were not opened until 1984.[10] As matters stand, Soviet education tends to produce a great many more technicians than intellectuals.

To their credit, Soviet authorities place great emphasis on education, spending approximately 14 percent of their total budget on it. Although teachers are poorly paid, they teach only three or four classes per day, and class sizes are generally smaller than in the United States. A high-school foreign language class in the United States may have as many as 35 or 40 students, whereas such a class in the Soviet Union may be limited to 10 or 12 students. Education remains free to all; the state assures that every

[9]Vera Rich, "Russia Seen Reforming Higher Education," *The Chronicle of Higher Education,* Nov. 5, 1986.

[10]Stephen F. Cohen and Katrina Vanden Heuvel, *Voices of Glasnost* (New York: W. W. Norton & Company, 1989), p. 116.

student receives a sound exposure to the basics of language, science, math, and vocational training. Those finding it impossible to attend school full time may complete their education in part-time or correspondence study.

On the other side of the ledger, however, Soviet students find themselves confronted with rigid discipline, enormous amounts of homework, and a great deal of pressure to conform and to succeed. Although the structure of the educational system is uniformly controlled by the central government, the quality of instruction, not unlike that in other societies, varies across the country, with the large urban areas enjoying the best education available. With prescribed texts, courses of study, syllabi, and teaching methods, little room is left for experimentation or innovation. Classes tend toward the "chalk/talk" method as audiovisual equipment and materials remain in short supply.

Because the number of students in higher education must be limited due to financial reasons, strenuous entrance examinations are given to applicants. Hence, late bloomers find it difficult to get a college education, thus reducing the talent pool from which the society can draw.

Although the Soviet system is unable to prevent high-status families from enjoying an advantage in admission to and success in post-secondary education, it has made college education available to more children from farms and the worker class than many Western systems provide. Additionally, about 50 percent of all college students are women, and most ethnic minorities encounter few impediments to seeking a higher education.

For most of its history, Soviet academies have been controlled by the state, but Gorbachev's reforms are reducing this debilitating restraint. Reflecting its continued interest in science, but also its new willingness to encourage individualism, the government has changed its policy of giving grants to the heads of institutes and letting these people, often political hacks, dole out the money to researchers as they saw fit. Since 1988 the government has given 70 percent of its research budget to individual scientists on a competitive basis, and the remainder of the budget goes to the institutes who must also compete for the grants. Further, the **Academy of Sciences,** the most prestigious scholarly institution in the country, is now allowed to elect its leadership by secret ballot, without government or party interference. The academy has long chosen its membership by secret ballot, but its leadership—those who controlled its funds and activities—were always party loyalists.

On balance, one must conclude that the Soviet system of education is a success. Within a very short time it has become capable of adequately servicing the needs of a highly complex industrial society. It has created a literacy rate that stands among the highest in the world, and it is available to all.

YOUTH GROUPS

Not content to leave the task of formal political socialization solely to the schools, the Soviets maintain three youth groups. Although the youth groups are technically not a part of the party or the schools, they work closely with both in efforts to develop model Soviet children, preparing them to become loyal, contented citizens.

The Little Octobrists and the Young Pioneers

All schoolchildren are inducted into the **Little Octobrists,** an organization roughly equivalent to the Cub Scouts and Brownies. The Little Octobrists provide a variety of out-of-school activities for youngsters under 10 years of age. The children learn handicrafts, games, songs, and stories; and they are taken on outings and shown films. The objective of their training is to acquaint them with proper personal, social, and political attitudes. The nation's heroes and history are lionized; members are encouraged to sacrifice their own interests for those of the group and taught to practice personal hygiene and good manners.

When they enter the fourth grade, the children leave the Little Octobrists, graduating to the **Young Pioneers.** Like our Boy Scouts or Girl Scouts, the Pioneers wear uniforms. Theirs are white and blue, garnished with a red star pin featuring Lenin's bust laid over an eternal flame. The ensemble is embellished by a red neckerchief knotted at the front.

Composed of older, more mature children than the Octobrists, the Pioneers experience a more heavily structured and more intensely instructional program. The children of each school are organized into a Pioneer brigade: Each grade level is combined into a detachment, and classrooms are divided into "links" of about a dozen students each. The links are the principal organizational units, and they practice "socialist competition" by vying with one another in scholastics, athletics, and personal conduct. As one might expect, the links that excel are assigned the task of helping the others improve. The link leader not only heads his or her particular unit but also reports to the teacher on the conduct and accomplishments of each member. Uncooperative students are shamed and pressured by their fellow link members to conform to the expectations of the school.

Pioneers are encouraged to demonstrate their devotion to the state by participating in various "socially useful" campaigns, such as cleaning up their school or neighborhood, aiding the aged, standing guard at a national monument, or agitating against smoking and excessive drinking.[11] Pioneers are also expected to hold to the rather puritanical moral code endorsed by Soviet authorities. Among the desired attitudes are good manners, respect for elders, mutual aid, willingness to work hard, frugality, and modesty.

The Pioneer organization maintains a large number of trade-union–supported facilities for its members. In the cities there are Pioneer palaces where youngsters can learn folk dances, music, art, crafts, and athletic skills. In the countryside a large number of Pioneer camps receive thousands of children each year; the camps, which operate during summer recess from school, reinforce the state's ideas about good conduct, morality,

---

[11]While riding a riverboat on the Dnieper near Kiev, I spotted in the passenger section a plaque exclaiming that the boat was made of scrap metal collected by local Pioneers.

and recreation. Pioneers also join parades during national holidays; enjoy outings to museums, monuments, and other places of interest; and take tours of the Soviet Union and occasionally even Eastern Europe.

Upon reaching age 15, students leave the Pioneers, and rather than being automatically inducted into the third and last youth group, they find themselves confronted with the choice of whether or not to continue their affiliation with the state's socialization network.

The Komsomol

Founded in 1918, the Young Communist League, better known as the **Komsomol,** is the oldest Soviet youth organization. In its early years the Komsomol was an idealistic and radical organization devoted to doing its part to lead the Soviet people to communism. In fact, the Komsomol was, for a time, more radical than the party itself; its members supported Trotsky during the early stages of his struggle with Stalin. Gradually, however, Stalin came to dominate the Komsomol, purging his enemies and appointing his supporters to its leadership. Its radicalism tamed, the Komsomol maintained its idealism, plunging into the modernization programs of the new five-year plans. Its members formed "shock brigades" that entered the factories and the countryside urging personal sacrifice and greater productivity. Komsomol zealots were also among those who carried out the brutal farm collectivizations that resulted in the Siberian exile or murder of millions of kulaks (well-to-do peasants). The Soviet effort during World War II was also enhanced by Komsomol activists who made great sacrifices for the motherland. Since World War II, however, the Komsomol has suffered a serious decline in the idealism and commitment of its members.

Contrary to the implication of its formal name, Komsomol members are not necessarily members of the Communist Party. It is not technically a party agency, although it is certainly controlled by the CPSU. Predictably, the organizational structure of the Komsomol is similar to that of the party. It is founded on a base of about 450,000 PPOs in military units, factories, apartments, offices, schools, and collective farms. Each level of government is flanked by a committee that governs the Komsomol units within its jurisdiction. This structure is capped by a central committee at the national level. Almost all Komsomol leaders are party members who are specially trained to work in the youth group. The most important Komsomol leaders are members of the Central Committee of the CPSU. Like the party, the Komsomol receives a large share of its revenue from publishing 238 youth magazines and newspapers. Its major organ is *Komsomolskaya Pravda,* a daily with a circulation of 17.6 million. It has become one of the most reform-oriented and liberal newspapers in the Soviet Union.

As indicated previously, the Komsomol differs from the other two youth groups in that its membership is selective. Instead of being automatically inducted along with the rest of one's class, as is done in the Little Octobrists and the Young Pioneers, one must apply for membership in the Komsomol. Aspirants must be between the ages of 14 and 28 and enjoy a good reputation in their neighborhoods, schools, and work places. Moreover, they must be sponsored for membership by members of the Komsomol or by a party member.

Komsomol members are expected to be model youth. They are to lead exemplary lives and work conscientiously to improve their productivity. Taking their cue from the party, they are expected to encourage their peers to follow accepted patterns in dress, manners, conduct, recreation, and social relationships. Consistent with the busybody nature of Soviet society, Komsomol units may be assigned to inspect dormitories for cleanliness and propriety, to conduct shame sessions for errant members, or to attempt to ameliorate family disputes.

Besides being productive at school or on the job, Komsomol members are expected to spend their spare time in socially useful endeavors. Some of them are assigned to spend their leisure hours counseling and leading Young Pioneer units, helping to clean up the streets, painting buildings, or trimming public gardens. They may be asked to agitate against unsafe driving, alcoholism, or juvenile delinquency; to serve on voluntary police forces (the *druzhina*); to help turn out people for parades on holidays; to march in parades; or to conduct propaganda and agitation for the party or the government. During the summer months, thousands of Komsomol members go to Siberia, Central Asia, or rural parts of the European Soviet Union to help with planting and harvests or with construction of roads and buildings.

When the party dropped its *nomenklatura* lists and withdrew from direct supervision of the government, the Komsomol was directly affected. Previously, career advancement was dependent on Komsomol membership, since it helped people achieve party membership later, and it was almost always required for admission to universities and institutes. The elimination of these advantages, along with its ideological training, its requirement for many hours of social work, and its puritanical rules of deportment, have left few modern youngsters attracted to the organization. Consequently, its membership began falling off steeply in 1987. Once boasting a membership of about half the Soviet people between the ages of 14 and 28, it now has only about 28 million members. Astonishingly, over four million members quit the organization in the first six months of 1990 alone. Attempting to reverse this trend, Komsomol leaders have tried to make group activities more relevant to the Soviet youth, even going to the point of creating job placement offices. Their prospects for rebuilding their membership seem bleak, however.[12]

Scouting

As the Komsomol has become unpopular (a 1990 poll found respondents less trustful of the Komsomol than of the KGB), many people turned

---

[12]Elizabeth Christie, "Discredited Communist Youth Group Finds New Life in the Job Market," *The Los Angeles Times,* July 31, 1990.

A young student guards the Tomb of the Unknown Soldier in Kiev.

to a different model: *scouting.* Founded in England in 1909 by Sir Robert Baden-Powell, scouting had spread to Russia by the time of the 1917 revolution. However, because Baden-Powell had been a British spy in Russia in 1886, and because many scout leaders supported the White cause during the Civil War, the Soviet government abolished scouting in the mid-1920s, sending many of its leaders to prison.

With the liberalization of the late 1980s, however, several people independently organized local troops, and in 1990 they founded the Russian Union of Scouts. Their success in attracting young people has not been lost on other groups, however. The leadership of Komsomol has expressed an interest in forming its own scout troops, and the xenophobic, anti-Semitic group, Pamyat, has also looked to the scouting model in an effort to lure youth to its reactionary cause.[13]

[13]John-Thor Dahlburg, "Scouting, Snuffed Out in '20s, Rekindled in Russia," *The Los Angeles Times,* Nov. 11, 1990.

THE MEDIA

In the Soviet Union, as in Western society, young and old alike are strongly influenced by the media. Information is generally recognized as a major source of power in any society. This realization is certainly a part of the Soviet consciousness, as it was in tsarist Russia. Controlling information through propaganda, censorship, and inordinate amounts of secrecy is a practice stretching far back into Russian history, long predating the Soviet era. Yet, use of modern technology and ideological commitment combined to give Soviet leaders a formidable capacity to control what their people knew.

Propaganda, Censorship, and Secrecy

The leaders of the Soviet Union, like those in many other nations, view propaganda as a legitimate activity in the socialization of their society. Putting a desirable spin on information is not uncommon among politicians even in the United States. Indeed, governments and other large organizations in every society employ legions of people—press secretaries or public information officers—to try to manipulate information for the benefit of their employers. In the Soviet Union, however, the propaganda effort was, until recently, extraordinarily intense. The media were required to report the current party line, which invariably placed the best possible light on the Soviet Union, even as it dwelled upon the most negative aspects of its adversaries. Since only the party line was regarded as true, Soviet officials contended that it would be irresponsible to suggest that opposing points of view might be correct.

The Soviet people were not unaware of the slant placed on the official news. This now dated joke demonstrates their shrewd comprehension:

> President Kennedy and First Secretary Khrushchev ran a race. When Khrushchev came across the finish line after Kennedy, the Soviet press is supposed to have reported, "Our beloved Nikita Sergeivich won a respectable second place, but the American President finished next to last."

Censorship, which Marx condemned as hypocrisy, is another major tool to control information. Before the late 1980s, no official publication or broadcast was free of the censor's blue pencil. Every book, article, journal, radio broadcast, and television script had to be submitted before publication to the scrutiny of *Glavlit* (the Chief Administration of Literary and Publishing Affairs), the official censorship agency. Soviet writers and broadcasters familiarized themselves with a list of thousands upon thousands of forbidden topics that were to be published only with special permission. The Ministry of Culture even had a department of jokes, through which Soviet comics had to clear their material.

Soviet writers must belong to a trade union, and membership in the party is also advisable. Both of these institutions also exerted pressure encouraging compliance with official norms for publication. More than the institutional checks on Soviet writers, however, the most efficient censors were the writers themselves. Unwilling to jeopardize their careers by writing about a forbidden topic or arousing suspicions among their superiors by not showing the expected political discretion in their articles, Soviet writers were extremely cautious about the material they submitted to official censors for approval. Hence self-censorship assured that a good deal of the spontaneity and breadth of coverage common in the West was absent from Soviet publications.

Heading the list of motivations for Soviet control of information was secrecy. Like their tsarist predecessors, Soviet rulers shunned openness, preferring to give vent to an exaggerated suspicion about the harm large amounts of information could do the society. Even some of the most mundane kinds of information were classified and thus withheld from publication. Timely and complete information about natural disasters, crime, and even personal details about the leadership often did not appear in Soviet publications. For example, the Soviet people, and the world at large, were forced to wait for several days before the authorities published detailed accounts of the nuclear power plant accident at Chernobyl. During the first critical hours after the explosion releasing deadly radiation from the plant, Radio Kiev, only 60 miles from the accident, broadcast this terse announcement:

> There has been an accident at the Chernobyl nuclear power plant in the Ukraine. One of the nuclear reactors has been damaged. Measures for eliminating the consequences of the nuclear accident have been undertaken and victims are being rendered assistance.[14]

By contrast, however, the Soviet people were among the world's best informed people—that is, on matters their government wished them to know about. The same instruments of propaganda, secrecy, and censorship used to deny information were also employed to inculcate the citizenry with desired knowledge and attitudes. Accordingly, the Soviet people were treated to numerous explanations of government policies and frequent campaigns mobilizing the people to increase productivity, to drive more carefully, to conserve energy, and so on. Besides the press, the Soviet government used party agitators to speak to the workers on the farms, at the offices, in the factories, and at the schools. Every city or village has a house of culture where the party line was absorbed by the people while they engaged in recreation or entertainment. While commercial advertisement was almost unknown on Soviet billboards, every Soviet city was festooned with large signs, usually in red and white, which proclaimed slogans and goals the leadership wished presented.

[14]"Radio Kiev Skims Over News, Moves to Sports," *The Los Angeles Times*, May 1, 1986.

Glasnost. Very soon after he became the Communist Party general secretary, Gorbachev realized that the muted circumstances in the Soviet Union must be changed. Science and high-tech productivity are dependent upon the free flow of information and the exchange of ideas. More specific to the Soviet Union, silence about the Stalinist era prevented the society from facing the truth about its own history and compelled it to live a lie. The Brezhnev era, now called the period of stagnation, had become mired in lethargic corruption and thus obscured understanding about its present and about the future. Information and travel had been strictly controlled since tsarist times, but Stalin's paranoia and Brezhnev's conservatism had exaggerated this control beyond reason until telephone books were issued only to government offices and Soviet-made maps were deliberately distorted and inaccurate. The absurdity of the Soviet fetish for secrecy, long obvious to many outsiders, became clear to Gorbachev and his supporters in the mid-1980s. Accordingly, Gorbachev called for **glasnost** (openness), and a new era was born in the Soviet Union.

Although the parameters of glasnost are still not completely clear, the policy has engendered unprecedented candor in the society. Among the primary targets Gorbachev set early on was debunking Stalinism, or **de-Stalinization.** The media became the most important instrument for executing this policy, although the urban press seems to be much more comfortable in that role than more provincial publications.[15] In 1988 Khrushchev's secret speech to the Twentieth Party Congress detailing Stalin's crimes was published in the Polish weekly, *Polityka,* apparently with Soviet approval. The contents of the speech had long been known in the West and among Soviet intellectuals, but it had never before been officially published in the communist bloc. The publication was quickly followed by revelations of NKVD (the Stalinist secret police) executions of millions of people and the unearthing of mass grave sites of Stalin's victims across the country. The people were first shocked by the seemingly interminable revelations, but eventually they appeared to become anesthetized or even bored by them, according to a former Soviet pollster.[16] Undeterred, the debunking campaign continued. Films, plays, television programs, and books critical of Stalin's policies were presented; old Bolsheviks who had been vilified and disgraced were rehabilitated—even Trotsky was mentioned in *Pravda* and other media in sympathetic articles, and some of his works were published in the Soviet press. Finally, the Central Committee of the Communist Party recommended that the government pass a law rehabilitating millions of Stalin's victims, and it publicly supported erecting monuments to those who were persecuted and killed during the terror.

Beyond Stalinism, the spotlight of the media has been turned on virtually every problem in the Soviet Union. Once forbidden topics like official corruption, negligence, nepotism, poverty, homelessness, crime,

---

[15]See Walter Laqueur, *Stalin: The Glasnost Revelations* (New York: Charles Scribner's Sons, 1990).

[16]Vladimir Shlapentokh, "Soviet Citizenry Grows Restless," *The Los Angeles Times,* Aug. 28, 1989.

prostitution, AIDS, natural and human disasters, and so on are exposed and analyzed in the press. The growing power of the press as a check on the government is articulated by this Soviet riddle:

> What does a butterfly and a government minister have in common?
> They both can be killed by a newspaper.

Soviet maps are now accurate; the government has stopped jamming Radio Liberty, Radio Free Europe, and other foreign broadcasts; Voice of America now even has offices in Moscow. Telefax machines are used by newspapers, businesses, and a few private individuals, and the government no longer tries to regulate the use of copy machines. Until 1989 the Ministry of Interior required the registration of all copy machines and strict control of their use. Now, with this restriction gone, private journals and newsletters, called **samizdat,** flood the streets and are sold in the open.

Gorbachev's strategy was to use the press to combat self-indulgent and insensitive bureaucrats. But, as the Russian proverb reminds us, "When you chop wood, chips fly." Before long, glasnost went farther than the general secretary had anticipated. The people undoubtedly profit by having access to more information, and they also no longer exhibit much concern about openly talking to foreigners or expressing their views. Suddenly the former practice of "kitchen glasnost" (candor in the privacy of one's home) has been replaced by public complaints about declining economic conditions, the rising crime rate, and ethnic unrest.

The Soviets have become inveterate pollsters as public opinion (usually negative) on one thing or another is published daily in the press. Glasnost also cuts two ways. The conservatives have used the new freedom to criticize Gorbachev's policies, even as the reformers have begun to do the same from the other side of the political spectrum. Stung by complaints from all sides, in 1989 Gorbachev called together editors of the leading magazines and newspapers to angrily assert that some of them were going too far and that they should focus more on the positive achievements of his programs than on their failures. Two radical reformers, Vladislav A. Starkov, editor of *Argumenty i Fakty* (Arguments and Facts), and Vitaly A. Korotich, editor of *Ogonyok* (Little Light), were particularly singled out as offenders.[17] Many observers were concerned that this outburst might signal a reversal of glasnost, but such has not yet been the case, and criticism of Gorbachev and his programs mounts. Indeed, reflecting both the new freedom of the press and the growing economic crisis, a new joke is making the rounds.

> It is more interesting to read in the Soviet Union than to live in it.

[17]John-Thor Dahlburg of the Associated Press, "Gorbachev Turns About-Face on Practitioners of Glasnost." *Escondido Times-Advocate,* Oct. 17, 1989.

Yet, other Soviet humor suggests that perhaps glasnost is more permissible for the press than it is for the individual.

> "Volokya," asks Ivan, "have you read the latest issue of *Moscow News?*"
> [*Moscow News* is a leftist newspaper.]
>
> "No, Ivan. What does it say?"
>
> "It's not something we can talk about on the phone," Ivan responds. "I'll bring it over."

Despite the new freedom of glasnost, however, the press has also had its problems. The 1991 Soviet clampdown in Lithuania is a good example. Although many in the media supported the action, the radical press did not, with *Moscow News* calling Gorbachev's government criminal. In an angry response, Gorbachev called on the Supreme Soviet to suspend the freedom of press law it had passed only six months before. This is but one of many moves to the right by Gorbachev since the summer of 1990, but the Supreme Soviet has so far refused to approve Gorbachev's request.

Soviet writers still claim that censorship is not completely eliminated. Glavlit continues to operate, although now the editors have the last word about what will be published—except where military secrets and pornography are involved. Previously, editors could blame deletions on the censors. Now, however, since the editors are usually the ultimate judge of what is published, they find themselves the object of the writers' wrath that was previously directed at Glavlit. **Self-censorship** is still a problem, however. Because of reflexes developed from years of having to please the censors, or because of fear that glasnost might be rescinded, many Soviet journalists are still cautious about what they submit for publication under their names. So even though Glavlit is no longer as powerful as it once was, the "inner censor" tends to inhibit many writers.

One place where the inner censors and the outer censors have each been very unsuccessful is in the field of pornography. Since glasnost was invoked, "girly literature," films, and videos have flooded the market. This in a society that was previously noted for its straight-laced approach to sex. Soviet officials estimate that the pornography market now generates about 9 billion rubles in profits annually. There are over 25,000 video salons alone, nationwide, featuring programs heavily ladened with sex and violence.

Demands for control over pornography from certain elements of the public have flooded into the government, while at the same time an apparently equal number of people want it left alone. Gorbachev created a Committee for Public Morals late in 1990 to fight against the objectionable material. In 1991, however, the Supreme Soviet refused to pass censorship laws relating to pornography. Instead, it created a government panel to develop and promulgate the distinction between acceptable and unacceptable exhibitions of nudity and sexual acts.[18]

---

[18]Carey Goldberg, "Soviets Act on Furor Over Pornography," *The Los Angeles Times,* April 13, 1991.

The Print Media

The Soviet press is among the most extensive in the world. In 1989 the Soviet Union published 8,500 newspapers with a circulation of 200 million.[19] By comparison, in 1988 there were 1,642 daily newspapers in the United States with a circulation of only 62.7 million.[20] Passionate readers, the Soviet people are served by three official news services, thousands of newspapers, and hundreds of periodicals, journals, and magazines. Like the Associated Press, United Press International, and Reuters in the West, Soviet news agencies supply the Soviet and foreign press with some of their copy. Two news services, TASS (Telegraphic Agency of the Soviet Union) and Novosti (News), have correspondents throughout the world. TASS, a government agency, is the more authoritative news service. Novosti is ostensibly not a government agency, but it is clearly subject to the same checks and constraints as TASS. A third news agency, Interfax, is associated with Radio Moscow and recently became the source of some of the most revealing stories about the Soviet Union. In an ominous move, the government tried to shut down Interfax in 1991, but it was reopened because of the insistence of its employees. Some of the popular fronts have also developed their own private news agencies, reporting on developments in the provinces. Rukh Press International is the most noteworthy of these.

Before glasnost, news was distributed on a need-to-know basis. Consequently, even most government and party officials—to say nothing about ordinary people—were allowed to see only those items thought appropriate for them. TASS, for example, released three daily versions of the news; they were named for the color of paper used. The "blue TASS" was for general consumption and was void of anything that the leadership felt was critical of the Soviet Union or the party. Usually the only controversial articles published were those that the leadership planted to signal the demotion of an official or to call attention to a problem the government wanted people to deal with, like alcoholism. Reports about foreign events were also heavily censored. The "white TASS" went to middling party and government officials, and it contained a greater number of articles on a broader range of topics, foreign and domestic. Finally the "red TASS" went to the leading party and government people and included stories from the foreign as well as the domestic press; virtually no important subject was deleted from it.[21]

The Soviet press was used to mold public attitudes and opinion and to mobilize the public to accomplish the goals the leadership had set. Speaking to this point, the conservative *Pravda* editor, Viktor G. Afanasyev, who has since been replaced, said, "Our job is to help organize the masses to fulfill the party's wishes, to shape and reflect public opinion."[22]

[19]*USSR '90 Yearbook*, p. 200.

[20]*Statistical Abstracts of the United States* (Washington, DC: US Department of Commerce, 1990), p. 555.

[21]Hedrick Smith, *The Russians* (New York: Ballantine, 1976), pp. 474–495.

[22]Philip Taubman, "Soviet Newspaper *Pravda* Reflects a New Openness," *Escondido Times-Advocate*, Feb. 15, 1987.

Clearly, matters have changed since 1987 when Afanasyev made this statement.

The Soviet Union has over 8,000 newspapers, with a total circulation of 200 million. Besides Russian-language newspapers, there are newspapers in about 60 other languages. Home delivery is uncommon, so most Soviet citizens must buy their newspapers on the streets. Paper sales are ubiquitous and prices are kept down to about 10 cents for a copy of *Pravda*. Playing on the low price of *Pravda* (which means "truth" in Russian) and winking at its credibility, Soviet wags often quip that

> Truth is cheap in the Soviet Union.

To further increase their readership, newspapers are displayed on bulletin boards throughout the city for passers-by to peruse.

Pravda, established by Lenin in 1912, is the Communist Party paper and until recently it was the largest, most authoritative publication in the country, but since 1987 its circulation has plummeted from 11.1 million to 6.5 million in 1990. Essentially, its pages are viewed as little more than the mouthpiece for a discredited party. It has also made some critical errors. Most notably it took on Boris Yeltsin, the country's most popular politician. The paper printed an unsubstantiated Italian newspaper's account of Yeltsin's exploits on a 1990 visit to the United States. The article claimed the Russian leader had made a fool of himself by being drunk during most

Public bulletin boards are located throughout Soviet cities where daily papers are posted for passers-by to read. In this picture a Soviet woman reads a copy of *Pravda*. (Photo provided by Louis and Helen Van Moppes.)

of a tour in the West. The public uproar in support of Yeltsin cost Afanasyev his job, and since then the new editor, a philosopher and the former editor of *Kommunist,* reformer Ivan T. Frolov, now a Politburo member, has tried to change the paper's image. He changed its format: It now uses color on Sundays; it includes some advertisements for the first time—even some advertising Western products; and it now carries more interesting and controversial articles—some of which even criticize the party. Until the party itself becomes more acceptable in the eyes of the people, however, *Pravda's* circulation is not likely to increase by much.

   Izvestia is the official government newspaper. It used to be conservative and hackish, but since glasnost it has become one of the most respected and professional journals in the country. Efforts in 1991 by conservative officials to transfer its senior editor, Igor N. Golembiovsky, were foiled by protests among the *Izvestia* staff.

   The largest number of Soviet newspapers address regional or local issues. There are, however, several well-known national papers besides *Pravda* and *Izvestia.* Most of these are dailies published by the major interest groups in the society. *Trud* (Labor), for example, is published by the nation's trade unions, *Krasnaya Zvezda* (Red Star) by the military, and *Komsomolskaya Pravda* (Komsomol Truth) by the Komsomol. The newspaper with the largest current circulation is *Argumenty i Fakty* (Arguements and Facts). (See Table 7–1.) Its editor, Vladislav A. Starkov, built its readership from 1.4 million in 1985 to almost 30 million in 1990, making it the most widely read newspaper in the world. The secrets to its success are aggressive editorials and short, hard-hitting articles about problems in Soviet society, including Stalin's purges, unemployment, nuclear weapons, housing shortages, poverty, crime, and official corruption. Called the people's newspaper, its muckraking pages spare no one—not even Gorbachev. In 1989 the paper conducted a poll of the country's most popular politicians: Gorbachev was not listed among them. Angered by the "negativity" of *Argumenty i Fakty,* Gorbachev called for Starkov's resignation, but so far the pugnacious editor continues at his post.

   Before glasnost, Soviet newspapers were dull sheets. News items were brief and uninformative, causing people to "read the white spaces" (read between the lines) to get a realistic idea of what was going on. This reality left them largely dependent on supposition, inference, and especially rumor. So serious were some of these whispering campaigns in their effect on the public mood that the press was sometimes forced to publish denials of stories they never reported. Long pieces lauding the productivity of various segments of the economy appeared. These articles resembled brag sheets more than news articles, for they extolled the efforts of heroic workers in the Uzbekistan cotton fields or the voluntary sacrifices made by Siberian coal miners to increase production. Official editorials outlining party and government policy were ubiquitous. Newspapers also included feature articles, public interest stories, sports, and television listings. There were no advertisements, advice columns, comic strips, horoscopes, or classified ads. Of course, much has changed recently and many of the once absent features are now regularly carried in the Soviet press, to say nothing about the numerous articles on controversial subjects. Letters to the editor

TABLE 7–1   Circulation of Leading Soviet Newspapers and Magazines (in millions of copies)

	1985	1986	1987	1988	1989
Newspapers					
Argumenty i Fakty	1.4	1.9	3.2	9.1	20.5
Trud	16.4	18.2	18.2	19.0	19.5
Komsomolskaya Pravda	13.2	14.6	17.0	17.6	17.6
Izvestia	6.7	6.9	8.0	10.4	10.1
Pravda	10.5	10.8	11.1	10.7	9.7
Selskaya Zhizn	9.1	9.0	8.8	7.5	6.6
Literaturnaya Gazeta	3.0	3.0	3.1	3.8	6.3
Sovetsky Sport	4.6	4.6	4.8	5.2	4.7
Sovetskaya Rossiya	3.6	3.6	4.6	5.2	4.2
Krasnaya Zvezda	2.2	2.3	2.3	2.0	1.4
Sotsialisticheskaya Industriya	1.3	1.3	1.3	1.5	1.0
Ekonomicheskaya Gazeta	0.7	0.7	0.8	0.7	0.7
Magazines					
Krestyanka	14.3	16.4	17.4	18.9	20.4
Rabotnitsa	15.9	17.3	17.5	19.8	20.4
Zdorovey	16.6	15.9	15.6	16.8	15.5
Roman-Gazeta	2.0	1.8	2.5	3.5	3.8
*Ogonyok**	1.5	1.5	1.5	1.8	3.4
Smena	1.1	1.1	1.3	2.0	2.4
Politicheskoye Obrazovaniye	2.4	2.5	2.6	2.3	1.9
Novy Mir	0.4	0.4	0.5	1.1	1.6
Agitator	1.5	1.6	1.6	1.4	1.2
Druzhba Narodov	0.2	0.2	0.2	0.8	1.1

*Its circulation has been artificially limited by recalcitrant bureaucrats.

Source: *USSR '90 Yearbook* (Moscow: Novosti Press Agency, 1990), p. 201.

were sometimes interesting as they often complained about inefficiency and corruption. It is suspected, however, that many of these were planted by the leadership to call attention to a problem it wanted highlighted. Still, millions of letters to the editor were, and are, received by the press each year. Until 1988 Western newspapers and magazines were very difficult to come by in the Soviet Union. Now, however, they are sold along with Soviet journals at *kiosks* on the street.

Over 5,000 magazines are published in the Soviet Union with annual printings of 3.7 billion copies. These are usually keyed to specific interests, ranging from women to farmers, chess to travel. Perhaps the most entertaining magazine in the USSR is *Krokodil* (Crocodile), a humor magazine. Founded in 1922, it is the oldest extant magazine in the Soviet Union. Although its editors had to be careful to observe the conventions imposed on all publications, *Krokodil* was able to do with humor what other media could not: sharply criticize the system. It poked fun at the generation gap, alcoholism, the foibles of bureaucrats, the ethnic problems, and the scarcity of consumer goods. With many of the traditional taboos now abolished, the magazine is able to take even closer satirical aim at the society and its institutions.

A number of Soviet magazines focus on current affairs, but the most authoritative magazine on ideological questions is *Kommunist*. Once enjoying wide circulation, this magazine is a major vehicle by which the party expresses its ideological interpretations on current affairs. Its popularity, however, has gone the way of *Pravda* and the party itself. A magazine achieving recent popularity is *Ogonyok*. Previously a mundane publication, its new editor, Vitaly Korotich, responding to Gorbachev's policy of glasnost, has made it a muckraking journal that reports on many formerly taboo subjects, and the public has received the change with enthusiasm. A thorn in the side of conservatives and bureaucrats, *Ogonyok* experienced an attempt to limit its circulation. In 1990 the government suddenly raised the journal's annual subscription rate to 51 rubles, a very high figure. Undaunted, Korotich and his staff fought back, finally pooling their money and buying the magazine from the government. However, it is having trouble purchasing newsprint, and getting the government houses to print the weekly is a constant struggle. Korotich is seeking an independent source of printing and newsprint; he even contacted *Time-Life* and *Reader's Digest* in this regard.[23]

Soviet magazines such as *Soviet Life* and *Sputnik* are also available in the United States. Although they are specifically designed for Western readers, one can sample their technical quality (which is quite good) and gain some insight into the style employed by Soviet publishers.

A wide variety of professional journals are also published. With its fetish for secrecy, the government classified most new scientific findings, thus sheltering them from the view of Western scientists but also denying them to their own researchers and scholars. Herein was one of the troublesome flaws in the Soviet system. To prevent foreigners from profiting from Soviet research, the authorities also denied it to their own people, thus tending to hinder the scientific and technological progress the economy so desperately needed. Recognizing this problem and hoping to enlist the intellectuals in support of his economic and social reforms, Gorbachev made several important efforts to relax censorship and to encourage the flow of information within the society.

In June 1990 the Supreme Soviet passed a long-awaited law guaranteeing freedom of the press and establishing criminal punishment for people who violate the law. Further, journalists are now free to remove their names from articles that contradict their personal convictions. Although it is laudable, this statute is apparently limited in at least one important respect. The month before it was passed, the Supreme Soviet passed another statute making it a criminal violation to "insult or slander" the

---

[23]John-Thor Dahlburg, "Fiery Soviet Magazine Flies Free of Party Ties," *The Los Angeles Times,* Aug. 4, 1990.

president of the Soviet Union. Passed in response to the 1990 May Day parade when protesters marched through Red Square reviling Gorbachev and other Soviet leaders, this law seems to be a throwback to a former, less tolerant era. So far, the law has not been enforced, but if it is, a private person can get as much as three years in prison and up to three more if the offending remarks are carried in the media. Newspapers and television programs that are twice found to publish such statements can be suspended or shut down.

With this exception, however, the Soviets so far seem to be taking their freedom seriously. The printed media is divided on the question of Gorbachev's reforms, although not every publication has entered the debate. Among the most conservative publications besides *Pravda* are *Moskovskaya Pravda, Sovietskaya Rossiya, Literaturnaya Rossiya, Molodaya Gvardia,* and *Nash Sovremennik.* Ranged against them are the reformist publications *Ogonyok, Mosokvskiye Novosti* (Moscow News), *Komsomolskaya Pravda, Argumenty i Fakty,* and *Novy Mir,* the only major publication to have a non-party member as editor, Sergei Zalygin.

The Electronic Media

Soviet leaders once thought radio was a good way to reach vast numbers of people. Swift electrification of the country after the Civil War was followed by an effort to make radio receivers available to Soviet consumers. Until Stalin's death, most receivers were closed-circuit instruments that had to be wired into government-controlled broadcasts. The introduction of wireless receivers not only increased the availability of receivers but also opened the Soviet audience to broadcasts from outside the USSR. This situation brought pause to the leadership, a concern that was amplified by the West's efforts to broadcast programs rivaling the propaganda level of Soviet offerings. Until the late 1980s, the Soviets tried to jam most foreign broadcasts, but an estimated 20 percent of the people listened to some kind of foreign broadcast each week. Glasnost has brought an end to the jamming. At the same time the Soviet Union is the largest international broadcaster in the world, transmitting 240 hours of programming a day in 77 languages.

Domestically Soviet radio broadcasts over 1,400 hours of programming daily. These programs are in 67 of the languages used in the country. Television is also widely used, with 4,000 hours of programs transmitted each day in 45 languages. Television has been met with wide popular acceptance and has become a major feature in the society. Enjoying precious few outlets for entertainment and relaxation, the Soviet people have become devoted television viewers. The authorities were quick to appreciate the opportunity television offers. Having a weaker signal than radio, television was especially convenient as it limits the vast majority of citizens to domestic programming. Access to television from the West was enjoyed only by viewers in the Baltic region which receives a signal from Finland. Now, however, Western programs can be relayed into most of the European union republics from Eastern European transmitters.

Presently there are about 350 television stations across the land, and a vast network of booster stations carry Moscow programming throughout the populated sections of the country. The extensive broadcast coverage is accompanied by an unusual attention to the consumer. Unlike most Soviet consumer goods, television sets are of remarkably good quality, and their cost is kept to reasonable levels. A black-and-white set costs approximately 160 rubles, the equivalent of just over three weeks' wages. To date, about 90 percent of Soviet households have television sets as compared to about 98 percent in the United States. Only about 30 percent of Soviet television sets are color, however. Quality color sets cost almost five times as much as black-and-white sets.

Soviet radio and television were censored as rigorously as printed materials. Although the technical quality of programs was good, the content quality was mixed. News broadcasts, like articles in the press, were usually brief and unrevealing. Live interviews and programming were rare as the censors wanted to preview all items before they were transmitted. There were special channels carrying educational programming for both adults and children. (Soviet children watch television an average of 21 hours per week, compared to American youngsters who watch an average of 30 hours.) Another channel was devoted exclusively to sports. Regular programming featured drama, ballets, concerts, operas, films, amateur hours, travel logs, and economic and social themes laced with propaganda.

Today, however, programming is less political and more varied. In addition to the types of programs mentioned before, programs featuring topics from aerobics to game shows to faith healers are shown. The Soviet Union is even showing American television programs, including "Barnaby Jones," "Love Boat," and "Dallas." While some eyebrows might be raised concerning the dramatic quality of these selections, the fact that Western programs are being aired on Soviet television is a major step forward for glasnost. Indeed, if negotiations are successfully completed, Seventh Day Adventist George Vandeman will broadcast his religious series, "It Is Written," in weekly programs on Soviet nationwide television. In 1988, Robert Schuller of the Crystal Cathedral was broadcast in the Soviet Union, but the show was canceled by the Soviets after only a few weeks.

Like the printed media, radio and television broadcast programs about Stalin's use of terrorism, drug abuse, alcoholism, juvenile delinquency, official corruption, and so on. "Pyatoye Koleso" (Fifth Wheel), broadcast from Leningrad, is similar to the CBS program, "60 Minutes," and is watched weekly by avid viewers. "Vremya," out of Moscow, is the most popular newscast. "Vzglyad" (Viewpoint), the most popular and radical television news magazine, ran afoul of the authorities by interviewing several aides of Eduard Shevardnadze, in an attempt to find out why he resigned as foreign minister. The program was taken off the air in 1991. This action and the attempted closing of the news agency Interfax have stimulated serious questions about whether glasnost is being abandoned.

Considerable controversy surrounds television broadcasting because it is so popular. (On average, 100 million people watch it each night.) Critics complain that the government and party continue to use it for their own purposes. For example, in 1990 the television broadcast of Moscow's May Day parade was shut off after protesters began to shout unpleasant, angry slogans at Gorbachev and other leaders. Similarly, Gorbachev's criticism of Boris Yeltsin given at the Russian Congress of Peoples' Deputies was aired in its entirety, while no part of Yeltsin's remarks of the previous day was shown. Some candidates for the CPD of the USSR also complained that they were not given the air time the election rules guaranteed.

To deal with the controversy, Gorbachev issued a presidential decree in July 1990 that henceforth Soviet television and radio were to be unbiased in their coverage. Further, he authorized union republics, local governments, and even political parties to establish their own radio and television stations and to use state facilities for their broadcasts. Even so, official coverage of the 1991 military crackdown on Lithuania was decidedly pro-Soviet. Furthermore, Gorbachev's appointment of conservative party member, Leonid P. Kravchenko, as Chairman of the State Committee for Television and Radio has caused considerable concern among many people in the media. Kravchenko has ordered the electronic media to become more circumspect in its criticisms of Gorbachev's policies. Refusing to cooperate with what he believed to be a retreat from the freedoms of glasnost, Vladimir Pozner, the most widely known Soviet commentator in the West, abruptly resigned his post with the committee in 1991. He complained that Kravchenko was transforming the committee "from state television and radio, which is tolerable, into presidential television and radio, which isn't."[24]

CULTURE

Soviet culture was also closely controlled by the party, the state, and the trade unions. Artists were told where and what to perform. **Socialist realism** was required of all artists. This concept demanded that Soviet society be portrayed not as it was, but as it would be. Hence, the truth in art became obscured by the bureaucrats' mandates. Soviet humorists have not let such obfuscations pass without comment. Asked to describe various art forms, a Soviet artist is supposed to have said

> "Expressionism is painting what you feel, impressionism is painting what you see, and socialist realism is painting what you hear."

This bit of levity, however, should not obscure the bitterness artistic people felt at the imposition of socialist realism. Their creativity stifled during the Brezhnev period, musicians, writers, artists, dancers, and other artistic people fled the Soviet Union, robbing it of richness, sensitivity, and depth.

---

[24]Michael Parks, "TV's Face of Glasnost, Vladimir Pozner, Quits as State Tightens Reins," *The Los Angeles Times*, April 27, 1991.

When Gorbachev launched glasnost, the first group he turned to were the intellectuals and the people in the creative community, and some of them have been quick to respond. Elem Kilmov, the film director and an outcast during Brezhnev's era, led a political drive to take control of the Filmmakers Union in 1986. He immediately released films that had been forbidden for decades, including Andrei Tarkovsky's *Andrei Rublev,* Tengiz Abuladze's *Repentance, The Commissar* by Alexander Askoldov, Eralii Kvirikadze's *The Swimmer,* and his own films *Farewell* and *Agony.* Since then several interesting new films have also been produced, including modern social commentary in *Is It Easy to Be Young?* and *Little Vera,* and comedies like *Lovely Women Searching for a Life Companion.*

An opening in literature also took place with the publication of Roy Medvedev's *Let History Judge; Children of the Arbat* by Anatoly Rybakov; Alexander Solzhenitsyn's *First Circle, Cancer Ward,* and *The Gulag Archipelago;* and *Forever Flowing* and *Life and Fate* by Vasily Grossman. Each of these works is deeply critical of Soviet politics and society. This passage from *Forever Flowing* is an example. Grossman writes,

> What hope is there for Russia if even her greatest prophets cannot tell freedom from slavery? What hope is there for Russia if her greatest geniuses see the bright gentle beauty of her soul made manifest in her submissive acceptance of slavery?

As valuable as these works are, however, they are all the products of previous eras. Little of great quality has yet come from post-glasnost film or literature. The same is true of Soviet theater. Theater critic Igor Shagin recently complained, "Our artists now have freedom, more money, the right to travel abroad and meet foreigners here. People want to know where all the masterpieces are."[25]

There are of course writers of quality in the Soviet Union. Chingiz Aitmator depicts the ecological and social problems suffered in Central Asia in *The Place of the Skull; Fire* gives vent to Valentin Rasputin's populist and reactionary ideas; and the enduring poet, Yevgeny Yevtushenko, continues to write powerful and thoughtful verse. Yevtushenko claims that poetry played a special part in making the current liberalization possible. "The poetry of our generation," he said "was the cradle of glasnost." Whether a correct assessment or not, poetry is given a prominence in Soviet society that is equaled in few and surpassed by none.

In art, too, the recent opening is making way for the showing of previously forbidden works—those of Kasimir Malevich, for example. Yet, although contemporary art is produced in the Soviet Union, it finds a greater market among Western collectors than among Soviet buyers. On the other hand, Soviet posters have gone through a great renaissance, abandoning the pseudo-heroic figures of socialist realism for more imaginative and realistic portrayals.[26]

---

[25]John Kohan, "Freedom Waiting for Vision," *Time Magazine,* April 10, 1989.
[26]See Victor Litvinov, *The Posters of Glasnost and Perestroika* (New York: Penguin, 1990).

Perhaps the greatest cultural revival of glasnost so far is to be found among Soviet youth. Bizarre costumes and punk hair are now in fashion. Rock music is as popular among Soviet youth as with youngsters in the West. Once forced to go underground, rock bands now abound and public concerts are common in most cities. DDI, Black Coffee, Time Machine, and many other groups sing and gyrate irreverently with the best of them. Their music focuses on contemporary themes and people. One group, Grand Prix, has even introduced a song entitled "Gorbachev." The youth culture is expressing itself in other ways. Soviet film heartthrob Natalia Negoda posed seductively for *Playboy Magazine* in 1989, and soon a Disneyland-style theme park is supposed to be completed in Moscow.

But the exuberance of the freed youth and the resurrection of old masterpieces, which never should have been buried by censors in the first place, do not obscure the regrettable fact that glasnost has yet to produce a large amount of excellent serious art. The reason for this cultural deficit is not clear. It could be that the works are in progress and that expecting them to materialize immediately is unfair. It could also be that such works are still subtly discouraged. As late as 1987, a Soviet citizen was arrested and prosecuted for distributing copies of *Lolita,* the great psychoerotic novel by Vladimir Nabokov, and Glavlit tried unsuccessfully to discourage the publication of Yevtushenko's epic poem, *Fuka,* at about the same time. Academia also seems to withhold its potential. As historian Yuri Afanasyev laments, "There is more perestroika and glasnost in the media than in academics."[27] For whatever the reason, glasnost has yet to give vent to the abundance of cultural achievement that the society has provided in the past. In hopeful anticipation, the world awaits.

TRADE UNIONS

The first Russian trade unions were organized in the tumultuous days of the 1905 revolution. There had been several attempts to organize unions before that time, but each failed. Even so, workers' strikes were relatively common as protests against the exploitative conditions in which the laborers were forced to toil.

Once organized, unions grew rapidly. By 1907 there were 625 trade unions, with a total membership of 245,000 workers, and by the summer of 1917 union membership had grown to 1.5 million. As the Kerensky government unsuccessfully struggled for control against the workers' soviets, trade union membership expanded, until it reached almost 3 million in October 1917.

Quick to seize the opportunity of growing labor unrest, the Mensheviks established themselves at the head of the trade union movement. Their indecisiveness about further steps, however, proved debilitating in the face of the growing Bolshevik aggressiveness. "All power to the Soviets" and "Workers take the factories" were slogans Lenin used to bring workers

[27]Cohen and Heuvel, p. 114.

to his camp. By October 1917 the workers and the military around Petrograd had united behind the Bolshevik banner and marched on the Winter Palace, bringing the Kerensky government down. But the question of labor's position in the new society was yet to be determined when the Bolsheviks came to power. Should the trade unions remain independent of party and government control, should they be managed by the state, or, indeed, should they exist at all?

Having encouraged the workers' independence before the revolution in order to destabilize the Kerensky government, after the revolution Lenin needed to consolidate the situation so as to restore productivity. Hence, he supported a policy of subjecting the independent workers' councils to trade union control. This objective accomplished by 1919, the Bolsheviks faced an even greater problem: controlling the trade unions themselves.[28] The issue, precipitated by Leon Trotsky, who was responsible for Soviet railroads at the time, erupted in 1921 at the Tenth Party Congress. Trotsky argued that because workers now controlled the state, trade unions had become unnecessary. Labor affairs, the energetic Bolshevik leader suggested, should be handled through normal government channels.

Resisting Trotsky's plan, a group of union leaders organized a faction that came to be known as the *Workers' Opposition.* The trade union leadership was given to syndicalism, by which the economy would be organized and administered by the trade unions. Shunning party control and government authority, the Workers' Opposition insisted that a true workers' state would be one that remained under direct control of the laborers, unimpeded by party or government.

Entering the debate with a third alternative, Lenin ameliorated the situation by advocating a compromise. Following Lenin's proposal, the Tenth Party Congress agreed that, as the party leader said, "the trade unions are a school of communism" and as such should enjoy a unique place in society.[29] They could retain their distinct structure and identity, but at the same time they were to be subordinate to the will of the party and government.

With the critical juncture of the Tenth Party Congress, Soviet trade unions gradually fell more and more under the control of the party. By the 1930s the trade unions, as virtually every other institution in the country, became completely subordinate to Stalin's personal will. Still, they have maintained their identity and today are somewhat more independent than during Stalin's time, performing an important and unique role in the society.

Trade Union Structure and Functions

Until recently Soviet trade unions were controlled by the party and functioned largely as an arm of the state. Although they certainly did not

---

[28]Isaac Deutscher, *Soviet Trade Unions: Their Place in Soviet Labour Policy* (London: Oxford University Press, 1950), p. 1.

[29]A. Zaichikov, *USSR: Trade Union Activity* (Moscow: Novosti Press, 1977), p. 23.

ignore the needs of the worker, they were primarily engaged in increasing labor productivity. Then, as now, trade unions also provided the society with the bulk of its social services.

Trade unionism in the Soviet Union is syndical in nature. That is, all employees in a given industry—including management—belong to the same union, regardless of trade or work performed. There are 708,000 local trade unions in the country and 31 syndicates, umbrella nation-wide unions, with which the local unions affiliate. Virtually all workers belonged to one of these unions until the very late 1980s when many of them disaffiliated and formed their own independent unions. Virtually every occupation, from agricultural workers to writers, communications and transportation workers to artists, geological prospectors to government workers, is unionized.

Union membership is theoretically voluntary, but in fact almost all people join the union because they are bound to the labor agreements negotiated by the unions and because the unions dispense a wide variety of social and fringe benefits. Union dues are nominal, coming to about 1 percent of the average worker's income. Students, pensioners, and people temporarily unable to work pay token sums. Although dues represents only a minor expense for the individual worker, it and union income from publications combine to help fund the extensive services and benefits the unions bring to the workers.

The organizational structure of Soviet trade unions follows approximately the same format as that of the Communist Party. (See Figure 7–2.) The lowest body is the *Profgrup*, which is responsible for mobilizing workers to accomplish production objectives on a daily basis. New union members are usually inducted into these bodies. If a particular work station or shop has as many as 100 members, the workers may choose to elect a *shop committee* to represent their interests and to coordinate their productivity. All elections within the union are by secret ballot, and consistent with Gorbachev's call for democratization, trade union leaders are now elected by contested ballots.

The most important of the local organizations is the *factory committee*. This elected body deals directly with management of the enterprise, setting goals and bonus levels, handling grievances, establishing and administering social benefits, and training workers. This committee is the foundation of the entire union structure.

The factory committees elect delegates to attend regional union congresses and delegates from these congresses are elected to attend union congresses at the union republic and national levels. These congresses are responsible for the general administration of union activities within their jurisdictions. They also elect a central committee and secretariat to administer their affairs between the infrequent congress meetings.

Each of the 30 all-union trade union congresses used to send delegates to the All-Union Congress of Trade Unions, which capped the entire union structure, consolidating it into one giant labor federation. This body was the administration's heart of the traditional trade union movement, and its leader was a ranking member of the CPSU. Soviet Vice President

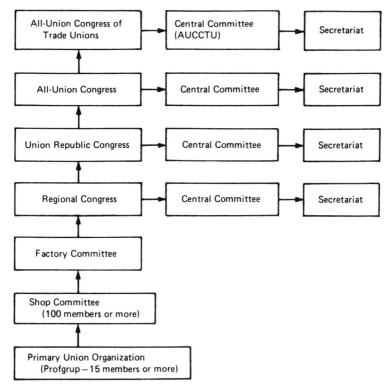

FIGURE 7-2   Trade union organizational structure.

Gennady Yanayev was chairman of the AUCCTU before he entered the Politburo and finally the government. In October 1990, however, this organization collapsed and voted itself out of existence due to the pressure from the growing number of independent unions.

The trade unions used to be governed by the principle of democratic centralism and, as a result, they were closely controlled by the leadership. The party was also careful to maintain control over the unions. Gorbachev's reforms, however, have encouraged the unions to become much more independent of the state and party, and contested elections have produced a leadership that is increasingly responsive to the membership.

Soviet trade unions are much more central to Soviet society than they are in the West. Before perestroika, the trade unions were a major instrument by which the party and the state socialized, mobilized, and controlled the labor force. Describing this **political function,** A. Zaichikov wrote before the reforms, "They cultivate in the working people a conscientious attitude towards work and care of public property, and promote the molding of the new man—well educated, conscientious, diligent and morally sound."[30] The

[30]Zaichikov, pp. 23–24.

unions were a major communicator between state and people. The government and party frequently interrupt production to give the workers lectures and presentations about ideological, political, and economic matters. At the same time, workers were allowed during these sessions to vent their frustrations about social problems, conditions of work, salary, and management practices. The major purpose of the meetings, however, was to motivate the workers politically and to encourage productivity. This political function, and the close coordination between the unions and the party, have significantly abated since the Gorbachev reforms.

The economic functions of the trade unions involve them in more traditional union activities. The principal instrument for implementing the trade unions' economic function is the collective agreement. This agreement is developed by means of negotiations between the factory committee and the factory management—themselves union members. The collective agreements are usually concluded in February and apply to all union and nonunion workers alike. They are composed of several parts: One section lists the obligations and rights of management; a second section lists the same for labor. Additional sections list the production goals for the office, farm, or plant, as well as the wage scale for the employees.

Although other benefits were always negotiated, wage levels used to be set by the state, but now managers have more latitude in negotiating pay issues. Accordingly, there are provisions in the collective agreements regarding pay, bonuses, work hours, production processes, and rest periods. Additional provisions specify the amounts to be spent on new technology, labor safety, and in-service training. The collective agreements may also commit enterprise funds to facilities it maintains for its workers—for example, housing; cultural, social, and sports facilities; and garden plots.

With the agreement reached, the trade unions assume a policing role. They regularly inspect facilities to assure compliance with health and safety regulations. They receive and process complaints and requests from workers regarding such issues as management relations, job assignments, and work load.

Trade unions also play an important role in labor disputes with management. Upon receiving a formal complaint from a worker or from management, the factory committee (on which management may also serve) convenes to seek amelioration of the situation. If this step fails, the controversy can be taken to a labor dispute board composed of equal numbers of workers and managers. Most disputes are settled at this point, and perhaps surprisingly, far more decisions favor workers than managers. This was true even before Gorbachev's reforms.[31] If the worker remains dissatisfied after these two steps, he or she may take the matter to the people's court.

Trade unions are also deeply involved in the staffing process. No worker may be reassigned or fired without the approval of the trade union except for excessive alcoholism, and even then the worker can appeal to the people's court for reinstatement if he or she wishes. Such appeals are

[31]Mary McAuley, *Labour Disputes in Soviet Russia, 1957–1965* (Oxford: Clarendon Press, 1969), p. 156.

frequently honored, resulting not only in reinstatement but in the award-ing of back pay. The economic reforms passed in 1987 address labor disci-pline and productivity. They provide that workers will be paid on the basis of their productivity, and job security is also affected. Trade unions can be instrumental in securing the dismissal of management personnel as well. If managers violate collective agreements or abuse workers, factory commit-tees can vote no confidence in them and have them dismissed.

The *social task* performed by Soviet trade unions is generally not du-plicated by labor organizations in the West. Soviet trade unions are the chief purveyors of social benefits in the society. Each factory committee consults with management about needed social insurance benefits. The benefits afforded the workers, as detailed in law and in the collective agree-ments, are locally administered by the factory committee. Trade unions also maintain a huge network of entertainment, social, and recreational facilities for their workers and their workers' families. Among the facilities maintained by the unions are theaters, cinemas, stadiums, playgrounds, nursery schools, vocational educational centers, Young Pioneers' camps, and some housing. The trade unions fund and administer cultural palaces, sports clubs, and chess clubs, as well as holiday resorts, rest homes, medical centers, and sanitariums. All of these are made available to the workers, and indeed the society as a whole, free of charge or at nominal cost.

Labor unrest.   Walter Laqueur reminds us that we know less about the workers in the Soviet Union than any other class.[32] Job security, a major provision of the Soviet social contract, has long been an important objec-tive. Much of Soviet production is **labor extensive** (using large numbers of workers to sustain high productivity rather than using **labor intensive** means, such as mechanization) not only because of an inability to produce enough capital to mechanize, but also because of a commitment to assuring employment for all. This policy, however, also ensures that a large amount of the production tasks (40.1 percent) are done by manual labor. In fields like construction and agriculture, the percentage is even higher. As a re-sult, jobs have been plentiful and worker turnover is also relatively high. In 1984, 19.3 percent of the workers changed jobs—almost one-fifth of the labor force.[33] Such fluidity not only indicates a high degree of dissatisfac-tion among labor about the jobs it holds, but also, on the more positive side, it reflects a general economic mobility.

Gorbachev's perestroika reforms have considerably destabilized the labor force, however. His policy of increasing productivity and enterprise (business) profitability means that labor will have to work harder and that **redundant labor** (workers who are employed in excess of the number needed to accomplish the tasks) will become unemployed. Being required to work harder is not popular among people in any society, but the growing

[32]Walter Laqueur, "Soviet Politics: Future Scenarios," in *Soviet Union 2000: Reform or Revolution,* ed. Walter Laqueur (New York: St. Martin's Press, 1990), p. 56.

[33]Mikhail S. Bernstam, "Trends in the Soviet Population," in *The Future of the Soviet Empire,* eds. Henry S. Rowen and Charles Wolf, Jr. (New York: St. Martin's Press, 1987), p. 212.

unemployment is potentially a greater problem for the Soviet Union. Since the Soviet population growth rate is declining, jobs for all workers will eventually be found. However, the trauma and inconvenience of losing one's job, together with the fact that there are few social programs to help unemployed workers because there have not been any in the Soviet Union for decades, are causing insecurity pangs throughout the society. These feelings are exacerbated by the fact that wages are relatively low and prices have begun to rise sharply in response to other perestroika reforms.

Matters came to a head in 1989. Strikes were long forbidden by Soviet law, although wildcat strikes sometimes occurred.[34] Even though these work stoppages were annoying to the leadership, they did not threaten the stability of the political system. In 1989, however, strikes erupted in every part of the country and among a wide variety of occupations including bus drivers, railroad workers, air traffic controllers, masons, teachers, and so on. The worst blow, however, was landed by the nation's coal miners.

Soviet coal miners have a life expectancy only three-fourths as high as the national average. The average miner dies at 48 years of age. Retirement age for miners is 55, but few of them manage to survive to enjoy it. Each year about 800 Soviet miners die in industrial accidents alone (55 United States coal miners died of accidents in 1988); many died in cave-ins due to the lack of timber to shore up the mines—an ironic situation in a country that has immense forests. Large numbers of other miners die of respiratory problems and many just wear out because of hard conditions.[35]

Fed up with their conditions and threatened by unemployment, high prices, and greater production goals, the miners in Siberia's Kuznet fields, the country's second largest, called a strike that soon spread to the Ukraine and elsewhere. Demanding job security, better food in the shops, safer working conditions, more housing, environmental clean-ups, and re-formed administration, half of the nation's 1 million coal miners refused to work for three weeks. This work stoppage was the most threatening since the 1920s. Even local party officials and mine managers joined the strike, and companion strikes in other fields of work swept the country.

The strike threatened the energy supply for the approaching winter, so the situation was serious. Gorbachev, while trying to get the workers back on the job, sympathized with their plight and sent high-ranking officials to negotiate with the disgruntled miners. Finally a settlement was reached, marking the first known time that the government gave in to strikers' demands. The central government agreed to give more authority and responsibility to the local governments, and it pledged to spend tens of millions of rubles to improve the miners' working and living conditions. In the fall of 1989 the Supreme Soviet also adopted a law legalizing strikes. The Ryzhkov government originally proposed that all strikes be suspended until 1991, but the Supreme Soviet refused. The law requires workers to go through various stages of mediation and arbitration before they may strike,

[34]Leonard Schapiro and Joseph Godson, *The Soviet Worker: Illusions and Realities* (London: Macmillan, 1981), p. 122.

[35]"Notes from the Underground," *The Los Angeles Times,* July 22, 1990.

and it leaves to the courts, not the government—a significant change—the refereeins of disputes. If these measures do not work, however, most workers (about 65 percent) may now strike. Strikes for political or ethnic reasons and work stoppages against government bodies are still forbidden. Also, strikes remain prohibited in key industries like transportation, communications, energy, and defense. These prohibitions, however, apparently have not discouraged illegal strikes.

In the spring of 1991, perhaps as many as 500,000 coal miners went out on strike again. They complained that the government had not delivered on its 1989 promises. Furthermore, the miners demanded political changes at the highest levels of government, including Gorbachev's resignation. Eventually offered a 100 percent pay increase, the miners refused, pressing their demands for other economic reforms and insisting on Gorbachev's resignation. As the situation grew critical, the Supreme Soviet took new steps to legally curb such political strikes and the chief executives of 9 union republics, including the Russian SFSR, called for the coal miners to return to work. Although money was collected nationwide to supplement the strikers' income, almost two months without paychecks and the mounting political pressure forced the strikers to leave the picket line without making significant economic gains. Even the wage increases the government had offered earlier were withdrawn. A commitment was made, however, that the coal mines in Russia would be placed under the jurisdiction of the Russian SFSR government. This transfer was completed in May 1991. Further, the miners were promised that with the transfer of authority, they would be given greater say in the management and ownership of the mines.

At the same time as the coal strike, workers in Georgia went on strike to protest Moscow's ethnic policies in the republic and tens of thousands of workers in Byelorussia repeatedly refused to work in protest of the huge price increases on consumer goods raised in April 1991. The strikes in Byelorussia were perhaps the most politically disquieting to the government since that republic is traditionally the most tranquil and conservative in the union. Assorted strikes were also launched at various locations throughout the country.

Although Gorbachev managed to weather this wave of strikes, he can take little solace from the victory. The workers have become increasingly bold and political, and their demands have not been satisfied. Indeed, even the trade unions which remain affiliated with the Communist Party have publicly protested several of Gorbachev's economic policies, and his conservative opposition has made numerous overtures to labor for an alliance to bring down his government. The May Day celebration in Moscow on April 1, 1991, the first not choreographed by the party, was a sullen affair. Organized by the trade unions, it drew only 50,000 workers in Moscow and 20,000 in Leningrad. The parade in Moscow had no floats or marching troops and it was almost bereft of color and smiling faces. The speeches were short (Gorbachev, virtually the only Soviet leader to attend the Moscow fete, did not even speak) and they lacked the usual hyperbole about the achievements of Soviet labor. When the speeches were over, the workers simply walked away from Red Square without the usual cheers or the obligatory rousing chorus of the *International.*[36] Clearly, the mood of labor in the workers' state is short-tempered and politically dangerous.

Dissatisfaction with conditions and with the traditional trade unions has resulted in new independent labor unions being formed. The **United Workers' Front** headed by a conservative, Verimin Yarin, is attracting workers with its anti-perestroika message. The All-Union Congress of Trade Unions, once the handmaiden of the state and the party, also tried to regain the workers' support by opposing perestroika's move toward a market economy. Protesting that the government was moving in dangerous uncharted directions, Gennady Yanayev, when he led the group, said "We know more about space research than we do about the market," and "We don't seek equality in poverty." As you know, its effort to recuperate from devastating losses to the independent unions failed and the All-Union Congress of Trade Unions ceased to exist in 1990. Other groups are forming, however. Finding the government's promises largely unfulfilled, the Donetsk coal miners in the Ukraine (the country's largest coal field) formed the Congress of Soviet Miners in June 1990. They also called a 24-hour strike, but this time their demands were different. Having lost faith in the party, they called for the disassociation of the party with the coal miners, and some of them even physically removed party offices from mine facilities. This action led to widespread public demands that the party be forced out of all work places and that its property (worth about $8 billion) be forfeited to the state.

A peasant union also organized to resist perestroika. This conservative group offered its highest post to Yegor Ligachev, one of Gorbachev's conservative opponents, but he declined. Finally, delegates from fledgling independent unions formed the Soviet Council of Independent Trade Unions and demanded government policies to protect the workers.

At present, the labor movement is in such flux that it is impossible to determine where it is headed. One thing is certain, however, Soviet labor has mobilized as one of the most formidable opponents of Gorbachev's programs. The workers fear the consequences of developing a market economy and of increasing labor efficiency. We now turn to a further examination of the economy and of Gorbachev's policy of perestroika.

[36]Michael Parks, "No Hoopla on a Sullen Moscow Day," *The Los Angeles Times*, May 2, 1991.

chapter 8

The Economy and the Government

Perhaps no society is more completely devoted to attaining economic productivity than is the Soviet Union. In his theory of historical materialism, Karl Marx stated that socialism would be the most productive of all economies and the most fair because it would apportion equally the product of people's labor. Capitalism, by contrast, was viewed as exploitative and unjust.

Although Soviet leaders have made many adjustments to the specific elements of Marx's theory, they have, until recently, remained true to the fundamental principle that socialism is beneficial and capitalism is evil. Anatoly Yesipov, a Soviet economist, summed up the Soviet views as follows:

> Under capitalism all production is subordinated to the purpose of enriching the capitalists. That is quite logical, because who owns the means of production will want to appropriate the fruits of labour. Consequently, the purpose of capitalist production is to obtain the highest profits possible. It is developed only to ensure the highest profits.
> The socialist economic system is founded on other principles. The overall objective of socialism is to satisfy to an increasing extent the material *and*

spiritual requirements of the people through the steady development and improvement of social production.[1] [emphasis added]

Apart from the general theme of this quotation, two features within it are worthy of special attention. First, one will note that socialism, at least as Soviet ideologues have understood it, addresses more than just the material needs of its practitioners; it also ministers to their spiritual needs. Second, Yesipov's statement pays particular attention to the ownership of the means of production, arguing that private ownership breeds exploitation and implying that public ownership does not. Today however, faced with virtual economic collapse, the Soviet leaders are changing the rules.

Gorbachev claims to retain his commitment to socialism, but he also believes that the economic mechanism put in place by Stalin has long since outlived its usefulness and is actually counterproductive. So Gorbachev is trying, in effect, to become the Soviet equivalent of Franklin D. Roosevelt. Roosevelt's 1930s New Deal policies may have saved capitalism from disaster, tempering its greatest excesses by integrating enough socialism within it (Social Security, welfare, government regulation of business, protection of the workers from exploitation, etc.) to give it a human face. For his part, Gorbachev hopes to modify the Soviet economic system with enough of the market economy to increase productivity and reduce bureaucratic insensitivity, thus casting out those elements of the system that have become obsolete, while preserving its humane parts. Before we examine the present Soviet economic structure in detail, however, let us briefly review the history of Soviet economics.

ECONOMIC HISTORY

Idealistic in the extreme, the Bolsheviks anticipated creating an entirely new, more prosperous, more humane economic system, one that would become the model for a new era throughout the world. Since their 1917 accession to power, the rulers of the Soviet state have sought to devise models of economic activity that will accomplish their goals. Although the profound idealism of its early leaders has long since given way to more practical approaches, the quest for an economic system that remains true to socialism is still very much a part of the Soviet goal.

After the catastrophic failure of Lenin's attempt to completely socialize the economy in a single fell swoop, he recapitalized a large segment of the economy with the **New Economic Policy (NEP),** calling it a "temporary retreat" from socialism. The NEP succeeded in restoring productivity to pre–World War I levels, but Stalin, calling for a "second revolution," abandoned the NEP and resocialized the system. Economic planning was introduced, industries were nationalized, and farms were collectivized. So well had Stalin done his work, that today the economic system remains, in

---

[1]Anatoly Yesipov, *How the Soviet Economy Is Managed* (Moscow: Novosti Press Agency Publishing House, 1975), p. 9.

most fundamental respects, as he left it. Even so, the Stalinist model demonstrated signs of obsolescence even before the dictator's death, and his successors attempted to reform it.

Khrushchev and Brezhnev grappled with the stifling impact of overcentralized economic control, worker alienation, shoddy goods, shortages, poor service, and a host of other maladies seemingly endemic to the Stalinist model. Each of Stalin's successors has tried in his own way to increase the worker's personal commitment to production, initiative, and inventiveness, but these efforts went unrewarded. Brezhnev's Premier Alexei Kosygin also tried to liberalize the system in the mid-1960s, but his reforms were also aborted.

These attempts to decentralize the system failed largely because they were foiled from within the economic system itself. Half-hearted rewards for the plan's success were insufficient to induce plant managers to abandon the system that, while inefficient, was the one they regarded with favor. Not only were they accustomed to the old system, but they had been successful in it. As you will see later, the present system is so bureaucratic that it is relatively easy to escape responsibility for failure. The decentralizing reforms devolved power, but they also focused responsibility on the managers. The ministries likewise resisted the reforms; they were understandably resistant to changes that decreased their control over the economy. Hence, in each case, the ministry personnel who were given the task of executing the reforms were in ideal positions from which to assure their failure. The decentralization of the economy was evaded from within by the very people whose support was needed to effect it.

The failure of Kosygin's reforms persuaded the conservative Brezhnev to leave things as they were. From the late 1960s the system was allowed to stagnate and stultify. The Stalinist approach of increasing growth by pouring more and more people and resources into production was no longer adequate as each of these assets became more scarce. Further, the infrastructure was ignored as increasing amounts of resources from a slowing economy had to be devoted to simply maintaining the socioeconomic status quo and building up the nation's military capacity. Roads were not paved; the railroads were ignored; and communications, storage, and distribution facilities went unmodernized. By the early 1980s it became apparent that the economy was exhausted and that profound changes had to be made.

Building on Andropov's brief efforts to reform the economy, Gorbachev has tried to initiate sweeping, even "revolutionary" changes in the economic system. Using the rubric of perestroika (restructuring), he has called for vast innovations, including sanctioning some private enterprises, giving more control to plant and farm managers and less power to the central planners, using supply and demand to establish some prices, and assessing production success by profit margins rather than by gross output. His plan also includes allowing workers to periodically elect their superiors, adjusting wages so as to reward productive workers, and cracking down on shoddy products, alcoholism, absenteeism, malingering, and other manifestations of poor labor discipline. He also recommends allowing unproductive firms to go bankrupt and freeing some Soviet firms from the government's monopoly in foreign trade.

Given past experiences with economic reform, one may wonder about the potential success of these policies. Once again, the very ministries that have the most to lose from devolving power are charged with executing the reforms. Some managers and workers are resisting being made responsible for production. The public balks at increased prices and unemployment. Elements of the military and heavy industry oppose transferring scarce resources to the consumer sector of the economy.

Yet, there are some important differences between the current situation and the past. First of all, the economic situation is more grave than ever before. Following a period of steady decline, the production growth of the early 1980s was lower than at any time since World War II. These and other bleak prospects may persuade some who might otherwise be hesitant that dramatic remedies must be employed to reverse a dangerous and embarrassing trend. Further, although the economic reforms appear to be liberal, they are combined with disciplinary moves against slovenly labor, crime, and corruption, which the conservatives appreciate. The need to reform the economy as an abstract proposition is not really at issue. Serious questions persist, however, about whether the ministers, bureaucrats, managers, and the people themselves are willing to suffer the sacrifices incumbent in effecting meaningful change to the system. Indications are that they want the problems fixed by the leadership, but with no inconvenience to themselves. Yet they are cynical about their leader's approaches to the economy, as illustrated by this joke.

A train carrying the nation's leaders stops because there are no more tracks before it. How to resolve the problem? Lenin suggests a *subbotnik* (a voluntary day of labor) to finish the line. Impatient with this solution, Stalin advises that every peasant in sight should be shot and that prisoners be brought in to complete the line. Shunning such brutality, Khrushchev recommends the problem can be solved by taking rails from behind the train and laying them in front. Rejecting this approach, Brezhnev's suggestion is to pull down the curtains and pretend that the train is moving. Finally, when asked for his proposal, Gorbachev jumps from the train and yells, "No rails! No rails!"

Sardonic humor aside, changing the Soviet economy is a monumental task because, as in any system, when inefficiency is rooted out, lives are changed. Although people suffer under the present system, they have made adjustments and accommodations to it (discussed in the next chapter) and reform threatens to negate even these modest advantages without giving absolute assurance that things will get better. In fact, the economic conditions have so far grown much worse under Gorbachev. Furthermore, the attitudes and institutions fundamental to the present system are deeply rooted in the society, and modifying or eliminating them is a wrenching, painful process. Our endeavor to understand the Soviet political system requires that we now examine some of these factors.

PRIVATE PROPERTY AND PROFIT

The Soviet economy is, at least officially, virtually controlled by state authorities. Eighty-five percent of the workers in the Soviet Union are employed by state-owned and state-operated enterprises or farms. The bulk of the remaining 15 percent find themselves on collective farms, which, although technically independent, are actually controlled almost as closely by the government as the state farms. A tiny percentage of workers belong to cooperatives, in which they ply their skills as artisans, work as repair persons, or perform other services, and of course there are the advocates in their collegia.

There are basically three kinds of ownership in the Soviet Union: state ownership, collective ownership, and private ownership. Throughout Russian history the state, in the person of the tsar, always owned a large share of the land and industry in the country. As great as state ownership under the tsars was, however, it never came close to equaling the amount of property held by the contemporary government. Over 90 percent of all capital property is now **nationalized,** that is, owned by the state outright. This state ownership includes all the land in the Soviet Union, the bulk of the factories and machines, and almost all the natural resources.

Collective ownership is practiced on collectives—most frequently farms, repair shops, or groups of artisans. The members of these producers' cooperatives collectively own the tools of their trade, the buildings perhaps, and the machinery used in their economic pursuit. The members govern their collectives democratically, at least in theory. They elect their managers, and they determine important financial goals, such as production quotas, wages, and capital investment.

The third form of ownership, **private ownership,** is very restricted. Individuals may own clothing, furniture, savings, appliances, food, and other items necessary for personal use. A few well-to-do people own private automobiles, condominiums, and small weekend cottages called *dachas.*

Until recently Soviet law forbade private ownership of the means of production. Beginning in 1987, however, Gorbachev's perestroika reforms began experiments with small-scale individual or family private enterprise; cooperative enterprises are also encouraged. Although the buildings and other capital equipment for these enterprises are usually rented from the state, private individuals may now own the tools and machinery necessary to run car repair shops, restaurants, hairdressing businesses, and small-scale manufacturing concerns. Still, most Soviet people work for the state; and all banks, land, mines, and common carriers are owned by the state, while most factories, service industries, and so on, also remain in public hands.

The Soviets have traditionally been opposed to allowing private ownership of the means of production (e.g., factories, land, and machinery) because of their socialist ideology. Individual profits were considered exploitative because the owner of the means of production—the employer—paid the workers less value than they produced. Thus, simply because the employer owned the means of production, he or she presumed to take value that someone else *worked* to create. This expropriation was viewed as exploitative in the belief that each worker should, in some manner, receive the value he or she created. Since capital investment is necessary in order to create and sustain the means of production, profits made by state-owned enterprises were legitimate because they were eventually returned to the society as a whole, with no individual receiving unearned value by virtue of the fact that he or she privately owned the machines and factories necessary for the workers to create value. Thus, profit was appropriate only if it was public profit; private profit had been forbidden. Even this sacred principle is being abandoned by *perestroika,* however. Even though private entrepreneurs are still severely limited as to the size of their operations and the number of people they may have in their employ, the strongest philosophical wall dividing socialism and the market economy has been breached.

The bulk of Soviet enterprises and farms is still in the hands of the state, however; and these entities are, in large measure, governed by economic planning.

PLANNING

Regardless of proposals for reform, planning remains the most important single element in the Soviet economy. Significantly, planning has nothing whatever to do with Marxism. Marx spent most of his time analyzing capitalism. Indeed, he wrote precious little about socialism in general terms and did not address such specific mechanisms of fiscal administration as planning. Nor was Lenin the founder of the planned economy. Lenin did play a part in planning, however. In 1920, proclaiming that electricity was socialism's power source, Lenin established the State Commission for Electrification, giving it the responsibility of bringing electricity to the entire country. To accomplish the goal of this crash program, the commission employed planning techniques that at the end of the decade would be used for the economy as a whole. In 1928 Stalin assigned the commission, which had been renamed the **State Planning Commission (Gosplan),** the responsibility of developing the five-year plans. Today Gosplan employs thousands of people in Moscow and in its branch offices throughout the Soviet Union and remains the principal planning agency in the country.

Planning is a monumental effort in the Soviet Union. It attempts to mandate the production, allocation, distribution, and prices of most goods and services in the society. In doing so, it tends to ignore the market forces of demand. In a capitalistic society, the market, or consumer demand, determines the production, allocation, distribution, and prices of most goods. The prices of these goods and services are established by the dynamic of supply and *demand*. Thus, it is said that capitalist economies are **demand economies.**

By contrast, the Soviet economy is often referred to as a **command economy** since the quantity, variety, and cost of goods are established by central planners (Gosplan) and may bear little relationship to the demand for them. The planners determine, for example, how much rolled steel will be produced each year, and they allocate it to automobiles, appliances, and armaments based on the leadership's perception of the society's *need* for, rather than on the society's *wish* for, these products. As a consequence, demand for automobiles may be far greater than supply. The prices for automobiles are fixed by the government, and one must wait for four or five years for a turn to buy a new car.

By the same token, the government has determined that certain goods are essential to the well-being, if not the political stability, of the society. It makes very substantial efforts to provide these goods—bread, for example—in relative abundance and at prices far below their true value. Much more will be said later about the problems created by planning. For now it is sufficient to understand that the Soviets consider economic production and distribution much more a matter for public policy than a mechanism of private satisfaction. It should also be recognized that some things are not limited by the plan. The black market and other illegal activities are, of course, quite independent from the dictates of the plan. Many legal economic activities are also left to the individual. Besides the recent experiments with small-scale private enterprises, you will recall that people may pursue whatever occupation they wish, assuming they have the requisite skills. Minimum wages are mandated by the state, but managers are allowed to pay more if they wish. And although prices are fixed by the state, people have the option of refusing to buy goods they find unappealing. These and other exceptions to the "command" rule tend to modify the planned economy with muted, but important, market pressures.

Developing and Administering the Plan

Developing the plan is an enormous undertaking, involving millions of people at one stage or another. Although Gosplan actually drafts the plan and is therefore very influential in its development, it does not do so in a vacuum. Actually, the planning process involves virtually every level of the economy and is touched in some way by almost every employed person in the Soviet Union.

To begin with, the basic parameters of the plan, its fundamental goals, are established by the government, after consultation with its economic experts. These agencies have previously consulted with lower echelons, including trade unions and plant managers, who have in turn consulted with foremen and shop stewards, who have previously consulted with the workers themselves.

Based on the information obtained, the government establishes fundamental priorities for the distribution of goods among the military, consumers, and social programs, ascertaining the desired level of capital investment by taking into consideration such variables as the desired growth rate and relative needs of various regions of the country. Then, as Gosplan begins to develop the details of the plan, a whole new round of top-to-bottom—bottom-to-top consultations begins. The consultations take on several forms. Some are exchanges of information: "We must have timely delivery of these materials if we are to meet our goal," or "This is how much we anticipate our plant can produce this year," or "We must invest so much in machinery this year to maintain productivity."

Other consultations are more like negotiations. Ministry officials, plant managers, union officials, and the workers themselves share a common interest. The material well-being and career potential of each is, to some extent, dependent on successful completion of the plan. Thus, they are each interested, to a degree, in assuring that the production quotas are set as low as possible. Arrayed against them is Gosplan, representing those who wish to maximize production. However, once the plan is adopted, Gosplan itself shares in its colleagues' interest that the plan is successfully completed. Hence the planning agency is also partially motivated by the desire to keep goals low enough to be easily reached. It should be obvious by now how complex the process of developing the plan is, and it should be equally apparent that the procedure is heavily influenced by politics as well as by economics.

When completed, the plan is divided into two gigantic portions. Group A is basically heavy industry, including mining, most military production, energy production, steel-making, and automobile production. This element of the economy, referred to as the "heavy boys," has always been given the greatest amount of attention and the vast bulk of the capital investment and resources. Group B is composed of light industry. The vast majority of goods in Group B are consumer goods, including textiles, appliances, and food. Recent five-year plans have called for more rapid growth in Group B, but in actuality these objectives have seldom been achieved. Historically, Group B has consistently been slighted in favor of Group A. Perestroika and Gorbachev's redirection of military production to consumer goods has somewhat changed this traditional pattern.

Although the basic economic document is the five-year plan, other plans of varying lengths of time are developed as well. Some very general forecasts, projecting growth over 15 to 20 years, are maintained. Yet the five-year plans remain the fundamental planning instrument. The five-year plans are amazingly specific, but they are divided into even more detailed annual and monthly plans. The results of production during shorter periods are then used as indicators for necessary modifications in the base of five years.

Since 1987, Gosplan has been supposed to remove itself from economic micromanagement, focusing instead on broader economic questions, but in large measure, little has changed except the vocabulary. Instead of "quotas" being handed down to the farms, offices, and enterprises, the government now makes orders for goods and services by way of commercial contracts or goals. The contract goals, however, are treated like quotas and so the system, which is supposed to encourage more individual incentive for plant and farm managers, lumbers along pretty much as it always has.

When completed, the plan sets policy for over 350,000 enterprises and farms. Its calculations include the following categories: labor (jobs, skills, education, and location), finance (capital investment, prices, credit, and minimum wages), productive properties (arable land, factories, machinery and shops), power (energy plants, power lines, and booster stations), transportation (air, trucks, rails, shipping, pipelines, and automobiles), trade (foreign and domestic), and consumption. The plan is then remanded to the agencies responsible for its execution.

Although Gosplan supervises the administration of the plan in a general way, the government ministries bear principal responsibility for its administration. Indeed, seeing to the plan's fulfillment is practically the sole responsibility of the ministries. As you know, the Soviet Union includes both national and union republic ministries. National, or all-union, ministries generally concern themselves with heavy industry and matters of broad concern, including the aircraft industry, heavy machinery, oil, chemicals, and foreign trade. Headquartered in Moscow, they maintain regional offices throughout the country. The less-centralized union republic ministries are also headquartered in Moscow, but they relate to corresponding ministries in their respective union republics. Even more local government agencies tend to such things as housing, food, civil construction, fisheries, and public service industries.

Below the administrative level is the one actually responsible for carrying out the plan: the plant managers and local soviets. Managers are perhaps the most important link in the economic chain since they are most directly responsible for production. Served by a staff of management experts including a chief engineer, an economist, and a personnel manager, each plant manager has considerable authority over day-to-day affairs of the enterprise.

Plant managers suffer considerable restraints as well as enjoy great power. They must cooperative with the trade unions in employment practices and benefits, and they must constantly deal with the pressure brought to bear by Gosplan and the ministries. Yet, their role is crucial to the system. It is they who must ensure production if enough goods are to be available to sustain the system.

The local governments (local soviets) also play a vital economic role. Whereas the managers command the artillery of production, the local soviets captain the logistics of consumer goods. Generally, it is the local soviets that are responsible for housing, retail shops, intracity public transportation, and all the other day-to-day facilities so necessary to any society.

Success of the Plan

Historically, the Soviet economy must be considered an amazing success. It is a unique economic system in four important respects. First, the Soviet Union originated the concept of planning and has employed it since 1929. Second, the economy grew with extraordinary speed. Between 1929 and 1939 the Soviet Union catapulted from a backward, preindustrial state to an economic giant, even as the West languished in the economic dissipation of the Great Depression. Third, Soviet economic success was achieved virtually without foreign aid and in the face of concerted Western attempts to impede its development. Almost as remarkable, the Soviets used planning to rapidly rebuild their economy again after World War II. One can argue that the goods and factories the Soviets expropriated from Germany and Eastern Europe after World War II were a kind of extorted foreign aid. But the Soviet people respond that the Nazi invaders destroyed or carted off vast amounts of their economic capacity, and their own later expropriations were nothing more than a partial repayment for the brutal and wanton destruction wrought by the Nazi aggressors. Fourth, the Soviet economy is the first modern economy to develop in the virtual total absence of private capital.

No objective observer could fail to appreciate the magnitude of the Soviet economic achievement. Analysis of the phenomenon suggests four factors that have made this economic success possible. To begin with, the Soviet Union enjoys abundant natural resources and, until recently, a huge population that could be mobilized into the work force. Its government has traditionally been able to enforce its will regarding the production and distribution of goods. The idealism of revolutionary goals has, until recently, created a disciplined work force that more or less willingly sacrificed the production of consumer goods for capital and military investment. Finally, the plan itself has been vital. With it, the Soviet government found the tool by which to organize and execute its economic goals.

Planning also affords certain other efficiencies not enjoyed by Western economics. Taking a rational approach to the economy, planning can avoid waste through overproduction. It can husband resources and channel goods and resources to the sectors most in need of them. The wasteful aspects of competition are avoided. Labor can be educated for and directed toward needed jobs, and until recently, strikes and other work stoppages were held to a minimum. Committed to economic equality, the leadership used the plan to narrow the gap between the haves have-nots in society, to provide employment to all of its workers, and to hold inflation to an enviable minimum.

Problems of the Plan

The phenomenal economic growth during the 1930s and the late 1940s was followed by a slower, but still impressive advance. In the three decades between 1950 and 1980 the Soviet economy quadrupled. Exploiting its treasure of natural resources, the Soviet Union has become the world's most self-sufficient industrial country as far as raw materials are concerned, and it leads the world in production of oil, natural gas, steel, coal, fertilizers, and other essential products. At the same time the Soviet standard of living tripled between 1950 and 1980. The Soviet people enjoy many advantages, including inordinate job security; low-cost staple foods, housing, and utilities; an admirable literacy rate; and free education and medical care. All of this was accomplished as the Soviet Union poured 15 to 17 percent of its GNP into the military, becoming the world's second superpower. Yet, having apparently reached the limits of its progress, the Soviet economy is now in serious jeopardy.

The economic growth rate has declined from the 1950s, when it averaged an annual increase of about 6 percent. In the 1960s and 1970s the annual growth rate averaged about 5 and 4 percent, respectively. The 1980s saw a sharp decline in its GNP growth rate; by 1984 it had fallen to only 3.1 percent, yielding a GNP of about $2 trillion, or 54 percent of the U.S. GNP.[2] In the late 1980s the GNP grew by only about 1 percent annually, and real income has actually declined by an average of about 2.3 percent per year since 1985.[3] In 1990 the Soviet economy suffered the worst year since World War II, according to an official Soviet report. The GNP actually declined by 4 percent. Some Western analysts estimate that it may actually have fallen by 5 percent. Labor productivity was down by 3 percent, and almost no enterprise managed to fulfill its production target.[4] At the same time, inflation skyrocketed. (See Figure 8-1.)

Reflecting their bitterness over the declining productivity in their own country and mocking the Soviet decline relative to the states it once dominated, this story is related by humorists about an imagined negotiation between Gorbachev and Chinese leader Deng Xiaoping.

Deng: "Before relations between our states can improve, you must sell us 100 tons of coal."

Gorbachev: "Done."

Deng: "And 20 new cargo ships."

Gorbachev: "Agreed."

Deng: "And 100 million bicycles."

Gorbachev: "Impossible, Bulgaria does not make bicycles."

The reasons for the economic turnaround in the Soviet Union are systemic; planning was useful in building an industrial economy, but it seems incapable of sustaining, to say nothing about increasing, productivity. Its difficulty is compounded by the development of high-tech, informative-processing economic models. Stalin's successors, it will be recalled, have been engaged, unsuccessfully to this point, in trying to find an economic model suited to the contemporary task. The Stalinist model was effective during an era when crash programs to build productivity were necessary. Basically it is a *labor-* and *resource-extensive* system, one that in-

[2]Henry S. Rowen, "The Soviet Economy," in *The Soviet Union in the 1980s*, ed. Erik P. Hoffmann (New York: The Academy of Political Science, 1984), p. 36.

[3]"Gorbachev's Greatest Gamble," *The Economist,* March 24, 1990.

[4]John-Thor Dahlburg, "Soviets Call Economic Output Worst Since 1945," *The Los Angeles Times,* Jan. 27, 1991.

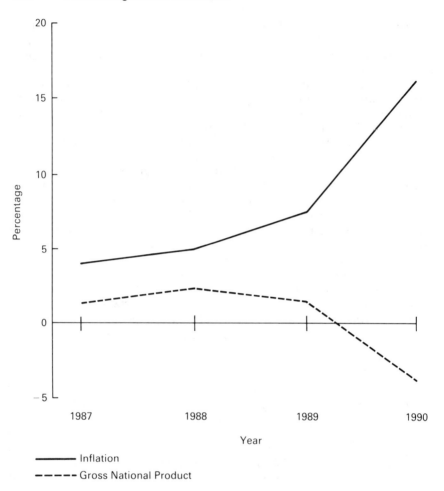

FIGURE 8–1   Soviet gross national product and inflation performance.
Source: Extrapolated from "The Soviet Economy," *The Los Angeles Times,* April 6, 1991.

creased production by applying ever more workers and materials to the task. At present, however, the Soviet economy is mature. It has no more excess labor with which to increase production, and it must begin to conserve its resources if these vast reserves are not to be further squandered. Put simply, it is past time that the Soviet Union adopt *labor-* and *resource-intensive* measures, increasing the productivity of the individual worker and making more efficient use of its precious resources. Soviet labor productivity is only about half that of workers in West Germany, Japan, and the United States. Although lack of mechanization accounts for much of the discrepancy, Soviet labor discipline is also clearly at fault as evidenced by a joke frequently heard among workers:

A Kiev retiree earns extra money and remains active by weighing people for three kopecks each.

"The government pretends to pay us, so we pretend to work."

The solution to Soviet economic difficulties is simply stated but far from easily accomplished. Planning in the Soviet Union includes a number of vexing inefficiencies, including inflexibility, impediments to innovation, discouragement of efficiency, and a lack of spontaneity. These systemic problems, together with Brezhnev's "don't rock the boat" policies, resulted in the serious decline in the growth rate already discussed. The downward spiral of Soviet economic growth has tended to exacerbate the difficulties, thus making recovery increasingly elusive. Consider this "Catch-22" statement found in a United States Defense Intelligence Agency analysis of the Soviet economy: "A vicious cycle has appeared; low economic growth requires more capital investment, which reduces consumption, which reduces incentives, which reduces labor productivity, which reduces growth."[5]

A closer look at the Soviet economic model reveals several serious weaknesses. To begin with, the rationalist might be tempted to think that planning the exploitation, allocation, and distribution of goods and services offers the best means of efficient economic management. Yet, enormous difficulties present themselves when the central planners attempt to rationalize the huge number of variables incumbent in a national economy the size of the Soviet Union's. For example, perhaps the most difficult problem planners face is to assure that all expected outputs are supplied with the needed inputs in timely fashion. If a tractor factory is to meet its

[5]*The Soviet Union* (Washington, DC: Congressional Quarterly, Inc., 1982), p. 94.

goal, it must receive the materials and labor necessary for the job. This means that planners must attempt to coordinate dozens of different enterprises, including mining, steel plants, and shipping, so that the tractor goal can be met. Try as they may, however, they are not always successful. One can view the Soviet economy as a giant factory with thousands of intersecting conveyor belts. If production or distribution is delayed at any particular point, it will have dilatory consequences all the way along the line. If the tractors are delayed, the crops may not be harvested. Lacking tractors, the authorities may find it necessary to mobilize factory workers, sending them into the fields to harvest the crop. If laborers are taken from the factories, industrial production is delayed, thus starting a whole new chain reaction.

Any delay in the system can result in other unfortunate, and unplanned, consequences. To meet the goal called for in the plan, plant managers may have to authorize shortcuts in production and quality control. Hence, shoddy goods are common. Ironically, the removal of the party from the day-to-day operation of the economy has exacerbated the problem of coordinating supplies. In the past, powerful party leaders could be relied upon by plant managers to pull strings, thus getting needed materials to plants so that production goals could be reached. Now such political influence no longer exists, so plant managers are left to their own resources to fill orders.

Because prices are arbitrarily fixed by the state and because the planners are more sensitive to government-set priorities than to consumer demand, shortages of goods are a consistent fact of Soviet life. Fixed prices and shortages of goods inevitably spawn corruption, theft, and black market activities.

Planning also stifles economic spontaneity, which is perhaps the most creative single feature in the capitalist system. On a 1976 visit to the Soviet Union, I stayed in a hotel that had been built only three years before. My room was small but clean and well appointed. The furniture was fashioned of lovely lacquered wood, the plumbing worked, and the floor was carpeted, albeit with a rather unattractive rust-colored indoor-outdoor fabric. In front of my bed lay a beautiful four-by-three–foot carpet made in the mills of Central Asia.

As I left my room one day, I looked down while opening the door and noticed that there was no doorstop. Instead, the workmen had nailed a small square of wood into the floor of this brand new hotel. This episode sent my mind into a flurry of speculation. Either the needed doorstops had not arrived in time to be installed, or, more likely, the planners had chosen to use the materials for some other object enjoying greater priority than doorstops. In any event, there on the floor of a lovely, new hotel was a makeshift doorstop.

In our society, some enterprising person would likely have noticed the need for doorstops, produced them, and soon built a thriving industry responding to a legitimate need. In the Soviet Union, on the other hand, sufficient doorstops will be made and distributed only if the central planners are persuaded that they are needed above requirements for other goods.

During the Brezhnev era, the economic system became moribund because as long as people remained politically orthodox, almost no one was held responsible for economic incompetence. With but rare exception, seemingly no infraction or incompetence could cost a minister or plant manager, or worker for that matter, his or her job. The phenomena common to bureaucracies everywhere—inertia, covering up mistakes, needless staff expansion, and resisting threatening change—compounded to an absurd degree as ministers remained in their positions for 10, 15, and even 20 years. Resolved to create a more responsive and efficient economy, Gorbachev has seen dozens of ministers, hundreds of managers, and thousands of other party and government officials fired for corruption, negligence, irresponsibility, and ineptitude. So far, however, the situation has not seemed to improve, even though the consequences of slovenly work are well known, as reflected in this joke.

A new manager of a factory finds two letters on his desk from his predecessor who was fired for incompetence. The instructions were that the new manager was to open the first letter in the event that productivity continued to decline. When the plant failed to meet its goal, the manager opened the first letter which read, "Blame it on me." He did so, thus buying time. However, as the enterprise failed to meet its goal a second time, the manager opened the next letter which instructed him to "Prepare two letters."

Perhaps an equally humorous, but real example of the unconscionable inefficiency of the bureaucracy is found in the way the state has managed the time of day. In 1930 the state decided to go on to daylight savings time, so it ordered the clocks moved up one hour in March. However, when fall came, no order was given to move the clocks back, thus the country's winter days were one hour earlier than planned. So it remained, until in 1981 the government decided to correct the mistake, but the error was not completely understood, so in March the clocks were set ahead by another hour. Now Soviet time was one hour ahead in summer and two hours ahead in winter. Finally the government decided in 1991 that the clocks would not be set ahead in the spring, thus returning to the original daylight savings time. At this writing, it is too early to tell if the government will remember to set the clocks back one hour in fall 1991, however, the growing independence of the union republics has some of them (Estonia, Latvia, Lithuania, and Moldavia) ignoring the order not to set the clocks forward, while Tadzhikistan and parts of Kazakhstan have actually decided to set their clocks back one hour in March 1991.[6]

The systemic inefficiencies of the Soviet economic plan do not end at the planning level. Indeed, they filter all the way down through manage-

[6]"Soviets Get Clocks Back on Track—and It's About Time," *The Los Angeles Times,* March 22, 1991.

ment to the workers themselves. One of the fundamental problems of Soviet planning is that successful completion of the plan is usually measured in gross product or gross weight. *Perestroika* is supposed to move the system toward cost accounting and profitability as success indicators, but little progress has yet been made in this transformation. Using gross measures tends to work against quality control, and it encourages very wasteful uses of materials.

In industries where gross weight is used as a measure of success, managers are encouraged to make goods out of iron and steel rather than converting to plastic. Hence, Soviet plants continue to use up the nation's iron ore by producing iron pipes rather than plastic tubing. Extra-thick glass is used in window production, and items like chandeliers are made of heavier material than necessary. Goals of this sort can much more easily be met by producing a few heavy items rather than several more useful items. Hence, it is better to produce whole tractors than tractor parts; as a result, farm machinery and other vehicles lie idle for lack of spare parts.

> Reflecting the absurdity of this situation, the Soviet humor magazine *Krokodil* once pictured a plant having met its quota by producing one enormous spike rather than nails of various sizes.

The rush to produce the required number of goods is equally fraught with difficulties. Since managers, workers, and quality-control inspectors are all dependent on completing the goal if their bonuses are to be paid, poorly made goods easily reach the market. The process of "storming the plan" is a notorious source of badly made goods, a procedure which Gorbachev railed against in a speech to the Twenty-seventh Party Congress. The inevitable delay in delivery of materials, drunkenness on the job, absenteeism, and general malingering usually force a rush in the last ten days of the month if the goal is to be fulfilled. At these times, workers literally throw things together in frenzied production. So many items are being produced that production lines often spill out factory doors, exposing goods to the elements. Soviet shoppers have learned to avoid buying goods made during the last 10 days of the month.

Managers know that much of their product is defective, but they also know that the consequences of failing to produce sufficient quantities are far greater than neglecting quality. The defective goods are simply passed on. They either pile up in warehouses and on store shelves because they can find no buyer, or they are purchased by shoppers who either are oblivious to the flaws or simply have no alternative. Such negligence is common even in vital public services. For example, Gorbachev himself recounted this foul-up at a meeting of the CPSU Central Committee. In 1989 the Ministry of Health imported 30 million syringes, an item in critical deficit (the term Soviets use to signify shortage). A second ministry was supposed to produce the needles for the foreign syringes, but it failed to do so. Having to satisfy its contract for providing this vital necessity, however, the Ministry of Health simply shipped the useless syringes throughout the country, thus meeting its goal.[7]

As part of his *perestroika* reforms, Gorbachev has created *Gospriemka*, an agency that specializes in quality-control inspections. Its agents are sent into plants to assess the viability of items produced, and they have the power to pass the goods on or to reject them. The losses are supposed to be made up for with money that management would have used for bonuses. Although the inspectors have helped improve the quality of goods sent from the factories, their numerous rejections have exacerbated shortages, and the inspectors have aroused the enmity of consumers, managers, and workers alike.

Fulfilling the plan's requirements is a universal objective, and its mandate touches virtually every Soviet citizen in one way or another. The goals must be reached; managerial positions and workers' bonuses depend upon it. Yet, as pointed out above, many things can interfere. The weather can slow deliveries, parts can be misrouted, workers can be temporarily sent to the fields for the harvest, machines can break down, materials can spoil en route, and so on and so forth. Yet, the plan must be completed!

If the plan is to remain inflexible, the people who must fulfill it inevitably become "flexible." If objectives are not met and all else fails, management often resorts to illegal or unethical techniques in order to satisfy superiors. Virtually every conceivable technique is used to mask failure to meet the plan. Managers appeal to planners to adjust their goals downward; they lie about production figures and write off the differences as breakage or spoilage. They pad their accounts, called "cooking the books." If they exceed production quotas, they store the surplus either as a hedge against a future shortfall or as a precaution to avoid having their quotas raised by the planners.

Managerial and ministerial record falsification can progress to absurd degrees, even to the point of falsely reporting the successful construction of factories and production that did not exist. In other cases, whole trains and their cargoes have been lost and records of the disappearances were destroyed by negligent or corrupt functionaries.[8]

Besides questions of outright fraud or incompetence, innovation is complicated by the system itself in that new techniques require extra preliminary costs, and a temporary decline in productivity will result from retooling and adjusting to more efficient measures. The plan rewards short-run success but penalizes those who would try to innovate long-run efficiency. Besides, it is far easier to meet the plan by producing the same products in the same old way rather than taking the chance of failure by trying something different.

Responding to these and other problems, Gorbachev has pressed for reforms he hopes will make managers more directly responsible for production but which also give them more control over production, prices, and

[7]Michael Parks, "Gorbachev Says Backsliders Imperil Reform," *The Los Angeles Times,* April 27, 1989.

[8]"Soviet Train Lost in Paper Blizzard," *The Los Angeles Times,* June 3, 1985.

disbursal of profits. So far, however, these changes have had disappointing results and one questions the long-term prospects for their success. Not only is economic reform difficult to achieve in such a heavily bureaucratic system but also, one must remember, the Soviet people are themselves profoundly conservative. This natural reluctance to change is magnified by the fact that, being accustomed to the system, the ministers, managers, and workers do not wish to see the system change since it presently requires so little personal responsibility.

FINANCE

Two rules were, until recently, absolute governing principles of Soviet finance. First, private capital was forbidden, and second, the Soviet Union tried to be as economically self-sufficient as possible, eschewing the intermingling of its economy with that of countries outside Comecon (the economic unit within the Soviet bloc). Each of these sacred rules has been abandoned by Gorbachev, however, and he now hopes to make the Soviet economy competitive and integrated with the world economic community.

Revenues paying for the annual budget come from two major sources: taxes and profits from government enterprises and farms. Profits currently account for about 27 percent of the budget, down from 31 percent only a few years ago. Taxes raise most of the remainder. The principal tax, accounting for about 32 percent of all revenue, is an indirect assessment called the **turnover tax.** Similar to Europe's value-added tax and some of our excise taxes, the turnover tax is assessed at the production level. Its cost is then added to the price the consumer pays at time of purchase. The turnover tax is very high, often reaching 50 percent of the purchase price. The turnover tax is not only an important source of revenue, but it is also used to regulate demand by artificially increasing prices.

The largest direct tax paid by Soviet citizens is the personal income tax, yielding about 9 percent of the total government revenue. The income tax, which is withheld from the worker's pay, is progressive, ranging from 10 to 13 percent depending on the level of income earned. However, in 1988 a new graduated income tax was imposed on people working for cooperatives. It can reach as high as 90 percent of the earnings of the highest paid co-op workers. People earning less than 70 rubles per month are exempted from the tax altogether. A new corporate income tax was also passed when the government began to allow private enterprise. Perhaps because citizen behavior has been easy to control, no government agency with the awesome powers of the American Internal Revenue Service exists, but clearly that void will have to be rectified soon.

President Gorbachev, exercising the powers of decree on economic matters given him by the Congress of Peoples' Deputies, assessed a sales tax in 1991. This 5 percent levy was added to all consumer goods,[9] but in a

[9]Carey Goldberg, "Gorbachev Hits Soviets with 5% Sales Tax," *The Los Angeles Times,* Dec. 30, 1990.

compromise with the chief executives of the union republics, Gorbachev later agreed to rescind the unpopular tax. Other revenues come from an assortment of direct taxes, indirect taxes, and nontax sources, such as social security payments, tariffs, and auto registration fees. Revenues are also expected to increase as the government sells off many of the enterprises it now controls. It plans to use 20 percent of this money to pay for social programs, and the remaining 80 percent will go to help defray the growing budget deficits.

Until 1988 the government denied that it ran budget deficits, but in that year it announced that indeed it had suffered consistent deficits since the mid-1970s. It generally covered the shortfalls by printing more paper money, thus inflating the currency, until people now refer to their currency as the "wooden ruble."[10] With Gorbachev's reforms, the deficit jumped from 3 percent of the GNP in 1980 to a whopping 13 percent in 1989. The deficits have grown not only because productivity has declined even as government expenses have increased (some 24,000 government enterprises ran losses in 1989), but also because the government has allowed enterprises to keep more of their profits and the anti-alcohol campaign, which was ended in the late 1980s, reduced the government's tax revenues.[11] In 1989 the government budget was $804 billion, of which it borrowed $160 billion, or almost 20 percent. By contrast, the United States, whose national budget is a far smaller portion of its GNP than is the Soviet budget, borrowed only 12 percent of everything it spent in 1989. (See Figure 8-2.)

Now that it has admitted such huge deficits, the government is trying to find ways beyond the defunct sales tax to bring them down. Government expenses are being cut, including leaving the Mir space station vacant for a few months in 1989. The Soviets hope to recover some funds from the money owed it by Third World countries. The Supreme Soviet is also considering selling bonds to finance the debt and raising taxes on tobacco and spirits.

Currency and Banks

The basic units of Soviet currency are the ruble and the kopeck. There are one hundred kopecks to the ruble. The ruble has no international standing, although there are indications that Gorbachev may soon seek such status. At present it cannot be exchanged in foreign banks, and it is not accepted in the West in payment for goods. Smirking at their money which no one else will accept, Soviet jokesters say

> The ruble is our greatest patriot. It never sells itself to the enemy.

[10]See Judy Shelton, *The Coming Soviet Crash* (New York: The Free Press, 1989).
[11]"Russia Twixt Scylla and Charybdis," *The Economist*, March 31, 1990.

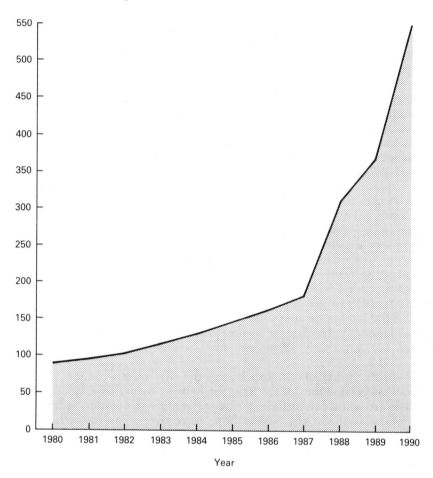

FIGURE 8–2 Soviet annual deficit.
Source: "The Soviet Economy," *The Los Angeles Times,* April 6, 1991.

The ruble's value against the dollar, in which the Soviet planners calculate foreign trade, is arbitrarily set by the Soviet government. It is a violation of Soviet law to carry rubles in or out of the country. Still, some rubles manage to appear in the West but find few buyers except among people who wish to buy them for pennies and smuggle them back into the Soviet Union. The government estimates that as many as 7 billion rubles may be held abroad.

In 1989 the government split the value of the ruble. For purposes of foreign trade, it kept the existing rate of $1.60 to the ruble; but for tourist and businesspeople, it devalued the currency by 90 percent, to 0.63 rubles per dollar. In 1990 it devalued the currency again, but kept the split values. People in the Soviet Union can now buy rubles for 18 cents each, while business transactions use a rate of 56 cents per ruble, a 69 percent devaluation. It is hoped that these policies will eventually lead to the ruble being accepted in international trade, but they still have a long way to go since foreign banks estimated the ruble as worth only between 5 and 7 cents in 1990.[12]

The government also does what it can to induce owners of hard currency (tourists, diplomats, journalists, and Soviet citizens) to spend it. The famous *Beryozka* (birch tree) shops are a good example of the Soviet proclivity for hard currency. These stores accept only foreign currency. Prices in the *Beryozki* are considerably lower than in regular Soviet shops, and the shelves are stocked with many Western goods, including tape re-corders, scotch, and appliances that are simply unobtainable in the regular stores. The *Beryozki* are frequented primarily by foreign tourists, diplo-mats, businesspeople, and journalists. However, since 1990 Soviet citizens who have foreign currency may spend it in special shops and may open hard currency accounts in Soviet banks. Soviet citizens can come by hard currency in a number of ways. Some of them receive money from relatives in the West, while others—diplomats, artists, seamen—bring it in upon returning from abroad. An additional ready source of hard currency is the black market. Few foreign visitors have not been approached on the streets, in stores, and even in their hotels by someone asking if they wish to ex-change their hard currency for rubles. The going rate in this illicit trade can be as little as 4 cents to the ruble. The rate seems to depend on the use the vendors have for the hard currency. If they want to use it to buy objects available only in the *Beryozka,* one can bargain for the highest rate since rubles are virtually worthless in pursuit of these goods. It was estimated by Soviet authorities in 1990 that some $324 billion worth of hard currency is held by Soviet citizens, and with the sharply falling value of the ruble, the dollar and other major foreign currencies are now being used among pri-vate citizens as mediums of exchange. In 1990 the government also opened markets in each union republic capital where enterprises wishing to engage in foreign trade may buy foreign currency with rubles.[13]

Even though some items are not available in Soviet stores, one may wonder where the money comes from to squander on popular Western goods. In fact, there is a surplus of money in the hands of Soviet con-sumers. The government's policy of printing money to cover its huge defi-cits has inundated the country with rubles. People carry large amounts of money on their persons, and Soviet savings accounts, totaling about $670 billion in 1990, have never been so full. Regular bank accounts fetch only about 2 percent interest, but in 1990 Gorbachev decreed that banks could offer much higher rates for long-term accounts. Some rates have gone as high as 10 percent.

However, in 1991 the state caused a financial crisis by suddenly and without warning declaring the old 50 and 100 ruble notes void, giving people only three days to exchange them for new notes. In addition, people were allowed to exchange no more than 1,000 rubles unless they could prove the money was obtained legally. The intent was to deny black

[12]Michael Parks, "Gorbachev Orders Ruble Devalued 69%," *The Los Angeles Times,* Oct. 27, 1990.

[13]"Soviets Will Open Domestic Money Exchange," *The Los Angeles Times,* Aug. 8, 1990.

marketeers their ill-gotten profits, but many innocent people were hurt; and there is speculation that black marketeers managed to protect their assets through bribery and other means.

Until now, the Soviet banking system has been much less complex than the one in the West. *Gosbank,* the central bank, controls the money supply and handles most of the financial transactions in the country. It maintains several thousand branches, which make short-term loans to enterprises and farms. Its associate, *Stroibank,* negotiates long-term loans with enterprises; foreign trade finance is administered by the *Vneshtorgbank,* Bank of Foreign Trade. In addition to its branches for business loans, Gosbank also maintains offices that handle private savings accounts. Like almost everything else in the Soviet Union, these banks are controlled by the government and are subject to the Council of Ministers. If an enterprise spends beyond its budget, the government can order Gosbank to loan it money, regardless of the financial viability of the enterprise. When Gosbank exhausts its saver's deposits in these transactions, it is authorized to release new money and thus add to the country's inflation.

Late in 1990, however, the Supreme Soviet voted to approve a new banking system. Gosbank is supposed to become independent of the government and to enjoy powers similar to the American Federal Reserve System. Thus, Gosbank, not the government, will be given the power to regulate the monetary policy of the Soviet Union. To date, the system has not yet been put in place. If it is, and if it works, another large step away from the "command-administrative economic system" will be taken. However, one wonders whether it will work. To begin with, Soviet bankers have no experience with monetary control. Also, it is hard to imagine the government allowing its banking system to plunge the economy into a recession in order to accomplish the arcane objective of monetary stability, as did the American Federal Reserve System in 1981–1982. Much more likely in a society that has known only socialism for decades, the political leaders will intervene. In fact, in a 1991 effort to bring down inflation and control the black market, Gorbachev decreed that citizens could withdraw no more than 500 rubles per month from their savings accounts. The decree was supposed to last for six months but it could be extended.

Whatever the case, personal credit has been rare in the Soviet Union. Except for those individuals who take out 15-year loans on condominiums, people pay cash for almost everything. VISA and MasterCard have been used for some years, but ordinary Soviet citizens have not taken to them so far. In 1988 Gosbank introduced its own SovCard, but it too is largely ignored by Soviet shoppers. Checking accounts were also introduced in 1988, but most people still use cash. Workers are paid in cash, and they usually carry enough money to buy the goods they need.

FOREIGN TRADE

Not unlike any other nation-state, the Soviet Union uses foreign trade for political reasons. Because of its own reluctance and owing to Western economic boycotts, the Soviet Union engaged in very little foreign trade during the first several decades of its existence. However, having emerged from World War II the leader of a bloc of communist states, Stalin took on new responsibilities in international trade. In 1949, he also forged an economic association known as *Comecon*, which was established as a response to the Marshall Plan. Even so, apart from the aid received from the Allies during World War II, the Soviet Union did not join in wide-scale trade outside its own sphere until after Stalin's death.

Soviet trade with Western Europe, the United States, and Japan began in earnest in the 1960s, when the Soviet Union opened its doors to Western companies, many of which maintain offices in the USSR. In turn, Soviet trade has established itself in the West.

Finding markets for Soviet industrial products outside the Eastern bloc countries has not been easy because of their poor quality, and the problem persists even though the best goods are marked either for the military or for foreign trade. Consequently, the Soviet Union finds itself exporting few industrial goods but large amounts of raw materials. Its major exports include oil, lumber, metal ores, chromium, coal, natural gas, and cotton. The finished goods it does find markets for are varied in number, but they are not great in terms of the total amount of revenue generated. They include military equipment, tractors, automobiles, airplanes, and mineral fertilizers.

All of this commerce still falls short of providing the Soviet Union with enough foreign currency to satisfy its Western shopping list. In a desperate attempt to increase their hard currency income, Soviet planners have all but cleared domestic shelves of luxury items associated with Russia, including furs, good vodka, caviar, and crab. These products are presently seldom found anywhere in the Soviet Union except in the *Beryozki* and the special shops for the elite of the society. The Soviet Union has also found it necessary to sell vast quantities of gold and diamonds to satisfy its needs.

Self-sufficient in raw materials and energy, the Soviet Union is virtually unique among industrial states. Yet, the money it saves by using its own raw materials is more than offset because its technological level is not consistently high and its agricultural production remains low, thus forcing it to buy grain and costly high-tech equipment from the West. Besides the massive quantities of grain necessary for sustaining its population, the Soviet Union also imports electronic equipment, computers, oil and gas development paraphernalia, machine tools and even whole factories to produce cars, trucks, steel, and canned goods.

Unable to balance its foreign trade deficit, the Soviet Union is incurring unprecedented (for it) foreign debts. One should be careful not to overemphasize the economic importance of foreign trade, however. Jealously protecting its essential independence from foreign markets, Soviet foreign trade, important though it is, amounts to less than 3 percent of its gross national product.

Even so, Gorbachev has publicly announced his wish to integrate the Soviet Union with the world economic system. He has applied for admission to the General Agreement on Tariffs and Trade (GATT), the United Nations Food and Agricultural Organization (FAO), the World Bank, and the International Monetary Fund (IMF). In 1990 the Soviet Union was invited to assume observer status in the IMF with full membership pending, and in 1991 it was given special membership status in GATT.

The Soviet Union also wants to trade with other countries much more heavily than it did before. In 1989, the European Community agreed to gradually reduce its tariffs on Soviet goods. It has also agreed to economic cooperation with the Soviet Union on a broad scope in areas including science and technology, banking, transportation, agriculture, environmental protection, energy, raw materials, and mining. This agreement excludes trade in strategic goods. Although the Soviet Union buys huge amounts of grain from the United States, the total amount of trade between the two economic giants is not large. The Soviet Union wants the United States to grant it **most favored nation** status (meaning that Soviet goods would not be tariffed any higher in the United States than are the goods of the United States' best trading partner). Since the United States has given most favored nation status to the People's Republic of China, there is some criticism that the United States is treating the Soviet Union with a double standard. (See Table 8–1.)

In trying to build trade with the West, the Soviet government has encouraged joint ventures. Originally, the majority share in these endeavors had to be Soviet-owned, but now foreign corporations may own majority interests. Some examples of joint ventures are McDonald's, Pizza Hut, shoe manufacture, fertilizer manufacture, computer software sales, oil drilling endeavors, X-ray equipment, blood analyzers, and ink jet printer

TABLE 8–1   United States–Soviet Trade in 1988 (in millions of dollars)

Year	Soviet Imports of U.S. Goods	Soviet Exports to the U.S.
1984	3,284	554
1985	2,423	409
1986	1,248	568
1987	1,480	424
1988	2,768	578*

Leading Soviet Exports to the United States in 1988		Leading Imports from the United States in 1988	
Petroleum products	182	Corn	888
Silver, plutonium	114	Wheat	750
Chemicals	79	Animal feeds	247
Scrap metal	29	Fertilizers	223
Vodka, beverages	28	Oil seeds	158
Fertilizers	24	Rubber or plastics	54
Furs	17	Fruits and nuts	43
Pig iron	11	Cotton	31
Uranium	11	Measuring instruments	29
Crude oil	10		

*About the same amount as imported by the United States from the United Arab Emirates.

Source: U.S. Commerce Department

manufacture. Also, since 1990 businesses that are 100 percent foreign-owned may establish themselves in the Soviet Union.

Western firms have encountered serious problems in developing these concerns, however. The Soviet bureaucracy is far from facile in developing these arrangements. Contracts take years to negotiate (McDonald's spent 13 years creating its joint venture in which the City of Moscow owns 51 percent). Red tape and delays plague the process, so that only a small number of the joint venture agreements are actually operative so far. The number of Soviet agencies and companies with which foreign firms must deal for even the most temporary transactions is daunting. Soviet accounting practices are inefficient and not conductive to the cost accounting approach. There are certain words that are common to Western business transactions that have no Soviet counterparts, so contracts must be negotiated, translated into Russian, and then translated back into English, to assure that they are understood correctly.[14] Getting copy machines and other equipment for Soviet-based business offices is difficult, and keeping Western employees in the Soviet Union is expensive. Apartments must be renovated to bring them up to Western standards; ordinary necessities like toothpaste, toilet paper, fresh fruit, and vegetables must be imported to assure their availability; and employees must be allowed several trips home each year so that they will not go stir-crazy in bleak Soviet cities. Advertising is also a problem in this noncommercial society. Perhaps most difficult is the problem of taking profits out. Since the ruble is not convertible, profits must be spent in buying Soviet goods that can be taken to the West. Pepsico, which has done business in the Soviet Union since 1974, trades its cola for Stolichnaya vodka to sell in the West. It also recently agreed to buy 10 Soviet-built freighters and tankers.[15]

Unable to exchange its currency on the international market, the Soviet government is desperate to earn hard currency for its purchases abroad. Beginning in the 1980s it has purchased more abroad than it has sold, thus incurring an unfavorable balance of trade. This deficit has been exacerbated by lower oil prices and by its recent need to buy consumer goods from the West in addition to its usual purchases of grain and technology. Although its trade deficit is not yet high by Western standards, almost $54 billion, it is falling behind on interest payments. In 1990, for example, it was unable to pay $2 billion in interest on its foreign loans. This is extremely unusual because the Soviet Union has always been scrupulous about paying its debts. Complicating matters, the Soviets have also agreed to make good on the tsarist bonds held in the United States and Britain. Although this agreement was necessary to settle old outstanding accounts, it is not helpful for the beleaguered Soviet economy.

The sale of energy (oil, coal, natural gas) provides the bulk of the

---

[14]The United States, Western Europe, and Japan have sent hundreds of businesspeople to the Soviet Union as consultants to teach how business is done in the West. These people instruct Soviet businesspeople on everything from contract negotiations to accounting to the proper clothing to wear in a business setting.

[15]John-Thor Dahlburg, "Pepsico Will Swap Cola for Soviet Ships, Vodka," *The Los Angeles Times*, April 10, 1990.

Soviet Union's hard currency. Over half of all hard currency earned by the Soviet Union comes from the sale of oil alone. Experts anticipate that as Soviet oil production levels off and domestic demand increases, Soviet access to hard currency will decline. Since Khrushchev's time the Soviet Union has sold oil to Eastern Europe, Cuba, and other friendly states at below market prices and taken back overpriced and poorly made industrial goods and agricultural commodities. This amounted to huge subsidies of the economies of the states in its trading sphere. Since 1990, however, as Eastern Europe has become more independent of the Soviet Union, the Soviets have demanded hard currency for oil.

The Soviet Union is the world's largest producer and exporter of oil. Since 1989, however, its oil production has declined sharply, largely because it lacks modern technology. Joint ventures with major Western oil companies promise to improve the situation. With the warming relations between East and West, even as the Middle East becomes increasingly unstable, Soviet oil production may become even more important to the United States and its allies, and as the Soviet economy becomes increasingly integrated with the Western economies, its oil industry will become even more central to its foreign trade.

Foreign Aid

The Soviet Union first accepted foreign aid in 1988 to cope with the earthquake in Armenia. In 1990 the strain caused by its transition from a planned to a market economy led Gorbachev to request massive amounts of additional aid from the West. The figure needed is not completely clear, but most experts agree that such a huge economy could not be helped with much less than $100 billion, and perhaps much more is needed. The United States balked at giving aid on grounds that the Soviet Union still assisted Cuba to the tune of about $5 billion annually. West Germany and France, however, hoping to stabilize European politics, were much more sympathetic. They each negotiated favorable trade agreements and pledged shipments of aid to the USSR. The collapse of the Soviet food distribution system in the winter of 1990–1991 brought even more aid activity. A newly United Germany sent 300,000 metric tons of food and other supplies. Ironically, these supplies had been stored in West Berlin to be used during the Cold War in case of a Soviet attack. Private relief drives were also sponsored across Europe. Even India, a nation that often encounters difficulty feeding its own 833 million people, but a state with long-standing warm relations with the Soviet Union, sent 24 million metric tons of food and medicine to the USSR. Private charities in the United States also sent help, but the Bush government demurred until December 1990. Finally, beginning in 1991, President Bush agreed to give loan guarantees, agricultural support, technical assistance, and most favored nation trade status. Yet the amount of Western aid was still insufficient to the Soviet need and Gorbachev was once again moved to plead for help in April 1991. He warned that the West has an important stake in the success of his reforms and that perestroika will be severely jeopardized if sufficient aid is not forthcoming.[16]

This aid, although critically needed in 1990–1991, is but a fraction of what must be done if the Soviet economic situation is to be improved in a fundamental way. Even so, it has met with serious problems. The Soviets, a proud people, are embarrassed that their country has had to go hat in hand throughout the world. The poet Yevgeny Yevtushenko frustratedly said in 1991, "We are the richest beggars in the world." Quite beyond hurt feelings, an even greater problem exists. The food shortage in 1990–1991 was not caused by low productivity, indeed Soviet food production was unusually high in 1990. The crisis arose from a collapse of the distribution system. More will be said in the next chapter about this paradoxical circumstance, but for now it is enough to note that the huge foreign aid deliveries were also delayed by an inefficient and corrupt system of distribution, and many experts question if large amounts of future aid might also be wasted. At the heart of the Soviet economic failure and a major factor in its future development is the Soviet transportation system.

TRANSPORTATION

Besides its low per-capita productivity and its relatively low technological capacity, no other single factor vexes the Soviet economy as does its problems with transportation. Most of its industry is in the western part of the country, while the bulk of its resources are in the east. Harsh weather during the long winter months presents hazards not only to travelers and transporters but to the roadbeds, ships, and landing strips, necessitating inordinately expensive maintainance budgets. Even the sheer vastness of the land presents a serious problem to transportation and communication.

No summertime visitor to the Soviet Union could fail to be impressed by the huge amount of commerce plying its large rivers. Furthermore, an extensive network of strategically placed canals connects the Baltic and White seas of the north with the Black Sea to the south; additionally, canals link the Ob and Yenisei rivers in Siberia and other major waterways. Extensive though it is, most of the river transport is forced to stop almost completely by November or December as the waterways turn white with ice.

In recent years the Soviets have made an enormous investment in merchant ships, many of which are constructed in foreign yards. Soviet transport firms have bitten deeply into the sea cargo trade. About 90 percent of all its own foreign sea trade is carried in Soviet holds, while its low-cost shipping logs almost 30 percent of the sea trade between North America and Europe. Even so, Soviet sea transport is of limited usefulness to its domestic commerce because so few of its ports can be relied upon to remain ice-free the year round.

The Soviet Union has long taken a keen interest in air travel and has

[16]John Thor-Dahlburg, "Gorbachev Urges World to Help Save Perestroika" *The Los Angeles Times,* April 18, 1991.

produced several pioneers in that field. It was first to deploy a successful international jet aircraft passenger service, and its supersonic transport was used in domestic flights between Moscow and distant provinces for several years. It also maintains a fleet of large civilian and military cargo transports. Aeroflot, its sole airline, flies to most of the major countries of the world and enjoys a monopoly on domestic passenger flights. Relative to Western rates, air travel is inexpensive in the Soviet Union, and Aeroflot's service is very extensive, making it the world's largest passenger airline.

Important though it is, air travel is expensive compared to other modes of transport and is thus of limited utility for this vast country. The key to Soviet transportation is its surface facilities. Yet, here too we find serious difficulties. The Soviet road system, suffering from inhospitable construction conditions, as well as decades of official neglect, is completely inadequate to the nation's needs. There are basically three kinds of road surfaces in the country: pavement, gravel, and dirt. Hard pavement is restricted to streets in the major cities and to highways linking metropolitan areas. In 1990 the Soviet Union had only slightly more than a half million miles of paved streets, roads, and highways in the entire country. By contrast, California alone had about 40 percent as many miles of paved transportation surface. Soviet graveled roadways are sufficient only for light traffic. The largest percentage of roads are simply dirt, which turns to impassable mud in spring and autumn. Dirt roads are seen everywhere—in the countryside, where only the major thoroughfares are paved, and even in the suburbs of major cities. The lack of adequate surface transportation in the countryside is one of the major causes for agricultural shortfalls. Crops often spoil before they reach market, and fertilizer sometimes dissipates at railroad sidings while awaiting transport to the fields.

The countryside between Moscow and Suzdal. Note the paved highway in the foreground but the dirt roads leading to interior villages.

Railroads are the mainstay of the Soviet transportation system. The rails carry almost 80 percent of all Soviet freight and about 40 percent of all intercity passengers. While boasting the largest system of electric lines in the world and the world's longest single line (the Trans-Siberian line, which measures some 6,200 miles), the Soviet rail system does not compare favorably with that of the United States. The total Soviet rail line mileage comes to something over 90,000; American mileage exceeds 200,000.

Traditionally, Soviet officials have lauded their rail system as the most advanced and most efficient in the world. Since Gorbachev's succession, however, focus on ministerial inefficiency has revealed many serious difficulties in the system. Besides reporting the loss of whole trains, newspaper campaigns blame poor organization and the indifference of stationmasters for people waiting many hours in uncomfortable and dirty stations as nearly empty trains depart. Railroad workers are criticized for demanding bribes to perform their work, allowing lavatories to become filthy and devoid of toilet paper, refusing to clean compartments, and serving "inedible" fare while stealing the best food for sale on the black market.

In 1989 railroad mismanagement, strikes, and ethnic strife saw the system come to a veritable halt. At one point over 500 trains with 25,000 fully loaded boxcars were backed up by stoppages as their cargoes spoiled. At the same time, $16 billion worth of foreign consumer goods bought with precious hard currency were delayed in East European rail centers as the Soviet railroad traffic jam prevented their delivery.[17] Trouble with the railroad system also helped cause the food shortages of 1990–1991.

Railroad safety is another problem. Maintenance of the heavily used lines is substandard and negligence by managers and workers is commonplace. The aging rolling stock is being replaced slowly, but unmet production goals for locomotives and boxcars are frustrating this effort, resulting in frequent mechanical breakdowns and serious safety problems.

In the 1970s and 1980s the Soviets built a major addition to the Trans-Siberian line. Concerned that the Eastern portion of the line lay too close to unfriendly China, the Soviet leadership ordered a new line to be built to the north. Called the **Baikal-Amur Mainline (BAM),** it begins at Taishet and runs north of Lake Baikal, ending at Sovietskaya Gavan opposite Sakhalin Island on the shore of Tatarsky Proliv, the northern end of the Sea of Japan. Three spurs connect it with the old Trans-Siberian line, and the project took a half million workers 10 years to build—it was finished in 1984 at a cost of $10 billion. Sixty new settlements were built along its remote course and one million people were relocated there. The BAM has not yet equaled the expectations it inspired, however. Relations with China have improved, meaning that the old line still carries the bulk of the cargo, and people have resisted living in BAM's remote, inhospitable environs.

The Soviet Union also has an extensive system of pipelines, totaling about 30,000 miles and carrying over 12 billion tons of natural gas, oil,

[17]Michael Parks, "Soviet Railway System Crippled by Strikes, Blockades, Mismanagement," *The Los Angeles Times,* Oct. 24, 1989.

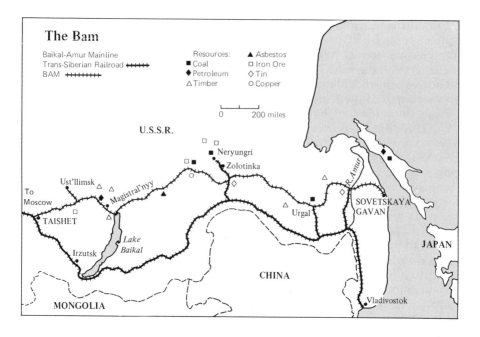

ammonia, and petrochemicals annually. In the 1980s a line tapping the Urengoi natural gas fields was built. Stretching for 2,759 miles from the Siberian Yamal Peninsula, it links up with pipelines in Eastern Europe. The Soviet Union provides about 25 percent of the natural gas used in Western Europe, and these sales bring in billions in needed hard currency. Yet, Soviet pipelines make the country increasingly dependent on Western technology. It spends billions in dollars in the West for equipment to maintain its lines. Even the pipe for the new Yamal line was made in the West.

The safety of the huge Soviet pipeline system is also in need of attention. In June 1989 a huge explosion killed over 600 Soviet passengers and injured hundreds more in the Ural Mountains. As one passenger train sat on a siding to allow a second train to pass, a spark set off a conflagration that flattened trees for two miles. The explosion with the force of a 10,000 ton bomb occurred because of a leak in a pipeline carrying liquid petroleum. Workers who detected the leak simply increased the pressure in the line, instead of tracing and fixing it. The explosion destroyed 800 yards of track and demolished every car of the two trains.[18] This tragic episode illustrates many of the problems in the Soviet economy and why Gorbachev has so energetically tried to reform it.

PERESTROIKA

Finding the economy stagnant when he became general secretary, Gorbachev first thought that the situation could be reversed with a few minor

[18]Masha Hamilton, "Raid Disaster Negligence, Gorbachev Says," *The Los Angeles Times,* June 6, 1989.

adjustments. As he became increasingly conversant with the economic problems, however, and as he studied the successful reforms in China and Hungary, Gorbachev ultimately concluded that the society needed to be completely restructured. Many of his perestroika reforms have already been examined and more will be dealt with later, so only a general overview of them is necessary here. Essentially, Gorbachev wants to relegate planning to long-term general design making, while allowing the economy to evolve market mechanisms to carry out the details. He wants to conserve natural and human resources by shifting from extensive to intensive production techniques and by encouraging economic experimentation to develop among the various union republics. At the same time, however, he hopes to preserve and enhance the fundamental social services that the people have come to appreciate and expect. To accomplish this enormous task, Gorbachev called upon his people to develop new attitudes about production and consumption and to accept short-term sacrifices—painful sacrifices—so as to reap future rewards.[19] Unfortunately, to date the reforms have had disappointing results. Production is down; taxes, inflation, and unemployment are on the rise. The people resent the prices charged and the profits made by entrepreneurs, even as they oppose the additional work necessary to meet new economic goals. At the same time, 25 percent of the government budget goes to subsidize prices for housing, food staples, and unprofitable enterprises.

Even though most people agree in general terms that the system must change, they resist the reality of it as it affects their individual lives. Socialism is more deeply rooted in the Soviet Union than in Eastern Europe or elsewhere. Most Soviet citizens have no experience with other systems and they fear the consequences of fundamental change. At the same time, the Soviet people have often been promised future advances for immediate sacrifice, and they have frequently been disappointed; so they are wary about such additional claims, even from Gorbachev. Perestroika threatens risk, while the Soviet people have been taught to expect a risk-free life. The people resist the responsibility it places on them, preferring instead the old system which asked of them no such commitment. They remain uncommitted to its goals although they desire its promised benefits. Not even the nation's youth have risen to its support. Indeed, the leading reformers in the society, the *perestroishchiki*, are, like Gorbachev, "children of the Twentieth Party Congress" in their 50s and 60s.

In 1989 as the economy unraveled, Gorbachev began to pay the price for failing to secure deep public support for his programs. Although Gorbachev adviser Alexander Yakovlev apologized for growing popular unrest about perestroika by saying, "It is like repairing a house or an apartment. Living becomes better only after the reconstruction is complete,"[20] the situation is much more serious. The public, after six years of reform with little apparent payoff, is becoming conservative—it is joining with the right

[19]See Able Aganbegyan, *The Economic Challenge of Perestroika* (Indianapolis, IN: Indiana University Press, 1988).

[20]Stephen F. Cohen and Katrina VanDen Heuvel, *Voices of Glasnost* (New York: W. W. Norton, 1989), p. 59.

wing ideologues, the military, and the bureaucrats against further reform. Grimacing about the economic failures, Gorbachev himself engaged in telling a joke at his own expense.

> President Mitterrand has, they say, 100 lovers, and one of them has AIDS, but he doesn't know which one.
>
> President Bush has 100 bodyguards, and one of them is a terrorist, but he doesn't know who it is.
>
> And Gorbachev has 100 economists, and only one of them has any brains, and he, too, doesn't know which one.

"I liked that one," he said.[21]

Jokes aside, the matter came to a head in the summer of 1990. The radicals, led by Russian SFSR President Boris Yeltsin, demanded a crash program to switch to a market economy in 500 days, while the conservatives demanded caution. Gorbachev, perhaps remembering Peter the Great's lament, "Even if it is good and necessary, yet be it novel, our people will do nothing about it unless they are compelled," chose to take a more temperate course, but the situation continued to degenerate at an increasing pace. Finally, in April 1991 Gorbachev decided that decisive action had to be taken. Letting his new prime minister, Valentin S. Pavlov, take the lead in the matter, a series of price increases was announced. Claiming that to end the spiraling budget deficits, the government had to drastically reduce the subsidies (240 billion rubles in 1991, or $384 billion by the official rate of exchange) it paid to support low prices for consumer goods. Furthermore, it was claimed that the reason such great shortages existed in the country is that the low prices charged for consumer goods discouraged their production. As a consequence, prices were increased by 50 to 70 percent on average, and some goods, like wheat bread—the price of which had not been increased for decades—climbed by almost 400 percent. Prices for staple goods like flour, sugar, meat, and milk continue to be set by the state, albeit at much higher rates than before, while prices for other goods are allowed to float upward until they reached state established ceilings. To soften the blow of such inflation on living expenses, the government announced an average monthly wage supplement of 60 rubles ($96), but this stipend is far short of the amount necessary to cover the entire shortfall.[22]

Understandably, the price increases were met with protests and grumbling across the country. Strikes broke out, the most serious of which were in Byelorussia. Undeterred, Gorbachev and Pavlov announced even more far-reaching reforms. Announcing in April 1991 that in the first quarter of that year the productivity of the country had dropped by an alarming 12

[21]Carey Goldberg, "Hey, That's Funny, Mikhail—Now Did You Hear the One About . . . ," *The Los Angeles Times*, Nov. 28, 1990.

[22]Elizabeth Shogren, "Soviets Get Allowances, Starting Now, to Ease Impact of Price Boosts," *The Los Angeles Times*, March 21, 1991.

percent, the two leaders initiated a crash program by which the economy is to abandon state-owned and operated enterprises and adopt a market system in much of the economy over a six-month period. Farmers are to be afforded loans and subsidies to buy land and equipment. Stores, factories, homes, vehicles, and other assets in the cities are to be sold to private owners, and state monopolies are to be ended in many commercial fields. Anticipating high unemployment throughout the transition, huge government job retraining programs are planned. At the same time, prices are expected to rise even more because the reform proposes that almost all state price controls are to be abandoned within 18 months of the reform's beginning. Finally, to combat the inflation caused by the government covering budget deficits by printing more money, Gorbachev invoked a tight money policy. Such a drastic endeavor will not go without serious resistance, but the leadership believes that the economy is at a desperate impasse. Hence, Pavlov gave ominous warnings that labor unrest, strikes, and ethnic violence would not be allowed to impede the progress of the reforms.[23]

These astonishing policies not only attest to how profound the economic failure of the Stalinist economic model is, but they also give insight into Gorbachev's political character. Sometimes mistakenly read as a devoted liberal reformer, Gorbachev is much more a pragmatic politician who sees it to be his task to lead the Soviet Union to modernization. Bending to the resurgent power of the right, he has allowed something of a retreat from the political freedoms of glasnost. Yet he sees no viable alternative to immediate economic liberalization, since the old system has collapsed and his more moderate efforts at reform have failed. At the same time, however, he proposes to meet debilitating ethnic violence and labor unrest with a state clampdown reminiscent of former eras in Soviet history. Seemingly devoid of ideological fixation, Gorbachev is determined to take whatever steps appear necessary to save the Soviet Union from economic and political disaster. He swerves to the left and right with equal ease when he sees the necessity of doing so. How successful this political wizard's economic policies will be remains to be seen, but objective observers must conclude that the prospects are not encouraging.

The preceding pages show, in broad terms, both the successes and failures of the Soviet economy. Yet, no analysis of Soviet political society would be complete without an examination of the economy as it affects the people themselves.

[23]Michael Parks, "Gorbachev Plans Tough Recovery Steps," *The Los Angeles Times,* April 10, 1991, and Carey Goldberg, "'Old-Style Coercion' Is Soviet Premier's Cure," *The Los Angeles Times,* April 23, 1991.

chapter 9

The Economy
and the People

Approximately 49 percent of the Soviet people have full-time jobs. Since almost all people of working age are employed, the remaining 51 percent are either infants, retirees, or students. Of these "nonworkers," a large percentage of the adults have part-time jobs or work in the fields for a few weeks during the harvest. About 73 percent of the full-time labor force is engaged in producing material objects, while the remainder provide services. Soviet publications list 61.8 percent of the labor force as workers, 26.2 percent as office employees, and 12 percent as farmers.[1] More will be said later about agricultural labor; for now we will concentrate on the urban work force.

INDUSTRIAL LABOR

Since the Soviet Union pictures itself as the workers' state, it is important that we take a brief look at the labor force in the country. Soviet policy

---

[1]This figure includes only those who work on collective farms. Actually, about one-fifth of the labor force is engaged in agriculture.

requires that all working-aged adults who are not in school be employed. The average workweek is 41 hours spread over five days. The average industrial wage is about 217 rubles per month. The worker's base pay, however, is augmented by bonuses paid for fulfilling the plan; the bonuses, sometimes called the "thirteenth month pay," can equal as much as 20 to 30 percent of the base wage. In addition to their normal work, laborers are obliged to exercise their "socialist obligation," which may require them to help with the harvest or participate in a *subbotnik*, an unpaid day of labor cleaning up the city. The word *subbotnik* comes from the Russian word for Saturday—*subbota*. A *subbotnik* is usually scheduled on the Saturday closest to Lenin's birthday, but plant managers also schedule them throughout the year, depending upon whether the plants need more time to meet their production goals.

In large plants groups of workers are separated into production brigades. Each brigade has a leader and is assigned production goals. However, although workers are encouraged to pressure laggards in their brigade, individuals may take little interest in production since they bear no individual responsibility. Relations between labor and management are not the most amicable. Workers are often heard carping about the "bosses" who wear business suits and are driven around in big black Volga limousines.

In an attempt to improve labor-management relations and to increase productivity by giving the workers a stake in production, a law was passed in 1987 that required managers to be elected by the workers. This approach, as it turned out, was a mistake. Workers tended to elect managers who gave big bonuses and little work. The problem faced by Soviet authorities is that if the management of plants is too centralized, workers become alienated and indifferent about their jobs. Yet, when they are allowed to elect their managers, they tended to emphasize personal convenience with their votes, rather than the general good.

In June 1990 a new "law on state enterprises" was passed. It leaves the question of electing managers vague. Essentially, it allows each factory to decide for itself if managers are to be elected. More importantly, it changes the decision-making process. Councils of employees are now elected by the workers to join management in developing production goals. Factories have the right to modify goals in the plan handed down from the ministries, yet the income of the workers is determined by the amount earned in sales, so it is in the workers' interests to maximize quantitatively and qualitatively.

The new approach is patterned after the Japanese industrial model which the Soviets admire, and it also roughly parallels the principle of democratic-centralism. Management calls a meeting of the employees' council to explain the production goals suggested in the plan. The council then takes the information to the workers and discusses its viability. When consensus is reached, the employees' council returns to management with a counterproposal which management considers. Finally, management announces its decision. It can ignore the workers' advice, but it must take responsibility for the decision. Although this process is time-consuming, if it encourages workers and managers to become more cooperative and if it helps increase the workers' interest in production, it will be worth the cost. The new procedure has not yet had enough time to allow for an assessment of results, but early indications are that it may improve the situation.[2]

As we learned in a previous chapter, the right to strike is now assured to most Soviet workers and they have used it with a vengeance. Strikes have been used not only to pressure for better working conditions and higher wages, but as you learned in the last chapter they have also been used to protest neglect of the environment, Communist Party interference with the economy, and government corruption. Better social and recreational facilities, more abundant housing, and variety in the shops have also been demanded by strikes. Responding to the growing disruption of productivity by incessant work stoppages, Gorbachev called for a moratorium on strikes in 1991. There is little chance that his appeal will be honored, however, and Prime Minister Pavlov has advocated the use of force to deter debilitating walkouts.

Another serious problem concerning industrial labor is plant safety. For many years labor safety did not enjoy high priority, and workers suffered many preventable deaths and injuries. The net result was, of course, lowered productivity. As part of the present reform package a new emphasis on labor safety has been instituted. *Trud*, the labor daily, has engaged in a campaign pointing to needed modifications in plants, and Soviet officials have created a national program involving hundreds of research institutes and dozens of ministries to devise methods of improving safety for the workers. And Gorbachev himself has enjoined trade union leaders to be more energetic in assuring the rights of workers.

Unemployment

One of the most enviable accomplishments of the Soviet economy is that, until recently, it had virtually eradicated unemployment. In the 1920s the government, announcing that unemployment was nonexistent, abolished unemployment benefits but also committed itself to maintaining permanent full employment for its workers. Since that time, while Western capitalist countries saw a quarter or more of their work forces idle during the 1930s and grappled with high unemployment figures during the 1970s and 1980s, the people of the Soviet Union have enjoyed unprecedented job security, have become increasingly free to change jobs at will, and have seen their wages rise as demand for labor has grown faster than supply. These facts are indeed salutary, contributing to the considerable amount of personal security afforded Soviet citizens. It would, however, be a mistake to appreciate the Soviet employment record only on face value. Indeed, the remarkable record of full employment registered by the Soviet economy is not unencumbered, for it includes several serious disadvantages and economic glitches.

As previously observed, the Soviet economy is labor extensive. That is to say, increases in productivity have been achieved largely by adding more people to the work force rather than by devising other methods such as increased mechanization and incentives to raise the productivity of each

[2]"Perestroika in the Factory," *The Economist*, June 9, 1990.

individual worker. The former approach was adopted in part because the technology and resources needed for mechanization were diverted to specific areas like space, the military, and public transportation. One should hasten to add, however, that failure to mechanize has also occurred because of government efforts to maintain full employment.

The question of incentives has also been particularly nettlesome. In trying to build a collective society, Soviet authorities often ignored individual rewards and responsibilities. In addition, by attempting to divert the people's interest from personal gain, Soviet leaders often tried to satisfy workers with such morale-building rewards as medals, praise, and patriotic hoopla. These policies have not always been successful. The state also offered material incentives but these too were insignificant.

Another complication confronting planners is the serious decline in the birthrate. Although Western experts have long recognized the problem, Soviet authorities were slow in admitting it. With the Slavic birthrate barely equaling Slavic deaths, the authorities are finding it hard to staff mills and factories. By contrast, the fastest growing population center in the Soviet Union is Central Asia, which has relatively little industry, but it does have the greatest unemployment problem. A simple solution to the problem might appear to be either to move factories to Central Asia or to resettle Central Asians in European Russia. Yet, neither of these options is palatable since the Central Asians resist immigration from their ancient homelands and the authorities are hesitant to shift Soviet economic power to that unassimilated and restive section of the country. Added to the logistics of this problem is the general disquiet among Russians, who see their status as the majority population eroding even as the numbers of Central Asians grow.

Even though there was no overt unemployment before Gorbachev's insistence that farmers, offices, shops, and plants become more efficient, there was, and continues to be, a serious problem with "hidden unemployment."

Soviet managers are notorious for overstaffing their plants. The need to employ more workers than ordinarily required stems from several inefficiencies in the system. First of all, extra workers are needed to make up for the drunks, absentees, and malingerers—or for those workers who quit or become ill. Also, the necessity to shore up production (storming the plan) at the end of the month demands extra hands. Managers who have excess workers will often lend them to other plants in exchange for scarce supplies or for a favor returned later on. Finally, managers are occasionally required to provide workers for the harvest or to help construct public works. Each of these circumstances causes featherbedding, or redundant labor, which in turn results in an inefficient use of labor and retards productivity. It will be recalled that the Soviet worker produces only about half as much as the American laborer, and some authorities estimate it is actually closer to 40 percent;[3] only a portion of this low productivity can be blamed on the lack of machinery.

[3]Gur Ofer, "The Future of Economic Reform," in *Soviet Union 2000: Reform or Revolution,* ed. Walter Laqueur (New York: St. Martin's Press, 1990), p. 83.

A sobering result of Gorbachev's new labor policies is the expectation that between 13 million and 19 million workers may be laid off as the factories become more efficient. Trying to reverse the disincentives that presently exist, Gorbachev has initiated inducements to increase the efficiency of the workers, thus eliminating the need for redundant labor. His original plan was to have these programs going full force by the mid-1990s, but worker anxiety and conservative pressure have slowed the process considerably. If the perestroika reforms are ever allowed to proceed, however, the impact of such heavy unemployment will send shock waves throughout the system, threatening social and political destabilization. Job retraining and relocation programs are planned and the government has given assurances that high unemployment figures would be only temporary, yet people are understandably concerned. In 1989 *Pravda* reported that unemployment had reached the 3 million mark and that it is heaviest in Central Asia. In response, the government slowed the reforms, but while this measure helped stem increasing unemployment, it left the economy in an ambiguous situation; the old command system was disrupted but a new market system was not allowed to replace it. Consequently, productivity declined and prices increased in a classic example of what is called in the United States *stagflation*. Finally, in April 1991 Gorbachev embarked on a series of massive reforms to convert the economy to private ownership and the market dynamic, but unemployment is expected to rise again as a result.

Labor Discipline

No reasonable amount of mechanization or reformed management techniques will, in itself, solve the labor productivity problem. In fact, worker morale is lower than ever before. Ironically, the workers' state seems to have spawned a "don't work" ethic among its citizens. Although this sad attitude stems from complex sources, the impediments to real incentives—extreme job security and the disappointing consumer goods market—must account for a large measure of the problem. Fearing that their goals might be increased, workers deliberately discourage good work habits by shaming their industrious peers.

Evidence of the bad attitude Soviet labor has toward work is perhaps most clear in shops and restaurants. Fortified by an ideology implying that waiting on anyone is demeaning, Soviet service personnel are deliberately dilatory and rude. One can stand for several frustrating minutes while clerks, who do not care whether or not they make a sale, fuss with meaningless tasks, talk to friends, read, or simply look off into space with typical Slavic stoicism. After waiting patiently to be seated in an empty restaurant, one can spend additional time while waiters find their way from the back of the room to the table. Having ordered, one waits again, only to find that the desired fare, although it appears on the menu, is not available. Such frustration causes Soviet diners to grumble that

"When the doors open, the restaurant closes."

Beyond these and other deliberate efforts to slow productivity, Soviet workers find themselves in impossible circumstances. The utter lack of variety and shortages in shops force people to duck work periodically so that they can go shopping in the city. Fruit- and vegetable-hungry northerners pay high prices for produce, so Azerbaijans, Uzbeks, Georgians, Armenians, and Moldavians skip work to fly north and sell their privately cultivated foods.

Most women in the Soviet Union work. Since refrigerators are small and men do little shopping, women must shop daily. If they wait until the workday is over to go to the store, they may have to stand in line for an hour—only to find the shelves empty. Consequently, workers use company time to shop during the day. When word circulates that scarce items are in the shops, some workers will cover for their peers, who rush out to buy goods for everyone in the plant. To combat such absenteeism, managers have taken to establishing shops in their plants where workers can at least buy staple goods before they leave for the day, thus somewhat reducing the absenteeism.

Yet the plants cannot stock everything the workers need, and leaving work for personal errands—even beyond shopping—has become standard behavior for many workers. It is quite common for workers to duck out to visit friends, attend weddings, take in a film, lounge in the public baths, drink in pubs, or see a doctor.

Andropov tried relatively heavy-handed methods to increase labor productivity. He launched an anti-alcohol campaign and sent police to sweep shops to discourage shopping during work time. Neither of these approaches was very successful and each angered the public. For a while Gorbachev redoubled his predecessor's effort to discourage heavy drinking but the campaign was a complete failure, and it also seriously reduced government revenues from the sale of spirits, thus aggravating the budget deficit.

Other policies have met with more success. Shops have been required to remain open later to accommodate workers. Laws have been passed punishing violators with extra work hours or less vacation time should they miss work or be found drunk on the job. Plant managers have been empowered to assess fines for damage caused by alcoholics or, in some cases, to fire inebriated offenders on the spot without trade union approval. Additional penalties see pay reductions imposed for sloppy work, and "work jumpers" now must give two months' notice rather than the previous two weeks' warning of their intention to quit. But positive reinforcement accompanies these negative measures. Good workers are to be rewarded with two extra vacation days per year with a choice of good resorts, and they are to be given priority for new apartments and other amenities.

Although these policies have had some salutary effects, labor discipline is still abysmal and the recent food shortages have simply increased the time people must spend as hunters and gatherers. It is hoped that recent changes in management decision making will improve worker attitudes and production, but given the level of alienation and indifference that has existed since the Brezhnev era, one wonders how successful they will be. Dismal as it is, however, industrial productivity is not the greatest problem faced by Soviet leaders. To study the most serious problem, we must leave the cities and go to the countryside.

AGRICULTURE

Russia has always depended heavily on its agricultural base for sustenance. No class paid more dearly for the luxuries of the tsars than the serfs. Combatting oppressive weather conditions and exploitative landlords, they eked out a living while watching their goods being carted off for taxes. With the emancipation in 1861, the newly freed peasants found that they had simply exchanged their aristocratic masters for bondage to the mir and that they often had less land to farm than before.

The Stolypin reforms at the turn of the century and the policies of the NEP in the 1920s were but brief exceptions to the rule of collective farming that the peasants had endured for centuries. Ending the NEP, Stalin reimposed collectivized farming upon a reluctant and even insurgent peasantry, and only the most brutal efforts induced the peasants to abandon private ownership and return to the collectives.

In a strange way, Stalin could be said to have reestablished the tsarist system. Making the party the new aristocracy, he restored the bureaucracy, the secret police, and the military to their accustomed place of dominance—to say nothing of making himself the single, all-powerful ruler. He even reinvigorated the Russian Orthodox Church to some extent during World War II. Most importantly for purposes of this discussion. Stalin returned agriculture to its traditional structure and role. The recollectivization of agriculture made the peasants virtual serfs by denying them domestic passports and the freedom to move. And he gave agriculture the task of paying for the prosperity of the system.

Stalin's intention was to build a modern industrial state. To the extent that he succeeded, the bill was paid by the Soviet people. But the burden of cost was not borne equally throughout the society. Stalin's policies clearly favored heavy industry first and urban works second; last of all came the peasants.

Peasants have always suffered an ambiguous place in Marxist ideologies, except for Mao Tse-tung's theory giving the peasants the dominant revolutionary role in China. Marx himself seldom discussed their role in the new society. In applying Marxist theory, Lenin made an attempt to integrate those wielding the sickle with those swinging the hammer, but even he was oriented toward the urban worker.

Stalin paid little more than lip service to equality for the peasantry; his policies were clearly biased against them. During his long rule, agriculture was squeezed and squeezed again for products, the value of which was poured into the industrial base. The farms were starved of capital investment, fertilizer, transport, roads, skilled managers, buildings, machinery, storage facilities, social benefits, and adequate wages.

Hence, like planning and industry, agriculture rests on the foundation and assumes the structures Stalin created for it. As a result, it has been the unrivaled Achilles' heel of the Soviet economy. So profound are its systemic problems that it has failed to respond to substantial efforts by Stalin's successors to cure its ills.

Farm Structure

Today there are essentially five basic farm structures producing food and fiber for Soviet markets: state farms, military farms, collective farms, private plots, and cooperatives.

State farms. The **state farms,** or *sovkhozy,* are the largest agricultural establishments in the country. First appearing in the 1920s, their number was not important until Khrushchev embarked on a massive program of consolidating collective farms into giant "agricultural factories." Averaging about 50,000 acres each and numbering approximately 23,300, these state farms occupy more than half the total arable land.

The state farms are administered by the State Commission for Foods and Procurements and by related agencies at the union republic level. They are managed by professional administrators who may be elected by the workers. The *sovkhozy* workers enjoy the same status as industrial workers. They are considered workers, not farmers. They are paid fixed wages depending upon the skilled tasks they perform, and they are entitled to the full array of social services available to urban workers. State farms usually specialize in one or two particular items—vegetables, livestock, cotton, dairy products, or grain.

Military farms. **Military farms** are a state secret, so little is known about them. Their size and numbers are not precisely known, but recent evidence indicates that since 1965 they have been increasing. Managed by the Ministry of Defense, these farms are similar to the *sovkhozy* in structure and are used to produce a portion of the food consumed by the military, thus enhancing its status as a society within a society. The successive agricultural failures of the late 1970s and early 1980s apparently induced the leadership to demand that these special farms become even more productive, thus relieving the pressure on civilian food markets.

Collective farms. The structure of the **collective farms,** or *kolkhozy,* is significantly different from that of the *sovkhozy.* Collective farms are theoretically voluntary associations of previously independent farm workers. The state owns the land on which the farm is situated, but the *kolkhoz* is given the perpetual right to farm it, rent free, in exchange for selling requisite amounts of its products to the state at fixed prices. The members of the *kolkhoz* collectively own the tools, machines, stock, seed, and buildings. The farmers may own their own cottages, although the land upon which they rest belongs to the state.

Each collective farm is run by the mandates of the general meeting. Attended by every worker 16 years or older, the general meeting convenes periodically throughout the year to decide democratically on policy. Member workers elect a chairperson of the farm, a management committee, and an auditing commission. Collective farm managers used to be on the party's *nomenklatura* lists, but supposedly this is no longer so. Still, the party remains a powerful institution at the local level, so regional first secretaries appear able to influence collective farm management elections. Like state farms, the *kolkhozy* must fulfill state orders for their products. When these goals are exceeded, however, the collective farms may now sell their surplus to the state or on the open market. Proceeds from these sales are divided among the workers in accordance to the units of work performed.

Collective farms, about 27,000 in number, average only 15,000 acres and thus are much smaller than the state farms. Unlike the state farms, they do not usually specialize, preferring to raise several different crops, maintain small herds, and produce eggs and dairy products on the same farm. Yet, the work conditions are not a great deal different from the state farms. Both state and collective farms assign workers to brigades of perhaps 100 persons. These brigades, headed by manager-appointed or worker-elected leaders, are assigned to work details. One day they may find themselves weeding a given section of the farm, the next day they may be moved to fence mending elsewhere, and a third day they may be assigned to plowing yet another field. Having no particular responsibility for a given crop or field because they are shifted from one seemingly meaningless task to another, farm workers demonstrate little interest in their jobs. Trying to increase the farmers' feelings of personal involvement with production, Soviet managers on both state and collective farms have recently begun experimenting with assigning particular workers to specific sections for the duration of a season. These efforts, however, have not had the desired result since the farmers know that they may be assigned to work a different section the following season.

Attempting to improve conditions for the collective farmers, the Brezhnev government raised wages and extended many previously forbidden privileges to these hapless souls. In 1964 collective farmers, previously left to their own resources in old age, were integrated into the social security system, assuring them a small pension upon retirement. Two years later the state bestowed on them a guaranteed minimum wage, thus making them somewhat secure from the severe economic plight that usually followed periodic poor harvests. Indeed, perhaps no element in Soviet society enjoyed a greater improvement in living standards under Brezhnev's stewardship than the collective farmers. However, their income still remains the lowest in the society, currently averaging about 178 rubles per month. Moreover, collective farmers, similar to peasants of old, remain bound to the land as no other person in the society. Even though they have now been issued internal passports, making it easier for them to leave the farm, they must secure the permission of the farm chairperson, the general meeting, and the local police chief in order to quit the collective farm legally.[4]

[4]Konstantin M. Simis, *USSR: The Corrupt Society*, trans. Jacqueline Edwards and Mitchell Schneider (New York: Simon & Schuster, 1982), pp. 180–181.

Private plots.   Originally created by Stalin as a grudging concession to recalcitrant farmers resisting collectivization, the **private plot** has become a vital source of food in this socialist country. Collective farmers were allowed to farm a small plot of land (between one-half and one full acre) and dispose of its yield as they wished—either consuming it themselves or selling it at the market, pocketing the proceeds from whatever price demand allows. The private plot was firmly rooted in the countryside by the time Khrushchev became the leader. The new party secretary, however, fought against this pocket of free enterprise, attempting to strangle it by reducing the size of the plot and the number of animals each family was allowed to own.

The anti–private plot policy was quickly revised by Brezhnev, however, when crop failures in the early 1970s threatened the land with famine. Since then the government has generally pursued policies encouraging the development and increased production of the private plots. Industry was ordered to produce adequate numbers of garden tools and small farm machinery for use on these plots. Government subsidies were established, encouraging construction of single-family dwellings behind which the plots are found. State farm workers are allowed to till small plots; city dwellers may cultivate empty lots or buy cottages on the outskirts of towns to raise gardens.

Only about 3 percent of all the cultivated land in the Soviet Union is designated for private plots, yet they produce about 30 percent of the country's produce. In 1990 these plots were estimated to produce 27 percent of all meat, milk, and eggs; 28 percent of all vegetables; 55 percent of all potatoes; and 70 percent of all fruit consumed in the country.[5]

Before he came to Moscow, Gorbachev was noted for his agricultural innovations in Stravropol, where he was the party first secretary. When he became general secretary of the CPSU, he quickly encouraged the private plots. He increased the land devoted to them, encouraged farm managers to cooperate with the peasants by lending them materials and equipment to use on the private plots, and he demanded that the party not interfere with private plot cultivation.

Today's farmers assume the same attitude about working collective lands as Russian peasants have had for centuries; it is a kind of dues paid so that they may be allowed to till their own bit of land. The private plots, however, are not only important economically, providing peasants with a good share of the food they consume and augmenting their incomes, they also have profound social and psychological significance. They constitute the first introduction to the land for the farmers' children, they give the aged a meaningful occupation after retirement, and they are one of the few places where people can feel like they are their own bosses.

Generally disinterested in their work on the public fields, farmers husband their own crops and animals with meticulous care. Proving that Soviet farmers are quite capable of performing intensive farming, they maximize the productive capacity of every inch of ground allotted to them.

---

[5]*USSR '90 Yearbook* (Moscow: Novosti Press Agency, 1990), p. 235.

In somewhat less laudatory behavior, farmers often sneak off from their assigned chores to put more time into their gardens, and they pinch the government's fertilizer and other materials to lavish on their own crops.

Interestingly, Soviet working-age men do not contribute most heavily to the private plot. Soviet studies indicate that only 9 percent of the men's work time goes to the private plots, while over one-third of the women's work time is devoted to these small plots. The remainder of the work is done by the very old and the very young of the household.

Although more will be said later about the farmer's markets at which the produce from these plots is sold, we should briefly note here one more social phenomenon related to the private plots. Life on Soviet farms is crushingly boring. Consequently, one of the benefits of the private plot is that it offers the farmer an occasional opportunity to escape the tedium of the village and visit the city, which by comparison is exciting and entertaining. Early spring finds the greatest number of people engaging in this happy pilgrimage. The cities are filled with recently arrived people from such exotic places as Uzbekistan, Armenia, Moldavia, Georgia, and Azerbaijan, hawking their flowers, fruits, wines, and vegetables. At any time of the year, however, one can visit the open markets to find recently arrived peasants in rented stalls selling rabbits, poultry, honey, radishes, carrots, dill, and other farm products.

These commercial forays also give rural people the opportunity to shop in the city for things that are unobtainable in the hinterland. Visions of hundreds of peasants laden with recent purchases riding home from the cities on olive-drab Soviet railroad cars inspired this riddle.

> What is long and green and smells like sausage? A train leaving Moscow.

Cooperative farms. These new experiments will be discussed in detail later in this chapter in the section on economic reform. For now I will just point out that Gorbachev has encouraged farmers to rent, lease or buy land from the state and to run it as family or cooperative enterprises. So far, however, Soviet farmers have not taken to the idea with much enthusiasm.

Farm Production

No economy, regardless of how advanced or how heavily industrialized, can be confident of a secure future without an abundant supply of agricultural goods. Agriculture is, in fact, the foundation of any national economy—except perhaps that of the oil-rich states. Even they, however, must have a ready supply of agricultural goods if they are to enjoy the bounty of their other natural resources.

This inescapable fact, perhaps more than any other, places the Soviet economy in jeopardy of stunted growth. Even as industrial production has increased more than a hundredfold since 1917, Soviet agriculture has increased at only a snail's pace. As one might expect, Soviet farms changed little during the neglectful years of Stalin's rule, but between his death and 1980, even in the face of massive commitments of resources and money, Soviet agricultural production increased at an average annual rate of only about 3 percent. Recently Soviet planners have invested 20 percent of their labor force (agriculture uses 3.6 percent of the labor force in the United States) and 25 percent of its capital investment (4 percent for the United States) in agriculture. Still, Soviet food production has barely kept pace with the population growth. Even more serious, since the early 1970s the Soviet government has had to squander precious hard currency to import massive amounts of grain from the West because of Soviet agriculture's inability to satisfy domestic needs. In the decade between 1972 and 1982, Soviet grain imports increased by 1,000 percent, and in 1985 alone the Soviets imported $11 billion worth of grain, an amount equal to its total foreign sale of natural gas. Good weather, technological improvements, and management changes saw the grain harvest of 1986 rise to 210 million metric tons, the largest since 1978, but poor weather and bad management saw grain production decline again throughout the last years of the decade. Not until 1990 did Soviet grain production climb again. Yet, expectations of new shortfalls and the incredible inefficiency in getting food to market before it spoils, for which Soviet agriculture is noted (60 percent of the 1990 bumper crop of vegetables spoiled before they could be consumed) caused the government to agree to buy large amounts of grain from the United States between 1991–1995. As a result the Soviet Union has become our largest foreign grain customer; it also buys large amounts of grain from Canada and Argentina.[6]

Compared with other countries, Soviet farm labor is incredibly unproductive. A Soviet farmer feeds himself or herself and four other people; an American farmer will feed 50 people including himself or herself and then produce a huge surplus. To make matters worse, young Soviet men are leaving the farms in droves. Having gotten a glimpse of the big city while in the military, young men find little to attract them back to the lonesome, boring life of the farm. Attempting to forestall their migration, authorities usually give young men the best paying jobs, jobs that involve the use of machinery. Hence, Soviet agriculture is caught up in an interesting irony. Women do most of the drudgery of manual labor on the farms, while the men straddle tractors and combines.

The poor showing of Soviet agriculture is caused by many factors that have parallels in other parts of the economy. The plan's rigidity prevents farm workers from enjoying the flexibility necessary for efficient operation. For instance, the plan specifies when the harvest will occur, and the appropriate machinery is scheduled to enter the fields at the designated time. Workers are ordered to harvest grain even though the fields may be wet, causing damage to both crops and machinery. Fertilizer is delivered on the plan's schedule. If it is not needed at that time, it is often allowed to stand in uncovered piles, dissipating in the elements. Management is too

[6]Art Pine, "Soviets Approve 5-Year Deal for American Grain," *The Los Angeles Times,* March 3, 1990.

centralized; commands are passed up and down the line, wasting valuable time. Workers have little incentive to toil efficiently or to take personal interest in their jobs since they are not personally responsible for the production of any particular crop, field, or herd. Additionally, the growing season is very short, limiting the size and number of crops that can be planted. Monumental efforts must be made each year if crops are to be harvested before being devastated by rain or cold. Only about 10 percent of the land area of the country is suitable for even marginal farming, and two-thirds of its farmland is highly susceptible to erosion. Almost all the best land suffers from erratic rainfall. The rich black earth lands are parched by drought once in every three years on average. These unhappy facts necessitate costly irrigation projects and fertilizers if production is to be maintained. Even so, about two-thirds of all Soviet wheat is winter wheat. As any Dakota farmer can tell you, if the snow is too early or too light, the crop can fail, and no human device can effectively substitute for an uncooperative winter.

Those problems nature spares the people are often caused by planners or the people themselves. With inordinately poor soil, except for the black earth region in the Ukraine and Kazakhstan, fertilizer is an absolute necessity. Soviet factories produce substantial amounts of fertilizer, even more than is produced in the United States. Most Soviet fertilizer is of poor quality, however, and it is packaged indifferently, subjecting it to the elements. Much of it is wasted by inadequate transit, and the peasants sometimes resist its use.

Until now the increases in Soviet agricultural production have been accomplished largely through "land-extensive" measures, bringing more and more acres under the plow. This approach is perhaps natural in a land that has such massive expanse. Clearly, however, it is past time for the Soviet farmers to begin to make each acre more productive by farming intensively. Intensive farming, while it probably demands fewer people, is expensive in fertilizer, herbicides, energy, and machinery costs, so Soviet leaders have preferred to find a variety of ways of expanding Soviet acreage. Khrushchev and Brezhnev each opened vast new farmlands to the plow. These measures were somewhat successful but not spectacularly so. Another, less successful, approach was tried by Stalin and Khrushchev. This method involved applying the theories of Trofim D. Lysenko, a geneticist who dominated Soviet biological science for decades, retarding it severely.

Extrapolating from Marx's social theories about people adjusting to their environments, Lysenko speculated that plants could do the same thing. Thus he hypothesized that by raising generation after generation of wheat in arctic climes and by husbanding those shoots that survived the extreme cold, a genetic transformation would gradually occur, resulting in the evolution of a whole new breed of wheat that would resist the harsh cold of the snow-blanketed fields in the north. No such transformation has yet taken place, but occasionally one still reads of isolated experiments with Lysenkoism in remote parts of the Soviet Union.

Pending the unlikely success of Lysenko's unorthodox theories, the Soviet leaders will be hard-pressed to achieve major improvements in agricultural production unless they address their problems of transportation and mechanization. Although Soviet industry produces more tractors annually than are produced in the United States, the best of them are exported, thus leaving farmers with poor quality equipment and a shortage of machinery. Furthermore, much of Soviet agricultural machinery is ill suited to its task. Combines and potato harvesters are notorious for damaging crops, and the lack of sufficient machinery leaves crops to rot in the fields. Spare parts, a valuable commodity in the Soviet Union, are so scarce that crops are left to spoil while machinery sits idle, awaiting repair. Farm mechanics sometimes strip perfectly good machines for parts that cannot be duplicated. Many machines are left exposed to the elements for lack of adequate barn space, thus causing their premature demise. At the same time, perfectly good equipment, tools, and facilities are often poorly maintained by disinterested workers.

Crop handling, transport, and storage are also terrible problems. At best, one-quarter of all Soviet food crops fail to reach the table because of needless waste and spoilage. Soviet statistics reveal that 50 percent of its potatoes and 20 percent of its grain are lost because of negligence, fuel shortages, inadequate transportation, poor storage facilities, and chaotic distribution. One-fifth of its sugar beets, cabbage, carrots, and onions, and almost as much of its fruit, is lost through spoilage or waste.

These incredible losses occur for a number of reasons. First, workers are careless in harvesting and handling crops. (It should be remembered that many of the people who help with the harvest are transplanted students, urban workers, and soldiers who, being forced to work temporarily in the fields, often resent the interruption of their normal lives.) Because of their carelessness, moisture, dirt, and chaff adulterate grain and produce. Packaging is also a serious problem. Shortages of boxes and bags cause fruit, potatoes, tomatoes, and other vegetables to be either ruined by improper packaging or left in the fields to spoil. Rigid and slow to respond to changing conditions, the plan limits the number of workers and equipment that may be used for a task. If the elements combine to produce a bumper crop, as happened in 1990, much of the surplus will go unharvested because of shortages of machinery, labor, and packaging materials.

> Lamenting the irregularities of planning for agriculture, Soviet farmers tell the fictitious story about the peasant who had raised three pigs but whose farm manager had reported to the local Gosplan agent that the peasant had actually raised five. The local Gosplan agent told his oblast superior that the number was eight, and the oblast Gosplan reported to Gosplan in Moscow that this fine peasant farmer had raised ten pigs. Moscow's response was to send the following message to the peasant: "Good work, comrade peasant! Send us only three of your pigs; you may keep the rest."

Storage facilities are primitive in many cases. Canning equipment, grain elevators, food bins, drying facilities, and refrigerated storage are insufficient to the task. Sixty percent of all potatoes and much of the cabbage, carrots, and beets are stored over the winter in the same fashion as has been used by peasants through the centuries. Huge trenches are dug, and the produce is poured inside and covered with dirt. One need only visit a Soviet store to see the poorly stocked bins of dirt-encrusted, half-spoiled radishes, potatoes, and carrots to realize that vegetables receive precious little of the care common in the United States.

Transportation problems cause much additional waste. Since most of the roads are dirt, they become impassable when the rains come. As trucks bog down in the mud, their cargo rots. Trying to avoid places in the road that have become deep holes of ooze because of rain and heavy usage, truck drivers sometimes find it easier to divert across fields, destroying unharvested crops en route. The drivers' goals, after all, call for a requisite number of miles logged and delivery of crops; that these detours destroy other crops is not the drivers' affair.

Even in the years of poor grain harvest, a visit to the country reveals a roadside strewn with tons of grain that blew away from uncovered transport. Refrigerated trucks and railroad cars are in very short supply, so perishable goods must be transported long distances in vehicles ill suited for their delicate baggage, resulting in more waste. Railroad cars in sidings emit the stench of crops spoiling because they somehow were not routed to their destination in timely fashion.

The horror stories of Soviet agriculture are endless. Tales of waste, corruption, and senseless spoilage abound not only in the Western media, but also in outraged tones in the Soviet press itself. Given the expensive imports the Soviet government must buy to maintain the meager diet its people enjoy, Soviet agriculture is truly facing a problem of crisis proportions, a problem demanding extensive remedial efforts.

Reforms

Impeded by their ideological convictions and influenced by their proclivity for bigness, the Soviet leaders find themselves severely limited in the kinds of changes they will accept in efforts to improve agricultural production. Knowing that agriculture's problems are so profound that meaningful improvement can be made only at the risk of imposing deep social transformation, the leadership seems indecisive, incapable of committing to a course that is rigorous enough to make much improvement.

Khrushchev, you will recall, eliminated the Machine Tractor Stations, increased the size and number of state farms at the expense of the collective farms, and expanded into the virgin lands of Kazakhstan, but none of these reforms made more than marginal improvements in Soviet agriculture. Although Brezhnev encouraged cultivation on the private plots and poured capital investment into agriculture and farm wages and benefits, his major thrust was not much different from Khrushchev's. He continued to rely principally on a land-extensive approach to increase production. Reaching north into the nonblack earth region, he resettled a half million people in a newly cultivated area four times the size of Texas. These lands have rather poor soil, necessitating extensive fertilization, but unlike the black earth region to the south they enjoy abundant rainfall. Even so, the increase in agricultural production was disappointing in the extreme. Unwilling to discipline party and state officials for corruption and incompetence, Brezhnev saw his agricultural policies fail as food production declined over the 1970s.

Although Gorbachev quickly lashed out at ineptitude, negligence, and corruption on the farms, his first structural reform in agriculture was securely within the tradition of his predecessors. He consolidated a number of government ministries dealing with agriculture into one giant bureaucracy: the *Gosagroprom.* Unfortunately, but predictably, this mammoth agency performed sluggishly and it was abandoned in 1989.

Other reforms to date are also disappointing in performance, but they have promise of long-term improvement. Beginning in 1986 farmers were allowed to sell about 30 percent of their crop on the open market, yet bureaucratic resistance to this plan has been fierce. Moreover, the imperatives of the plan have been relaxed, giving farmers more say in what will be planted and when it will be harvested. To answer farmers' objections that higher pay for their work is meaningless as long as the shops are empty, the government has tried unsuccessfully to increase the availability of consumer goods in the rural areas, and it has promised to pay farmers in hard currency for part of their crop.

In 1989 a major new reform became effective. It allows farmers to lease land for up to 50 years and farm it as their own, and it gives these farmers tax deductions if they are ecologically responsible. These leases can be willed to heirs, given away, or subleased, but they can be revoked if they are misused. In response to pressure from the union republics for more autonomy, this program has been given to them to administer directly. Farmers, however, have not flocked to this seeming new opportunity largely because local bureaucrats are apparently sabotaging it. Few lease contracts have been approved for longer than three years and automatic renewal rights are usually not granted. Hence, farmers may find themselves forced to take marginal land during the next contract period. Banks are reluctant to loan money to these farmers and the farmers have also had trouble buying insurance on their crops. There is no retirement plan for private farmers; they are the last to receive improvements like roads and schools; they have had trouble getting timely deliveries of machinery, fertilizer, and veterinary services—and they find themselves charged more for these services than is charged to state and collective farms.[7]

Until 1991, Gorbachev remained adamantly opposed to allowing farmers to own their own land. Boris Yeltsin and the Supreme Soviet of the Russian SFSR, however, did take the fateful leap to private ownership in late 1990. Russian law was modified to allow peasants to buy land and equipment from the state.[8] At the same time, conservative farmers have organized the Peasants' Union of the Soviet Union. The advocates in-

[7]Dmitri N. Shalin, "For Soviets to Master the Land, Land Must Be Given to Masters," *The Los Angeles Times,* March 16, 1989.
[8]Carey Goldberg, "Russia OKs Private Farms—With Limits," *The Los Angeles Times,* Nov. 4, 1990.

creased state benefits and protections for Soviet farmers, while looking askance at private farming. Still, agriculture continued to produce sluggishly. Finally, in April 1991 Gorbachev himself announced government low interest rate loans and subsidy programs to encourage farmers to buy state land and equipment in a belated and desperate attempt to privatize large sectors of Soviet agriculture. Since this reform was imposed from the top, there is little question that it will meet with the same bureaucratic resistance and peasant caution the 1989 reforms encountered. Hence, the prospects for success seem very tenuous.

The crisis into which Soviet agriculture has blundered clearly demands even more creative and energetic attention if the economy is to overcome its present stagnation. A major increase in labor efficiency and agricultural mechanization is essential if productivity is to be raised and the society desperately needs more agricultural production. At the same time, conditions on the farm must be dramatically improved if the current exodus of young people is to be stemmed. As things are, life on the farm is a dreary and tedious existence.

Living on the Farm

Even the shortest excursion away from the city into the vast countryside of the Soviet Union launches the visitor into a time warp, seemingly hurtling one back a century or more. Even before one reaches the outskirts of most cities, paved side roads end and dirt paths begin. The clothing of the people quickly transforms from moderately fashionable streetwear to awkward, faded, and ill-fitting but utilitarian garb of nondescript cut. Put plainly, living conditions in the countryside are, by modern standards, primitive. More than one writer has observed that the Soviet peasant leads a life-style more appropriate to residents of the Third World than to citizens of the world's second greatest industrial power.

The quaint *izbi*, low-slung log cabins often painted bright red, blue, yellow, purple, or green, look charming from afar. The windows are often festooned with potted plants and lace curtains, and electric lines bring power for television and lights. On closer inspection, however, the *izbi* appear to be quite primitive. The outside wells reveal that the cottages have no plumbing, and the small size allows for no more than a couple of rooms. Even so, the peasants fiercely resist periodic attempts to move them from their aging cottages to farm apartment complexes. Owning a single-family dwelling is a rare luxury in the Soviet Union except in the countryside. These ground-level houses may have dirt floors and may lack many modern amenities, but they are preferred to the communal buildings. The *izbi* give residents a measure of privacy, as well as the convenience of having a private plot just outside the back door.

Deep ruts in the roads in front of these houses eloquently testify to how difficult it is to move about when the rains come. Villages may have a meeting hall where people gather in their leisure or for general meetings, but movie theaters or other entertainment facilities are rare. Similarly, schools and medical facilities are substandard, and telephones are almost nonexistent. Isolated from the world by distance, inconvenient travel, and social custom, the peasants find little to do in their free time save gossip and drink, drink and gossip—and drink.

The tedium of farm life is perhaps interrupted, but not relieved, by the farm work. A majority of the work on Soviet farms is done by manual labor. It is common on Soviet farms to see most feeding, picking, milking, planting, and weeding done by hand. Women carrying heavy buckets of milk and water dot the rural landscape. As indicated earlier, most of the hard manual work is performed by women since the men are enticed to remain on the farm by being given jobs using machinery. Even so, the farm population is aging as the youth flee the rigors and boredom of farm life for the excitement, comfort, and better jobs of the city.

Something of a social class system exists on each farm. The elite include the chairperson, the party secretary, the chief agronomist, and the chief auditor. The middle class consists of other management personnel, labor brigade leaders, and machine operators. At the bottom of the ladder are those who perform manual work in the fields, stables, pens, and barns. Wages generally follow this class structure: The elite earn wages that can approximate those of plant managers, and machine operators' wages can equal those of the urban workers. Most farm workers, however, receive significantly lower pay than their urban counterparts. Currently the average industrial wage is about 280 rubles per month (about $448 by the official rate of exchange), while the average collective farmer earns only 230 rubles (about $368).[9] Besides this discrepancy in wages, it should be remembered that farm dwellers get less education, have less entertainment, receive poorer medical treatment, are allowed less freedom of movement, and generally enjoy less opportunity for excitement than their cousins in town.

Their meager wages are not even rewarded with attractive shopping opportunities. The typical village store is a dingy one-room affair dominated by bare, dusty shelves. Items usually found in these dreary shops include cigarettes, a few sewing materials, jarred vegetables (usually applesauce), matches, bread, sugar, some bins containing assorted vegetables depending on the season, a burlap bag or two of potatoes, perhaps some fatback or sausage on a rusted meat counter, an assortment of candy, and spirits, including vodka and brandy.

Such lean living conditions may lead one to the erroneous conclusion that the Soviet countryside is simmering with discontent. Peasants do occasionally exhibit animosity toward the system, as in 1990 when they threatened to withhold their crops unless they were provided with the fuel, vehicles, spare parts, and extra workers needed to complete the harvest. Such open defiance, however, is rare on the farms. Soviet peasants, like their predecessors of tsarist times, remain deeply conservative. Those seeking a more eventful life-style usually manage to leave the farms, while less

[9]Making ruble to dollar comparisons is not very helpful in assessing comparative standards of living because prices in the Soviet Union and the United States are very different. An analysis of the Soviet standard of living is made later in this chapter.

A Moldavian collective farm is served by an outside water well and deeply rutted dirt roads.

adventurous souls content themselves with the more tranquil and whole-some rural life. Imbued by a strong attraction to the land, the peasants see their circumstances gradually improving. Although their wages are low, their private plots, over which they have sole authority, provide them with fresh food and supplemental incomes. The boredom of their lives is occa-sionally interrupted by a foray into the city; meanwhile, they live in their

Soviet peasants in Uzbekistan gather around a tank of *kvas. Kvas* is a lightly fermented drink made by passing water through black bread.

snug *izbi,* close to the ground, avoiding the life of modern-day apartment dwelling experienced by their urban compatriots.

To say that the Soviet farmer (or any Soviet citizen for that matter) is basically satisfied with his or her lot is not to say that they are contented, nor is it to imply that the official Soviet economy provides all the needs of its citizens. Indeed, the official economy is but the first, albeit the most important, of the economies in the Soviet Union. Other, less approved economic activities run parallel to the first economy, and they deserve some notice as well.

COUNTER ECONOMIES

Anyone who has a passing acquaintance with conditions in the Soviet Union knows that it hosts a thriving "second economy," or black market. There is, however, also a "third economy," or "gray market," which also exists outside the official socialist economy. These counter economies are almost as varied and complex as the first economic system, and their extent, though less complete than the official economy, is pervasive indeed.

The Second Economy

On the first morning of my first visit to the Soviet Union, jet lag and excitement refused to let me sleep, so at 5:30 A.M. I dressed and left my hotel in Leningrad to stroll along the Neva River. In the distance, on the opposite side of the river, I could see the face of the Winter Palace. Directly across a canal from my hotel was the *Aurora.* Peter and Paul's Fortress was but three blocks away. As the minutes passed, the streets began to fill with people walking to work in brisk, businesslike cadence. Passing by some elderly men whose fishing poles stretched over the embankment, lines draped almost incidentally into the river (they never seem to catch anything), I paused to absorb the beauty and history of the city before me: capital of the tsars, birthplace of the revolution, survivor of the 900-day Nazi siege, hero city of the Soviet Union, noble and elegant—Leningrad. Leaning on the parapet of the river's embankment, thoughts spinning through my mind, excited and awed, I suddenly met my first Russian. (Before this, the only Russian I had encountered was the Intourist guide who had met me and the rest of my party in Moscow the night before and had escorted us to the lovely city built by Peter the Great.)

"American?" I heard someone say. Turning, I saw a short, slightly built man with the ruddy face and hard hands of a worker. "Yes I am," I responded. "I have beautiful icon—cheap," he said. "What?" I asked in surprise. "Icon, Russian icon—cheap," he said in a deep, "r"-rolling accent, "You want?' "Oh, no thank you," I said, remembering reading that Soviet authorities would not allow icons or other ancient works of art to leave the country. "Is beautiful. Is beautiful," he persisted. "But such things are against the law," I said. "I would not be allowed to leave the country with it. Don't you know such things are forbidden?" "Is okay, is okay. Is okay for

American tourist," he rejoined firmly after pausing long enough to figure out the substance of what I had said. "No thank you. I don't want it," I said without yet having seen the item under discussion. "But why do you take such chances? Won't you be punished if you are caught?" I asked. He paused again briefly, apparently for another mental translation. Then looking at me with softened face, a slight, friendly smile appearing, he shrugged with his arms bent at the elbow extending open palms and said, "*Nado zhit!*" (You have to live) and walked away.

Interesting as the encounter was at the moment, it was not until long afterward, following a much more thorough understanding of Soviet society, that I realized how significant it was that the second person I should meet in the Soviet Union, the first person I met by chance, should be engaging in the **black market,** or the shadow economy, as the Soviets like to call it.

Scarce goods and fixed prices are the natural ingredients of the black market borshch. Long before Soviet rule, Russians dealt with one another *na levo* (on the left). The striking thing is that after almost 70 years of Soviet government, the black market not only continues to thrive but has become a vital institution in the Soviet economy, distributing goods and services that the official economy cannot or will not market. The clandestine nature of the black market masks its extent. Estimates about its size vary greatly, not only because no official statistics about it exist, but also because authorities disagree about which items are appropriately included as black market trade. Andrei Sakharov once told *New York Times* correspondent Hedrick Smith that he guessed the black market accounted for at least 10 percent of the gross national product.[10] Other estimates are even higher. *The Wall Street Journal,* no ally of the Soviet economic system, claims that the black market comprises one-third of all commerce in the country.[11] Soviet estimates seemed to support the notion that a high percentage of the total economic activity was provided by the black market. Before many private economic activities were made legal, *Izvestia* estimated that as many as 20 million workers provided unofficial services valued at $8 billion. Indeed, it is guessed that almost half of all services in the city and about 80 percent of all services in the countryside were provided by the black market. In fact, no less than 40 percent of all car repairs were provided "on the left."[12] The situation has continued to worsen, until in 1990 the government announced that it estimated that half of the consumer goods produced in the Soviet Union reach the public through the black market.[13]

Quite apart from not having complete figures about the illicit trade in the society, we have difficulty defining the extent of the black market be-

---

[10]Hedrick Smith, *The New Russians* (New York: Random House, 1990), p. 266.

[11]David Brand, "Free Enterprise Helps to Keep Russians Fed but Creates Problems," *The Wall Street Journal,* May 2, 1983.

[12]William J. Eaton, "Soviets Allow a Little Private Enterprise—Warily," *The Los Angeles Times,* Dec. 15, 1986.

[13]Michael Parks, "Soviet Crackdown on Black Market," *The Los Angeles Times,* Oct. 23, 1990.

cause no one knows what specific activities should be included under this rubric. Is the sale of stolen goods part of the black market? Probably so, but is the theft itself also part of the black market? Bribery is another murky area. Bribery is rampant in the Soviet Union, but is all bribery part of the black market? Clearly, a bribe for an early peek at stolen university entrance examinations qualifies, but does a payoff for fixing a sentence for criminal activity satisfy the definition equally? How should one ascribe a bribe paid to a jailer for special privileges? Or a worker's kickback to provide a plant manager funds enough to bribe someone else so that needed materials are delivered in time to complete the production goals?

There is also a completely separate, unofficial, but legal—or at least semilegitimate—activity that will be dealt with in the next section. This kind of commerce, the third economy, is also difficult to separate from the black market. A person moonlighting on his or her own time is not in violation of the law, but if materials that have been pilfered from a state work site are used, all three kinds of activity are in play: the black market, other kinds of crime, and the third economy, or "gray market." It should also be noted that each of these three activities is essentially a nonsocialist activity since proceeds often evade the state, going directly into private purses.

Besides shortages and fixed prices, one other commodity is necessary if a black market is to pervade an economy: There must be a surplus of money. That is, the available money on the market must not be so small that it is all absorbed in the first economy. By steadily raising wages without increasing prices or the supply of consumer goods, and by releasing new money into the economy to cover the annual budget deficits, the government is not only creating inflation, but it is also providing the money supply necessary for a thriving black market.

Also, the Soviet black market tends to feed itself. Because black market prices are usually two to three times higher than the prices on the official market (one must remember that items may be low priced but unavailable on the official market, thus creating demand "on the left"), one who buys on the black market may also find it necessary to sell on the black market, thus earning the additional money necessary to sustain his or her illicit purchases. A favorite Georgian curse expresses the extent to which the Soviet people depend on the black market for sustenance.

May you have to live on your salary.

Moreover, the inflated prices on the black market tend to attract goods from the official economy into illicit trade. Soviet shoes are notoriously bad, so a shoe salesperson may buy up several pairs of imported shoes as soon as they reach the store, selling them on the black market for triple their official price and pocketing the difference.

The black market is so pervasive largely because it is ignored by law enforcement authorities. Unable to jail the millions of people engaged in the black market—perhaps not wishing to arrest the teenagers who openly bargain for jeans, records, cassettes, and stenciled T-shirts on the streets— and aware that the black market has a stabilizing effect on society by distributing goods that are unobtainable on the official market, the authorities wink at a huge portion of this clandestine enterprise. Evidence and logic also suggest that the authorities, from the local police to high-ranking party and state officials, are themselves participants in the underground trade.[14]

In the summer of 1986, however, a brief effort was made to clamp down on illicit commerce in the society. But officials apparently had to quickly relent as the flow of needed goods slowed and public outrage mounted. The authorities tactfully backed away from the campaign, contenting themselves with making legal, and therefore taxable, many pursuits that previously had been illegal: Taxi services using private automobiles, home and appliance repair businesses, and seamstress services are but a few examples.

Still, laws have been enacted in an effort to inhibit the really big dealers—often called "private millionaires" or "the mafia." In any purchase of items costing over 10,000 rubles—condominiums and expensive automobiles, for example—the buyer had to fill out a government form indicating where he or she got the money. Further, the 1986 law provided the death penalty for those convicted of large-scale speculation in foreign currency. Also, rumors persisted that the government planned to convert to a new currency, thus leaving the private millionaires holding the worthless, ill-gotten money. These efforts failed, however. In 1990 a new crackdown was announced. Decrying the involvement of organized crime in the illicit trade, the Supreme Soviet placed a penalty of up to 10 years in prison for anyone convicted of dealing in the black market. As has already been pointed out, in the following year the government took its most drastic step yet in trying to combat the shadow economy. Since most black marketeers hold much of their ill-gotten gains in 50 and 100 ruble notes, the government simply recalled the notes, replacing them with new ones. No one was allowed to exchange more than 1,000 rubles unless it could be proven that the money was legally earned. Only three days were allowed to make the exchange, and the economy was sent into an uproar. Black marketeers were not the only people who had large savings, and many honest people were affected. Given the extent of the shadow economy, however, one wonders how much impact such laws will have.

The growing shortages of goods and food force Soviet citizens to resort to the black market. The entire country is permeated with it, and it has even spread to international trade. In one sinister case, KGB investigators uncovered a cooperative business smuggling Soviet-made MIG-29 fighters and T-72 tanks abroad.[15] In another instance, fearing a repetition

[14]Vladimir Bukovsky, "The Political Condition of the Soviet Union," in *The Future of the Soviet Empire*, eds. Henry S. Rowen and Charles Wolf, Jr. (New York: St. Martin's Press, 1987), p. 38.

[15]John-Thor Dahlburg, "KGB Reveals Illegal Sales of MIG-29s, Tanks Abroad," *The Los Angeles Times*, May 11, 1990.

of the lost 1988 aid sent to relieve victims of the Armenian earthquake, Soviet authorities assigned KGB troops to guard 1990 aid shipments from the West to prevent them from falling into the hands of black marketeers. Even some of these goods, however, were diverted to the second economy. Less threatening, but just as brazen, Polish tourists flock to the Soviet Union laden with desirable items. They even use hotel rooms to show their goods. After selling their wares, they use the rubles to buy items that are scarce in Poland, like gold and electrical appliances.[16] Conversely, with Soviet travel restrictions liberalized, Soviet citizens also flock to Poland to trade government subsidized goods for hard currency and items that are in short supply in the Soviet Union.[17]

The sources of contraband goods are multitudinous, however, far exceeding the private stashes of foreign tourists. Underground factories using pilfered, embezzled, or even purchased materials turn out huge quantities of unofficial, unreported, and untaxed goods. Sometimes these factories are tucked into urban basements or secreted away in the countryside. More often, however, they are found in the state factories themselves, where people work after hours, turning out clothes, purses, shoes, sunglasses, handbags, and pirated Western pop music on disks or cassettes. Seamen, artists, dancers, athletes, state officials, and other Soviet citizens returning from abroad cart home thousands of sought-after Western goods, bribing their way through customs.

Black market items come from legitimate sources as well. Lucky shoppers chance upon scarce items. Buying them up to the limit their purses will allow, these fortunate people sell them to thankful friends and relatives at a profit. Items of personal property that are forbidden to be sold privately fetch handsome prices in the clandestine trade. Icons, rare books, pets, and many other items are exchanged for money or other goods all over the country, sometimes right under the noses of the authorities.

Other items are bootlegged—as when taxi drivers demand extra money if the prospective passenger is not to be left on the street, seamstresses make clothes to order on company time, and peasants sell moonshine (*samogon*) produced in rural stills. Services are bootlegged as well as goods. Repair shops are scarce, and one usually is placed on a waiting list extending for weeks. A few extra rubles can sometimes persuade the repair person to fix a television set, automobile, or watch immediately—without registering the transaction. A package of cigarettes, a lighter, or a ballpoint pen placed in full view on a restaurant table can help speed the otherwise dreadfully slow service. *Shabashniki* (fixers) hire themselves out to new apartment dwellers to fix the many unfinished or poorly completed things construction teams have overlooked. This moonlight activity is not in itself illegal, but often fixers use materials pilfered from state work sites or, as some suspect, they are the very people from the construction team who, only days before, deliberately left jobs undone so as to return and sell their

[16]Francine du Plessix Gray, *Soviet Women* (New York: Doubleday, 1989), pp. 158–159.

[17]Charles T. Powers, "Soviets Flock West to Poland, Eager to Wheel and Deal," *The Los Angeles Times*, April 13, 1991.

repair services to the apartment's newly arrived and disappointed occupants.

Often arguing that state property belongs to no one, citizens who would not think of taking another person's belongings feel little compunction at carting off government goods. Virtually no item is safe from people trying to turn an extra ruble at the state's expense. According to *Izvestia*, state gasoline siphoned by truck drivers or gas station attendants provided one-third of all gas used by Moscow's private cars in 1975. Drivers of cement trucks on their way to state building sites make unofficial deliveries at prearranged private locations. Butchers shortchange customers at the counter so that they can sell choice cuts and plump chickens *zadni khod* (out the back door). Such larceny does not stop at the professions. Teachers sell stolen examinations to eager students, and medical personnel pilfer drugs, medicine, and hospital goods to vend them on the street. Illegal abortions, often desirable because anesthetics are used, are performed—for a high price—by doctors during their off hours.

The ethnic strife in the Soviet Union is also fertile ground for the shadow economy. Guns and other weapons can easily be bought from "the mafia"; weapons can also be surreptitiously rented from larcenous soldiers. In 1989 the United States tightened up on the number of Soviet Jews who could emigrate to America, and a rush on the embassy soon exhausted its supply of application forms. Suddenly, these five-page forms became easily available on the black market. When the Soviet Union embargoed oil shipments to Lithuania in response to its declaration of independence, oil was sold to Lithuania "on the left" from Byelorussia. In 1989 trains destined for Armenia were stopped by militant nationalists in Azerbaijan. The cargoes were looted and sold illegally to a grateful Azerbaijan public.

More exotic cases find people buying diamonds stolen from Siberian mines; trading tsarist gold coins, gold bullion, and furs; or even visiting illegal gambling salons in Moscow apartments.[18] Furthermore, the illicit trade permeates the official sector when managers find it necessary to buy goods illegally in order to meet their goals. Engaging "pushers" (scroungers who seek out scarce materials), plant managers sometimes find themselves violating the law because the needed goods are to be found only on the black market. Similarly, often flouted by official suppliers, cooperative restaurants and other businesses are frequently forced to rely on black market purveyors for goods that they need to do business.

The list of contraband goods is seemingly endless. Besides the goods already mentioned, valued items include jeans (long the most treasured item among Soviet youth—they currently prefer Wrangler's), Western cigarettes (Marlboros are favored), chewing gum (Wrigley's is preferred), and even the labels from Western clothes. Stamps, videocassette recorders and films, paint, watches, automobile parts, pornographic literature and pictures, tape recorders, Sony Walkmen, every possible kind of clothing, footwear, cosmetics, fashion magazines, furs, automobile spare parts, narcotics, and guns are all valued items.

[18]Simis, pp. 171, 177.

The Third Economy

The third economy, or **gray market,** is primarily composed of the legitimate exchange of privately owned goods. By far the most prominent example of the third economy is the open markets (*rinki*) where farmers sell goods raised on their private plots. These markets are a mainstay of the Soviet consumer economy. During much of the year, the *rinki* are the only markets where people can find greens, tomatoes, melons, grapes, oranges, pomegranates, carrots, cheese, meat, nuts, sour cream, dried mushrooms, sour cabbage, pistachios, flowers, and dozens of other goods.

When these items are found in the state stores, their freshness and quality cannot compare with those of the open market. At the same time, however, the prices at the farmers' markets are much higher than in the state stores. Perhaps thinking of the tsarist peasants at market, Ivan Turgenev wrote in his famous novel *Fathers and Sons,* "A Russian peasant will get the better of God himself."

One can easily understand the motivation for this observation by watching the peasants sell their wares. In the midst of gossiping about events of the day, they will haggle with prospective buyers, saying, "No better quality can be found, these being the juiciest tomatoes" or "the freshest melons," or "Your husband will thank you for having the wisdom to buy these wonderful mushrooms," or "These grapes are the rubies of

A peasant market outside Leningrad. The fruits and vegetables grown on private plots are sold for much higher prices than are charged in the state stores. (Photo provided by Harriet C. Norris.)

Uzbekistan," or "Here, try one. You will see that I tell the truth about these fine dried apricots. There are no better."

In fact, the products are probably the best available, and they are often even better in some respects than produce in the United States because they are fresh and unadulterated by pesticides, preservatives, or color enhancers. Except for staples like bread, cabbage, potatoes, sugar, and butter, Soviet food is very expensive even in state stores, but prices in the *rinki* are usually three, four, or even more times as expensive.

So handsome are the profits to be made from the eager customers in Moscow and Leningrad that peasants from Moldavia, Uzbekistan, and Armenia can pack bags full of plums and peaches, fly to the distant cities, pay for hotels and food, and enjoy the city's entertainment before returning home with a tidy profit from the sale of their produce.

> Satirizing the exploits of these commercial folk, a popular story tells of an Armenian peasant seated on a plane headed for Moscow with a suitcase loaded with carnations. Suddenly, a young man jumped to his feet, pistol in hand, and ordered the pilot to take the plane to London. At his first chance, the Armenian overpowered the would-be hijacker and told the pilots to proceed to Moscow. News of the daring rescue preceded the plane's arrival in Moscow, and the Armenian was met by an honor guard and the city leaders. When asked why he decided to risk his life in the cause of the Motherland, the shrewd peasant responded, "What would I do with 5,000 carnations in London?"

A wide variety of other goods are legally sold on the private market. Government-run "consignment stores" sell used appliances, clothing, antiques, china, and other articles for private citizens, taking a 7 percent commission for the service. The shelves of these consignment stores usually feature the shabby and eclectic stock found in American secondhand stores, but one can sometimes spot a graceful old vase or an antique silver-plated samovar, causing one to speculate about the item's history and the story of the seller's life.

Less formally, swap meets and flea markets are organized in vacant lots where everything from caged birds to rabbits and from books to potted plants can be purchased from their private owners. In other vacant fields, people align cars they wish to sell. Although the price for used cars is fixed by the state, desperate buyers and wily sellers negotiate additional sums while taking the vehicles out on test drives. Since the waiting lists for new cars are several years long, used cars usually go for quite a bit more than the state-fixed price for current models. As with the second economy, many services can also be purchased on the gray market. Private typists, translators, and tutors are available for a price, as are private nurses. The gray market also provides private consultations with lawyers or surgeons.

Interestingly, according to some interpretations, even the government deals in the counter economy. Maintaining a number of special stores where only the elite can shop, the government sells items, often at reduced prices. The *Beryozki* also could be placed in this category. In another type of transaction, store managers often force ordinary shoppers to buy unwanted, spoiled goods along with desired scarce items. Thus, state stores vend goods no one would voluntarily buy by putting a pound of rotten apples together with two pounds of scarce oranges in a "package deal." Such practices are technically illegal, but few people do more than mutter under their breath because this is sometimes the only way they can obtain the desired goods.

Cooperatives and private businesses.   As a major step in perestroika, the USSR Supreme Soviet legalized the ownership of cooperatives and private business concerns in the late 1980s. What is more, these private businesses may borrow money to fund expansion or they may even sell stocks and bonds in their companies. The companies can be cooperatives in which the workers own the enterprise, or they can be owned by someone who then employs other people. The wages and working conditions of employees are regulated by the state. Although these enterprises are small, they cover a wide variety of fields, including a yellow page directory, pet grooming, auto and appliance repairs, computer maintenance, restaurants, hairstyling, wallpaper hanging, maid services, singles clubs, plumbing, and even pay toilets.

Although the profits of some of these businesses are huge, many people still hesitate to become involved in them. In 1989 there were 155,880 of them employing 1.4 million people,[19] only a tiny fraction of the Soviet economy. There is a lingering fear that the businesses may be renationalized someday, as they were when the NEP was abolished in the late 1920s. Also, the private businesses have had trouble with the bureaucracy. Some have been required to hire needless personnel in order to get or keep their licenses. Others have been shaken down by the police or forced to pay extortion by "the mafia." Several have been fire-bombed or seen their customers harassed, while the police looked on indifferently. The taxes on these firms have become very heavy, regulations are suffocating, and private businesspeople have found it difficult to legally buy the goods they need to do business, forcing them to bribe officials or to deal on the black market.

The public also deeply resents the entrepreneurs. Many people still have ideological qualms about private enterprise. They are envious of the nouveau riche "*yuccies*" (young upwardly mobile communists) and employees who make two, three, or four times the average wage. The people also resent what they consider to be price gouging. As goods became scarce in 1989, public passion rose against the private businesspeople. A box of detergent, for example, cost 62 cents in the state stores but was usually unavailable. The same detergent—coming from unknown sources—was

---

[19]Stephen F. Cohen and Katrina VanDen Heuvel, *Voices of Glasnost* (New York: W. W. Norton, 1989), p. 31.

abundant in private shops, but it sold for $9 a box.[20] To combat this commercial excess, the state has now established maximum prices private businesses can charge for certain goods and services. Although virtually everyone engages in the black market, the Soviet public, perhaps somewhat ironically, is enraged that it must pay exorbitant prices for goods in the private shops that, it suspects, came from the black market and were probably stolen from the state in the first place.

Still, as long as shortages exist in the state stores, as long as services are slow and poorly executed, as long as an over-abundant supply of money saturates the economy, the black market, the gray market, and the private firms will persist. Given the problems of the Soviet economy, one wonders how ordinary citizens contend with life in the Soviet Union. What travails do they suffer, and what advantages do they enjoy? In short, what conditions of life do they face?

CONDITIONS OF LIFE

Assessing the quality of life in the Soviet Union is a difficult enterprise because the Soviet economy is so different from our own. Many things that we take for granted either do not exist there or are in very short supply, while goods and services that absorb large portions of our personal income are either free to the Soviet people or sold at very low cost. Consequently, comparisons between the standard of living in the United States and the Soviet Union will likely result in error and inaccuracy. It is therefore better to analyze the Soviet economy on its own terms.

Wages and Prices

Initiating an idealistic egalitarian wage structure, the Bolsheviks paid workers virtually the same amount, regardless of task, throughout the 1920s. In the 1930s, however, Stalin moved away from egalitarianism and introduced wage differentials, heavily favoring the officer corps, professionals, and high-ranking government and party officials. Since Stalin's time, however, the gap between the highest paid people and the lowest paid (the collective farmers) has been gradually narrowed, thus improving the living conditions for the bulk of the people in the society.

Pleasant though the reequalization of wages may sound at first, this policy has caused some rather serious dislocations in the economy. The average wage for an industrial worker is roughly 280 rubles per month, counting the supplement given as a result of the 1991 price increases. Families with children also receive an additional sum of 50 to 70 rubles per month depending on the ages of the children. Yet, skilled workers are in some cases paid less than manual laborers, and doctors and teachers, who are poorly paid by any standard, may make less than a manual laborer.

[20]Michael Parks, "Private Business Profits Irk Soviet Lawmakers," *The Los Angeles Times*, Sept. 27, 1989.

Hence, a kind of "brain drain" is occurring within the country. Fleeing their prestigious but low-paying jobs, these *lumpenintellectuals* are abandoning their skilled professions to become house painters, taxi drivers, and factory workers. Additionally, the Soviet press recently lamented that some youths were avoiding professional jobs, preferring to become sales clerks, car mechanics, and sailors, because they can earn much more in those jobs through engaging in the black market.

Before reviewing the cost of goods the workers buy with their seemingly low income, I should introduce an important mitigating factor. The amount of wages does not necessarily correlate with an individual's purchasing power. Many luxury items, desirable goods from abroad, and other scarcities are not found in regular Soviet stores. They can, however, be found in special stores where only the elite may shop or, as mentioned earlier, in the foreign currency stores. Hence, although a distinguished scientist may earn as much as a ranking party or government official, for instance, the scientist may not enjoy the standard of living of the official unless he or she is privileged to frequent the special stores.

On the whole, most Soviet consumer goods are priced very high. Even though the government heavily subsidized the prices of certain commodities before 1991, food expenses still accounted for about one third of the average Soviet income. Since the 1991 price increases, food must take up an even greater share of the family budget because the government income supplements are too low to cover more than a fraction of the increased cost of living. Although almost all prices have been increased, the cost of staple foods is still held down by the government, so that bread, potatoes, beets, milk, cabbage, and carrots are still relatively cheap. (Before the 1991 price increases, the price of bread had remained unchanged for decades, selling for 8 cents a loaf. It was so cheap that peasants fed it to their stock rather than buying less heavily subsidized unprocessed grain, and children used hardened loaves for footballs). Other food items, however, including spirits, are very high indeed. Clothing is another costly item. Not only is footwear expensive, but Soviet-made shoes are, as previously mentioned, notorious for their poor quality. Undergarments and outerwear are all costly, forcing many Soviet citizens to shop for bargains in secondhand stores. Consumables like cigarettes, appliances, private automobiles, jewelry, ballpoint pens, and color televisions bite heavily into the worker's pocket, while furniture, books, and newspapers are cheap. In all, however, Soviet shoppers buy only about one-third of the number of consumer goods purchased annually in the United States.

Until recently, the government did an admirable job of keeping inflation down, but "invisible inflation" did occur. Old products were sometimes phased out and new, more expensive items were substituted. On the whole, however, prices were fairly constant, but this stability came at a high price. In order to keep prices down, the government subsidized the cost of staple foods, housing, utilities, and public transportation. These subsidies cost the government billions of rubles annually, thus forcing up its deficits and denying it funds for capital investment. In an effort to reduce the deficits, most of the price subsidies have been relaxed, and prices have shot up. The reduced subsidies, together with growing shortages and an exploding black market, have combined to visit a serious inflation on the Soviet economy. In 1989 the government estimated that inflation was around 8 percent. In 1990, however, it catapulted to over 16 percent. Private economists, taking into consideration the enormous increase in prices on the black and gray markets, estimate Soviet inflation may have been as high as 80 percent in 1990.

Still, the Soviet citizen pays little to nothing for some major items that cost Western consumers large amounts of money. You will recall that medical care is free; housing, electricity, water, and heating costs account for roughly 5 percent of the average worker's wage. Public transportation, private telephones—when they are available—insurance, bank loans, child care, dental care, and pharmaceuticals are all very inexpensive. It is estimated that the average Soviet citizen receives about 81 rubles, or about 40 percent above the average salary in free goods and services each month.

Marketing, Shoddy Goods, and Shortages

Shopping in the Soviet Union can be an adventure for the occasional visitor, but for the resident it is a grueling, unpleasant affair. Both economic necessity and ideological bias have caused Soviet authorities to ignore the etiquette of marketing and merchandising. Remember that in a land where waiting on other people is considered demeaning, Soviet clerks are often surly, indolent, and rude. Displays in shops are usually unattractive and untended. Often items displayed in windows cannot be found in the shop; they are in the window as *pokazukha* (only for show). Poor and dull packaging fails to attract buyers, causing needless waste. And there are very few self-help stores similar to Western supermarkets. The ubiquitous shopping lines, where the average Soviet consumer waits for almost 400 hours per year, are often lengthened by archaic merchandising techniques and featherbedding, as well as by shortages.

Shortages of consumer goods are both legend and legion in the Soviet Union.

> The bitter humor of Soviet shoppers tells of a woman who attended her 30-year class reunion. Asked to pick out her old boyfriend, she did so without hesitation. "How did you know who he was?" asked her companion. "I recognized his overcoat," the old woman replied.

The reasons for acute scarcities in the Soviet economy are complex and numerous. By and large, responsibility must be placed at the door of the planners. The system simply does not work well for consumers. To begin with, the Soviet economy has always been oriented toward Group A of the plan—military and heavy industry. The best items are appropriated by the military, industry, and foreign trade, thus leaving Soviet consumers with the inferior leftovers. Furthermore, even these poorly made goods are often in short supply. If goods are shoddy, as they often are, they tend to break down or wear out quickly, creating demand for more and thus making them all the more scarce. As explained earlier, any glitch in production causes slowdowns all along the chain. So when a Siberian plant fails to meet its goal of sulfanol, an ingredient in Soviet soap, the end result is a serious shortage of laundry detergent nation-wide. Careless production techniques cause needless waste, and incompetent distribution creates abundances in one part of the country and shortages elsewhere. Moreover, now that the enterprises are required to show profits, the low prices established for consumer goods by the state make it difficult for plant managers to keep their factory incomes above the margin, thus discouraging them from producing consumer goods. Additionally, the people tend to aggravate the problem themselves. Believing rumors that supplies of certain goods are dwindling, people hoard the supposedly scarce items, thus fulfilling the prophecy. Clerks and other distributors often siphon off the best goods to sell to friends or on the black market. Peasants trying to save kopecks feed their stock government-subsidized baked bread rather than the more expensive feed grain.

Whatever the cause, scarcity of consumer goods is commonplace. Paradoxically, while shoddy or unfashionable goods pile up on the shelves, Soviet shoppers must hunt high and low for commodities as mundane yet essential as light bulbs, pencils, saucepans, cosmetics, warm clothing, needles, thread, and aspirin. Such personal articles as soap, toothpaste, toilet paper, blankets, and diapers are also often in short supply. The planners' negligence results in car owners searching for gasoline and garages to protect their vehicles from the elements. Because planners failed to include garages in designs of apartment buildings, makeshift sheds appear in nearby vacant lots.

Although most shortages are accepted with forbearance by the Soviet people and cause no serious political problem, food shortages may be another matter. In a land that has known frequent famine and mass starvation, the Soviet government, since Stalin's time, has wisely placed a high priority on improving the diet of its citizens. In an unparalleled achievement, the Soviets have doubled food consumption since 1951. Even so, the Soviet diet remains heavy on starch and short on protein. Consuming only half as much meat, fruit, and vegetables as Americans, Soviet citizens eat unvaried, heavy meals of bread, sugar, potatoes, cabbage, beets, pickled mushrooms, and carrots. The average Soviet citizen consumes 240 pounds of potatoes ("Russian's second bread") per year; starchy meals result in obesity for 50 percent of the population. The meat deficiency in the diet, greater indeed than in any Eastern European country, has caused adoption of a substitute protein source. Soviet fishing fleets have expanded greatly, hunting for fish in all the world's seas. Indeed, the Soviets have vastly increased their consumption of fish over the last two decades, and the average Soviet citizen now consumers 39 pounds per year.

Despite these efforts, unfavorable weather and inefficient farming have brought the Soviet Union to a crisis. As the population increases by about 1 percent each year, food production, processing, and distribution cannot keep pace, resulting in shortages. Public protests of these shortfalls have occurred repeatedly, encouraging Gorbachev's focus on the problems.

Adjusting to a bad situation, the Soviet people do their best to make do. Soviet people are legendary for improvising when they cannot buy the things they need. Home recipes for making scarce items abound. Cottage cheese, caviar, bread flour, spirits, and so forth are all improvised or cleverly imitated with concoctions made of other, more readily available items. Soviet citizens have even used spare parts and stolen items to piece together medical instruments and automobiles.

Any visitor to the Soviet Union must be struck by the number of people carrying a bag or briefcase on the streets. Not all these people are students or businesspeople. Rather than being loaded with papers and books, these satchels are usually empty so that scarce goods, encountered by chance, can be purchased and toted away. If foreign goods arrive in the shops, word spreads rapidly among the people. Soviet consumer goods are so poorly made that any foreign product is preferred. Factory managers, attempting to keep their workers on the job, bring everyday items to their plants for sale after work. Peasants, called "paratroopers" by their urban cousins, stream into nearby cities on shopping forays, snapping up goods impossible to find in village stores.

Footsore, exhausted, clerk-abused shoppers put up with the shoddy goods and incessant shortages because the staples were usually available. In 1990, however, matters came to a critical point: A combination of factors created acute shortages that winter. These factors included quality control inspectors rejecting poorly made goods, farmers withholding crops, poor harvest management failing to bring in hundreds of tons of produce, and panic buying and hoarding caused by a government announcement of huge price increases (the price increases were later rescinded before they took effect, but by then the damage had been done). There was also a collapse in the distribution of goods due to poor management, disincentives for production, work stoppages, and, some suspect, deliberate sabotage by recalcitrant bureaucrats. In August 1990 a joint report to Congress by the CIA and the Defense Intelligence Agency claimed that only 200 out of 1,200 standard consumer goods were readily available in Soviet shops,[21] and the month before, the American press reported that a large Moscow supermarket had only 23 items on its shelves, including salted fish, bags of groats, pureed pumpkin, mashed onions, and some staples.[22] (See Table 9–1.)

To protect their citizens from scarcity caused by millions of "paratroopers" who come to the city to buy goods each month, the cities of Moscow and Leningrad required people to prove that they were residents in order to buy in the shops. In retaliation, provincial political and economic leaders refused to ship goods and produce to these cities. Also, it is suspected that conservative functionaries deliberately delayed shipments to these two cities because of the cities' radical local leadership. The result was that for the first time since World War II, Moscow and Leningrad had to

---

[21]Michael Parks, "Soviet Looks to the Past for Cure to Market Woes," *The Los Angeles Times,* Aug. 14, 1990.

[22]Carol J. Williams, "Moscow Shoppers Vent Ire Over Food Shortages, Costs," *The Los Angeles Times,* July 7, 1990.

TABLE 9–1 A Partial List of Items Reported
Scarce in Soviet Shops in 1990

Food	Other Goods
Meat	Cigarettes
Butter	Gasoline
Sugar	Children's clothing
Rice	School notebooks
Potatoes	Books
Bread	Toilet paper
Salt	Detergent
Macaroni	Shampoo
Tea	Condoms
Coffee	Pharmaceutical drugs
Candy	Cotton cloth

implement general rationing of consumer goods. For example, each adult was given monthly ration cards for 4.4 pounds of sugar, 2 pounds of meat, and 1 pound of cheese. The shortages became so serious that foreign tourists were allowed to take out no more than 100 rubles worth of goods, thus reducing the country's hard currency income. A city in the Ukraine, Stakhanov, eschewing money, gave toilet paper, towels, and bowls as prizes to winners of its lottery.

As you know, foreign countries have been generous with aid to prevent a catastrophe, but their help was not sufficient to make up for the shortages, and public outrage in the Soviet Union over the scarcity was palpable, although most needs were apparently satisfied by the black market. They claim that everything is in shortage, *except* the ruble. The ever-ready Soviet joke mill has also given vent to the public cynicism and frustration. For example:

What is 150 yards long and eats potatoes?

A Moscow queue waiting for meat.

Shopper: "I'll take half a kilo of beef today."

Without looking at his supplies the butcher said: "We have none."

Shopper: "Veal?"

Butcher: "None."

Shopper: "Chicken?"

Butcher: "None."

Shopper: "Pork?"

Butcher: "None."

Shopper: "Lamb?"

Butcher: "None."

As the shopper left the store she thought to herself, "What a memory!"

Boy: "What will communism be like when it is perfected?"

Father: "Everyone will have what he needs."

Boy: "But what if there is a food shortage?"

Father: "There will be a sign on the butcher shop saying, 'No one needs meat today.'"

A man orders a beer.

Bartender: "One ruble please."

Customer: "But last week a beer cost only 50 kopecks."

Bartender: "Ah, but that was before glasnost. Now there is a 50-kopeck charge for glasnost."

The customer pays the ruble and the bartender returned 50 kopecks to him but gives him no beer.

Customer: "What's this? You said I had to pay 50 kopecks for glasnost."

Bartender: "You do, but we have no beer today."

Poverty

For decades Soviet authorities claimed that they had eliminated poverty in the society. Although the gap between rich and poor has been significantly narrowed since the revolution, poverty remained a fact of life, and *glasnost* has brought some of the details about it to light.

In 1990 the poverty line was set at 68.75 rubles per month. By Soviet calculations, 41 million people lived on incomes at or below this level, and they included 50 percent of the nation's pensioners. In response to the public focus on the poor, the Supreme Soviet raised the pensions of the poorest citizens by as much as 40 percent. However, this program will cost billions of rubles and will exacerbate the state's fiscal problems. Even though there is no welfare per se in the Soviet Union, the poor suffer less stigma than their counterparts in the West and they receive special stipends from the government. These supplements were raised along with the 1991 price increases, but the added payments are not expected to fully cover the increase in the cost of living. Therefore, in the short run at least, one can expect that the Soviet poor will become worse off than before.

Another measure to combat poverty is the legalization of private charities. Until 1989 private charity was seen as remnant of bourgeois values, and it was forbidden. However, since then churches have been allowed to aid the poor and private charities have established soup kitchens and rehabilitation centers for veterans from Afghanistan.

A new kind of poverty has developed since perestroika and glasnost were invoked. Homeless people and beggars have begun to appear. Some of the homeless established themselves in shanties within sight of the Kremlin until they were forced to move by the authorities in December 1990. Some homelessness is caused by people leaving the farms and coming to the cities without finding lodging. They can be found sleeping in doorways and railroad stations. Other homeless people—perhaps as many as a half million—have fled north to escape the ethnic violence of Central Asia, Azerbaijan, Armenia, and Moldavia. Many of these people are ethnic minorities, but some of them are Russians as well. Still more homelessness is caused by the Soviet Union's bringing its troops and their families home from Eastern Europe. Housing is so scarce in the Soviet Union that many of these hapless people have been forced to live in dormitories or with friends and relatives.

The existence of widespread poverty in the Soviet Union should not obscure the fact that there are also many advantages for people in the society.

Benefits of the System

By certain measures, the average Soviet citizen, provided he or she does not fall afoul of the regime (most people in most societies are apolitical), has an enviable existence in many ways. To begin with, Soviet citizens experience far fewer insecurities than people in the West. Government policy assures most citizens an unusual degree of job security. The personal tranquillity of individuals is enhanced by free medical care and education, substantial maternity leave, and low-cost dental care, child care, and public transportation. Housing, all but ignored until the last four decades, is improving gradually. Although about 20 percent of the urban dwellers still share kitchens and bathrooms with neighbors in communal apartments, new apartment buildings dominate Soviet suburbs, providing private, albeit cramped, housing for increasing numbers of people. Additionally, the relative cost of housing has not increased since 1928, and the more affluent can buy condominiums on reasonable terms. Ranging in cost from 6,000 to 8,000 rubles, a condominium can be purchased with a downpayment of one-third and a 15-year bank loan at 2 percent interest.

Medical care is not only free, but it is relatively extensive. Emphasizing preventive medicine, the state encourages semiannual examinations. Clinics are located close to apartment dwellings, doctors make house calls to the bedridden, and an extensive ambulance service protects all but the most remote areas in emergencies. Still, the quality of Soviet health care is poor. Physicians are usually not well trained, and they are often indolent and unconcerned about patient care. Adequate drugs and medical equipment are frequently lacking and doctors sometimes demand bribes for prompt, professional service.

Vacations are a positive feature of the Soviet system. Not only do

Soviet citizens receive their regular wages while on holiday, but vacation expenses are absorbed by the state either entirely or to a minimum of 70 percent. Soviet workers usually receive 24 vacation days per year, but they can earn as many as 56 days per year in Siberia and in the far north. Retirement begins earlier in the Soviet Union than in most Western countries. Women may retire at 55 years of age, and men at 60. (There were 58.7 million pensioners in 1990.) Most pensions are quite low, but provisions are made for people to take part-time jobs that keep them in society's mainstream. Additionally, pensioners pay only 2.50 rubles per month for their apartments, and they enjoy reduced fees for public transportation, special medical benefits, and various programs provided by state associations that cater to their needs. The indigent old or those unable to care for themselves are kept in special state homes.

All in all, the Soviet socioeconomic system leaves much to be desired, but it also includes much to be envied. The paradox and contradiction in the system do not escape Soviet street humor. According to a current joke, just as Marx found contradictions in capitalism, there are six contradictions in the Soviet system:

1. There is no unemployment, but nobody does any work.
2. Nobody works, but each year the plans are fulfilled and exceeded.
3. The plans are always fulfilled, yet there is nothing to buy in the shops.
4. There is nothing in the shops, but the typical Moscow apartment refrigerator is loaded with delicacies that haven't been seen in the stores for months.
5. The people find ways of getting goods that are not for sale in the stores, but they still complain.
6. Everyone complains, but at elections they all vote yes.

Levity and cynicism aside, there are other matters besides economics that cause Soviet political society severe stress. Indeed, the society seems to be struggling for its very existence. These cultural and social factors should be examined at this point.

chapter 10

Cultural Stress Points

Always a country with one of the world's largest populations, the Soviet Union is currently experiencing dynamic demographic problems. Closely related to demographics, the question of the Soviet nationalities (ethnic groups) has become one of the country's most explosive issues. A third cultural stress point is religion. Although Gorbachev has decided to coexist with religion and even make use of it in some ways, the state is still officially atheist, and religion will continue to present fundamental complications to the government.

DEMOGRAPHICS

The most recent Soviet census (1989) revealed a population of 286,717,000, making the Soviet Union the third most populous country in the world, behind China and India. This fact is hardly consoling to Soviet leaders when the demographic trends are studied in detail, however.

Successive tragedies of World War I, the revolution, the Civil War, famine, collectivization, Stalin's great terror, and World War II depleted the population. More importantly, death fell most heavily upon Soviet males—

in 1946 there were only 59.1 men for every 100 women in the country.[1] By 1989 this disparity had been significantly reduced, with the census registering 127.8 million men to 159.2 million women. Further, it was clear that the bulk of the imbalance between the sexes was among those over 50 years old. In recent years, however, there has been an alarming increase in the death rate of young Soviet men. Young men are dying at three times the rate of young women, threatening a prolongation of and perhaps an increase in the disparity between the sexes at the age of greatest fertility. The reason for such a stunning difference in death rate is difficult to determine for certain, but leading American experts believe alcohol consumption to be a major contributor. Indeed, alcoholism has become so serious a problem with Soviet men that their life expectancy has dropped from 67 years to 61 years in just over two decades—a full 12 years lower than Soviet women. Gorbachev's attention to labor discipline, industrial safety, and alcohol abuse has somewhat reduced deaths by industrial accidents, but more time will have to pass to determine if these improvements are permanent.

The alarming death rate of young males, combined with a declining birthrate and an increasing infant mortality rate, has produced a disappointing growth rate for the Soviet Union of less than 1 percent annually. The Soviet infant mortality rate is three times higher than in the United States (which has far from the best record itself), and it is one of the world's worst. Ranking fifteenth in the world, 2.5 percent of Soviet infants fail to live for one year. The reasons for this dismal figure are the cumulative effects of alcoholism among expectant mothers, the consequences of heavy manual work by pregnant women, and repeated abortions. It is believed that numerous abortions, especially in the first few pregnancies, tend to reduce the mother's ability to carry children to term. Thus, in Moscow alone, 8 percent of all babies born are premature and weak, and one in five children nation-wide is born with abnormalities.[2]

The jeopardy for infants in childbirth, as well as other insecurities for the young, is reflected in the following Soviet joke:

QUESTION: Why are so many Russian children now born with nervous disorders?

ANSWER: The condition begins at conception. The first three months they are concerned about being aborted. The second three months they wonder whether their parents will marry. And the last three months they worry about whether their grandmother will still be around to take care of them.

[1]Gail Warshofsky Lapidus, *Women in Society* (Berkeley: University of California Press, 1978), p. 169.
[2]Francine du Plessix Gray, *Soviet Union* (New York: Doubleday, 1989), p. 21.

The reasons for the declining birthrate are also numerous. To begin with, urban families tend to have fewer children than rural households. Since 1917 the Soviet Union has urbanized at a faster rate than almost any other society. In 1917 only about 20 percent of the population lived in the cities; by 1990 the figure had increased to 67 percent. Additionally, abortions are readily available for unwanted pregnancies. Housing is cramped in the Soviet Union, and, as you will learn later, women are deterred from having children because their occupation and household duties are time- and energy-consuming. Moreover, Soviet families have become increasingly desirous of improving their living conditions; by limiting the size of the family, couples divide scarce resources among fewer people. Also, Soviet couples are tending to marry at a later age, reducing the time span in which children can be produced.

Alarmed by the declining birthrate and the slow overall growth of its population, the Soviet government has embarked on a number of policies to redress the situation. Women are exhorted to have many children and those who have 10 or more are decorated as Hero Mothers. Additionally, the government recently extended maternity leaves to a full year, allowing mothers to remain with their children throughout the first year of the child's life. In addition, women with several children are permitted flexible work schedules, and families with five or more children receive special stipends. Quite beyond these official efforts, Soviet scholars have suggested less orthodox methods of increasing the birthrate. For example, Soviet demographer Viktor Perevedentsev has encouraged young Russian couples not to attend night school but to start families instead. He also suggested that the society should take a more liberal view of the growing number of illegitimate children.

The Soviet concern is with more than sheer numbers, however. The shift in population has become even more of a problem. The six Slavic and Baltic republics (RSFSR, the Ukraine, Byelorussia, Latvia, Estonia, and Lithuania) grew by only 6.7 percent between 1979 and 1989, while the six Muslim republics (Azerbaijan, Uzbekistan, Kazakhstan, Kirghizia, Turkmenistan, and Tadzhikistan) grew at almost four times that rate, 23.8 percent. If present trends continue, the Muslim population will constitute more than 25 percent of the Soviet population by the year 2000, and it will be considerably younger than the European cohort. (See Table 10–1.) Aggravating this situation is the fact that people are moving away from the northern industrial areas toward less economically developed regions in the south and east. In 1940 only 18 percent of the population lived east of the Urals; by 1990 the figure had reached 28 percent.

Contrary to some impressions, Soviet citizens enjoy a great deal of mobility, with about 6 or 7 percent of the people moving from one place to another annually. As many of these people shift to the less economically advanced areas of the country, pressure will build on an already declining productivity rate.

As mentioned in an earlier chapter, the Soviet Union has used a labor-extensive approach (adding more and more workers to the factories) to increase productivity, rather than labor-intensive measures (increasing the

TABLE 10–1   Populations of the Major Soviet
Nationalities

Nationality	Population	Percent of Total Population
Russians	145,071,550	50.6
Ukrainians	44,135,989	15.4
Uzbeks	16,686,240	5.8
Byelorussians	10,030,441	3.5
Kazakhs	8,137,878	2.8
Azerbaijans	6,791,106	2.4
Armenians	4,627,227	1.6
Tadzhiks	4,216,693	1.5
Georgians	3,983,115	1.4
Moldavians	3,355,240	1.2
Lithuanians	3,068,296	1.1
Turkmen	2,718,297	0.9
Kirghiz	2,530,998	0.9
Latvians	1,459,156	0.5
Estonians	1,027,255	0.4
Total	257,839,481	90.0

Source: 1989 Soviet Census.

productivity of individual workers by mechanizing). The increase of factory workers has come from three basic sources: increases in the work-age population, workers previously engaged in agriculture, and women entering the work force. Expanding productivity by simply adding more and more people to the job is effective, however, only as long as vast reserves of nonworking people exist. When the supply of excess labor plays out, increases in productivity decline.

This unfortunate state of affairs is exactly where the Soviet Union currently finds itself. Not only did the annual growth of Soviet labor fall from 2 percent in the early 1970s to about 0.9 percent in 1989, but Soviet productivity also plummeted. Hélène Carrère d'Encausse forecasts that as Soviet labor needs become critical, Central Asia will be the only important source of new workers.[3] At the present rate, the Russian population is expected to grow by only 2.4 million people between 1979 and the year 2000, while the Central Asian minorities will expand by 20 million. Given the social and political stress among the nationalities, this dependence on Central Asian workers could portend serious problems for the Soviet Union.

For the past few years, the Soviet Union has contradicted its tradition of assuring full employment, accepting some unemployment, and after a brief effort to reduce the growing unemployment rate, in 1991 Gorbachev initiated a policy that will surely increase the problem significantly, at least

[3]Hélène Carrère d'Encausse, *Decline of an Empire,* trans. Martin Sokolinsky and Henry A. LaFarge (New York: Newsweek Books, 1979), p. 93.

in the short term. If the state ever returns to its labor-extensive policy, it will not only fail to increase productivity significantly but it will ultimately encounter labor shortages. Several remedial steps can be taken to mitigate a labor shortage, but none of them offers ideal solutions and each has undesirable side effects. The leadership could reach deeper into the ranks of the retired by postponing the retirement age or by inducing more retired people to take part-time jobs. The former policy could, however, have a demoralizing effect on workers who look forward to retirement. The latter alternative holds little promise, of course, since a large percentage of retired people already work. Students could be moved through school more rapidly so that they could join the work force at an earlier age, but such a measure might concern parents about increased pressure on their children. It could also result in lower academic achievement for future graduates, a dismal prospect for an advanced industrial state. A third possibility might be to reduce the term of military service, to draft fewer young men, or to eliminate the draft altogether. However, the military has recently expressed serious opposition to eliminating the draft and it has also resisted further cuts in its ranks. A final approach could be to increase mechanization and efficiency on the farm, thus releasing workers to enter the factories. But, as we learned in the last chapter, Soviet efforts to increase food output have yet to meet with much success.

Quite apart from its implications for productivity, the decline in the growth rate of the Soviet population means that the population is aging. Currently about 20 percent of the Soviet people are retired, and if present trends continue, the cohort of retired people will rise to 24 percent by the year 1999.[4] This figure would constitute a drop in the ratio of workers to retired people from 3.73:1 in 1979 to 2.95:1 in 1999. Hence, even if Soviet per capita productivity is increased by added mechanization, a substantial portion of the extra productivity will go to support the expanding, nonproductive segment of the society. Interestingly, the aging of the Soviet population is manifesting in the largest cities even more rapidly than it is in the population as a whole. As people in Moscow retire, for instance, they tend to remain there rather than move to less attractive areas. The authorities restrict emigration to Moscow in an attempt to control the capital's population; hence, its population is aging rapidly.

From the broad question of demographics, which threatens serious problems, we are led to the more specific and even more politically charged issue of the Soviet nationalities.

NATIONALITIES

The Soviet Union is one of the most diverse societies in the world. The government officially recognizes 128 distinct nationalities, but scholars dis-

---

[4]Calculated from a demographic table in Mikhail S. Bernstam, "Trends in the Soviet Population," in *The Future of the Soviet Empire,* eds. Henry S. Rowen and Charles Wolf, Jr. (New York: St. Martin's Press, 1987), p. 210.

agree as to the exact number, some putting the figure as high as 400. The Oroki, numbering 198 people, is its smallest national group. The Russians with 50.6 percent of the population are, of course, the largest. About 200 different languages and dialects are spoken. This diversity is, by itself, the source of many severe political complications. Yet, the difficulties are compounded by the fact that many of these people—the Finns, Armenians, Poles, Azerbaijans, Koreans, and Kazakhs—have brethren across the border in foreign lands. At the same time, many more nationalities are indigenous to the area in which they live. Both of these factors make assimilation of these diverse people into a Soviet nation a difficult, if not impossible, enterprise.

The Soviet Union, then, like the Russian Empire it succeeded, is a single state hosting dozens of nations of people. The Soviet record of dealing with the various people has been far from consistent as it has vacillated from liberationist to oppressive. The net result of these policies is also mixed.

History

Since Ivan IV's 1552 conquest of Kazan on the Upper Volga, Russia has been a multinational empire. Kazan's estates brought under the tsar's rule Udmurts, Chuvash, Tatars, Mordvinians, and Mari. Other distant and exotic people were subjugated as the tsar's minions pushed east beyond Astrakhan into the lands of the Bashkirs, Buryats, and Yakuts. Expansion to the West in the seventeenth and eighteenth centuries eventually incorporated Finns, Byelorussians, Ukrainians, Latvians, Estonians, Lithuanians, Poles, Jews, and Rumanians. Finally, in thrusts southward during the nineteenth century, the successive tsars came to rule people who had enjoyed great civilizations even before the Slavs left the banks of the Vistula—people like the Georgians, Armenians, Azerbaijans, Ingushi, Balkars, Kirghiz, Kazakhs, Tadzhiks, Ossetians, and Turkmen.

During the reigns of Nicholas I, Alexander III, and Nicholas II, energetic efforts were made to absorb the minorities by having them conform to the Russian image. Attempting to stifle local religions, customs, and languages, the Russian princes alienated their subjects, who became discontented with rule from St. Petersburg. Sensing the revolutionary potential of these disgruntled people, Lenin was quick to exploit their separatist desires. Indeed, as early as 1903, the Bolsheviks advocated autonomy for the minority nationalities, and by 1917 many minority nationalists had been drawn into the revolutionary movement and thus played a crucial role in the tsar's demise. Once Lenin found himself in power, however, and several minorities had broken with Moscow, he began to see the independence movements among the minorities as a political liability. Toward the end of the Civil War (1918–1921), Lenin realized that no proletarian revolution was imminent in the industrialized West; thus a consolidation of Soviet power was necessary. At the same time, some minority independence movements were aided by the bourgeois states, threatening Moscow. Hence

Lenin reversed himself and called for the conquest of the minority states that had established their independence.[5]

By 1922 the Soviet government had regained control of the Russian territories with few exceptions: Bessarabia was taken by Rumania; large portions of Byelorussia and the Ukraine were annexed by Poland; and Finland, Estonia, Latvia, and Lithuania successfully maintained their newly won independence with Western help. Consolidation of the re-absorbed minority peoples and their governance now loomed as a large problem. Stalin, who was ultimately placed in charge of the minorities question, leaned toward subjecting all the people to the dictates of a single central government. More sensitive to the rights of the minorities, Lenin gradually came to support a federal system. Torn between anxiety about "Great-Russian chauvinism" and the separatist impulses of the minorities, he struck a middle course. Although he hoped that ultimately a "new human community united in class solidarity" would be forged, he supported federalism as a way station on the road to building the "new socialist man." Stalin finally bowed to his superior and vowed that the Soviet Union would be "national in form but socialist in content." This new formula meant that while each minority would enjoy its own culture and language, Marxism-Leninism was to pervade all values and policy.

In 1922 the Union of Soviet Socialist Republics was formally given life by the signing of a treaty of Union. The constitution provided that the state be composed of four constituent parts: the Russian Soviet Federated Socialist Republic, the Transcaucasian Federation (including Armenia, Azerbaijan, and Georgia), the Byelorussian SSR, and the Ukrainian SSR. Since then, there have been several additions and modifications to the federation. (See Table 10–2).

In the mid-1920s the emphasis of the government was placed on developing many of the cultural attributes of the minority people. Dealing with civilizations ranging from very advanced cultures to primitive tribes, the Soviet government instituted policies most helpful to the less advanced people. Indigenous languages were encouraged by establishing schools teaching literacy in native tongues. The government authorities even went to the lengths of creating alphabets for the Uzbeks and other people who had none. Emphasis on the cultures and customs of these backward people instilled a fresh sense of national identification that, indeed, contradicted the state's ultimate goal of unifying all people into a single national entity. Herein lies a great dilemma that continues to confront the Soviet leaders. How does one create of such an ethnically and culturally diverse people a single nation, while at the same time making them comfortable with the state by pandering to their great differences?

Not noted for his patience with subtleties, Stalin reversed Soviet policy toward the nationalities in the late 1920s and 1930s. Collectivization on the farms was the beginning salvo. People who had farmed and herded on ancestral lands for millennia found themselves being rounded up and

[5]Richard Pipes, "Solving the Nationalities Problem," in *Man, State, and Society in the Soviet Union*, ed. Joseph L. Nogee (New York: Praeger, 1972), pp. 505–507.

TABLE 10–2   Development of the USSR

Year	Development
1922	The Union of Soviet Socialist Republics was created. It comprised the Russian Soviet Federated Socialist Republic (RSFSR), which included European Russia, Siberia, the Far East, and Central Asia; the Transcaucasian Federation, which included Armenia, Azerbaijan, and Georgia; the Byelorussian SSR; and the Ukranian SSR.
1924	The Turkmen SSR and the Uzbek SSR were separated from the RSFSR.
1929	The Tadzhik SSR was separated from the Uzbek SSR.
1936	The Kazakh SSR and the Kirghiz SSR were separated from the RSFSR, and the Transcaucasian Federation was divided into the Armenian SSR, the Azerbaijan SSR, and the Georgian SSR.
1940	The Karelo-Finnish SSR was created by severing the Karelian Autonomous Republic from the RSFSR; Bessarabia was taken from Rumania and combined with the western Ukraine, forming the Moldavian SSR; and the Baltic states were reconquered and joined to the USSR as the Latvian SSR, the Estonian SSR, and the Lithuanian SSR.
1956	The Karelo-Finnish SSR was collapsed back into the Karelian Autonomous Republic and restored to the RSFSR.

forced onto collective farms. Resistance brought only catastrophe to these humble but proud people. Perhaps the most striking case of Stalin's harsh treatment of nationalities was the slaughter of recalcitrant Kazakhs, whose numbers were reduced by perhaps one million—about one-fourth of the total population—because of their futile defiance of the state's collectivization policies. Such single-minded brutality was already foretold by Stalin's ruthlessness toward his own people when they resisted Soviet power; by unleashing the army on Georgia in 1921 and mercilessly purging its intellectual and political echelons, he startled his Bolshevik colleagues, causing Lenin to later suggest that Stalin be removed from power.[6]

In 1934 Stalin, now without peer in the Soviet leadership, took a crucial step in reversing the state's policy toward the minorities. Contradicting Lenin's old rejoinder, Stalin proclaimed at the Seventeenth Party Congress that "non-Russian nationalism" was, indeed, more dangerous to the state than Great-Russian chauvinism.[7] This unambiguous announcement served as a beacon for those who were trying to find their way in the shoals of the nationalities question. Conformity became the order of the day. Nationalist leaders were purged and killed, unique cultural events and customs were discouraged, and alphabets based on Latin, Mongolian, or Arabic were transformed to Russian Cyrillic.

[6]Carrère d'Encausse, pp. 17–18, 51.
[7]Pipes, p. 529.

At the close of the Great Patriotic War (World War II), Stalin made yet another unequivocal protestation of Great-Russian chauvinism in a 1945 toast celebrating victory. Giving the lion's share of credit to Russia for the victory, he proclaimed that Russia "had won the right to be recognized as the guide for the whole Union" and that the other nationalities should treat it not as an equal but as an "elder brother."[8] Backing his words with deeds, the *Vozhd*, suspecting the loyalty of several minority peoples, deported over one and one-half million souls during the war. Among those people moved east were the Kalmyks, Chechens, Ingushi,[9] Meshketians, Balkars, Karachai, Volga Germans, and Crimean Tatars.

Since Stalin's time, however, Soviet policy on the nationalities question has become more ambiguous. Khrushchev condemned his predecessor's russification policies. He found no merit in Stalin's claim that the deported minorities had been disloyal during the war. Thus, these people were "rehabilitated," and most were allowed to return to their ancestral homelands, with the noted exceptions of the Volga Germans and the Crimean Tatars. Although these two hapless peoples were absolved of wrongdoing, they were prevented from returning home. In 1988, however, following some Tatar protests, the government relented somewhat, agreeing to let the Tatars gradually return to the Crimea. Their lands have not been restored, however, and the 80,000 Tatars who have returned to the Crimea find themselves fiercely resisted by its new residents. The Volga Germans too are now allowed to return to their ancestral lands, but they are also refused reparations. Many of them have emigrated to Germany, almost 100,000 left the Soviet Union in 1990 alone.

Several of Khrushchev's decentralization reforms gave the union republics and their peoples greater autonomy, but these improvements were abolished after he was removed. Khrushchev also worked to include more minorities in the party, and Brezhnev did the same, although the percentages of minorities in the party has never equaled the percentage of non-Russians in the society as a whole. Even though Brezhnev was never enthusiastic about fostering the cultural and linguistic customs of his diverse people, public pressure made it impossible to subdue them. Indeed, ethnic identification and pride actually increased, and it has become a major political problem in the current era.

Contemporary Situation

Political. We have already learned that the USSR is divided into 15 "equal" union republics, 20 autonomous soviet socialist republics (ASSRs), 8 autonomous oblasts, and 10 national districts (okrugs). Most of the lesser jurisdictions, each of which envelops a distinct ethnic group, are in the RSFSR. (See Table 10–3.)

---

[8]Carrère d'Encausse, p. 34.

[9]The Chechen-Ingush men are noted for their pride and their headgear. At a party meeting, one of these fellows refused to doff his hat to Stalin saying, "Chechen-Ingush bow only before three things: the earth, a spring of water, and their mothers."

TABLE 10–3   Soviet Federal System

RSFSR	
ASSRs	Bashkir, Buryat, Chechen-Ingush, Chuvash, Daghestan, Kabardo-Balkar, Kalmyk, Karelia, Komi, Mari, Mordvin, No. Ossetia, Tatar, Tuva, Udmurt, Yakut
AOs	Adyge, Birobidzhan, Karachai-Cherkess, Khakass, and Upper Altai
Okrugs	Aga-Buriat, Chukchi, Evenki, Khanty-Mansi, Komi-Permiak, Koriak, Nenets, Taimyr, Ust-Orda, and Yamalo-Nenets
Azerbaijan SSR	
ASSR	Nakhichevan
AO	Nagorno Karabakh
Georgian SSR	
ASSRs	Abkhaz, Adzhar
AO	So. Ossetia
Tadzhik SSR	
AO	Gorno-Badakhshan
Uzbek SSR	
ASSR	Kara-Kalpak

Each union republic and most subordinate entities enjoy their own language, cultural facilities, schools, courts, economic agencies, and governmental institutions.

Before Gorbachev's reforms, these local governments were controlled from Moscow, but now they enjoy greater autonomy and many of them want even greater freedom from central control. Responding to the heightened national awareness among the minorities, Gorbachev, as you know, has restructured the highest echelons of the party and the government so as to give the minorities greater voice in the affairs of state: The party heads of each union republic now hold seats on the Politburo and the leading governmental officials of each union republic now sit on the Council of the Federation. Additionally, the Council of Nationalities in the USSR Supreme Soviet has a much more meaningful task than ever before in legislation relating to the country's various ethnic groups. Furthermore, although the leading party and government officials in the union republics were often Slavic before, today they are members of the national groups that they govern.

The political circumstances are not the only perspective from which the Soviet nationalities should be viewed, however. For a more complete sample of the situation, we should turn to other broader considerations.

Economic and cultural.   In previous chapters I have said a great deal about the Soviet economy, and a later section of this chapter will deal specifically with religion. Consequently, only general observations about the economy will be entered here, and I will limit discussion of the cultural area to those important aspects that do not bear upon religion.

Although the Slavs dominate the country politically and there have been several attempts to russify the nationalities, the minorities have not suffered economic exploitation at the hands of their more numerous siblings. In fact, the Baltic states, having been richer than their Slavic neighbors when they were annexed, continue to enjoy a higher standard of living than their political seniors. The Baltic people find little solace in this fact, however, since they tend to compare their lot with the wealthy Scandinavian states to the north and west. Still, the Baltic countries have not seen their salutary economic circumstances pilfered by the poorer Slavs.

The Central Asian union republics join Moldavia as the poorest in the land. Yet, perhaps no section of the country benefits more economically from the Soviet system than Central Asia. As David Lane puts it, "Central Asia has been transformed from a stagnant, illiterate, disease-ridden semi-feudal society to a modern, dynamic, progressive oriented society."[10] Furthermore, the usual measurement of relative economic well-being within the Soviet Union is somewhat deceiving. There are no limits on the size of private plots or animal herds in the south, as there are in the north. Ethnic minority farmers are better able to augment their incomes and diets than are the Slavic farmers.[11]

Indeed, the Soviet government must be credited with making sincere and determined efforts to enhance the economic well-being of all its citizens. It has done so through a number of methods. Vast capital investment has been poured into developing the natural resources of Central Asia and Siberia. Additional capital has been spent to build industrial plants in the distant provinces, and huge irrigation projects have been constructed to make the southern deserts bloom. Perhaps the Soviet government's greatest achievement in advancing the economic well-being of its citizens comes through its success in raising the educational level of the people and in maintaining educational opportunity. Although only the Jews, Russians, Armenians, Latvians, Georgians, and Ossetians maintain levels of education above the national average (and also dominate the professions), the Soviet accomplishment in education has been truly noteworthy and has been instrumental in increasing the wealth of its citizens. These and other efforts have caused the gap between rich and poor to decline markedly. At the same time, the geography of wealth has changed considerably. The west and north are still richer than other areas, but the difference is much narrower than it was before the revolution. Yet, it is clear that basically the same people—Tatars, Jews, Armenians, Georgians, Latvians, and Estonians—tend to be high-achieving minorities under Soviet rule, just as they were under the tsars.

Accompanying the rise in economic well-being is, of course, urbanization. The Soviet people continue their headlong rush toward the cities, a trend that began before the revolution. Between 1970 and 1979, 50 cities reached populations in excess of 100,000, bringing the total to 272 cities.

[10]David Lane, *Politics & Society in the USSR*, 2nd ed. (New York: New York University Press, 1978), p. 457.

[11]Bernstam, p. 201.

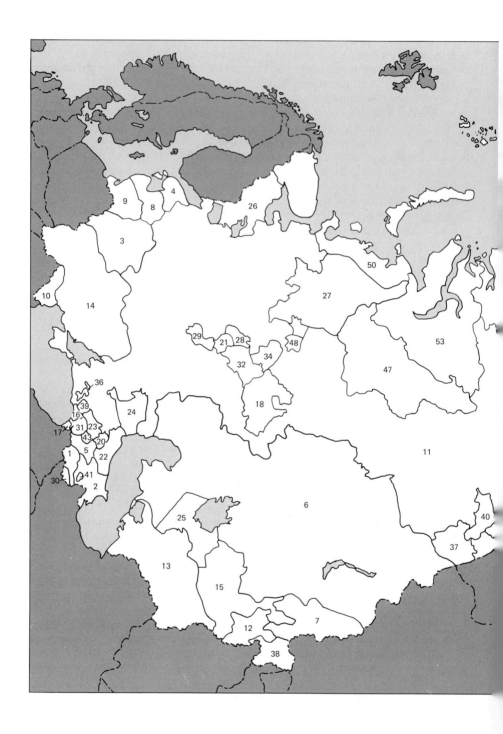

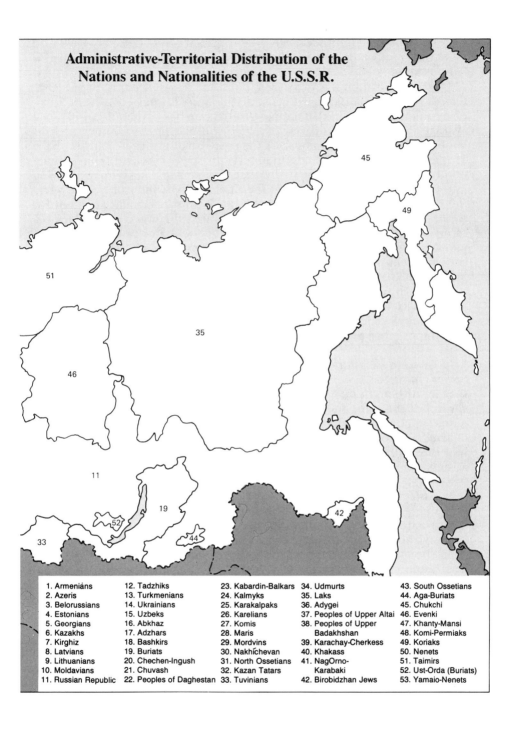

Administrative-Territorial Distribution of the Nations and Nationalities of the U.S.S.R.

1. Armenians
2. Azeris
3. Belorussians
4. Estonians
5. Georgians
6. Kazakhs
7. Kirghiz
8. Latvians
9. Lithuanians
10. Moldavians
11. Russian Republic

12. Tadzhiks
13. Turkmenians
14. Ukrainians
15. Uzbeks
16. Abkhaz
17. Adzhars
18. Bashkirs
19. Buriats
20. Chechen-Ingush
21. Chuvash
22. Peoples of Daghestan

23. Kabardin-Balkars
24. Kalmyks
25. Karakalpaks
26. Karelians
27. Komis
28. Maris
29. Mordvins
30. Nakhíchevan
31. North Ossetians
32. Kazan Tatars
33. Tuvinians

34. Udmurts
35. Laks
36. Adygei
37. Peoples of Upper Altai
38. Peoples of Upper
   Badakhshan
39. Karachay-Cherkess
40. Khakass
41. NagOrno-
   Karabaki
42. Birobidzhan Jews

43. South Ossetians
44. Aga-Buriats
45. Chukchi
46. Evenki
47. Khanty-Mansi
48. Komi-Permiaks
49. Koriaks
50. Nenets
51. Taimirs
52. Ust-Orda (Buriats)
53. Yamaio-Nenets

333

In the 1980s the country's largest cities grew fastest. Between 1979 and 1989 the number of Soviet cities with one million people or more grew from 8 to 24.

The population has urbanized, but it has also shifted south and east. Except for Georgia (0.9 percent) and Moldavia (1.0 percent), every European union republic has an annual growth rate below that of the national average (0.9 percent) and has provided the rest of the country with its largest number of immigrants. At the same time, however, natives of the Muslim union republics, loath to immigrate, have increased their population by almost 3 percent annually. The Russians and Ukrainians moving into Central Asia tend to settle in the cities, taking white-collar jobs, while the native populations remain on the farm, thus increasing potential for socioracial strife. Clearly, the Soviet leaders are confronted with a dilemma of major proportions. If they move industry south and east, following the people's migratory patterns, they will tilt the economic power in that direction and will also probably induce a speedup of the migration. If they induce the Central Asians to move toward the industrial northwest, racial tensions will surely increase there. If, on the other hand, they do nothing, productivity will almost certainly decline further, risking growing discontent. In any event, the Central Asians are not likely to approve of an ever-growing number of Europeans moving into their cities and taking the best jobs.

Current difficulties notwithstanding, over the span of its history, the Soviet Union has done a good job encouraging the economic growth of its people. Although the Russians have traditionally maintained firm political control of the state, they have not been guilty of rank exploitation of the ethnic minorities. Indeed, several minority populations have consistently enjoyed an economic situation far better than the Russians themselves. But how much progress can be charted toward the ultimate Soviet objective of assimilation?

Assimilation. The ultimate goal of the Soviet leaders is to create a new, single nationality unifying the many different peoples, creating a "new Soviet man." Yet, successfully accomplishing this goal in a society so diverse is an extraordinarily difficult, if not impossible, task.

Successful assimilation, at least to an important extent, means the russification of the Soviet minorities since the Russian language is to be the *lingua franca* of the society. The practicality of adopting the language spoken by the majority of the people rather than using Esperanto or some new international tongue is certainly understandable. Yet, language is so much a part of the culture to which it belongs—music, literature, poetry, values, nuance—that to adopt Russian as the first language could cost each minority at least a part of its own unique identity. Further, such a policy gives the Russian people an automatic advantage in the society, a fact not lost on the minorities.

Even though the Soviet constitution holds all languages equal, there can be no doubt that Russian is more equal than the others. A mandatory secondary language in all minority schools, Russian is almost the only language used in higher education. It is also preferred in party and government circles and used exclusively in the military. One who does not become proficient in Russian will find his or her professional and political horizons significantly reduced. There is also a kind of creeping russification in most national languages in two important respects. First, with but a few important exceptions, the Cyrillic alphabet is used in the written word. Second, virtually all minority languages borrow Russian terms for new technical concepts.

Soviet efforts to develop a national language have been directed toward bilingualism rather than toward abandoning the ethnic languages altogether. Success in developing a bilingual population has been important but far from spectacular. Bilingualism is greatest in Europe, except among the Russians themselves, of whom only 3 percent claim to be fluent in a second language. Among non-Russians, bilingualism is least well developed in Central Asia and in the Transcaucasian republics. Significant gains in bilingualism have been made, however. In 1959 only 41.9 million of the non-Russian people claimed Russian as a second language. By 1983 Soviet authorities claimed that 82 percent of the total population was fluent in Russian.[12] The 1979 census indicated that 93 percent of the total Soviet population considered its native tongue its first language, but the 1989 census showed that that figure had dropped to just over 89 percent. Most of those who did not express this preference claimed Russian as their principal language. Yet, attachment to the mother tongue seems to be increasing, especially in the Muslim and Transcaucasian republics.

Preference for the native language seems connected somehow to territorial identification. The titular nationalities of the union republics have very strong attachments to their languages, although the Byelorussians seem to be less committed than others. The people in the autonomous jurisdictions have much less protection of their language, and in most cases loyalty to the mother tongue has suffered. This is certainly not a universal fact, however, as is witnessed by the fierce nationalism and linguistic separatism of the Udmurts and the Tuvinians. It seems that the people who have no territory of their own are the most exposed. Although the Jews technically have a territory in the Birobidzhan Autonomous Oblast, very few Jews chose to live in that remote area. (About 10 percent of the Birobidzhan AO is Jewish.) Having long suffered from suppression of their schools and journals, they are losing their language. Currently only about 14 percent of the nation's Jews speak Yiddish, and even fewer speak Hebrew. Poles are also losing their language and their national identity. Both groups seem to be assimilating. Those Jews who resist assimilation are leaving the Soviet Union in large numbers. On the other hand, a majority of the Volga Germans, although denied their own territory since World War II, stubbornly hold to their national language.

If a people abandon their own language, it can be fairly assumed that

---

[12]Dan N. Jacobs and Theresa M. Hill, "Soviet Ethnic Policy in the 1980s: Theoretical Consistency and Political Reality," in *Soviet Politics*, ed. Joseph L. Nogee (New York: Praeger, 1985), p. 170.

they are on their way toward assimilation with another people. Bilingualism alone, however, does not necessarily imply loss of ethnic identity. As Richard Pipes points out, the Asian Indians have adopted English as a second language, yet they are certainly not assimilating with their former colonial masters.[13] Consequently, we must look beyond language preference to appreciate fully the success or failure of Soviet assimilation policies.

Other signs of assimilation are the interarea mobility of the minority people and intermarriage between ethnic groups. In each of these cases, there is scarcely more evidence of assimilation than we found in examining language patterns. The most migratory people in the Soviet Union are, indeed, the Russians and Ukrainians. They have emigrated in large numbers to the Baltic region and to Central Asia. Yet, as previously noted, they tend not to mix with their hosts, preferring the cities to the countryside— and the newer parts of the cities at that. In fact, every titular national group, with the exception of the Armenians, remains largely at home. Even though only 62 percent of the Armenians in the Soviet Union live in Soviet Armenia, 87 percent of the Ukrainians, 84 percent of the Uzbeks, 92 percent of the Turkmen, 94 percent of the Latvians, and 97 percent of the Georgians live on their native soil. These are certainly not figures that attest to a great deal of assimilation. (See Table 10–4.)

Soviet statistics indicate that while the number of new families has increased by 18 percent between 1959 and 1979, the number of ethnically mixed families shot up by over 200 percent.[14] But the greatest number of mixed marriages occur among the Slavs, Balts, and Jews. On the other hand, the Muslim and Transcaucasian peoples rarely intermarry, and when they do, they usually unite with people of neighboring nationalities, not with Slavs. When Muslims do marry Slavs, however, the children usually choose to identify themselves as Slavic rather than Uzbek, Kazakh, Kirghiz, Tadzhik, or Turkmen.[15] Yet, the largest number of minorities usually keep to their own people. From 75 to 94 percent of them, depending on the particular national group, live in ethnically homogeneous families.[16]

Unlike their tsarist predecessors, the Soviets have rarely tried to force people to abandon their nationality. Instead, they have generally attempted to persuade the minorities to adopt additional traits, such as the Russian language. The tools they have used to accomplish this task are varied and have met with mixed success. Clearly, they manipulate education and the media for the purpose. Bilingualism and intermarriage are enthusiastically encouraged by the state. Slavic emigration into the provinces has been substantial, and anyone wishing to advance very far professionally, in the party or in the government, must be fluent in Russian and would also do well to adopt other Russian behaviors, such as heavy drinking in social

---

[13]Pipes, p. 511.

[14]Jacobs and Hill, p. 171.

[15]Carrère d'Encausse, pp. 101, 250–253.

[16]Gail W. Lapidus, "The Nationality Question and the Soviet System," in *The Soviet Union in the 1980s*, ed. Erik P. Hoffman (New York: The Academy of Political Science, 1984), p. 105.

TABLE 10–4 Ethnic Distribution of the Union Republics (in percentages)

Russian SFSR	81.6	Russian	3.8	Tatar	3	Ukrainian	11.6	other
Ukraine SSR	72.6	Ukrainian	21	Russian	1	Jewish	5.6	other
Byelorussian SSR	77.8	Byelorussian	13	Russian	4.3	Polish	4.9	other
Moldavian SSR	64.5	Moldvaian	13.9	Ukrainian	13	Russian	8.6	other
Estonian SSR	61.5	Estonian	30.3	Russian	3.1	Ukrainian	5.1	other
Latvian SSR	51.8	Latvian	34.2	Russian	4.5	Byelorussian	9.5	other
Lithuanian SSR	80	Lithuanian	8	Russian	8	Polish	4	other
Georgian SSR	69.6	Georgian	8.1	Armenian	6.3	Russian	16	other
Armenian SSR	93	Armenian	3.3	Russian	0.5	Kurdish	3.2	other
Azerbaijan SSR	82.6	Azerbaijan	5.6	Russian	5.5	Armenian*	6.3	other
Kazakh SSR	39.7	Kazakh	37.8	Russian	5.4	Ukrainian	17.1	other
Kirghiz SSR	52.3	Kirghiz	21.5	Russian	12.9	Uzbek	13.3	other
Tadzhik SSR	61	Tadzhik	23	Uzbek	14	Tatar	2	other
Turkmen SSR	71.9	Turkmen	9.5	Russian	9	Uzbek	9.6	other
Uzbek SSR	75.3	Uzbek	7.7	Russian	4.5	Tadzhik	12.5	other

*Most Armenians have fled Azerbaijan due to ethnic violence.

Source: 1989 Soviet Census.

settings. Some scholars contend that the military is the principal tool of assimilation, but the ethnic violence and hatred in the ranks seem to contradict this notion.

The success of these tools of assimilation has been disappointing to the Soviet leadership. Efforts have been frustrated by three important factors. First, it is important to remember that, unlike the United States, which also has a large multiethnic population, most of the people of the Soviet Union are indigenous to their homeland. They did not have to break old ties to come to a new world. Rather, a new world is being imposed on ancient, deeply rooted cultures. Whereas immigrants in the United States sometimes feel they must prove themselves in the new environment, it is often the Russians, or at least the communists, who must prove that their way is better than the traditional one.

Second, since the 1960s a resurgence of nationalism has developed throughout the world. People are taking more interest in their heritage and becoming resistant to the loss of their traditional identity and cultural patterns. This trait has also influenced the people of the Soviet Union, and a new sense of national pride has emerged among many of its nationalities.

Third, the very policies of the Soviet government have tended, paradoxically, to awaken national pride among the minorities. Encouraging minority languages and culture, dividing the different peoples into the various administrative units, and requiring each citizen to declare his or her nationality at age 16 have all contributed to the national awareness of the various Soviet people.

Even so, some degree of assimilation is taking place. Those people who enjoy their own union republic seem very firm in their national identification. Some, however, like the Estonians and Latvians, seem condemned to extinction because of their inability to keep pace with the population growth of their union republic owing to Slavic immigration. Other less populous groups are also in some danger of disappearing as distinct cultures. Among them are Jews, Poles, Mari, Udmurts, Chuvash, Mordvinians, Finns, and several other peoples.[17]

With these few exceptions, however, the Soviet hope for assimilation has seemingly failed: The "new Soviet man" is nowhere in sight. To the contrary, the minorities are more concerned about preserving their unique identities than ever, and their agitation for autonomy, sovereignty, and even for independence seems to threaten to pull the Soviet Union apart and perhaps lead to civil war. Recognizing that the society is perilously close to disintegration, Soviet humorists say that cynical people are preparing themselves in one of two ways.

> The optimists are studying English, while the pessimists are learning Chinese.

[17]Pipes, pp. 501, 512.

Autarky

Upon becoming general secretary of the CPSU, Gorbachev launched an anti-corruption campaign that hit the minority populations particularly hard, even though it had no overt ethnic implications.[18] Traditions among some minority groups encourage favoritism, nepotism, and corruption; hence, Gorbachev's policies angered the minorities—they felt that they were being singled out. Gorbachev is the first general secretary who has not had experience working in minority regions and he clearly underestimated the resistance and animosity his policies would engender. In any event extensive purges of the party and government took place in Moldavia, Georgia, Armenia, Azerbaijan, Kirghizia, Uzbekistan, Tadzhikistan, and Kazakhstan. In fact, Gorbachev removed Dinmukhamed M. Kunayev, a Brezhnev crony, from the Politburo and replaced him as first secretary of the Kazakhstan Communist Party with a Russian in 1987. This move tripped off ethnic riots lasting for days in Alma Ata, Kazakhstan's capital.[19]

Glasnost and *demokratisiya* also evoked unforeseen consequences among the minorities. Emboldened by these reforms, the minorities gave vent to their frustrations with Soviet rule and they articulated separatist and chauvinistic ideas. Before long, popular fronts organized in every union republic. Originally these movements campaigned for perestroika, glasnost, and demokratisiya, but inevitably some of them became opposition parties contesting communist and even Soviet rule. It should be noted, however, that while the minorities resent Russian domination, many of them also have ancient hatreds of their closest neighbors. Consequently, as the dominant nationalities in the union republics manifest their desire for greater control over their union republic governments, less populous people within the republics agitate for autonomy or independence from the people who control the union republics. Additionally, some union republics, nursing long-held grudges, have come to the point of virtual war with one another. In addition to the economic reverses, Gorbachev and the reformers must be faulted for their failure in dealing with the nationalities. The current turmoil in the "periphery"[20] may be inevitable, however, as the economic system collapses. The necessary reforms that de-Stalinize the society and introduce some aspects of the market economy into the system have eliminated Marxism-Leninism as the unifying theme that held the Soviet Union together. With cohesion weakened, people have sought other unifying themes and different explanations to give meaning to life. Apparently finding few new ideas to satisfy their needs, many people have returned to old ones: nationalism and religion. Indeed, several nationalities have gone so far as to create illegal military units that are used against other nationalities, and occasionally even against the Soviet military.

---

[18]A term used to signify a system of national self-sufficiency.

[19]Bohdan Nahaylo and Victor Swoboda, *Soviet Disunion* (New York: The Free Press, 1989), pp. 254–257.

[20]Soviet leaders, reflecting the ancient tradition for centralization, often refer to Moscow as the "center" and to the union republics as the "periphery."

Forced by events, Gorbachev held a national referendum to address the issue of whether the people favored staying in the union. While some localities voted against the proposition, each of the nine union republics that held the election voted to remain in the union. The total vote in favor was 77.3 percent. Yet six union republics, the most recalcitrant areas, refused to hold the election. See Table 10–5.

Although the goal of the various separatist movements is broadly the same, the issues and the methods differ from one part of the country to the other. Accordingly, we should examine these movements in more detail.

The Baltics.   Being the most westernized and prosperous people in the Soviet Union, the **Balts** are unique. Indeed, Gorbachev hoped to use them as models of reform. He actually encouraged them to strike out on their own economically, thinking that they would most easily make the transition to a market economy. With their success, he hoped to more easily persuade other peoples to begin to modernize their economic patterns. The Baltic is unusual from another perspective. Although its peoples have

TABLE 10–5   Results of the National Referendum on Unity

The question: "Do you think it necessary to preserve the Union of Soviet Socialist Republics as a renewed federation of equal, sovereign republics in which human rights and freedom will be guaranteed for all nationalities?"

Republic	Percent of Yes Votes
Russian SFSR	74
Ukraine SSR	70
Byelorussian SSR	83
Moldavian SSR	Did not participate
Estonian SSR	Did not participate*
Latvian SSR	Did not participate*
Lithuanian SSR	Did not participate*
Georgian SSR	Did not participate*
Armenian SSR	Did not participate†
Azerbaijan SSR	89
Kazakh SSR	94
Kirghiz SSR	95
Tadzhik SSR	95
Turkmen SSR	95
Uzbek SSR	90

*Held its own referendum in which the majority voted for independence.
†Plans to hold its own referendum later.
Source: "Vote Backs Gorbachev But Not Convincingly," *The Los Angeles Times*, March 19, 1991.

lived next to one another for centuries, little of the jealousy and animosity found in other regions infects their relationships. Indeed, they have usually been quite cooperative with one another in efforts to relax the Soviet grip on their countries. Each of the three was forcibly annexed to the Soviet Union in 1940 and each suffered Stalin's purges, so they share a community of spirit.

In a series of very brave steps, Lithuania, Latvia, and Estonia each moved toward political independence in deed as well as in word. Estonia and Latvia have only declared that they will work toward independence, but Lithuania actually declared it on March 11, 1990, bringing down upon it a Soviet embargo of most goods including oil and natural gas. Lithuania refused to rescind its declaration, but after several months only Iceland had recognized its independence, so the Lithuanian government reluctantly agreed to postpone implementing the declaration, ostensibly until terms for its departure could be worked out. Similarly, Lithuania's and Latvia's communist parties have broken with the CPSU, but—with the election of **Sajudis** (Lithuania's Popular Front) founder Vytautas Landsbergis as president of the republic—Lithuania is the only Baltic state so far to be governed by a noncommunist. The three republics have created joint institutions to coordinate their political and economic policies; they tried to take control of the customs stations at their borders; and each of them has refused to cooperate in drafting the new Soviet treaty of Union because they claim that they are preparing to leave the Union to which they were originally forcibly annexed.

Space limitations prohibit a complete listing of their acts of defiance, but they include flying their traditional flags rather than the ones they were given when they entered the Soviet Union (each of these nationalist flags has since been officially recognized by the USSR), encouraging their young men to avoid the draft and hiding them from the authorities (perhaps as many as 50 percent of the Baltic youth refused to appear for the spring 1990 draft call), and organizing their own home guards in defiance of a Gorbachev edict. Lithuania has approved legislation giving its farmers land without charge; it fired the Moscow-appointed procurator and appointed its own (the original has been since reinstated by the USSR); and it passed legislation stating that future new residents would have to live in the republic for 10 years before they could become citizens and vote. Estonia is developing its own currency and tax system; it passed a law denying people who have not lived in the republic for at least five years the right to vote (this was since revoked under pressure); and it has required all workers to learn Estonian within four years. In a massive gesture of solidarity commemorating the fiftieth anniversary of the Hitler/Stalin Nonaggression Pact that eventually led the Baltic states to be annexed into the Soviet Union, over one million people in the three republics joined hands, forming a human chain running 370 miles from Vilnius, through Riga, to Tallinn, the republics' capital cities.

These actions have not gone without resistance, however. Opposition popular fronts have been organized—usually composed of Russians, Poles, Ukrainians, and other non-Balts—to resist many of these policies. Soviet troops have forced themselves into public and party buildings that the Balts took over, and they have interfered with the Balts from controlling customs offices at their frontiers. Finally, cooperating with an attempted coup by a virtually anonymous group called the Committee for National Salvation, Soviet troops seized the Vilnius radio and television center on January 13, 1991, killing 14 Lithuanians who attempted to block their path. Although the communications facilities were successfully occupied, the Lithuanian government blockaded itself inside the parliament building, so the coup failed.[21] This tragic episode interrupted what had been to that point an almost completely nonviolent independence movement. The violence was followed by a February 1991 Lithuanian popular, nonbinding vote in which 90.5 percent of a heavy voter turnout called for Lithuania's independence. Although the Lithuanian government remains intact and its people persist in their defiance, the national government continues to maintain a strong presence in the republic, and Soviet troops occasionally have been used to take over buildings and facilities, albeit not at the heavy cost of lives occasioned by the January 1991 action. Meanwhile, other violent acts took place in Latvia. Only days after the Vilnius tragedy, Black Berets attacked the Ministry of Interior building in Riga. After over an hour of fighting and six deaths, the building fell to Soviet hands. Implausibly, Gorbachev later claimed that he knew nothing about the military attack until after it was executed. He called for investigations of the actions, but he has supported them as legitimate. Bitter that the United States and the West have not been more supportive of their independence movements, the Balts grimly tell this riddle.

> Which is the best, Russia or the United States?
>
> Russia, they liberated us from the Germans while the damned Americans have not yet liberated us from the Russians.

In 1991, however, in an apparent response to the Soviet crackdown, the United States announced that it would send relief supplies directly to the Baltic and to the Ukraine, bypassing the Soviet government.

Moldavia.   Bessarabia, a Rumanian province, like the Baltic republics, was forcibly annexed to the Soviet Union in 1940 and renamed Moldavia. Indeed, Leonid Brezhnev himself was the leading Communist Party official in the republic before he was promoted to Moscow. The Moldavians have never been comfortable under Soviet rule, but until 1989 they remained sullenly quiet. On November 7, 1989, however, thousands of nationalists massed at the central square of Kishinev, obstructing the traditional Revolution Day parade and chasing the party first secretary from the reviewing stand. The demonstrators were eventually dispersed

---

[21]Elizabeth Shogren and John-Thor Dahlburg, "Gorbachev Says Local General Ordered Force," *The Los Angeles Times,* Jan. 15, 1990.

and extra troops were sent in to keep order. Meanwhile, the Moldavian popular front pressed for its goals in the republic's Supreme Soviet, finally winning a law making Moldavian (virtually indistinguishable from Rumanian) the national language; also the traditional blue, yellow, and red flag was officially recognized.

The nationalists' passions were fueled even more when late in 1989 the Rumanian dictator, Nikolai Ceaucescu, was forced from power. New cries for independence went up in Moldavia and people talked openly of leaving the Soviet Union and joining Rumania. In the spring of 1990, thousands of Rumanians and Moldavians crossed their common border, despite Soviet efforts to stop them. No violence ensued, however, and in the summer the Moldavian Supreme Soviet declared the sovereignty of the republic, claiming control over all its natural resources and land and pledging never again to celebrate the anniversary of Moldavia's annexation to the Soviet Union.

All is not united within Moldavia, however. The Gagauz, a Christian Turkish minority in southern Moldavia, declared its own republic within Moldavia. The Moldavians resisted this move with force and Soviet troops had to be sent in to restore order. In the eastern part of the republic, 300,000 Russians and Ukrainians also declared their independence from Moldavia. Eventually, Gorbachev decreed that each of these movements was illegal.

Transcaucasia. Georgia, the birthplace of Joseph Stalin, has always had a strong independent streak and Soviet tanks had to be sent to Tbilisi to put down massive riots in 1977 when the Soviets threatened to eliminate Georgian as the republic's national language.

Yet, even as Georgia has chafed under Soviet rule, its minorities, principally the Ossetians and the Abkhazians, have struggled under Georgian domination. In 1989 matters came to a head in the Abkhazian Autonomous Republic when the Georgians announced plans to build a university there at Sukhumi, a popular Black Sea resort. Since then, hundreds of people have been killed in ethnic violence. In April 1989 Soviet troops were ordered to suppress anti-Abkhazian demonstrations in Tbilisi. Twenty people were killed by troops using gas and shovels against the crowds. This brutal act galvanized the Georgians. Virtually in a single night, a majority of the people began to demand independence from the Soviet Union.

As the violence between Georgians and Abkhazians continues, the Georgian Supreme Soviet asserted its right to become independent and it created a commission to study processes that might be used to that end. Georgian nationalist extremists were still not satisfied. In August 1989 their demonstrations, boycotts, and blockades of the railroads forced the authorities to allow multiparty elections in the republic and the first elected noncommunist union republic parliament resulted. The non-communist ruling coalition, led by nationalistic extremist Zviad Gamskhurdia, held a referendum in which 98 percent of the people voted for independence. Accordingly, the government declared independence in April 1991. Like Lithuania, however, Georgia has not yet been able to withdraw from the union. Although the Soviet military has not occupied Georgian buildings or facilities, a tense stalemate exists while the two sides await developments.

In the meantime, ethnic violence flared up in a second part of the republic. In December 1990, after the Georgian parliament began to study the possibility of secession from the Soviet Union, the South Ossetian people, a Muslim minority living in Georgia's South Ossetian Autonomous Oblast, declared their wish to stay in the Soviet Union and asked that they be given full union republic status. Unwilling to grant their own minorities the same independence of action and political identity that they demand for themselves, Gamskhurdia and the Georgian nationalists have declared the South Ossetian Autonomous Oblast dissolved, and they have used force in a futile attempt to quiet the ethnic unrest. Sadly, since December 1990, over 100 people have been killed in brutal clashes. Gamskhurdia claims that the Soviet government is secretly encouraging and arming the South Ossetians and that Soviet troops will use the violence as a pretext to crush the Georgian independence movement.

Meanwhile, Armenia is restive as well. In 1987 the Armenians demanded that the Nagorno-Karabakh Autonomous Oblast just across the border in Azerbaijan be returned to Armenia. This enclave is about 80 percent Armenian and Christian, and the Armenians claim it has been theirs throughout the ages. Yet, the Muslim Azerbaijans also claim the territory as traditionally theirs and they refused to part with it. Riots and strikes ensued and scores of people were brutally murdered and maimed on both sides. After months of fighting, during which Moscow governed Nagorno-Karabakh directly, the USSR Supreme Soviet decided that that enclave would remain in Azerbaijan. Then, in December 1988, an earthquake measuring 6.5 on the Richter scale struck Armenia, killing 25,000 people and leveling whole cities. Gorbachev, who rushed to the scene, learned firsthand how deep the nationalist feelings were. Although stunned by the natural tragedy, the people castigated him for not resolving the problem of Nagorno-Karabakh, even though thousands of Azerbaijan government and party officials had been disciplined for not preventing the riots there, and Soviet troops had been sent to restore order.

Meanwhile, the Azerbaijans blockaded the railroads leading through their republic to Armenia and pillaged cargoes intended to relieve the Armenian earthquake victims. Armenia suffered from shortages of everything, and the blockade backed up hundreds of trains across the country.

In Armenia a militant Karabakh Committee was formed, and party and government officials joined the radicals. For their part, the Azerbaijan radicals took control of government and party offices. Each side organized private armies and vast stores of weapons and munitions were stolen from military bases as the region slipped toward civil war. The Karabakh Committee was arrested and the private armies were gradually disarmed, but the situation was far from resolved.

In January 1990 riots broke out in Baku and other Azerbaijan cities. Lasting for days, mobs slaughtered Armenians and mutilated their bodies. The violence was, of course, reciprocated in Armenia—hundreds were killed and perhaps a half million people fled these republics to escape the

These three stones, painted in national patterns, mark the point at which Armenia, Georgia, and Azerbaijan come together. Two Armenian radicals were killed and two others were wounded in a 1989 attempt to blow up this monument.

violence. To restore order, Gorbachev sent in the military; 130 people were killed and the port at Baku was blockaded while refugees were taken across the Caspian Sea to Central Asia. This migration, you will learn, tripped off additional ethnic violence there.

Secessionist support rose in each republic. Each declared its sovereignty. The Armenians refused to allow its youth to be drafted until their safety was assured. Azerbaijan reasserted its right to rule Nagorno-Karabakh and it declared null and void in its territory all Soviet laws with which it disagreed.

At the same time, separatists rose up in Azerbaijan's Nakhichevan Autonomous Republic, a small territory on the opposite side of Armenia. The Azers and the Nakhichevans are Shiite Muslims and have relatives across the border in northern Iran. In January 1990 thousands of people mobbed the frontier, destroying watchtowers and barbed wire fences, and crossed the border to visit their cousins in Iran. For a time the government completely lost control of the frontier and Iran as well as the Soviet Union became very concerned. Before order could be restored, the Nakhichevan Supreme Soviet declared its independence from the Soviet Union and appealed for help from the United Nations, Turkey, and Iran. Meanwhile, the conflict between Armenia and Azerbaijan continues to rage; wrenching violence recurs incessantly. Like the problems in Georgia, little hope is seen for a solution to the brutalities and killings. Indeed, the situation in Transcaucasia has become so severe that some authorities fear a "Lebanonization" (spasmodic civil war with little hope of resolution) of the area is developing. After repeated failed efforts to bring about a truce in the Armenian-Azerbaijan conflict, Gorbachev apparently decided to resort to tough military means. Troops were sent to occupy strategic locations along the borders of the two republics in May 1991. This new effort was greeted with defiance, however, with Armenia's nationalist leader, Levon Ter-Petrosyan, protesting that "The Soviet Union has declared war against Armenia." Such strong-arm policies may bring brief respite, but a permanent solution to the problem is not likely to be found with the use of troops. Indeed, if the area is truly becoming Lebanonized, a permanent solution will elude the antagonists for years.

Central Asia. The situation in **Central Asia** is perhaps less violent at the moment, but it is no less complicated, and it is potentially even more incendiary because the fanatic revolutions plaguing other parts of the Muslim world could spread to this huge area, which contains one-fifth of the Soviet population. Since the Soviet government has relaxed its control on religious practices, a new awakening of Islam got under way and some organizations have demanded that Arabic script be substituted for the Cyrillic alphabet that is presently used in the native languages. Economically, Central Asia is still heavily subsidized by Moscow, but since the "Sibaral" project to divert Siberian river water to the south has been scrapped, many Central Asians are concerned that the state has abandoned serious efforts to raise their standard of living. Beyond these economic concerns, there is a growing amount of talk of an Islamic union of the Soviet Muslim republics. Indeed, an Islamic Democratic Party has already been organized. Yet, such a union seems unlikely at least for now because relations among the peoples of the prospective union are so strained.[22]

Beyond question, Uzbekistan is the superbowl of corruption in the Soviet Union. The "cotton mafia," a consortium of government officials, party leaders, and farm and industrial managers, has for years embezzled billions upon billions of rubles from the government in schemes that reported far more cotton produced than was actually harvested. Gorbachev has tried to root out the swindlers. He has fired, arrested, imprisoned, and even executed some of them, but the problem persists; and the people resent their leaders being singled out.

Besides its difficulties with Gorbachev, Uzbekistan has had serious confrontations with its neighbor Kirghizia. Local squabbling has seen riots flare up on its borders that resulted in hundreds of deaths. Similar ethnic violence has occurred within the republic. In 1944 the Meskhetian Turks were forced to leave their homes in the mountains of Georgia and were resettled in Uzbekistan. The Uzbeks have never taken to these immigrants

[22]Walter Laqueur, "Soviet Politics: Future Scenarios," in *Soviet Union 2000: Reform or Revolution*, ed. Walter Laqueur (New York: St. Martin's Press, 1990), pp. 51–54.

and in 1989 mobs attacked the Meskhetians, killing over a hundred and forcing them to flee the republic. Since then they have tried to return to Georgia, but they are unwelcome there as well, so they have joined the growing number of homeless people in the Soviet Union.

Resentful over the anti-corruption campaigns and Soviet involvement in their ethnic struggles, the Uzbeks have developed a popular front called *Birlik* (Unity) to advocate for more autonomy. The Uzbek Supreme Soviet passed a declaration of sovereignty and it has taken up legislation to make Uzbek the national language. Furthermore, Uzbek authorities have refused to send food and industrial goods out of the republic to protest low state prices.

Kazakhstan has also had ethnic disturbances. The only union republic in which the namesake people are not a majority, it was the first republic to have major contemporary ethnic riots (when Kunayev was replaced). Its people contend that they are underpaid relative to other people in the republic, and youthful Kazakh gangs have attacked Armenians, Azerbaijans, and Lezghians. Much more important, however, is the Kazakh movement *Adilet* (Justice) against nuclear weapons tests in their republic at Semipalatinsk. Finding birth defects to be much higher than normal among people in the area, *Adilet* exerted heavy pressure and in 1990 finally succeeded in persuading the government to move its testing grounds to the far north.

Turkmenistan is the most tranquil of all republics, but even it has declared sovereignty and some of its people want its entire delegation to the USSR Congress of Peoples' Deputies recalled because of its obsequious compliance with Moscow. Kirghizia, on the other hand, has had serious problems, especially with its neighbors. In 1990 its citizens fell into pitched battle with Uzbeks in the holy city of Osh over land use. Several people were killed and many buildings were destroyed. The year before, Kirghiz people came to blows with their Tadzhik neighbors over precious water rights.

Tadzhikistan, however, is perhaps the most troubled Central Asian republic. It has the highest infant mortality rate in the country and yet its population is growing faster than any other—doubling in the past 20 years! Its standard of living is the lowest in the land, with rampant unemployment, and its average monthly wage is almost half of the national average. Of those who do work, the average per capita production is about 30 percent of Byelorussia's, the nation's highest. The most devout Muslim republic, gangs of youths have rampaged through its streets, attacking nonbelievers and humiliating women who do not follow the strict social code of Muslim tradition. In 1990 a mob of believers in Dushanbe, the capital, forced seasoned Soviet combat officers to kneel while a Mullah recited verses from the Koran atop the officers' vehicle.[23]

The officers were in Dushanbe to protect Armenian refugees from Azerbaijan who had been sent there for protection. Somehow a rumor

---

[23]David Aikman, "Karl Marx Makes Room for Muhammad," *Time Magazine*, March 12, 1990.

spread among the Tadzhiks that the Armenians were being given preference for scarce housing and a riot broke out, killing several of the hapless
refugees. Although order was restored, passions continued to build until
23,000 Russians were forced to flee and supported by the local popular
front, *Rastakhiz* (Renaissance), the Tadzhikistan Supreme Soviet placed an
embargo on the export of its food and legislated provisions to protect the
Tadzhik language from russification. Anti-Russian feeling has long been
high in Tadzhikistan and anti-Russian riots have often occurred; before
1990 the most serious one took place in 1978 in Dushanbe.[24]

The Slavs. Nothing approaching the violence in the south has yet
afflicted the Slavic areas of the country, but serious trouble is brewing there
also. Byelorussia, long the most compliant union republic, has been reluctant to assert its individualism, even though a number of its citizens have
demonstrated against Stalinism. However, in 1990 its Supreme Soviet declared its sovereignty and claimed supremacy over national law. Its popular
front *Adradzhen'ne* (Renewal) was mobilized by the Chernobyl nuclear accident and it advocates political pluralism and private property as well as
environmental issues. Also, the workers of Minsk and other Byelorussian
cities went out on strike to protest the consumer goods price increases of
April 1991. This broad-based show of disenchantment with the state's economic policies was unsettling to the leadership. Even so, the republic remains timid by contrast to other republics, and it is still controlled by
conservatives. When neighboring Lithuania declared independence in
March 1990, Byelorussia demanded that the lands it ceded to Lithuania
when Lithuania entered the Union be returned if it pulled out. Those
lands include Vilnius, Lithuania's capital.

Besides Russia, the Ukraine is the most important union republic in
the Soviet Union. It has 52 million people, and it produces about one-
quarter of the nation's food and one-third of its industrial products. Gorbachev himself has publicly stated that his reforms will fail unless they are
successful in the Ukraine, and he purged the old Brezhnev leaders of the
republic, replacing them with his own loyalists. He also had Ukrainian
Vladimir A. Ivashko elected to the new post of deputy general secretary of
the CPSU.

The Ukraine has many grievances against Moscow, however, including that its western territories were forcibly annexed from Poland at the
beginning of World War II (this area remains the most restive part of the
republic), its Catholic population has been systematically persecuted, millions of its people died in a 1930s famine deliberately created by Stalin,[25]
and the effects of the Chernobyl nuclear accident are still being felt.

While the eastern part of the republic apparently remains loyal to the
Soviet Union, the western Ukraine is seething with discontent. One hundred thousand Ruthenians who were forcefully incorporated into the Soviet Union after World War II demand to be rejoined to Czechoslovakia.

[24]Nahaylo and Swoboda, p. 203.
[25]See Robert Conquest, *The Harvest of Sorrow* (London: Oxford University Press, 1986).

More importantly, the Ukrainians themselves are restive. Their popular front, *Rukh* (Movement), has become increasingly radical. At first, it only called for a confederation of union republics with little power at the center, but later it demanded full independence from the Soviet Union. In January 1989, to commemorate the 1918 founding of an independent Ukraine, it organized a human chain of one million people stretching 300 miles from Lvov to Kiev, and it has led mass protests of the Chernobyl accident and the government's handling of the tragedy.

The union republic elections of March 1990 saw many radicals seated in the Ukrainian Supreme Soviet, including several former political prisoners. Since then the Supreme Soviet has voted to declare its sovereignty, to create its own armed forces, to remain neutral in foreign affairs, and to end deployment of Ukrainian troops outside of the republic; and it claims complete control over its industry, agriculture, and natural resources. With the exception of demanding that its troops be immediately brought home from Kirghizia, Armenia, and Azerbaijan, the Ukraine has committed to move toward these policies only gradually. On one policy it is adamant, however. It ordered the Chernobyl plant closed within five years, and it has created a commission to study the feasibility of closing its other 14 nuclear power plants within 15 years.

Finally, a profoundly conservative people, the Russians have been slow to react to Gorbachev's reforms and to adopt separatist attitudes about the society they themselves in large measure control. There has always been an extremist Russian nationalist movement that wants to retreat from the modern world and preserve a rural "Holy Mother Russia," but this group is not large—although it recently has begun to grow. More will be said about extremist Russian nationalism in the next chapter.

Since 1988, however, many Russians have begun to question the continued efficacy of the Soviet Union. As its external empire in Eastern Europe melted away, some people wanted to fight to preserve it, while others said good riddance to societies they saw themselves having to support economically and militarily. At the same time, many Russians began to feel that they too were captives of the Soviet Empire. Like virtually every union republic, the RSFSR believes that it gives more economically to the other republics than it gets in return, and it has also begun to resent the control of the USSR government. Many Russians complain that the central government is ignoring Russian rights in efforts to placate the minorities. They object to Russian troops being sent into harm's way in the southern republics to quell the ethnic violence, and many are now demanding that Russian soldiers be kept at home. They are stung by the anti-Russian feelings expressed in other union republics, and they bitterly resent seeing Russians forced to flee these areas to avoid being insulted, brutalized, and even massacred. What is worse, severe anti-Russian acts have even been perpetrated by minorities on Russian soil itself. In Tuva, an autonomous oblast 3,000 miles east of Moscow on the Mongolian border, the Tuvinians have long resented the Russian presence in their land. In 1990 violence broke out resulting in one death and the flight of 3,000 Russians. Moreover, the Udmurt ASSR has proclaimed sovereignty over its industry, agriculture, and natural resources, and the same has happened in the Karelian ASSR and the Tatar ASSR. Similarly galling, Gorbachev has made overtures to these national minorities within Russia, offering them increased autonomy within the Russian SFSR.

These episodes have stimulated a backlash among some Russians and the populist politician Boris Yeltsin has given voice to their concerns. Following the 1990 Russian parliamentary elections, Yeltsin was narrowly elected leader of the RSFSR parliament and he has led the republic to confrontations with Gorbachev and the USSR itself. In the meantime, voicing complaints about government and party corruption, economic woes, and ecological concerns, radicals were elected to several city soviets, including those in Moscow and Leningrad.

In May 1990 the Russian SFSR declared its sovereignty and that its laws are supreme within the territory. Claiming that its resources are being plundered, it wants to raise the price of its oil (it produces 91 percent of all Soviet oil) and other products. It believes it is being forced to subsidize the other union republics and it moved to void all contracts for the sale of its goods made by the USSR (a move Gorbachev declared was illegal). It claims to have legitimate control over all of its lands, factories, and transportation facilities, and it has negotiated bilateral trade treaties with other union republics, including the Ukraine and the Baltic states. Furthermore, it has threatened to withhold about 80 percent of its tax revenues from the USSR; it announced plans to import from the West sorely needed consumer goods; it tried to establish a Russian SFSR state bank; and it has adopted a policy that allows farmers to buy their land.

These policies have placed Yeltsin and Gorbachev against one another, and their mutual antagonism is exacerbated by several other political moves by Yeltsin. He has launched his own foreign policy, signing an agreement of friendship with Poland in October 1990, insisting that the Russian SFSR parliament must agree before the Soviet Union can cede to Japanese islands in the Kuril chain (these islands are presently part of the Russian SFSR), and calling for the formation of a RSFSR army. Yeltsin has even issued a decree forbidding Communist Party PPOs to be located at Russian enterprises, and informally suggested that the USSR government vacate Moscow and find a new location for its capitol. (Previously, Gorbachev recommended that Moscow be made a federal district, independent of the Russian SFSR government.) The two leaders, once political allies, became opponents in 1987 when Yeltsin was removed as the Moscow Party leader and as a member of the Politburo,[26] and they remained adversaries until 1991. In that year, Yeltsin was elected by a direct popular vote to the newly created post of President of the RSFSR. Since then, the two reformers have been more cooperative with each other in order to meet a resurgent conservative opposition.

The question of framing a new treaty of union has been central to the dispute between the two leaders. Originally, Yeltsin resisted certain provisions of the new treaty, and in a fit of rage over Gorbachev's centralizing

---

[26]See Boris Yeltsin, *Against the Grain* (New York: Summit Books, 1990).

policies, he even called for Gorbachev's resignation in February 1991. Only a month later, however, Yeltsin reversed course. Driven by the growing power and assertiveness of the Soviet right-wing, Yeltsin spoke out in support of Gorbachev's leadership, and he entered into a compromise agreement with Gorbachev and the leaders of eight other union republics pledging to work toward a speedy signing of the new treaty of Union. However, given the volatility of the Russian leader, the final agreement on a new union cannot be taken for granted.

If the worst happens, and Russia decides to pull out of the "tattered empire", and if it could do so, the very existence of the Soviet Union would be severely jeopardized. Similarly, although the departure of the Baltic states, Armenia, Georgia, and Moldavia would probably not be catastrophic, the secession of the Ukraine would be a serious blow. Whatever happens, barring a clampdown and a return to Stalinism, the Soviet Union is going to change, as its previous centralization has become untenable. The proposed new treaty of Union, giving much more cultural, political, and economic autonomy to the union republics is the minimum change one can reasonably expect. It is possible, however, that some republics may break away and that the remaining union will transform into a confederate system. Some decentralization is certainly desirable, but there is no assurance that the conservative elements in the party, military, bureaucracy, and public will accept such an arrangement. Furthermore, such an amorphous political structure in a state holding such massive nuclear weapons capability will be a matter of intense concern to the world at large.

RELIGION

One of the great ironies in history is that Marxism, an internationalist ideology, was first implemented in the Soviet Union, a multinational country of the first order. Equally paradoxical is the fact that Marxism, an atheistic theory, was first applied in a land inhabited by millions of believers practicing most of the world's great religions.

By far the largest number of believers practice the Russian Orthodox faith, but millions more are Muslims, Catholics, Protestants, and Jews. Additionally, many religions practiced on Soviet soil originated in this land before the revolution. Some of these indigenous religions are the Georgian Orthodox Church, the Armenian Apostolic Church, the Feodorist Crusaders, the Innocents, the Ukrainian Catholic Church (Uniates), the Old Believers, the Molokans, and the Dukhobors. Among the Protestant sects are Baptists, Methodists, Pentecostalists, Jehovah's Witnesses, and Lutherans. The Soviet Union also includes a sizable Buddhist population, a few Hindus, and even a tiny group of Hare Krishnas. Interestingly, besides its believers and its atheists, the Soviet Union also includes two pagan people, the Mari and the Tchememiss.

Into this labyrinth of religious sects the revolution was plunged. Viewing religion as an archaic remnant of a previous era, the Bolsheviks, following Marx, condemned it. They believed that religion did little save inducing people to tolerate their earthly squalor and hardship in exchange for the promise of a nonexistent reward in a mythical afterlife. Because the new government was based on an ideology that promoted a better life in the here and now, the leaders believed that the revolution had to eliminate religion and other "superstitions" for the good of all. The Bolsheviks did not immediately attempt to crush the faith. Instead, they reasoned that religion, like all other capitalist and feudal institutions, would atrophy and disappear as the new society was constructed.

Religious Persecution and Revival

Promulgating the right of all to "practice religious cults" in 1918, the state also moved quickly to divest the Russian Orthodox Church of its sources of power over the people. Church lands were nationalized, and religious schools were abolished. The clergy were branded as members of the deposed bourgeois elite and denied the right to vote; their children were barred from school beyond the elementary level; and priests were issued low-priority ration cards. The state took over the function of recording births, marriages, and deaths and made it illegal for clergy to teach religion to anyone below the age of 18.

After a few years of futile resistance, the Church was forced to cooperate, however grudgingly, with the state. By 1923 the Russian Orthodox Church's relationship with the state was remarkably stable. However, a major campaign to restrain religious practice was initiated in 1929. With

Kazan Cathedral on Nevsky Prospect in Leningrad is used as a museum on atheism.

Stalin's blessing, believers were attacked and imprisoned, clergy were killed, and nuns were disgraced. Churches, mosques, and synagogues were converted into warehouses, clubs, theaters, and even museums dedicated to atheism.

Religious persecution continued unabated until the Nazi invasion of the Soviet Union in 1941. Calling upon his people to defend the Motherland, Stalin made peace with the Russian Orthodox Church, and it cooperated against the common enemy. This symbiotic relationship continued throughout the remainder of Stalin's life, but things took a different turn when Khrushchev came to power.

Condemning Stalin's alliance with the Russian Orthodox Church, Khrushchev embarked on a new campaign to rid the land of "superstition." By the end of his tenure, about half of the country's remaining 20,000 churches had been closed, and many priests and believers were imprisoned or committed to mental institutions. The state machinery was all but closed to the religions as they found it increasingly difficult to publish literature or even apply successfully for the creation of new congregations.

Khrushchev's successors, perhaps less concerned with ideological consistency on this point, pulled back from the extremes of persecution. Brezhnev seemed content to contain religion, hoping it would gradually disappear. The government maintained very strict control of the officially registered religions and occasionally prosecuted those who refused to register with the government. At the same time the government continued a campaign of propaganda and mild harassment against the believers. These relatively benign policies witnessed the number of registered congregations increase somewhat since Khrushchev's time.

Faced with a religious revival and impelled by his own belief that religious faith among those who chose to exercise it is good for the moral substance of the society, Gorbachev committed himself to allowing more religious freedom than has previously been tolerated. In an unprecedented meeting with Patriarch Pimen, Gorbachev said the church had a role to play in helping the country restructure itself. He went on to say that mistakes had been made in past treatment of believers but that, in the future, they would be allowed to practice their faith.

Before religious freedom was granted, the state engaged in numerous practices to discourage believers. Religions were denied the right to practice charity, run hospitals, proselytize, or teach religion to minors. Prayer books and Bibles were kept scarce, services outside of houses of worship were forbidden, and clergy could not make political speeches. Parents were berated for baptizing their children; believers were chastised at work; and church leaders, chosen by the state, were usually selected on the basis of their willingness to cooperate with the authorities. No religious groups were well treated, but those with ties outside the country like the Jews, the Catholics, the Baptists, and the Pentecostalists suffered the most prejudice. The major exception to this rule was the Muslims with whom the state dealt gingerly because Muslim leaders were usually compliant, the Muslim people were numerous and potentially restive, and the Soviet Union did not want to alienate Muslim countries by mistreating their co-religionists.

The exact number of believers is not known. The state estimates that about 60 percent of the population are atheists, 20 percent are Orthodox, 10 percent are practicing Muslims, and the rest are distributed throughout the other religions. In the absence of a formal study, however, it is impossible to know their numbers for sure.

The state still holds a monopoly on the schools, and scientific atheism is taught at all grade levels. Church lands continue to belong to the state. Even so, the circumstances for religious worship have improved dramatically since Gorbachev became the nation's leader. Gorbachev, who was baptized as a child (although his children were not) and whose own mother is a practicing Orthodox believer, contends that Soviet society can benefit from the spiritual training of religion. Echoing this position, Yevgeny Yevtushenko said, "The real danger isn't people who believe in God but people who don't believe in anything."[27] Accordingly, in 1990 the Supreme Soviet passed a law guaranteeing freedom of religion. The state is prohibited from financing religious activity or "propaganda on atheism," but religious groups are allowed to worship as they choose and to teach religion in the homes.

Even before the law was passed, a great deal of freedom was allowed religions *de facto*. As you know, some clergy were elected to the Congress of Peoples' Deputies and a Christian Democratic Party has been founded. Bibles and other religious literature are freely distributed; thousands of copies are even given out free at the annual Moscow book fair. The conservative editors of *Naukai Religiya* (Science and Religion) were replaced with liberals. The journal still supports atheism, but the new editors are committed to a dialogue between atheism and religion, and it gives equal space to religious articles. Thousands of churches, mosques, and synagogues have been reconsecrated, including Uspensky Cathedral on the Kremlin grounds (the nation's most important church), St. Isaac's Cathedral in Leningrad, and the Pechorsky Monastery in Kiev. A new cathedral, the Holy Trinity, is being built in southeast Moscow. Scheduled to be completed in the year 2000, it is the first cathedral built in the Soviet Union in over 70 years. Catechism classes are given after school in rented classrooms. Soviet television regularly broadcasts religious programs; Alcoholics Anonymous has chapters in the Soviet Union, and it relies on religious themes in parts of its program; and Charles Colson's group, Prison Fellowship, gives Bible study classes in Soviet prisons.

A revival of religion was detectable before Gorbachev became general secretary, but now it is clearly growing. The reasons for the increased interest in religion are many. Some people who secretly believed all along are now able to publicly worship without fear. Even some Communist Party members attend church and have their children baptized.[28] Other people, as Gorbachev hoped, are turning to religion for renewed spiritual meaning. Ironically, these new converts are adopting religion for the very reason

[27]Stephen F. Cohen and Katrina VanDen Heuvel, *Voices of Glasnost* (New York: W. W. Norton, 1989), p. 270.

[28]Gray, p. 9.

that Marx gave for its stubborn resilience: He wrote that "Religion is the sigh of the oppressed creature, the heart of a heartless world, the spirit of soulless stagnation. It is the opium of the people."[29] A portion of these searching people are followers of Alexander Solzhenitsyn, who calls for a return to the religious purity of "Holy Mother Russia" and the rejection of sterile, foreign Marxism-Leninism. Other people are using religion in an effort to find their past. Intellectuals find religion fashionable and they collect icons and contribute to the restoration of old churches.[30] Finally, some people use religion as a political statement. Nationalism and patriotism have seldom been far removed from religious practice among the people. Young people wear crucifixes and cross themselves in public; they even go so far as to cynically part company with a group blessing as signs of contempt for the state's authority.[31]

Russian Orthodox

During its 1,000 year history, the Orthodox Church in Russia has often accommodated and augmented autocracy. Something of a junior partner, the Church was historically rewarded for its loyalty and service to the tsar with a number of privileges, including seats on local governing agencies and the Council of Ministers. The Church also enjoyed monopolies in giving religious instruction and publishing religious literature; children from mixed marriages were required to study the Orthodox catechism.

Reflecting the official mood of the time, the mainstream of the Russian Orthodox Church became increasingly reactionary during the early years of the twentieth century. It resisted demands for social, political, and economic reform, and it supported the pogroms against the Jews. With the revolution, the Church generally supported the White cause, although an element called "the Living Church" came out in favor of the social reforms of the Reds.[32]

The early years of the revolution were characterized by resistance from the Russian Orthodox Church, by subsequent arrests and executions of priests, and by persecution by the state. By 1923, however, Patriarch Tikon, canonized in the Uspensky Cathedral in 1989, was forced to capitulate and cooperate with the state. Stalin's policies of 1929 again brought the Church under great pressure until World War II, when a new accommodation was reached, allowing the election of a new patriarch, a post that had stood vacant for two decades. In return the Church called upon the faithful to support the communist side in the war, and it prayed for "our divinely protected land, and for its authorities headed by its *God given leader*"

---

[29]Charles W. Lowry, *Communism and Christ,* 2nd ed. (New York: Collier Books, 1962), p. 54.

[30]Laqueur, p. 25.

[31]Andrea Lee, *Russian Journal* (New York: Random House, 1981), pp. 97–98.

[32]Lane, p. 459–460.

[emphasis added].[33] Since then, except for the Khrushchev era, the Church has generally been able to abide the government in peace and cooperation.

During the Brezhnev era the Church kept a low profile. Because it was not allowed a social role, it had little on which to spend its money, thus becoming one of the wealthiest churches in the world. (Since the Church has been allowed to do good works, it has established charities and hospitals. A dozen churchmen, including Alexei II before he became Patriarch, visited Russian Orthodox communities in the state of Washington in 1989 to study how modern pastoral work is done.) Under Brezhnev, each year the Church gave millions of rubles to the government for historical restoration projects and for the government's "peace fund." Another, perhaps less pleasant, form of cooperation with the state was the Church's practice of disciplining clerics who resisted the government's authority.

In 1961 the Russian Orthodox Church joined the World Council of Churches, where it has often spoken forcefully in support of Soviet foreign policy, assuming the peace line of the Kremlin. However, it has demonstrated independence on occasion, as in 1980, when it did not oppose a council resolution expressing "serious concern" about the 1979 Soviet invasion of Afghanistan. Basically, however, the Church's policy has been to support Soviet interests.

In return, the Russian Orthodox Church enjoyed considerable support from the state. Its tradition of communal worship greatly differs from Catholic authoritarianism and Protestant individualism and is perhaps more compatible with socialism. In any event, the state afforded it more privilege than any other religion. Like all religions, it leases, free of charge, all church buildings and grounds. However, it alone accounts for about half of all the houses of worship in the land; its seminaries produce the greatest number of clergy. And the Church has gradually managed to induce the state to return to it many of its most revered churches and monasteries. Moreover, Russian Orthodox priests are usually allowed to live in considerable comfort, enjoying a standard of living usually reserved for the elite of the society. The closeness of church and state in the Soviet Union has long been a matter of great controversy. Precisely how much support the Russian Orthodox Church enjoys among the Soviet people is impossible to determine from available data. The number of regular practitioners is usually estimated to be between 30 and 40 million. Visits to church services reveal that most attenders are older women, although in the past decade congregations have become noticeably more youthful. The intense piety of many of the worshipers is striking. One sees people completely prostrate on the church floor, arms outstretched so as to assume the posture of a cross. Believers walk on their knees between icons which they queue up to kiss, as priests wipe the glass between worshipers. Something of the mysticism and ceremony of this ancient church is conveyed when one hears the lovely *a cappella* harmony of the congregation as it sings the beautiful music of the mass.

[33]Lane, p. 462.

No discussion of the Russian Orthodox religion is complete without a word about the *Old Believers*. Violently opposed to the modernizing reforms of Patriarch Nikon in the late seventeenth century, hundreds of thousands, perhaps even millions, of people refused to accept the authority of the established church. Suffering suppression and persecution during virtually the entire tsarist era, these hapless souls often preferred death to submitting to a "false faith." Mass suicides are recorded throughout their history. Believers were lowered into rooms without doors or windows to starve themselves to death; children were told that they would feast on sweet meat and honey in heaven, while men with clubs remained above to dispatch those who tried to escape. In other cases, whole congregations would collect in houses and churches, lighting them aflame and perishing in the infernos. The last recorded case of such fanaticism occurred in Tiraspol in 1897, when 28 people buried themselves alive rather than submit to being recorded in the census of that year. Despite these excesses, this stubborn faith has survived and even grown since the 1905 Edict of Tolerance ended their persecution. Today the Old Believers are thought to number about five million.

Armenian and Georgian Churches

The Armenian Apostolic Church, the world's oldest national Christian church, was founded in A.D. 301 upon the conversion of King Tridates III and his court by St. Gregory the Enlightener. After a dispute over the nature of Christ, the Armenian Apostolic Church became independent of other Christian sects in 451.

Seated but a few miles from Yerevan at the monastery of Echmiadzin

An Orthodox priest and a believer walk toward an active church at the ancient monastery of Zagorsk near Moscow.

(Christ came down), the Armenian Apostolic Church is the focus of Armenian national traditions and identification. The church is headed by the catholicos, Vozgen I, who presides at Echmiadzin. The seminary at Echmiadzin trains students for the priesthood who come from Armenian communities around the world.

The Church has traditionally enjoyed considerable independence from the state. It remained healthy even during the worst times of persecution, and today it claims the loyalty of over 70 percent of all Armenians. It is a strong nationalistic symbol, with fathers proclaiming after a child is baptized, "Now you are an Armenian." The national emblem is not the hammer and sickle, but a flowering cross conveying Christ's resurrection, and the Armenians still consider their alphabet a holy script.

The Georgian Orthodox Church enjoyed a less salutary history. Very similar to the Russian Orthodox faith, it struggled against efforts to merge it with the larger Church. Although it, like the Armenian Church, serves as a nationalistic symbol, its membership declined sharply until a recent revival of interest in it developed among Georgians. More bold than the Russian Orthodox leaders, the Georgian Patriarch in 1980 publicly condemned the 1979 Soviet invasion of Afghanistan.

Catholics

Soviet authorities estimate that there are about 13 million Catholics in the country: Eight million practice the Latin rite and five million are Uniates who will be discussed later. Of the Latin rite practitioners, the largest number are concentrated in Lithuania, but many are also found in the

Echmiadzin Cathedral outside Yerevan, Armenia. The local priests claim that this church stands on the foundations of the first Christian church ever built.

Ukraine and Byelorussia, and there are about 1.5 million in Central Asia. Catholicism has long been a critical factor in Lithuanian nationalism and the state responded by persecuting the Church. Seminaries, monasteries, and churches were closed (St. Casimir's, the national cathedral, was even made a museum to atheism for a time), and leading prelates were sent into internal exile. The government even tried to enter the confessional in Lithuania by demanding that priests require the people to include disrespect for state property in the catalogue of their sins.

In 1972 Lithuanian Catholics began to resist openly. Thousands signed petitions protesting the Church's persecution, and clandestine journals (*samizdat*) were published detailing offensive state policy. Throughout the 1970s these movements were suppressed by the KGB. Upon the accession of Pope John Paul II, however, the state became somewhat more restrained because of the pope's immense popularity in Eastern Europe, the Baltic states, the Ukraine, and Byelorussia. In 1983 it consented to the investiture of the Soviet Union's first Roman Catholic cardinal. Significantly, however, the person chosen was Bishop Julijans Vaivods of Latvia rather than a Lithuanian prelate. (Pope John Paul II, however, named Lithuanian Bishop Julijonas Stepanovicius cardinal *in pectore* [in his heart]. Stepanovicius had been held in interior exile for over 20 years at the time.) Since Latvia had only about 290,000 active Catholics, barely 10 percent of the number in Lithuania, it is speculated that the pope agreed not to appoint a Lithuanian in deference to Soviet concern for the political reverberations of such a choice.

Gorbachev has been even more accommodating of the Catholic Church than were his predecessors. St. Casimir's has been returned to the Church and long-closed churches, seminaries, monasteries, and convents have been opened. Bishop Stepanovicius was released from 27 years of interior exile and sent to Rome, and in 1988 Bishop Vincentas Sladkevicius, held in exile for 25 years, was allowed to be elected president of the Lithuanian Catholic Bishop's Conference. Furthermore, in 1989 the Lithuanian parliament declared December 25 a state holiday, one year before the USSR Supreme Soviet recognized Christmas as a national holiday. Gorbachev has also mended fences with the Vatican. In 1989 he visited the pope in the Holy See, and since then diplomatic relations—broken off in 1917—have been reestablished.

Uniates.   One of the issues discussed in Gorbachev's audience with the pope was the fate of the Ukrainian Catholics, or **Uniates,** who practice the Greek rite. This Church, which finds its roots in Greek Catholicism, is the center of a vehement Ukrainian nationalism. For this reason and because church members were suspected of collaborating with the Nazis, Stalin brutally suppressed it, destroying its facilities and executing its leaders. Its believers were ostensibly absorbed into the Russian Orthodox faith, but many of them continued to worship underground. It had a secret hierarchy with some of its prelates unknown even to Rome. With an estimated five million members, it was the largest banned religion in the world.

Until 1987 its members held mass in private houses, in the woods, and in other secret places. Since then, however, they have mobilized and gone public. They have created a Committee for the Defense of the Ukrainian Catholic Church. Hundreds of thousands in the western Ukraine, where the Church is most popular, have marched in demonstrations, and public masses attended by tens of thousands of people have been defiantly held. Finally, in 1989 several Orthodox priests announced their conversion to Ukrainian Catholicism and took over churches in Lvov and other west Ukrainian cities. This movement is attractive to Ukrainians of all ages, and it has become the focal point of Ukrainian separatism.

Russian Orthodox leaders opposed legalization of the Uniates sect. Over 1,000 churches and other properties are at issue. An Orthodox prelate who accompanied Gorbachev to Italy in 1989 did not go to the Vatican and was quoted as saying the Orthodox Church would not negotiate the transfer of property "at the muzzle of a gun."[34] Since Gorbachev's visit with the pope, however, the Uniates have been allowed to register and worship as Uniates, the Vatican has appointed an archbishop to negotiate outstanding issues with the Orthodox establishment, and in 1991 Cardinal Myroslav Lubachivsky—who has been exiled in the West since 1938—was allowed to return to the Soviet Union to lead his flock. The Soviet president, having been impressed by the pontiff's skill in moderating the situation in his native Poland, hopes that the pope will use his influence with the Ukrainian Catholics to temper their separatist activities.

Protestants

The **Lutherans** were treated considerably more gently by Gorbachev's predecessors than their Catholic fellows. Centered principally in Latvia and Estonia, they were less worrisome because their population (about one million) was smaller; the foreign Lutheran Church does not equal the Vatican in its ties to Soviet believers; and until recently, the Latvians and Estonians did not manifest nearly as much nationalistic vitality as did the Lithuanians. This compliant circumstance has changed, however, and the Soviet Lutheran Church is central to much of the political activity in the two Baltic states. Major concessions have been won by Lutheran believers, including courses in Bible study—listed as the history of religion—that are being offered in Riga high schools by Lutheran pastors. The courses are offered at the request of parents and attendance is voluntary.[35]

The same benign policy was not enjoyed by other important Protestant sects, however. The Lutheran Church is the only establishment Protestant religion with many adherents in the Soviet Union. All the other important Protestant sects are evangelical, thus causing them to balk at Soviet authority and bringing them into conflict with the state.

During the early days of the revolution, the **Baptists** were largely left alone since they were anti-tsarist. They supported many of the social re-

---

[34]William D. Montalbano, "Archbishop, Selected for Vatican-Kremlin Talks," *The Los Angeles Times,* Dec. 12, 1989.

[35]Michael Parks, "Soviets Allow Bible Study Classes in Some Latvian State Schools," *The Los Angeles Times,* Oct. 30, 1988.

forms of the Bolsheviks, and they shared a common puritanical aversion to sexual license, hooliganism, and drinking. Favored by the regime, they organized their own collective farms and were even allowed to sponsor their own youth movement—the Khristomol. In 1928, however, they found themselves pressured to join the state's collectives and they resisted, bringing the full force of Stalin's suppression upon them. World War II brought some relief from persecution, and at the war's end the Baptists and related faiths organized the All-Union Council of Evangelical Christians-Baptists (AUCECB). Composed of Baptists, Pentecostalists, Methodists, and some Mennonite groups, the AUCECB managed to demonstrate significant unity until the era of Khrushchev's suppression (1960–1964), when a schism occurred that continues to this day. Objecting to being forced to pay taxes on church income, to being denied the right to hold Sunday school for their youth, and to being forbidden to proselytize, a large component of the AUCECB abandoned the registered organization, becoming illegal faiths. These resisters have consistently ignored Soviet regulations and saw their leaders arrested in the process. They have seized every opportunity to publicize their plight, even going so far as to demonstrate at Baptist services during visits by Billy Graham and other Western clergy. In 1989 the AUCECB published estimates of the number of Baptist believers for the first time in over four decades. It listed 2,000 Mennonite Brethren in independent congregations and 260,000 Baptists distributed among 15,000 unregistered churches and 8,000 registered churches. Unofficial estimates speculate that the true number of Protestant fundamentalists could be four times larger.[36]

Perhaps the most nettlesome evangelical group is the *Pentecostalists*. There are perhaps 500,000 of these believers, but no more than 200,000 have registered with the government. The only religion brought to the Soviet Union after the revolution, Pentecostalism was established in the USSR by Ivan Voroniyev, who returned to his homeland from the United States in order to spread the good word. The Pentecostalists had an especially difficult time with the government because they are committed to proselytizing new members, to schooling their children in the faith, and to refusing to bear arms. Among their other beliefs are faith healing, speaking in tongues, exorcism, and prophetic utterances.

Their nonconformist practices visited upon them perhaps the most persistent and harsh persecution except for the ill-fated Uniates and the Jews. Thousands of Pentecostalists were killed under Stalin, and thousands more were deported from their native Ukraine to remote villages in Siberia and Central Asia. During the Brezhnev era they were harassed by the authorities, denied all but the poorest jobs, assessed heavy fines, placed in prison, and committed to psychiatric hospitals. In some cases, their children were taken away to be raised in state homes, and because Soviet law does not recognize conscientious objectors, their young men are forced to serve in the military. A sober, frugal, hard-working people, they usually prosper even under these repressive conditions, but Soviet authorities

---

[36]"Soviet Evangelists Detail Membership," *The Los Angeles Times*, July 15, 1989.

often whipped up local resentment against them by charging that their prosperity is the result of aid from the United States.

Persistent in their faith and in their defiance of the authorities, the Pentecostalists publicly demonstrated, contacted the Western press, appealed to President Jimmy Carter for help, and applied for visas to the United States—all to little avail, however. In the most celebrated case, two families sought refuge in the American Embassy in Moscow from 1979–1983. Finally, after a long hunger strike, they were permitted to immigrate to Israel.

Gorbachev's liberalization policies have considerably reduced the persecution of the Protestant fundamentalists. Yet, their individualism and resistance to state control continue to make them uncomfortable in the Soviet Union. Thousands of them have taken advantage of relaxed emigration policies and have left the country.

While some Protestant fundamentalists flee the country, however, others enter it. Followers of the Rev. Sun Myung Moon, derisively called *Moonies,* have entered the Soviet Union to proselytize, and they have attracted people in major cities. This religion maintains that Moon, an intractable anti-Communist, is the second Messiah. Moonie missionaries have been especially effective in recruiting students from Soviet universities. As part of the initiation, over 2,000 converts have visited the United States as Rev. Moon's guests. "Going abroad is the sweetest candy for a Soviet person," said a Soviet official while trying to explain the religion's sudden popularity among the student elite.[37] But as Christianity grows in the Soviet Union, another major religion declines.

Jews

Any discussion of the Jewish religion in the Soviet Union must also include an examination of the Jews as a people, whether they practice the faith or not. Judaism is both a religion and a nationality, and even though all Jews may not practice their parents' faith, most are influenced by their cultural heritage. Nowhere in the world has the heritage of the Jewish people been more important to their welfare in the society than in Russia and the Soviet Union.

The first large infusions of Jews into the Russian Empire occurred in the eighteenth century, when Catherine the Great annexed western territories in the Partitions of Poland. Resented because they were viewed as "Christ killers" and because a few Jews became wealthy financiers and merchants, the Jews suffered Russian prejudice almost immediately. The Jews found themselves restricted to living within the **Jewish Pale,** which included parts of Lithuania, Poland, Byelorussia, and the Ukraine. Jews also were found in parts of the Caucasus and Central Asia. Although segregated, the Jews were allowed to keep their own laws and to provide their own social services until 1884. They were not allowed to own farmland; thus, they turned to mercantile pursuits and congregated in urban commu-

---

[37]Elizabeth Shogren, "Moonies in the U.S.S.R.," *The Los Angeles Times,* March 4, 1991.

nities. Their prosperity and tranquility were periodically interrupted by outbreaks of rampant anti-Semitism, resulting in **pogroms** during which Jews were burned out of their homes, beaten, looted, and even killed. The regimes of Alexander III and Nicholas II, the last two tsars, were often supportive of these abominations, a fact that contributed to the radicalization of many Jewish youths.

When the revolution came, the Jewish community found itself divided. Many supported the radical call; some, including Leon Trotsky and Julius Martov, became important leaders of the movement. Most of these activists, however, had abandoned their traditional faith for new theories. When they came to power, therefore, they had little patience with their fellow Jews who refused to abandon their traditions. Ironically, it has been through the support of secular Jews that a good many transgressions have been perpetrated on believing Jews by the Soviet government.[38]

Although Stalin's anti-Semitism was made clear before World War II, he embarked on his most vehement attack on the Jews in 1948 in an "anticosmopolitan" campaign that threatened to destroy the culture by eliminating Yiddish and Hebrew instruction, journals, and theater. Khrushchev managed to quell the persecution when he gained power, but after his time anti-Semitic government policies reemerged, albeit in a more subtle manner, especially following the 1967 Arab-Israeli War.

Criticized for their "cosmopolitanism" (foreign ties and interests) and for their ethnic and cultural cohesion at the same time, the Soviet Jews are trapped in a no-win situation, as long as they wish to maintain their heritage. The government has, it is claimed, a secret policy of excluding Jews from certain sensitive jobs and limiting their entrance to universities, medical schools, and institutes.[39] Also a larger than proportionate number of Jews are convicted of economic crimes. This phenomenon may be a matter of persecution, or it may be that, being denied well-paying jobs, Jews may engage more than others in such crimes.

Ironically, Gorbachev's liberalization policies have in a way made life much worse for the Jews. *Glasnost* has allowed open anti-Semitic literature and speech, although *Pravda* and other official publications condemn it. The ethnic violence in Azerbaijan and Central Asia has been turned on Jews as well as other minorities, forcing thousands to flee. In Moscow itself, gangs of roughs—many claiming membership in *Pamyat,* a rabidly antiSemitic organization—have threatened and assaulted Jews on the streets, in their homes, and at meetings. In early 1990 a rumor spread that a pogrom would begin in May in Moscow and Leningrad. Although no such event occurred, the rumor, which many people thought was supported by powerful government and party officials, terrified many people. There was also a strong strain of anti-Semitism in the elections for the USSR Congress of Peoples' Deputies, with some people openly encouraging the electorate not to vote for Jewish candidates.

[38]Lane pp. 449–451.

[39]Konstantin M. Simis, *USSR: The Corrupt Society*, trans. Jacqueline Edwards and Mitchell Schneider (New York: Simon & Schuster, 1982), pp. 232–233.

Persecution and relaxed emigration laws has encouraged huge numbers of Soviet Jews to leave. Between the late 1960s and the early 1980s, some 300,000 Jews left the country, with 51,330 leaving in 1979 alone. After 1979, however, Brezhnev again tightened up on Jewish emigration, but under Gorbachev, increasingly large numbers have been allowed to leave, until in 1989 almost all impediments to emigration were abolished. In that year 70,000 Jews left the country and perhaps as many as 200,000 emigrated in 1990.

It was estimated in 1990 that perhaps 750,000 of the nation's 1.8 million Jews wanted to leave the Soviet Union. The number of emigres is so great that flight reservations must be made eight months in advance. Almost 300,000 requests for emigration visas to the United States were received in 1989. In response the United States, which had always implored the Soviets to allow all the Jews who wanted to leave it do so, drastically limited the number of Soviet Jews it would accept annually, and it also limited the number of Jews it would receive from third countries.

Even so, the Jewish population is rapidly declining in the Soviet Union. Indeed, it is the only major nationality whose numbers have declined since the turn of the century. Emigration is not the only reason for the decline of Jewish citizens, however. Assimilation is another major, and perhaps even greater, reason. In the Soviet Union, one may establish nationality by simply stating the national group with which one identifies. The loss of their cultural heritage, combined with Soviet persecution, have led to an unusually large number of Jews marrying out of their nationality, while presumably others have adopted another racial designation so as to escape further persecution.

As to the Jewish religion itself, the same disintegration seems to be occurring. Many Jewish people know little about the religion and have never been to a synagogue. An unusually large number of Jews (over 90 percent) list themselves as atheists, and studies indicate that many Jews who emigrate to the West do so for greater economic opportunity rather than for religious freedom, although many sectarian Jews begin to practice their faith once they have left the Soviet Union.

The scientific and intellectual background of large numbers of Jews undoubtedly accounts for a loss of religious commitment, but the damage done to the culture by Soviet policy must also take a large share of the responsibility. Until recently, it was forbidden to teach Hebrew and Yiddish in schools, except for a few major universities. Jewish theater, music, journals, and newspapers were also suppressed, and the number of synagogues was drastically reduced.

Happily, Gorbachev's reforms have seen these policies reversed. In 1989 a Jewish cultural center was established in Moscow, featuring a library with Hebrew and Yiddish collections. The center has classes in the two languages, a theater group, and an exhibit of the holocaust. A *yeshiva* has also been established to school boys in their religion and to train rabbis. Over a dozen Yiddish newspapers are now published, and in 1990 Moscow held a Jewish film festival. Jewish organizations are also being encouraged. *Vaad,* an umbrella council for over 160 Jewish organizations in 75 cities sponsored a 1989 congress in Moscow and B'nai B'rith, once reviled in the Soviet Union, has established a chapter in the capital. Furthermore, in an effort to improve relations with Israel, Gorbachev has released several leading **refuseniks** (Jews refused the right to emigrate for political reasons); the government has cooperated with efforts to trace Raoul Wallenberg (a Swedish diplomat who saved thousands of Hungarian Jews from Hitler's gas chambers and later disappeared into Soviet Gulags); and the Bolshoi Ballet toured Israel in 1989 (it had not visited Israel since 1967).

These improvements have not stemmed the tide of Jews wishing to emigrate, however. Indeed, an increasing number of other nationalities, hoping to escape the political turmoil and economic problems of the country, are joining the exodus, as this Soviet joke implies.

A Jew applied for emigration to Israel.

"Why do you want to leave?" the Soviet official asked.

"I don't want to go," replied the Jews, "but my wife and her family want to emigrate to Israel."

"So let them go and you stay," the official suggested.

"Impossible!" said the applicant. "I'm the only Jew among them."

Buddhists

The fate befalling the Jews may also await the Buddhists. In 1917 the Soviet Union counted perhaps as many as 16,000 Buddhist monks in over 40 temples. Currently they number approximately 60, and they worship in only two temples; there are about 50,000 Buddhists in the Soviet Union. Most of them are found among the Buryat people in eastern Siberia. A second small group of Buddhists, the Kalmyks, lives along the lower Volga. This interesting ethnic group is the only Buddhist people who are indigenous to the European continent. There is no Buddhist monastery in the Soviet Union to train novices, and Tibetan, the language in which ceremonies are conducted, is taught only in Leningrad, thousands of miles away from the Buddhist populations. Consequently, Soviet Buddhists wishing to become monks must travel to Ulan Bator, Mongolia, or to India to receive their religious training.

Muslims

Islam was brought to Central Asia in the seventh century by invading Arabs. Adopting the new faith with great fervor, the Central Asians quickly became full partners in the Muslim world, giving it some of its greatest thinkers and scientists. When Moscow was still a squat, logged outpost of the Kievan state, Bukhara had become the seat of Arab learning in the

East, and Samarkand boasted splendid palaces, lavish tombs, and lovely madrasahs.

Islam spread also to Azerbaijan, to the Crimean Khanate, and to Kazan. Indeed, it once threatened Christian Moscow itself. Years of struggle between the two great people and faiths ensued. In celebration of Christian victories over Islam, Russian Orthodox churches are often capped with crosses that include the Muslim half-moon at their base.

The long-standing historical difficulties between the Russian Orthodox and Muslims are not the only factors causing friction between these Oriental people and their European fellows. Islam has certain transcendental qualities that cause many Soviet Muslims to feel that they are part of a greater Muslim nation, far exceeding the boundaries of the Soviet Union. Additionally, Islam, perhaps more than any other religion in the Soviet Union, demands precise conduct of its followers during every aspect of their lives. Among the most persistent Muslim traditions are circumcision, arranged marriages, prepubescent weddings, kidnapping brides, ransoming fiancees, and self-immolation by disgraced women. Moreover, the intensely paternalistic Muslims will not allow their women to work out of the home, and they tend to follow the advice of powerful elders and shamans. Perhaps the most dangerous of all are the **Sufi.** These secret brotherhoods, complete with secret rites and discipline, are especially popular in the Transcaucasus, but authorities believe they are spread throughout the Soviet Muslim area. These ancient organizations are very popular, comprising perhaps half of all the believers in some areas. Conjecture about the political potential of these clandestine groups must trouble the Soviet leadership.[40]

Their estimated 50 million believers make the Soviet Muslims the fifth largest Islamic population in the world after Indonesia, Pakistan, Bangladesh, and India. Besides the Central Asians and Azerbaijans, there are many Muslims in Europe and Siberia, including the Tatars and Bashkirs. The Transcaucasus Muslims are mostly of the *Shiite* sect, whereas most of the others are *Sunni*. The Shiites have their headquarters in Baku; the majority Sunni sect is seated in Tashkent.

Today there are about 1,400 registered mosques, most of which have been opened since Gorbachev became general secretary. However, there are an estimated 18,000 mosques that have not been officially registered. Before the 1917 revolution there were over 26,000 mosques serving a much smaller population. The number of imams and mullahs is still very low, about 21,000, but recent relaxations of government policy have increased the number of students in the nation's madrasahs. Yet, Cyrillic translations of the Koran still do not exist. In 1990 Saudi Arabia sent one million copies of the Koran to the Soviet Union, but very few Soviet Muslims read Arabic. Muslim programs are regularly broadcast on Central Asian television transmissions, but only 25 to 30 pilgrims are allowed to travel to Mecca annually.

Muslim leaders have been among the most compliant and flexible in

[40]Carrère d'Encausse, pp. 246, 254–255, 260–261.

the Soviet Union. Claiming that there is no essential conflict between Marxism and Islam, the mullahs focus on such common beliefs as eliminating poverty and injustice and protecting women, children, and the elderly. The Soviet goals of freedom, equality, and fraternity are completely compatible, the mullahs say, with the Koran.

When Muslim practice has conflicted with Soviet law, the Muslim leaders have bent enough to satisfy the politicians. Veils and polygamy are forbidden, extreme fasting over Ramadan (a month-long period of abstinence) is discouraged, sacrificial slaughter of animals has been replaced by giving monetary offerings to the mosque of equal value to the spared animal, pilgrimages to Mecca may be made by proxy (unique in the Muslim world), and believers are required to pray only once a day rather than the usual five times so as not to disturb work schedules.[41]

These pragmatic compromises have alienated many believers from their religious leaders, which gives impetus to the Sufi and the large number of unregistered mosques. The people have taken matters into their own hands in other ways as well. In 1989 huge public demonstrations in Tashkent forced the removal of the chairman of the Muslim Board for Central Asia, an important religious governing agency. This government-approved functionary was obsequious with the authorities and he also drank heavily, a major violation of Muslim law. *Wahhabism,* a fundamentalist Muslim sect, is becoming very powerful in some parts of Central Asia, especially in Tashkent, the Soviet Union's fourth largest city. Extremists are demanding that there be no limit on the number of people who visit Mecca each year and some of them have called for the secession from the Soviet Union and the formation of an Islamic republic. Worse yet, gangs of fundamentalists have terrorized peaceful citizens. Enraged by the women not following the dictates of the true faith, they have attacked school girls who go out without veils and slashed the faces of women on the street who had no veils. The growing fundamentalism has also caused an increasing number of women to burn themselves alive when they were accused of disgraceful conduct, infidelity, or promiscuity. Between 1986 and 1987 alone, 270 women self-immolated.[42]

These fundamentalist stirrings have caused Soviet authorities considerable apprehension. Although it still seems unlikely that Central Asia will attempt to leave the Soviet Union, the growing unrest in the region and its burgeoning population demand serious attention.

In this chapter, we have studied two powerful influences of the diverse Soviet society: the nationalities and religion. In each of these areas we find powerful cultural forces at work, and each is rife with significant political implications. However, many social factors also must be addressed if the Soviet political society is to continue its modernization and viability. We shall now examine some of the most important of these social stress points.

[41]Carrère d'Encausse, pp. 231–235.
[42]Richard N. Ostling, "Islam Regains Its Voice," *Time Magazine,* April 10, 1989.

chapter 11

Social Stress Points

Having examined the most politically potent cultural factors in the Soviet system, we will now investigate the social factors that bear hard on the society. This chapter focuses on several social problems, including the status of women; the family; various dissident movements; and crime, vice, and corruption. Each of these seemingly disparate categories relates to the other in that each is, in part, a reflection of the political, cultural, and social reality unique to the Soviet Union and each gives insight to Soviet political society.

WOMEN

"A hen is not a bird, and a woman is not a person." This old Russian proverb gives us some idea of the position women, at least rural women, held in prerevolutionary tsarist society. The *Domostroi* (Law of the Home), which was written by a monk and widely distributed during the reign of Ivan the Terrible, instructed men to beat their wives and women were ordered to accept the discipline without complaint. A woman's position in the Muslim culture within the empire was even more subordinated.

Interestingly, however, the social condition of Russian women in the nineteenth century was in some ways advanced compared to that of women in the rest of Europe. Women were allowed by Russian law to own and inherit property.[1] Also, some Russian political activists preceded their Western counterparts in a concern for women's rights. Early reformers, including Alexander Herzen and Vissarion Bielinski, called for the liberation of women. However, the liberation of women was generally viewed in a larger context. It was usually seen as only a component of more general revolutionary goals. An inordinate number of women were involved in the radical cause during the Russian Revolution. Perhaps as many as 15 to 20 percent of the revolutionaries of Russia were women. Largely attracted to the *Narodniki* during the early period, female revolutionaries were generally accorded considerable respect and equality by their male counterparts.[2]

Among the best-known women revolutionaries were Yekaterina Breshkovskaya, Vera Figner, Olga Lyubatovich, Pvaskovya Ivanovskaya, Vera Zasulich, Elizaveta Kovalskaya, Aleksandra Kollontai, Inessa Armand, Yekaterina Kuskova, and Nadezhda Krupskaya (Lenin's wife). Not hesitating at the violent aspects of the revolution, many women were involved in assassinations and robberies for the cause. For example, Sofya Perovskaya aided in the 1881 assassination of Tsar Alexander II. Between 1880 and 1890, 21 of the 43 Russian radicals sentenced to hard labor for terrorism were women.

Women participated in large numbers in the tsarist labor force. Always active in agriculture, women were also heavily employed in industry. Russian factory owners often preferred women and children in the mills because they could be paid less than adult male workers and were usually more compliant with the pitiful conditions in which they were made to work. By 1913 women made up about one-third of the total industrial labor force. As World War I called more and more men to arms, women found themselves dominating professions like nursing and education. In all, they made up about 40 percent of the entire Russian work force. In fact, in some industries like garment and textile manufacturing, they constituted well in excess of a majority of all workers.[3]

When the Bolsheviks took power, they immediately set to the task of creating equal social conditions for the nation's women. They lionized the exploits of Civil War heroines like Maria Popova, who single-handedly turned back a White Army charge with a machine gun. The Bolsheviks abolished the veil in Central Asia and elevated women to positions of authority in the party, the government, and the economy. They were the first to declare the emancipation of women. Even so, the party believed that more had to be done if women were to be equal in the society. Harkening to Marx's call, they believed that women would have to become productive in the economy if they were ever to enjoy liberation. Even though women generally endured terrible suppression under tsarist employers, Lenin re-

---

[1] Gail Warshofsky Lapidus, *Women in Soviet Society* (Berkeley: University of California Press, 1978), p. 28.

[2] Marjorie Wall Bingham and Susan Hill Gross, *Women in the U.S.S.R.* (St. Louis Park, MN: Glenhurst Publications, 1980), pp. 98–106.

[3] Lapidus, pp. 31, 37–39, 49, 164.

garded the growing percentage of women in the prerevolutionary labor force as a positive step toward social equality. Once in power, he quickly proclaimed equal pay for equal work and equal educational opportunity for women.

Throughout the 1920s the mobilization of women in the work force was pursued as a social rather than as an economic policy; total equality for women was the ultimate goal. But in the 1930s, as Stalin transformed society with his five-year plans, the mobilization of women workers became an economic policy. Women were pressured to believe that if they were unemployed they were not complete persons and were setting a bad example for their children. Striving to create an industrialized economy, Stalin subordinated the social objective of women's equality to the production mandates of the plan.[4] During World War II women comprised over half of the entire work force, and because of the enormous number of male deaths during the war, women have remained numerically dominant in the work force ever since, except for a brief period after the war. Unfortunately, however, although Soviet propaganda makes much of the state's commitment to women's equality, the social goal has never again been as important as the economic motivations for employing women. One of the results of this economic emphasis is that since the 1920s men have seldom been encouraged to liberate themselves from their traditional chauvinism, and women continue to suffer oppression at their hands.[5]

Contemporary Trends

Women steadily increased as a percentage of the labor force from the time of the revolution, growing from 25 percent in 1922 and peaking in 1945 at 56 percent. After the war, the percentage declined a bit as men returned from battle (it must be remembered that many women also fought with the Red Army) and were absorbed into the work force. By the mid-1950s women constituted only 46 percent of the labor force. Yet, the need to increase industrial production called for a new infusion of workers in the factories since the Soviet government basically relied on a labor-extensive strategy. Throughout the 1960s women entered factories, offices, and the professions until in 1970 they leveled off at about 51 percent of the work force.

Currently the Soviet Union employs a greater percentage of its working-age women than any other industrial state. Of all Soviet women between 20 and 55 years old, almost 90 percent hold jobs. Indeed, very few women remain to be added to the labor supply except in Central Asia, where cultural biases still tend to dissuade many women from leaving the home to work.[6] Further, in 1928, 90 percent of all working women were

---

[4]Michael Paul Sacks, "The Place of Women," in *Contemporary Soviet Society*, ed. Jerry G. Pankhurst and Michael Paul Sacks (New York: Praeger, 1980), p. 234.

[5]Lapidus, p. 5.

[6]Dan N. Jacobs and Theresa M. Hill, "Soviet Ethnic Policy in the 1980s: Theoretical Consistency and Political Reality," in *Soviet Politics*, ed. Joseph L. Nogee (New York: Praeger, 1985), pp. 178–179.

employed in agriculture, while today the number has dipped to about one-third.[7] Approximately 48 percent of all factory jobs are held by women; women still hold about 56 percent of the jobs in agriculture.

The distribution of women in the labor force is also very interesting, if somewhat inconsistent. Generally, it can be said that women dominate the lowest-paying jobs. Yet, as a result of enhanced educational opportunities, Soviet women are also found in large percentages among the professions and semiprofessions. Women hold 60 percent of all post-secondary degrees.

In industry, women are found in large numbers among the lowest-paid and most physically demanding jobs. Soviet law prohibits women from doing some of the heaviest and most dangerous work, such as coal mining, but these laws are not strongly enforced. The Ministry of Railways, for example, reports that no less than 65,000 women are employed in laying and repairing track. Similarly, Soviet law prohibits women from being nighttime security guards, yet over 4 million women—many more than the number of men—have such jobs. Almost all of the nation's janitors and street sweepers are women.

Women take most of the jobs in public catering, textile manufacturing, and garment production. At the same time, women dominate low-level white-collar jobs and thus make up the bulk of nursery and elementary school teachers, clerks, telephone operators, postal workers, bank tellers, and insurance sales representatives. In the professions, women represent 25 percent of the judges, 38 percent of the secondary school directors, 44 percent of the engineers, 45 percent of the teachers in higher education, 50 percent of the specialists working in technical institutes, 75 percent of the dentists and public school teachers, 77 percent of the doctors, 86 percent of the economists and planners, and 98 percent of the nurses. Men dominate the legal professions and account for the majority of composers, artists, radiotelegraph operators, plumbers, wood workers, transportation workers, machine operators, and metallurgists.[8]

The large number of Soviet women in the professions is a testament to the policy of equal educational opportunity and to the openness of occupations that in other societies are monopolized by men. Another noteworthy achievement is the Soviet policy of paying its workers equally for equal work, regardless of gender. Regrettably, however, the Soviet employment record is not as enviable as it might appear. The fact is that whether at the menial or professional level, women tend to dominate in the low-paying job categories. Further, in almost every field, including those in which women dominate numerically, they tend to stay at the lower levels longer than men before being promoted, and their numbers tend to decrease dramatically as the responsibility and pay increase. Men tend to receive better assignments than women, resulting in a disproportionate number of women doctors, for instance, being assigned to work in rural areas while most male doctors are found in the cities.

[7]Lapidus, pp. 161, 167, 228.
[8]Sacks, pp. 237–238; Lapidus, p. 173.

Women make up 51 percent of the labor force, yet only 12 percent of the managers are women. They comprise 60 percent of all specialists with post-secondary degrees, but only 5.4 percent of all top executive positions. They hold 50 percent of the seats on the Academy of Sciences, but only 2 of its 28 section heads are women. This tendency is consistent even in industries in which women are numerically preponderant. For example, women constitute 85 percent of the labor force in textile manufacturing but hold only 15 percent of the assistant supervisor jobs. Looking at the situation in reverse, a full 70 percent of the women in the machine-construction industry occupied the least-skilled, lowest-paid labor categories, while only 17 percent of the male workers are found at the lowest levels of that industry.[9] While 77 percent of all Soviet doctors are women, only about 60 percent of all the chief doctors and hospital administrators are women, and women make up only 6 percent of the nation's surgeons.

This disparate situation is even more striking on the farms. We have already learned that young men who get a look at city life while serving in the military are often very reluctant to return to the tedium of the farm. To encourage them to "stay down on the farm after they've seen Smolensk," farm authorities give them favorable jobs, leaving the arduous and dirty tasks to women. Men receive the best training for jobs on the farm; indeed only 10 percent of the students in agricultural technical schools are women. There are very few female farm managers, and only 15 percent of the farm machine operators are women. Almost 86 percent of the women on the farms do the poor-paying drudgery of manual labor. Reviewing figures like this, Khrushchev was once moved to quip, "It turns out that it is men who do the administering [on the farm] and the women who do the work."[10]

It is clear that the Soviet system offers women a great deal of opportunity for employment. It is equally obvious that social mobility is available to women chiefly through achieving high levels of education, allowing them to move into professional fields. Unfortunately, most of the fields in which women are so numerous, including teaching, medicine, and dentistry, are low-paying occupations in "the workers' state." Further, once in a job or profession, women find it difficult to advance through the ranks into positions of authority and responsibility.

Women find themselves at such disadvantage in the Soviet Union for several reasons. To begin with, the notorious male chauvinism in the Soviet Union undoubtedly contributes a great deal to their difficulty. Also, women are generally perceived to lack initiative and ambition on the job. Few women express a desire to improve their careers. Rather, most women usually harbor little aspiration for advancement and cite economic rather than career reasons for taking employment. Women also carry heavy burdens at home, as we will learn in more detail later. The duties of child care and housekeeping do not lighten for the average working Soviet woman. With time and energy devoted to domestic chores, women find little oppor-

[9]Sacks, pp. 236–237.
[10]Lapidus, pp. 177–179, 188, 236–237.

tunity to prepare for advancement. Finally, women are not proportionately represented in the party; hence many important positions have traditionally been denied them.[11]

Women in the political elite.   Gail Lapidus finds that Soviet women tend to eschew politics and political power. Before open elections were allowed, the number of women in government positions was maintained at about 30 percent; recently the figure has fallen off steeply. The number of women in government at the union republic level is higher, but only about 16 percent of those elected to the USSR Congress of Peoples' Deputies are women. Only one woman presently sits on the USSR Council of Ministers and very few women have previously made it to such high government posts. Among them, Aleksandra Kollontai was the Peoples' Commissar of State Welfare in the early years of Bolshevik rule; later Maria S. Korigina was minister of health; Yekaterina Furtseva (rumored to have been Khrushchev's paramour) was minister of culture in the 1950s; and from 1988–1990 Aleksandra P. Biryukova was vice-chair of the Council of Ministers and chair of the Bureau for Social Development.

The statistics are about the same in the Communist Party. Even though about 30 percent of the membership is female, less than a dozen women sit on the Central Committee. Furtseva and Biryukova are the only women to have been elected to the Secretariat and they also held candidate positions on the Politburo. Galina Semyonova, elected in 1990, is the first woman to be a full member of the Politburo.

In addition to women who have reached prominence in formal office, Gorbachev's wife, Raisa, is also an important figure. The only first lady of the Soviet Union to become a public figure since Krupskaya (Lenin's wife), she is a well-educated person and frequently accompanies her husband on travels inside the country and out. She meets with first ladies in other countries, and she has been very active within the Soviet Union encouraging certain projects, especially in the fields of literature and art. Her prominence is somewhat resented in this paternalistic and conservative society. Some people criticize her fine clothes and her spending sprees abroad, while others grumble that the mere wife of a leader has no right to assume such a high profile. Mrs. Gorbachev has become so well known that the Soviets tell this joke.

> Gorbachev visited a factory and introduced himself to a worker, "I'm Mikhail Gorbachev."
>
> "Oh," said the worker, "I didn't recognize you without your wife."

Although their representation at the highest levels of government is not at all strong, Soviet women probably enjoy more influence in public affairs than is apparent upon superficial examination. Since 1920, when

[11]Sacks, pp. 233, 236; Lapidus, pp. 194–195, 227.

women made up only 1 percent of the local party leadership, their numbers have steadily increased until now the percentage of local party first secretaries who are female exceeds the percentage of women in the party. Furthermore, the preponderance of the nation's planners and economists (86 percent)—those people who develop the information by which policy is made and who make many of the important decisions about the administration of policy —are women.[12] Anyone who has a passing acquaintance with the workings of modern government cannot be unimpressed with the power enjoyed by the technical staff serving policy makers. This influence, enormous in Western societies, is undoubtedly even greater in the highly centralized and heavily bureaucratized Soviet system.

Even so, the fact remains that women are vastly underrepresented in the power elite of the Soviet Union. Quite beyond the question of a bias against women in positions of power, which may exist among the male elite who determine who shall join them in the upper echelons of the system, Gail Lapidus suggests several other reasons for this glaring deficit. Party work demands an enormous commitment of time, energy, and mobility if one is to advance through the ranks. The burden carried by women in the home (discussed in the next section) no doubt impedes all but the most talented and driven women from giving the necessary effort to distinguish themselves in the eyes of superiors. Although personal data about party members are scarce, the number of widows and divorced women who must care for their children could be another significant factor preventing them from being sufficiently mobile and committed to party work. Further, it is speculated that Soviet girls may suffer from early socialization biases that dissuade them from seeking political power. Finally, Professor Lapidus suggests that women, regardless of the educational opportunity and occupational mobility available, are too new to the Soviet infrastructure to provide a significant number of candidates to the power elite.[13]

Nevertheless, women enjoy many advantages in Soviet society. They benefit from virtually unparalleled educational and employment opportunities, although these are clearly tainted with inequities. They find themselves protected, albeit very imperfectly, from the heaviest and most dangerous occupations but are prominent in an enormous breadth of jobs from construction work to space flight, from hand-milking cows to doing advanced scientific research. They retire at age 55, five years earlier than most men, and they are consistently given lighter sentences than men for violations of the law. The courts also favor women in child custody battles during divorce hearings. Pregnancy brings up to a full year of maternity leave, and many children are cared for in nursery schools while their parents work. Yet, as extensive as these benefits and advantages are, they only partially mitigate what is an extraordinarily hard life for Soviet women.

The "Double Burden"

Women in Soviet society carry a "double burden," one of grueling proportions. Working a full day in the clinic, shop, office, factory, or field,

---

[12]Sacks, pp. 239–240.
[13]Lapidus, pp. 225–226.

the average woman returns home after spending an hour or so shopping. Once home, she usually is forced to plunge into the housework and cooking. She must not only make dinner but must also make lunches for the children, her husband, and herself for the next day. The typical Soviet husband does only a minimum amount of shopping and even less cooking or housework—these being "women's work." The new day sees the woman rise early to fix breakfast, get the children ready for school, and get herself ready for work. Then the cycle begins all over again. Weekends find women absorbed in cleaning chores that could not be done before—washing clothes, mending, and scrubbing. Some women call their household tasks their "second shift," and Soviet statistics indicate that more time is spent on household chores (275 billion hours annually) than on the job (240 billion hours).[14]

This arduous existence is the result not only of male chauvinism but also of too little effort and resources from the state to ease women's burden. Most women still do the laundry by hand; about 70 percent of the washing machines that do exist still have hand wringers. Refrigerators, although more plentiful than before, are small, necessitating daily shopping. Vacuum cleaners, sewing machines, clothes dryers, and dishwashers are archaic, scarce, or nonexistent. According to one study, only 15 percent of the housework is mechanized. Precooked or frozen meals are virtually unknown, and microwave ovens are a rarity.[15]

Additionally, the child-care facilities for preschoolers are inadequate in number and quality. Thus, a majority of mothers must rely on other methods for caring for their children while they are at work. Often expressing guilt about leaving their children, mothers turn their youngsters over to grandmothers or neighbors, if they are lucky. The less fortunate must sometimes leave their young charges completely unattended, creating legions of latchkey children.

Psychological anxiety and physical fatigue among Soviet women are compounded by considerable inconveniences and discomforts. Soviet women complain that foundation garments are unattractive, bulky, and ill-fitting. Sanitary napkins are very scarce. Instead, women use cotton battings that come in but a single size (as do Soviet intrauterine devices) or rags that are washed and used repeatedly. Gynecological care is often poor; one in three Soviet women has gynecological problems and miscarriages are common. Maternity wards are unsanitary and patient care is often haphazard, lackadaisical, and neglected—strange behavior in a society that wants to increase its birthrate. More than three times the percentage of Soviet women die while giving birth as in the United States. In 1989 and 1990 over 80 children contracted AIDS in Volgograd and Elista hospitals because they were given injections with syringes that had not been sterilized. Some of these children were nursing and passed the disease on to their mothers whose nipples had cracked.

[14]*USSR '90 Yearbook* (Moscow: Novosti Press Agency, 1990), p. 290.

[15]Robert Gillette, "Housework After Day at the Factory," *The Los Angeles Times*, March 9, 1982.

Francine de Plessix Gray reports that one of the most popular books of fiction is Natalya Baruskaya's *Nedelya Kak Nedelya* (A Week Like Any Other). It pictures Soviet women coping with all these problems without much help from their husbands.[16] Soviet women spend an estimated 30 to 40 hours per week performing household chores, child care, and shopping; Soviet men spend between one-quarter to one-half as much time in these pursuits.

> Spending their extra leisure at sporting events, visiting with friends, or all too often sleeping off binges, Soviet husbands joke about their wives' unfortunate circumstances by quipping that "a woman's nightstand is a stove."

Beleaguered though they are, Soviet women struggle to assert their identity, and they have begun to virtually glorify the distinctive traits of their gender.

Feminityism and feminism. Soviet women have recently become obsessed with increasing their femininity or "womanliness." They increasingly complain about the heavy work they are assigned in fields and factories and they are becoming very fashion and diet conscious. More women have their hair done professionally now than at any previous time, and cosmetics, perfume, and fashion magazines are in high demand.[17] Many women also want to be freed from the work place so that they can spend more time in the home and with their children. These desires led to Gorbachev's 1987 statement about "what we should do to make it possible for women to return to their purely womanly mission."[18] This comment was widely interpreted in the West as chauvinistic, but actually it was a response to a deeply felt desire among Soviet women. Paradoxically perhaps, Gorbachev has also called for more women to be elevated to responsible positions in the party.

Although "feminityism" has attracted a wide distaff following, feminism has not. No state in history has done more in formal policy to liberate women from second-class status. Yet, most of these policies have suffered under the pressure of economic expedience and deep-rooted social bigotry. In the words of one frustrated and exhausted Soviet mother, "They emancipated us but forgot to tell the men." A short-lived effort to organize a Western-style women's liberation movement ended abruptly with the 1980 exile of its three leaders. Even with Gorbachev's liberalization policies, however, feminism has not taken hold. Perhaps the disinterest in feminism accrues from the fact that Soviet women have already achieved the occupational mobility sought by many Western women. Indeed, they have been

[16]Francine du Plessix Gray, *Soviet Women* (New York: Doubleday, 1989), pp. 28–29.
[17]Lapidus, p. 232.
[18]Jill Smolowe, "Heroines of Soviet Labor," *Time Magazine,* June 6, 1988.

"liberated" into unhealthy levels of physically hard work and, between their homes and outside jobs, 16-hour workdays. Hence, the movement is toward "womanliness" rather than feminism.

On the other hand, Soviet women often hold men in contempt and frequently express such feeling among themselves—to say nothing about sharing their abjuration with their husbands. Francine du Plessix Gray suggests that there is a deep-seated feeling of superiority over men felt by Soviet women that may be traceable to ancient times. Women were very powerful in the Slavic tribal communities and their pagan religion worshiped a self-inseminating "Great Mother" god, and male gods were inferior to her. Russian folklore is replete with heroic female figures and powerful witches. The Russian Orthodox priests warned of the power women had as sexual temptresses, but at the same time, the virgin mother is perhaps more prominent in the Russian Orthodox religion than in any other Christian sect. Even today, the people refer to "Mother Russia" and to the Volga River as the "little mother."[19] Women, according to Gray, despise the Slavic male tendency toward passivity in domestic relations, yet she quotes a University of Leningrad professor, Elvira Ossipova, as saying "Russian women have a need to control that verges on the tyrannical, the sadistic . . . like no other women I can think of in history."[20]

Underscoring their contempt for their menfolk, Gray recounts an anecdote Russian women tell comparing the clumsiness of Russian men with the style of Georgian men—notorious philanderers.

> A Georgian man will have a dozen mistresses and keep all of them hidden from his wife, thus preserving his marriage. A Russian man will bring his mistress home and ask his wife to polish the woman's shoes. Then he will torment himself about which woman to keep and which to turn out. Finally, in a fit of indecision, he will commit suicide.

Government Policies for Women

Overtly feminist or not, Soviet women have begun to loudly voice their discontent with the socioeconomic system. They want more control over their lives, flexible work and schedules, part-time as opposed to full-time jobs, time-saving household appliances, supermarkets where they can buy what they need in a single stop, and so on. Gorbachev, paying more attention to women than any Soviet leader since Lenin, has heard their demands. At the Twenty-eighth Party Congress (1990) he chided his colleagues for not electing more women (less than 10 percent of the congress members were women) and called for more women to become involved in politics. "I think we should be ashamed of ourselves now that we see

---

[19]Andrew Katell of Associated Press, "Consumerism, Not Love, Rules Soviet Marriages," *Escondido Times-Advocate,* June 17, 1990.

[20]Gray, p. 17.

women take an active part in many countries," he told the congress. "Just take a look at the assembly—how many women are there among the delegates?" To back up his words, he secured the election of Galina Semyonova, the first full member of the Politburo. Her portfolio is expressly women, children, and the family, and she has since played an active part in public affairs.

Gorbachev has also encouraged the activities of the newly reinvigorated Soviet Women's Committee. Composed of 240,000 women's councils across the country, this organization has several important goals, including

> Assuring that divorced men pay child support
>
> Giving women paid time to upgrade skills and education
>
> Establishing retraining programs for unemployed women (Soviet expectations are that more women than men will be unemployed by perestroika's reforms)
>
> Improving the environment to protect unborn children
>
> Achieving reform in the military so that recruits are not brutalized by peers or superiors
>
> Fostering professional advancement for women
>
> Changing school curricula so that boys, as well as girls, learn to do household chores
>
> Encouraging sex education classes
>
> Promoting fatherhood instruction for young men.

Gorbachev has also increased maternity leave benefits and child-care subsidies, and he has encouraged plant managers to develop flexible work schedules (some are experimenting with six-hour workdays for women) and part-time jobs for women. Additionally, he has given women's interests a dedicated voice on the Politburo.

THE FAMILY

These difficult conditions, together with other economic and social pressures, place enormous stress on the Soviet family, forcing the divorce rate to its highest point in the history of the land. Taking their signal from Marx and Engels, the Bolshevik leaders at first assaulted the family as an anachronistic bourgeois institution. Aleksandra Kollontai, an Old Bolshevik and government minister who became notorious for her views on free love, said in 1919 that "the family is ceasing to be a necessity for its members as well as for the state."[21]

Motivated by revolutionary verve, the state promulgated incredibly lax divorce, abortion, and legitimacy laws. Stalin's puritanical values led him to tighten up, and women found themselves forced to bear more than their share of the social responsibility for marriage and child care, while

---

[21]"Sex in the Kremlin's Shadow," *Time Magazine*, July 23, 1979.

A young Uzbek woman in traditional dress sits in the garden of an active mosque in Tashkent. (Photo provided by Louis and Helen Van Moppes.)

they were simultaneously urged to take jobs in order that they contribute to national productivity. Although the balance between men's and women's rights and responsibility has been redressed somewhat, much more is obviously left to be done.

Quite aside from government policy, however, the forces of urbanization and modernization are bringing social pressures upon the family, wresting it asunder. The extended family has always been an important social institution in the Soviet Union, as it has been throughout Europe. Yet, this stabilizing phenomenon is disintegrating as children leave their parents on the farms to go to the cities and as young couples seek to improve their lives by moving out of their parents' cramped apartments. The *babushki*, the custodians of Russian children for the past millennia, are less and less able to tend their former charges as grandparents find themselves living at increasing distances from their progeny. Denied the warmth and security of loving but stern grandparents, children find little comfort in the home where both parents have to work to make ends meet.

Squeezed into tiny apartments, families often share quarters with relatives and friends; some must even share kitchen and bathroom facilities with neighbors. As often as not, the family outgrows its apartment, forcing parents to share their bedroom with children or permanently use the couches as beds. Virtually living on top of each other, family members endure serious stress. Children hear parents argue over money, drink, or other problems; adults become frustrated at their private lives being necessarily tempered and muted because of family members sleeping close by; and young couples, lacking private automobiles or apartments, find it almost impossible to be alone in this land of busybodies. The dearth of entertainment and other psychological outlets forces the family back upon itself, spending its time walking together in parks, watching television, or talking together at the tiny kitchen table. All these things, and more, demand an amount of mutual respect and consideration that would test even the most loving family. No wonder that Soviet family members—father, mother, sisters, and brothers—frequently take separate vacations, or that the family seems to be disintegrating, or that the divorce rate is skyrocketing.

Marriage, the cement of most families, has had a controversial and varied history in the Soviet Union. From a society that often relied on such traditional institutions as matchmaking, the people of the Russian Empire were thrust into the most radical social experiments attempted to that date. In Bolshevik law, marriage was made virtually superfluous; only cohabitation was needed for a legal union. Furthermore, divorce could be accomplished through the mails; abortion was permitted for any reason; and bigamy, incest, adultery, illegitimacy, and homosexuality were officially winked at by a benevolent legal code. Yet, the Stalinist era brought a deliberalization in social matters. Formal marriage and divorce were required again; legal abortion was made more difficult; illegitimate children lost their property and family rights; and male homosexuality was punished. After Stalin, the laws were relaxed somewhat, but the family and marriage have remained important institutions in Soviet law.

Both government policy (because of the declining birthrate) and societal pressure encourage women to marry early. Mothers and peers warn unwed female teenagers that because of the shortage of men, if they are not married by age 21, they may never be. Also, there exists the feeling that unwed women are morally suspect. As a consequence, the average age for girls to wed is falling. In 1988 the average woman married three years younger than two decades before; one in four girls wed at eighteen.[22] As shortages of consumer goods increase, some young people are apparently getting married, or at least filing papers to do so, in order to get preference at certain stores. *Gemini,* a chain of shops for brides and grooms with an unusual selection and abundance of goods, accepts purchases only from officially betrothed couples. Consequently, some young people pay the 15 ruble fee to apply for a marriage license and are issued a *Gemini* coupon booklet; they then shop for scarce items in the special stores. If they do not wish to marry, they simply let the license expire without appearing for the ceremony. Many youngsters apparently go through this charade time and again.[23]

[22]Gray, p. 59.

[23]Murray Seeger, "Russian Families, Once Bulwark of Society Gaining More Attention from Regime," *The Los Angeles Times,* April 11, 1981.

Since Stalin's time, the position of women has improved legally but perhaps has been retarded socially. In fact, contemporary Soviet law, unlike some Western jurisprudence, leaves women's rights virtually untouched by marriage. Women may withhold sexual privileges from their husbands; they are not legally obliged to perform households tasks; they enjoy equal property rights; and they may refuse to accompany their husbands should they change domicile. Although men are required to pay child support, they are not obliged to provide financial support for their wives since women are supposed to be self-supporting and independent—thus liberated.

Society, however, still demands the traditional roles of women, as one might gather from preceding sections of this chapter. To make matters worse, the devastation of males during Stalin's purges, World War II, and the rising death rate among young males leave women with few choices for husbands, forcing them to settle for conditions in their marriages that they might otherwise have avoided. Women have found themselves caught up in unequal unions, making life more difficult than it might otherwise have been.

Among the most unsatisfying aspects of married life for women appears to be sex. Madam Kollontai once said that sex should be "as free as a glass of water," yet an unusually high percentage of Soviet women are frigid. The director of the Zhordania Institute for Human Reproduction in Tbilisi, Georgia, claims that an extraordinary percentage of Soviet women have never had an orgasm.[24] This abnormality is attributed to psychological repression among women who have been taught that sex is "dirty." It was a forbidden topic before glasnost, with the media being forbidden even to mention masturbation or prostitution. Also, women are sometimes traumatized by the brutal sexual aggression of their mates. Not only are Soviet men often unschooled in lovemaking, but many attack their spouses in drunken rages.[25]

Even so, a growing fascination with sex seems to be occurring. Underground pornographic literature, called *sexizdat,* enjoys relatively wide circulation. Since the glasnost reforms, this literature is openly sold on the streets, and Soviet films, television, and art shows have begun to present nude scenes. *Advice to Young Couples,* a book featuring explicit sex, was a best seller in 1989, and lonely hearts ads and columns are commonly found in the popular press. At the same time, the number of people engaging in premarital sex has soared. A sociological journal, *Sotisologicheskoe Issledovaniye,* reported in 1988 that 60 percent of the young men and women polled regularly engage in premarital sex. Premarital sex is also increasingly common among teenagers.

One of the consequences of this growing promiscuity is an increase in the rate of illegitimate children born into the society. Indeed, 10 percent of all babies born in the Soviet Union each year are illegitimate, a distinct

[24]Gray, pp. 13, 19.
[25]Gray, pp. 19–20.

increase over that of the 1960s. Perhaps the most interesting thing about this development, however, is that the greatest increase in this phenomenon is among adults between 20 and 29 years of age rather than among teenagers. Since abortion is inexpensive and easy to arrange, most illegitimate births among adults would appear to be deliberate. A growing number of women in their twenties and early thirties are opting to have families without encumbering themselves by marriage. As one young woman told Francine du Plessix Gray, "I, personally, wish to bring up a child by myself, without a man. A man! Who needs a *second* child?"[26] The state so desperately wants its population to grow that it has actually begun to modify its cool attitude toward illegitimate births. Some authorities asked people to change their attitude about illegitimate children and accept them as wanted members of society.[27]

Child care in the Soviet Union is very traditional by contemporary standards. Many Soviet infants are still swaddled by their parents. Babies are bound in a tight wrapping called a *kosinka* to protect them from scratching or otherwise injuring themselves. Fearing that they will suffocate on their stomachs, Russian parents always lay babies on their backs. The Soviet people believe in natural feeding; almost all Soviet babies are breast-fed. So convinced are they that natural milk is the proper nutrient for their young, the Soviet government has established maternal milk stations at some clinics. Here women with excess milk can sell it for a small fee, and mothers with nursing problems can purchase it for the same price for their babies.

Life for Soviet children, although not idyllic, is much less harsh than it used to be. The privations of famine and war have been avoided since 1945, and children generally profit from the growing affluence of their parents. Yet, the tendency of having only one child denies many youngsters the camaraderie of siblings and the comfort of aunts and uncles. Many children suffer the loneliness of being abandoned daily by their working parents. A growing number of children are orphaned because of alcoholic parents and others are simply given up due to economic problems or alcoholism. However, most Soviet parents deeply love their children and even dote on them. Strolling for miles on sidewalks, in parks, and along river banks is a common family activity. Fathers who often refuse to do any housework at home are very often the principal custodian of the children on these outings, walking hand in hand or carrying on their shoulders little girls wearing frilly dresses and huge bows in their hair and little boys sporting miniature sailor or soldier caps.

Loving their children, however, does not successfully encourage Soviet families to have more. The tendency toward having only one child is very pronounced and is persistently enforced by birth control measures. Contraception is not a popular form of birth control, however; Soviet birth control pills are scarce and often produce adverse side effects. Intrauterine devices are also unpopular since, being produced in only one size, they are often ill-fitting and uncomfortable. Soviet condoms are unreliable and

[26]Hedrick Smith, *The New Russians* (New York: Random House, 1989), p. 266.
[27]Lapidus, p. 240.

hard to get. Until recently, Soviet authorities refused to make available birth control information for fear that it would further slow birthrates. As a result, Soviet women sometimes resort to "folk methods" of birth control, like douching with lemon juice and jumping from refrigerators when their periods are late.[28]

> Soviet husbands, perhaps only half-jesting, sometimes joke that the most common birth control devices are the complete absence of double beds in the society and the utter exhaustion of their wives.

In fact, abortion remains the principal form of birth control in the Soviet Union. The typical Russian woman has between 6 and 9 abortions, but some claim to have had over 30. *Meditsinsyaya Gazeta* reported that there were 105 legal abortions to every 100 births in 1988, and *Moscow News* estimated that 90 percent of all first pregnancies are aborted. Between 7 and 8 million legal abortions are performed each year, about 4 times the number in the United States. A legal abortion cost 5 rubles and is accompanied by a 3-day leave from work. Wishing to increase the population and suspecting that repeated abortions are part of the cause for the increasing rate of infant mortality, Soviet doctors now try to discourage abortions by giving stern lectures to women requesting the procedure. If the women remain unpersuaded, the doctors comply with the request.

Abortion clinics are often understaffed and are run like assembly lines with rude, rough doctors and primitive facilities.[29] Furthermore, anesthetics are not usually used in state-subsidized abortions. For these reasons, and because abortion is socially frowned upon in the southern union republics, many women pay for illegal abortions. Exact figures do not exist, of course, but some Soviet officials estimate that between four and eight million illegal abortions are performed annually.[30] (Some observers claim that birth control methods are deliberately discouraged and legal abortion clinics are purposely mismanaged by doctors who want to augment their incomes by performing illegal abortions.) In any event, the high number of abortions is blamed for the unusually high Soviet incidence of infertility, gynecological diseases, infant mortality, miscarriages, and birth defects.

Unfortunately, as the average size of the Soviet family dwindles, the success ratio of Soviet marriages is also declining. Divorce rates have steadily climbed throughout Soviet history. Between 1975 and 1980 alone divorces increased by 30 percent; today they occur in almost four of every 10 marriages. The divorce rate is highest in the cities; Moscow registers a 50 percent divorce rate, for instance. Each year almost 600,000 children are

---

[28]"Soviet Union's Women Fighting Battle of the Bottle," *The Los Angeles Times*, May 12, 1976.

[29]Gray, pp. 157–166.

[30]Mikhail Gorbachev, *Perestroika: New Thinking for Our Country and the World* (New York: Harper & Row, 1987), p. 117.

left in single-parent homes, and one-sixth of all families have but one parent in residence.

Soviet divorce laws treat men and women about equally, giving the woman an advantage only when she is pregnant. Child support is usually awarded to the mother along with custody of the youngsters. However, alimony is usually not awarded except when a spouse is handicapped. A man may not divorce his wife without her permission while she is pregnant or before their youngest child has reached one year of age.[31]

These laws have basically been in force since 1968. Although the ease with which people can dissolve their marriages may encourage some percentage of the current divorce rate, the reasons for its growing frequency are much more complex. Something over half of all Soviet divorces are initiated by the woman, a phenomenon that can be viewed in one of two lights: Either the partnership is more intolerable for the woman than for the man or women are sufficiently independent from men that they can feel free to end an unhappy marriage.

The most commonly stated reasons for divorce cited by women are the alcoholism and cruelty of their spouses. Men most frequently cite the wives' frigidity and interfering mothers-in-law (Soviet women—especially Russians—are unusually close to their mothers). Both genders also frequently give as reasons infidelity, loss of affection, incompatibility, lack of privacy and crowded living conditions, arguments over household chores, and persistent physical exhaustion of the wives. There are about one million divorces annually nation-wide. Wife beating has been a long, sad tradition in Russia, a custom that is celebrated by the proverb "If he doesn't beat you, he doesn't love you." In fact, although it accounts for less than 10 percent of the reasons given for divorce, abuse by drunken husbands is one of the most frequently heard complaints among disgruntled women. By contrast, increasing numbers of men indicate that they find it difficult to accustom themselves to their wives' professional success when it exceeds their own. Sexual frustration is also an increasingly frequent reason given by people of both genders. Women complain that their husbands are poor lovers and brutalize them, while men aver that their wives are unfeminine.

Another problem that is beginning to concern Soviet officials is the growing rate of alcoholism among women. Verging on epidemic proportions among men, alcoholism is considerably less widespread among women. Yet, it is becoming a serious concern because it is increasing and because it is believed to have a far more serious effect on women. Tolerated among men, alcoholism among women tends to be scorned. Hence, Larisa Kuznetsova, a Soviet sociologist, said that the woman alcoholic is "more alone, more rejected, more bitter, more coarsened" than the alcoholic man.[32] Further, Soviet authorities attribute a portion of the responsibility for sharply increasing rates of child beating and infant mortality to alcoholic mothers. In an effort to combat the problem of alcoholism among women, Soviet authorities have established clinics specializing in this field.

[31]Gray, p. 115.
[32]Gray, p. 48.

Many of the problems encountered by the Soviet family are addressed in the platform of the Soviet Women's Committee (outlined on page 378). Besides this attention, no other group has risen to advocate family issues. There are, however, several groups organized to demand solutions to other, broader social and political problems. Some of these groups have attacked the system so profoundly that they are known as dissident movements.

DISSIDENT MOVEMENTS

Resistance to the Soviet government, like that in any modern state, reaches as far back as its history goes. You will remember that the Bolsheviks were a tiny minority in the country when they took power, but they succeeded in felling the Kerensky government because they were able to mobilize the workers and military in certain key cities. Resistance to Bolshevik rule erupted in a civil war, while internally the Bolsheviks found themselves confronted with radicals of every stripe, each urging that the revolution be taken in a different direction. Finally concluding that the Bolshevik way was the only way for the revolution, Lenin authorized the purge of the dissident elements and gave Feliks Dzerzhinsky authority to institute the Red Terror.

Policy debate continued to rage within the party, however, until finally in 1921 the Tenth Party Congress adopted a resolution forbidding criticism of the formal party line. With the adoption of this prohibition of opposition even within the party and with the rise of Stalin, dissident elements within the society became muted for decades. During the long period of Stalin's ascendancy, opposition for the tyranny was seldom openly expressed and was quickly stifled when it did become overt.

Khrushchev's liberalization policies and de-Stalinization campaign, however, encouraged many who had remained silent to speak out. Intellectuals, students, artists, and even some ordinary people joined in the debate about the propriety of Stalin's policies. Permitting such political criticism, Khrushchev encouraged others to chance remarks and demands for additional causes. Troubled by the 1956 uprising in Hungary and by the extent to which some critics were going in his own land, Khrushchev began to retract some of the freedoms he had fostered. Yet, it was not until after Khrushchev's fall from power that suppression began in earnest.

In 1965 two authors, Andrei Sinyavsky and Yuri Daniel, were arrested and brought to trial for having written pieces that were critical of the Soviet Union and for having smuggled them to the West for publication. The trial attracted a great deal of attention as citizens, enjoying their new liberty, became alarmed by the thought that they might be lost in a new repression. Bravely expressing their views, many writers and intellectuals wrote to the authorities demanding a fair trial for the two authors.

However, the court insisted upon having its way. Sinyavsky was given seven years and Daniel got five for spreading "anti-Soviet agitation and propaganda," a violation of the infamous Article 70 of the RSFSR Criminal

Code. The trial failed to have the desired results, however. Rather than quiet its critics, the party actually emboldened them by creating a focal point, a symbolic standard behind which dissidents could rally. Indeed, the trial was of such importance that many authorities date the beginning of the modern dissident movement from that event.

A young Russian/Jewish libertarian who became one of the most celebrated dissidents—Alexander Ginzburg—wrote and circulated an account of the trial. This early *samizdat* work ultimately cost Ginzburg years in the camps, but it also became a prototype of hundreds of secretly written, self-published (painstakingly copied by hand) critical tracts. Among the most important of these defiant works is the *Chronicle of Current Events,* a journal whose numerous issues enjoyed wide circulation and a reputation for accurately reporting Soviet suppression of dissidents.

In 1970 several prominent scientists, mathematicians, and social scientists formed the Soviet Human Rights Committee. One of the committee's members was Andrei Sakharov, perhaps the best known and most courageous of all Soviet dissidents. Sakharov, a major figure in the development of the Soviet hydrogen bomb, was made the youngest member of the Soviet Academy of Sciences at age 32. During the 1960s he began to question the wisdom of Soviet domestic and foreign policy and quietly petitioned the leadership to take a more enlightened course. These efforts were fruitless, so in 1968 Sakharov published the paper "Progress, Coexistence, and Intellectual Freedom" in which he called for intellectual freedom in the USSR and for a convergence of East-West economies. This paper and Sakharov's subsequent activities on behalf of human rights brought down upon him an increasing amount of state suppression.

The activities of individual dissidents were closely monitored by the KGB for several years, as were the activities of the Human Rights Committee and the publishers of the *Chronicle of Current Events.* In 1973 the KGB launched a crackdown, infamously known as "Case 24," which devastated the ranks of the dissidents. With the arrest of its editors, the *Chronicle* was silenced for awhile. Other dissidents were rounded up and, following a series of trials, were imprisoned, sent to labor camps, committed to psychiatric hospitals, or exiled.

The Soviet police, like their tsarist predecessors, maintain a large network of informers and agents provocateurs. One could never be sure about the loyalty of one's colleagues, and betrayal among conspirators was not unusual. Perhaps celebrating the dangers posed by even their friends, as well as all the other adversities they faced, Soviet dissidents saluted each other with the following toast:

"We drink to the success of our hopeless cause."

Set back by the purge of 1973, the dissident movement rebounded three years later. In May 1976 a group of prestigious persons organized the *Helsinki Group.* Its self-appointed task was to monitor Soviet compliance with the human rights provisions of the Helsinki Accords, which the Soviet government had signed the year before. Led by physicist Yuri Orlov, the group also included Yelena Bonner (Sakharov's wife), Pyotr Grigorenko, Anatoly Shcharansky, and Alexander Ginzburg. The group soon developed sister organizations throughout the Soviet Union, including the Ukraine, Latvia, and Georgia. The Helsinki Group alarmed the authorities because it showed promise of uniting many of the disparate dissidents behind a single objective. Consequently, a new crackdown was staged in 1977, and within a year of its founding virtually all of its leaders had been arrested and given stiff sentences. Undaunted, the tiny covey of dissidents who remained free, including Yelena Bonner, continued their work until finally disbanding under pressure in September 1982. More than 50 group members had been arrested by then, and only three remained at liberty. During its life, the Helsinki Group had made almost 200 statements to the Western press reporting Soviet violations of the human rights provisions in the Helsinki Accords.

The 1977 crackdown was so complete that it denied dissidents virtually all of their foremost leaders. Western observers speculated that the sweep's thoroughness was motivated by the government's wish to remove the dissident leaders from society before the 1980 Moscow Olympic Games.

By 1980 virtually all the well-known dissident leaders had been banished from the land or had been incarcerated in the camps or in psychiatric hospitals—all, that is, except for Andrei Sakharov and Yelena Bonner. Sakharov had lost his right to work with secret information since the 1968 publication of his paper calling for liberal reform of the Soviet government. He worked for human rights from that time, and, with his marriage to Yelena Bonner in the early 1970s serving as added inspiration for him, he came forward as the country's leading spokesperson for individual liberty.

Sakharov was one of the most distinguished Soviet scientists. He had been decorated with the Hero of the Soviet Union three times and remained a member of the prestigious Soviet Academy of Sciences. Voting in secret, that body stubbornly refused to expel him, even in the face of party pressure to do so. In 1975 Sakharov was chosen to receive the Nobel Peace Prize but was denied permission to go to Oslo, Norway, to collect it. Bonner, who was in the West for medical treatment, accepted the prize for him.

Persisting with his defiant work for human rights and publicly criticizing the 1979 Soviet invasion of Afghanistan, Sakharov was finally arrested in January 1980. Without benefit of trial, he was exiled to Gorky, an industrial city about 250 miles east of Moscow, a city Western journalists were not permitted to visit. There he was harassed by the police and kept under virtual house arrest. Even so, he continued to struggle with the authorities while they attempted to discredit him with slander and with suggestions that he was mentally ill.

In 1984 Soviet authorities clamped down on Bonner's dissident activities, sending her into exile with her husband. Sharing the indignities and harassment with Sakharov, Bonner's health deteriorated. Sakharov's own health was poor from stress and previous hunger strikes, but he began yet another hunger strike, demanding that Bonner be allowed to travel to the West for medical treatment. He was hospitalized, and videotapes were secretly made by the authorities in an attempt to assuage the growing international concern for his health. Finally, after going to the extreme of refusing medical help and resigning his membership in the prestigious Soviet Academy of Sciences, Sakharov secured the release of his wife. She went to the West for medical treatment, and in 1986, after her return, Sakharov himself was freed by Gorbachev's orders. Although Sakharov said he wanted to spend the remainder of his days on scientific projects, he could not refuse appeals that he continue the struggle for human rights. In 1989 he was elected to the USSR Congress of Peoples' Deputies and became a leading member of the Inter-Regional Group. Renowned throughout the world for his uncommon courage and indefatigable commitment to human rights, and regarded as the "conscience of the Soviet Union," Andrei Sakharov died in December 1989 while writing a speech he was to deliver to the CPD.

While Sakharov—brilliant and gentle but firmly committed to his humanist principles—became the international symbol of Soviet dissidents, thousands of other brave people defied the authorities for their own causes. Religious dissidents struggled for freedom of conscience, people joined in illegal protests to march for peace, and workers formed illegal unions. Perhaps the most articulate protests of Soviet repression were expressed by the creative community. Seeking artistic freedom, a huge number of Soviet ballet dancers, musicians, and writers abandoned their homeland for the West. As a consequence, their families were persecuted and the defectors lost their citizenship and were denied the right to return ever again to the Soviet Union. Soviet humor, ever fruitful, took account of this artistic drain by asking,

---

How do you define a Russian "musical trio"?

It is a quartet returning from the West.

Seldom citing ideological or economic reasons for leaving their country, these people, who were members of the highly privileged Soviet elite, gave artistic freedom as the reason for defection, complaining that they were forced to perform in provincial towns instead of in major cities, that their selection of material was often overruled by petty party officials, and that they were often denied the freedom to experiment with new forms of artistic expression. A partial list of Soviet artists to defect or who were exiled since 1961 includes writers Alexander Solzhenitsyn, Andrei Sinyavsky, and Viktor Nekrasov; musicians Viktoria Mullova and Vado Jordania; and ballet greats Rudolf Nureyev, Mikhail Baryshnikov, Natalia Makarova, Aleksandr Godunov, Yuri Stepanov, and Yuri Aleshin. The loss of these creative people not only constitutes a tremendous blow to Soviet prestige, but it also costs the Soviet people the priceless talents of some of their finest artists and results in a great deficit to their cultural enrichment.

Russian Nationalists

The nationalist movements have already been dealt with in considerable detail in the last chapter, but one group should be examined here: the **Russian nationalists.** As you know, reaction to the vilification the Russians have received at the hands of the minority peoples and frustration with Soviet nationalities policy have given new impetus to extreme Russian nationalist movements.

Essentially, these Russophiles hold traditional Russian culture to be superior to all others. They reject Western political and economic ideas as decadent and corrosive of Russia's spiritual purity; they renounce both individualism and communism. They want to stop the environmental deterioration of the Russian landscape. They want to restore ancient churches and return the ancient names to cities, rivers, and mountains, forsaking the names the communists have given them. Reminiscent of the *narodniki,* they tend to regard the peasant life as the purest existence and look back nostalgically at the ancient Russian village life. Fundamentally, this movement rejects things modern. It is reactionary in the purest sense of the term and it is often referred to as "red fascism." This movement is far from united as to what its followers want to replace the current system, however. Some wear buttons depicting St. George slaying a dragon (St. George is a patron saint of ancient Russia) and wave the tsarist flag. These monarchists include the Russian Monarchist Party and *Otechestvo* (Fatherland), and they would restore the imperial system and would ally with the Russian Orthodox Church to recreate "Holy Mother Russia." These people often claim Solzhenitsyn as their intellectual leader.

Others favor a new Stalinist-type dictatorship, but without the ideological corruption of Marxism-Leninism. A third group would divest Russia of the minority areas, send home all non-Russians and encourage Russians in the periphery to return to a motherland secure in its isolation from the corrupting influences of the "mongrel" peoples of the old empire and isolated from the West, other foreign people, and their ideas.

All these strains, although divided in their wishes about the future, agree in their passionate anti-Semitism. Reminiscent of ancient Russian hatred for the "Christ killers," current Russian nationalists believe the Jews are the most corrupting influence in society. The most active anti-Semitic organization in the Soviet Union is a coalition of six extreme rightist organizations called *Pamyat* (Memory). Composed of perhaps 5 percent of the Russian population, this group has lately been growing rapidly. In a 1990 poll, 19 percent of the Moscow respondents said that they approved of *Pamyat*'s activities.

Founded in 1979 as a cultural and historical preservation society attached to the Ministry of Aviation Industry, Pamyat quickly became independent of the government. It opposes Western influence, the "yellowing of the population," free masonry, drunkenness, and environmental deterioration. But its greatest interest is anti-Semitism. With a Judophobia rivaling Adolph Hitler's, it claims that the Jews are responsible for almost every conceivable evil including the tsarist pogroms, the Bolshevik Revolution, the murder of Tsar Nicholas II and his family, the rise of Hitler and his invasion of the Soviet Union, the holocaust (it is thought to have been a plot by powerful Jews to weed out the weak among them), and Stalin's terror, to say nothing about all the current problems in the Soviet Union.

Pamyat toughs vandalize property, terrorize people, and assault others. Following their charismatic leader, Konstantin Smirnov-Ostashvili, *Pamyat* ruffians broke up a 1989 meeting of Soviet writers in Moscow. Although no one was hurt badly, it was the first time *Pamyat* had been bold enough to disrupt such an important public meeting. Perhaps remembering similar acts by the Nazis during their rise to power, the government acted swiftly. Smirnov-Ostashvili became the first person to be prosecuted for violating a new law against inciting ethnic violence. His trial had to be postponed on its first day because of the rowdy behavior of his supporters in the courtroom, but eventually he was convicted and given two years at hard labor.[33] Smirnov-Ostashvili committed suicide in prison in 1991. His fate has not dampened *Pamyat*'s spirits, however, as it continues to agitate against and harass Jews, thus reinforcing their wish to leave the country. Indicative of the hopeless economic and political situations of Soviet Jews is this joke.

> A Jew applying for emigration was asked by the official, "Why do you want to leave the Soviet Union?"
>
> "Two reasons," the Jew responded. "Every night my neighbor, a member of *Pamyat*, pounds the wall and yells 'as soon as we put an end to the Soviet regime we'll take care of you Jews.'"
>
> "Relax,": said the emigration officer. "The Soviet regime will last forever."
>
> "That's my second reason," said the Jew.

Russian nationalism is, of course, opposed by other political movements. The **liberals,** originally led by Sakharov and now finding voice through Yuri Afanasyev, Boris Yeltsin, and others, advocate individualism; freedom of speech, press, and religion; national self-determination among the various ethnic groups; and better conditions for women, children, and labor. This group is particularly opposed to bureaucratic obstructionism, and it wants to severely limit the power of the military, while developing a multiparty parliamentary democracy. The liberals oppose traditional Russian secrecy in government and want the national legislature to adopt the Soviet equivalent of the American Freedom of Information Act. To reveal in full measure the deepest of Soviet secrets, these reformers have founded the Memorial Society, which publicizes the Stalinist terror and erects monuments to its victims across the land. The penchant for official secrecy has

---

[33]Elizabeth Shogren, "Russian Nationalist Gets 2 Years for Anti-Semitism," *The Los Angeles Times*, Oct. 13, 1990.

not escaped the cynical attention of Soviet humorists, as evidenced in this old joke.

> A man was said to be running through Red Square yelling, "Brezhnev's a fool! Brezhnev's a fool!" Arrested and tried, the errant critic was given ten years in the camps: five years for disturbing the peace and five years for disclosing a state secret.

There are also a decreasing number of **Marxist-Leninist purists** led by historian and former political outcast, Roy Medvedev. Members of this faction object to the tortuous distortions made to Marxism-Leninism by Stalin and his successors. They advocate a socialist, internationalist society that respects the rights of its people and is devoted to the concepts of human equality.

Ranged against all of these dissident factions are the **conservatives** who are most powerful among the bureaucracy, the party, and the military. Recognizing that change must occur, they are willing to accept only so much as will make possible the preservation of a strong, united Soviet state.

Gorbachev, of course, has answered critics of the system with unprecedented reforms and liberalizations. Besides the policies of *perestroika, glasnost,* and *demokratisiya* already mentioned in other chapters, he has relaxed travel restrictions on Soviet citizens both abroad and domestically. Many formerly banished or self-exiled people have been restored to citizenship and may return to the Soviet Union. Soviet citizens now enjoy unparalleled freedom to speak out, public demonstrations are common with hundreds occuring each year, and the Soviet Union has accepted World Court authority over five major human rights treaties, ending 40 years of resistance to the court's jurisdiction. As indicated elsewhere, however, the Soviet president has recently turned to, or been forced to, the right and more time is needed to determine whether this represents only a tactical maneuver or a permanent shift.

Besides the plight of its women and its dissident movements, the Soviet Union also has very severe difficulties with social deviance. These problems have become so numerous and widespread as to expose the society to potential chaos and to threaten the collapse of civility.

CORRUPTION, CRIME, AND VICE

Corruption

Among an increasing number of Soviet people there is the growing feeling that their society is void of meaning, that it lacks moral justification, that it is in ethical decay. Responses to this attitude are varied. Some people turn to their national traditions or religion for solace; others look back nostalgically to the Stalinist era, admiring its discipline and sense of purpose; some accept it cynically, not troubling themselves with introspective reflection but simply coping with the system on its own terms in the belief that the society is doomed to moral bankruptcy.

It seems premature to agree with this bleak assessment, although many observers have done so. More optimistic people believe that there is still much about Soviet society that is good. If it is currently caught up in a moral crisis, if its internal integrity is in jeopardy, the causes could be put to a temporary relaxation as people adjust to and consolidate the strengths of the new social order. Or, perhaps this debilitation stems from the trauma of revolutionizing this fundamentally conservative people. Another explanation could be that the current malaise is a natural reaction to the urbanization and industrialization of a society that only a few decades ago was mired in an archaic feudal monarchy. These and several other rationalizations can be used to explain the present quandary of spiritual stagnation seen by so many Soviet people, and these rationalizations can be used to suggest that the problem is temporary, not fatal. The nature of the problem and how deeply it is engrained in Soviet society can accurately be assessed only after the passage of more time, for the Soviet Union is still a comparatively new state. We must remember that the changes it has wrought are more fundamental than those imposed upon most other societies born of revolution.

Yet, although it might be too soon to assess accurately the problem of moral stagnation, it is not too early to recognize that Soviet society does indeed face an ethical malaise of serious proportions. Corruption, that is, a fundamental dishonesty in social and economic relationships among people, does indeed permeate the system. It touches the young and the old, the rich and the poor, the weak and the powerful.

Privilege. Although the Soviet system has done a remarkable job at narrowing the gap between the haves and the have-nots, a privileged class or classes do exist. These elite groups, consisting primarily of political leaders, the officers' corps, plant managers, scholars, athletes, and artists, enjoy a bounty denied to the vast majority of people in the society. Although such favoritism is technically legal, the egalitarian ideology espoused in the society makes the privileges enjoyed by the elite implicitly dishonest. Thus, they are included in this section, for ideological dishonesty is a perversion, a corruption of a fundamental sort in a society so overtly given to its philosophical goals. It should also be pointed out that, rather than follow Lenin's Spartan example, the members of the Soviet elite have deliberately rewarded themselves with great advantage, thus setting an example of corruption for those below.

Although the best available goods are reserved for the elite, all of its members do not share equally in the bounty. There is a very clear pecking order, with the quantity and quality of goods and services increasing as one travels up the social pyramid. Perhaps the most obvious status symbol for the elite is the state-owned *dacha*. Ordinary people can own dachas, but these are usually humble structures. The state-owned dachas, situated in secluded, exclusive locales, are usually of excellent quality and can be quite luxurious. The same rule applies to state-assigned automobiles, special clinics, exclusive clubs, special shops, and travel. The most elite among the privileged class enjoy the best, and such amenities as chauffeurs, maids, gardeners, and state-owned antique furniture and flatware are reserved for the most influential people. The elite also enjoys its own sanatoriums, vacation spots, ticket agencies, theaters, book stores, pharmacies, repair shops, and tailors.[34]

A striking example of the stratification among the Soviet elite can be seen in the Kremlin office buildings. They include snack bars on three different floors. Not only is the best quantity and quality reserved for the highest floor, which caters only to the most important people, but the prices of goods are also lowest on the highest floor.

The special stores, where the elite can buy goods unavailable to ordinary Soviet citizens, do not usually accept currency. Instead, they barter for special vouchers that are given to the elite in strict relationship to status. Those at the highest echelons enjoy a limitless supply of the certificates, but lower ranking functionaries have to be content with monthly chits ranging in value from 80 to 140 rubles.

In the provinces the circumstances are similar. The elite eat in special rooms at the best restaurants and are served special food. State and collective farms make regular deliveries of fresh vegetables, eggs, meat, fish, honey, and wine to the homes of the elite. For recreation they enjoy automobiles and other diversions, including special clubs that may feature saunas, reading rooms, theaters, and other facilities.

Of course, the salaries of the elite are much higher than those of ordinary people, and their pensions are also augmented. They are assigned roomy apartments in special buildings that often include restaurants, garages, and theaters. The highest-ranking officials are driven to work in Moscow by chauffeurs who use special lanes in the middle of the street reserved for them alone; they enjoy special private facilities at home and on vacation. Their elite status follows them even to the grave, as they are buried in special cemeteries, such as the Novodevichy Convent and the Kremlin Wall.[35]

One of the most vexing problems facing the elite is that since it is difficult to own land or large enterprises, it is hard to pass their privileged status along to their children. The best they can do is to shower their children with material goods (clothes, tape recorders, travel, money) and to assure that they go to the best schools and secure good jobs. Raised in an environment of privilege and plenty, these young people act much like rich children elsewhere, flaunting their advantages and taking them for granted. According to Milovan Djilas, former Yugoslavian political figure and social philosopher, these "golden youth," as they are called, have evolved into a "new class" of elite who were born to the purple and who expect to continue enjoying their exalted status. This is a sobering thought

---

[34]Konstantin M. Simis, *USSR: The Corrupt Society*, trans. Jacqueline Edwards and Mitchell Schneider (New York: Simon & Schuster, 1982), pp. 39, 43, 242.

[35]Simis, pp. 40–46, 73.

given the egalitarian goals of the society. The opulence of the elite and its hypocritical implications are pressed home by this old story.

> Brezhnev was showing his mother around his sumptuous apartment. He proudly introduced her to his fine furniture, his huge wardrobe, and his famous collection of luxury automobiles. "This is all very nice, my son," the old woman told him, "but what will happen to you if ever the Communists take over the country?"

Overt corruption.   Certainly not limited to the elite class, corruption is a fact of life over the length and breadth of the society. In Chapter 9 we studied the black and gray markets. The same ingredients that make up the black market (fixed prices, scarce goods, and too much money in circulation) contribute to the existence of other kinds of corruption.

Because the economy distributes goods so inefficiently, many Soviet people feel that corruption is necessary in order to succeed. In the words of one frustrated Russian intellectual, "Everyone knows that to get ahead in the country, it is almost required that you be a liar or a cheat—often a swine. We keep going backwards in the qualities on which social progress depends."[36] Yet, it should be stated at the outset that, pervasive though corruption is in the society, not everyone submits to it. Millions of people do their best in the society, eschewing illicit or even questionable activity. Time and again I have encountered cab drivers and clerks who refused money, valued ball-point pens, chewing gum, or American cigarettes as tips, and hotel maids who rushed down to the lobby to return a bottle of perfume and other trinkets we had left as tips but which they thought had been forgotten on the bed tables. Street artists and other isolated vendors have scorned dollars (hard currency!), accepting only rubles for their goods. On two different occasions I inadvertently left my Japanese camera, a treasured object in the Soviet Union, in hotel lobbies. The first time I discovered it missing after about an hour and hurried to where I had left it, hoping against hope that it would still be there—and it was. The second time, a knock at my door led me to discover a doorman who had seen me leave my camera behind and followed me to my room to return it. Similarly, one day on a Leningrad trolley when a friend did not have the correct change for the fare, she put a large coin in the coin box (Soviet citizens are on the honor system to pay trolley fares). Thinking no more about it, we sat back to enjoy the ride. Presently we noticed two *babushki* collecting fares from subsequent passengers instead of allowing them to deposit the money in the unattended coin box. When they had collected enough money to make change for my astonished friend, they pressed it into her hand.

Hence, one should be careful not to overgeneralize about corruption in the Soviet Union. It is indeed widespread, but it certainly is not universal, although it has grown much worse since severe consumer goods short-

---

[36]George Feifer, "Russian Disorders," *Harper's Magazine,* Feb. 1981, p. 50.

ages set in. Like the black market, all accounts place the greatest excesses of corruption in the Transcaucasus and Central Asia. But, to lesser extents, people trying to make a fast ruble can be found in virtually every part of the land.

Bribery is one of the most common forms of corruption. As with Mexico's *mordida* ("the bite"), the Soviets have their *vzyatka* ("the take"). Bribery runs the full length of the society, from top to bottom. Judges have taken bribes to lighten sentences and heads of union republic supreme soviets have sold pardons. Officials of OVIR (the MVD agency that issues visas) have accepted under-the-counter payments to expedite exit papers, customs officials close their eyes to illicit imports—for a price—and government ministers have been known to take money from Western business for smuggling out valuable goods like top-quality caviar in sardine cans.

Lofty offices are not alone in corrupt activities. Middle-ranking party authorities extort bribes for favors in order to augment their modest incomes. Plant managers find it impossible to run their enterprises without *vzyatki*. Bribes are necessary to ensure timely delivery of raw materials, to buy off auditors who discover false production reports, or to grease the palms of quality inspectors. By the same token, businesspersons traveling the country carry "gifts" of perfume, candy, and food to "impress" their associates.[37]

In addition, university entrance exams are sold; places for children in the most prestigious Pioneer camps can be bought; nurses and doctors demand payment for drugs, anesthetics, and attentive care; and linen changes on some trains are withheld until the head conductor is "remembered." With the "proper consideration," one can get teeth capped sooner, obtain permission to build on a private plot, get dry cleaning done early, secure a plump chicken, buy imported shoes, have an appliance repaired ahead of others, and be issued a driver's license. Policemen can be "persuaded" to look the other way and taxi drivers pay local authorities to keep the number of cabs down and the prices up.[38]

Besides bribery, there are a multitude of schemes to illegally increase incomes, including kickbacks from foreign businesses in exchange for government contracts. There are skimming operations, for example, the watering of beer and the use of low-quality flour in high-priced bread. State property is "diverted" to private use by people at virtually every level of the society, customers are shortchanged at stores, labels are changed on goods, funeral wreaths are used more than once, and "left-hand work" is performed on company time using state goods but paid for under the table.[39]

The level of corruption has risen to such a point that it has become a national disgrace. Rising to power on something of a reform platform, Andropov moved quickly to punish some of the worst offenders; his government appealed to the public to work harder and to eschew corruption.

[37]Simis, pp. 128–129, 135–136, 138, 140–141.
[38]Ester Dyson, "Three Weeks That Shook My World," *Forbes*, June 2, 1989.
[39]Simis, pp. 221, 229–235, 247, 261.

After Chernenko's brief rule, during which time Andropov's policies were allowed to cool, the Gorbachev government has lashed out at corruption with new vigor, dismissing, imprisoning, and even executing some party officials, government ministers, plant managers, police officials, shop clerks, and many others for such transgressions. Unfortunately, however, little improvement has been made. In 1989 two Soviet legal officials who successfully prosecuted several people in Uzbekistan's "cotton mafia"—including Brezhnev's son-in-law—were suddenly suspended from their jobs, removed from the party, and charged with improprieties when they claimed that some people in the Politburo itself were engaged in corruption. The two prosecutors became popular heroes, however, and were subsequently elected to the Congress of Peoples' Deputies by overwhelming margins.

Crime

Crime has always been a difficult factor to deal with in the Soviet Union. Marx believed that crime was caused by social stress resulting from a maldistribution of property within the society. Consequently, it was speculated that as the nation's wealth was equitably apportioned among the citizens, the crime rate would decline until it ceased being a concern.

Accordingly, in the 1920s crime was seen more as the product of an economically warped society than as a matter of individual responsibility. Sentences tended to be light, the courts forgiving. The Stalinist era brought more emphasis on the individual's responsibility. Sentences were stiffened, more acts became illegal, and the age for legal responsibility was lowered from 16 to 12. With the ascendance of Khrushchev, the penalties were relaxed again, and the age of legal responsibility was raised to 14. Stalin's successors also revived the previously ignored field of criminology, as well as other sociological subjects. Although statistics on crime used to be very difficult to find—even for Soviet criminologists—some important work was begun in the 1960s on the study of social deviance.

Even during the early stages of glasnost, Soviet crime statistics were only irregularly reported. The authorities usually published reports only about crimes upon which they wished to focus public attention—juvenile delinquency, embezzlement of state property, official corruption, and bribery, for example. When Vadim Bakatin became minister of internal affairs, however, data on crime poured forth into the media. Suddenly it became publicly known that the Soviet Union had one of the world's fastest growing crime rates. Some of this growth is undoubtedly due to increases in crime reporting and better accumulation of statistics, but it is clear that the society is beset by a major crime wave. In 1988 the crime rate grew by about 18 percent and in 1989 and 1990 it catapulted to over 30 percent annually. (See Table 11–1.) The largest increase in crime is occurring in the major cities and in certain union republics like Moldavia, Estonia, and Latvia. The rise in crime has become so serious that, for the first time, people are expressing anxiety about walking the streets at night, neighborhoods are organizing their own vigilante groups, and in 1990 the U.S. State Department issued warnings to tourists to watch out for thieves. Even so, the

TABLE 11–1   Soviet Crime Statistics for 1988

Crime	Percentage Increase over 1987
Murder and attempted murder	+14
Aggravated assault	+32
Rape and attempted rape	+ 5
Violent robbery	+43
Theft of public property	+25
Theft of private property	+44
Fraud	+10
Corruption and embezzlement	+10
Black market, speculation	+ 4

Source: Michael Parks, "Kremlin Reveals Details on Rising Crime Rate," *The Los Angeles Times*, Feb. 15, 1989.

crime rate in the Soviet Union remains far below that in the United States. In 1988 there were 657 crimes per 100,000 people in the Soviet Union; the figure was 5,550 per 100,000 in the United States—745 percent greater than the Soviet rate.

Furthermore, this comparison holds even though the Soviet Union recognizes several kinds of crimes that are not viewed as such in Western law. Some acts that are considered little more than rude conduct in the West are considered criminal violations in the Soviet Union, and in a few cases, the Soviets punish activities for which our society rewards its citizens. For example, rowdyism may be punished as disturbance of the peace in the West, but it is often overlooked. Soviet authorities, on the other hand, claim that, together with traffic violations, **hooliganism** is the most frequent infraction. People with no visible means of support in the West are occasionally prosecuted under vagrancy laws, although our courts are taking an increasingly jaundiced view of such statutes. Yet, **parasitism** is seen as a serious violation of the Soviet social norms.

Even so, the Soviet people have no experience with the rate of crime that has developed in their country, and it is a source of embarrassment that resulted in Bakatin's removal. Soviet jokesters greet the increasing crime rate with their usual levity, however.

> "We must have the richest country in the world!" the Soviet joke goes.
>
> "For 70 years everyone has been stealing from the state, and there is still something left to steal."

As the joke implies, there is an enormous amount of pilfering from the state. In some years, one-quarter of all crime involved theft of state property. Some people resent their low wages and help themselves to government property to get even; others tend to view state property as no one's property and thus as fair game.[40] Usually people simply walk off the job with state goods, but cases of truck hijacking, burglary, and wholesale theft of government goods have been reported. Even poaching rare animals is becoming a serious problem. Bank robbery, extortion, and smuggling are also increasing. In fact, in 1982 Brezhnev's daughter Galina was indirectly involved in a massive smuggling scandal; a crackdown at the Moscow circus revealed that several of her friends were stashing millions in diamonds, gold, and contraband goods.

As the nation becomes more affluent, a rise in certain kinds of crimes can be expected. Car theft is a case in point. As the number of private automobiles increases and as the going price of used cars remains higher than the official cost of new cars, it is inevitable that car thefts will mount. Indeed, car theft has already become such a problem in Moscow, where the largest number of private cars are found, that the police have established a special section for this crime alone. Because spare parts are so scarce, a great premium exists for accessories. Accordingly, drivers regularly remove windshield wipers and sideview mirrors and lock them inside the car before leaving the automobile parked on a public street. Hijacking has become a greater problem in the Soviet Union than in any other society. Between 1989 and 1990 no fewer than a dozen hijackings or attempted hijackings were reported, with one case involving domestic passengers who became angry about delays. They seized a plane and demanded to be taken home.[41] Most Soviet hijackings are attempts to leave the country, however. Suicide is also increasing, with the Soviet rate almost two-and-one-half times higher than the United States rate in 1988.[42]

Organized crime has also become a serious problem in the Soviet Union—the word "mafia" has become a comfortable part of the Soviet vocabulary. National networks deal in luxury goods, ancient art works, and narcotics. They have even connected with Soviet émigré criminals in the United States and elsewhere.[43] The Soviet police have been implicated in cooperating with organized crime and private businesspeople have been shaken down or their establishments fire bombed. Organized crime is heavily into smuggling valuables, and important people who are suspected of dealing with them have disappeared. The honest authorities are combating the "mafia" as well as they can under the circumstances. Police investigators who specialize in organized crime are harassed and have suffered several attempted assassinations.[44] The Soviets are seeking help from abroad to combat organized crime. Recently some Soviet police officials traveled to Chicago to study the latest crime-fighting techniques.[45]

---

[40]Simis, pp. 114, 252–253, 298.

[41]"Travelers, Angry at Delays, Seize Plane," *The Los Angeles Times,* Sept. 1, 1990.

[42]"High Soviet Suicide Toll Cited, Called Past Peak," *The Los Angeles Times,* Jan. 16, 1989.

[43]Carrol Bogert, "On Reform: Prime Time for Crimes," *Newsweek,* June 4, 1990.

[44]Charles P. Wallace, "Soviet Racketeers Muscle in on Growing Number of Private Businesses," *The Los Angeles Times,* Jan. 14, 1989.

[45]"Soviets Turn to Home of Al Capone for Help," *Escondido Times-Advocate,* Aug. 19, 1990.

For all crimes, the most alarming increase is among juveniles, although the proportion in the Soviet Union falls far short of that found in the West. Over 50 percent of all the crimes in the Baltic republics are perpetrated by juveniles. Blaming parental permissiveness and contact with decadent Western standards, Soviet authorities grudgingly reveal that juvenile crime is increasing across the board, from hooliganism to rape, from robbery to senseless slayings. Soviet criminologists identify most delinquents as the children of alcoholic or divorced parents. Delinquents tend to be poorly educated and idle. Yet, a growing number of them are among the "golden youth," those who come from homes of the elite.

The profile of Soviet criminals is ordinary in some respects and unusual in others. As in other societies, Soviet criminals are overwhelmingly male. Women account for only 12–18 percent of all offenses, and they tend to commit economic crimes as opportunity arises rather than on a premeditated basis. Men tend to commit most violent crime, with 98 percent of all open stealing and armed robbery being committed by males. Although women account for no more than 17 percent of all Soviet prisoners, they make up 36 percent of all those serving time for theft of state property. Most juvenile delinquents are also male, with fewer than 10 percent being female.

Alcohol is, by far, the most common contributor to crime. Eighty percent of all juvenile crime is perpetrated by youngsters under the influence. Further, over three-fourths of all violent crime (murder, rape, robberies, assault) is committed by people after they have been drinking. More will be said about the problem of alcohol later.

Not unusually, the crime rate in rural areas is much lower than in urban areas, with the urban rate exceeding the rural rate by about 40 percent. The most common crimes in rural areas are making and selling bootleg spirits (usually a woman's crime) and stealing state property. Crimes against individuals are also proportionately higher in rural areas than in urban settings, yet urban centers experience the greatest percentage of crime against personal property.

These trends are not unique. Indeed, they mirror the trends of most rural and urban societies. However, the geography of urban crime is somewhat surprising. Most societies suffer the greatest crime rate in their largest and oldest cities. Although most crime is committed in the older parts of Soviet cities, the crime rates of Moscow, Leningrad, and Kiev—three of the oldest and largest cities—are actually lower than those of newer, middle-sized cities. The reasons for this interesting contradiction are unique to the Soviet system. Most crime is committed by young males, particularly those who have recently changed residences. Soviet policy encourages young people to move to Siberia and other remote areas to help develop the nation's resources. Conversely, Soviet officials try to discourage people from moving into large, crowded cities. Also, people convicted of serious crimes are usually banished to the provinces. Hence, Soviet demographic policies inadvertently direct its criminal element away from its largest cities and towards its medium-sized centers.

Also, unlike in the West, where the criminal element tends to inhabit the central districts of cities, Soviet criminals tend to live in the suburbs.

Housing in the city is hard to come by, so young, recently arrived people—those who make up the largest proportion of the criminal element—usually live in suburban apartments, far away from work or school.[46]

Criminal penalties.   As we learned earlier, education and leniency play a major role in the Soviet legal system. The court gives relatively light sentences to first-time offenders of most crimes. Also, women consistently receive lighter sentences than men, and pregnancy or motherhood is often accepted as a mitigating factor in sentencing.[47] Soviet penalties range from correctional tasks (extra work assignments for minor offenses) to prison confinement, to labor camp terms, to death by shooting. The most extreme penalties follow from political offenses and large economic crimes. The death penalty, you will recall, is given for treason, espionage, sabotage, premeditated murder, and heinous rape. Minors under 18, women, and men over 60 years old may not be executed.

Juvenile offenders are handled by the Commission on Juvenile Affairs. The commission administers punishment not only to youthful offenders but also to their parents if it is thought appropriate. First-time offenders of ordinary crimes are usually given a stern lecture and a suspended sentence. Those youths who receive a sentence are usually confined in special labor camps until their sentence is finished or until they are old enough to be sent to an adult institution.

Blanket amnesties are not unusual, except for political prisoners, serious offenders, and recidivists. For example, in 1975 amnesty was given to a large number of women in honor of International Women's Year, and in 1977 the Sixtieth Anniversary of the Soviet Union brought a similar blanket pardon for female and male prisoners. Between 1986 and 1989 some 600,000 prisoners, amounting to about one-third of the total Soviet prison population, were given amnesty. Recidivism of Soviet criminals is estimated to be about 35 percent, about half that of the United States. The conditions in Soviet prisons and labor camps are hard.[48] Soviet officials have expressed some interest in improving matters, but few definite corrective policies have yet been adopted.

Vice

Vice, including illegal activities such as gambling, is a relatively minor problem in the USSR. Indeed, gambling is little more than a slight embarrassment in this puritanical society. Many Soviet citizens are avid horse racing fans, and gambling is allowed at the tracks. Also, the state administers a fairly popular lottery. Beyond these diversions, however, gambling is not an important element in Soviet life.

---

[46]Louise Shelley, "Crime and Delinquency in the Soviet Union," in *Contemporary Soviet Society,* ed. Jerry G. Pankhurst and Michael Paul Sacks (New York: Praeger, 1980), pp. 212–221.

[47]Lapidus, p. 240; Shelley, p. 223.

[48]Shelley, p. 222.

Illicit drugs present something of a more serious problem, but still one of very minor proportions when compared to the West. Official Soviet interest in the drug problem began in 1974 when poppy cultivation, a traditional practice in Central Asia, was made illegal. Even so, however, until the introduction of glasnost, the official line was that drug abuse was basically a problem in the decadent West and that it was negligible in the Soviet Union. Official attention focused on the problem in 1985, however, because of an increasing frequency of soldiers' using hashish after returning from Afghanistan, and because of alarm for the potential spread of AIDS (Acquired Immune Deficiency Syndrome)—the Russian acronym is SPID.

Recent Soviet studies put the number of drug addicts at 46,000, with an annual increase of 2,500–3,000. Since United States statistics list 30 million of its citizens as users of narcotics, the magnitude of the Soviet problem is indeed small by comparison. Yet, it is growing, and some authorities have called for an anti-drug program similar to past anti-alcohol campaigns. Indeed, some authorities suggest that the anti-alcohol measures have caused some alcoholics to turn to drugs as a substitute. Between 1985 and 1987 Soviet authorities claim that alcoholism declined by 17 percent (a questionable figure) but that drug use increased by 150 percent. Police sweeps through Soviet cities have netted hundreds of drug users, and in 1990 Leningrad authorities discovered two underground factories producing a psychedelic drug known as trimetil phentonil, worth 16,000 rubles per gram on the street. So far, however, few illicit laboratories have been found.[49]

Another illegal activity previously downplayed in importance but now spotlighted because of glasnost and because of concern over the spread of AIDS is homosexuality. Although no specific numbers have been published, recent Soviet publications have identified homosexuality as a growing phenomenon. Approaching the problem as a question of choice rather than as a physiological disorder, the authorities maintain that homosexuality can be eradicated with education and proper upbringing. Interestingly, only male homosexuality is illegal; lesbians are either ignored or are treated in psychiatric hospitals.[50]

Although the authorities are becoming very concerned about the potential spread of AIDS in the society, it has yet to rise to significant proportions or to attract much public attention. While some Soviet journals published stories suggesting that AIDS resulted from American experiments with biological warfare, the Soviet scientific community has firmly denied such a link. As a precaution against the disease, in 1987 the government began a mandatory testing program of all people suspected of carrying the infection. In 1989 a Ukrainian woman with AIDS was given four years in prison for refusing to abstain from having sex. Because of the dearth and unreliability of condoms in the Soviet Union, practicing safe sex is very

[49]Bogert, p. 24.
[50]Gray, p. 96.

difficult. As you know, large numbers of children and nursing mothers have also contracted the disease in Soviet hospitals.

Concern about AIDS and the new freedoms of glasnost has focused attention on another previously ignored problem: prostitution. Recently described in the Soviet media as a "national disgrace," prostitution is now the subject of considerable scrutiny. Although some accounts stress that Soviet women pander to foreign clientele, additional reports point to prostitution afflicting the general population, and there have even been accounts of prostitutes joining extortionist rings and blackmailing unsuspecting officials whom they are able to lure into compromising situations.[51]

Konstantin Simis, an émigré lawyer, reports that prostitution is relatively common in the Soviet Union. According to Simis, because all people are compelled to work, most prostitutes hold down a full-time job and engage in the world's oldest profession in their off hours. The prying eyes of apartment neighbors and laws forbidding unwed people to register in the same hotel room prevent the existence of brothels. So, finding a place to ply her trade can give a prostitute some difficulties. Simis suggests that parked taxicabs are often used, the driver being bribed to leave his car on a dark street for a predetermined period of time. Prostitutes—even a rare male prostitute—can be found working the streets, train stations, and the better hotels. The most expensive women are found in the hotels, and the women in train stations are considered to be at the bottom of their profession.[52]

As with gambling and drugs, however, prostitution is thought to be considerably less prevalent in the Soviet Union than in the West. Alcohol abuse, on the other hand, is altogether a different story.

Alcohol abuse. Lenin voiced his ideological convictions by saying, "The proletariat is an ascending class. It needs no intoxication by alcohol." Needed or not, the Soviet proletariat drinks heavily, as do its intellectuals, its farmers, its men, its women, its children, and its leaders. (Brezhnev had a serious drinking problem according to Andrei Gromyko.) Considerably less imbued with ideological conviction than Lenin, Soviet cynics tell this riddle.

> What is the transition stage between capitalism and communism?
> Alcoholism!

The proportions of alcohol abuse in the Soviet Union are simply overwhelming. One-third of all consumer spending in food stores, before the Gorbachev era, was said to go toward the purchase of alcohol. Nearly 15 percent of the average family budget goes for drink, and the figure

[51]William J. Eaton, "Sexy 'Robot' Is Convicted of Blackmail," *The Los Angeles Times,* April 18, 1987.

[52]Simis, pp. 276–292.

climbs to as high as 40 percent for families with alcoholics in residence. The Soviet Union ranks first in the world for the consumption of hard liquor, with the per capita consumption at about 50 liters per year—the equivalent of just over one quart per person per week. The impact of this figure is magnified even more when one realizes that the Muslim people in the Soviet Union drink very little or not at all, and although alcohol abuse among children is a growing problem, most of them do not drink; thus, the consumption of northern adults assumes immense proportions.

It should be remembered that people in all Nordic countries tend to drink heavily and that Russia has traditionally had a problem with alcoholism. Yet, the problem lingers and is increasing, even in the face of concerted Soviet efforts to arrest it. In 1925, 11 percent of the workers were thought to drink to excess, but by 1980 the figure had reached 37 percent. Between 1965 and 1979 the per capita consumption of alcohol increased by 50 percent, and by 1984 the production of alcohol had increased at twice the rate of the population growth. The number of alcoholics, as distinguished from those who simply abuse alcohol on occasion, was estimated to be over 20 million in 1990. In 1987 the U.S. Department of Health and Human Services estimated that the United States had only about half that number. Some authorities fear that the Russians may be drinking themselves into extinction. Signs that pandemic alcoholism is threatening the genetic pool are alarming. Eight of every 100 children suffer some degree of brain damage due to their mothers' alcohol abuse and over 50 percent of the high school students have difficulty mastering their lessons.[53]

The causes for such excesses are deeply rooted in the social and cultural system. Boredom, loneliness, depression, crowded living conditions, and limited sources of entertainment seem to be major contributors to the problem. Additionally, drink is a lubricant for social relationships, especially among men, many of whom regard drinking with friends as their favorite leisure pastime.Unless one drinks with others, it is difficult to get beyond the stern Russian veneer. Former Soviet newspaper correspondent Alexander Yanov once told me that party and government officials would not trust him unless he drank with them. Thus, in response to my question about what was the most difficult thing about being a newsman in the Soviet Union (I expected him to say something like "dealing with the censors"), Yanov replied, "Avoiding alcoholism."

Social tradition condones heavy drinking by males. Russians seldom sip their drinks at cocktail parties. Rather, they drink heavily at dinner, throwing back straight shots of vodka in between eating bread, butter, meat, and potatoes. Eating while drinking is one of the secrets to their monumental capacity for hard drink. Frequent practice is another. Once a bottle is opened, tradition demands that it be emptied. Hence, most vodka bottles in Soviet stores do not even have corks. They are sealed with a foil

[53]Alex Alexiev, "Life-Death Struggle for the Soul and Center of Soviet Union," *The Los Angeles Times*, March 25, 1990.

lid that is destroyed in the opening. Virtually no event passes without being toasted multiple times. Soviets drink to holidays, birthdays, weddings, funerals, weekends, and paydays. Drinking for social pleasure, for many, is perhaps only the excuse for drinking to get drunk, which Soviet drinkers often do. One need only walk down a central street in any major city to find drunks sleeping it off in doorways while others stagger uncontrollably. Such sights are not everyday occurrences, but they are frequent enough to alert even the most casual observer to a serious social problem.

We have already learned that drunkenness among women is a growing problem. The same is true among the youth. The legal age for drinking is 21, and drinking under age is not uncommon for Soviet youth, often occurring with the encouragement of adults—even parents. In fact, over the past decade the average age of registered alcoholics has dropped by five years, and one-third of all alcoholics report that they began drinking before the age of 10.

The social costs of excessive drinking are horrendous. Eighty percent of all violent crime is attributed to drinking, as are 40 percent of the divorces, 30 percent of traffic accidents, and 25 percent of all industrial accidents. Drink is the country's third largest killer (over 40,000 people a year die of alcohol poisoning alone) behind heart disease (which is in part attributed to alcohol abuse) and cancer. Alcohol is also blamed for most of the suicides and for much of the mental illness in the country.

Quite apart from personal tragedies, the economic costs of alcohol abuse are enormous. Large sums are spent on police control, sobering-up stations, and treatment spas. It has been estimated that Soviet industrial production could be increased by 10 percent if alcohol-related tardiness, absenteeism, breakage, accidents, and shoddy production were eliminated. The problem is just as serious, or perhaps worse, in the countryside. The amount of *samogon* (moonshine) produced almost equals the amount of legal vodka turned out annually, and the lion's share of the illicit hooch is made in the countryside. A half million people were prosecuted for *samogon* production in 1987. Spirits, legal or not, double as a medium of exchange on the farms. In fact, they are often the only currency in circulation among peasants. Of course, spirits are used for something besides barter. Having little to do on the dreary farms, peasants drink. Drunken tractor drivers destroy crops, field hands plant uneven rows, and peasants leave livestock to starve or freeze while they enjoy their stupors. Report after report tells of whole villages going on week-long binges while crops wither and animals die of neglect.[54]

Unlike other social problems that have, until recently, been ignored, alcoholism has long been featured in the press as a debilitating affliction. Campaign after campaign against drunkenness is launched; and party members, plant managers, schoolteachers, military commanders, and union leaders hammer away at the people to change their ways. Repeated drunkenness can bring pay cuts, extra work assignments, lost vacations, or

[54]Simis, p. 81.

dismissal. The government has raised the price of spirits, limited the hours during which they can be sold, reduced the alcohol content in popular brands of vodka, stopped selling vodka by the glass at kiosks, and made it illegal to sell alcohol in close proximity to schools, factories, and construction sites.

The Commission for the Struggle against Drunkenness, with chapters throughout the country, tries to combat the problem. Unlike the usual punitive methods, it uses persuasion as its major approach. Additionally, in 1987 the Soviet American Alcoholism Center was opened in Moscow, and since then Reverend J. W. Canty, an Episcopal priest from the United States, has opened Alcoholics Anonymous chapters in the Soviet Union. These organizations, with Soviet support, use religious belief as part of their treatment. In other cases, ambulances pick up drunks off the streets, taking them to sobering-up stations. The errant one is then sobered up, showered, fined, and reported to his or her employer. Frequent repeaters may be required to take treatment in drying-out clinics run by the MVD. In these hospitals, alcoholics are often treated with sulfazine, a strong drug that induces high temperatures, sweating the alcohol out of their systems. Western physicians refuse to use the drug.

Gorbachev launched an anti-alcoholism campaign as his first social program. Although the new program promised additional medical help to alcoholics and more recreational facilities to youth, the major thrust of the campaign was punitive. The legal age for drinking was raised from 18 to 21 years; a reduction in the production of spirits was announced; the penalties for drunk driving and public drunkenness were toughened; drinking at official banquets was prohibited; the hours during which alcohol could be sold (previously 11 A.M. to 9 P.M.) were changed to 2 P.M. to 7 p.m.; and the production of spirits was cut back by almost 40 percent.

Although the government claimed that crime, divorce, industrial and traffic accidents, and premature deaths declined as a result of the program, the public was outraged. The sale of cologne and other alcohol-based products shot up, together with an enormous increase in the production of *samogon,* depleting supplies of yeast and sugar. The people also fought back with their usual biting humor as they told one another

> Eat a large breakfast because lunch won't be served until 2 P.M.

Playing off the ironical effects of glasnost and the anti-alcohol campaign, disgruntled drinkers averred,

> In 1939 when the police came to the door, you hid the political tracts and brought out the vodka. Now when the police come, it's just the opposite!

Finally, in 1988 the government capitulated. The number of liquor stores was increased, the beer and wine bars were reopened, and spirits were sold in grocery stores once again. The authorities protested that they still wished to encourage sobriety, but that henceforth education and rehabilitation would be used to discourage drinking. Western experts suggest that Soviet officials face uncommonly difficult obstacles in their struggle against alcohol abuse. To begin with, heavy alcohol use is deeply ingrained in the social and cultural patterns of the country, making it extremely difficult to eradicate. Additionally, there are paradoxes in the Soviet approach to the problem. They tend to treat alcoholism as a habit rather than a disease. Hence, they try to persuade, scare, intimidate, or bully alcoholics into giving up drink. Moreover, the government finds itself in an ambiguous position on the question. A huge percentage of its tax revenues is raised from the sale of alcohol. When it cut back on alcohol production, its revenues plummeted, exacerbating the annual budget deficits. Thus, the government is caught in a squeeze: The citizens demand spirits; the official efforts to reduce alcohol consumption have failed; and the government, in any case, is tempted to push booze in order to increase revenues. These factors hardly portend well for successfully addressing a problem that has assumed epidemic proportions, and with this seemingly insoluble problem added to all of the other complex difficulties facing the country, one wonders about the prospects for Soviet political society.

chapter 12

Prospects

In assessing the Soviet achievement, many Western observers either ignore or ridicule the herculean effort undertaken by Lenin and his successors. This oversight is regrettable, for it denies the Soviet people and their leaders credit for a noble, if somewhat idealistic, effort. They tried to recast human nature, turning it away from what they consider shortsighted, selfish, and exploitative individualism to a collective approach in a society that sees each person working toward and sacrificing for the greater good–a revolutionary and noteworthy goal, but one that is perhaps too visionary.

The Soviet people have accomplished much in their brief experiment, but they have so far fallen short of the objective set by their founder. Indeed, the evidence detailed in the preceding chapters indicates that the Soviet leaders erred more seriously than simply not reaching their goal; it seems, instead, that they actually veered away from it.

Trying to apply Marxism—a revolutionary, atheistic, internationalist, and industrial-oriented philosophy—in Russia, Lenin had indeed assumed a monumental task. The application of any theory to a practical situation necessitates creativity and modification, but Lenin's objective of bringing socialism to Russia—a feudalistic, rural, multinational state of deeply religious people—seemed an impossible enterprise. Only by having a profound commitment to the revolution, by calling upon the force of his masterful intellect, and through implementing policies that Marx had not anticipated did Lenin launch the Soviet Union toward its collectivist goals.

Tragically, this great revolutionary did not have time to become more than the midwife of the expected new era. His death and the fateful rise to power of Joseph Stalin signaled a new course for the revolution, one that, if not abandoning Marxism-Leninism entirely, certainly truncated it. Stalin, another powerful personality, did more than simply mold social institutions to his liking. He actually transformed the revolution from a radical movement to a different, but no less revolutionary, reactionary phenomenon. Thus, he set in motion the "second revolution." By the time of the *Vozhd's* death, however, his intransigent stance had become obsolete, and Khrushchev, a third strong personality, desperately tried to chart a leftward course. Unfortunately for the cunning peasant politician, Stalin's bureaucratic model was too deeply entrenched to be reformed, and Khrushchev was replaced by a new kind of leader—the organization man.

Brezhnev was a cautious man. One of his favorite proverbs was "Always measure the cloth seven times before cutting it." Governing the Soviet Union with a steady but undramatic style, Brezhnev saw the system atrophy and stagnate. Although he attempted to duplicate for himself the personality cult enjoyed by his predecessors, Brezhnev could not fool the pundits among Soviet intellectuals. Shrewdly analyzing his failure at personal leadership, they observed that

> Brezhnev could not develop a *personality cult* until he first developed a *personality*.

Brezhnev's forte was indeed not in personal leadership. Rather he became a master power broker, balancing the competing and conflicting social and political groups that had emerged after Stalin's death. In doing so, however, his "steady as you go" policies signaled the death—or perhaps only the coma—of the revolution. Following the brief tenures of Andropov and Chernenko, Gorbachev began cautiously to address the enormous issues facing the system. Soon, however, it became obvious that profound change was necessary and he embarked on a social and political transformation the likes of which few societies have endured without widespread violence.

Although little doubt remains that Gorbachev is sincere in his efforts to modernize the system, there is serious question about whether he will be able to carry it off. Faced with a privileged party, a ponderous bureaucracy, a pampered military, a slovenly economy, and a profoundly conservative public, Gorbachev and his supporters confront a challenge of mammoth proportions. These entrenched elements have frustrated attempted changes since Stalin's time. Seemingly cast in iron, the Soviet system has developed a momentum of its own, one that has been far more powerful than the strength of personal leadership. Indeed, the Soviet system may have matured to the point that no single person, or even a small group of people, is able to force it to change substantially. If any potential for fundamental change exists, it depends on the cooperation of thousands of functionaries, many of whom stubbornly refuse to disrupt society or, indeed, to modify their own personal lives enough to rescue a floundering political and economic system.

In short, the Soviet Union has evolved from revolution to corporate state, from dynamic personal leadership to bureaucratic functionalism, and from radical ideological commitment through reactionary retrenchment to conservative pragmatism. Structurally it seems checked—perhaps checkmated—against itself. It seems to be a prisoner of a framework that plays one role to perfection, that of self-preservation.

For their part, the Soviet people, after several years of only half-hearted cooperation with reforms that never seem to improve matters but only cause social turmoil and increased economic entropy instead, have become more and more frustrated. Traditionally they have displayed an almost legendary forbearance toward their government. Public acceptance of the system is based on a tacit social contract in which the people will accept a rigid political system in exchange for the government providing jobs, social progress, and material well-being. We in the West, schooled in the virtues of free political expression and activity, are sometimes tempted to believe that such values are natural and that they are shared by everyone on earth. The people of the Soviet Union, however, have almost no tradition for liberalism, and because life has been hard, they have been willing to trade personal liberties for security. Liberal democracy is a foreign concept, poorly understood and deeply desired by only a few in the Soviet Union. The tradition for strong leadership is much more widely and deeply appreciated. Unaccustomed to taking responsibility for public policy, the people demand that their leaders somehow solve their problems for them, causing at least one obscure poet in 1989 to scrawl this verse on a central Moscow wall, "I love Russia with a heavy heart. I hate our untalented leadership. But we, because of our obedience, are to blame."

The people of the Russian Empire traditionally had an uncommon desire for order, and at least some observers believe that their conservatism has only been increased by the Soviet experience. Although they have been heroic, at the same time they display "slavish obedience, and blind self-satisfaction."[1] Hence, they preferred to accept the privations imposed upon them by government inefficiency and bureaucratic corruption, rather than risk the disruption and uncertainty incumbent in trying to change the system. Although they have had to deal with red tape, shoddy consumer goods, scarcities, and the like, they developed ways of working around these problems. Beating the system through bribery, black marketeering, and numerous other ingenious maneuvers is something of a national sport. Moreover, the Soviet people had only one direct experience with which to compare their present circumstances: the Russian imperial regime. On the whole, the tsarist government was no less bureaucratic, no less slow, no less corrupt than the Soviet government. Further, it can be argued that the

---

[1]Andrei Sinyarsky, *Soviet Civilization: A Cultural History*, trans. Joanne Turnbull and Nikolas Formozov (Boston: Little, Brown, 1990), p. 268.

imperial government was far less sensitive to the material privations of ordinary people. Finally, the Soviet system offered an idealism that attracted many people. Marxism held out the promise of egalitarianism and social progress, and the Soviet version of it promised security through military might.

Most of these unifying factors, however, are currently in jeopardy and the system appears to be teetering on the verge of collapse. The generation that could remember tsarist oppression has largely passed from the scene. The long, moribund Brezhnev era sapped society of its ideological commitment and its pride in the system. The social contract seems violated as shortages of critical staple goods have become commonplace and as unemployment and inflation—virtually unknown before—are threatening the commonweal, even as society is humiliated by having to accept economic aid from abroad. Even though the Soviet Union may be more secure now than ever before from foreign aggression, its economic plight makes it impossible to maintain its current military stature, and the feeling that the society is in decline is palpable among the public.

In trying to rescue the economic system from its downward course, Gorbachev has asked the bureaucrats and the people to make sacrifices that they seem unwilling to accept. The functionaries resist the loss of power and the people refuse to believe the promises that the system will only become more productive when they work harder, give up redundant jobs, and pay higher prices and taxes. Bitterly disappointed that the new freedoms have not brought economic plenty, Soviet people growl

> The leash is longer, but the dish is still empty.

At the same time, *glasnost* and *demokratisiya* have encouraged former allies to abandon the Soviet Union, and its internal unity is crumbling as the nationalities vent pent-up frustrations and strain to loosen themselves from the center. These outbursts have mobilized a conservative backlash, until the middle ground upon which compromise might be based is eroded. Gorbachev accumulates more and more power but he seems increasingly unable to manage a system that appears to be spinning out of control, and people on the street and in the corridors of power openly talk about the possibility of civil war.

The looming problems of the Soviet Union must be addressed. Productivity must be increased, not only to raise the GNP but also to reduce the huge government subsidies now necessarily paid to buttress failing enterprises and to make Soviet goods competitive on the world market. Consumer goods production must be multiplied to satisfy the expectations of increasingly acquisitive consumers. Public health must be improved to stem rising death rates and birth defects. Alcoholism must be curbed if the society is to fulfill its human potential and stop the enormous current waste of life and resources. Corruption must be curbed if the growing moral malaise is to be stemmed. The national minorities must be accommodated if the Soviet Union is to avoid a civil war. The lot of women must be improved if the nation's majority is to fulfill its potential. The people must be allowed meaningful choices of political leaders and economic managers if the "workers' state" is ever to become more than an idealistic dream. And individual liberty must be expanded if cultural impotence is to be checked and if the society is to flourish.

A further complication faces the Soviet leadership in that the once great commitment of the people to the goals of the revolution has vanished. Captivated by Lenin's idealism, millions of people joined the Bolshevik effort to build the new world. The willingness or the necessity for self-sacrifice was sustained throughout the terrible travail of the Stalinist era. Even later Khrushchev was able to call upon the Soviet people to work enthusiastically to open the virgin lands as another step on the road to communism. Although popular commitment to the revolution was certainly not universal, it was real and profound among many.

The Brezhnev era, with its attendant stagnation, corruption, and malfeasance, seems to have stifled popular verve even though it increased the economic well-being of the majority of its citizens. Having lost its ideological consensus, the society is atomizing, losing its once powerful collectivist spirit and becoming materialistic and selfish, unwilling to sacrifice or to share.

Such a spiritual decline would be serious for any society, but the individualization occurring in the Soviet Union, a society striving to build socialism, clearly is a development of profound proportions. Indeed, the spiritual malaise is so fundamental that no meaningful advancement toward socialism can possibly precede its reversal. Herein lies perhaps the greatest single challenge to the Soviet leadership: How can ideological commitment be restored among a people who have lost it?

It would appear that the chances of doing so are slim indeed without setting in motion a new radical movement as Lenin did or a reactionary hysteria of the Stalinist type. Russian and Soviet history offers only five examples of revolutionary leaders. Of these titans only three, Ivan the Terrible, Peter the Great, and Joseph Stalin were afforded enough time in power to do more than simply set their schemes in motion. Lenin took power and began developing the new state, but it was left to Stalin to actually mold the society. And Khrushchev, the only liberal reformer of the five, was ousted, his policies dismantled. Tellingly, each of the three who successfully revolutionized their respective societies resorted to brutality as the principal governance mechanism. Given this historical example, one might be excused for suffering some skepticism about the potential for Gorbachev's rationalist and pragmatic effort. Progressivism has never been a successful vehicle in Russian or Soviet history for driving modernization programs. To make matters worse, while Gorbachev's policies promise great advances over the long term, in the short run they threaten reduced privilege, harder work, lowered wages, rising prices, and mounting unemployment. So far the Soviet public seems nonplussed by calls for renewed sacrifice and the conservative nature of the Soviet people, leadership, and institutions again seems to divide the system against itself. Recognizing the dilemma, Gorbachev frustratedly wrote in *Perestroika,* "We have to overcome our own conservatism."[2]

Yet, it is too early to sing Gorbachev's requiem. His recent turn to the right distresses many in the West as well as in his own country. However, it must be remembered that he is a practical politician of the first order. Rather than being an ideologue, Gorbachev is fixed on a pragmatic objective: to bring about the modernization of the Soviet Union. If he is successful, he will inevitably see the system decentralize and liberalize even more than it has already. Many reformers see his recent policies as a return to the old, Stalinist methods. But in the words of Alexander Dzasokov, the Communist Party secretary in charge of ideology, "If we were using the old methods, then everything would have been resolved months ago."[3]

But no leader can ignore compelling political forces, and Gorbachev apparently feels that at this juncture some retrenchment and consolidation are necessary. It is of course possible that he has completely capitulated to the right so far as political policy is concerned, but such behavior is completely out of keeping with his previous actions and with his current economic reforms. More likely he is bending to the winds of conservatism long enough to exhaust their fury, so that later he may continue his modernizing policies. Whatever his intention, however, there is no assurance that he will succeed and indeed he may be replaced. If he is, however, the fundamental dilemmas remain and cry out for solutions that a lesser person may be unable to provide without resorting to traditional methods that are, in the long run, doomed to repeat the mistakes so often made in the past.

Regardless of who holds the reins of power, the basic demeanor of both the state and the population must change if the society is to overcome its present problems. The present competition between the system and the citizen must be arrested if society is to advance. As things stand the system tries to create legal institutions to channel public conduct, and, in turn, the people devise ways to defeat the system. Thus we find that in many aspects of ordinary life, the state and the people are working against each other, creating another systemic check.

Our own ideological biases encourage us to hope that the Soviet Union will become more like us. To expect, however, that the Soviet leaders will solve their problems as we think they should, or even that they will adopt policies that please us more than current conditions, is to miss the point. As I have tried to demonstrate in this book, the Soviet people, their history, their traditions, their physical environment, their economic conditions, and their political system are very different from our own. They will, after all, act in accordance with their own experience. Hence, their perceptions of society and their approaches to solving its problems will be as they have always been—unique.

---

[2]Mikhail Gorbachev, *Perestroika: New Thinking for Our Country and the World* (New York: Harper & Row, 1987), p. 65.

[3]Michael Parks, "Kremlin Still on Road to Reform, Official Says," *The Los Angeles Times,* Jan. 28, 1990.

Created by radical conflict, the Soviet order became stagnant, resistant to change, even though the need for transformation soon became painfully clear. Extremist in form yet traditional in substance, again and again Soviet society assessed its conditions but recoiled from solutions. Forged by Stalin's "second revolution," the Soviet Union has long since abandoned its Leninist ideals and sacrificed its legitimacy at the alter of an orderly, bureaucratic state. Now, however, it is impossible to delay any further. Impulses of racism and nationalism combine with articulate demands for economic improvement and moral purposefulness to make change—profound change—inevitable. The only question remaining is what kind of change will occur? Conceivably, the society could, even at this late date, rally behind a new set of common goals, thus pulling itself together and emerging stronger than before. This prospect, however, is becoming increasingly remote. On the other hand, parts of the country could spin off on their own, leaving the remainder to forge a union with a new consensus and a renewed commitment to the future. Having apparently failed at the former scenario, Gorbachev seems to be desperately trying to salvage the latter.

A much less pleasant set of possibilities also presents itself, however. As has happened so often in the past, the polity could find itself terrorized and forced by a reactionary police state to conform to the stifling dictates of a new totalitarian order. Or, failing attempts at compromise, consolidation, or coerced discipline, the society could collapse altogether, with its various constituent parts falling into violent conflict with one another. Civil war, as frightening as it may be, is by no means impossible. Indeed, some observers consider it likely. This last traumatic possibility threatens not only the tranquillity and existence of the Soviet Union, but it poses serious jeopardy for the entire world community. One thing seems clear: Lenin's grand experiment has failed. Bolshevism, at least for the moment, is discredited, leaving the Soviet people facing a series of fateful decisions. If they ignore Gorbachev's moderate path, they leave themselves only a choice between another era of mind-numbing suppression and years of spasmodic self-consuming bloodshed, and they risk fulfilling the prophecy of the early Soviet poet:

> Thus will Rus forever keep:
>   With hopsacks and hurrahs!
> While in its crumbling gutters,
>   People Weep.
>   *Sergei Esenin*

Glossary

AUCECB. (All-Union Council of Evangelical Christians-Baptists). The official union of fundamentalist Protestants. A large number of fundamentalists refuse to be regulated by the AUCECB, thus making the practice of their faith illegal.

Agitation. Short-term campaigns led by the rank and file to accomplish certain specific objectives (i.e., agitating for greater sobriety at work, for more care in driving, or for public condemnation of the nuclear weapons buildup of the United States).

Andropov, Yuri (1914–1984). Long-time head of the KGB who rose to lead the party after Brezhnev's death in 1982. Andropov began many reforms designed to increase productivity, but none was completed by the time of his death in 1984.

Apparatchiki. A term referring to the ranking members of the Communist Party and its professional party functionaries.

April Theses. A list of 11 policy steps Lenin advocated just prior to coming to power. This specific plan of action made Lenin appear decisive and strong in the face of the Kerensky government's ineptitude and inaction.

Autonomous oblast (AO). An autonomous province that enjoys a government of its own. The autonomous oblasts are organized to accommodate specific small nationalities. There are eight autonomous oblasts.

Autonomous Soviet Socialist Republic (ASSR). One of 20 governments that are subordinate to the union republics in which they are housed. ASSRs enjoy separate governments because they serve certain medium-sized nationalities within the union republics.

Babushki (grandmothers). Grandmothers traditionally care for their grandchildren while the children's parents work. *Babushki* exert a great influence on everyday life in the Soviet Union.

Beryozka (Birch Tree). A store where foreign tourists, journalists, businesspersons, diplomats, and other "elite" are allowed to shop. *Beryozki* take only foreign currency, and they feature many items that are unavailable in regular Soviet stores.

Bloody Sunday (January 9, 1905). Marks the beginning of the Russian Revolution. On that day a large, peaceful group marched to the Winter Palace to ask the tsar for certain reforms. Instead, the protesters were brutally cut down in the street.

Bolsheviks. Meaning "those in the majority," this term was adopted by the Russian Marxists who followed Vladimir Lenin.

Bonner, Yelena (Born 1923). A courageous dissident and the wife of Andrei Sakharov. In 1984 she was sentenced to a five-year exile in the city of Gorky for her dissident activities. She and her husband were released from confinement in 1986.

Boyars. The ancient high nobility of Russia. Claiming to be descendents of the Viking rulers of the Kievan state, the boyars enjoyed great privilege in the realm. The struggle between tsar and boyars for control of the society dominated the era between the reigns of Ivan the Great (1462–1505) and Peter the Great (1682–1725).

Brezhnev, Leonid (1906–1982). Replacing Nikita Khrushchev as the head of the party in 1964, Brezhnev gradually increased his power until he became the dominant person on the Politburo. His era (1964–1982) was noted for its unwillingness to discipline errant party leaders and government officials. Consequently, malaise, corruption, and irresolution developed in the society.

CPSU. Communist Party of the Soviet Union.

Capitalist encirclement. Stalin's theory that the Soviet Union was threatened by capitalist enemies from all sides. Thus, he reasoned, the Soviet Union had to enter a crash program (the first three five-year plans) to modernize and build a strong defense.

Catherine the Great (1762–1796). Catherine II was a German princess who adopted Russia as her own after her marriage to Peter III, then the pretender to the Russian throne. An enlightened despot, Catherine achieved spectacular successes in foreign policy but failed to accomplish serious domestic reform. By the time of her death, the ancient institution of serfdom had enveloped almost the entire Russian peasantry.

Central Committee of the CPSU. The executive committee of the Party Congress. The Central Committee meets biannually, and it has the power to make party policy that is inevitably ratified by the Party Congress during its infrequent meetings. The Central Committee also elects the Politburo and the Secretariat to administer party policy.

Cheka. The first Bolshevik secret police, led by Feliks Dzerzhinsky. The word *Cheka* is an acronym drawn from the formal title of the police unit, the Extraordinary Commission for Combatting Counterrevolution and Speculation.

Chernenko, Konstantin (1911–1985). A stalwart of the party bureaucracy rather than a leader who supported reform, Chernenko was passed over for succession to Brezhnev in favor of Yuri Andropov in 1982. Andropov's 1984 death, however, saw Chernenko succeed him as general secretary of the party. He held that post until his death in March 1985.

Civil War, Russian (1918–1921). The war between the Reds, or Bolshevik supporters, and the Whites, their opponents. Terribly destructive, this war gave the Bolsheviks control of most of the former Russian Empire.

Collective agreement. The labor contract or agreement arrived at through discussions among government officials, plant managers, and trade union officials. The agreement usually includes statements about production goals, wages, benefits, and working conditions.

Collective farm. See Kolkhoz.

Collegium. An administrative unit in Soviet government composed of the deputy ministers and other ranking bureaucrats in a ministry. The collegium advises the government minister, but the minister is free to ignore its counsel.

Comecon (Council for Mutual Economic Assistance). An economic pact organized in 1949 among the Soviet Union and its closest allies. Comecon was originally developed as a response to the Marshall Plan for European recovery and was dissolved in 1990.

Comintern (Communist International). Organized by Lenin and first led by Grigory Zinoviev to encourage workers' revolutions throughout the world. It was also called the Third International.

Command economy. An economy that is organized to respond to a central plan rather than to consumer demand.

Committee for Constitutional Compliance. A quasi-judicial body, it has the authority to declare certain laws and actions unconstitutional.

Comrades' courts. Informal judicial bodies that attempt to solve such local problems as drunkenness, absenteeism, and marital difficulties. The comrades' courts are not a part of the formal judiciary but are more like neighborhood arbitration committees.

Congress of Peoples' Deputies (CPD). Created in 1989, it meets on occasion during the year. The constitution recognizes the CPD as the highest authority in the land; it elects the Supreme Soviet which meets throughout the year. The CPD can overrule legislation of the Supreme Soviet.

Cosmopolitanism. A Soviet euphemism for the activity of Jews whose loyalty is questioned. The term implies that Jews have divided loyalties between the Soviet Union and Israel.

Cossaks. A group of runaway serfs, peasants, debtors, and criminals who inhabited the lower reaches of the Volga, Don, and Dnieper rivers during the fourteenth, fifteenth, and sixteenth centuries. At first a thorn in the tsar's side, the Cossacks eventually became staunch supporters of the regime.

Council of Ministers. The Soviet cabinet comprising more than one hundred ministries and state committees. An inner circle of the most powerful members of the council forms the Presidium of the Council of Ministers.

Council of the Federation. The leading advisory body to the president of the Soviet Union. It is composed of the leading government officials of the 15 union republics.

Cyrillic alphabet. An ancient Slavic alphabet thought to have been developed by Saint Cyril. It is presently used in Russian and most other languages in the Soviet Union.

Dacha (a country cottage). Dachas have become status symbols for the Soviet elite.

Dedovshchina. Brutal hazing of military recruits by their peers.

Demand economy. An economy where prices, wages, and production are determined by consumer demand. It is contrasted with a command economy in which central plans set the economic course of the country.

Democratic centralism. The mechanism of party government developed by Lenin and still applied. Theoretically, democratic centralism has party leaders elected by their subordinates, and it provides for open policy debate within the party. Decisions are then made by the leadership, and all party members are expected to obey the decisions without question.

Demokratisiya. Gorbachev's democratization reforms. It includes contested elections among competing political parties, workers' electing their managers and trade union leaders, and Communist Party members' electing their leaders.

De-Stalinization. A movement begun by Khrushchev in 1956 to eliminate the effects of Stalin's personality cult. The movement attempted to expose Stalin as a demented villain. It was abandoned after Khrushchev's fall from power in 1964. Gorbachev later began a new program to debunk the old dictator that has become very extensive.

Détente. Refers to a relaxation in United States–Soviet tensions. It was especially prominent during the early 1970s because of the policies of Richard Nixon.

Dictatorship of the proletariat. The political system that Marx predicted would serve as the transition from capitalism to socialism. Lenin used it as a justification for capping Russian society with the Communist Party dictatorship.

Doctor's Purge. In 1953 Stalin seemed about to start a new blood purge on the pretext that a group of doctors—mostly Jews—was plotting to assassinate the top leadership, including Stalin himself. The new purge was averted because of Stalin's death.

Druzhina. A volunteer police force whose members (*druzhiniki*) encourage citizens to keep streets clean, take drunks to police stations, and generally help to keep order. They can be identified by the red armband they wear.

Economic determinism. The Marxist theory that economics—the relationship of technology to raw materials and of people to the means of production—predetermines the structure and style of all societies.

First secretary of the CPSU. See *General secretary of the CPSU.*

GNP (gross national product). An estimate of the value of goods and services produced in a country within a year's time.

GRU (Chief Intelligence Directorate). The Soviet military intelligence agency.

General secretary of the CPSU. Created in 1922, this position of party leader became crucial. From 1952 to 1966 the title was changed to first secretary, but the original title was readopted under Brezhnev.

Glasnost (openness). Gorbachev's reform that encourages more candor regarding the social and political factors in the society.

Glavlit (Chief Administration for Literary and Publishing Affairs).   This is the principal censor of published works in the Soviet Union.

Gorbachev, Mikhail (Born 1931).   Early in his career, Gorbachev profited from the patronage of Mikhail Suslov and Yuri Andropov. He joined the party in 1952 and was rewarded for diligent service by being made first secretary of the party in the Stravropol Krai in 1970. In 1978 he was promoted to the Secretariat, and two years later he advanced to full membership of the Politburo. In March 1985, only seven years after coming to Moscow, he succeeded Konstantin Chernenko as general secretary of the CPSU. Cautious at first, Gorbachev has initiated many important reforms. Among them are democratization, glasnost, and perestroika.

Gosbank (the central bank of the Soviet Union).   Gosbank controls the money supply and administers most major financial transactions within the country.

Gosplan (State Planning Committee).   This agency is the principal planning body in the system.

Gray market.   Also called the third economy. The gray market is usually composed of legal private enterprise, for example, people working after hours to augment their income or selling their cars, pets, furnishings, or food raised on private plots on the private market.

Great Patriotic War.   The name the Soviets have given to World War II. For the Soviet Union, the Great Patriotic War began with the 1941 Nazi invasion and ended with the defeat of Germany and Japan in 1945.

Great Purges (1936–1939).   Sometimes called the *yezhovshchina*. During this period millions of people were sent to labor camps or executed as Stalin attempted to eliminate any possible opposition to his regime.

Great-Russian chauvinism.   Russian nationalism. Lenin feared that it would destroy socialism if allowed to develop. Stalin, however, encouraged its development both during and after World War II.

Gulag.   An acronym for the Main Administration of Correction Labor Camps. *Gulag Archipelago* is the title of a book by Alexander Solzhenitsyn about the chain of Stalinist labor camps.

Helsinki Accords.   A 1975 agreement about the structure of post–World War II Europe. The accords, signed by the Soviet Union and many other states, included a series of provisions on human rights.

Helsinki Group.   A group of liberal Soviet dissidents who from 1976 to 1982 tried to monitor Soviet violations of the human rights provisions of the Helsinki Accords. Eventually all its members were jailed, exiled, or sent to camps and psychiatric hospitals.

Hooliganism.   A term given to a large number of petty crimes, including vagrancy, vandalism, and drunken disorderliness. Hooliganism is one of the most frequent crimes in the Soviet Union.

Inter-Regional Group.   Composed of liberal and radical reformers, it is the first legislative opposition group allowed in the Soviet Union since the 1920s. It was founded by Andrei Sakharov, Boris Yeltsin, Yuri Afanasyev and others.

Izbi.   Small log cabins in which Russian peasants have traditionally lived.

Izvestia.   The official government newspaper in the Soviet Union. *Izvestia* means "news" in Russian.

Jewish Pale.   An area consisting basically of Lithuania, the Ukraine, and Byelorussia. From the time of Catherine the Great, the imperial government would not allow Russian Jews to live outside the Pale.

KGB (Committee for State Security).   The Soviet secret police. The KGB also includes several hundred thousand troops in the border guards.

Kerensky, Alexander (1881–1970).   Leader of the Labor Party, Kerensky rose to power in the chaotic months of 1917 that followed the tsar's abdication. In October 1917 Kerensky was deposed by Lenin and the Bolsheviks.

Khrushchev, Nikita (1894–1971).   A long-time protégé of Stalin, Khrushchev became an important reformer when he succeeded Stalin. Khrushchev's greatest accomplishment was that he ended government by terror.

Kolkhoz.   Collective farm. Theoretically the farmers elect their own managers and collectively decide policy for the kolkhoz. In reality, these decisions are largely made by the plan. Collective farmers use government land, but they own their own buildings and machinery.

Komsomol (Young Communist League). A voluntary youth group for people from age 15 to 28. Before the late 1980s Komsomol membership was a prerequisite for membership in the Communist Party and for admission to the university.

Krai. A territory used to administer remote and sparsely populated areas of the USSR.

Kulaks. Well-to-do peasants who were exterminated during Stalin's collectivization policies of the first two five-year plans.

Lenin, Vladimir Ilyich (1870–1924). Lenin, whose real name was Vladimir Ilyich Ulyanov, became a revolutionary in his youth and ultimately led the movement that ousted Kerensky in 1917 and founded the Soviet state.

Links. Small labor units whose members are given responsibility for a specific part of a plant or piece of land.

Little Octobrists. A youth group to which all Soviet schoolchildren belong until they reach age 10.

MTS. Machine tractor station.

MVD (Ministry of Internal Affairs). The MVD administers the militia (police) and other control agencies.

Malenkov, Georgi (1902–1988). Premier after Stalin's death. Malenkov was ousted by Khrushchev in the mid-1950s.

Medvedev, Roy and Zhores (Born 1925). Twin brothers who lead the "new-left" dissidents. Claiming that the CPSU has abandoned Marxism-Leninism, the new left calls for a return to these principles, Zhores, a scientist, now lives in exile in England; Roy, a historian, remains in Moscow and has been elected to the CPD.

Mensheviks. Meaning "those in the minority," the Mensheviks were Marxist followers of Georgi Plekhanov. They held rather orthodox Marxist views and opposed Lenin's revisions of the German master's theories.

Militia. The Soviet uniformed police. The militia is administered by the MVD.

Mir. An ancient Slavic collective farm. In Russian, the word *mir* is also used to mean "world" and "peace."

NATO. North Atlantic Treaty Organization.

NEP (1921–1928). New Economic Policy. With this policy, Lenin abandoned the radical economic policies of War Communism and recapitalized much of the Soviet economy. A return to socialism was intended as soon as possible. The NEP ended in 1928 with Stalin's five-year plans.

NKVD (People's Commissariat for Internal Affairs). The organization that served as the secret police during Stalin's regime.

Nagorno-Karabakh. An autonomous oblast in Azerbaijan, which is populated mostly by Armenians. The Azerbaijans and Armenians have been fighting a virtual civil war over its control.

Narodniki. Populist radicals who, in the mid-1800s, romanticized about the peasants, contending that they were the source of all goodness in Russia. These idealists were ultimately replaced by more practical revolutionaries.

New socialist man. The objective of Marxism-Leninism is to transform human beings into people who practice the socialist ethic—people who want to work and who freely share the products of labor among all people in society. If successful in accomplishing this objective, the CPSU will have created the "new socialist man."

Nihilism. A form of anarchism that developed in Russian in the mid-1800s. The Nihilists believed that Russian society was so corrupt that improvement could be accomplished only through its destruction.

Nomenklatura. Party lists of positions in the military, government, schools, farms, plants, and other institutions that can be held only by people who are cleared by the party.

Novosti. A Soviet news agency. *Novosti,* like *Izvestia,* means "news" in Russian.

OGPU (Unified State Political Administration). A secret police unit created in 1922 to replace Cheka.

OVIR. The Soviet agency that issues exit visas. It is administered by the MVD.

Oblast (province). There are about 120 of these administrative units in the Soviet Union.

October Manifesto. Promulgated in October 1905 by Nicholas II, this document granted a Duma and certain protection of civil liberties.

Okhrana. The secret police under Nicholas II.

Okrug (national district). Okrugs enjoy separate governments because of the discrete nationalities they serve. There are 10 okrugs in all.

Old Believers. See *Raskolniki.*

Old Bolsheviks. People who were Bolshevik revolutionaries before the revolution. Most of these people were killed by Stalin in the Great Purges of the 1930s.

PPO (Primary Party Organization). The PPOs are the most basic units in the party. All party members must belong to a PPO.

Pamyat. A militant Russian nationalist movement that is particularly active in anti-Semitism.

Party Conference. A meeting of party leaders that is sometimes held in the interim between Communist Party Congresses. The last one, the Nineteenth, was held in 1988.

Party Congress. Party Congress is technically the highest party organ in the Communist Party. It elects a Central Committee to administer party affairs in its absence. Some important party congresses include the Second (1903), in which the Bolsheviks and Mensheviks first split; the Ninth (1920), during which the trade unions were subjected to party control; the Tenth (1921), which disallowed factions within the party; and the Twentieth (1956), at which Khrushchev condemned Stalin for "crimes" against the Soviet people. The Twenty-eighth Party Congress was noted for its open debate.

Party self-criticism. The process by which party members are supposed to debate the administration of policy and to focus on personal failure to achieve objectives.

People's assessors. Lay people who sit with professional judges to hear civil and criminal cases.

Perestroika (restructuring). Gorbachev's reform that encourages economic managers to be more efficient and workers to be more productive.

Permafrost. Permanently frozen ground. In Siberia the permafrost has been measured to 1,000 feet deep.

Personality cult. The image manufactured by a leader to persuade the people of his power. Stalin, Khrushchev, and Brezhnev are each accused of trying to establish a persona that appears to be all-knowing and always right.

Peter I "the Great" (1682–1725). The tsar who finally managed to subdue the boyars. Peter used his advantage to modernize Russia, to turn it toward the West, and to institutionalize the power of the tsar.

Planning. The procedure by which the exploitation of resources and the production and distribution of goods are organized. Soviet authorities use the five-year plans as their basic planning units.

Pogroms. Incidents during which Jews were murdered, brutalized, robbed, and terrorized by their neighbors. Many pogroms were openly sanctioned by the tsar's government.

Politburo. The leading Communist Party agency. Until 1989–1990 it made the basic policy decisions for the government, but it since has become much less central. It is now composed of Communist Party leaders of the union republics.

Pravda. The official party newspaper. *Pravda* means "truth" in Russian.

Private plots. State-owned land that peasants and workers are allowed to farm; the crops may be kept or sold on the open market. Only about 3 percent of Soviet farmland is in private plots, but almost one-third of all Soviet meat and table vegetables come from this source.

Procurator general. The head of the Soviet judicial system and the chief procurator of the Soviet Union.

Proletariat. Industrial workers.

Propaganda. Ordinarily, propaganda can be defined as a one-sided argument. In the Soviet Union, however, it has a special meaning. The term refers to the party function of explaining party and government goals.

Provisional Government (February 1917–October 1917). The government that ruled Russia between the abdication of Nicholas II and the Bolshevik seizure of power. Both Prince Lvov and Alexander Kerensky were premiers during this period.

RSFSR (Russian Soviet Federated Socialist Republic). One of the 15 union republics in the USSR.

Raion. An administrative unit approximate to a county in rural areas and to a ward or borough in cities.

Raskolniki (Old Believers).   People who rejected the modernization of the Orthodox Church that Patriarch Nikon initiated in the seventeenth century.

Red Terror (1918–1919).   The purges conducted by Feliks Dzerzhinsky's Cheka to rid the Soviet Union of those whose loyalties were suspect.

Redundant labor (featherbedding).   Workers who are employed beyond those necessary to accomplish production tasks.

Refuseniks.   Soviet Jews who have been refused permission to emigrate to the West.

Rinki.   Free markets where peasants sell produce from their private plots.

S-Rs (Socialist-Revolutionaries).   Led by Viktor Chernov, the S-Rs were successors to the *Narodniki*, becoming the strongest proponent for Russia's peasants. The radical wing of this group, the Left S-Rs, briefly entered into a coalition government with the Bolsheviks in 1917–1918.

Sakharov, Andrei (1921–1989).   Father of the Soviet hydrogen bomb, he became a leader of Soviet advocates for human rights. He displayed extraordinary courage and persistence in the face of government suppression, and he became an international symbol for the struggle for human freedom.

Samizdat.   Literally meaning "self-published," *samizdat* is political and religious literature duplicated by carbon copies and circulated privately throughout the country.

Samogon.   Moonshine spirits, usually produced and sold by female peasants.

Second economy.   The black market.

Second Revolution.   The economic, social, and political transformation attendant to the first two five-year plans (1929–1939).

Secretariat.   The agency charged with administering the Communist Party. It is headed by the general secretary.

Shchit (shield).   An organization of reformers within the Soviet military. It is mainly composed of junior officers.

Shiite Muslims.   A Muslim sect found mainly in Azerbaijan whose religious beliefs are similar to those of the Ayatollah Khomeini of Iran.

Social Democratic Labor Party, Russian.   Founded in Minsk in 1898, the original Marxist party in Russia.

Socialism in one country.   Stalin's imperative that the Soviet Union should be made strong and impregnable before it brings on socialist revolutions elsewhere in the world.

Socialist competition.   Competition among workers to increase productivity. The idea is that workers should compete, not to prove who is better, but to establish the best means of production and to teach them to others. The same concept is used in Soviet schools to motivate students.

Socialist realism.   The doctrine calling upon artists to portray the Soviet Union as it *will* be when communism is achieved rather than as it actually is.

Solzhenitsyn, Alexander (Born 1918).   Exiled author and social critic. Solzhenitsyn leads the dissident Russian nationalists who want a return of the moral integrity of "Holy Mother Russia."

Soviets.   The term "soviets" is used to refer to legislatures and local government agencies.

Sovkhoz (state farm).   Sovkhoz workers are like factory workers in that they work for the state. The state owns all land, buildings, and machinery. Managers are appointed by the government, and the farms produce according to the central plan.

Speculation.   Buying cheap and selling dear. Speculation is a crime in the Soviet Union since it is assumed that the profit made by the middleman is actually value taken at no compensation from the worker.

Stalin, Joseph (1879–1953).   Totalitarian dictator of the Soviet Union between the late 1920s and 1953. Stalin's policies revolutionized Soviet society, establishing many economic and social patterns that remain in effect today.

State committees.   Agencies of government that do not hold ministerial rank but are still very important. The KGB and Gosplan are examples of important state committees.

State farm.   See Sovkhoz.

Steppe.   A vast area below the taiga and north of the deserts of Central Asia. Stretching from the Ukraine to northern Kazakhstan, this area is comprised of the famous black earth, the richest soil in the world. Erratic rainfall prevents this rich agricultural area from developing its full potential.

Subbotnik.   Derived from the Russian word for Saturday, this is a free day of "voluntary" labor that workers "give" to the state, usually on the Saturday closest to Lenin's birthday.

Sufi.   Secret Muslim societies.

Sunni.   A Muslim sect. Soviet Sunni are found east of the Caspian Sea.

Supreme Soviet of the USSR.   Elected by the Congress of Peoples' Deputies from its membership, this legislative body meets in several sessions throughout the year. Its actions can be overruled by the CPD.

TASS.   (Telegraph Agency of the Soviet Union).   The principal news agency of the Soviet Union.

Taiga.   A vast forest area stretching the entire width of the Soviet Union. The taiga is found in latitudes south of the arctic tundra and north of the fertile steppe.

Technicum.   A technical school in the Soviet educational system. Students may spend their eighth and ninth school years in technicums, learning such job skills as nursing and machine-tool technology.

Testament, Lenin's political.   A document written by Lenin the year before his death in which he criticized Stalin and asked for his removal from authority in the party.

Third economy.   See *Gray market.*

Trans-Siberian Railroad.   The longest single railroad line in the world, stretching for 6,200 miles, from Moscow to Vladivostok.

Trud.   The Soviet trade union newspaper.

Tundra.   Arctic wasteland.

Turnover tax.   Similar to a value-added or excise tax, the turnover tax is assessed on goods not only to raise revenue but also to regulate demand by adjusting the prices of items.

Two-stage theory.   A theory held by Georgi Plekhanov suggesting that Russia, a feudal society, would have to pass through a capitalist stage before socialism would be possible.

USSR.   Union of Soviet Socialist Republics.

Uniates.   Greek-rite Catholics of the Ukraine. Stalin brutally suppressed these believers after World War II.

Union republic (Soviet Socialist Republic [SSR]).   One of the 15 constituent parts of the Union of Soviet Socialist Republics.

Vanguard of the proletariat.   According to Marx, a category of people who, because of their perceptiveness, could see the focus of history leading to a proletarian socialist state. Lenin later used this concept to justify a Bolshevik-led revolution before Russia had developed a capitalist economy. Once in power he used the concept to dignify Communist Party members as those who were leading the worker toward the utopia.

Virgin lands.   Vast acreages of the eastern steppe that Khrushchev put to the plow in a desperate attempt to increase agricultural production.

Vozhd.   Russian for "boss" or "leader." Stalin was often called *Vozhd.*

War Communism (1917–1921).   The first Bolshevik attempt to socialize all land and factories. It failed because peasants and workers refused to cooperate with the state. War Communism was replaced by the NEP.

Warsaw Pact.   The Soviet Union uses this 1955 military alliance between the USSR and its Eastern European satellites as a countermeasure to the Western NATO alliance. It has virtually collapsed since 1989.

Yeltsin, Boris.   Once a member of the Communist Party Politburo and first secretary of the Moscow party, he has since left the party. He is president of the RSFSR. Perhaps the most popular politician in the Soviet Union, he is an opponent of Gorbachev.

Yezhovshchina.   The Great Purges of 1936–1939. The name was taken from Nikolai Yezhov, the head of the NKVD at the time.

Young Pioneers.   A youth group composed of all Soviet children between the ages of 10 and 15.

Zampolit (Deputy Commander for Political Affairs).   Political officers in the Soviet military. Although they are responsible for the political training of the troops, the political officers have no military authority.

Zionism.   A movement among Jews to return to their homeland in Israel. During periods of anti-Semitism, Soviet authorities have equated many ordinary Jewish cultural practices with Zionism and have persecuted Jews as disloyal citizens.

Bibliography

Aganbegian, Able G. *The Economic Challenge of Perestroika.* Bloomington, IN: Indiana University Press, 1988.

Allworth, Edward. *Soviet Nationality Problems.* New York: Columbia University Press, 1971.

Andrew, Christopher, and Oleg Gordievsky. *KGB: The Inside Story.* New York: HarperCollins, 1990.

Arbatov, Georgi, and Willem Oltmans. *The Soviet Viewpoint.* New York: Dodd, Mead & Company, 1983.

Azrael, Jeremy R., ed. *Soviet Nationality Policies and Practices.* New York: Praeger Publishers, 1978.

Bandera, V.N., and Z. Melnyk, eds. *The Soviet Economy in Regional Perspective.* New York: Frederick A. Praeger, 1973.

Barghoorn, Frederick C. *Politics in the USSR,* 2nd ed. Boston: Little, Brown, 1972.

Barry, Donald D., and Carol Barner-Barry. *Contemporary Soviet Politics,* 2nd ed. Englewood Cliffs, NJ: Prentice Hall, 1982.

Billington, James H. *The Icon and the Axe: An Interpretive History of Russian Culture.* New York: Random House, 1966.

Bingham, Marjorie Wall, and Susan Hill Gross. *Women in the U.S.S.R.* St. Louis Park, MN: Glenhurst Publications, 1980.

Black, Cyril E., ed. *Russia: On the Eve of War and Revolution.* Princeton: Princeton University Press, 1961.

Breslauer, George W. *Khrushchev and Brezhnev as Leaders: Building Authority in Soviet Politics.* London: George Allen & Unwin, 1982.

Carr, E.H. *Socialism in One Country 1924–1926.* Baltimore: Penguin Books, 1970.

Carrère d'Encausse, Hélène. *Decline of an Empire,* trans. Martin Sokolinsky and Henry A. LaFarge. New York: Newsweek Books, 1979.

Clarkson, Jesse D. *A History of Russia,* 2nd ed. New York: Random House, 1969.

Cockburn, Andrew. *The Threat: Inside the Soviet Military Machine.* New York: Random House, 1983.

Cocks, Paul. *Controlling Communist Bureaucracy.* Cambridge, MA: Harvard University Press, 1977.

Cohen, Stephen F. *Rethinking the Soviet Experience.* New York: Oxford University Press, 1985.

————, **and Katrina VanDen Heuvel.** *Voices of Glasnost.* New York: W. W. Norton, 1989.

Conquest, Robert. *Power and Policy in the USSR: The Struggle for Stalin's Succession, 1945–1960.* New York: Harper Torchbooks, 1967.

————. *The Conscience of the Revolution.* Cambridge, MA: Harvard University Press, 1960.

————. *The Harvest of Sorrow.* New York: Oxford University Press, 1986.

————. *Stalin and the Kirov Murder.* New York: Oxford University Press, 1989.

Cox, Arthur Macy. *Russian Roulette: The Superpower Game.* New York: Time Books, 1982.

Crankshaw, Edward. *Khrushchev.* New York: The Viking Press, 1966.

Deutscher, Isaac. *Russia, China, and the West, 1953–1966,* ed. Fred Halliday. Middlesex, England: Penguin Books, 1970.

————. *Soviet Trade Unions: Their Place in Soviet Labour Policy.* London: Oxford University Press, 1950.

————. *Stalin,* 2nd ed. New York: Oxford University Press, 1967.

Dijlas, Milovan. *The New Class.* London: Unwin Books, 1966.

Dmytryshyn, Basil. *A History of Russia.* Englewood Cliffs, NJ: Prentice Hall, 1977.

————. *USSR: A Concise History,* 4th ed. New York: Charles Scribner's Sons, 1984.

Dobson, Richard B. "Education and Opportunity." In *Contemporary Soviet Society,* ed. Jerry G. Pankhurst and Michael Paul Sacks. New York: Praeger Publishers, 1980.

Draitser, Emil. *Forbidden Laughter.* Los Angeles, CA: Almanac Press, 1978.

Dukes, Paul. *A History of Russia.* New York: McGraw-Hill, 1974.

Dziewanowski, M.K. *A History of Soviet Russia,* 2nd ed. Englewood Cliffs, NJ: Prentice Hall, 1985.

Engel, Barbara Alpern, and Clifford N. Rosenthal, eds. and trans. *Five Sisters: Women Against the Tsar.* New York: Schocken Books, 1977.

Field, Daniel. *Rebels in the Name of the Tsar.* Boston: Houghton Mifflin, 1976.

Fletcher, William C. *The Russian Church Underground, 1917–1971.* London: Oxford University Press, 1971.

Garthoff, Raymond L. *Soviet Military Policy.* London: Faber & Faber, 1966.

Geiger, H. Kent. *The Family in Soviet Russia.* Cambridge, MA: Harvard University Press, 1968.

Goldman, Marshall. *The Spoils of Progress.* Cambridge, MA: M.I.T. Press, 1972.

Gorbachev, Mikhail. *Perestroika: New Thinking for Our Country and the World.* New York: Harper & Row, 1987.

Gray, Francine du Plessix. *Soviet Women: Walking the Tightrope.* New York: Doubleday, 1989.

Harasymiw, Bohden, ed. *Education and Mass Media in the Soviet Union and Eastern Europe.* New York: Praeger Publishers, 1976.

Harcave, Sidney, ed. *Readings in Russian History.* New York: Thomas Y. Crowell Company, 1962.

Hazard, John, and Isaac Schapior, eds. *The Soviet Legal System,* 2nd ed. Dobbs Ferry, NY: Oceana, 1969.

Hendel, Samuel, ed. *The Soviet Crucible,* 5th ed. North Scituate, MA: Duxbury Press, 1980.

Hoetzsh, Otto. *The Evolution of Russia,* trans. Rhys Evans. London: Harcourt Brace Jovanovich, 1966.

Hoffmann, Erik P. ed. *The Soviet Union in the 1980s.* New York: The Academy of Political Science, 1984.

_____, and **Robbin F. Laird, eds.** *The Soviet Polity in the Modern Era.* Hawthorne, NY: Aldine Publishing Co., 1984.

Hollander, Gayle Durham. *Soviet Political Indoctrination: Developments in Mass Media and Propaganda since Stalin.* New York: Frederick A. Praeger, 1972.

Jacoby, Susan. *Inside Soviet Schools.* New York: Hill and Wang, 1974.

Kaiser, Robert G. *Russia: The People and the Power.* New York: Atheneum, 1976.

Karnet, Roger E., ed. *Soviet Foreign Policy in the 1980s.* New York: Praeger Publishers, 1982.

Kelley, Donald R., ed. *Soviet Politics in the Brezhnev Era.* New York: Praeger Publishers, 1980.

Kennan, George F. *Russia and the West: Under Lenin and Stalin.* New York: Mentor Books, 1961.

Khrushchev, Nikita S. *Khrushchev Remembers,* trans. and ed. Strobe Talbott. Boston: Little, Brown, 1970.

_____. *Khrushchev Remembers: The Last Testament,* trans. and ed. Strobe Talbott. Boston: Little, Brown, 197

_____. *Khrushchev on Khrushchev.* Boston: Little, Brown, 1990.

Klose, Kevin. *Russia and the Russians: Inside the Closed Society.* New York: W. W. Norton, 1984.

Kort, Michael. *The Soviet Colossus: A History of the USSR.* New York: Charles Scribner's Sons, 1985.

Kruglak, Theodore E. *The Two Faces of TASS.* Minneapolis: University of Minnesota Press, 1962.

Lane, David. *Politics & Society in the USSR.* 2nd ed. New York: New York University Press, 1978.

Lapidus, Gail Warshofsky. *Women in Soviet Society.* Berkeley: University of California Press, 1978.

Laqueur, Walter. *Stalin: The Glasnost Revelations.* New York: Charles Scribner's Sons, 1990.

_____, **ed.** *Soviet Union 2000: Reform or Revolution.* New York: St. Martin's Press, 1990.

Lawrence, John. *A History of Russia,* 2nd ed. New York: Mentor Books, 1969.

Lee, Andrea. *Russian Journal,* New York: Random House, 1981.

Levytsky, Borys. *The Use of Terror: The Soviet Secret Police, 1917–1970.* New York: Coward, McCann and Geoghegan, 1972.

Litvinov, Victor. *The Posters of Glasnost and Perestroika.* New York: Penguin, 1990.

Lowry, Charles W. *Communism and Christ,* 2nd ed. New York: Collier Books, 1962.

MacKenzie, David, and Michael W. Curran. *A History of Russia and the Soviet Union.* Homewood, IL: The Dorsey Press, 1977.

McAuley, Mary. *Labour Disputes in Soviet Russia, 1957–1965.* Oxford: Clarendon Press, 1969.

_____. *Politics and the Soviet Union.* Middlesex, England: Penguin Books, 1977.

Marshall, R.H., ed. *Aspects of Religion in the Soviet Union, 1917–1967.* Chicago: University of Chicago Press, 1971.

Massie, Robert K. *Peter the Great: His Life and World.* New York: Ballantine Books, 1980.

Matthews, Mervyn. *Privilege in the Soviet Union.* London: George Allen & Unwin, 1978.

Medish, Vadim. *The Soviet Union,* 2nd ed. Englewood Cliffs, NJ: Prentice Hall, 1984.

Medvedev, Roy. *Let History Judge.* New York: Knopf, 1971.

_____, **and Zhores A. Medvedev.** *Khrushchev: The Years in Power,* trans. Andrew R. Durkin. New York: Columbia University Press, 1976.

Medvedev, Zhores A. *Andropov.* New York: Penguin Books Ltd., 1984.

_____. *The Legacy of Chernobyl.* New York: W. W. Norton, 1990.

Minan, John H., ed. *Law in the Soviet Union.* San Diego, CA: Professional Seminar Consultants, 1984.

Murphy, Paul J. *Brezhnev: Soviet Politician.* Jefferson, NC: McFarland & Company, 1981.

Nahaylo, Bohdan, and Victor Swoboda. *Soviet Disunion.* New York: The Free Press, 1989.

Nettl, J.P. *The Soviet Achievement.* San Diego, CA; Harcourt Brace Jovanovich, 1967.

Nove, Alec. *An Economic History of the USSR.* Middlesex, England: Penguin Books, 1972.

————. *The Soviet Economy: An Introduction,* 3rd ed. London: Allen & Unwin, 1969.

Oliva, L. Jay, ed. *Russia and the West: From Peter to Khrushchev.* Boston: D.C. Heath and Company, 1965.

Osborn, Robert J. *The Evolution of Soviet Politics.* Homewood, IL: The Dorsey Press, 1974.

Pankhurst, Jerry G., and Michael Paul Sacks, eds. *Contemporary Soviet Society.* New York: Holt, Rinehart and Winston, 1980.

Pipes, Richard. *Russia under the Old Regime.* New York: Charles Scribner's Sons, 1974.

Pokshishevsky, V. *Geography of the Soviet Union.* Moscow: Progress Publishers, 1974.

Rabinowitch, Alexander. *The Bolsheviks Come to Power.* New York: W. W. Norton, 1976.

Raeff, Marc. *Imperial Russia 1682–1825.* New York: Knopf, 1971.

————. *Origins of the Russian Intelligentsia.* San Diego, CA: Harcourt Brace Jovanovich, 1966.

————. *The Red Army.* Boston: World, 1981.

Reshetar, John S., Jr. *The Soviet Polity,* 2nd ed. New York: Harper & Row, 1978.

Rothman, Stanley, and George W. Breslauer. *Soviet Politics & Society.* New York: West Publishing Co., 1978.

Rowen, Henry S., and Charles Wolf, Jr., eds. *The Future of the Soviet Empire.* New York: St. Martin's Press, 1987.

Rubinstein, Alvin Z. *Soviet Foreign Policy since World War II.* Cambridge, MA: Winthrop Publishers, 1981.

Salisbury, Harrison E. *Black Night, White Snow: Russia's Revolutions 1905–1917.* New York: Doubleday, 1978.

————. *The Nine-Hundred Days: The Siege of Leningrad.* New York: Harper & Row, 1969.

Schapiro, Leonard. *The Communist Party of the Soviet Union.* New York: Random House, 1960.

————, **and Joseph Godson.** *The Soviet Worker, Illusions and Realities.* London: Macmillan Press Ltd., 1981.

Shabad, Theodore. *Geography of the USSR: A Regional Survey.* New York: Praeger Publishers, 1951.

Sharlet, Robert. *The New Soviet Constitution of 1977.* Brunswick, OH: King's Court Communications, Inc., 1978.

Shelton, July. *The Coming Soviet Crash.* New York: The Free Press, 1989.

Shevchenko, Arkady N. *Breaking with Moscow.* New York: Knopf, 1985.

Shifrin, Avraham. *The First Guidebook to Prisons and Concentration Camps of the Soviet Union.* New York: Bantam Books, 1980.

Shipler, David K. *Russia: Broken Idols, Solemn Dreams.* New York: Penguin Books, 1983.

Shub, David. *Lenin.* Middlesex, England: Penguin Books, 1966.

Simis, Konstantin M. *USSR: The Corrupt Society,* trans. Jacqueline Edwards and Mitchell Schneider. New York: Simon & Schuster, 1982.

Smith, Hedrick. *The Russians.* New York: Ballantine Books, 1976.

————. *The New Russians.* New York: Random House, 1990.

Solzhenitsyn, Alexander. *The Gulag Archipelago,* trans. Thomas P. Whitney. New York: Harper & Row, 1973.

————. *One Day in the Life of Ivan Denisovich,* trans. Max Hayward and Ronald Hingley. New York: Frederick A. Praeger, 1963.

The Soviet Union. Washington, DC: Congressional Quarterly, Inc., 1982.

Stephan, John J. *The Russian Fascists.* New York: Harper & Row, 1978.

Strong, John W., ed. *The Soviet Union under Brezhnev and Kosygin.* New York: Van Nostrand Reinhold Company, 1971.

Sunyavsky, Andrei. *Soviet Civilization: A Cultural History,* trans. Joanne Turnbull and Nikolai Formozov. Boston: Little, Brown, 1990.

Tokes, Rudolf L., ed. *Dissent in the USSR.* Baltimore: Johns Hopkins University Press, 1975.

Tucker, Robert C. *The Marxian Revolutionary Idea.* New York: W. W. Norton, 1969.

Ulam, Adam B. *The New Face of Soviet Totalitarianism.* New York: Frederick A. Praeger, 1963.

————. *The Russian Political System.* New York: Random House, 1974.

Von Laue, Theodore H. *Why Lenin? Why Stalin?* Philadelphia: J.B. Lippincott Company, 1971.

Von Rauch, Georg. *A History of Soviet Russia,* 6th ed., trans. Peter and Annette Jacobsohn. New York: Praeger Publishers, 1972.

Voslensky, Michael S. *Nomenklatura: The Soviet Ruling Class,* trans. Eric Mosbacher. Garden City, NY: Doubleday, 1984.

Wren, Melvin C. *The Course of Russian History,* 3rd ed. London: Macmillan, 1968.

Yakir, Pyotr. *A Childhood in Prison.* New York: Coward-McCann, 1972.

Yanov, Alexander. *Détente after Brezhnev,* trans. Robert Kessler. Berkeley: Institute of International Studies, University of California, 1977.

————. *The Russian New Right: Right-Wing Ideologies in the Contemporary USSR,* trans. Stephen P. Dunn. Berkeley: Institute of International Studies, University of California, 1978.

Yarmolinsky, Avrahm. *Road to Revolution.* New York: Collier Books, 1962.

Yeltsin, Boris. *Against the Grain.* New York: Summit Books, 1990.

Zaichikov, A. *USSR: Trade Union Activity.* Moscow: Novosti Press Agency Publishing House, 1977.

Index

Magazines, 212, 233, 237
Main Administration of Corrective Labor Camps (Gulag). *See* Labor camps
Main Political Administration, 180
Makarova, Natalia, 388
Male chauvinism, 370, 375
Male gods, 377
Male prostitution, 402
Malenkov, Georgi, 83, 84, 85, 155, 178
Malevich, Kasimir, 241
Malinovsky, Marshal Rodion, 178
Mamaev Hill, 76
Manchuria, Japanese invasion of, 67
Mao Tse-tung, 290
Marbury v. Madison, 171
Mari people, 326, 338, 351
Marketing, 314
Marriage, 380, 381, 383, 384
Marshall Plan, 273
Martial law, 140
Martov, Julius, 363
Marx, Karl, 33, 42–43, 44, 45, 47, 61, 64, 96, 108, 163, 164, 228, 251, 256, 290, 296, 320, 351, 355, 378, 396, 407
Marxism, 210, 256, 351, 367, 407, 410
Marxism-Leninism, 95–96, 104, 221, 327, 339, 355, 389, 408
Marxist-Leninist purists, 390
Marxist platform, 102, 112
Masonry, 389
Massachusetts Institute of Technology (MIT), 194, 219
Mass arrests, 202
Massive nuclear retaliation, 89
Mass, Russian Orthodox, 356
MasterCard, 272
Matchmakers, 125
Matthews, Mervyn, 105, 109, 177, 178, 182
May Day, 207
  celebration of 1991, 249–250
  parade of 1990, 238, 240
McAuley, Mary, 201, 246
McDonald's, 274, 275
Mecca, 366, 367
Media, 209, 210, 228–240
  electronic, 238–240
  print, 233–238
Medical care, 261, 319
Medical supplies, 209

Mediterranean Sea, 34, 75
Mediterranean zone, 18, 21–22
Meditsinsyaya Gazeta, 383
Medvedev, Roy A., 71, 84, 86, 90, 99, 111, 148, 241, 391
Medvedev, Vladim, 112, 151, 152
Medvedev, Zhores A., 84, 86, 90, 99, 111
Memorial Society, 390
Mennonites, 361
Mensheviks, 44, 45, 59, 70, 110, 200, 242
Mental illness, 404
Meskhetian people, 329
Meskhetian Turks, 346–347
Messiah, second, 362
Methodists, 351, 361
Mexico, 66, 395
Meyer, Stephen, 194
Middle East, 16, 191, 276
MIG-29, 187
Military, 106, 114, 118, 159, 176, 196, 200, 209, 254, 257, 258, 278, 287, 290, 291, 314, 325, 346, 351, 361, 391, 408
  alcoholism, 183
  bases, 186
  budget, 191
  civilian academics, 190
  colleges, 187
  conditions in the ranks, 182–187
  construction battalions, 185
  coup, 196
  doctrine, 191
  draft, 185–186
  equipment, 273
  farms, 291
  food, 183
  GNP percentage, 188
  Gorbachev, 188–196
  heroes, 107
  investment, 260
  Party control of, 179, 180
  political commissars, 178
  political revolt, 179
  privilege in, 180–182
  racial tension, 185
  racism, 184–185, 186
  science, 219
  structure, 179–180
  training, 187–188
  units, 146
  women, 185

Parent-teacher conferences, 215
Parthian Empire, 31
Partisans, 80
Partitions of Poland, 362
Party bureau, 108
Party Communist. *See* Communist Party of the Soviet Union
Party conference. *See* All-Union Party Congress *and* Party Congress
Party Congress, 110, 113, 116, 123, 161. *See also* All-Union Party Congress
  First, 44, 110
  Nineteenth, 111, 137
  Ninth, 111
  Second, 110
  Tenth, 98, 111, 243, 385
  Twentieth, 111, 230
  Twenty-eighth, 87, 102, 111–113, 115, 377
  Twenty-seventh, 114, 266
  Twenty-sixth, 111
Party Control Commission, 113, 114, 116
Party control of military, 179, 180
Passport, internal, 6, 197
Pasternak, Boris, 60, 87
Patriarch, 138. *See also* Nikon, Pimen, Tikon, *and* Alexander II
Patriotism, 211
Patriot missiles, 192
Pavlov, Valentin S., 152, 158, 282, 283, 286
Peaceful coexistence, 88
Peace fund, 356
Pearl Harbor, 74
Peasant rebellion, 47
Peasants, 37, 44, 50, 62, 63, 68, 69, 85–86, 290, 292, 293, 302, 316
Peasants' Union, 299
Peat bogs, 27
Pechorsky Monastery, 354
Pedagogical approaches, 213
Pedagogy, 219
Peipus, Lake, 9
Penitentiaries, 173. *See also* Prisons
Pentagon, 190
Pentecostalists, 351, 353, 361–362
People's assessors, 163, 165, 169, 170, 172
People's Commissariat of Internal Affairs (NKVD), 197, 201, 202, 230

People's Commissar of State Welfare, 373
People's Control Committee, 108, 139
People's court, 169
  judges of, 145, 169
People's Republic of China, 191, 274. *See also* China
Pepsico, 275
Perestroika (restructuring), 150, 198, 242, 247, 248, 250, 253, 255, 256, 266, 267, 277, 280–283, 288, 311, 319, 339, 391, 412
  anti-*perestroika* message, 250
Perestroishchiki, 281
Perevedentsev, Viktor, 323
Permafrost, 8, 17
Permanent revolution, 45, 65, 88
Perovskaya, Sofya, 369
Persia, 29, 33
Persian Empire, 29
Persian Gulf War, 192
Persian lineage, 32
Peter and Paul Fortress, 174, 303
Peter I (the Great), 37–38, 89, 130, 200, 212, 303, 411
Peter III, 38
Petrograd, 52, 53, 54, 55, 56, 58, 243. *See also* Leningrad *and* St. Petersburg
Philby, Harold "Kim", 204
Physical education, 218, 221
Pilsudski, Marshal Joseph, 61
Pimen, Patriarch, 137, 353
Pioneer camps, 224, 395
Pipelines, 280
Pipes, Richard, 327, 336
Piskarevskoye Cemetery, 77
Pizza Hut, 274
Place of the Skull, The, 241
Plan, Group A, 258
Plan, Group B, 258
Plan, problems of, 260
Plan, success of, 259–260
Planners, 287
Planning, 256–268. *See also* Gosplan
Plant managers, 258, 392
Playboy magazine, 242
Playgrounds, 161
Plays, 230
Plekhanov, Georgi, 43–45
Pluralism, 125, 348